HISTORIC CONTACT

CONTRIBUTIONS TO PUBLIC ARCHEOLOGY

HISTORIC CONTACT

INDIAN PEOPLE AND COLONISTS
IN TODAY'S NORTHEASTERN
UNITED STATES
IN THE SIXTEENTH THROUGH
EIGHTEENTH CENTURIES

BY ROBERT S. GRUMET

FOREWORD BY
FRANCIS JENNINGS

PREFACE BY
JERRY ROGERS

UNIVERSITY OF OKLAHOMA PRESS : NORMAN AND LONDON

By Robert S. Grumet

Native Americans of the Northwest Coast: A Critical Bibliography (Bloomington, 1979)
Native American Place Names in New York City (New York, 1981)
The Lenapes (New York, 1989)
(ed.) *Northeastern Indian Lives* (Amherst, 1995)
Historic Contact: Indian People and Colonists in Today's Northeastern United States in the Sixteenth through Eighteenth Centuries (Norman, 1995)

This book is published with the generous assistance of Edith Gaylord Harper.

Library of Congress Cataloging-in-Publication Data

Grumet, Robert Steven.
   Historic contact : Indian people and colonists in today's northeastern United States in the sixteenth through eighteenth centuries / by Robert S. Grumet ; foreword by Francis Jennings ; preface by Jerry Rogers.
      p.   cm.—(Contributions to Public Archeology; 1)
   Includes bibliographical references and index.
   ISBN 0-8061-2700-7 (alk. paper)
   1. Indians of North America—Northeastern States—Antiquities—Collection and preservation. 2. Indians of North America—Northeastern States—History—Sources. 3. Indians of North America—Northeastern States—Government relations. 4. Excavations (Archaeology)—Northeastern States. 5. Ethnohistory—Northeastern States. 6. Northeastern States—Antiquities—Collection and preservation. I. Title.
   E78.E2G78   1995
   974'.02—dc20   94-41591
                                                                     CIP

Text design by Brad Price.

Historic Contact: Indian People and Colonists in Today's Northeastern United States in the Sixteenth through Eighteenth Centuries is Volume 1 in the series Contributions to Public Archeology.

Published 1995 by the University of Oklahoma Press, Norman, Publishing Division of the University. All rights reserved. Manufactured in the U.S.A.

1 2 3 4 5 6 7 8 9 10

In Memory of Bert Salwen

TABLE OF CONTENTS

LIST OF FIGURES

LIST OF
MAPS

All maps prepared for this volume depict relative distributions rather than actual locations of Historic Contact period archaeological sites and structures in the Northeast. This is done to respect the privacy of property owners and to maintain the confidentiality of site location data in existing inventories. A random number of dots indicate approximate site locations that range in size from one to two miles in diameter—"approximate" in that some of the dots appear five to ten miles from actual locales in order to further safeguard site locations. All numbered dots are keyed to tables listing site names, site numbers (when known), county, state, date range, National Register (NR) status, and major citations.

MAP TABLES

Properties listed on the maps include standing structures and archaeological sites and districts known to contain tangible deposits dating to the first three centuries of contact in the Northeast. Sites included in the lists have been found to contain original fabric, radiometrically datable deposits, clearly sealed stratigraphic deposits, or clearly related assemblages of Indian and European materials dating to the Historic Contact period. Inventory listings include both existing and since-destroyed documented sites.

Every effort has been taken to make these listings as complete as possible. Despite these efforts, many known sites do not appear in these tables. Some are not listed because investigators have not yet fully verified their age or affiliation. Others do not appear because their documentation has not yet been located in inventory folders, file cards, or computerized data base records.

MAP TABLE KEYS

SITE NAME

Historic names used to identify properties listed in the National Register of Historic Places, state registers, and other federal, state, or professional listings, surveys, and inventories are employed wherever known. Modern orthographies and site-name variants also are noted where appropriate. Smithsonian trinomial designations and other site numbers are included if known.

LOCATION

As noted above, exact information delineating property locations is not provided in order to safeguard archaeological sites. Inventories list only county and state.

DATE

Dates presented in each inventory listing have been drawn from the most authoritative available sources. Although archaeologists have worked hard to establish accurate chronologies and dating systems, few absolutely dated deposits associated with historic contact have been found in the region. Most dates represent "guesstimates" or approximations. The majority are TPQ (terminus post quem) determinations reflecting the earliest possible appearance of particular diagnostic artifacts. Radiometric dates are listed as cited in original sources. Calibrated dates are used whenever known. Terms such as "historic," "contact," and "protohistoric" reproduce nomenclature appearing in original inventory records.

NATIONAL REGISTER STATUS

Properties listed in the National Register of Historic Places are indicated by an X in the column headed "NR".

SOURCES

All cited sources are listed in the bibliography.

LIST OF SIDEBARS

FOREWORD

This theme study was made both to identify archaeological sites for special attention by the National Park Service and, as Jerry Rogers writes in his preface, to reflect 'critically significant advances in our understanding of archaeology.' My concern as a historian is primarily with the latter goal.

The study achieves that goal. It has turned up much new information and has identified innovative methods adopted by archaeologists everywhere. Everyone will agree that the tasks ahead are immense and that the passage of time makes them harder, but the giant strides already made are statistically measurable in the study's bibliography. Slightly less then half of its entries refer to publications issued since 1978: 553 compared with 558 in all the years before 1978.

By this bibliographical measure, work in the field proceeded at a steady pace until 1973, when it began to pick up, accelerating in 1978, and again in 1985. This is not a bell curve. Archaeology is coming into its own not a minute too soon, and this theme study reveals its importance to scholarship in all disciplines related to human culture.

A major question for which answers are to be found in the evidence concerns precontact Amerindian populations. We know from written documents that many epidemics swept away Indian peoples after the introduction from Europe and Africa of diseases new to the 'Americans.' Was there one giant pandemic ravaging the entire continent before Europeans were present to describe it? Only the evidence in the earth can answer.

What do we know about how and when North America originally was populated and how its peoples moved about and dealt with each other, not to speak of how groups made a living? Nobody wrote any of that down. Long after Europeans first reached the continent large regions remained unknown to them; consequently, our only sources of information are orally transmitted texts and artifacts marking routes of passage. Some scientists are dubious about oral traditions; the artifacts confirm or refute such traditions.

What intertribal trade networks existed before 1492, when the introduction of European goods created new systems of exchange? And what do those networks imply about the lives and psychologies of the people? When did particular tribes begin to trade with Europeans, and how were their cultures affected by this novelty? The men who recorded the trade—not all wanted it known—were wholly uninterested in its effects on Indian culture. For that information we must go to the material evidence.

Questions such as those posed above are relatively new to archaeology—and to history. They require patient examination of surviving artifacts. Scholars are far from consensus about the interpretation of much evidence. For example, I witnessed a heated argument between two serious, well-informed archaeologists about the disappearance from history of Saint Lawrence Iroquoians. Because the vanished people's ceramic pots traveled in one direction and their smoking pipes another, the debaters could not agree which direction had been taken by the Indians. The solution to the debate is found in the written evidence.

On the other hand, the findings of this study demonstrate the falsity of certain written documents. For centuries it had been assumed that the Delaware Indians had been conquered and made 'women' by the Iroquois and so had become incompetent to own land or decide weighty matters of war or peace. This assumption was central to nearly all historical and anthropological studies of the Delawares (and of colonial Pennsylvania) until recently. It had been supported by Seneca oral tradition. Nobody noticed that the 'tradition' itself derived from a written document that originated as an English diplomatic ploy against France.

How could archaeology resolve such a muddle? By confirming two other tribal traditions: a Delaware tradition and a Cayuga tradition. These traditions agreed that the Delawares were 'women' in the special context of eastern tribal cultures. They had been recognized by all the easterners as peacemakers, a role attributed to women. Now archaeologists find that tribes on the north and south of the Delawares lived in concentrated fortified villages, always prepared for war, but that the Delawares themselves lived dispersed, without fortifications. Obviously from such evidence, they were spared the fear of war, a finding that perfectly supports their own version of what 'women' status meant.

One exciting feature of this book is the attention it gives to other disciplines relevant to archaeology. The days are past when 'diggers' measured and weighed objects and tried to determine their age without looking beyond the findings of their technologies. There can be no doubt whatever that such basic data are needed. (Is calling it 'necessary spadework' too awful a pun?) But people outside the profession ask, 'Why bother?' and archaeology has suffered much public neglect because its practitioners long ignored such questions.

Now, however, as this study clearly demonstrates, the diggers have lifted their sights and joined interdisciplinary discourse about the peoples of America, especially those invisible to historians. As these peoples emerge, histories must be revised to take account of them.

Sorry to say, technicalities still mar the scene—though there are fewer than formerly. An outsider must plead for mercy and enlightenment when battered with terms like 'concave-based Levanna projectile points,' 'Niantic-series globular collared Hackney Pond and other terminal Windsor wares,' and 'Bowmans Brook/Overpeck.' Such jargon, probably meaningful to the initiated, certainly is mysterious to outsiders. It cannot be said too often that the language of interdisciplinary communication is Standard English. Jargon draws a curtain.

All disciplines have been handicapped because, as Robert Grumet reports here, 'no general archaeological synthesis of eighteenth-century North Atlantic life has yet been attempted.' We owe congratulations and gratitude to the National Park Service for providing us with this new approach to such a synthesis for the sixteenth and seventeenth centuries as well as the eighteenth.

It hardly needs to be added, but it won't hurt to say it plainly: Historians must pay serious attention to this new fund of archaeological evidence and must incorporate it in their own work.

FRANCIS JENNINGS

Chilmark, Massachusetts

PREFACE

The Historic Sites Act of 1935 declared historic preservation a policy of the federal government. It authorized the Secretary of the Interior, through the National Park Service, to make 'a survey of historic and archaeologic sites, buildings, and objects for the purpose of determining which possess exceptional values as commemorating or illustrating the history of the United States.' The Secretary designates as National Historic Landmarks those properties found to possess exceptional historical significance. Ideally, these nationally significant properties are identified through 'theme studies' that evaluate surviving structures and sites within the context of our national history and archaeology.

The first theme studies in archaeology were undertaken between 1958 and 1962, and they resulted in the designation of seventy-four archaeological landmarks. I regret that no such studies were done in the three decades that followed. For this reason the present theme study of the Historic Contact period, covering the Northeastern United States, represents an important initiative. For the first time in thirty years critically significant advances in our understanding of archaeology are reflected in the results of the National Historic Landmarks Survey.

I am confident that this vanguard survey will encourage land-planning agencies at all levels of government and preservation organizations both public and private to adapt the methodology of this survey to their special needs.

JERRY ROGERS

Associate Director,
Cultural Resources
National Park Service,
Washington, D.C.

ACKNOWLEDGMENTS

This book is a revised abridgement of a National Park Service National Historic Landmark theme study (Grumet 1992). Begun in 1989 and completed in 1993, the study identified, evaluated, and nominated seventeen new National Historic Landmarks associated with historic contact in the Northeastern United States. I conducted the research under the supervision of Lloyd N. Chapman as a major program initiative of the National Park Service's Mid-Atlantic Region Cultural Resource Planning Branch. Representatives of the seventeen state historic preservation offices in the branch's service region, National Park Service Cultural Resource Management program staff, the Society for American Archaeology's National Historic Landmark Committee, and members of the region's academic and preservation communities furnished information, reviewed project products, and provided vital technical assistance.

This volume presents the results of this multiyear cooperative effort—though, as an extensive revision undertaken after the completion of the initial report, it does not follow that report's administrative format and regulatory nomenclature.

Like many other federally funded archaeological research projects conducted in the Northeast during the last ten years or so, this study owes much to Lloyd N. Chapman. As chief of the Cultural Resource Planning Branch, Mid-Atlantic Region, National Park Service, Lloyd first suggested the project some months after I joined his staff in 1988. In the intervening years he has persistently supported the project's development in the face of shifting priorities, uncertain resources, and an always exacting workload. Whatever success this study encounters as a comprehensive preservation-planning document may be attributed directly to the support provided by Lloyd, Departmental Consulting Archaeologist Francis P. McManamon, and Katherine H. Stevenson, Associate Regional Director for Cultural Resources for the Mid-Atlantic Region.

Their vision also inspired Senior Historian Ben Levy of the National Park Service's History Division in Washington to support this first attempt to use a National Historic Landmark theme-study framework as a vehicle for a regional-scale preservation-planning historic context. Working closely with us at every stage of project development, Ben played a major role in adopting the new National Register of Historic Places Multiple Property Documentation Form as the theme-study presentation format, while seeing to it that all project products met National Historic Landmark program standards.

Richard C. Waldbauer, of the Archaeological Assistance Program's Washington office, also provided crucial technical support from the very beginning of the project. De Teel Patterson Tiller, Chief of the Washington office's Preservation Planning Branch, and Jan Townsend, of the National Register Branch, also gave much-needed technical assistance. Significant help was also provided by National Park Service Interagency Resources Division staffers John Knoerl, of the Geographic Information System Branch, and Susan L. Henry, of the Preservation Planning Branch.

Representatives from all Mid-Atlantic Region state historic preservation offices provided essential support. Each supplied data, verified product adequacy and accuracy, and served as liaisons among state, local, and tribal governments, specialists, and other members of the preservation community. Especially significant assistance was provided by David Poirier, of the Connecticut Historical Commission; Richard B. Hughes, of the Maryland Historical Trust; Charles Florance, then of the New York State Historic Preservation Field Services Bureau; Alice Guerrant, of the Delaware Bureau of Archaeology and Historic Preservation; Kurt Carr, of Pennsylvania's Bureau of Historic Preservation; Paul A. Robinson, of the Rhode Island Historical Preservation Commission; and E. Randolph Turner III, of the Virginia Depart-

ment of Historic Resources. Society for American Archaeology National Historic Landmarks Committee chair David S. Brose and committee members Stanley A. Ahler, Jeanne E. Arnold, Albert Dekin, Jr., and Tim A. Kohler reviewed project materials. Mid-Atlantic Region National Register Programs Division colleagues Tina C. LeCoff, Bert Herbert, John Hnedak, Dennis Montagna, and Charlene Smith provided further technical support and guidance.

Three people I had come to depend on for advice and support—Bert Salwen, James G. E. Smith, and my mentor, Eleanor Burke Leacock—passed away just before or shortly after the project got started. Luckily, Bruce J. Bourque, Robert L. Bradley, Alaric Faulkner, Herbert C. Kraft, Robert F. Maslowski, Kevin A. McBride, Martha L. Sempowski, and Dean R. Snow stepped in to provide much-needed direction during critical early phases of project development. Later on, Monte R. Bennett, James A. Brown, Colin G. Calloway, Dena F. Dincauze, Gregory E. Dowd, William E. Engelbrecht, David N. Fuerst, Charles T. Gehring, George R. Hamell, Robert J. Hasenstab, Paul R. Huey, Francis Jennings, William C. Johnson, Richard S. Kanaski, Alice B. Kehoe, Barry C. Kent, Howard A. MacCord, Sr., Adrian O. Mandzy, Ronald J. Mason, Henry M. Miller, Larry E. Moore, Cheryl Ann Munson, James F. Pendergast, Stephen R. Potter, Harald E. L. Prins, Patricia E. Rubertone, Donald A. Rumrill, Patricia Kay Scott, Ralph S. Solecki, R. Michael Stewart, Peter A. Thomas, Elisabeth Tooker, E. Randolph Turner III, and Clinton A. Weslager took the time to extensively review early document drafts, suggest prospective National Historic Landmark property nominees, direct attention to over-looked sites and sources, correct errors big and small, and generally see to it that the information contained within these pages was as accurate and precise as possible. Lisa Anderson, Joseph A. Baker, Gary Shaffer, D. Noël Strattan, Stephen G. Warfel, and Beth Wellman provided vital last-minute inventory data, photo-documentation, and other information.

John N. Drayton, Editor-in-Chief of the University of Oklahoma Press, over-saw the transformation of the original government report into a published book. Associate Editor Sarah Iselin provided crucial assistance through the editing and production phases. The project was particularly well served by the careful and capable copy-editing of Ursula Smith. The maps were produced by William L. Nelson. Patsy Willcox over-saw production of the volume.

Bruce J. Bourque, Robert L. Bradley, Ellen R. Cowie, Leon E. Cranmer, Alaric Faulkner, David B. Guldenzopf, Mary Ellen N. Hodges, Paul R. Huey, Jerome Jacobson, Douglas Knight, Herbert C. Kraft, Kevin A. McBride, Martha W. Mc-Cartney, Francis P. McManamon, Henry M. Miller, James B. Petersen, Patricia E. Rubertone, Patricia Kay Scott, Dean R. Snow, Ralph S. Solecki, E. Randolph Turner III, and Lorraine E. Williams extended assistance by furnishing documentation, reviewing nomination-form drafts, and providing other technical support for nominations of the seventeen National Historic Landmarks designated through this initiative.

Others responding to the many calls for comment and technical assistance made by our office and the state historic preservation office coordinators include Kathleen M. Allen, David W. An-thony, Barbara Applebaum, Michael B. Barber, Alex W. Barker, Carl Barna, Louise Basa, Alan D. Beauregard, Bar-bara H. Bell, Charles A. Bello, Nels Bohn, Marie Bourassa, James W. Bradley, Susan Branstner, Janet G. Brashler, John B. Brown, Hetty Jo Brumbach, Ian C. G. Burrow, Anne-Marie Cantwell, Ronald Carlisle, John A. Cavallo, Scott M. Chapin, Paul B. Cissna, Charles E. Cleland, Dennis Connors, Edward R. Cook, Lauren J. Cook, C. Wesley Cowan, Jay F. Custer, Thomas Cutter, Thomas E. David-son, Mary Davis, Joseph E. Diamond, Anne S. Dowd, Ethel Eaton, Keith T. Egloff, Leonard Eisenberg, William N. Fenton, Charles Fithian, Jonathan Gell, Hugh Gibbs, Virginia Gibbs, Frederic Gleach, Roy Goodman, Jeffrey Graybill, James B. Griffin, Daniel Griffith, Donald A. Grinde, Laurence M. Hauptman, John Haynes, A. Gwynn Henderson, Curtiss Hoffman, Edward J. Johannemann, Eric S. Johnson, Michael Johnson, Kurt Kalb, Albert Klyberg, Robert D. Kuhn, Ed-ward J. Lenik, W. Frederick Limp, Eliz-abeth A. Little, Barbara Luedtke, Nancy O. Lurie, Ronald J. Mason, John McCar-thy, John H. McCashion, Leslie Mead, William P. Miles, Jay Miller, Roger W. Moeller, J. T. Moldenhauer, John Moody, E. Pierre Morenon, L. Daniel Mouer, Stephen Mrozowski, Daniel Murphy, Ed Natay, Antony F. Opperman, Daniel Pa-gano, Elizabeth S. Peña, Lynn Pietak, Ruth Piwonka, John Pratt, Peter P. Pratt, Stuart Reeve, J. Daniel Rogers, Nan A. Rothschild, David Sanger, Sally Sappey, Lorraine P. Saunders, Ellen-Rose Savulis, M. Patricia Schaap, Kent Schneider, Mar-vin T. Smith, William A. Starna, David M. Stothers, John A. Strong, Lynne P. Sul-livan, Joseph Tainter, Len Tantillo, Ronald A. Thomas, Linda Towle, Alden

T. Vaughan, Nina Versaggi, Wilcomb E. Washburn, Laurie Weinstein, and Ronald Wyatt.

As I look at this list of some of the finest minds working in Northeastern archaeology and ethnohistory today, I feel that my role in this project has been more than anything else like that of a conductor of a huge and magnificently talented ensemble. Like all conductors worth their salt, I have struggled to listen attentively to each ensemble member as we have worked to bring out the piece's best qualities. Fully accepting my responsibility for all errors great and small, I hope that you, and they, will lend a patient ear to the piece's occasional discordant notes as you enjoy its more harmonic passages.

ROBERT S. GRUMET

Cultural Resource Planning Branch
Mid-Atlantic Region
National Park Service
Philadelphia

HISTORIC CONTACT

MAP 1: NORTHEASTERN UNITED STATES

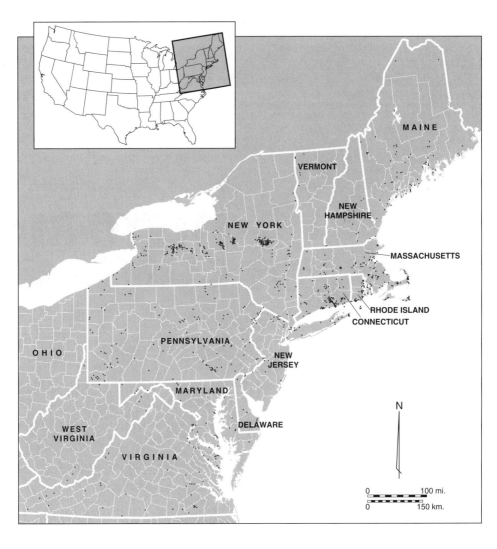

INTRODUCTION

Research for this book was conducted as part of a National Historic Landmark theme study on historic contact in the Northeastern United States; the study was carried out by the Cultural Resource Planning Branch of the Mid-Atlantic Region, National Park Service, United States Department of the Interior, between 1989 and 1993. The study area lies within the region defined as the Northeast in volume 15 of the *Handbook of North American Indians* (Trigger 1978b). Although Canadian data are mentioned, statutory limitations have precluded inclusion of eastern Canada within the study area. Time and resource limitations also prevented inclusion of two other areas (the Great Lakes/Riverine and coastal Carolina regions) defined as parts of the Northeast in volume 15 of the *Handbook*.

Research in the thirteen-state study area (a region largely extending along the eastern slope of the Appalachian Mountains from Maine to Virginia) was completed just as people throughout the world finished observing two major commemorative events associated with contact between Indian people and colonists from Europe and Africa. The first,

the 1992 quincentenary of Columbus's first voyage, marks the 500th anniversary of an event that brought people on both sides of the Atlantic into a world wider than any known by their ancestors. Whether people lionize Columbus as a noble hero or vilify him as a rapacious exploiter, most agree that his voyage symbolizes the resumption of sustained contact between the peoples of the Eastern and Western Hemispheres largely broken off some ten thousand years earlier.

The other observance, the 1993 United Nations International Year of the World's Indigenous People, reminds us of the costs and consequences of contact. Relations between Indians, Europeans, and Africans established in the years following 1492 transformed the lives of people throughout the Atlantic world. Like all new beginnings, such contacts were a mixed blessing. Those regarding the contact as a good thing can find ample reason to celebrate the opening of a wider world. Others look back on the last five centuries as an era marked by oppression, devastation, and exploitation.

However they regard the event, peo-

The National Historic Landmarks Program

Established by the United States Congress under the terms of the Historic Sites Act of 1935 (P. L. 74-292; 49 Stat. 666; 16 U.S.C. 461 et seq.), the National Historic Landmarks Program was given the mission to identify, evaluate, designate, and encourage the preservation of "historic sites, buildings, and objects of national significance for the inspiration and benefit of the people of the United States." The History Division of the National Park Service, which administers this program, primarily uses scholarly surveys known as *theme studies* and other special studies to compile and evaluate extant information on groups of thematically related properties and to provide a contextual framework for evaluating the national significance of these properties.

As stated in the program's regulations (36 CFR Part 65.4), "the quality of national significance is ascribed to districts, sites, buildings, structures, and objects that possess exceptional value or quality in illustrating or interpreting the heritage of the United States in history, architecture, archeology, engineering and culture and that possess a high degree of integrity of location, design, setting, materials, workmanship, feeling and association." Six criteria are used to evaluate the "national significance" of nominated properties:

Criterion 1: That are associated with events that have made a significant contribution to, and are identified with, or that outstandingly represent, the broad national patterns of United States history and from which an understanding and appreciation of those patterns may be gained; or

Criterion 2: That are associated importantly with the lives of persons nationally significant in the history of the United States; or

Criterion 3: That represent some great idea or ideal of the American people; or

Criterion 4: That embody the distinguishing characteristics of an architectural type specimen exceptionally valuable for a study of a period, style, or method of construction, or that represent a significant, distinctive and exceptional entity whose components may lack individual distinction; or

Criterion 5: That are composed of integral parts of the environment not sufficiently significant by reason of historical association or artistic merit to warrant individual recognition but collectively compose an entity of exceptional historical or artistic significance, or outstandingly commemorate or illustrate a way of life or culture; or

Criterion 6: That have yielded or may be likely to yield information of major scientific importance by revealing new cultures, or by shedding light

ple inspired by renewed worldwide interest in the causes and consequences of intercultural relations see both commemorations as an opportunity to take a new look at contact. Perhaps nowhere else have the problems and opportunities of relations between people belonging to vastly different cultural traditions been more extensively documented or more energetically discussed than in the history of the earliest phases of the ongoing encounter between Indian, European, and African people in what is today the Northeastern part of the United States. Reinterpreting old data or discovering new sources, scholars studying intercultural relations in the region are writing for colleagues and a general upon periods of occupation over large areas of the United States. Such sites are those which have yielded, or which may be reasonably expected to yield, data affecting theories, concepts and ideas to a major degree.

Ordinarily cemeteries, birthplaces, graves of historical figures, properties owned by religious institutions or used for religious purposes, structures that have been moved from their original locations, reconstructed historic buildings and properties that have achieved significance within the past 50 years are not eligible for designation.

The National Park System Advisory Board, a committee of scholars and interested citizens appointed by the Secretary of the Interior, applies the criteria and recommends properties for designation; the final decision, however, rests with the Secretary.

Upon designation, National Historic Landmarks are listed in the National Register of Historic Places. Established through the Historic Preservation Act of 1966 (P. L. 89–665; P. L. 96–515; 80 Stat. 915; 16 U.S.C. 470 et seq.), the National Register currently contains 61,000 listings recognizing the local, state, regional, or national significance of more than 90,000 individual cultural resources. Fewer than 2,100 of these properties are National Historic Landmarks.

National Historic Landmark designation not only aids planning by federal, state, and local agencies, tribal govern-

ments, and private organizations, it is also one of the major tools used for scrutinizing areas proposed for inclusion within the National Park System and for nomination to the World Heritage Site listing of internationally significant sites and areas maintained by the United Nations.

The nineteen National Historic Landmarks highlighted in these pages represent properties currently recognized as possessing nationally significant information that illustrates aspects of life in the Northeast during the Historic Contact period. Two of these properties, the Accokeek Creek and Boughton Hill Archeological Sites, were recognized between 1964 and 1976 for their national significance to the Historic Contact theme. The remainder were identified, evaluated, and designated between 1989 and 1993 for values associated with the Historic Contact period. Three of these properties—the Camden and Saint Mary's City Historic Districts and the Old Fort Niagara Historic Site—had earlier been designated for their associations with other themes in American history. The rest are newly designated properties. Collectively, these nineteen National Historic Landmarks represent some of the best-preserved and most extensively documented historic resources illustrating relations between Indians and colonists in the Northeast.

public increasingly interested in the subtle complexities characterizing contact between all people.

The following pages primarily focus upon the ways people initially established and responded to sustained intercultural contact in the Northeast during the sixteenth, seventeenth, and eighteenth centuries. Events described in

this volume involve people of different ethnicities, genders, races, classes, and conditions. However, in the pages that follow we do not focus on such categories and abstractions; emphasis is placed instead on the people themselves and on the events in which they were involved.

This emphasis is expressed most

graphically in the terms chosen for use in this study. The term *country,* for example, is used in preference to more customary usages like "tribal homeland" or "territory" to identify particular regions. This choice underscores the viewpoint adopted in this study regarding geographic areas primarily as places where people belonging to different, diverse, and changing societies and cultures come in contact with one another. Places are thus seen more as arenas of interaction than as locales occupied or invaded by static cultural, social, or political entities.

Terms used to identify individuals and groups in this study also have been chosen with an eye toward emphasizing people's roles as active rather than passive participants in contact events. To bring this point home, personal names are used to identify individuals whenever possible. Individuals acting in particular roles are specifically referred to as diplomats, administrators, or townsfolk; people associated with particular groups or locales are identified as such rather than as anonymous representatives of undifferentiated collectivities. Moreover, plural rather than singular forms (i.e., "Shawnees" or "the Shawnees" instead of "the Shawnee") are used wherever possible both to affirm the collective aspects of identity and to more emphatically situate people as active participants in events.

No satisfactory substitutes for terms like prehistory, protohistory, ethnohistory, history, or historic contact have yet emerged. *Prehistory* (the period in which archaeological materials and, to a lesser extent, oral accounts are the only known evidence) and *protohistory* (the interval between the first archaeolog-

ically or orally documented contacts between natives and newcomers and the initial appearance of written records of such encounters) are not used in this volume. Although specialists continue to use these terms as referents noting the presence or absence of various types of empirical evidence, most other people generally regard them as pejorative expressions suggesting that only literate people have history (Axtell 1989).

This study uses the term *history* in its broadest sense, as the study of the past. Seen in this light, archaeological remains, oral narratives, linguistic documentation, environmental information, architectural structures, ethnographic data, artifacts, and written records all constitute historical evidence.

No adequate term identifying the specific span of years extending from the first documented contacts in the Northeast between people from both hemispheres to the end of the American War for Independence presently exists. "Ethnohistory," a term used by scholars to define studies of Indians and other people producing few or no written records of themselves, most appropriately refers to a method rather than to a period of study. Other terms, like "colonial period" or "age of exploration," all too obviously emphasize only one side of the encounter. Used alone, the term "contact" just as obviously is a generic term delineating relationships between all people. As used in this study, the term *Historic Contact period* represents the least problematic referent, succinctly describing intercultural relations in the region from the sixteenth through the eighteenth century.

Particular meanings also are assigned here to other terms currently subject to wide variations of definition and interpretation. The term *tradition,* for example, is presently most widely used to signify a sense of heritage. In this study the term is used in its specialized archaeological form. Identifying Late Woodland, Monongahela, Ontario Iroquois, and other traditions, the term delineates distinctive groupings of artifact types, features, and settlement patterns within particular areas and time periods. Masculine possessives are used here with comparable specificity—that is, they are used only in reference to males.

Terms like "red," "white," and "black" will appear only in describing colors; they will not be used to classify and thus objectify people. Words like "gardening," "horticulture," "village," and "explorer" also will not be found in these pages. Each of these is increasingly regarded as a part of conquest cant that intentionally or unintentionally minimizes or diminishes the lives and achievements of native people. Less loaded terms like "cultivation," "community," "town," and "traveler," will be used in their place.

As Mary W. Helms (1988) has recently pointed out, people have always been fascinated by travel. Conjuring up images of foreign lands and exotic customs, travel brings people into contact with those defined as "other." Growing awareness of multicultural diversity and increasing interest in recognizing differences that make us all "other" have, in a sense, brought contact home. Linked more closely than ever before within our electronic global village, we realize that we live among "strangers."

Everyone knows about strangers. No matter what they do or how they do

it, strangers are different. Symbolically, strangers embody the uncertainties inherent in all contacts with the unknown or the unfathomable. Regarded with fascination, fear, or indifference, strangers are, by definition, aliens, somehow different from family or friends.

Nevertheless, we need strangers. Allies or adversaries, they furnish what family and friends alone may not provide. Formulating this idea as one of the first great guiding principles in anthropological theory, pioneer ethnologist Edward S. Tylor stated that we must marry out or die out (Tylor 1889). Other basic human institutions, such as trade, diplomacy, and war, also trace their origins to the common human need to deal with strangers. Although different people handle the problem in different ways, all people try to get what they want while avoiding whatever is thought or felt to be dangerous or undesirable.

No matter how much we come to depend upon strangers or how familiar they eventually become, we can never be entirely sure that they think about or feel things in quite the same ways we do. The expression "creative misunderstanding," which conveys the fact that no two people perfectly understand one another, can perhaps be used to characterize relationships between strangers who succeed in meeting each other's expectations, often for entirely different reasons.

Contact with people one can only "creatively misunderstand" almost always arouses strong emotions. Some people deal with their feelings by trying to drive away, dominate, or destroy strangers. Others work to turn strangers into family and friends. Rituals, such as modern international diplomatic protocols or the wampum exchanges used nearly everywhere in the Northeast throughout the Historic Contact period, are meant to lessen tensions somewhat by regulating contacts between strangers in orderly, predictable ways.

But not all people use ritual to formalize foreign relations. Some people try to avoid all contacts, while others, like the central African Mbuti people—who reputedly receive *all* visitors as friends and family—evidently choose to dispense with formalities altogether.

No matter how they are regulated, most contacts between strangers are indirect. In their most extreme form, they can occur as a type of blind barter, in which trade partners never meet one another face-to-face. Most people, however, conduct business with strangers through special intermediaries thought to possess unusual powers or abilities. Specialists skilled in dealing with strangers exist in every society. Called "culture brokers" by anthropologist Eric Wolf (1959), such individuals manage relationships along the boundaries that separate strangers belonging to different cultural, ethnic, or political groups.

Whether contacts occur in face-to-face meetings or as indirect transactions knowingly or unknowingly brokered by intermediaries, all encounters between strangers move ideas, people, and things across cultural divides. The meanings of things and words change as they pass from one person or place to another. Things like shell or glass beads, regarded as mundane utilitarian objects by one people, for example, may be regarded as priceless treasures by others. Studies by Ceci (1982b) contrasting Indian and European use of wampum shell beads and similar studies by Hamell

(1983, 1987) comparing differing views of glass beads exemplify analyses seeking to chart and explain variations in the symbolic significance of particular artifacts to different people.

Acts associated with the process of contact itself are subject to differing interpretations. Transactions regarded as trade by one party, for example, may be regarded as extortion, theft, or worse by another. One person's raid, by extension, can be another's war. Like "prehistory" and other terms discussed earlier, words like "trade," "diplomacy," "war," and "raid" rarely pass easily or unchanged across cultural or personal divides.

Such uncertainties make contact a volatile phenomenon whose causes and consequences are neither predictable nor controllable. Under certain conditions, for example, new ideas, materials, and technologies may revolutionize societies and overturn established orders. Under other conditions, contact seems merely to reaffirm people's most cherished notions of themselves and their place in the world.

Few people in history have come to appreciate the volatility of contact more than the Indians, Europeans, and Africans who met one another in Northeastern North America in the centuries immediately following Columbus's voyage. Rarely have greater numbers of strangers belonging to different cultural traditions tried to live with one another in one place and time. Clinging to established practices or embracing change, people throughout the Northeast struggled to survive, endure, and prosper in the tumultuous era that was symbolically bounded by the first documented contact between Italian navigator Gio-

Historic contact in New Sweden, ca. 1640. This woodcut, complete with palm trees and vignettes of warfare and burial adapted from earlier illustrations from other locales, was produced for Thomas Campanius Holm in 1702 to illustrate an account of New Sweden written by his grandfather during the mid-1640s (Holm 1702). *Courtesy Library Company of Philadelphia.*

vanni da Verrazzano and his crew and Indian people along the mid-Atlantic coast in 1524 and the close of the American War for Independence in 1783. Small wonder, then, that artifacts, documents, orally transmitted texts and narratives, and other evidence of this era continue to fascinate people everywhere up to the present day.

Perhaps as many as 250,000 Algonquian-, Iroquoian-, or Siouian-speaking people, tracing descent from ancestors who first came to the region 10,500 or more years before, were living in the area of the United States bounded today by Maine in the north, Virginia on the south, and the Pennsylvania-Ohio border on the west when western European navigators began sailing to the area with some regularity during the 1500s. Speaking different languages and belonging to distinct social and political groups, all of these people shared a broadly similar way of life known to archaeologists as the Late Woodland Tradition.

People in this cultural tradition used broadly similar types of stone tools, clay pots, and other domestically produced implements and weapons to feed, shelter, and clothe themselves and their families. Many of their tools and techniques had been in use in the Northeast in one form or another for thousands of years. Other developments, such as corn, bean, squash, and tobacco cultivation and new weapons like the bow and arrow, were more recent innovations, probably first introduced into the region when the Late Woodland way of life first emerged in the Northeast about A.D. 900.

Verrazzano was not the first European encountered by Northeastern Late Woodland people. Indian people living in Labrador and Newfoundland first met Norse voyagers about A.D. 1000. Basque, Breton, and Norman sailors were fishing off the Grand Banks of Newfoundland when Giovanni Caboto, an Italian in English employ more widely known as John Cabot, made the first recorded European visit to these latitudes in modern times while searching for a western route to China in 1497.

More sustained contact between Northeastern Indian people and Euro-peans did not start until Spanish, Portuguese, French, Basque, English, and other voyagers began traveling to North Atlantic shores in ever-increasing numbers during the following century. The effects of these encounters ultimately were felt throughout the Northeast and the rest of North America. Like people everywhere, Indian people probably greeted word of contact with everything from profound excitement to complete disinterest. Whatever they thought about the newcomers, neither awareness of the existence of Europeans nor direct or indirect acquisition of their iron, glass, or textile objects resulted in immediate technological transformation or social revolution for native peoples. Although they almost assuredly regarded objects originating in Europe as fascinating, they were rarely fascinated enough to immediately abandon trusted tools and traditions.

Contact was seen as significant enough, however, to cause Indians as well as Europeans to extensively document the process. Indian people generally have regarded the story of initial contact as parable and prelude. Drawing from their own literature, many Indian commentators have recognized and expressed enduring themes of conflict and cooperation in contact-event narratives and often use these narratives to trace the origins of present-day conditions to the earlier events.

Drawing similar conclusions based upon their own cultural experiences, newcomers generally view contact history from either a romantic or a rationalist perspective. People emphasizing the romantic viewpoint traditionally regard the Northeast as a stage where struggles between noble savages and heroic pioneers (e.g., the mythical Chingachgook and Hawkeye) or between real people (e.g., Pocahontas and John Smith) have been played out against a dramatic backdrop of unspoiled natural splendor and international intrigue.

Contrasting European and American romantic and rationalist viewpoints, Bruce G. Trigger (1991a) notes that present-day romantics tend to idealize Indian people as natural ecologists, spiritually superior, and more socially astute than non-Indians. Such people, explaining Europeans' apparent inability to emulate more positive aspects of these societies, portray Indian cultures as uniquely and ineffably different, incomprehensible in any but their own terms.

Rationalists, for their part, have also helped shape our view of contact in the region. Ambitious entrepreneurs like William Penn and hardheaded imperial expansionists like Sir William Johnson regarded the land and its people as exploitable resources providentially placed to provide unlimited opportunities for growth and development. Since earliest colonial times, pamphleteers have flooded newsstands and mailboxes with brochures touting the value of Northeastern real estate. Rationalistic scholars have sought to explain the causes and consequences of contact between natives and newcomers by weighing economic, social, political, and other measurable factors impacting people and land.

The general dimensions of historic contact in the Northeast—mutual discovery, conflict, accommodation, military and political subjugation of Indian people, and their continuing struggle to preserve their various cultural heritages—are well known and extensively documented (Leacock and Lurie 1988; Trigger 1978b; Washburn 1988). Although the complexities of this encounter are widely acknowledged, the contacts between Indians, Europeans, and Africans in the region are at present most commonly regarded as an invasion of one hemisphere by people from the other (Jennings 1975).

Seen from the vantage point of the present day, European contact with the Northeastern Indians certainly can be conceptualized as a devastatingly invasive onslaught mounted on a continental scale. European people first arrived uninvited to the region's shores during the last decades of the fifteenth century. Although several attempts were made to colonize the coast at that time, none succeeded until the following century. Taking advantage of new developments in sail, ship, and gun technology, the latercomers built their largest settlements around Massachusetts Bay, in the Connecticut River Valley, along the lower reaches of the Hudson and Delaware Rivers, and around Chesapeake Bay.

Expanding outward from these centers, the new settlers soon found themselves embroiled in conflicts with native people as both struggled for sovereignty and survival. The initial phase of this struggle ended when rebellious Americans wrested control of the region from Great Britain and began asserting sovereignty over all Indian people living on lands claimed by the new republic. By then, most surviving native people had been dispossessed of all but the poorest of their lands. Denied representation in new American legislatures and forced to accept the unsolicited and frequently meager protections of American law, most Northeastern native people had to acquiesce to the realities of life with the foreigners or move.

In hindsight, the defeat and dispossession of Northeastern Indians by the invaders seem to have been the inevitable outcome of inexorable historical processes. Possessing seemingly superior tools and weapons, and exploiting (often inadvertently, but, on occasion, deliberately) the devastating effects of new epidemic diseases, newcomers settling along the Atlantic seaboard achieved overwhelming numerical superiority over neighboring Indian people by 1700. Eighty-three years later, when the new American republic won its independence from Great Britain, nearly 2.5 million newcomers lived in the region. Slightly less than 1.9 million of them were Europeans. The rest, more than 500,000 men, women, and children, were people of African ancestry (McCusker and Menard 1985). By contrast, Northeastern Indians had dwindled to fewer than 50,000 in number. Thousands of people of mixed parentage, born to unions between Indian people and settlers of European or African descent, became members of existing communities or formed small multicultural enclaves of their own.

A closer look at records produced at the time shows that the outcome of early contacts in the Northeast was neither irrevocable nor inevitable. Colonial documents reveal that people rarely took the future for granted. Although nearly all recorded Indian opinions reflect anger or apprehension, native people confronting military, cultural, and pathogenic invasions evidently continued to hope for the best as they prepared for the worst. The writings of most newcomers generally expressed confidence and assurance, but experience showed even the most optimistic that many of the advantages they perceived were more apparent than real.

Inspired and energized by vigorous political ideologies and strong spiritual beliefs, most settlers looked to their numbers, iron axes and plows, and newly developed guns, sails, and ships to overcome the land and its original inhabitants. But no matter how strong their belief in themselves and their tools, most ultimately had to adjust to prevailing conditions. And although they belonged to societies reckoning populations in the millions, settlers trying to colonize Indian lands neither instantly nor invariably outnumbered native people. Although they had achieved preponderance along a narrow strip of Atlantic coastline by the mid-1600s, they did not enjoy numerical superiority everywhere in the region. People of African origin became majority populations in many locales around Chesapeake Bay during colonial times. Farther west, beyond the Appalachians, native people overwhelmingly outnumbered newcomers until the end of the American War for Independence.

No matter what their numbers, Indian people at the time of first contact possessed their own considerable resources, and nearly every Indian community maintained the ability to feed, clothe, and shelter its members throughout the Historic Contact period. Most, moreover, maintained forms of governance responsive to their wants and needs. Indian leaders skilled in consensual politics struggled to preserve the health and welfare of their people by cannily bargaining with strangers and by playing foreign rivals off against one another.

Many of these leaders were women. Some, like Awashonks, Quaiapan, Weetamoo, and other Coastal Algonquian sunksquaws or "squaw sachems," wielded power directly (Grumet 1980). Others, like the Iroquois women who had the authority to choose or remove sachems, exerted strong influence in community councils (J. K. Brown 1970; Spittal 1990; E. Tooker 1984a).

Civil chiefs schooled in the skills of forest diplomacy—such as the above-mentioned sunksquaws, the Powhatan paramount werowance Wahunsonacock, the Eastern Abenaki chief Madockawando, the Hackensack sachem Oratam, and the noted Onondaga diplomats Daniel Garacontie and Teganissorens—tried to secure advantages for themselves and their people while stemming the tide of colonial expansion. Striving for peace, they continually reminded strangers that their warriors and military leaders could be formidable adversaries in battle. When more peaceable expedients failed, war chiefs like Pontiac and Joseph Brant used weapons and tactics adapted to the conditions of forest combat to war against their enemies.

Like the newcomers, Indian people also drew upon considerable spiritual resources. Most continued to honor the ways of their ancestors during the first centuries of contact (M. R. Harrington 1921; Speck 1931; E. Tooker 1979). Later, prophetic reformers such as the Delaware prophet Neolin and the Seneca prophet Handsome Lake (A. F. C. Wallace 1970), and native missionaries like the Presbyterian Mohegan minister Samson Occom (Blodgett 1935) recast old beliefs or brought promises of new religions to embattled believers.

Even in defeat, with prophets discredited and leaders killed or compromised, many Indian people avoided domination or destruction by moving beyond the limits of colonial settlement. Settling among other Indian people or establishing expatriate communities of their own as far away as northern New England, the Ohio Valley, and the Great Lakes, many exiled native Northeasterners resisted foreign attempts to dominate, destroy, or drive them away during several decades following the American War for Independence.

Unable to anticipate the scope or impact of contact developments, natives and newcomers alike struggled to adapt to changing and uncertain conditions (Kupperman 1980; Morrison 1984). Forced to adjust to the realities of their situation, Indians, Europeans, and Africans continually moved back and forth across cultural divides in the region, carrying with them tools, goods, and ideas that they used in new, different, and unforeseen ways. To this day the stream of ideas, products, and people flows undiminished both ways across the Atlantic Ocean. Whether contact is judged an invasion or a case study in symbiotic relationships, this "Columbian exchange" transformed the world in ways not yet fully understood or appreciated (A. Crosby 1972, 1986).

ESTABLISHING A CONTEXT FOR HISTORIC CONTACT IN THE NORTHEAST

The national significance of the Columbian encounter is well known and widely appreciated. Scholars sifting through masses of written, architectural, ethnographic, and archaeological evidence have studied nearly every aspect of contact. Results of recent research have been particularly productive. But despite these efforts, the overall record of contact in the region remains tantalizingly incomplete. Most physical evidence consists of scattered and often enigmatic archaeological or written materials. Much oral literature remains uncollected or unstudied. Little of the record of contact has survived intact. What has survived often is inadequately surveyed or incompletely analyzed.

These problems are not unique to contact studies. Researchers investigating the past always face formidable obstacles. Archaeologists dedicated to finding and interpreting physical evidence that would connect a locale with known events, for example, continually labor to extract additional information from already known sites while working to find and protect new resources. Ethnohistorians trying to deal with incomplete or inconsistent bodies of documentation work to overcome the limitations of time, space, and theory. To complicate matters further, investigators working in one field often refrain from crossing disciplinary lines. Even when they do, few agree on facts or interpretations.

People trying to understand relations between natives and newcomers in the Northeast face particularly vexing challenges. Investigators working to bridge the cultural gap separating our time from the Historic Contact period rarely agree on matters of chronology, geography, or interpretation. Most are keenly aware that the volatile nature of contact events caused conditions to change considerably, often in unexpected ways.

Scholars, limited by the fragmentary nature of surviving resources and viewing events from different theoretical, cultural, and personal perspectives, have not yet agreed on any single interpretive or organizational scheme. Many investigators, for example, accept the proposition that the end of the American War for Independence marks the close of the earliest phases of the Historic Contact period in most parts of the Northeast. By contrast, there is general disagreement on when or where contact began. Some writers believe that contact between the hemispheres began with ancient arrivals of Celts, Iberians, Africans, and other ancient outlanders traveling to American shores. Others trace contact to the time of the first Norse voyages. Most people agree that the modern Historic Contact period began when Spanish, Portuguese, Basque, French, and English sailors began traveling to the Northeastern coast during the 1490s.

While the exact beginnings of contact remain unclear, the consequences of the Columbian exchange are well known. Contact changed very nearly every aspect of life in the North Atlantic world. Collectively these changes represented only the most recent of a long chain of events that had been transforming life on both sides of the Atlantic since the fourteenth century. These changes did not occur overnight nor did they unfold in orderly, predictable ways. Instead they resulted from complex processes whose impacts were felt differently by people in different places and times.

Not all change, however, was random. Archaeological evidence indicates that Indian life in all but the northernmost reaches of the region began focusing around increasingly large and centralized settlements as Europeans were moving through the Renaissance during the fourteenth and fifteenth centuries. Most of these people began crafting new and distinctive forms of pottery, stone tools, and shell ornaments as they produced more substantial crops of corn, beans, and squash.

Other evidence suggests increased trade, warfare, and migration throughout much of the region as explorers sailing for newly emergent European nations began charting Atlantic shores during the 1500s. Some goods, like the copper or brass discs found at the Port Tobacco ossuary and the Trigg site in Southern Appalachian Highlands Country, represent evidence of long-distance networks extending across entire regions (Waselkov 1989). Archaeologists are developing increasingly more effective stylistic and chemical analyses to trace origins, ranges, and mechanisms of exchange in the Northeast.

Written records chronicling the early decades of the 1600s corroborate archaeological evidence that these and other developments intensified as Europeans established their first permanent footholds on the Atlantic seaboard. Archaeological remains, written documents, and oral literature show that as the seventeenth century wore on, Northeastern Indians who adopted European imports gradually shifted production from stone tools, clay pots, and other aboriginal manufactures to trade commodities such as beaver pelts and wampum shell beads. Importation of European manufactures gradually led to dependence as native people, abandoning ancestral skills, found themselves unwilling or unable to live without foreign goods. Ironically, most Northeast-

ern Indians ultimately became dependent upon imports at the same time that settlers, struggling to reduce their own dependence on home-country markets, freed themselves from direct European political control.

These changes occurred as demographic shifts of unprecedented size and scope transfigured the Atlantic community. The movement of millions of Europeans and Africans to the Northeast was part of a more massive series of voluntary and forced migrations that had begun at about the time of the first transatlantic contacts. Epidemic contagions spread by migrants killed hundreds of thousands of people on both sides of the Atlantic. Bubonic plague from Asia joined with syphilis and other Western Hemisphere diseases to ravage western Europe while Indian people, struck by smallpox, measles, and other new maladies against which they had no natural immunities, sickened and died in unnumbered thousands (A. Crosby 1969; Dobyns 1983; Elting and Starna 1984; McNeill 1976; Ramenofsky 1987; Snow and Lanphear 1988; Spiess and Spiess 1987).

Countless thousands more were killed on both sides of the Atlantic in wars whose ferocity rose as technical, logistic, and tactical developments made violence a more efficient and lethal business. In Europe, struggles such as the Thirty Years' War—which caused the deaths of perhaps two-thirds of the entire German Rhineland population between 1618 and 1648—ravaged entire regions. During the same period, colonists devastated the Pequots of Connecticut and the Powhatans in Virginia, while warriors of the Iroquois confederacy depopulated much of the country surrounding their central New York homeland.

Although nations such as the Iroquois were able to maintain their numbers for a time through wholesale adoption of captives and other means, Indian communities generally could not replace population losses as quickly as could Europeans. More importantly, no Indian community could draw upon the vast number of potential migrants available to the colonizing powers. Colonists settling along the Atlantic coast took advantage of this situation by establishing many of their first communities on recently depopulated Indian lands. Chronicling this process, Francis Jennings (1975) has shown that, while colonists naturally regarded the sparsely inhabited territories they moved to as "virgin land," they actually were settling upon newly desolated "widowed lands."

Wherever they moved, newcomers struggled with Indians and each other for land and what it provided. Mohawk and other Iroquois nations, eager to maintain secure borders and adequate supplies, created buffer zones around their heartlands by driving away or incorporating Indian neighbors. No less concerned with political and economic security, provincial authorities tried to obtain all the territory they could acquire.

Many colonists used force against Indians and each other to seize land. Contending colonial administrators bickered over provincial boundaries and spheres of influence while their home countries fought one another for control of the continent. Indian people ultimately were unable to avoid being embroiled in the wars growing out of these disputes. Some of these conflicts ended in devastating European victories that opened vast tracts of Indian land to colonial settlement. Others, however, produced far less decisive outcomes.

More thoughtful leaders warily weighed costs of war against potential benefits. Then as now, wars were disruptive and expensive. Their outcome was seldom certain or conclusive. Only a few struggles, such as the Pequot and Powhatan defeats, were clear-cut conquests. Most others dragged on interminably. French and English colonists battled one another off and on for more than one hundred years while embittered, dispossessed Indian nations like the Abenakis and the Shawnees waged implacable war against invading settlers. More like feuds than wars, these imperial colonial struggles ended only after Americans imposed centralized authority over most of the region after 1800.

War played an increasingly prominent role in native life throughout the region during the Historic Contact period. Iroquois warfare has attracted particular attention. Surveying extant sources, scholars have attempted to understand the economic (G. Hunt 1940), sociopolitical (Snyderman 1948), and emotional (Richter 1983) motivations impelling Iroquois warriors and their communities to go to war against their neighbors. Growing numbers of scholars also are surveying tactical, technological, and sociological aspects of Indian warfare in New England (Hirsch 1988; Malone 1973, 1991).

People anxious to avoid the costs and uncertainties of armed struggle looked for less disruptive ways to expand their borders and defend what they already had. Most ultimately turned to diplomacy to come to terms with each other.

Negotiations between Indians and colonists often were complicated affairs. Negotiators used highly stylized diplomatic models blending European and Indian rhetorical forms to reach agreements. Skilled forest diplomats, like Teganissorens and William Johnson, held forth at treaty conferences, negotiated covenant agreements, and affixed their names or marks to deeds. Agreements reached at these meetings established or maintained more-or-less stable relationships by settling disputes, formally transferring land rights, and defining borders, rights, and obligations of treaty signatories.

Colonists began to use deeds to legitimate acquisition of Indian lands as early as the 1620s. Although Indian people did not believe in individual land ownership, all recognized corporate land and resource rights. Such rights generally were transferred peaceably in ritualized negotiations or were seized forcibly in often no less ritually organized military encounters. Unlike Indians, who used wampum and other mnemonic devices to jog memories of past agreements, colonists employed written deeds to record title transfers.

Colonial authorities used deeds as a vehicle to extend sovereignty as well as ownership (Jennings 1975; Springer 1986). Like earlier unwritten agreements, deed negotiations between natives and newcomers were ritualized transactions. More than a few guaranteed continued Indian rights to lands and resources within purchased tracts. When used in this way, Indian deeds served as a form of treaty as well as a type of title transfer.

No matter how deeds worked, few colonists found Indian people eager to sign papers surrendering their birthrights. Although few Indians probably appreciated the full consequences of the first sales, they soon established creative misunderstandings with colonists interested in acquiring their lands. Even after establishing this relationship, most Indians initially refused to sell all but the smallest portions of ancestral domains. Even fewer were willing to move among strangers after running out of land to sell.

In the end, however, all Indians were forced to acknowledge that they could not stop settlers from taking their territory. Unwilling to capitulate outright to European demands, most gradually accepted the political realities of their situation by doing their best to slow rates of land loss. Records of thousands of Indian deeds in archival repositories throughout the Northeast show that many succeeded in buying time by selling as little land as possible while extracting the maximum number of concessions from purchasers (Baker 1989; Grumet 1979; Springer 1986).

Ultimately, even such stratagems failed. By the time the new United States took its place among the world's nations in 1783, newcomers had used deeds to extend sovereignty over most of the Indian lands within modern state boundaries east of the Appalachians. Like other dispossessed peoples, Indians forced to part with their lands had to remain on small reservations or missions, establish homes on land owned by other people, settle on vacant or unwanted territory, or move elsewhere.

Once land was obtained, speculators, powerful proprietary lords, and government administrators competed for the labor of settlers, servants, and slaves to make it productive. New landowners from Maine to Virginia used African

American, Indian, and European slaves; indentured servants; and hired laborers to clear brush from former Indian fields, cut down forests, and plant crops. Laborers also worked to dig mines and canals, build mills and roads, and erect townsites. New roads and old waterways were used to link newly emerging colonial communities throughout the region. Many aspects of these and other economic developments have been extensively examined (e.g., Land, Carr, and Papenfuse 1977; McCusker and Menard 1985; J. M. Smith 1959). Not surprisingly, much of this documentation has focused upon colonists and their activities. (See Cronon 1983 for a particularly useful bibliographic survey of sources for the North and Middle Atlantic regions.)

Recent studies of the period no longer concentrate solely on the settlers. Among the landmark events that have generated intensifying waves of interest in Indian heritage are the enactment of the 1934 Indian Reorganization Act, the creation of the Indian Claims Commission in 1946, the Indian Power and ecology movements in the 1960s, the passing of the National Historic Preservation Act of 1966, and the more recently enacted Archaeological Resource Protection and Native American Graves Protection and Repatriation Acts. In the Northeast the focus of contact studies has gradually shifted. Writers of early American history traditionally portrayed Indian people as bit players in the colonial drama. No longer satisfied with that view, growing numbers of people are laboring to construct a different picture of events.

Inspired by the work of anthropologists William N. Fenton (Fenton 1940,

1948, 1951a, 1957), Eleanor Burke Leacock (Leacock 1954; Leacock and Lurie 1988), Nancy O. Lurie (Lurie 1959; Leacock and Lurie 1988), historian Robert Berkhofer (Berkhofer 1973), and other proponents of what is today called the New Indian History, increasing numbers of investigators are undertaking ethnohistorical studies that creatively synthesize the disciplines of anthropology and history. The more influential of these studies are moving Indians from the periphery of contact to center stage. See, for example, Trigger's (1985) reconsideration of early Canadian Heroic Age history before 1663 and Francis Jennings's (1975) and Neal Salisbury's (1982a) pathbreaking ethnohistorical reevaluations of intercultural relations in early New England. By depicting Indians as active participants in contact rather than passive victims inexorably caught in irresistible historical processes, these and similar studies are transforming our views of the American past.

Archaeologists, of course, have been studying the material remains of the Indian side of historic contact for more than a century. Although written records and oral literature provide otherwise unobtainable contextual information, archaeology provides tangible physical evidence available nowhere else (Lowenthal 1985). Textual data tend to represent or reflect views or interests of particular individuals or groups. Although graves and other deposits frequently reflect people's intentions as well as ideals, most archaeological deposits tend to represent actual conditions at various times of occupation and abandonment.

Forces of decomposition and dissolution at work in most archaeological sites rarely respect human wishes or honor human intentions. As a result, archaeological deposits rarely precisely mirror social realities. Redistribution systems extensively chronicled throughout the Northeast, for example, generally make it difficult to equate the relative quality and quantity of deposits with social status or role. Inadvertent abandonment; the desire to provide for spiritual contingencies, reuse, and ritual or functional disposal of goods or other materials; and other archaeological-site-formation processes also affect what is preserved (Schiffer 1987).

Archaeological deposits nevertheless generally tend to represent all site occupants or users rather than an articulate or favored few. As such, the archaeological record can often present more inclusive, physically verifiable views of events than those chronicled in oral or written literature.

Excited by the possibilities offered by the study of such deposits, investigators inspired by the New Archaeology of the 1960s turned their attention from descriptive culture histories to formulation of testable scientific hypotheses capable of revealing and explaining cultural phenomena (Redman 1991). Today nearly all archaeologists continue to employ the explicitly scientific, problem-oriented approaches advocated by New Archaeologists.

Postmodernist contextual archaeologists are building on the New Archaeology. Representing the recent wave of revisionism, they deconstruct the work of their predecessors by stressing symbols, political orientation, gender, and other less tangible phenomena downplayed or ignored by their more materialist forebears. Unlike the New Ar-

chaeologists, postmodern contextualists self-consciously stress the social, political, and economic contexts of all intellectual projects. They also increasingly employ critical archaeological frameworks to focus attention on women, Indians, African Americans, impoverished immigrants, and other people regarded as "disenfranchised, destroyed, encompassed, colonized, or silenced in some way" (Leone and Potter 1988). In the Northeast, archaeologists concerned with elucidating processes of domination and hegemony are reexamining what some call Indian burial programs and other unrecognized or undervalued sources of evidence for Indian resistance to foreign intrusion (Gould and Rubertone 1991; Rubertone 1990).

No matter whom they study or how they interpret their findings, an increasing number of scholars interested in contact are adopting interdisciplinary perspectives. They are using a wide range of evidence to show how Indian people struggled to maintain time-tested ways of life as they found themselves progressively enmeshed in the emerging world-system (Wallerstein 1974; Wolf 1982).

Much of this research is documenting Indian involvement in the region's growing cash economy as hunters, traders, guides, soldiers, herbalists, laborers, servants, millworkers, whalers, and artisans. Other studies are showing how Indian people produced wampum and other aboriginal manufactures for new commercial markets or peddled homemade splint baskets, straw brooms, beadwork, and other handicrafts modeled after European prototypes to settlers and each other.

Many writers have documented the

Conjectural reconstruction of Indians selling handicrafts in Brooklyn, ca. 1720. Pen-and-ink illustration by William Sauts Netamuxwe Bock, 1985. *Courtesy Brooklyn Historical Society.*

trapping and fishing Indians did for newcomers. Most ethnohistorians emphasize the exploitative aspects of these activities. Nearly all call attention to their many deleterious impacts upon native provisioners. Most archaeological evidence relating to these activities is preserved in the forms of metal traps, fish hooks, gunflints, musket balls, gun parts, and other fishing and trapping gear. Although the circumstances of their use or deposition generally are unclear, new research may provide insights into the causes and consequences of Indian employment as trappers and fishers.

Several studies detail Indian involvement in the colonial whaling industry. Numerous references to Indian whaling are found in colonial records. Ethnohistorian Elizabeth A. Little (1981b,

1988a), for example, has located and analyzed especially detailed archival sources documenting eighteenth-century Nantucket Indian whaling. By studying Indian and European account books, she has shown that rather than being "indebted servants obliged to return their earnings to their masters," Indians often were successful whalers earning "up to four times the annual wages of a Boston seaman" (Little 1988a). Other written sources document Indian whaling at Nantucket and other places. An extensive body of Indian oral literature further commemorates the lives and exploits of Indian whalers. Collectively, these sources describe the full range of Indian participation in onshore and blue-ocean whaling ventures.

Relatively few sources focus on Indian

participation in the region's offshore fishing fleets, shipbuilding industry, or privateering enterprises (F. Harrington 1985; Vickers 1983). Extant documentation chronicles notable events, like the assemblage and destruction or recapture of Abenaki fleets consisting of numbers of shallops, sloops, whaleboats, and ketches seized from English sailors in Maine during King Philip's War in 1676 and Dummer's War between 1722 and 1727.

Evidence of more-everyday maritime activities in the form of fish bones and scales, hooks, netsinkers, and ship's furnishings have been found at many locales along the Atlantic coast. Whalebone, baleen, bone or metal harpoons, and other artifacts associated with whaling also occur in archaeological deposits.

Existing records show that not all Indian labor was free. Indian people falling into debt often were forced into indentured servitude. Others apprenticed themselves or were apprenticed to colonial masters. Both natives and newcomers often enslaved prisoners (Kawashima 1986, 1988b; Lauber 1913; Starna and Watkins 1991).

African captives represented the overwhelming majority of people enslaved and forced to work in the Northeast. Sold into slavery throughout the Atlantic seaboard, they became majorities around Chesapeake Bay and other places farther south. By 1783 more than 500,000 people of African-American descent lived in the region in slavery and freedom. Long ignored by all but a few scholars, African-American history finally drew the attention of investigators inspired by the Civil Rights and Black Power movements during the 1960s. Al-

though many studies since have described African-American contributions to American history, comparatively few have examined relations between African Americans and Indians.

Gary B. Nash's *Red, White, and Black* (1982) continues to be one of the best general overviews of the subject. Other surveys have been written by Craven (1971), Ferguson (1992), and Forbes (1988). Aspects of intermarriage, legal status, and labor in New England have been addressed (Greene 1942; Kawashima 1986; Piersen 1988; Woodson 1920).

Reports on archaeological investigations of sites associated with contact between African-American and Indian people, such as Kenneth Feder's excavations at the multiethnic Lighthouse community (Feder 1993), are only now beginning to appear in print. Written records document the existence of several communities like Lighthouse in various places throughout the Northeast. Although archaeologists have conducted excavations at many of these locales, few have found evidence dating to Historic Contact times. Most, instead, have found deposits associated with later nineteenth- and twentieth-century occupations.

Perhaps the most striking finding to emerge from recent studies is the growing awareness that the circumstances of contact compelled native people and newcomers to deal with one another as members of sovereign independent nations. On the face of it, this would seem to be obvious. To Indian people long accustomed to coping with strangers, Europeans and Africans must have seemed to be simply other foreigners. Colonial administrators in Europe, for their part, formally refused to recognize the legitimacy of Indian governments. Colonists living among Indian people and dependent upon them for success or survival, on the other hand, frequently adopted a more pragmatic attitude. Acknowledging the realities of contact, provincial authorities in the colonies often dealt with powerful native nations as sovereign states while denying that they were doing so.

Much scholarship reflects the European tendency to regard native people as passive reactors to dominant or domineering European invaders. That this is so should not be surprising; the cant of colonial conquest invariably characterizes Indians as subservient peoples. Actual relations between Indians and settlers in the Northeast were far more subtle and complex. Most Coastal Algonquian groups forced to submit to colonial authority by 1700, for example, found ways around colonists intent upon dominating their lives. People from unconquered communities, such as those Iroquois belonging to the Anglo-Indian Covenant Chain alliance that linked the Five (later Six) Nations and their Indian clients with New York and nearby British colonies, vigorously pursued their own interests as independent and autonomous nations while perfunctorily pledging fealty to foreign sovereigns thousands of miles away. Just as Europeans treated Indian polities as sovereign powers while denying they were doing so, many Indian people who otherwise refused to recognize the validity of the commoditization of land and labor in their cultural frameworks repeatedly sold land and worked in the colonial wage economy.

Many Indian people remaining in the Northeast after 1783 continued to conduct relations with the new American government as sovereign powers. Federal authorities acceded to this state of affairs by according constitutionally guaranteed special status to federally acknowledged Indian tribes. Today the federal government maintains a government-to-government relationship with several hundred Indian tribes. Although the form and tenor of this relationship has changed since the young American nation began to assert exclusive jurisdiction over Indian lands, people, and property, its constitutional basis has remained unchanged over the course of the past two hundred years.

The following pages survey much of the known written and physical record documenting the earliest phases of this relationship. As mentioned earlier, historic contact was only one expression of a larger process that neither began in the region nor ended with the close of the colonial era. The earliest verifiable contacts between Indian people, Europeans, and Africans within the territorial limits of the United States during modern times occurred farther south or north of the region. Although it has changed considerably in its particulars, contact continues between Indian and other American people to the present day.

Contact experiences vary in relation to changing times, places, and circumstances. Despite this fact, all people experience contact in broadly similar ways. Scholars like Edward H. Spicer (1961), Eleanor Burke Leacock and Nancy Oestreich Lurie (1988), and Edward M. Larrabee (1976) have developed systematic frameworks to organize and explain regularities and differences observed in

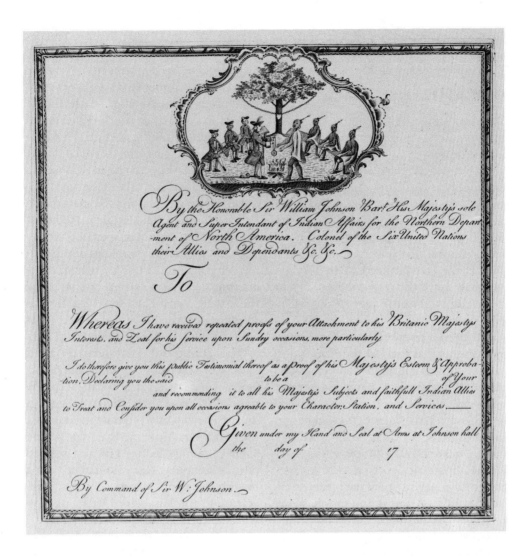

By the Honorable Sir William Johnson Bart His Majesty's sole Agent and Super Intendant of Indian Affairs for the Northern Department of North America. Colonel of the Six United Nations their Allies and Dependants &c. &c.

To

Whereas I have received repeated proofs of your Attachment to his Britanic Majesty's Interests, and Zeal for his Service upon Sundry occasions, more particularly

I do therefore give you this public Testimonial thereof as a Proof of his Majesty's Esteem & Approbation. Declaring you the said   to be a   of Your   and recommending it to all his Majesty's Subjects and faithfull Indian Allies to Treat and Consider you upon all occasions agreable to your Character, Station, and Services ____

Given under my Hand and Seal at Arms at Johnson hall the   day of   '7

By Command of Sir W. Johnson

1770 engraving based on a drawing by Henry Dawkins showing a medal presentation at a treaty ceremony beneath a Great Tree of Peace that commemorated the Covenant Chain of Friendship linking the Iroquois and their allies with the British. Sir William Johnson, British superintendent of Indian affairs for the Northern Department, presented certificates embellished with this engraving when giving medals to Covenant Chain Indian allies. *Courtesy John Carter Brown Library at Brown University.*

records of contact relations. Mark Leone and Parker Potter (1988), Patricia Rubertone (1990), and others are looking into the ramifications of meaning, trade, adaptation, gender, ethnicity, inequality, and other less tangible aspects of contact. These and all other interpretive frameworks continue to be the subjects of intense scholarly discussion and debate. Consequently, an eclectic approach drawing upon a variety of theoretical and methodological considerations guides what follows.

ORGANIZING SPACE

Although most writers agree in principle that a Northeastern region exists, few agree on its boundaries. Even fewer, moreover, classify its constituent geographic, historical, and cultural components in quite the same way. To minimize confusion, this study adopts the generally accepted geographic boundaries, cultural divisions, and ethnic nomenclature standardized in the *Northeast* volume of the *Handbook of North American Indians* (Trigger 1978b) whenever possible.

But even a framework as supple and inclusive as that used in the *Handbook* cannot answer all needs. For example, although its general parameters have been adopted, aspects of its regional organization have been reworked herein to reflect recent advances in knowledge. Unlike the *Handbook,* which uses ethnic, linguistic, and cultural categories to organize regional data, this document uses an organization emphasizing relationships between different people in particular times and places.

This volume also does not fully adopt the *Handbook*'s Coastal Region boundaries. As defined in the *Handbook,* the Coastal Region encompasses the single largest collection of documented locales associated with the Historic Contact period anywhere in North America. Far too massive and diverse to be effectively treated as a single area, the region has been divided in this document into two regions. The more northerly of these regions takes its name and, in large part, its boundaries from the National Park Service's North Atlantic Region. This region includes culturally, linguistically, and historically related groups from New England and the upper Hudson River valley.

Information associated with Indian people living farther south is presented in the Middle Atlantic section. This area includes the historic homelands of Munsee, Delaware, Nanticoke, Piscataway, Powhatan, and other Eastern Algonquian–speaking people; Siouian-speaking people from the Virginian Piedmont Country; the Iroquoian-speaking Nottoway and Meherrin people of southeastern Virginia; and the Susquehannocks, another Iroquoian group living along the Atlantic seaboard but classified as residents of the Saint Lawrence Lowlands in the *Handbook* (Trigger 1978b).

The *Handbook* classifies the Saint Lawrence Lowlands Region as the homeland of Northern Iroquoian–speaking people and their Algonquian neighbors on the north. Only the northernmost of these Iroquoian people lived within the Saint Lawrence Valley. The rest resided near Algonquian- or Siouian-speaking neighbors along rivers flowing westward into the Mississippi Valley or eastward toward Atlantic shores.

To complicate matters further, people from other places later moved into this region. Although most agreed to submit to some form of Iroquois authority prior to their move, few spoke Iroquoian languages. In light of this information, the area is termed the Trans-Appalachian Region in this study.

Like all boundaries, those used in this book reflect a series of compromises. Every effort has been made to accommodate the wide variety of opinions and viewpoints expressed by scholars, avocationalists, and cultural resource managers in the region. Because these views are constantly changing, the boundaries used here should be viewed as provisional constructs. Borders shift with time, changing political fortunes and customs, and differing perceptions. As anthropologist Jack Campisi (1974) has shown among the Oneidas, social, religious, and political boundaries frequently are neither universally shared nor fully accepted by a community or its neighbors.

People belonging to the Iroquois confederacy, for example, generally stressed political boundaries between themselves and others. Recent scholarship has shown that the force and form of these boundaries shifted over time. European documents corroborate more recent oral literature affirming that individual Iroquois nations, communities, and political factions often acted independently. Many formed temporary coalitions with particular Iroquois communities. Others formed close relationships with non-Iroquois people.

Archaeological evidence may reflect these patterns of shifting alliances. Similar incised pottery motifs used by Mohawk people and their more easterly Algonquian-speaking neighbors, for example, may physically document archivally recorded Mohawk tendencies to pursue their own interests in relations with Indians and Europeans along the Hudson River Valley.

Extant evidence sometimes obscures boundaries. Most eighteenth-century Iroquois site assemblages containing large amounts of European imports, for instance, are very nearly indistinguishable from those left by non-Iroquois Indians or settlers. Networks connecting families, friends, and strangers from differ-

ent communities, moreover, frequently blur boundary distinctions. Travel, migration, and population dislocation caused by changing economic patterns, warfare, land loss, and other factors also affect depositional and symbolic expressions of group identities and sociopolitical boundaries.

Such conditions affected all people living in the region. Established by charter or decree in Europe, many colonial provincial boundaries were based upon incomplete or inaccurate knowledge of the region's geography. Other documents, such as Virginia, Massachusetts, and Connecticut charters granting extravagant domains stretching from sea to sea, reflected unrealistic expectations.

Settlers frequently embroiled Indian people in their boundary disputes. Most provincial authorities tried to secure land claims by relentlessly working to bend Indian people to their wills. Some Indians gave in to these pressures and became clients or wards of particular colonies. Others resisted or moved elsewhere. Virtually all Northeastern Indian people choosing to remain in the region were forced to place their lands and lives under some degree of foreign control by 1783. Even so, Indian boundary concepts almost never entirely conformed to those held by colonists. Working to exploit boundary disputes whenever possible in order to protect their own interests, Indian people often cultivated alliances with different and sometimes mutually hostile natives and newcomers.

Many Indian people, such as the Iroquois and their Algonquian clients, closely aligned themselves with particular European nations, provincial governments, or interest groups. People living in the northernmost Munsee communities, for example, closely affiliated themselves with New Yorkers claiming sovereignty over their lands. Farther south, other Munsee people formed alliances with the New Jersey and Pennsylvania governments. Reflecting this state of affairs, New Jersey colonists often referred to their clients as "Jersey Indians" while Munsee people living on the north came to be called "New York Indians."

Most northerly Munsee people forced from their homelands gradually joined Mahican and New England Indian communities in exile during the middle years of the eighteenth century. Those living farther south generally affiliated themselves with the Delawares. Today, most people tracing Munsee and Delaware descent live in exile in Ontario, Wisconsin, Kansas, and Oklahoma.

Decades of separation have taken their toll on these people. Although most Munsees and Delawares recognize their common origins, few presently regard themselves as a single nation. While most descendants of New York Indians generally acknowledge their Munsee ancestry, most people tracing descent to the more southerly branches of their family tree regard themselves as Delawares.

Temporal and spatial distance does not always sunder tribal ties. Mohawk people living in New York and Quebec, for example, are citizens of different nations. Despite this fact, most Mohawks continue to regard themselves as a single people.

These are only a few of the many examples illustrating the extraordinary range of territorial diversity expressed by the native inhabitants of this region. Collectively they present an almost kaleidoscopic network of divergent borders, changing political forms, and shifting alliances. To best reflect this complexity, this volume employs a geographic framework emphasizing dynamic relations between different people in particular areas rather than the more static if more widely used approach that classifies according to ethnic or political boundaries.

ORGANIZING TIME
TYPES OF TIME

"Time," as the saying goes, "is what keeps everything from happening at once." Concepts of time, and chronologies based on such ideas, vary from culture to culture (Whitrow 1988). Some people believe that history is an orderly and inevitable process. Others, envisioning the universe as an arbitrary, disorderly place, think of history as a series of random and unique events.

Whatever their philosophy of history, all people recognize cyclic and linear aspects of time (Eliade 1959). Cyclic time expresses repetitive, unchanging rhythms such as the passing of seasons or the timing of religious festivals. Linear time, on the other hand, associates specific dates with particular points of time occurring on linear continua.

Every society mixes cyclic and linear time. No two, however, combine them in quite the same way. Societies honoring the ways of ancestors (e.g., Northeastern Indians during the Historic Contact period) tend to emphasize cyclic aspects of time. Industrial states requiring careful coordination of vast, disparate populations and systems (e.g., modern American society) generally organize time in more linear ways.

Different types of historic records

reflect different concepts of time. Some orally transmitted texts, such as sagas and epics, may order events within linear continua. Most oral literature, however, stresses cyclic aspects of time. Written records, for their part, can emphasize either or both types of time. People writing memoirs and other accounts meant to provide object lessons or moral guidance often recount and interpret events cyclically. Other writers, in setting down journal entries, court proceedings, or treaty minutes, almost exclusively express themselves in linear time. No matter how carefully writers work to anchor dated events firmly to specific points of time, few can prevent speculation, interpretation, and other nonlinear inferences from creeping into the record.

Archaeologists, by contrast, have traditionally tended to regard their data as moments frozen in time. Although inferences stressing such cyclic notions as normative laws or evolutionary development can be derived from archaeological remains, most archaeologists conceptualize deposits as evidence of discrete dated events.

People tend to organize time in ways reflecting the temporal emphases of their subject matter. Keepers and students of oral literature, for example, generally emphasize cyclic aspects of history. Historians using written documents, like ethnologists analyzing field data, tend to mix aspects of linear and cyclic time. Archaeologists emphasizing the linear nature of time, for their part, regard chronological ordering of discrete events as the necessary first step for all analysis.

Scholars view linear time in two ways. Absolute dates express time in specific units of measurement—days, weeks, or years—within a chronological framework anchored to a fixed point in time. Relative dates, in contrast, express time in free-floating temporal markers—"older," for instance, or "younger."

Relative dating sequences require radiocarbon or other absolute dates to anchor them in linear chronological frameworks. Investigators studying historic contact in the Northeast use a wide range of absolute and relative dating techniques. Excellent descriptions of many of these techniques may be found in current anthropology and archaeology textbooks (Haviland 1988; D. Thomas 1989). Although radiocarbon assays and document-verified terminus post quem (TPQ) that establish initial appearances of artifact types continue to be the most widely used of these techniques, new advances in tree-ring dating techniques hold much promise for future use in the region (Stahle and Wolfman 1985).

Chronologies and other temporal information presented here stress linear aspects of time. Although materials contained in this book may illuminate events in other times and places, particular data and findings developed here directly bear upon events and properties dating to the first three centuries of contact during the modern era in the Northeast. This period began to the north of the United States with the first known voyages of modern Europeans to Newfoundland and the Gulf of Saint Lawrence undertaken during the last decade of the 1400s. Commencing in the United States about the time of the first documented contacts between Indian people and the crew of Giovanni da Verrazzano's ship in 1524, the period ended in most areas of the region by

1783 when the newly independent United States began restructuring relationships with Indian people.

COMPETING CHRONOLOGIES

Most scholars agree that the Historic Contact period in the Northeast spans the years between the first encounters of natives and newcomers during the early 1500s and the final subjugation or expulsion of most of the region's native people by the end of the American War for Independence. At the time of this writing, eight states within the National Park Service's Mid-Atlantic external program service region have developed frameworks placing the Historic Contact period within chronological continua. These states and their Historic Contact period frameworks are

Delaware	1500–present (Custer 1986a)	
Massachusetts	1500–1775 (Bradley 1984)	
New Jersey	1500–1800 (L. Williams and Kardas 1982)	
Ohio	1600–1750 (Brose 1985)	
Pennsylvania	1600–present (Raber 1985)	
Vermont	1607–1767 (A. Dowd 1990)	
Virginia	1607–1750 (VDHR 1991)	
West Virginia	1050–1690 (Graybill 1986)	

As with other aspects of contact, these frameworks reflect the already noted fact that few regional specialists exactly agree on chronological specifics. Despite their differences, most would support the idea that historic contact neither began nor ended at the same time everywhere in the region. In the North Atlantic and Middle Atlantic regions, for example, most scholars think that contact began during the first decades of the sixteenth century. Farther west in Trans-Appalachia, most scholars believe that the earliest phases of contact began and ended somewhat later. No matter when it began, most scholars would agree that

contact affected different communities in different ways at different times.

These complexities make it difficult to clearly define broad patterns of contact, identify causes and consequences of culture change and stability, or organize time into discrete phases or periods. Patterns of local and regional culture change and continuity are complex. Many are incompletely documented. Available documentary, oral, and archaeological information often is fragmentary, contradictory, or inconsistent. As a result, existing chronological frameworks continue to exhibit wide ranges of variation. Oral and documentary evidence indicates that people belonging to Indian communities also used frameworks of their own to organize and understand contact events. Most of the scanty evidence recorded by scholars emphasizes cyclic aspects of time.

The Iroquois League historical framework recorded by William Fenton (1988) is one of the few Indian chronologies organizing time along more linear lines. Noting that many "Iroquois annalists periodize their culture history by the achievements of prophets," Fenton writes that the earliest phase of Iroquois history is associated with the culture hero Sapling, known as He Who Grasps the Sky, or Sky Grasper. The period of the confederacy is marked by the advent of its founder, Deganawidah. More recent history is known as the time following the resynthesis of the Longhouse religion by the Seneca prophet Handsome Lake during the late 1700s and early 1800s.

Most tribal and regional chronological frameworks used by scholars have been developed by archaeologists or ethnohistorians. Archaeologist James W.

Bradley (1984), for example, divides the Historic Contact era in Massachusetts into three periods:

Contact Period	1500-1630
Plantation Period	1630-1675
Colonial Period	1675-1775

Other scholars, having access to more complete bodies of data, often construct more tightly defined chronologies. Archaeologist Barry C. Kent (1984), for example, has formulated the following ten-stage framework based on cultural history to organize information drawn from such excavated historic lower Susquehanna Valley Susquehannock towns as the Schultz, Strickler, and Byrd Leibhart sites:

Same roots as the Iroquois	–1450
Proto-Susquehannock	1450-1525
Early Schultz and migration	1525-1575
Schultz	1575-1600
Washington Boro	1600-1625
Transitional: Billmyer and Roberts	1625-1645
Strickler	1645-1665
Leibhart: defeat and turmoil	1665-1680
The void (no known information)	1680-1690
Conestoga and other Indians	1690-1763

Many scholars rely primarily on documentary sources. Fenton (1988), for example, used written materials to organize the culture history of the Iroquois League of Five (later Six) Nations into the following five stages:

Formation of the League	ca. 1450-1600
Impact of Colonial Civilization	17th century
Forest Diplomacy	1701-1776
American Revolution	1774-1783
Reservation Period	1784-1967

Working with similar records, anthropologist Theodore J. C. Brasser (1988) has developed the following Coastal Algonquian Historic Contact period chronology:

First Contact (traders phase)	ca. 1550-1700
Shrinking of a World (settlers phase)	ca. 1620-1700
Behind the Frontier (integrative phase)	ca. 1650-1800

These frameworks closely reflect developments associated with particular areas or cultures. Interested in developing more comprehensive regional chronologies necessary for broader comparative analyses, Leacock and Lurie (1988) combined Coastal Algonquian and Iroquoian chronologies with others to produce the following temporal thematic arrangement:

Phase I Late Precontact
      Coastal Algonquian, 1500-1524
      Iroquois, 1500-1535
Phase II Early Contact
      Coastal Algonquian, 1524-1740
      Iroquois, 1535-1740
Phase III Competition and Conflict
      Coastal Algonquian, 1637-1740
      Iroquois, 1740-1800
Phase IV Administrative Stabilization
      Coastal Algonquian,
      1740-present
      Iroquois, 1800-present

These are only a few of the many documented chronologies constructed for the Historic Contact period in the region. Their range and diversity are as much a function of the social and cultural complexity of the period as they are a reflection of divergent methods, conflicting theoretical orientations, and diverse and often contradictory source materials.

Investigators interested in understanding the complexities of culture change and continuity among the Northeastern Indians face challenges similar to those confronted by archaeologists compelled to deal with highly complex or ambiguously delineated strata. Both

Detail of the Nova Belgii map. *Courtesy Geographical Society of Philadelphia.*

frequently solve such problems by excavating data at arbitrary levels. Just as archaeologists often try to dig in particular increments, data presented in this document are organized into 100-year chronological strata. Each stratum generally reflects regional chronological developments. Tighter temporal controls are employed whenever possible.

Extant archaeological, documentary, oral, and other material dealing with relations between Indians and colonists in the North Atlantic, Middle Atlantic, and Trans-Appalachian Regions is reviewed in the following pages. All inventoried archaeological sites and standing structures are listed and mapped. Nearly eight hundred places containing resources associated with the Historic Contact period in the Northeast have been identified during project development. The overwhelming majority of these are archaeological sites or districts. Seven hundred and forty of these properties represent locales where In-

dian people lived, worked, or worshipped. The rest are colonial forts, trading posts, or other places figuring prominently in relations with Indian people. This inventory represents only a fraction of the total number of properties capable of documenting historic contact in the region.

Cartographic studies, such as Helen Tanner's *Atlas of Great Lakes Indian History* (Tanner 1987), Campbell's (1965) study of the Jansson-Visscher maps of New England (more widely known as the van der Donck or Nova Belgii maps), McCary and Barka's (1977) analysis of Virginian Indian settlement locations on the John Smith and Zuñiga maps, and Barry Kent, Janet Rice, and Kakuko Ota's (1981) survey, *A Map of 18th Century Indian Towns in Pennsylvania,* show that Europeans documented thousands of Indian communities during early stages of historic contact in the region. Locations of thousands of others are uninventoried or unrecorded. Archaeologists believe that more than a few sites, both chronicled and unchronicled, remain to be found. Although this may be the case, large numbers almost surely have disappeared.

ASSESSING PREVIOUS RESEARCH

Archaeological, archival, and other materials summarized in this volume show that a vast corpus of data documents contact relations between natives and newcomers in the Northeast. Archaeological evidence of contact has been found in nearly every area of the region. Indian accounts of the coming of foreigners to their lands have remained staples of native oral literature (Axtell 1989; Simmons 1986). Native Northeastern material culture has fascinated Americans ever since European travelers first met Indian people. Written accounts of Indian appearance, tools, foods, social life, and other aspects of native life were the stuff of American literature long before James Fenimore Cooper (1826) popularized the romantic image of the Woodlands Indian in his novel *The Last of the Mohicans*.

THE WRITTEN RECORD

As mentioned earlier, Italian navigator Giovanni da Verrazzano (1970) wrote the first known account documenting direct contact with Indian people in the region. Verrazzano and other early voyagers were followed by colonial entrepreneurs whose promotional advertisements describing the virtues of newly founded colonies often included descriptions of the Indians of the country. The more observant of these, like Samuel de Champlain (1922–1938), Marc Lescarbot (1907–1914), William Penn

(1912), Roger Williams (1973), and William Wood (1977), wrote accounts that remain essential for an understanding of Indian culture and customs during the earliest phases of historic contact.

Military men, like Virginia's John Smith (1624, Barbour 1986) and New England's John Mason (1736), also wrote accounts of their exploits in wars against Indian people. Politicians and statesmen, like New York's Cadwallader Colden (1747), Pennsylvania's Benjamin Franklin (1764), and Virginia's Robert Beverley (1947), expanded on these and other sources as they wrote their own political histories based on provincial documents and eyewitness accounts during the eighteenth century.

Captivity narratives recounting actual or imagined experiences of prisoners taken by Indians in wars with colonists were widely printed and avidly read (Washburn 1975–1979). Many scholars today regard these extraordinarily popular accounts as the first distinctively American literary form (Levernier and Cohen 1977; Vaughan and Clark 1981). More than a few of these accounts were inaccurate or sensationalized. Others were blatant fabrications. The better examples of this genre, such as James Smith's (1799) account of his captivity among Ohio Valley Indian people and Mary Jemison's story of her life among the Senecas (Seaver 1992), furnished unparalleled insights into many aspects of Northeastern Indian life.

Scholarly organizations, such as Philadelphia's American Philosophical Society and the Massachusetts Historical Society in Boston, began sponsoring research on Indian history and culture during the late 1700s. Since that time, succeeding generations of investigators

Arthur C. Parker. *Courtesy New York State Museum.*

have built upon scholarly foundations first laid by such pioneering early–nineteenth-century students of Northeastern Indian life as Moravian missionary John Heckewelder (1819), government Indian agent Henry Rowe Schoolcraft (1851–1857), and ethnographer Lewis Henry Morgan (1851). Several of their intellectual descendants, anthropologists like J. N. B. Hewitt (Tuscarora), William Jones (Fox), and Arthur C. Parker (Seneca), were themselves Indians.

Scholars inspired by the example of Morgan and other ethnological pioneers have written thousands of studies based upon archival sources or ethnographic fieldwork conducted in the region during the past century (Murdock and O'Leary 1975). Specialists fascinated by contact continue to gather compen-

dia of written records documenting relations with Northeastern Indian people. The better known of these, such as *The Jesuit Relations* (Thwaites 1896–1901) and the *Guide to the Ohio Valley-Great Lakes Indian Ethnohistory Archive* on file at Indiana University's Glenn A. Black Laboratory of Archaeology (D. Miller 1979), are essential reading in the field. Other compendia include Fliegel (1970); Purchas (1625); and Quinn, Quinn, and Hillier (1979).

Many of these documents were written or compiled by missionaries. Well-documented biographies of several of these figures—Massachusetts Puritan ministers John Eliot (Francis 1836) and Thomas Mayhew (Hare 1932) and Moravian missionaries John Heckewelder (P. A. W. Wallace 1958) and David Zeisberger (De Schweinitz 1870)—have been published.

Many missionary enterprises in the region also have been subjected to extensive ethnohistorical examination. Most of these studies focus upon the effects of missionization upon Indian people (Beaver 1988; Campeau 1988; Gray and Gray 1956; Lewis 1988; Ronda 1983). Others detail the ways mission activities furthered colonial expansion (Jennings 1971; Salisbury 1974, 1982a; Von Lonkhuyzen 1990). Increasing attention is being directed toward studies emphasizing Indians as active contestants in an ideological struggle involving all peoples in colonial North America (Axtell 1985; Bowden and Ronda 1980; Goddard and Bragdon 1988; Simmons 1986).

A great deal of physical evidence associated with missionization survives. The silver communion service donated by Queen Anne to the Mohawk Indian congregation during the early eighteenth century, for example, remains with Mohawk descendants in Canada. Religious medals, rings, and rosary beads are found in many archaeological sites (A. Wood 1974). But these artifacts are not uniformly distributed throughout the region; Jesuit finger rings and medals, for example, are almost never found in sites in Maine (Bourque 1989b).

Archaeologists also continue to search for house patterns, foundations, burying grounds, and other deposits associated with Natick, Massachusetts, and other mission towns (Carlson 1986). Printed Bibles and other religious tracts translated into Delaware, Massachusetts, Mohawk, and other Northeastern Indian languages are preserved in many archival repositories (Goddard and Bragdon 1988).

Extensive descriptions of many mission settlements survive. Several descriptions, like that of Stockbridge, Massachusetts, are intensively documented and clearly mapped (Colee 1977; Frazier 1992; Mandell 1992). Other missions are less well known. Cemeteries and buildings associated with several mission settlements survive to the present day. Although many such sites have been architecturally or archaeologically surveyed in Ontario, Quebec, Florida, and points west, comparatively few sites in the Northeast have received the systematic study accorded mission properties around Massachusetts Bay (Carlson 1986).

Compendia of original or primary sources and secondary sources based upon primary documentation provide a wide range of information on many aspects of contact in the region. Major microfilm compilations of largely unpublished primary documents include the Newberry Library's Documentary History of the Iroquois project (a guide to which may be found in Jennings et al. 1985), the University of Wisconsin's Lyman Draper Papers, and the Moravian Archives (Fliegel 1970). Published compilations of primary documentation include Browne et al. (1883–1970), Gehring (1977, 1980, 1981), Hazard et al. (1852–1949), O'Callaghan (1849–1851), O'Callaghan and Fernow (1853–1887), Quinn, Quinn, and Hillier (1979), and W. Robinson (1983a, 1983b).

Investigators using these and other written sources have produced a vast secondary literature: hundreds of books, monographs, and dissertations; thousands of articles; and tens of thousands of unpublished reports and scholarly papers. Citations to some of the more prominent of these studies may be found in sources such as Murdock and O'Leary's *Ethnographic Bibliography of North America* (1975) and Trigger's *Northeast* volume of the *Handbook of North American Indians* (1978b). More specialized surveys appear in Newberry Library critical bibliographies written by Frank Porter (1979), Neal Salisbury (1982b), Elisabeth Tooker (1978c), and C. A. Weslager (1978b).

Historical surveys of various aspects of Northeastern colonial life include Carr, Morgan, and Russo (1988), C. E. Clark (1970), Eccles (1969), Gipson (1936–1970), Jordan and Kaups (1989), Land, Carr, and Papenfuse (1977), Leach (1966), Lemon (1972), McCusker and Menard (1985), E. Morgan (1975), R. Morton (1960), Rink (1986), Sobel (1988), Wacker (1975), Weslager (1967), and Weslager and Dunlap (1961). Summations of the current status of scholarship in colonial North America may be seen in Cooke (1993).

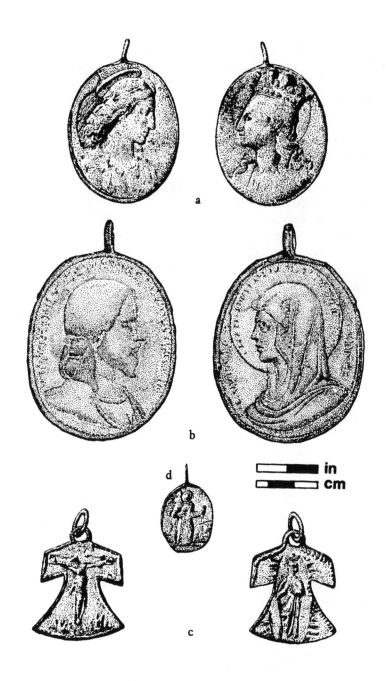

Catholic religious medals from seventeenth-century sites in Onondaga Country: (*a*) Shurtleff site; (*b*) Carley site (RMSC 10172/217);
(*c* and *d*) Lot 18 site. Illustrations by Patricia L. Miller (J. Bradley
1987a, fig. 15, p. 138). *Courtesy James W. Bradley.*

Journals such as *Ethnohistory, Northeastern Anthropology* (formerly *Man in the Northeast*), and *American Indian Culture and Research Journal* regularly publish articles dealing with historic contact in the Northeast. Although history journals such as the *William and Mary Quarterly* and the *Journal of American History* increasingly publish ethnohistorical articles, major journals in other fields presently do not regularly print articles on the Historic Contact period in the region.

Most of these writings traditionally examine groups, events, or issues. Scholarly biographies generally have focused on prominent figures like Sir William Johnson (M. Hamilton 1976) and Joseph Brant (Kelsay 1984). Biographies of less well known people generally were the province of local historians (Huston 1950; Seaver 1992; Sipe 1927), but scholars are increasingly focusing on such largely overlooked historical figures as the Powhatan leader Opechancanough (Fausz 1981), the Pamunkey Queen, Cockacoeske (McCartney 1989), the Mohawk medicine woman Coocoochee (Tanner 1979), Moses Tunda Tatamy (W. Hunter 1974), Pennacook sagamores Wannalancet and Kancagamus (Calloway 1988), and the New Jersey Indian sachem Taphow (Grumet 1988). These scholars, coordinating biographical data with other information, are developing more detailed views emphasizing the complexity and variety of Historic Contact period events in the Northeast.

THE ARCHAEOLOGICAL RECORD

Until recently most scholarly studies conducted in the region centered on ethnographic accounts or reconstructions of one sort or another. Minimal attention was paid to Historic Contact period archaeological locales. Stimulated by the general expansion of archaeological interest nationwide, scholars have worked to change this pattern by reporting on excavations at hundreds of archaeological sites associated with historic contact throughout the Northeast. Even so, relatively few sites were studied extensively until the 1970s. Even fewer were reported in scientific journals (Gibson 1980; W. Ritchie 1954; Simmons 1970; Solecki 1950). Until recently, most archaeological projects were sparked by scholarly or avocational interests, but today the majority of work published is the result of surveys or salvage excavations done on threatened sites.

Several factors account for the slow development of Historic Contact period archaeology in the region. As elsewhere, personnel and funding shortages restricted the scope and intensity of archaeological investigations. Then too, natural processes of erosion or decay and cultural factors such as development and looting destroyed many sites. Insufficient amounts of institutional support and insufficient scholarly interest in historically oriented anthropological archaeology in the United States also discouraged research in the region (Fitzhugh 1985).

Renewed interest in regional archaeology has overcome many of these obstacles in recent years. Inspired by this resurgence, archaeologists are turning their attention toward studies of evidence associated with the Historic Contact period in the Northeast. Although much of this work is being done by professional archaeologists, large numbers of avocationalists are also making significant contributions. The works of such investigators as Charles F. Wray (1973, 1985), who developed the early postcontact Seneca sequence; Monte R. Bennett (1973, 1979), who has identified many sites in Oneida Country; and Mohawk Valley archaeologist Donald A. Rumrill (1985) are benchmarks in the field.

Studies conducted by these and other investigators have resulted in listings of many archaeological sites on state inventories since the 1960s. Findings from these surveys have become integral parts of a growing literature synthesizing archaeological, documentary, and ethnographic data. Among the more prominent of these are studies by Ceci (1977), Engelbrecht (1985), Kent (1984), Kraft (1986), Potter (1982, 1993), Salwen (1978), P. A. Thomas (1991), Trigger (1980), Turner (1976), and L. Williams (1972).

Investigators publish their findings in many venues. Many produce reports for professional journals. Others publish in various series edited by state or regional archaeological societies. More than a few appear as contract reports. Other information appears in newspapers, magazines, and local histories. Care must be taken to substantiate all information encountered in these latter sources. Many are written by uninformed reporters; others are based on local folklore, hearsay, documentary inferences, or inadequately synthesized data and must be verified independently. Reanalysis of fifty-nine coastal New York sites listed by Ceci (1980a) as Historic Contact period sites, for example, indicates that more than half either postdate the eighteenth century or exist

only as place-names on colonial maps and documents (Wyatt 1990).

Most archaeological deposits in the Northeast are nondescript artifact scatters of indeterminate age and unclear cultural affiliation. Each state lists hundreds of such sites in its inventories. Although a certain percentage of these locales may date to the Historic Contact period, sites lacking diagnostic artifacts cannot be definitively associated with historic Indian people. Developments in chemical analysis and other techniques may allow future archaeologists to make such connections more confidently. Until then, deposits lacking diagnostic time-marker artifacts or datable organic materials cannot be associated with the Historic Contact era or any other time period with any degree of reliability.

Survey inventories generally represent the single most reliable source of information on Historic Contact period archaeological sites. All state historic preservation offices and many museums and universities maintain site inventories. Although many of these inventories contain files on tens of thousands of sites, few list more than a small number of Historic Contact period properties. Several factors account for this state of affairs. First, many areas that might contain deposits dating to this period have not yet been surveyed by state historic preservation offices. Few of these offices have specifically targeted Historic Contact period sites in thematic surveys, focusing instead on precontact archaeological sites or historic architectural properties.

This does not mean that states and other agencies lack data on the subject. Much of what they gather is published in limited-distribution reports known as gray literature. The bibliographic section of the National Park Service's computerized National Archeological Database (NADB) provides a guide to much of this literature. The NADB bibliographic section can be a significant research tool. A recent query of the 9,864 records on file in fifteen state historic preservation offices located in the Northeast revealed the existence of eighty-two documents filed under the keyword references "Protohistoric" and "Historic Native American" in the current Mid-Atlantic Regional Office's NADB database. Although many of these records were planning documents or historic surveys, eleven contained otherwise unavailable information on Historic Contact period sites.

Information on Historic Contact period deposits inventoried in state and other surveys can also be hard to find. Much inventory data is entered on report sheets, file cards, and other forms of hard copy. Searches conducted in manual inventories consume considerable amounts of time. The Virginia Department of Historic Resources manual file inventory alone contains more than twenty thousand entries. Nor is quantity the only obstacle facing researchers. For example, although forms generally list property time periods, few file systems are intensively cross-indexed. Others are plagued by significant numbers of data-entry errors. Often, therefore, researchers must go through entire file systems in order to find what they are looking for.

Computerization solves many of these problems. Most state historic preservation offices and other facilities are computerized. Despite this fact, only a few currently operate automated site-specific

databases. Those that do have not yet completely transferred data from earlier systems. Others are in the process of refining program and data-retrieval routines. More than a few concurrently run different databases. Funding, personnel, and technical considerations also influence computerized data-retrieval speed and efficiency.

These problems are exacerbated by other shortcomings. Many computerized inventories simply automate existing manual files. Such databases often omit critical information, such as property type and cultural affiliation, not listed in hard files. Others enter unverified or obsolete information. Few records, moreover, are entered with specific regions, times periods, or site types in mind. Data-entry errors also present problems. More than three-quarters of Historic Contact period sites listed in a computerized printout from one inventory, for example, were found to be entry errors caused by the extension of tops of checkmarks noting precontact sites into the box marked "Contact."

Many inventoried sites can no longer yield additional information. Large numbers have been obliterated by construction or vandalism. Moreover, collections once gathered from these and other sites have often been lost or dispersed.

Many factors have contributed to this state of affairs. Northeastern cities and towns have grown on or around Late Woodland Indian settlements. Other sites, located on fertile croplands, have been damaged or destroyed by farming. Gravel quarries, landfills, and other industrial developments also have claimed their share of Historic Contact period deposits in the region.

Locations of many Historic Contact

period sites on or near bays and rivers have made such deposits particularly susceptible to damage from shoreline development and erosion. Many Indian sites in and around New York Harbor, for example, have been scoured away or lie buried beneath layers of fill. In Maine, beach erosion seriously threatens most surviving coastal archaeological sites (Bourque 1989b).

Artifact hunters also continue to loot Historic Contact period sites. Motivated by the desire to possess a bit of history in the form of glass beads and other objects, many of these people seek out Historic Contact period sites. The very rarity of these materials increases their value in the booming artifact market.

The destruction of Historic Contact period sites is affecting the ability of scholars to reconstruct past lifeways by correlating archaeological and archival data. Many of the earliest of these efforts used the direct historical approach to identify the ethnicity of site occupants. Arthur C. Parker (1907), for example, using historic documents and cartographic materials, associated a site in Ripley, New York, with archivally documented Erie Indians. Another early practitioner, Donald A. Cadzow (1936), used written documents to link archaeological materials found along the lower reaches of the Susquehanna River with chronicled Susquehannock communities.

Today archaeologists directly or indirectly inspired by New Archaeology's call for greater emphasis on scientific understanding of culture and society are employing increasingly sophisticated interdisciplinary techniques to understand archaeological manifestations relating to such sociocultural intangibles as ideology, symbolism, kinship organization, and spiritual beliefs. Trigger's (1981) article, "Prehistoric Social and Political Organization: An Iroquoian Case Study," contains a useful overview of methods used by archaeologists to identify and analyze material evidence of precontact sociocultural lifeways.

For a long time many archaeologists have used assemblages of distinctive types of clay pots and stone tools as sociocultural indicators. Investigators commonly regard perceived similarities in pottery types and attributes as indices of ethnic identity or cultural affiliation. Most focus upon differences in pottery shape, decoration, temper, or paste. Less widely known are studies correlating impressed cordage twist directions with particular cultural traditions or time periods (Carr and Maslowski 1991).

Much attention has been devoted to aboriginal Historic Contact period ceramics in recent years. Studies such as Keith Egloff and Stephen R. Potter's (1982) examination of coastal-plain Virginia wares, the 1979 Iroquois Pottery Conference papers (Hayes 1980), Lucianne Lavin's (1986) analysis of southern New England pottery styles, and James B. Petersen and David Sanger's (1989) Maine and Maritime aboriginal ceramic sequence are refining pioneering stylistic and chronological frameworks developed by such scholars as Carlyle S. Smith (1950), Richard MacNeish (1952), and Clifford Evans (1955).

Colono wares found in later Historic Contact period sites south of Chesapeake Bay have attracted a particularly large amount of scholarly attention in recent years. Investigators focusing on data from North Carolina and points south hold that Colono pottery primarily was made by people of African descent (Deetz 1988; Ferguson 1978). Investigators examining archaeological and documentary data from Virginia and Maryland think Colono wares derive from local aboriginal pottery traditions (Binford 1965; Nöel-Hume 1962). Other archaeologists believe that these wares represent a syncretic development of aboriginal, African, and European ceramic styles, materials, and modes of manufacture (Henry 1992). Analysis of deposits found at locales like the Pamunkey Indian Reservation promises to provide new information on the role of Colono wares and other pottery forms in relationships among people in the Northeast.

Lithic technologies also are extensively examined in the existing site literature. Larger-scale lithic analyses frequently focus upon diagnostic bifacially chipped projectile points or knives (Justice 1987; W. Ritchie 1971). More recently, scholars have begun to devote increasing amounts of attention to smaller-scale patterns of wear, acquisition, distribution, and classification of all types of aboriginal lithic technology (Dincauze 1976b; Lavin 1983; Luedtke 1979).

Ceramics and lithics are not the only archaeological materials being studied for their ability to reveal information illuminating early aspects of conflict, conquest, and accommodation in the region. Archaeologists are using archival and excavation data to assess chronological characteristics of objects made from shells, like gorgets (Brashler and Moxley 1990) and beads (Sempowski 1989).

The effects of contact on these and other aspects of native material culture remain incompletely understood. Recent studies are contributing new data that trace impacts of European metal tools and techniques on Iroquoian and North Atlantic Algonquian basket production (Brasser 1975; Handsman 1987; McMullen and Handsman 1987). Other studies promise to more fully explicate effects of European materials and ideas on material and symbolic aspects of Indian production, distribution, and consumption of goods not wholly replaced by European imports.

The form and function of European materials themselves have been extensively studied. Well-documented technologies used as diagnostic time markers—such as glass beads (Kidd and Kidd 1970; Rumrill 1991b); European white-clay pipes, often called kaolin or ball clay pipes (Binford 1962; Omwake 1972; Walker 1977); and other forms of European ceramics—have received much scholarly attention in recent years. Firearms and constituent parts like gunflints and flintlocks have also been the subject of numerous studies (M. L. Brown 1980; T. Hamilton 1985; Hayes 1985; Malone 1973; Puype 1985; Rumrill 1991a). Other technologies such as iron axes and knives (Feder 1984; Hagerty 1963; Kidd 1955), native and European textiles (Welters 1985), and cloth seals (Endrei and Egan 1982) are subjects of extensive analysis. Further research is needed on Indian use and adaptation of glassware; copper, brass, and iron kettles; and other known European manufactures.

Archaeologists often regard discoveries of European imports and exotic, domestically produced pottery and stone tools as evidence of intercommunity trade, exchange, warfare, or postmarital residence patterns. Concentrations of ceramic artifacts associated with women or chipped-stone artifacts believed to be residues of more masculine activities within particular living floors or activity

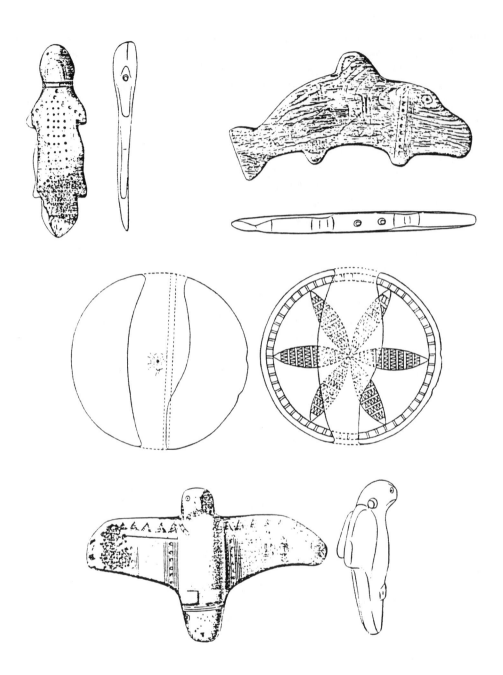

Shell artifacts recovered from Minisink National Historic Landmark archaeological deposits: *top left*, fish pendant; *top right*, beaver pendant; *middle*, restored gorget; *bottom*, bird pendant (Heye and Pepper 1915).

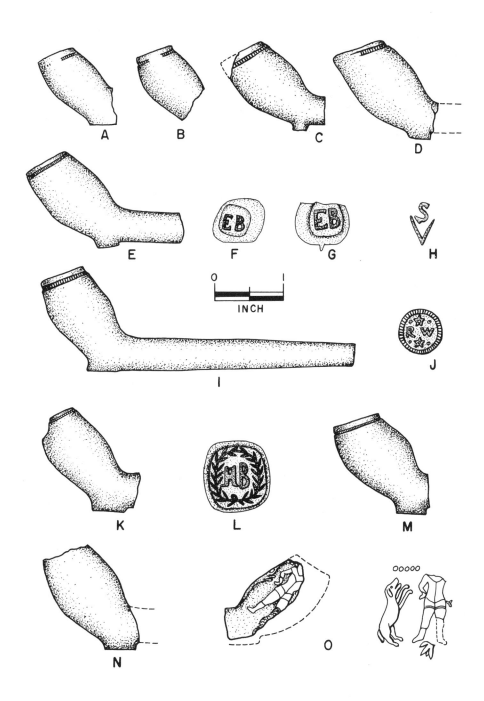

Seventeenth-century European white-clay tobacco-smoking pipes excavated from Feature 1221, Village Center site, Saint Mary's City Historic District National Historic Landmark, Maryland: *(a-e, i, k,* and *m-o)* pipe bowls, *(f-h, j,* and *l)* heel marks (depicted twice the size of the pipe bowls) identifying pipe makers (H. Miller 1983, fig. 20, p. 72). *Courtesy St. Mary's City Commission.*

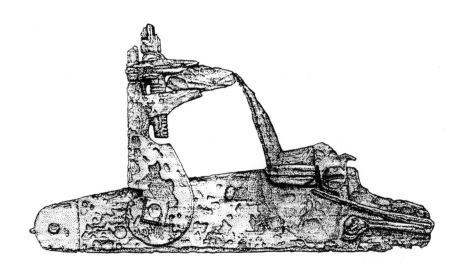

Top: drawing of a flintlock (catalog no. AR 18431), ca. 1655–1670, found at the Dann site in Seneca Country; Pen and ink by Patricia L. Miller (Puype 1985, fig. 37, p. 43). *Bottom:* gunflints; *left,* spall type; *right,* flake or blade types (T. Hamilton 1985, figs. 1 and 2, pp. 73 and 74). *Courtesy Rochester Museum and Science Center, Rochester, New York.*

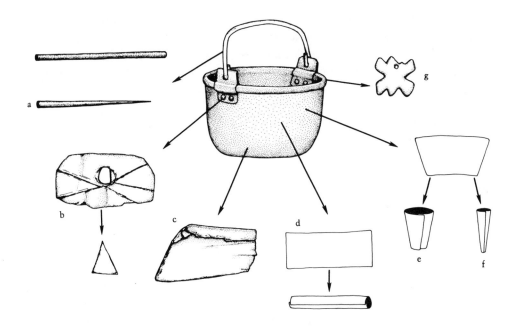

Recycling a copper kettle: *(a)* iron handle removed and ground into an awl; *(b)* heavier-gauge metal from a lug scored and cut into triangular projectile points; *(c)* sheet metal, from the body of the kettle, converted into a knife blade; *(d)* a tubular bead; *(e, f)* a conical bangle or pipe-bowl liner; and *(g)* a pendant. Illustrations by Patricia L. Miller (Bradley 1987a, fig. 13, p. 131). *Courtesy James W. Bradley.*

areas frequently have been interpreted as evidence of work-team organization, indications of sexual divisions of labor, or intimations of family, household, or community organization.

Although Indian people generally object to their disturbance or removal, human remains can provide information of great potential significance about individual and social patterns of age, health, diet, and disease. This information can provide data needed in addressing current medical problems. Recent studies conducted on archaeological remains associated with ancestors of modern Pima people in the Southwest, for example, have found evidence linking incidence of diabetes among Pima people, among the highest in the world, to more recent dietary changes.

Studies of human remains in association with other archaeological evidence also can be used to develop better understanding of personal and tribal economic, social, and political life. Archaeologists often believe that burials containing remains of healthy, well-nourished people accompanied by numerous or costly funerary offerings are graves of individuals possessing higher social status than burials not having such items. Following this line of reasoning, archaeologist Martha L. Sempowski (1986) has suggested that the more poorly furnished graves of early postcontact Seneca women do not reflect the higher status attributed to them in ethnohistoric and ethnographic sources. Another archaeologist, Elise M. Brenner (1988), has explained variations in the number and quality of goods in different seventeenth-century New England Indian graves as postmortem displays of power and wealth produced during a time of profound social and political change.

Burial data can reveal other information. Sempowski suggests that detected physical similarities shared by individuals buried near one another may be indicators of marriage or postmarital residence patterns. Seneca burials containing groups of physically similar men, for example, may consist of members of a closely related gene pool, suggesting a patricentered social order. Excavated burials containing graves of physically similar women, on the other hand, may represent evidence of an uxorilocal residence pattern that required men to move to households of wives and their female kin. Citing a seventeenth-century Jesuit report noting that Indian people put European goods into graves for the use of ancestors who had died before such goods became available in this world and the next, Dean R. Snow (1992) has raised a cautionary note about the usage of funerary offerings in analyses of status and role.

Some native communities, like the Narragansetts of Rhode Island, are working closely with archaeologists to preserve and study ancestral burials and cemeteries (P. Robinson 1988). Information from this collaboration is creating a database of past and present patterns of health and disease potentially of great use to the Narragansett people (Kelley, Barrett, and Saunders 1987; Kelley, Sledzik, and Murphy 1987).

Scholars working with Indian people on projects like these are developing new ways to reconstruct aspects of Indian social structure and political life from fragmentary archaeological deposits. Such developments are significantly raising the level of scholarly discourse throughout the region. Burials present particularly vexing challenges to archaeologists. Legislative acts regulating treatment of human remains are increasingly affecting the ways archaeologists study burials. Physical characteristics of burials themselves present further challenges. Preservation conditions differ widely. The circumstances of burial, moreover, vary tremendously. Information contained within graves may reflect ideals rather than realities. Certain societies emphasizing economic redistribution in this world or social equity in the next, for example, may furnish graves of less influential people more richly than those of individuals who wielded greater power or influence in life.

Deposits believed to preserve remains of other aspects of social or political life are subject to similar vagaries. Archaeological sites are dynamic locales. Almost every archaeological locale is the site of housecleaning, reuse, and episodes of renovation or rebuilding. Circumstances of abandonment also vary considerably. Postdepositional disturbances, such as rodent activities, frost heaves, and alluvial deposits of water-borne mud that cover earlier land forms, can alter locations of ceramic or lithic concentrations thought to represent work areas or labor organizations.

Natural forces of dissolution and decay at work in every site particularly affect the visibility of deposits containing evidence of less tangible elements of culture, such as social role or political organization. Archaeologist E. Randolph Turner III (1986), for example, has shown how deterioration of perishable featherwork, textiles, and wooden carvings and structures used by Powhatan Indian people as status markers has made it difficult for archaeologists to corroborate the extensive archival documentation of the politically complex Powhatan chiefdom.

Powhatans did not construct elaborate earthworks or other architectural monuments. Their craftspeople did not produce large amounts of sumptuary metalwork or stone jewelry. Thus, although colonial records clearly show that Powhatan sociopolitical organization was complex and highly hierarchical, presently available archaeological evidence suggests a more egalitarian social order.

Archaeological materials believed to have the capacity to reveal chronological information also must be used with care. Triangular stone projectile points or knives (often notched outside this region, farther west), collared or collarless globular or conoidal shell or grit-tempered clay pots, clay and stone pipes, and disc-shaped or tubular shell beads generally are regarded as the predominant diagnostic artifact types associated with most Late Woodland Northeastern native cultures.

Certain attributes of stone tools, such as the shape, dimensions, or characteristics of knapped edges of triangular, chipped-stone projectile points and knives, may represent temporal indicators. Findings of small, finely crafted, triangular, chipped-stone projectile points or knives indistinguishable from those

traditionally associated with Late Woodland occupations in earlier deposits containing Beekman, Hunter Brook, and Jack's Reef types, however, call the diagnostic efficacy of such artifacts into question (Dincauze 1976b; Kraft 1975a; R. M. Stewart 1990; Wingerson and Wingerson 1976).

Attempts to assign specific chronological or cultural associations to generally equilateral, straight-based, Madison-type triangular projectile points and more-concave-based isosceles Levanna types also have been inconclusive. Madison types, for example, have not been shown to be older than Levannas (Kraft 1975a). Although many archaeologists have suggested that Madison types occur with greater frequency in interior areas than in coastal regions, assertions suggesting that "Madison points were the exclusive Iroquois projectile style" await confirmation (Haviland and Power 1981). Existing studies indicate that both Madison and Levanna forms generally were contemporaneous in most areas of the Northeast between A.D. 900 and 1750.

At present archaeologists generally regard aboriginal pottery as the only class of artifact capable of revealing particular cultural or ethnic identities or affiliations. Along with European goods, aboriginal ceramics can also be used as diagnostic chronological markers. Aboriginal pottery types and styles continue to be particularly highly regarded diagnostic markers of Indian occupation. Yet recent analysis of Late Woodland pottery from upper Delaware River Valley sites indicates that archaeologists need to exercise caution whenever using pottery as a chronological tool. Discovering older pottery types mixed together with later types in pits at several sites, archaeologists have concluded that the valley's occupants added new types and styles while retaining older variants (Kraft 1975a; Moeller 1990). Hence archaeologists using pottery as diagnostic markers in areas where such patterns have been identified should use assemblages rather than individual types to determine site age or cultural affiliation.

Typological issues also affect the ability of ceramics to reveal temporal or chronological information. Many archaeologists focusing upon small-scale social processes, for example, emphasize unique attributes of each ceramic type variation in order to establish locally distinct pottery types. Such local types often are associated with small social units—families, bands, or corporate kin groups. Other archaeologists, studying larger-scale processes, work to develop more comprehensive typologies that encompass many related variations in order to identify tribal identities or delineate interaction spheres of widely shared symbols, beliefs, and trade networks (Caldwell 1964).

Most archaeologists are reluctant to merge typologies at high levels of abstraction. Many remember graduate seminars recounting problems caused earlier in the century by lumping all collared globular pots as "Iroquoian" and all collarless conoidal pots as "Algonkian" (Parker 1922; Wintemberg 1931). Subsequent research showed that this simplistic typology erroneously lumped together many distinct and unrelated cultures, social groups, time periods, and ceramic styles (Brumbach 1975; MacNeish 1952).

Overly simplistic or naive lumping must be avoided. Caution is advised in such fast-developing fields as ceramic analysis, where new information is changing hypotheses on an almost daily basis. Reluctance to develop more comprehensive typologies can also limit comparative analyses. Archaeologists, whether lumpers or splitters, should consider project scope and scale when developing or analyzing typologies and nomenclatures for ceramics and other artifacts.

Although great advances have been made in recent years, much remains to be done in this field. Developments in artifact typology, dating techniques, and chemical analysis promise to provide archaeologists with more and better cultural and temporal diagnostic indicators (Kuhn 1985, 1989; Kuhn and Lanford 1987; Trigger et al. 1980).

The results of research conducted by professional and avocational investigators strongly suggest that many native people encountered by sixteenth-century European explorers had been living in their ancestral homelands for more than a millennium before 1492. The origins of historic Northeastern native communities are the subject of much speculation. Investigators long have tried to link precontact cultures to historically chronicled Indian nations, Eastern Hemisphere civilizations, or otherworldly visitors.

The overwhelming preponderance of evidence indicates that historic native Northeastern societies developed from local antecedents. Pottery-type seriations performed by archaeologists William A. Ritchie and Richard S. MacNeish (1952; W. Ritchie and MacNeish 1949) permitted formulation of the "in situ hypothesis," which holds that people belonging to communities constituting the historic Iroquois League of Five Nations probably had lived in New York for at least four hundred years prior to European contact. At or about the same time this hypothesis was developed, archaeologist Donald A. Cadzow (1936), noting the presence of European materials in many lower Susquehanna Valley Indian sites, began to link his archaeological discoveries with the historic Susquehannocks.

MUSEUM COLLECTIONS

Thousands of objects collected from Northeastern Indian people presently are in museums, libraries, historical societies, and private collections. The earliest of these collections, gathered together by seventeenth- and eighteenth-century visitors to the region, generally are located in Europe. Collections gathered in more recent times, many containing paintings or artifacts specially produced for ethnographers by native people, may be found in American and Canadian facilities.

The largest of these institutions, like the National Museum of the American Indian, the Canadian Museum of Civilization, the American Museum of Natural History, and Chicago's Field Museum of Natural History, employ curatorial specialists to catalogue, conserve, exhibit, and study the vast Northeastern collections under their care. These collections are an enormous and relatively untapped source for future studies of Northeastern historic contact.

LINGUISTIC STUDIES

Many anthropologists use linguistic data to reconstruct patterns of Northeastern Indian sociopolitical life. Archaeologist Stuart Fiedel (1987), for example, employs glottochronological techniques measuring what are believed to be constant rates of linguistic change to derive approximate determinations of how long speakers of related Eastern Algonquian languages have been separated from one another. Other studies, such as Goddard and Bragdon's (1988) analysis of Massachusett texts, combine linguistic data with ethnographic, archival, and other materials to construct configurations of aboriginal culture and society.

ORAL LITERATURE

Although most archaeologists now work closely with historians and ethnologists, few consult folklorists or other specialists in oral literature. Most students of Indian narratives tend to focus on symbolic or literary values (Foster 1974; Thompson 1955). Increasing numbers of investigators, inspired by work in other disciplines, are beginning to study Northeastern native narratives for the light they can shed on Indian perspectives on historic contact events. Gordon M. Day's (1962) analysis of a narrative transmitting an Abenaki eyewitness account of Robert Rogers's 1759 raid on the town of Saint Francis is an outstanding example of the potential usefulness of Indian texts in historic contact studies.

The text gathered by Day tells a much different story than the tale of colonial triumph published by Rogers himself. The story, told to the informant's mother by her mother during the nineteenth century, reveals that Rogers's Rangers failed to achieve surprise and succeeded in only partially destroying the Abenaki town before withdrawing precipitately in advance of an imminent counterattack. Studies such as Day's and William S. Simmons's (1986) landmark survey of the adaptive significance of New England Indian oral literature provide a glimpse of the potential insights to be obtained from native narratives.

THE ARCHITECTURAL RECORD

Relatively little attention has been directed toward architectural evidence of historic contact in the Northeast since the publication of pioneering studies by David Bushnell (1908), Lewis Henry Morgan (1881), and Charles C. Willoughby (1906). Building materials used by Indian people to construct their houses were flammable and rotted easily. Susceptible to decay and vulnerable to accidental house fires and enemy incendiaries, most Northeastern Indian buildings and structures left little more than post-mold patterns, hearths, pits, and foundations as physical evidence of their existence. Although written documentation of Indian associations with colonial trading posts, houses, forts, and other properties generally is skimpy and incomplete, other sources, such as maps and journals, more amply record locations of Northeastern Indian towns and houses.

Indian settlement patterns changed dramatically during the colonial era. Many members of groups thought to have been more sedentary during the centuries immediately preceding European contact, such as Delaware people on the Atlantic coast, adopted more mobile lifestyles as changing patterns of trade, war, diplomacy, depopulation, and dispossession transformed their ways of life. Other people, such as the Mohawks of the Iroquois confederacy and the Susquehannocks of Pennsylva-

nia, initially responded to the same challenges by moving into larger and more densely populated settlements than those built by their ancestors.

Several factors induced most of these people to adopt more dispersed town plans during the late seventeenth century. Wooden fortresses vulnerable to attacks from enemies intent upon burning entire communities frequently became deathtraps after warfare intensified throughout the region during the mid-1600s. Formal declaration of Iroquois neutrality after 1701 ushered in a period of relative peace that made the construction of such fortresses less necessary in the confederacy heartland.

New organizations of space within settlements also appeared. Many communities established separate burial grounds for the first time. Some ultimately constructed mills, barns, and blacksmith shops. Many Northeastern Indian people gradually planted orchards and erected fences around their fields.

House types also changed. Wattle-and-daub houses disappeared in the upper Ohio Valley. Wigwams covered with bark and grass mats remained in use, but their numbers dwindled as the Historic Contact period wore on. People living in wigwams increasingly furnished them with wooden doors, tables, chairs, and other European housewares.

Log cabins or wooden-frame houses gradually supplanted bark-and-grass structures in most Northeastern Indian communities. Increasing numbers of new building types, such as mills, schoolhouses, and churches, also appeared. A large body of archaeological and written evidence documents these changes. Archaeological evidence such as post-mold patterns, midden deposits, pit and hearth features, and artifact concentrations associated with Indian occupations have been recovered at many locales.

Large numbers of European illustrations, maps, and written descriptions abundantly record information on Historic Contact period Indian architecture. Maps represent a particularly valuable resource. Several projections, such as Champlain's 1606 map of Indian plantations surrounding Nauset Harbor, Massachusetts (Salwen 1978), and the 1657 Bressani map showing an Iroquois longhouse (Heidenreich 1978), contain unique images of early postcontact Northeastern Indian housing.

Data describing house types, architectural details, building materials, and furnishings may be found in Indian and European oral narratives. Surviving standing structures, such as the Indian Mission House National Historic Landmark in Stockbridge, Massachusetts, and Mary Jemison's log cabin in Letchworth State Park, New York, are rare living examples of housing associated with Historic Contact period Indian people.

The chapter entitled "Wigwam and Longhouse: Northeast and Great Lakes" in *Native American Architecture* (Nabokov and Easton 1989) provides an unparalleled overview of the subject. Comprehensive and well illustrated, the chapter describes all known aboriginal and European building types, styles, methods, and materials used by Northeastern Indian people during the Historic Contact period. The volume's bibliographic essay contains an excellent critical review of key published sources. Useful studies of Scandinavian and Central European log cabins adapted by colonists and Indians alike to Northeastern conditions appear in Weslager (1969) and Jordan (1985).

Despite the large number of published sources on the subject, much remains to be learned about Indian architecture in the region. Archaeologists need to corroborate more fully the written records describing aboriginal structures such as the longhouse recorded by Jasper Danckaerts (1913) at the town of Nayack in Brooklyn, New York, in 1679, or the wigwams equipped with tables and other European furnishings drawn by Ezra Stiles at Niantic, Connecticut, in 1761 (Sturtevant 1975).

More information also is needed on Indian adoption of log houses, frame structures, and other European house types and building styles. Presently undiscovered written records may help future scholars better understand house patterns discovered during excavations of Historic Contact period components at Norridgewock and other sites.

ENVIRONMENTAL STUDIES

Renewed interest in environmental issues has resulted in several studies tracing ecological relationships in the Northeast during the Historic Contact period. Influential works of historians William Cronon (1983) and Alfred W. Crosby, Jr. (1986) have shown how Indian and European people affected and were affected by the environment in the North Atlantic region. Inspired by their example, historian Timothy Silver (1990) examines ecological relationships among Indian people, colonists, and African Americans along the South Atlantic seaboard below Pennsylvania.

Richard White and William Cronon (1988) have delineated three major

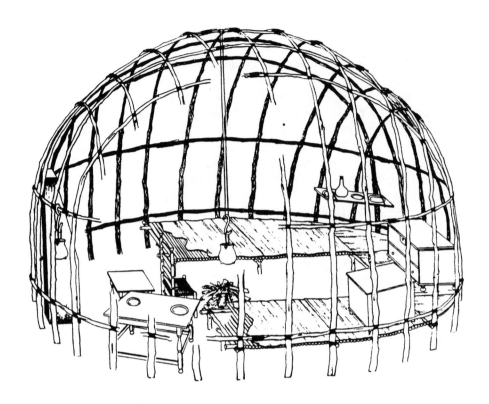

Reconstruction of a Western Niantic wigwam, 1761, based on notes and measured sketches by Ezra Stiles. Drawing by Edward G. Schumacher, under the direction of William C. Sturtevant (Sturtevant 1975, fig. 2c).

themes in extant literature documenting the environmental history of Indian-colonial relations. Both scholars have noted the enduring persistence of myths identifying Indian people as natural conservationists inhabiting a pristine wilderness. Calling attention to the growing recognition of Indian influence upon the historical landscape of North America, they have noted the increasing inclusion of environmental change as a factor in studies of Indian-colonial relations.

ETHNOGRAPHIC STUDIES

As the preceding pages show, most interpretations of past lifeways in the Northeast are guided by ethnographic findings. Scholars gathering information by direct observation or from the memories of informants have conducted ethnographic fieldwork among Northeastern Indians since the nineteenth century. Much of the history of anthropological field inquiry in the region is summarized by Elisabeth Tooker (1978a), who traces developments in Northeastern ethnographic fieldwork from early contact through the Jeffersonian years and the mid-to-late-nineteenth-century research of Lewis Henry Morgan and Bureau of American Ethnology investigators to the twentieth-century field studies of Alanson B. Skinner, Frank G. Speck, A. Irving Hallowell, Anthony F. C. Wallace, and their colleagues and successors.

The tradition of ethnographic scholarship has broadened in recent years. Anthropologists like Jay Miller (1973), who has worked with Oklahoma Delaware Indian elders to obtain new insights into their views of family life, social organization, and religion, continue to conduct ethnographic inquiries. Increasing numbers of scholars from other fields also have turned their attention toward Northeastern field studies in recent years. Historians studying existing ethnographic sources today work to develop more historically sensitive approaches to ethnography in the field and in such study centers as the D'Arcy McNickle Center for the History of the American Indian in the Newberry Library.

Historical linguists are also conducting ethnographic fieldwork. Linguist Michael K. Foster (1984), for example, has worked with the Cayuga chief Jacob E. Thomas to reconstruct diplomatic protocols in four speech events documenting councils held between Iroquois people and colonial authorities dating from 1736 to 1756. Growing numbers of ethnoarchaeologists, for their part, are using ethnographic observations to develop middle-range theories reconstructing and explaining archaeological data (Binford 1981, and 1983; Trigger 1991b).

ETHNOHISTORY

Investigators have struggled to use ethnographic, written, oral, linguistic, architectural, environmental, and other data to find and understand archaeological deposits for more than three centuries. Most recently, ethnohistorians combining anthropological and historiographical skills have been working to develop the interdisciplinary approaches needed to understand Indian life in the region (Axtell 1981; Simmons 1986; Trigger 1985).

Many of these scholars "upstream" findings of ethnographic field-workers by tracing written or oral evidence of sociopolitical continuity and change from the present to the past. As William N. Fenton (1957), its most articulate and influential advocate has noted, this technique, also known as the "direct historical approach," was first employed systematically by archaeologists William Duncan Strong (1940) and Waldo R. Wedel (1936, 1938) in their reconstructions of Indian culture history sequences on the Great Plains.

Fenton (1957, 1978) and Arthur C. Parker (1907, 1916), the first modern anthropologists to use this technique in the Northeast, produced comparative studies that have become models of ethnohistorical scholarship contrasting archaeological and ethnographic field data with archival records. Although uncritical application of this method can result in invalid inferences, ethnohistorians carefully extending other data have provided significant insights into patterns of conflict, diplomacy, trade, exchange, and settlement in the region. The following pages present some of the results of interdisciplinary research in the Northeast inspired by Fenton and his colleagues some forty years ago.

PART ONE

THE NORTH ATLANTIC REGION

MAP 2: THE NORTH ATLANTIC REGION

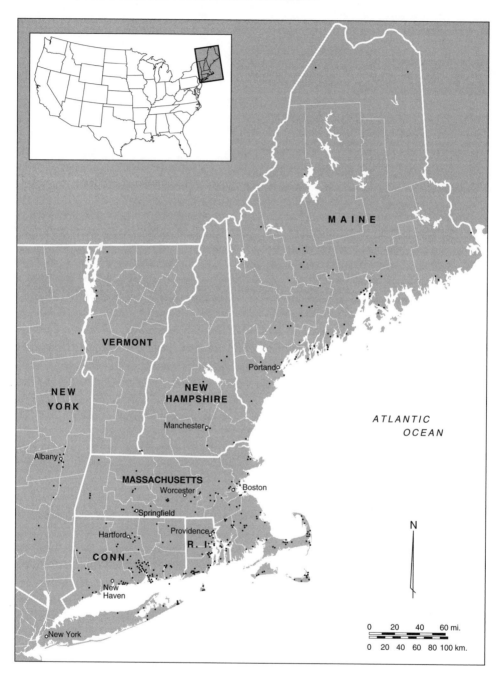

AN OVERVIEW
OF THE
REGION

At its widest extent, the North Atlantic region encompasses the northeastern United States, the Canadian Maritime provinces, and eastern Quebec. In the United States, the region extends across New England from Maine west to the Lake Champlain drainage and the upper Hudson River Valley. This area, which encompasses the northeastern portion of New York, a state often categorized by geographers and historians as part of the mid-Atlantic region, also includes Connecticut, Maine, Massachusetts, New Hampshire, Rhode Island, and Vermont.

This region has long been home to a diverse group of Indian communities. Passamaquoddy, Maliseet, Micmac, Penobscot, and other native people of Eastern Abenaki Country live in an area stretching across the present state of Maine from the Canadian border west to the Saco River Valley. Farther west, Western Abenaki people trace ancestry to the original inhabitants of New Hampshire and Vermont and more recent immigrants to those states. Many of these immigrants were forced from homes in Agawam, Pocumtuck, Woronoco, Norwottuck, Squakheag, and other communities in Pocumtuck-Squakheag Country by New England settlers moving onto their lands in central Massachusetts and adjacent portions of Connecticut, New Hampshire, and Vermont during the middle years of the seventeenth century. Others came from Nipmuck Country in the lake district of Worcester County, Massachusetts, and northeastern Connecticut. Still others immigrated from Pennacook-Pawtucket and Massachusett Countries along the Atlantic coast from the Saco River Valley south to Massachusetts Bay.

Descendants of the original inhabitants of Wampanoag Country, an area extending across southeastern Massachusetts from Cape Cod and the offshore islands to Rhode Island Sound, continue to live in places like Mashpee on Cape Cod and Gay Head on Martha's Vineyard. Nearby Narragansett Country stretches across the state of Rhode Island from Rhode Island Sound west to the Connecticut border and south to Block Island.

The native people of Mohegan-Pequot Country live in eastern Connecticut between the Pawcatuck and Thames river valleys. Descendants of such closely related communities as the Quinnipiacs,

Podunks, and Hammonosetts continue to live in portions of their Lower Connecticut Valley Country homeland. On the south, Shinnecock, Montauk, and Poosepatuck people still make their homes in Montauk Country on eastern Long Island. Farther west, Mahican Country stretches across the upper reaches of the Housatonic and Hudson river valleys.

Available evidence indicates that almost all North Atlantic region Indians spoke closely related Eastern Algonquian languages at the time of contact. Although each community maintained its own distinct dialect, social organization, political network, and system of spiritual beliefs, all participated to one extent or another in a generally shared regional cultural tradition.

Most followed the Late Woodland way of life that first emerged in the region sometime around A.D. 900. Like Late Woodland people elsewhere, members of North Atlantic Late Woodland communities used similar types of tools, weapons, and ornaments crafted from stone, wood, horn, bone, and shell, made and exchanged stylistically similar collared and uncollared pottery, and lived in grass- or bark-covered conical wigwams, dome-shaped roundhouses, and rectangular longhouses.

Contact with Basque, English, French, Spanish, and Portuguese mariners sailing to North Atlantic shores during the 1500s began to change the lives of these people. Slow at first, rates of change increased as Europeans began to permanently settle in the region during the 1600s. Adjusting to local environmental, social, and political conditions, French, English, Dutch, and other colonists supplanted or began crowding out Indian communities along the North Atlantic coast by the mid-1600s. Struggling to live with their new neighbors, Eastern Algonquian people worked to adapt old ways to new situations while reconciling new objects and ideas with established customs and practices.

Relying on established methods or inventing new ones, Indians throughout the region tried to respond creatively to challenges posed by economic and political shifts, demographic upheavals, land loss, and other changes brought on by direct contact with Europeans during the seventeenth century. Devastated by war, disease, and dispossession, many North Atlantic Indian people left ancestral lands to make new homes farther north or west. More than a few of these people moved north to previously sparsely settled areas of northern New England. Others moved even farther north to French Acadia or Quebec or emigrated west to the Susquehanna and Ohio river valleys.

Some emigrants, like Mahican and Western Abenaki people repeatedly forced from their homes by periodic warfare with the Mohawks, their Iroquois confederates, and European colonists, returned when peace was restored. Other emigrants—like many Central Connecticut Valley people, who by 1666 had been forced from their homes by Mohawk attacks, or numerous Nipmuck, Massachusett, and Wampanoag people, who were driven from their lands by English settlers during King Philip's War ten years later—remained exiles in foreign lands. Those unwilling to abandon their homelands for the uncertainty of exile moved to Christian mission settlements like Natick, Hassanamisco, and Mashpee, which were built in the heart of ancestral territories.

Life in the North Atlantic region changed dramatically during the next century. Disease, warfare, and out-migration caused already depleted native populations to plummet. Missionaries did their best to blot out native religions and spiritual beliefs, while provincial administrators struggled to force Indian people to submit to colonial authority. Native languages, religions, manufacturing skills, and other aspects of Indian heritage began to disappear, as distinctive customs were suppressed and elders died without passing on their knowledge.

New strategies emerged as old ways of doing things fell from use. Some were almost wholly derived from European or African models. Others reflected creative adaptations artfully blending existing customs and practices with innovations.

Not surprisingly, Indian people living closest to European settlements were almost always most deeply affected by the changes transforming their societies during the 1700s. Those continuing to live near centers of colonial expansion on the coast or along tidewater sections of the Merrimack, Connecticut, and other rivers were increasingly compelled to submit to some form of colonial supervision. Provincial authorities set aside small reservations on or near ancestral lands for some of these people. Missionaries settled in existing communities or established new settlements in ancestral homelands.

Increasingly pressed by colonists intent upon acquiring their remaining lands, growing numbers of Indian people signed away the titles to their last pieces of property and moved elsewhere during these years. Some joined friends and relations living in Indian towns far from the British settlements. Others, like Mahican and Housatonic Indians from western Connecticut and eastern New York, moved to the Protestant Stockbridge mission community established in 1736 in western Massachusetts on the still sparsely populated borderlands separating New France, New England, and New York.

Caught between colonial and Indian rivals struggling for control over a hotly contested frontier, Indian people found little peace in places like Stockbridge. Unwilling to submit to French, British, or Iroquois overlords, most of these people ultimately were forced to move farther north or west. Some joined friends and kinsfolk living on reservations or in other mission communities. Others moved to nearby unwanted or unoccupied mountain valleys, swamps, and pinelands.

Many of these people left the region during the decades following the end of the American War for Independence. Others refused to leave, and people tracing descent to the region's original inhabitants continue to live today in North Atlantic states and adjacent Canadian provinces.

THE SIXTEENTH CENTURY

As mentioned earlier, extant archaeological and documentary sources indicate that all Indian people living within the North Atlantic region at the time of initial contact generally followed the widespread Late Woodland way of life. These same data also indicate that people living in different parts of this region used different settlement-subsistence strategies.

People living in the northernmost reaches of the region, for example, tended to follow more mobile lifestyles based on hunting, fishing, and foraging. Those living farther south and west, for their part, generally lived more settled lives in larger, decentralized communities. Like their neighbors on the north, most people living in these larger communities would move to smaller hunting, fishing, and foraging camps at various times of the year. Unlike their northerly neighbors, however, they also grew corn, beans, squash, tobacco, and other crops at favorable locales (Salisbury 1982a contra M. K. Bennett 1955; A. Silver 1981 contra Ceci 1980a).

Available archaeological information supports early written accounts indicating that most North Atlantic Indians organized their social and political lives around interlocking networks of families, friends, and associates. Aided by councils of elders and talented men and women, North Atlantic leaders worked to achieve consensus among followers. Persuasion and peer pressure rather than force were used to develop support. Not bound by community decisions, people disagreeing with particular policies could refuse to participate in actions they found objectionable, or they could move elsewhere.

Leaders attracted followers by skillfully manipulating factions and by meeting the needs of individuals and interest groups. The more successful of these leaders built up large followings among people from many communities. Although some of these coalitions outlived their founders, many disbanded as members left to follow other leaders.

Like people everywhere, native Northeasterners employed marriage ties, friendship, and other relationships to recruit new members, increase the range and effectiveness of their networks, and circulate goods, ideas, and people. People traveled from place to place within this circle of kinsfolk, friends, and associates as changing climatic, economic, social, and political conditions allowed.

Linguistic analyses building from studies first undertaken by Rhode Island founder Roger Williams, Puritan missionary John Eliot, and others during the 1630s and 1640s indicate that the region's native people spoke related Eastern Algonquian languages at the time of contact (Goddard 1978a; Goddard and Bragdon 1988; R. Williams 1973). Archaeologists studying sites occupied by these people have unearthed evidence indicating that the particular types of ceramics, tools, foods, and housing they used generally appeared in the region several centuries before contact with Europeans.

These Indians used a technology based upon raw materials of stone, clay, shell, bone, antler, wood, sinew, and skin. As elsewhere, North Atlantic Late Woodland people used a wide range of stylistically similar chipped- and pecked-stone implements. Most crafted chipped-stone triangular projectile points from locally available materials. People living along the southern New England coast also continued to use narrow-stemmed points made from quartz or other stones. Farther north, Indians in Maine crafted more broadly stemmed projectile points and knives.

North Atlantic people also made and used clay pots throughout much of the Late Woodland period (Petersen and Sanger 1989). For reasons still unknown, hunting and gathering people living in more northerly portions of Maine seem to have abandoned pottery production just before 1600. Other people living farther south and west continued to make aboriginal ceramics up to the end of the seventeenth century.

Archaeological and archival evidence documenting North Atlantic aboriginal ceramic-distribution patterns highlights problems encountered by archaeologists using particular pottery types or styles to identify specific ethnic, linguistic, or economic relationships. Writing in 1634, Puritan colonist William Wood noted that Massachusett Indian people frequently used pots obtained from Narragansett people (W. Wood 1977). Archaeologists, for their part, have found distinctive incised, collared ceramics generally associated with Late Woodland Mohawk and Saint Lawrence Iroquoian people in contemporary deposits in the region.

Archaeologists Hetty Jo Brumbach and Herbert C. Kraft, for example, have found that people living in Mahican Country and their nearby Munsee neighbors both made pottery nearly identical to that produced by residents of Mohawk Country during Late Woodland times (Brumbach 1975; Kraft 1975b). Similar pottery has been found in sites as far east as Massachusetts Bay (E. Johnson and Bradley 1987). And pottery of the type made by Saint Lawrence Iroquoian people living along the banks of the upper Saint Lawrence Valley and eastern Lake Ontario has been found in sites located in Maine and Vermont (Cowie and Petersen 1992; Petersen 1989; Petersen and Sanger 1989; Pendergast 1991b).

These findings clearly indicate that people speaking different languages and belonging to different political and social groups often made or used similar types of pottery. The reasons for this finding, however, remain less clear. No known evidence indicates that Mohawk or Saint Lawrence Iroquoian people ever controlled or even colonized North Atlantic communities. Niantic, Shantok, and other pottery resembling Iroquoian wares found in North Atlantic sites may simply reflect expressions of regard or admiration for Iroquoian ceramics. Discoveries of Saint Lawrence or Chance Incised ceramics in North Atlantic sites, for their part, may represent evidence of visits or intermarriage or the presence of captives or refugees.

New findings are sharpening our understandings of relationships between pottery and people in this region. Archaeologists are developing chemical analyses capable of identifying distinctive signatures revealing sources of clays used to craft clay smoking pipes and pots (Kuhn 1985; Snow 1980). Other archaeologists, discovering particularly high numbers of subtle but distinctive "ladder" motifs in assemblages of castellated pottery from upper Hudson Valley sites, for their part, may have found a way to distinguish Mahican and Munsee pottery from Mohawk wares (Bender and Brumbach 1992; Diamond 1991).

Although archival records chronicle earlier contacts farther north in Canada, Giovanni da Verrazzano's journal of his 1524 voyage contains the first written record of a meeting between Europeans and Indian people in the portion of the North Atlantic region now within the borders of the United States. Other Europeans, like Jacques Cartier, who established contacts with Saint Lawrence Iroquoian people living at the present sites of Montreal and Quebec City in 1534, soon followed Verrazzano in search of gold, furs, slaves, and a western route to Asia.

Failing to find their Northwest Passage, English, French, Basque, Spanish, and Portuguese sailors making landfalls from Newfoundland to Virginia instead brought fish, pelts, gold, and slaves back to Europe. Voyages made by these men marked the beginning of more-or-less regular direct contact between both peoples in the region. Most of the small number of objects of European origin found in sixteenth-century North Atlantic Indian archaeological sites probably came from contacts with these early visitors. Much of this material may have come from contacts with Europeans sailing to North Atlantic shores; other glass beads and European brass or copper beads or scraps may have been carried into the region along Indian trade routes from the south by Indian people in contact with Spanish, English, and other Europeans making landfalls along the South Atlantic coast from Florida to Chesapeake Bay (Waselkov 1989).

Most documents written by early European visitors are little more than sketchy reports of brief encounters (Quinn 1977, 1981; Quinn, Quinn, and Hillier 1979). Other information appears on sixteenth-century globes, atlases, and maps. None of these sources contain detailed descriptions of Indian people or societies. Only a few mention Indian individuals by name, and virtually none identify communities or political groups. Collectively, these documents furnish only the most impressionistic glimpses of sixteenth-century Indian life.

Extant native texts describing initial contacts, for their part, often tend to reveal more about what the descendants of sixteenth-century Indian people feel about newcomers than about contact events themselves. Many accounts describe initial meetings with Europeans (Calloway 1991; Morrison 1984; Simmons 1986). Although all of these provide valuable information, none can clearly be dated to the 1500s.

Archaeologists familiar with the equivocal nature of available sixteenth-century written and oral sources tend to use the direct historical approach correlating historically chronicled people and practices with sites and site functions or use middle-range theory to develop analogies linking sites with ecological and other factors. Lynn Ceci, for example, used later documents to locate and interpret the function of sixteenth-century site deposits on Long Island (Ceci 1980a). Building upon earlier work by ethnographer Frank Speck, Dean R. Snow has tried to show that environmental conditions in Maine led Indian people to develop social, political, and economic practices within particular river-drainage systems (Snow 1978a, 1980). Although these and other studies have succeeded in shedding new light on many aspects of sixteenth-century North Atlantic Indian life, archaeological evidence for the most part continues to provide only marginally more informative material than written and oral sources.

Several factors account for this state of affairs. Most known sites in the region have been destroyed or substantially disturbed. Much of what is known has been salvaged from threatened locales. Although many professional and avocational archaeologists have systematically surveyed many properties, much recovered information remains scattered, unanalyzed, and unpublished.

Many scholars currently are working in the region. Although most of these people maintain meticulous field notes, few are publishing their findings. Much of their work appears in the form of cultural resource management reports printed in very limited editions. Anxious to do anything they can to stop looters from pillaging sites, many archaeologists are refraining from publishing any information of potential use to pothunters (Dincauze 1991).

Even so, many new discoveries are being made. An extensive suite of radiocarbon-dated deposits within the Nauset National Historic Landmark in the Cape Cod National Seashore, for example, preserves a significant record of Late Woodland Coastal Algonquian Indian life. Other deposits located within the Mashantucket Pequot National Historic Landmark give evidence of the gradual introduction of small amounts of European goods among Pequot people during the first century of direct contact with Europeans.

Settlement patterns identified at these and other known sixteenth-century sites confirm written accounts indicating that the region's Indian people generally lived in small, decentralized settlements. Assemblages of European artifacts found in these sites usually consist of little more than a few glass beads, some smelted-metal tubular beads, or scraps of brass, copper, and iron.

Clearly datable sixteenth-century European artifacts are most frequently found in human graves in this region. Their almost exclusive occurrence in such contexts may indicate that the impact of European technology was largely limited to ceremony and ritual at this time. Brass, copper, and iron kettles, firearms, and other evidence of more intensive contact have not yet been found in any sites unequivocally dating to the sixteenth century.

THE SEVENTEENTH CENTURY

Most available evidence indicates that all aspects of North Atlantic Indian life were irrevocably transformed by contact during the 1600s. Indian people only dimly aware of Europeans during the 1500s were forced to contend with new neighbors, tools, and ideas as wars, disease, and dispossession devastated their communities. Recognizing the far-reaching effects of changes brought on by these developments, many scholars identify the 1600s as a distinctive postcontact colonization or plantation phase (Bradley 1984; Brasser 1988).

Sustained contacts between natives and newcomers in the North Atlantic region began when European traders established posts and forts at favorable locations on the coast and along navigable rivers during the first decades of the seventeenth century. The pace of European settlement at these locales initially was very slow. Although records are incomplete, extant evidence indicates that fewer than a thousand newcomers lived in the few scattered year-round outposts on the North Atlantic seaboard by 1630.

Claiming to settle virgin or uninhabited land, Europeans actually moved to or near populous Indian communities. Although early investigators given to minimizing Indian numbers suggested total regional native population figures as low as 25,000 (Mooney 1928), more-recent scholars, who believe aboriginal populations to have been far larger, have suggested estimates ranging from 60,000 to 200,000 people (S. F. Cook 1976; Jennings 1975; Salisbury 1982a).

Whatever their actual number, North Atlantic Indian populations declined disastrously as Europeans migrated to the region. The first recorded pandemic in the region, a still-unidentified disease that ravaged communities between Cape Cod and Maine's Penobscot Valley from 1616 to 1622, may have killed as many as 90 percent of the people living at some locales (Spiess and Spiess 1987). The next reported episode, a smallpox epidemic, intermittently ravaged communities farther south and west from 1631 to 1634 (S. F. Cook 1973a). Although evidence is unclear, contemporary sources suggest that these and subsequent epidemics killed thousands (Dobyns 1983; Ramenofsky 1987).

Wars killed or drove away hundreds more. Indian people throughout the region adopted new weapons, developed new tactics, and acquired new reasons for fighting. Conflicts between native people, such as the wars between the Tarrantines (today's Micmac people) and Indian people living around Massachusetts Bay, became increasingly lethal (Siebert 1973). Farther west, Mohawk warriors and their allies repeatedly forced people living in Western Abenaki and Mahican countries to withdraw from settlements within range of their war parties (Calloway 1990; Trelease 1960; Trigger 1971).

Wars with settlers set new standards for ferocity and destructiveness. The first major conflict between Indian people and settlers in the region, the Pequot War, fought between Pequot Indian peo-ple and New England settlers and their Indian allies from 1636 to 1637, resulted in the defeat and devastation of the Pequot nation (S. F. Cook 1973b; Hauptman and Wherry 1990; Jennings 1975; Vaughan 1979; Washburn 1978). Thousands of New England natives were killed, enslaved, or driven into exile during King Philip's War (named for the Wampanoag sachem known to his own people as Metacomet or Matacam) between 1675 and 1676 (Baker 1986; Jennings 1975; Leach 1958; Vaughan 1979).

Indian, English, and French people became embroiled in seemingly incessant warfare along the region's borders during these years. On the north, fighting along the Acadian border beginning in the late 1670s finally compelled most Europeans to abandon settlements between the Kennebec and Penobscot river valleys for much of the remainder of Historic Contact period. Farther west, columns of French soldiers and Indian warriors striking out from New France attacked isolated English outposts strung out along the northern borders of New York, New Hampshire, and Massachusetts when the first of the four imperial wars fought between France and Great Britain for control of the region broke out in 1689.

Farther south and west, wars with the Mohawks and the Dutch ravaged Indian communities along the upper Hudson, Housatonic, and Connecticut river valleys. By the end of the century, these wars and epidemics had reduced overall native population to less than a tenth of its pre-1600 level.

In contrast, European population rose dramatically during this same period. The vast majority of these immigrants came from the British Isles. The "Great

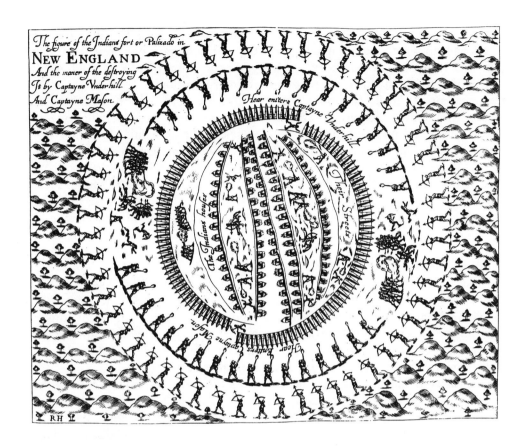

The May 26, 1637, attack led by Capts. John Mason and John Underhill on the Pequot fort at Mystic, Connecticut, has become an enduring symbol of the brutality of English troops in the Pequot War and in subsequent conflicts with Indian people. This engraving, first published in Underhill's 1638 account of the war, diagrammatically represents musket-bearing English settlers, backed up by bow-and-arrow-armed Mohegan and Narragansett warriors, firing on resisting bow-and-arrow-armed Pequot warriors and unarmed people fleeing from the invaders, who had penetrated to the community's residential core.

Migration" of English settlers into southern New England raised settler population in Massachusetts Bay from one thousand to eleven thousand between 1630 and 1638. In one area alone, three thousand settlers arriving between 1630 and 1633 overwhelmed the few hundred Massachusett and Pawtucket people known to have survived Micmac raids, sporadic attacks from Plymouth settlers, and earlier epidemics (Salisbury 1982a).

Thousands of other settlers had poured into Rhode Island, Connecticut, and nearby sections of New Hampshire and southwestern Maine by the 1640s. Still others moved westward beyond the Connecticut Valley toward the Hudson River and Long Island to lands claimed by the Dutch.

Total English population in New England had grown to nearly ninety-one thousand by 1700. The number of African people living in this area, by contrast, remained small. No more than seventeen hundred people of African descent were enumerated in New England in 1700 (McCusker and Menard 1985). Many probably were new arrivals. Others had almost certainly been born in the region. Although nearly all were slaves owned by European settlers, some of these people began living with and marrying Indians.

French numbers never approached those of the English during this period. Establishing their first settlements along the Gulf of Maine in 1604, their sphere of influence never extended beyond the upper Champlain Valley and the Acadian border in modern Maine. The French built forts, settlements, and missions at carefully selected strategic locales along this border to screen their main settlements in Acadia and Quebec. Living on the lands of Indian people who vastly outnumbered them, the few hundred French soldiers, traders, and missionaries occupying these posts relied more on diplomacy than force to secure their main settlements and project power outward.

Dutch West India Company officials began settling colonists from a number of northern European countries along the Hudson River after 1624. Stretching from the Connecticut River to Delaware Bay, the Dutch called their colony New Netherland. No more than ten thousand people, a figure that included six hundred people of African descent, were living on the Hudson when English troops conquered New Netherland in 1664 (Rink 1986). Dividing the former Dutch colony into two parts, the English named the northern portion "New York" and gave the name "New Jersey" to the southern section.

Initial English control over the area was not secure. As vulnerable to Dutch attack as it had been to English assault, New York surrendered to a Dutch squadron during the Third Anglo-Dutch War in 1673. Holding the Hudson and Delaware Valleys for nearly a year, the Dutch finally surrendered the area for the last time under the terms of the Treaty of Westminster that ended the conflict in 1674.

The total population of settlers in the Hudson Valley had risen to thirty thousand by 1700. More than three thousand of these people were Africans brought into or born in the area (McCusker and Menard 1985).

As these figures show, colonial population grew at increasingly faster rates everywhere in the region during the 1600s. Although war and disease claimed the lives of many newcomers, immigration and natural increase more than made up for all losses. Rising from almost nothing in 1600, total European and African population in the North Atlantic had increased to more than 130,000 by the end of the century.

Overwhelmed by these numbers and forced to contend with seemingly endless waves of warfare and epidemic disease, Indian people rarely were able to replenish their own losses. Europeans relentlessly pressed survivors of such disasters to convey title to their lands and move elsewhere. Although most sold land, few, if any, did so freely. All realized that they had to sell or see their lands forcibly seized. Many managed to slow the pace and extent of the loss by limiting sales to small tracts. Others did their best to play rival land claimants off against one another, supporting one faction or another in colonial courts. Despite these efforts, Europeans managed to obtain title to much of the most desirable land along the region's rivers and coasts by 1700 (Baker 1989; Jennings 1975).

Demoralized by the loss of land and loved ones, many Indians, seeking visions, conviviality, or consolation, began to drink heavily. Taking on the appearance of an epidemic by the end of the century, alcohol abuse devastated families and ravaged entire communities already reeling from the effects of war, disease, and division.

Nevertheless, Indians struggled to respond to the challenges. Many moved to new places. Others explored new ways of living. Old backcountry Indian towns far from colonial settlements, like the upper Kennebec Valley community of Norridgewock, were renovated and reoccupied. New towns were built. Of the people who left the region entirely, some moved north to the Saint Lawrence Valley, and others settled farther west in the Susquehanna or Ohio valley. But they tried to remain on or near ancestral lands whenever possible. Those forced to sell their homes moved to more remote places unwanted by colonists. Others settled in Christian mission towns or moved onto small reservations set aside by provincial authorities. Some people, like Western Pequots, who were granted a reservation at Mashantucket by Connecticut authorities in 1666, managed to hold onto some of their land. People living in what became known as Western Abenaki Country and other native people unwilling to be confined to reservations or missions increasingly found themselves living in territories that had become borderlands separating contending provincial, imperial, and Indian rivals.

Archaeological evidence indicates that Indian people throughout the region began moving from scattered settlements to larger, more compact, and occasionally fortified towns as the goals of warfare shifted from vengeance and glory to conquest, slave-taking, and annihilation during the early decades of the century. Proving vulnerable to determined attackers willing to burn or besiege such places, Indian people throughout the region gradually stopped building walled residential towns like the Pequot fort destroyed by New England settlers at Mystic in 1637. Although Indian people continued to construct fortified refuges when war threatened, most chose to live in small, decentralized towns and hamlets during times of peace.

Housing styles also changed during these years. Although many North Atlantic Indian people continued to live in bark- or grass-mat-covered, sapling-framed housing, growing numbers began moving into log or frame homes similar to those built by their English, French, and Dutch neighbors.

Only a few of the hundreds of seventeenth-century Indian towns documented in regional European written records have been archaeologically identified. Those that have been found generally contain scanty, scattered, or disturbed deposits. Cemeteries, like those found at Burr's Hill, RI-1000, and Pantigo, appear with increasing frequency during this century.

These and many other known seventeenth-century archaeological locales in the region have been damaged or destroyed. Most of the relatively few sites that have been systematically, if hurriedly, excavated have been unearthed by dedicated amateurs or contract archaeologists trying to keep ahead of bulldozers or looters.

Archaeologists have found unprecedentedly large and diverse assemblages of European goods in many of these locales. Although discoveries of European goods in graves located at the sites show that Indian people continued to use foreign imports as mortuary offerings, recovery of such materials in pits, midden layers, hearths, living floors, and other features attest to their growing importance in everyday life as well.

Important as they became, European imports did not impel abandonment of tried-and-tested tools and weapons. Many Indian musketeers, for instance, continued to use bows and arrows. New materials or techniques often improved old technologies. Metal arrowheads cut from kettles or copper sheets gradually replaced stone and antler projectile points. Other metal tools proved their worth to Indian woodcarvers, clothes makers, canoe makers, cooks, basket makers, and wampum manufacturers.

European demand for Indian goods also stimulated production of aboriginal manufactures. Many Indian people responded to new market opportunities by producing moccasins, wooden bowls, snowshoes, splint baskets, straw, brush, or birch splint brooms, and other objects for export. Herbalists concocted pharmaceuticals while doctors and midwives ministered to colonial clients. Others served as hired scouts, warriors, and hunters. Selling or bartering goods and services, Indian people had become

regular consumers of imported goods by the end of the century. Only small amounts of aboriginal manufactures have been recovered from places like Burr's Hill, the Fort Shantok National Historic Landmark, and other late seventeenth-century sites (Gibson 1980; Salwen 1966).

Evidence preserved at these and other sites further shows that their occupants found new uses for old commodities. Archaeological remains of wampum manufacture found at the Fort Corchaug site on eastern Long Island, for example, corroborate written records chronicling increased use of wampum shell beads as a medium of exchange among European and Indian people during the middle decades of the 1600s (Ceci 1980b, 1982b).

Such evidence attests to the dramatic change in Indian material culture during the seventeenth century. The changes do not mean that the region's original inhabitants somehow lost their identities or abandoned cultural traditions during these years. Although many aspects of their lives changed, Indian people themselves did not disappear. Surviving wars, epidemics, and dispossession, native people endured. Testifying to Indian persistence, written and archaeological records show how native people struggled to adapt creatively to drastically changing conditions.

THE EIGHTEENTH CENTURY

The already rapid pace of change in Indian culture accelerated throughout the region during the 1700s. Aboriginal social and cultural life was transformed as Indian people struggled to contend with colonists intent upon their assimilation, subjugation, dispossession, dispersal, or disappearance. Population statistics for the period tellingly reveal the toll these transformations took on native societies.

Available population records indicate that North Atlantic Indian population, already in sharp decline by the late 1600s, continued to dwindle precipitously as the 1700s wore on. No fewer than ten episodes of epidemic disease are recorded in Hudson Valley records alone between 1703 and 1767 (Grumet 1990). Hundreds of other Indian people perished in the nearly incessant wars that devastated Indian and European communities in frontier areas.

Land sales and oppressive provincial policies forced Indian people to leave their homes. Many fled to New France. Others moved farther west. The few thousand remaining in the region by the end of the century were forced to accept American control over their lives or move elsewhere.

European and African population, in contrast, increased exponentially during the same period. Total colonial population in the region rose from 130,000 in 1700 to 630,000 by the time the British captured most of New France at the height of the Seven Years' War in 1760 (McCusker and Menard 1985). These numbers would grow to more than 1,150,000 by the close of the American War for Independence. Fewer than fifty thousand of these people were Africans or descendants of African people. The rest were almost all immigrants from western Europe.

Warfare raged across the region's borders while France and Great Britain continued their contest for supremacy and survival in North America. Although the British finally forced the French to sur-

render Canada at the end of the Seven Years' War (1755–1762), their triumph was short-lived. British need to repay debts incurred in securing their empire soon limited their ability to hold it together. Shortsighted attempts to make colonists pay part of the price of empire turned New England into a hotbed of revolutionary ferment. Discontent finally turned to rebellion. Within ten years, Britain was at war with her colonies, and by 1783, the British were forced to surrender the region to the newly independent United States.

Immigrants moving to North Atlantic provinces during these years were quickly embroiled in these struggles. Tensions deepened and widened as landlords, merchants, provincial functionaries, royal administrators, and residents from neighboring provinces sought advantage over one another throughout the eighteenth century. Struggling to retrieve their steadily deteriorating position in any way possible, Indian people sided with one faction or another in many of these disputes.

No matter how they struggled among themselves, settlers generally shared the common goal of securing complete control over Indian people and land. Intent on realizing that goal, provincial governments throughout the region presided over the purchase or confiscation of nearly all North Atlantic Indian lands by the time the new American nation declared its independence in 1776.

Although Indian people in the region suffered devastating losses during these years, few were completely dispossessed from ancestral lands. Provincial governments set aside small reservations at places like Shinnecock on eastern Long Island and Charlestown in southern

Rhode Island. Powerful landowners occasionally also deeded small tracts to Indian people. Long Island manor lord William Smith, for example, signed over 175 acres in four tracts near Mastic to Indian people in 1700. This act established a reservation that endures today as the modern Poosepatuck community (Gonzalez 1986).

Indian people also continued to move to mission settlements. Some of these settlements, like the Massachusetts Bay Puritan Praying Indian towns, decreased in importance as the century wore on. Others, built in more remote frontier areas, grew in influence during these same years. Some missionaries, like Sébastien Râle, the French Jesuit administering the Norridgewock mission between 1695 and 1724, called on converts to openly serve imperial interests. New Light Presbyterian ministers, inspired by the wave of religious fervor known as the Great Awakening, which swept across Protestant communities throughout British North America during the 1730s and 1740s, established mission towns of their own at Schaghticoke, Connecticut, in 1734 and Stockbridge, Massachusetts, in 1736. Others, like pacifistic Moravian missionaries, established multiethnic utopian communities among Mahicans in the uplands of Dutchess County, New York, during the 1740s.

Affected by the policies and actions of missionaries, provincial magistrates, and imperial officials, North Atlantic Indian people radically changed most aspects of their way of life during this turbulent century. Observations entered onto trade ledgers, probate records, and other documents corroborate archaeological records showing that Indian abandonment of earlier aboriginal man-ufactures, already well along by 1700, was virtually complete by midcentury.

Collapse of the New England fur trade and the breakdown of the Indian real estate market following the sales of much of their remaining lands forced growing numbers of Indians into marginal sectors of the colonial wage economy. No longer employed as soldiers and guides after the end of the colonial wars, many of these people ultimately became laborers, seafarers, or servants.

Forced to live on relatively unproductive land and often compelled to travel long distances in search of work, food, and supplies, many Indians took up a wandering way of life. More than a few of them had become nomads in their own homelands by century's end. Unable to find spouses in their own shrinking or scattered communities, many married non-Indians or Indians from other groups.

Depending on where they lived, many native people learned to speak one of the trade jargons that had arisen in various parts of the region during the preceding century. As contact became more intensive, North Atlantic Indians also learned to speak English or French. Speaking these and other foreign languages, they generally became more aware of foreign ways. Many were taught new languages and customs by knowledgeable kinsfolk, neighbors, and missionaries.

Increasing numbers of Indian people also learned to read and write in native and European languages. English or French gradually supplanted native languages as elders grew old and died. Many aspects of established ways of life were transformed or abandoned by young people who chose to follow new ways of life they considered more in tune with changing times. In the process, several languages, such as Montauk, Massachusett, and Mahican, virtually disappeared.

These changes are reflected in the alteration or disappearance of many personal, ethnic, and tribal names as Indian people assumed European names or took as surnames the names of venerable ancestors or respected leaders.

People also assumed different ethnic identities. Many Eastern Niantics, for example, came to identify themselves as Narragansetts following their acceptance of Indian refugees from that tribe at the end of King Philip's War. In the same way, some southern New England Indian refugees, moving to the Schaghticoke community set up in 1676 by New York authorities on land long regarded as Mahican territory, later became known as Mahicans.

As with other changes noted earlier, a shift in naming practices does not signify the wholesale disappearance of cultural patterns or people so much as it reflects the Indian struggle to adapt creatively to the effects of dispossession, relocation, and social reorganization that marked the later phases of contact in the region.

SOURCES

A vast literature documents relations between Indian people and colonists in the North Atlantic region, yet no single study comprehensively surveys the archaeological, archival, and oral record of contact in the area.

Much of the documentation presented in this overview has been drawn from Brasser (1978a); Conkey, Boissevain, and Goddard (1978); Jennings (1975); Kraft (1989a, 1989b); Prins (1988a, 1991a, 1991b); Prins and Bourque (1987); Salisbury (1982b); Salwen (1978); and Snow (1980).

Several studies document early encounters. Some of the more accessible of these are Brasser (1978a) and Kraft (1989a, 1989b). More extensive examinations may be found in Morison (1971); Quinn (1977, 1981, 1985); Quinn, Quinn, and Hillier (1979); and Scammell (1981).

A number of studies focus more intensively on particular aspects of sixteenth-century contact. Ethnologist Bernard G. Hoffman (1961) examined evidence of early-sixteenth-century contacts along the northern coast. Lawrence C. Wroth has written a detailed analysis of Verrazzano's 1524 journal (Verrazzano 1970). Lynn Ceci (1977) chronicled early European voyages to southern New England predating Henry Hudson's 1609 voyage to the river today bearing his name. Laurier Turgeon (1990) has explored the potential of Basque, Norman, and Breton archives to reveal new information on sixteenth-century trade along North Atlantic shores.

A large body of written records documents relations between Indian people and colonists in seventeenth-century New England. General overviews synthesizing major aspects of this literature are published in Jennings (1975), E. Johnson (1993), Salisbury (1982b), and Salwen (1978). Extracts from primary sources documenting events in the North country are presented in Calloway (1991). Salisbury's detailed narrative (1982a) provides insights into the causes and consequences of contact events in and around southern New England during the first half of the century. Conkey, Boissevain, and Goddard (1978) synopsize information documenting relations in the years following King Philip's War.

Large numbers of more specialized studies document particular aspects of seventeenth-century North Atlantic intercultural relations. Studies such as those of Prins (1988a, 1991a, 1991b), Prins and Bourque (1987), and Snow (1980) present contrasting views of contact developments in Eastern Abenaki Country. English Indian policies are covered in Jacobs (1988). Leach (1988), Washburn (1978), and Malone (1973, 1991) document seventeenth-century warfare in the region.

Grumet (1980) surveys records documenting the role of women in Coastal Algonquian political, economic, and spiritual life during the Historic Contact period. Puritan-Indian legal relations in Massachusetts Bay are summarized in Kawashima (1986, 1988a). Particularly useful studies contrasting Indian and English society and material culture in the region may be found in Ceci (1980b, 1982b), P. Thomas (1985, 1991), and Fairbanks and Trent (1982).

A substantial literature is devoted to English and French Christian Indian missionization efforts. Axtell (1985) provides an excellent overview of the subject. Other valuable sources on seventeenth-century missionary efforts in the North Atlantic include Brenner (1980, 1984), Beaver (1988), Campeau (1988), Goddard and Bragdon (1988), Jennings (1971), Lewis (1988), Ronda (1983), Salisbury (1972, 1974), and Von Lonkhuyzen (1990). A particularly exhaustive survey of documentary and archaeological evidence associated with the first seven Massachusetts Bay Praying Indian towns may be found in Carlson (1986).

Surveys written by Haviland and Power (1981) and Snow (1980) describe much of what is known about seventeenth-century Indian archaeology in the region's more northerly reaches. Papers by Bradley (1983, 1987b) provide useful overviews of developments farther south.

The large number of site reports produced in the region provide an array of archaeological documentation for colonial North Atlantic Indian life. Contributions in the Burr's Hill site report (Gibson 1980), for example, present particularly detailed studies contrasting the wide range of seventeenth-century aboriginal and European technologies found in Burr's Hill mortuary contexts with contemporary assemblages elsewhere. Other site data sources include works by P. Robinson (1987, 1990), Simmons (1970), P. Thomas (1991), Turnbaugh (1984), L. Williams (1972), and Young (1969b). Studies presenting data on North Atlantic Indian place-names recorded by Europeans during the seventeenth and eighteenth centuries include those by Eckstorm (1978) and Huden (1965).

No general study synthesizing archaeological, archival, and oral evidence for North Atlantic Indian life during the eighteenth century has yet been attempted. Conkey, Boissevain, and Goddard (1978) survey general trends in eighteenth-century southern New England Indian life. More detailed information on eighteenth-century Indian life in the Massachusetts Indian towns of Hassanamisco, Natick, Punkapoag, and Stockbridge appears in Mandell (1992). Other useful sources include Beaver (1988), Calloway (1990), Kawashima (1986), and Salisbury (1982b).

EASTERN ABENAKI COUNTRY

Eastern Abenaki Country extends across most of the state of Maine. Starting from the Saint Croix River on the Canadian border, this area stretches westward across the Penobscot, Kennebec, and Androscoggin Valleys to the Saco River drainage.

THE SIXTEENTH CENTURY

Extant archaeological, archival, and oral documentation indicates that this area was home to a number of different Eastern Algonquian-speaking Indian communities when Giovanni da Verrazzano made the first recorded European voyage to North Atlantic shores in 1524.

The fragmentary and often ambiguous nature of this evidence has sparked lively scholarly debate over the distribution and identities of these groups. Some investigators believe that the area's physiographic setting, a series of roughly parallel river drainages separated from one another by barren lands or rocky uplands, generally restricted settlement to particular drainage systems (Snow 1968; Speck 1915). Calling attention to more widespread relation-ship patterns documented in later seventeenth- and eighteenth-century European written records, other scholars believe that Indian people living in this area belonged to flexibly interlocking networks of kin and clients stretching across river valleys (Bourque 1989a; Prins 1986b, 1991a, 1991b; Prins and Bourque 1987).

No known written document currently clearly chronicles the identities or affiliations of Indian people living in Eastern Abenaki Country during the 1500s. The name Abenaki itself (sometimes written Wabanaki), an Algonquian word meaning "Easterners" or "Dawnlanders," first appears in early seventeenth-century French records as a general term for northern New England Algonquian-speaking Indian people.

Archaeologists investigating sites in this area have found that most Indian people living between the Androscoggin and Penobscot Valleys during the sixteenth century made collared, incised pottery and triangular, chipped-stone projectile points resembling types and styles used by other Indian people living farther south and west. Contemporaries living on the north and east of Penobscot territory also made side-notched projectile points similar to others found in sites located in Nova Scotia and southeastern Quebec.

Although some people living along the westernmost reaches of this area planted corn, beans, and squash, most of the inhabitants of Eastern Abenaki Country primarily made their living by hunting, fishing, and foraging. Stone or bone harpoons, fishing gear, barbed arrows and spears, and remains of fish, shellfish, and sea mammals found in shell heaps and middens at sites like ME 17.076/ME 410-3, Pejepscot, and Sargentville show that people living along the coast drew much of their livelihood from the sea. Discovery of stone projectile points, knives, and scrapers in sites like Cobbosseecontee Dam located farther inland attest to the importance of hunting, trapping, and collecting.

Few as these known sixteenth-century sites are, their distribution and content suggest that most of the area's native people continued to follow the nomadic way of life that had first emerged in Maine thousands of years earlier. Gathering at certain times of the year to meet neighbors or take advantage of short-lived resource opportunities, most of these people pursued a highly mobile lifestyle. The small number of metal scraps and glass beads found with aboriginal stone, bone, and ceramic artifacts in sixteenth-century Eastern Abenaki Country archaeological deposits indicates that European contact had little impact on Indian technology in the area. Other effects of contact during these years are less clearly understood at the present time.

THE SEVENTEENTH CENTURY

Samuel de Champlain and other French explorers sailing to the shores of this area during the first decades of the seventeenth century noted that people identified as Etchemins and Souriquois lived in small communities along eastern Maine shores. Contrasting French and English written sources with recently discovered archaeological evidence, Bruce Bourque and Harald Prins have attempted to determine the identities of the Indian peoples living in Maine during the seventeenth century (Bourque 1989a; Prins 1991a, 1991b; Prins and Bourque 1987). They have found data indicating that most descendants of Souriquois people later came to be known as Micmacs. Although most Micmacs today live in New Brunswick and Nova Scotia, a small community of people tracing descent to Micmac ancestors still exists in the northern reaches of Aroostook County (Prins 1988a; Whitehead 1988).

Many speakers of the Micmac language continue to live in Canada's Maritime Provinces. The exact meaning of their group name remains unclear. Although some linguists think that the name comes from a French word for "nonsense speaker," most scholars trace the term's etymology to an Algonquian expression meaning "allies" or "kin-friends."

Identifying Etchemins as Maliseet people living along the Maine coast east of the Kennebec River, Bourque and Prins have further shown that these people joined with members of Caniba communities living on the upper Kennebec River and Pigwacket people living farther south to form a loose confederation

MAP 3: EASTERN ABENAKI COUNTRY

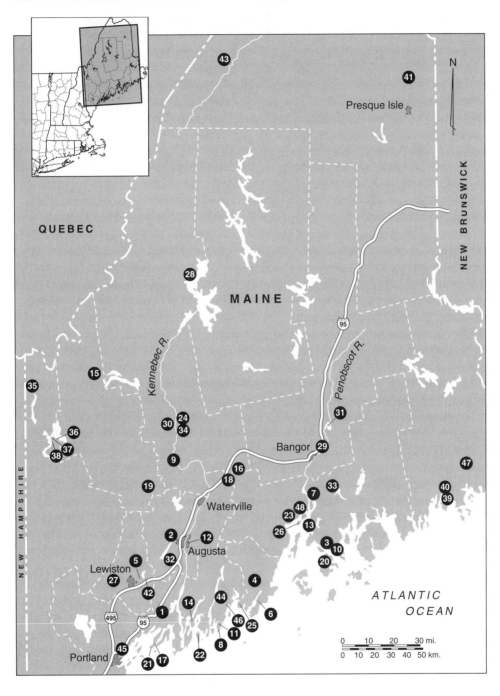

QUEBEC

MAINE

NEW BRUNSWICK

NEW HAMPSHIRE

Presque Isle

Kennebec R.

Penobscot R.

Bangor

Waterville

Augusta

Lewiston

Portland

ATLANTIC OCEAN

N

95

495

95

0   10   20   30 mi.
0 10 20 30 40 50 km.

Map 3 Historic Contact Sites

Map Number	Site Name	County	State	Date	NR	Source
1	Pejepscot (ME 14.108)	Cumberland	ME	1400–1550	X	MHASI; Spiess 1987
2	ME 37.5	Kennebec	ME	1500s	X	Bourque 1975
3	Sargentville	Hancock	ME	1500s–1600s		Moorehead 1922
4	ME 27.059	Knox	ME	1500s–1600s		MPASI
5	UMF 202	Androscoggin	ME	1500s–1700s		MHASI
6	ME 17.076 and ME 410-3	Knox	ME	1590–1620	X	MHASI; MPASI; A. Spiess 1983
7	Sandy Point	Hancock	ME	Early 1600s		Bradley 1983; Moorehead 1922
8	Nahanada (ME 16.090 and ME 058-3)	Lincoln	ME	1600–1625	X	MHASI; MPASI; A. Spiess and Bradley 1979
9	Norridgewock NHL Old Point (ME 069-2) Tracy Farm (ME 069-11) Sandy River (ME 069-24)	Somerset	ME	1614–1754	X	Cowie and Petersen 1992; Prins and Bourque 1987
10	Bridges Point (ME 059-3)	Hancock	ME	1620–1675		MHASI
11	Pemaquid NHL (ME 058-1)	Lincoln	ME	1625–1759	X	Beard and Bradley 1978; Camp 1975
12	Cushnoc NHL (ME 021-2)	Kennebec	ME	1628–1670	X	Cranmer 1990; Prins 1986a, 1987
13	Pentagoet NHL Fort Pentagoet (ME 084-3) Saint-Castin's Habitation (ME 084-7)	Hancock	ME	1635–1700	X	Faulkner and Faulkner 1985
14	Clark and Lake (ME 015-1)	Sagadahoc	ME	1654–1676	X	Baker 1985
15	ME 149-1	Franklin	ME	1600s(?)		MPASI
16	ME 068-1	Waldo	ME	Late 1600s		MHASI
17	Haskell Island	Cumberland	ME	1600s		MHASI
18	Ferguson's Rips (ME 068-2)	Waldo	ME	1600s		MHASI
19	ME 130-1 RSPF	Franklin	ME	1600s		MHASI; Prins 1988b
20	Pond Island District (ME 120-2)	Lincoln	ME	1600s	X	MHASI
21	ME 9.12	Cumberland	ME	1600s		MPASI
22	ME 16.119/ME404-2	Lincoln	ME	1600s		MHASI; MPASI
23	ME 41.053	Waldo	ME	1600s		MPASI
24	ME 69.005	Somerset	ME	1600s–1700s	X	A. Spiess 1986
25	ME 163-2 and ME 17.071	Knox	ME	1600s–1700s	X	MHASI; MPASI
26	Sears Island (ME 385-3 and ME 41.043)	Waldo	ME	1600s–1700s		MHASI; MPASI
27	ME 24.027	Androscoggin	ME	1600s–1700s		MPASI
28	ME 117.072	Somerset	ME	1600s–1700s		MPASI
29	Negas (ME 446-04)	Penobscot	ME	1700–1723		A. Faulkner 1988; MHASI
30	Hogdon (ME 69.004 and ME 146-1)	Somerset	ME	1700–1725		A. Spiess 1980
31	Indian Island Complex (ME 324-2)	Penobscot	ME	1723–present		MHASI; Snow 1980
32	Yale (ME 246-1)	Kennebec	ME	Early 1700s		MHASI
33	Bald Mountain (ME 119-1)	Hancock	ME	1700s		MHASI
34	ME 69.6	Somerset	ME	1700s		MPASI
35	Grassy Island	Oxford	ME	1700s		MHASI
36	Metallak Island	Oxford	ME	1700s		MHASI
37	Mill Brook West	Oxford	ME	1700s		MHASI
38	Portland Point	Oxford	ME	1700s		MHASI

Map Number	Site Name	County	State	Date	NR	Source
39	ME 61.026/ME 003-1	Washington	ME	1700s		MHASI; MPASI
40	ME 61.032/ME 003-1	Washington	ME	1700s		MHASI; MPASI
41	ME 177.001	Aroostook	ME	1700s		MPASI
42	ME 378-1	Androscoggin	ME	1700s		MHASI
43	Big Black	Aroostook	ME	Historic	X	Sanger 1975
44	Damariscotta	Lincoln	ME	Historic	X	Holstrom 1969a
45	Scitterygusset	Cumberland	ME	Historic		MPASI
46	ME 17.011	Lincoln	ME	Historic		MPASI
47	ME 78.001	Washington	ME	Historic		MPASI
48	ME 151/10 RSPF	Waldo	ME	Historic		MPASI

sometime during the late 1600s. The people of this confederation gradually came to be known collectively as Abenakis or Wabanakis.

Intensive contacts between Indian people living in Eastern Abenaki Country and Europeans began when explorers like Samuel de Champlain and John Smith journeyed to this area during the first decade of the seventeenth century. Although precise figures do not exist, the total number of Indian people living in Eastern Abenaki Country at the time probably did not exceed twelve thousand.

Archaeological evidence found in deposits dating to the early seventeenth century at sites like ME 17.076/ME 410-3, Nahanada, and Sandy Point indicates that these people continued to live much as they had in earlier times. Testing at Nahanada has revealed the presence of a thick midden layer containing post molds, pits, and numerous European artifacts predating the establishment of nearby English settlements in 1625 at what is today the Pemaquid National Historic Landmark. Sadly, erosion has all but obliterated Nahanada. Sandy Point, for its part, has been destroyed by erosion and development. Better-preserved sites containing small assemblages of contemporary European and Indian artifacts have been found at the aforementioned ME 17.076/ME 410-3 site, at Bridges Point, Murray Hill Portage, and several other locales.

Later seventeenth-century sites, like the Saint-Castin's Habitation in the Pentagoet National Historic Landmark and several locales within the Norridgewock National Historic Landmark, graphically show how Indian life changed as the fur trade came to play an increasingly important role in the lives of Indian people throughout the area. Journeying inland from the coast, French and English traders established permanent posts at various locales within Eastern Abenaki Country. Archaeological evidence of stone forts, substantial house foundations, and other features found at places like Pentagoet and Pemaquid shows that these Europeans intended to stay.

Though slow at first, the pace of change quickened when native people throughout the area found their lands turned into battlegrounds as France and England used the area's forts in their struggles for control of the continent. As elsewhere in the Northeast, Eastern Abenaki Country people responded to challenges and opportunities presented by war and trade by playing adversaries off against each other whenever possible. Most Indians living between the upper Kennebec and Penobscot Valleys at the flashpoint separating the frontiers of

New England and Acadia did their best to accommodate their often mutually hostile neighbors. Farther west, people living along the lower Kennebec River and the Androscoggin Valley worked to establish close ties with Plymouth and Massachusetts Bay traders, who provided comparatively better and cheaper English goods at what is today the Cushnoc National Historic Landmark and at other posts during the 1630s.

This commerce soon affected established modes and relations of production. Men and women, who had earlier often worked together in cooperative groups, began to work separately. Small groups of men began traveling longer distances in search of furs and other commodities. Remaining at home, women forged new roles for themselves as they turned their energies to community affairs, pelt processing, business, and crop cultivation. These changes ultimately transformed the relative status and role of men and women in Indian communities throughout Eastern Abenaki Country.

Most native people living in these communities were drawn into the fur trade by the middle decades of the 1600s. Mahicans and other Indian refugees moving to missions at Amesokanti at Farmington Falls and other locales in Maine between 1676 and 1725 later joined in the commerce (Bourque 1989a; Prins 1988b). A number of these people initially set up households near European posts, but they were subject to epidemic contagion and attacks by rivals while at these posts, and as the fur trade collapsed during the waning decades of the century, they gradually left for less volatile locales farther from European settlements.

The process of coalition building alluded to earlier began as people living in Eastern Abenaki Country searched for ways to respond to challenges posed by war, depopulation, and uncertain economic conditions. A 1625 source—evidently based upon information furnished by Indian people kidnapped by English ship captain George Weymouth in 1605—noted that twenty-one native communities located on eleven rivers in an area called Mawooshen that extended from Penobscot Bay to Massachusetts were organized into a loose federation led by a man named Bashaba or Betsabes (Eckstorm 1978; Prins 1991a, 1991b). Sometime later, most Indian people living in this area established the already-mentioned Wabanaki confederacy.

Unity was sorely needed as English colonists compelled individual Indian communities to sell and vacate increasingly larger expanses of coastline. Relations worsened as epidemics, Mohawk raids, dishonest traders, several murders, and other provocations angered and alienated Indian people everywhere in Eastern Abenaki Country.

In 1675, English settlers, alarmed by the widening King Philip's War, demanded that Indian people in the area surrender their firearms. Refusing to render themselves defenseless, most people living near English towns simply moved farther east to Penobscot territory. Outraged by the murder of the infant child of a Saco Indian leader and inspired by Indian successes against the English in King Philip's War then raging farther south in New England, most of these people finally went to war against the English in 1676.

Indians launched attacks against New England settlements everywhere in Eastern Abenaki Country. Cutting off the more isolated communities, they soon forced abandonment of Arrowsic, Cushnoc, and Pemaquid. Treaties signed in 1676 and 1678 only temporarily stopped the fighting in the area. Primarily focused upon halting hostilities, these treaties did little to address the causes of hostility and did not prevent most Indians in the area from striking out against English settlers moving back to the area when war broke out between France and England in 1689.

Indian attacks again devastated the English settlements. An Indian force supported by the French sacked Pemaquid and assaulted nearby Fort William Henry just as the war began. A larger force returned in 1696. Coordinating their efforts with three French warships, the warriors captured the town, sent their prisoners back to Boston, and razed both fort and town. So decisive was this attack that thirty-five years would pass before New Englanders tried to reoccupy the locale.

Indian relations with the French missionaries, traders, and government officials, by contrast, grew closer during these years. Pentagoet first became an important French administrative center when Sieur Charles d'Aulnay, the commander of Acadia, built a fort on the banks of the Bagaduce River in the modern town of Castine, Maine, in 1633. Captured and occupied by the English in 1654, the fort was returned to France in 1670. Rebuilt and refurbished at that point, Pentagoet subsequently served as the capital of Acadia until its final destruction by Dutch privateers in 1674. Refusing to abandon the area, Jean Vincent Abaddie de Saint-Castin established a trading post most widely known as Saint-Castin's Habitation in a nearby Etchemin town in 1677 (Faulkner and Faulkner 1987). Operating from places like Saint-Castin's Habitation and the Norridgewock mission established a few years later in the upper Kennebec Valley, missionaries and traders acted as agents of the French government. Working to secure the exposed frontiers of Acadia and New France, they helped Indian people to defend their own lands in Eastern Abenaki Country.

THE EIGHTEENTH CENTURY

Many aspects of native life in Eastern Abenaki Country had changed dramatically by the beginning of the eighteenth century. Hundreds of Indian people had been killed in the wars and epidemics that had raged across Eastern Abenaki Country during the 1600s. Colonists pouring into the area relentlessly pressed survivors to give up their lands. Giving in to these pressures, many leaders had already sold much of the coast below the Kennebec River to English purchasers by 1700 (Baker 1989). French authorities, for their part, regarded the land to the north of the Kennebec as theirs. No matter how they felt about each other, both nations continued to claim sovereignty over all Indian land in Eastern Abenaki Country up to the final French defeat in America in 1760.

Although all Indian people living in Eastern Abenaki Country continued to pursue their mobile way of life, many spent increasingly larger amounts of time in a few permanent towns. Some of these communities contained as many as fifty bark-roofed log houses. Centers of larger towns like Norridgewock often were enclosed by palisaded stockade walls.

Cushnoc Archeological Site National Historic Landmark

Archaeological remains of the trading post of Cushnoc, established by the Plymouth (Massachusetts) colony, are preserved on the banks of the Kennebec River in the city of Augusta, Kennebec County, Maine. Cushnoc, one of the most important seventeenth-century English outposts in Eastern Abenaki Country, was situated in the heart of the territories of people identified by Europeans as "Abenaquiois" or "Caniba"; it sat at a critical juncture on the strategic Kennebec-Chaudière River corridor connecting Acadia, northern New England, and New France.

Upper Kennebec Archaeological Survey researchers jointly funded by the Maine Historic Preservation Commission and the City of Augusta found the post-mold pattern of an earthfast building, remains of a palisade trench, and almost forty-five hundred artifacts dating to the mid-1600s during excavations conducted at the locale between 1984 and 1987. Contrasting their findings with extant archival data, researchers established the identity of the site, traced its boundaries, outlined its documented history, and analyzed its archaeological deposits.

Plymouth merchants operated Cushnoc as a small, year-round trading post from the 1620s to 1661. Although scholars continue to debate the exact dates of Cushnoc's construction and abandonment, most agree that the post was located, as the translation of its name from an Abenaki expression meaning "where the tide runs no higher up" suggests, at the head of navigation just below the first falls of the Kennebec River (Prins 1987:12). Several archival

Aerial photograph of the Cushnoc locale, Fort Western National Historic Landmark appears in the foreground; the Augusta, Maine, city hall is on the upper left. Photograph by Lynn Gustin, Litchfield, Maine. Courtesy Maine Historic Preservation Commission.

references, like Gen. John Winslow's December 30, 1754, letter stating that he had built Fort Western "at a place called Cushenoc Near the Spot where one hundred years ago the late Plymouth Colony had a Garrison," clearly place Cushnoc within the present Augusta city limits.

Other documents reveal that Cushnoc was the second of five trading posts built by Plymouth colonists along the New England frontier between 1626 and 1632. It was meant to support the economically hard-pressed colony during its critical formative years between 1620 and 1640, and Plymouth traders working at Cushnoc and other posts exchanged corn, peas, and English goods for furs and other Indian products. Inadequately supplied and located on hotly contested frontiers, most of these posts had been abandoned or seized by competitors by midcentury. Cushnoc, the longest-lived of these posts, was finally sold to four Boston merchants in 1661.

Most of the artifacts dating to the mid-1600s at Cushnoc were found beneath layers of plow zone and fill within sandy subsoil strata overlying culturally sterile, hard-packed, coarse, gray gravel, rock, and clay fluvial sediments. Although artifacts were found in most areas of the site, much of the diagnostic mid–seventeenth-century assemblage of hand-forged nails, white-clay European tobacco-smoking pipes, European ceramics, bottle glass, lead shot, gunflints and European flint-working debris, and glass beads was found in and around a wooden-plank–lined cellar feature within a post-mold pattern identified as the remains of a twenty-foot by forty-four-foot cross-passage earthfast structure. Testing also uncovered portions of a trench line believed to represent remains of the stockade wall surrounding the site.

Absence of a fire pit or hearth and discoveries of concentrations of daub in the cellar hole and the western end of the house indicate that building occupants used a wattle and daub smoke hood in place of a chimney. The uneven distribution of these daub concentrations, coupled with the discovery of nearly a thousand hand-forged nails associated with this and perhaps another undiscovered structure, indicates that the house walls were covered with clapboards or weatherboards rather than wattle and daub.

Analysis of the artifact assemblage found in and around this building affirms that it was occupied by people almost wholly dependent upon English manufactures during the middle decades of the 1600s. Slightly less than half of the 3,156 ceramic sherds found at the site consist of utilitarian redwares ($n = 1,055$), Spanish olive jars ($n = 467$), delftwares ($n = 33$), and French earthenwares ($n = 3$) excavated elsewhere in seventeenth-century contexts. All of the 647 sherds of green case bottle glass and twelve of the fifteen glass beads found in Cushnoc de-

posits also resemble glasswares recovered from other seventeenth-century Northeastern sites.

Other portions of Cushnoc's Historic Contact period diagnostic assemblage provide more precise date ranges. A datable lead cloth seal bears a motif known to have been in use from 1649 to 1660. Analysis of bore-diameter measurements taken from 725 of 2,000 European white-clay tobacco-smoking pipe stem fragments render a mean adjusted Binford formula date of 1650. The presence of eleven pipe bowls bearing marks dating from 1610 to 1680 and the absence of red-clay tobacco pipes generally dating to the last quarter of the seventeenth century further confirm the above-mentioned date range.

Further analysis of data collected at Cushnoc can shed light on several significant questions. What effect, for example, did the establishment of Cushnoc have on Indian life in the area? How did Cushnoc traders adjust to and influence political, social, and economic relationships in the Kennebec Valley? And why were the English unable to reoccupy Kennebec territory for nearly seventy-five years after being forced to abandon the region when King Philip's War spread north in 1676? Answers to these and other questions will illuminate many poorly understood aspects of early relations between Indians, Acadians, New Englanders, and settlers from New France in Eastern Abenaki Country.

The Cushnoc Archeological Site was listed in the National Register of Historic Places in 1990 and designated a National Historic Landmark on April 12, 1993. Artifacts recovered from the site currently are curated in the nearby Fort Western Museum.

Unless otherwise cited, information presented here is abstracted from Cranmer (1990).

Although their technology remained largely unchanged, people living in places like Norridgewock used imported European materials to craft utensils, clothing, ornaments, and weapons.

The inhabitants of these towns found it increasingly difficult to produce or acquire the commodities they needed as the century wore on. Much of their most productive fishing and foraging places along the coast and lower river valleys had already been sold or expropriated. Indian hunters and trappers, for their part, had long since extirpated beavers and other fur-bearing animals in territories close to their main settlements.

For their European goods, the Indians came to rely increasingly on gifts from missionaries and colonial administrators. They also worked for colonists as laborers, guides, and servants. Generally finding the French more generous than the British, many Indians developed close relationships with their Acadian neighbors.

Most Etchemins living along what the French regarded as the western borders of Acadia came to be known as Maliseets, Saint John's Indians, or Passamaquoddys during these years. Living in settlements on the north and east of the Penobscot River, they and Indians living farther west in the Kennebec Valley tried to remain neutral as tensions between France and Great Britain increased. Living between the competitors, they had suffered grievous losses while fighting with the French against the English during King William's War. Now forced again to choose, most sided once more with the French when war broke out in 1702.

Launching raids against British settlements along the coast (Bourque 1989a), they were forced to retreat in the face of British counterattacks, fleeing north toward Quebec or west to Norridgewock. Although some of these refugees remained in Quebec when the war ended in 1713, the majority returned to their homes in Eastern Abenaki Country. Some, like those people returning to homes around Sebago Lake in the Presumpscot Valley, moved back to communities close to coastal English towns. Others moved to places like Norridgewock far from all European settlements. Located on the border separating French and British spheres of influence, Norridgewock dominated communications along the Kennebec River. Commanding the invasion route to Canada that Benedict Arnold would use in 1775, the town also served as a springboard for military operations against New England.

Sébastien Râle, the Jesuit who established the Catholic mission at Norridgewock in 1695, continually worked to secure the friendship and support of the Kennebec Indian community. Recognizing the strategic importance of the town, Massachusetts officials periodically tried to draw Norridgewock's inhabitants to the English side. Town leaders did their best to manipulate this situation. Maintaining their French alliance, they supported trade with the British and allowed Massachusetts authorities to send carpenters to rebuild their town after it was burned by raiding New England troops in 1705.

That raid was the first of three attacks launched against Norridgewock by the British during the first quarter of the eighteenth century. The other two— a raid that resulted in the pillaging of the town while its occupants were off hunting in 1722 and a substantial attack made two years later that razed the town and left Father Râle and as many as forty of the town's inhabitants dead—occurred during Dummer's War (Eckstorm 1934), a war named for the Massachusetts lieutenant governor and commander of provincial troops and fought (1722–1727) to end French influence along the border with Acadia. Unlike other border wars of the period, Dummer's War was not part of a wider international conflict. Dragging on for several years, this local struggle finally ended when Eastern Abenaki leaders concluded a treaty nominally acknowledging British sovereignty over their territories.

Emulating successful French policies that used trade as a diplomatic tool, Massachusetts authorities established provincially regulated "truckhouses" at several locales near the mouths of rivers flowing to their coastal settlements in 1726. Although these posts helped to draw some Presumpscot and other Eastern Abenaki people back to their old homes, most Indians chose to establish new households at safer locales farther from the New England frontier. Many people moved to Saint Lawrence Valley missions like Bécancour and Saint-François de Sales, known to the Abenakis as Odanak and to the British as Saint Francis. Others settled in the Western Abenaki Indian community at Missisquoi at the northern end of Lake Champlain.

Indian and British people lived in uneasy proximity along the Presumpscot River for many years. Relations threatened to explode into war when settlers claiming Indian land built a dam blocking migrations of fish upriver. Meeting with Presumpscot leaders who came to Boston in 1739, Massachusetts authorities recognized the validity of their title to the land and ordered the demolition of the offending dam. Supported by provincial officials, this small group of Presumpscot families continued to live along the banks of Sebago Lake up to the outbreak of the Seven Years' War.

Farther east, the Kennebec Valley gradually became a hunting ground and communications route as most Norridgewock people moved elsewhere, either north to Canada or farther east in the Penobscot Valley. As the century wore on, leaders of Indian communities along the Penobscot came to represent the Maliseet, Passamaquoddy (a Maliseet community on the Saint Croix River that split off from the main group during the early 1700s), and other native communities in Eastern Abenaki Country in councils with colonists and imperial officials. Traveling to colonial towns or holding meetings in their own communities at Old Town, Pleasant Point, and Kingsclear, these people represented native communities of Maine in a Wabanaki confederacy that gradually expanded to include Huron, Ottawa, and other French Indian allies.

Locating their "Great Fire" at Caughnawaga just outside Montreal, leaders of the Wabanaki confederacy worked to coordinate efforts of many Indian people unwilling to accept British rule over their homelands. Supported by the French, most Wabanaki confederates sided with their allies when the Seven Years' War broke out between France and Great Britain in 1755.

Those Indians living closer to British settlements along the Penobscot River tried to remain neutral when the fighting started, but attacks on British towns launched by their Wabanaki confederates soon forced them to take sides. Fighting alongside their Wabanaki allies,

Norridgewock Archeological District National Historic Landmark

The three sites constituting the Norridgewock Archeological District are located at the confluence of the Kennebec and Sandy Rivers in Somerset County, Maine. Two of the district's three properties, the Tracy Farm and Sandy River sites, are located in the town of Starks on the west bank of the Kennebec just above the mouth of the Sandy River. The third property, the Old Point site, preserves remains of the Norridgewock Indian Jesuit mission community on the east bank of the Kennebec in the town of Madison.

Norridgewock is the most extensively described Indian community in the North Atlantic region. The town was first identified by name in 1625. Discoveries of post molds, daub, hand-forged nails, and other building debris amid dense deposits containing large numbers of European and aboriginal artifacts at Old Point corroborate written

Woodcut by James Franklin, Boston, 1724, depicting the August 12, 1724, British attack on Norridgewock. The flag in the woodcut matches a written description of a Jesuit flag that flew at the locale (Prins 1984, p. 8). Courtesy Harald E. L. Prins.

eyewitness accounts describing at least two successive nucleated communities on the spot. The first of these, built sometime between 1693 and 1695, was described by Massachusetts troops who burned the place in 1705:

> [T]he Head Quarters of the Eastern Indians, who advise of a large fort, Meeting-house & School-house that were there erected, the Fort encompassed 2 quarters of an acre of ground built with Pallisado's whearin were 12 wigwarms . . . The Meeting-house was built of Timber 60 Foot long, 25 Foot wide, & 18 Foot studd ceiled with Clapboards, in it were only a few old Popish Relicks; the School-house lay at one end distinct, all which they burnt, near to it was a Field of Corn ungathered.

Rebuilding their town between 1708 and 1713, Norridgewock people surrounded the main settlement with a palisade wall described by a visiting British chronicler in 1719 as "built with Round Loggs nine foot Long and set into ye Ground; [it] is 160 foot Square with 4 Gates but no bastions." This observer further noted that "within are Twenty six Houses Built much after the English manner, the streets reguler, yt from west Gate to ye East is 30 foot wide; Their Church stands 4 perch without ye East gate, And their men able to Bear Arms, are about three score."

Discoveries of sacramental objects, crucifixes, and other religious artifacts at the Old Point site corroborate documents chronicling the history of a Jesuit mission maintained at Norridgewock at various times between 1646 and 1754. The first Catholic church at Old Point, built by Fr. Sébastien Râle in 1698, was destroyed in 1705. A second church, rebuilt by the British in 1713 and finished by Father Râle in 1720, was destroyed with the rest of the town when Massachusetts troops killed Râle and at least forty other people and drove away the surviving defenders on August 23, 1724, during Dummer's War.

Largely abandoned after most Indian people left the area for the last time in 1754, Norridgewock again became a center of attention when Bishop Fenwick of Boston erected a monument to Father Râle's memory in 1833 near the spot where he was thought to have been killed. The Old Point locale has since been promoted by the Maine Historical Society and other organizations as one of the state's most notable historic sites.

Warren K. Moorehead conducted extensive excavations at Old Point in 1921. Long aware of the site, local collectors have found Râle's writing box, several crucifixes, the mission bell, iron fishhooks, gun parts, iron axes, copper or brass tinkler cones, metal shears, a claw hammer, chisels, a rasp, nippers, pliers, pewter sacramental objects, lead shot, lead bale seals, gunflints, a rapier fragment, European ceramics, and glass beads in deposits containing aboriginal stone and clay artifacts.

Surveying the general area during the early 1980s, Harald E. L. Prins and Bruce J. Bourque reconstructed Norridgewock's documented history, discovered the Tracy Farm and Sandy River sites, and arranged for the study of site collections. Field crews under the direction of University of Maine at Farmington archaeologist James B. Petersen subsequently conducted systematic subsurface test excavations at all

Longhouse post-mold pattern at the Tracy Farm site, in Norridgewock National Historic Landmark, 1990. Courtesy Ellen R. Cowie and James B. Petersen, Archaeology Research Center, University of Maine at Farmington.

three Norridgewock sites between 1988 and 1991. Funded by the Central Maine Power Company in compliance with the Weston Project Federal Energy Regulatory Commission relicensing process, University of Maine at Farmington field crews made several notable discoveries. Extensive assemblages of diagnostic terminal Late Woodland ceramics, chipped-stone triangular projectile points, glass beads, European white-clay tobacco-smoking pipes, metal tools, and other diagnostic artifacts dating to the Historic Contact period were found with well-preserved floral and faunal remains in or near intact pits, hearths, midden layers, and sealed strata.

Datable pieces of carbonized corn, beans, squash, and nut shells preserve evidence of the northeasternmost extent of aboriginal food production in North America. Discovery of 342 post molds representing evidence of an 82-foot-long and 16.4-foot-wide round-ended longhouse at the Tracy Farm site is the first discovery of its kind in and around Eastern Abenaki Country. A line of post molds with three-inch-wide diameters is believed to mark the structure's outer wall. A line of five or six larger post molds running through the center of the structure is thought to represent the remains of central support posts. Two parallel lines of post molds running along the northern side of the structure preserve evidence of what investigators believe was an interior platform or insulating wall.

One storage or refuse pit containing clearly identifiable deposits dating to the Historic Contact period was found inside the post-mold pattern. Measuring seventeen inches in diameter at its top, this pit was located inside the house's southern wall some twenty-three feet from its western end. Archaeologists excavating this feature recovered a European white-clay tobacco-smoking pipe bowl tentatively dated to between 1700 and 1770, four glass beads, and charred floral and faunal remains. Two other pits and the base of a hearth located in or near the structure also may be associated with the occupants of this longhouse.

Materials recovered during Weston Project investigations presently are curated in the University of Maine's Farmington Archaeology Research Center. Other collections from the Norridgewock locale are stored in the Maine State Museum and the Madison Public Library.

The Old Point site was listed in the National Register of Historic Places on April 2, 1973. The Norridgewock Archeological District was designated a National Historic Landmark on April 12, 1993.

Information presented here is abstracted from Cowie and Petersen (1992) and Prins and Bourque (1987).

---

they carried on their struggle against the British even after the French in Canada were forced to surrender in 1760. Making a separate peace with Massachusetts authorities, the people of Penobscot had to give up much of their land along the river in 1763. Two years later, Massachusetts officials compelled them to acknowledge the province's sovereignty over their remaining lands in Maine.

Never completely accepting British authority, most Penobscot people joined other Wabanaki confederates supporting the colonists' rebellion against British rule in 1775. Warriors from the Penobscot Valley served with colonial units as guides, batteaumen, hunters, and soldiers throughout the war. Although rebel authorities appreciated their help, their war record did not stop the victorious Americans from trying to take what remained of the lands of their erstwhile Indian allies once the fighting stopped.

Massachusetts authorities, for example, acted quickly to take control of all Indian land in what was then the northernmost part of their state. Interpreting the wording of the 1763 treaty as an Indian agreement to surrender title to their remaining lands in Maine, state commissioners claimed all land along the Penobscot except Old Town and a few small islands along the river and off the coast.

Sites located within the Old Town reservation preserve the most complete known archaeological record of eighteenth-century Indian life along the Penobscot River. Other deposits containing archaeological evidence documenting Indian life in Eastern Abenaki Country during the eighteenth century are preserved at the Norridgewock National Historic Landmark and at smaller sites like Negas, Grassy Island, and Portland Point.

SOURCES

Much of the information presented in this section has been drawn from Bourque (1989a), Prins (1986b, 1988a, 1988b, 1991a, 1991b), Calloway (1991), and Prins and Bourque (1987).

All reconstructions of Historic Contact period life in Eastern Abenaki Country depend upon Speck's pathbreaking ethnographic work (1915, 1940) in the area. Pertinent archaeological studies include Snow's overviews (1978b, 1980), Petersen and Sanger's ceramic analysis (1989), and detailed site reports written by Baker (1985), Cranmer (1990), and the Faulkners (1985, 1987).

Several of the most significant primary documentary sources recording European observations of Indian life in the area are published in Calloway (1991). Kenneth Morrison (1984) uses these and other texts to contrast spiritual and economic motivations affecting political relations between Indian people and colonists in the area. Ghere (1988) draws on a wide range of government records and other contemporary documents in his survey of colonial-era political relations in Eastern Abenaki Country.

Studies analyzing the relatively small amount of known documentary information chronicling Maliseet and Micmac life in Maine's Aroostook County include B. McBride and Prins (1991), Prins (1986b, 1988a, 1991a, 1991b), Nicholas and Prins (1989), and Wherry (1980). Accounts describing the culture and history of the main Micmac community in Nova Scotia may be found in Bailey (1969), Bock (1978), Bourque (1989a), B. Hoffman (1955), Nietfeld (1981), and Wallis and Wallis (1955).

WESTERN ABENAKI COUNTRY

At its widest extent, Western Abenaki Country stretches from Vermont and New Hampshire north and west to adjacent parts of New York and Quebec. Archaeologists have found evidence documenting the emergence of Late Woodland lifeways in various parts of Vermont and New Hampshire sometime after 1100. Recent discovery of corn in deposits dating to the twelfth century at the Skitchewaug site, for example, suggest that Indian people began growing maize in Vermont less than a century after it was first introduced into the more southerly Hudson and Mohawk Valleys.

THE SIXTEENTH CENTURY

Triangular, chipped-stone projectile points and clay pots similar to others found elsewhere in the north country have been recovered from sites along the Champlain and Connecticut River valleys. Some archaeologists regard differences in distributions of these and other artifacts as reflections of postcontact-chronicled ethnic boundaries. Analyzing stone tools found in Vermont and New Hampshire sites, Haviland and Power (1981) suggest that discoveries of

concave-based Levanna projectile points similar to those found in the Hudson, Housatonic, and Connecticut river valleys point to close relationships with people from those areas. Relative scarcities of straight-based Madison triangular projectile points generally found farther west, by contrast, are seen as evidence of less intensive contact with people from those areas.

Not all scholars agree with such findings. One study contrasting attributes of a large sample of triangular projectile points drawn from many sites conducted by archaeologists William Ritchie, Dean Snow, and Robert Funk, for example, failed to differentiate Madison from Levanna points (P. Thomas 1991).

Discoveries of castellated globular pots similar to others used by Indian people living in the Hudson and Mohawk valleys suggest relations with neighbors to the south of Lake Champlain (Haviland and Power 1981). Findings of wares closely resembling Saint Lawrence Iroquoian pots at various locales in Vermont, New Hampshire, and Maine, for their part, indicate connections with Indian people living farther north and west (Pendergast 1990).

Saint Lawrence Iroquoian-style clay pot, seven inches high, found in Colchester, Vermont. *Courtesy Fleming Museum, University of Vermont, Burlington.*

Chipped stone and other archaeological evidence have been found in most locales known to have been occupied by people living in Western Abenaki Country during the Historic Contact period. None of these sites contain intact deposits clearly associated with Indian occupation at this time. Analyses contrasting seventeenth-century sites with evidence from earlier locales in Vermont and New Hampshire indicate that people living in Western Abenaki Country during the 1500s followed a way of life similar to that pursued by other Late Woodland people on the east, north, and west.

THE SEVENTEENTH CENTURY

Written records and orally transmitted texts affirm that diverse communities consisting of Indian people from different places made their homes in Western Abenaki Country during the seventeenth century. Many were descendants of people who had long been living in the area. Others were closely related Central Connecticut Valley Sokoki people from Pocumtuck-Squakheag Country, Pennacook people from the upper Merrimack River Valley in New Hamp-

MAP 4: WESTERN ABENAKI COUNTRY

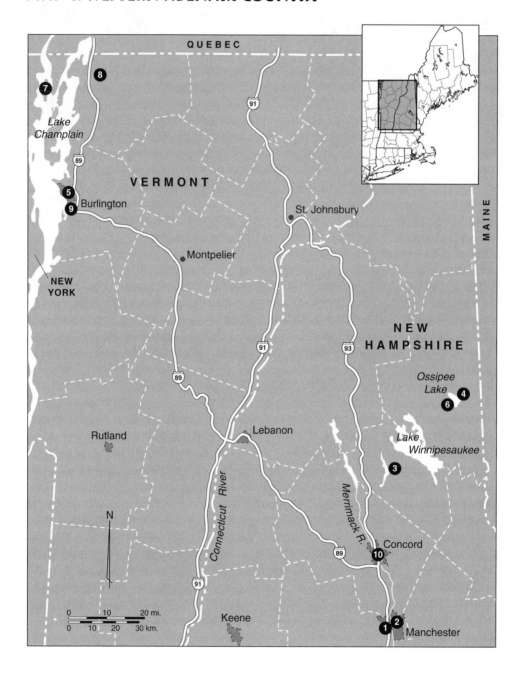

Map 4 Historic Contact Sites

Map Number	Site Name	County	State	Date	NR	Source
1	Smythe (27HB76)	Hillsborough	NH	Late 1500s		Bradley 1983; D. Foster, Kenyon, and Nichols 1981; Willoughby 1935
2	Union Cemetery	Hillsborough	NH	Late 1500s		Lamson 1895
3	The Weirs (27BK3)	Belknap	NH	Early 1600s	X	Sargeant 1974
4	Hormell (27CA15)	Carroll	NH	1610–1640		Boisvert 1993
5	Winooski	Chittenden	VT	1640–1680		VAI
6	Ossippee Lake	Carroll	NH	Mid-1600s		Bradley 1983
7	Fort Anne	Grand Isle	VT	1600s		VAI
8	Monument Farm	Franklin	VT	1600s		VAI
9	Howe Farm	Chittenden	VT	1720		VAI
10	Pennacook (27MR81)	Merrimack	NH	Historic		Simpson 1984

hire, and Pigwacket people from Maine's upper Saco River Valley. These and other people living along the fringes of Western Abenaki Country were compelled to relocate their main settlements more deeply into the Western Abenaki heartland during King Philip's War and subsequent struggles with New England settlers.

Scholars estimate that from five thousand to ten thousand people may have lived in Western Abenaki Country at the dawn of the seventeenth century. Most, if not all, spoke related Eastern Algonquian languages (Day 1975, 1981). Like their neighbors on the east in Eastern Abenaki Country, people making their homes in the Western Abenaki heartland moved from large towns to small camps at various times of the year.

In the Champlain Valley, people lived in communities on Grand Isle and at the mouths of rivers like the Missisquoi, Lamoille, and Winooski. Farther east, people living along the more northerly reaches of the Connecticut River in places like Cowasuck maintained close relations with Sokoki and Pocumtuck people living farther downriver. On the east, people living in Winnepesaukee and Pennacook communities along the upper Merrimack Valley were closely related to neighbors living closer to the coast at places like Accominta, Piscataqua, Pigwacket, and Pawtucket.

European white-clay tobacco-smoking pipes dating to the years 1610–1640 have been found with brass or copper triangular projectile points and a wide range of Late Woodland chipped-stone bifaces and ceramics in midden deposits preserved at the recently discovered, multicomponent Hormell site near Ossippee Lake, New Hampshire (Boisvert 1993). Glass beads and bird-shaped copper gorgets have been found with sheet-metal projectile points and aboriginal ceramics similar to types found in more southerly sites in disturbed, uppermost topsoil levels in the multicomponent Smythe site, which lies in the heart of Pennacook territory at Amoskeag in present-day Manchester, New Hampshire (Foster, Kenyon, and Nicholas 1981). European documents note that Amoskeag was a popular Pennacook fishing place during the early seventeenth century. Other records note the

A cache consisting of one copper and two brass triangular projectile points recovered at the Hormell site (27CA15), Freedom, New Hampshire. A fourth projectile point was found immediately above this cluster (ref. no. FSS6-6). Photograph by Richard A. Boisvert, 1993. *Courtesy New Hampshire Division of Historical Resources.*

Three-inch-high cut-copper bird effigy found at the Smythe site, Manchester, New Hampshire. Photograph by Richard A. Boisvert, 1990. *Courtesy New Hampshire Division of Historical Resources.*

presence of an early–seventeenth-century English trading post at the locale. Archaeologists have not yet found evidence of either occupation in or near known deposits at the Smythe site.

Small amounts of material of European origin dating to the middle decades of the seventeenth century unearthed at the Winooski site in Vermont and at The Weirs in New Hampshire provide evidence of otherwise-undocumented contact with English traders operating from posts first established in Pocumtuck-Squakheag Country during the 1630s. A ledger maintained by one of these traders, a Massachusetts man named William Pynchon, contains the earliest known record of direct contact with people from the southern borders of Western Abenaki Country. A notation in Pynchon's book lists one "Asquamme of Sowquakeaks" as a man who traded two beaver pelts for two blue cloth coats in 1648.

Western Abenaki people regarded the deep valleys between the Merrimack River and Lake Champlain as home. Other people living along its borders looked upon Western Abenaki Country as a mountainous frontier. New Englanders living on the south, for example, regarded Western Abenaki Country as a buffer zone separating their towns from those of the French colonies. On the west, New Yorkers and Mohawks both treated the area as a frontier shielding their eastern borders.

This singular position helped Western Abenaki people limit European penetration into their country during the seventeenth century. The French managed to erect small outposts like Fort Anne on the banks of Lake Champlain. While they welcomed a modest French presence along the lake, Western Abenaki people discouraged the French from establishing other posts deeper in their country. English settlers, for their part, did not succeed in purchasing their first small tracts of land on the southernmost fringes of Western Abenaki Country until the third quarter of the seventeenth century.

The mountain walls of Western Abenaki Country could keep European settlers out of their heartland. They could not, however, stop the ravages of war and epidemic disease from devastating their communities. Smallpox and other diseases afflicting communities everywhere in the Northeast struck Western Abenaki Country. Wars with the Mohawks and New England settlers killed hundreds and forced wholesale abandonment of entire towns and their hinterlands for years at a time.

Sokoki and Mahican people driven from their lands by Mohawk warriors moved to Western Abenaki Country during the early 1660s. In 1669, warriors from these communities joined other Western Abenakis in forming part of a larger force of New England Algonquian warriors invading Mohawk Country. This force was disastrously defeated and forced to retreat after suffering heavy losses. Two years later, Sokoki people then living at Cowasuck and other locales began selling land in their old homeland to English settlers moving up the Connecticut Valley.

Most Western Abenaki people tried to remain neutral when King Philip's War broke out in 1675. But they were unable to stay out of the war as the conflict spread, and many of them were killed in battles with New Englanders and their Mohawk allies before the fighting ended in western New England in 1676.

Survivors of English and Mohawk attacks moved north to refugee communities in northern Vermont and along the Saint Lawrence River. More than a few of these people subsequently joined other southern New England Algonquian emigrés at the earlier-mentioned Schaghticoke settlement established in 1676 by New York's Gov. Edmund Andros to guard the province's northern border from French attack.

Many Indian people forced from Pennacook and other places along the southern reaches of Western Abenaki Country tried to return to their homes after King Philip's forces were defeated. Others tried to live quietly in communities at Ossippee Lake, Missisquoi, Winooski, and Cowasuck deeper in the heart of their country.

Peace did not return to Western Abenaki Country when King Philip's War ended. Mohawks intent upon driving Western Abenaki people from their hunting and trapping grounds continued to launch attacks against their communities. Mohawk raiders forced the inhabitants of Winooski to temporarily abandon the place in 1680. Other attacks forced people living at Cowasuck to move farther north and east.

Seeking vengeance, embittered refugees living in Western Abenaki Country also continued to raid New England settlements after the war ended. Many of these people subsequently sided with the

French when King William's War began in 1689. Joining columns attacking English and Iroquois towns or fighting on their own, warriors from Western Abenaki Country fought on until the war ended in 1697.

THE EIGHTEENTH CENTURY

Warfare continued to ravage Western Abenaki Country as France and England renewed their struggle for control of the region after a brief hiatus between 1697 and 1702. Caught between the contending powers when Queen Anne's War began, Western Abenaki people were trapped in a seemingly relentless cycle of retreat and reoccupation.

Once again, warriors from Western Abenaki Country attacked the New England frontier. Outlying farms were burned while border towns like Deerfield were devastated or destroyed. Retreating from British counterattacks, most Western Abenaki people were again forced to take refuge in New France until the war ended.

Like their friends and relatives in Eastern Abenaki Country, many Western Abenaki families chose to remain in New France following the restoration of peace in 1713. Most moved with other refugees to missions like Saint Francis at Odanak and to Bécancour along the Saint Lawrence River. Marrying men and women from other native groups at these locales, these people formed strong attachments to their new neighbors. Regarding the towns as safe havens, most of them periodically moved back to old homes in Vermont and New Hampshire as conditions permitted.

Resentment of the New Englanders who were expanding north along the Connecticut and Merrimack Rivers drew many Western Abenaki people into Dummer's War in 1722. Warriors led by Gray Lock, himself a refugee from Massachusetts, harried British frontier settlements across the southern borders of Western Abenaki Country. Following a policy established nearly fifty years earlier during King Philip's War, neighboring New York remained neutral throughout the conflict. The French pursued a somewhat less passive neutrality. Declining to send troops against the New Englanders, they sheltered Western Abenaki families while furnishing arms, ammunition, provisions, and safe havens to Western Abenaki warriors.

Most Western Abenaki people maintained strong ties with the French when the war ended inconclusively in 1727. Resenting construction of British posts like Fort Dummer and Fort Number 4 on their southern borders, they allowed the French to establish new forts and missions along the strategic Lake Champlain–Richelieu River corridor on their western frontier. Several of these posts— most notably Fort Saint Frederic, established in 1731 at Crown Point, New York, near the southern end of Lake Champlain, and the Missisquoi mission established by Fr. Etienne Lauverjat in 1743 near Gray Lock's fort at Lake Champlain's northern end—became important gathering and trading places for many Indians in Western Abenaki Country.

Most of these people continued to actively support their French allies when they again took up arms against the British during King George's War (1744–1748) and the subsequent Seven Years' War (1755–1762). Again, Western Abenaki warriors joined French and Indian columns devastating British settlements along the New England frontier. And, as in earlier wars, Western Abenaki people withdrew to communities in northern Vermont and Quebec as British counterattacks drove deeply into their territory.

Indian population in Western Abenaki Country dwindled disastrously during these years. Many warriors died while fighting far from their towns during the border wars. Men, women, and children were killed in Robert Rogers's 1759 attack on Saint Francis and other raids launched from posts ringing the southern frontiers of their country. Substantial numbers of people died in epidemics like the smallpox outbreak that forced the temporary abandonment of Missisquoi in 1730. Still others succumbed to the stress of repeated relocation or the ravages of alcohol peddled in open defiance of laws prohibiting such trade.

Almost all documents mentioning Western Abenaki people in eighteenth-century Vermont and New Hampshire focus upon diplomatic negotiations or military campaigns. Very little archaeological or documentary evidence directly chronicles the domestic life and affairs of these people. Neither the few Frenchmen living among the Western Abenakis at places like Missisquoi nor the even-fewer British travelers passing through the North country left much in the way of literary accounts or written observations. Fragmentary archaeological deposits preserved at the Howe Farm site, for their part, contain the only clearly identifiable physical evidence of eighteenth-century Indian life in Western Abenaki Country.

What is known indicates that most aspects of native life changed dramatically during these years. Largely abandoning stone tools and aboriginal ceramics, nearly all Abenakis had adopted or adapted European technology to meet their own needs by the middle years of the century. Christianity also became a dominant force in Abenaki life during these years. A shrine to Sainte Anne de Beaupré was erected on Isle La Motte at a place long regarded by Indian people as a spiritually significant locale. Becoming a place of pilgrimage, the shrine draws Abenaki people to the present day.

Rebuilding Saint Francis after Rogers's attack, many Western Abenaki people returned to their homes in Vermont and New Hampshire following the fall of New France in 1760. British settlers moving north into the upper Connecticut and Champlain Valleys increasingly pressed Western Abenaki people to give up their lands. While recognizing Caughnawaga Mohawk claims to the North country by right of conquest, royal officials challenged Western Abenaki rights to their homeland. Caught up in wrangling over land, many Abenakis sold or leased their property and moved elsewhere.

Most Western Abenaki people tried to remain neutral when the American War for Independence broke out in 1775. Many waited out the war at Odanak and other locales in Canada. Angered by the accelerating pace of American occupation of their lands in Vermont and pressed by the British and their Indian allies to enter the war, some Western Abenaki warriors launched raids against colonists moving onto their lands.

Doing as they had done so many times before, many Abenakis returned to homes at Missisquoi, Cowasuck, and other places in northern Vermont and

New Hampshire when the war ended in 1783. This time, they found Americans living in their most cherished townsites. Not recognized as aboriginal owners by the American government, Western Abenaki people could not prevent the occupation of their lands. Discouraged, many of them returned to Canada. Those remaining on ancestral lands moved to remote valleys or back lots unwanted by the new settlers.

Many Abenakis married non-Indian neighbors. Although most children born to these couples learned the customs and languages of non-Indian kinsfolk and neighbors, few forgot their Abenaki heritage, and many people tracing descent to Western Abenaki ancestors continue to live today in various parts of Vermont, Quebec, and adjacent areas.

SOURCES

Most of the historical documentation in this section is abstracted from Calloway (1990). Other material has been drawn from Calloway (1991) and Day (1978). Archaeological data presented in this section largely have been drawn from Haviland and Power (1981), Pendergast (1990), Snow (1978a, 1980), and P. Thomas (1977, 1985, 1991).

POCUMTUCK-SQUAKHEAG COUNTRY

Pocumtuck-Squakheag Country encompasses the present-day central Massachusetts counties of Franklin, Hampden, and Hampshire and adjacent sections of Vermont, New Hampshire, and Connecticut. Stretching across the broad central valley of the Connecticut River, the area extends from the Worcester highlands west to the Berkshire Mountains.

THE SIXTEENTH CENTURY

Very little is known about the sixteenth-century inhabitants of this area. Sites containing ceramics associated with terminal Late Woodland occupations have been found in several locales. Small amounts of European artifacts found at two of these locales, the Indian Crossing and EPA sites, represent the only known archaeological materials dating to the sixteenth century in the area (Bawden 1977; Ulrich 1977).

THE SEVENTEENTH CENTURY

William Pynchon and other New England traders moving to the greater Springfield area during the mid-1630s penned the earliest known references to Pocumtuck-Squakheag Country Indian communities in Massachusetts at Agawam (present-day Springfield), Woronoco (Westfield), Quabaug (Brookfield), Norwottuck (Northampton), Pocumtuck (Deerfield), and Squakheag (Northfield).

Not much is known about Indian people living in these places. Preoccupied with trade and more concerned with security than ethnography, Pynchon and his contemporaries wrote little about the languages, customs, or beliefs of Indian neighbors in their ledgers, journals, correspondence, and reports. Letters and dispatches written by Dutch traders at Fort Hope (modern Hartford) and Fort Orange (in modern Albany) indicate that warfare and epidemic disease ravaged Indian communities throughout the area just before New Englanders began settling in the broad meadows around modern Springfield, Massachusetts.

Closely allied with Mahican friends and relatives living farther west, Pocumtuck-Squakheag Country Indians abandoned small scattered settlements vulnerable to Mohawk assault during the first Mohawk-Mahican War (1624–1628). Many of these people moved to more defensible fortified towns at Agawam and other locales. Crowded in behind town walls, they proved particularly susceptible to smallpox epidemics ravaging the region from 1631 to 1634.

Those surviving these twin disasters soon moved elsewhere or settled in small towns near newly established English towns. Archaeologists have found the sites of several of these communities. Guida Farm site deposits preserve remains of what is believed to be Woronoco town (Byers and Rouse 1960). The Bark Wigwams site in Northampton contains deposits associated with the Norwottuck community (E. Johnson and Bradley 1987). The Fort Hill site in Springfield, also known as Long Hill, contains remains of a fortified town built for Indian people by local settlers in 1666 (Pretola 1985; H. A. Wright 1895; Young 1969a).

Archaeological deposits discovered at the Fort Hill site in New Hampshire preserve the most complete known physical record of Pocumtuck-Squakheag Country Indian life during this time. A small hilltop fortification located atop a narrow bluff overlooking the Connecticut River in southern New Hampshire at the northernmost reaches of Squakheag territory, Fort Hill was built by Sokoki people forced to leave their main settlements around Northfield, Massachusetts, through fear of Mohawk attack at the beginning of the second Mohawk-Mahican War (1662–1675). Analysis of site deposits indicates that as many as five hundred people had crowded within the town's palisade

wall when Mohawk warriors finally assaulted the place in December 1663 (P. Thomas 1991). Withstanding a brief three-day Mohawk siege, the Sokoki people abandoned their fort a few months later.

Storage pits excavated at the site were found to contain large amounts of deer, bear, and dog bones; nuts; dried berries; and carbonized corn remains. Measurements of the storage capacity of these pits indicates that they could have held from thirty-two hundred to four thousand bushels of corn. French and English muskets, munitions, glass beads, metalware (including several Jesuit rings and medallions), and ceramics found at the site attest to the range of trade and other contacts maintained by town residents.

In the wake of the Mohawk siege, the Sokokis scattered to different places. Some moved farther north to the communities of the Cowasucks and other friends and kinsfolk in Western Abenaki Country; others moved farther north to towns near French settlements along the Saint Lawrence River; still others settled in Pennacook towns or moved south to Pocumtuck and nearby native communities.

The sites where they settled have yielded various deposits containing iron knives, axes, and other metal tools, together with copper or brass triangular or conical projectile points, gun parts and flints, glass beads, European white-clay tobacco-smoking pipes, aboriginal ceramics, chipped-stone triangular projectile points, and other stone tools. Stylistic analyses of Guida Farm wares suggest similarities with other pottery produced by people living south and east of Pocumtuck-Squakheag Country.

MAP 5: POCUMTUCK-SQUAKHEAG COUNTRY

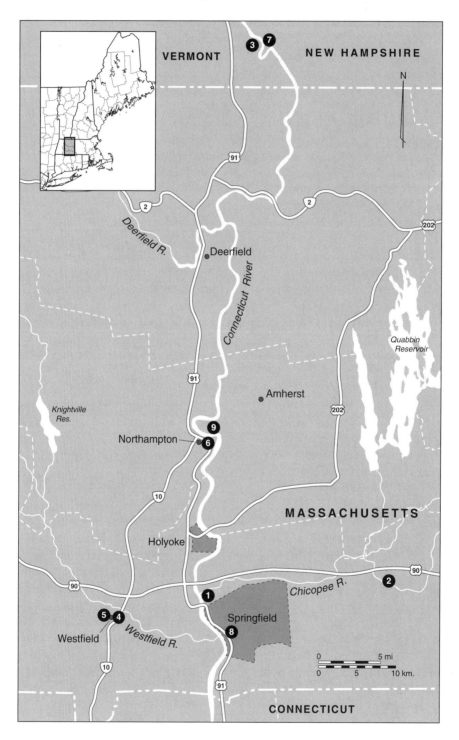

Map 5 Historic Contact Sites

Map Number	Site Name	County	State	Date	NR	Source
1	Indian Crossing	Hampden	MA	1500s		Ulrich 1977
2	EPA	Hampden	MA	1500s		Bawden 1977
3	Great Bend	Windham	VT	1600s		VAI
4	Palmer	Hampden	MA	Early 1600s		Bradley and Childs 1987; E. Johnson and Mahlstedt 1985
5	Guida Farm	Hampden	MA	1600–1675		Byers and Rouse 1960
6	Bark Wigwams	Hampshire	MA	–1654		E. Johnson and Bradley 1987
7	Fort Hill (NH) (27CH85)	Cheshire	NH	1663–1664		P. Thomas 1991
8	Fort Hill/Long Hill	Hampden	MA	1666–1675		Pretola 1985; H. A. Wright 1895; Young 1969a
9	Fort River	Hampshire	MA	Historic		Young 1969a

Discovery of a 3¼-inch-high European-style pottery mug made and decorated like incised Guida Farm collared wares at the Fort Hill site graphically shows how Central Connecticut Valley people creatively used time-tested techniques to manufacture new products.

Absence of artifacts postdating 1675 in deposits containing aboriginal ceramics and lithics at these sites corroborates reports written by settlers stating that most Indian people had abandoned their Pocumtuck-Squakheag Country homes by the end of King Philip's War. Other records indicate that most moved to new homes in nearby areas. Some settled with other refugees at Puritan Praying Indian Towns like Hassanamisco and Ockocagansett in nearby Nipmuck territory on the east. Others moved farther east to Catholic mission communities like Amesokanti in Eastern Abenaki Country. Still others moved west to the Schaghticoke community in New York. Most, however, moved north to Western Abenaki Country.

THE EIGHTEENTH CENTURY

Situated at the northwestern edge of New England on the New York, Canadian, Mohawk, and Western Abenaki frontiers, Pocumtuck-Squakheag Country became a hotly contested borderland during the eighteenth century. Wars embroiled British settlers, French colonists, and Indian people in a seemingly interminable series of hostilities between 1702 and 1762. Towns along the area's northern reaches like Deerfield were repeatedly devastated by parties of French soldiers, Canadian militia, and Indian warriors bypassing Fort No. 10, Fort Massachusetts, and other outposts established for their protection. Local militia units used these posts as springboards for their own assaults against French and Indian enemies.

Treaties signed in Europe ending wars between France and Britain failed to satisfy Indian people and settlers mourning losses of homes, friends, and loved

Sheet brass and copper artifacts collected by Walter S. Rodimon at the Bark Wigwams site. These artifacts are presently curated at the Springfield Science Museum. Photograph by Gail Gustafson. *Courtesy Department of Anthropology, University of Massachusetts at Amherst.*

ones. Seeking their own vengeance, native people fought the New Englanders openly in times of war and waged a covert struggle sporadically marked by assaults, thefts, and murders during times of peace.

Little is known about the few Indian people who chose to live within their ancestral homeland under such difficult conditions during the 1700s. Available documentation indicates that individuals and small families struggled to live quietly in and around colonial towns and farms. Continuing to hunt, fish, forage, and farm, many of these people found work as laborers, servants, or artisans. As elsewhere, most adopted the tools, technology, language, and religion of their non-Indian neighbors as elders died and young people married outside of their communities.

Many of these people had moved elsewhere or had been assimilated into New England society by the time the American War for Independence began in 1775. Although some people tracing descent from Pocumtuck-Squakheag Country Indian people continue to make their homes in the area, most live in exile farther north and west.

Portion of the large block excavation at the Fort Hill site, New Hampshire, after plow-zone removal. Circular stains are unexcavated pits; stakes mark possible post molds. Photograph by Peter A. Thomas. *Courtesy Peter A. Thomas.*

SOURCES

Much of the historical information presented in this section has been drawn from Bradley (1984); Conkey, Boissevain, and Goddard (1978); Melvoin (1989); P. Thomas (1991); and Salwen (1978). Sources for archaeological data appearing here include Byers and Rouse (1960), E. Johnson and Bradley (1987), P. Thomas (1991), and Young (1969a).

MAP 6: NIPMUCK COUNTRY

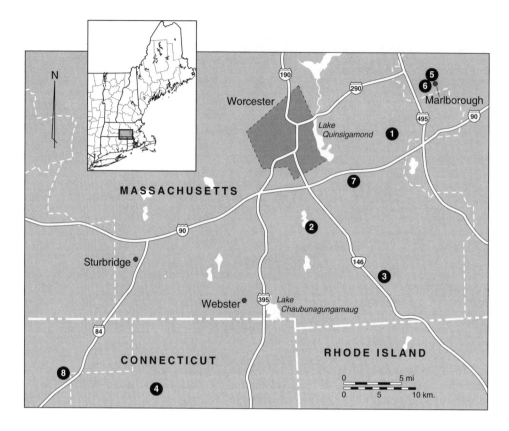

Map 6 Historic Contact Sites

Map Number	Site Name	County	State	Date	NR	Source
1	Cedar Swamp 4	Worcester	MA	1500s		C. Hoffman 1987
2	Bear Hollow	Worcester	MA	1500s–1600s		Cox et al. 1982
3	Hartford Avenue	Worcester	MA	1500s–1600s		D. Ritchie 1985
4	Stafford Brook	Windham	CT	1600s		K. McBride 1984
5	Forest Street Indian Burial Ground	Worcester	MA	Mid-1600s		Carlson 1986
6	Ockocagansett	Worcester	MA	Late 1600s		Carlson 1986; C. M. Hudson 1862
7	Hassanomisco Indian Burying Ground	Worcester	MA	1600s–1700s		Carlson 1986; Mulholland, Savulis, and Gumaer 1986
8	Snow Hill	Tolland	CT	Historic		CAS

NIPMUCK COUNTRY

Nipmuck Country encompasses the lake country at the headwaters of the Quinnebaug, Blackstone, and other coastal rivers flowing south into Block Island and Rhode Island sounds. This area of low, rocky uplands and dense forests extends across modern Worcester County in Massachusetts to adjacent portions of Franklin, Hampshire, and Hampden Counties on the west and parts of northeastern Connecticut and northwestern Rhode Island on the south.

THE SIXTEENTH CENTURY

Very little is known about sixteenth-century Indian life in this area. Archaeological evidence recovered from the few sites dating to the 1500s indicates that lifeways similar to those chronicled by English colonists moving to Massachusetts Bay during the 1620s and 1630s had first emerged in the area sometime between two hundred and three hundred years earlier. Stone tools found at the Bear Hollow, Cedar Swamp 4, and Hartford Avenue sites show that their occupants hunted, fished, and foraged for food much as their ancestors had.

Ceramics found at some of these sites indicate that their inhabitants made globular and conoidal pots. Some of these vessels were collared, decorated with incised designs, and surmounted with castellations similar to others made by people living farther south and west in the Connecticut and Thames river valleys. Others were conoidal wares similar to those found in sites elsewhere in southern New England and eastern Long Island.

THE SEVENTEENTH CENTURY

The few written records documenting Indian life in Nipmuck Country during the seventeenth century almost entirely focus upon political, military, and missionary affairs. Colonial chroniclers noted that Nipmuck people were compelled to pay some form of tribute to Massachusett, Wampanoag, Pequot, Mohegan, and Narragansett overlords at one time or another during the 1600s. Other sources document the Nipmuck struggle to resist subjugation by their Indian neighbors and by English colonists expanding westward from today's Greater Boston area to new settlements established at Brookfield, Lancaster, Mendon, and Worcester between the 1640s and 1660s.

Documents recording the efforts of John Eliot and other Puritan missionaries in this area note the establishment of the Hassanamisco Praying Town at Grafton in 1654 and the subsequent erection of other missions in Massachusetts at Chaubunagungamaug near Webster, at Manchaug, at Ockocagansett in Marlborough, at Pakachoag in Auburn, and at Waentaug in Uxbridge and in Connecticut at Maanexit in Thompson, at Quabquisset in Woodstock, and at Quantisset in Pomfret.

Beside these mission communities, Nipmuck settlements—all in Massachusetts—included Nashaway in Lancaster, Quabaug in Brookfield, Quinsigamond in Worcester, and Waushacum in Sterling. All of these communities, and those of English settlers moving to Nipmuck Country, were abandoned and destroyed during King Philip's War. Many people on both sides were killed in the fighting as Indian and English raiding parties laid waste to the entire area.

Many Nipmucks who survived these attacks were captured and sold into slavery. Those avoiding English captivity moved farther away to Western Abenaki Country, to Maine, or to Hudson Valley Indian towns. Few returned to Nipmuck Country after the war ended. One group of Praying Indians reestablished settlements along the banks of Chaubunagungamaug Pond. Another group moved back to an eight-thousand-acre "plantation" reserved for their use by Massachusetts authorities at Hassanamisco in 1693. Other Nipmuck people returning to their lands generally camped briefly on old homesites before moving on to new homes farther from English settlers, who rapidly reoccupied the area after 1680.

The archaeology of seventeenth-century Indian life in this area is poorly known. Avocationalists have reportedly found artifacts and intact deposits at the documented locales of the Hassanamisco and Ockocagansett mission towns (Carlson 1986). Fragmentary remains possibly dating to the seventeenth century have also been recovered from the Snow Hill and Stafford Brook sites in Connecticut (CAS; K. McBride 1984).

THE EIGHTEENTH CENTURY

Very little has been written about Indian life in Nipmuck Country during the eighteenth century. Both the Hassanamisco and the Dudley Indian community at Chaubunagungamaug continued to shrink in size as non-Indian overseers sold off or lost portions of their lands. Many of the few Indian people remaining at Hassanamisco moved away after much of the money obtained by the sale of their lands by Massachusetts authorities in 1728 was stolen or lost. The state of Massachusetts subsequently set aside 11.9 acres for their use in 1848.

Having sold most of their remaining lands at Chaubunagungamaug in 1797, Dudley Indian people continued to hold onto a small, twenty-six-acre tract until local authorities moved them into a building on a one-acre plot in town. People tracing descent to these and other Indian communities continue to make their homes in various places within Nipmuck Country today.

SOURCES

Much of the data appearing in this section has been drawn from Bradley (1984, 1985). Other pertinent sources include Carlson (1986); Conkey, Boissevain, and Goddard (1978); Connole (1976); Mandell (1992); and Salwen (1978).

PENNACOOK-PAWTUCKET COUNTRY

The Pennacook-Pawtucket Country extends along the Atlantic coast from the Saco River Valley in Maine across coastal New Hampshire to northeastern Massachusetts.

THE SIXTEENTH CENTURY

Almost nothing is known about Indian life in this area during the 1500s. Little more than a few smelted-metal fragments have been found with aboriginal ceramics and stone tools at the ME8.001 and Quick Water sites. Although other terminal Late Woodland sites in the area lacking European goods also may date to early Historic Contact times, further research is needed to establish their chronological and cultural positions.

THE SEVENTEENTH CENTURY

As elsewhere, Europeans sailing to the Atlantic coast during the early 1600s penned the first documents identifying the names of Indian people and places in this area. Writing in 1605, Samuel de Champlain distinguished corn-cultivating people he called Armouchiquois living from the Saco River to Cape Cod

from hunting, fishing, and foraging people he identified as Etchemins living farther east. Writing during the late 1600s, Massachusetts Bay Indian superintendent Daniel Gookin used Pawtucket, the name of a local community in the vicinity of modern Lowell, Massachusetts, as a general term largely encompassing the same area covered by Champlain's Armouchiquois.

Extant documents indicate that several distinct groups devastated by epidemics during the early decades of the 1600s had been joined together in series of loose confederacies in this area as English colonists settled on Massachusetts Bay shores during the 1620s and 1630s. Scholars have not been able to clearly define the boundaries, identities, and affiliations of these confederacies and their constituent groups. Archaeologists, for example, have thus far been unable to link fragmentary and incomplete ceramic, lithic, faunal, and floral assemblages found in most of the area's sites with chronicled ethnic groups. Written records, largely produced after epidemic disease ravaged communities everywhere in the area, document overlapping aboriginal territorial boundaries, changing ethnic identities, and shifting alliances and affiliations. Often regarded as a evidence of the disruption and dissolution of rigidly defined tribal territories brought on by contact, the kaleidoscopic nature of this data may just as easily suggest the existence of flexible network systems.

Available documentation indicates that the people of Pennacook-Pawtucket Country lived in the easternmost portions of Champlain's Armouchiquois territory. The northern reaches of this country stretched from Accominta near the mouth of the Saco River and Pigwacket territory farther upriver across Piscataqua land on the New Hampshire coastal plain to Pennacook territory along the middle reaches of the Merrimack River below Amoskeag in modern Manchester, New Hampshire.

Relationships between this latter community and people living at the town of Pennacook farther upriver in modern Concord are not clearly understood. Noting that Pennacook people living below Amoskeag maintained close affiliations with Pawtuckets and other neighbors on the south, some scholars distinguish the lower Merrimack group from the Western Abenaki upper Pennacook community (Salwen 1978). Others lump all of these people into a larger Pennacook confederacy (Calloway 1988).

Pawtucket communities extended along the Massachusetts coastal plain from the lower Merrimack River estuary around Lowell, Lawrence, and Haverhill to Cape Ann and the Ipswich River drainage between Agawam in modern Ipswich south to the Naumkeag lands on the northern shore of Massachusetts Bay.

Prominent leaders, like the Pawtucket chief Nanepashemet, the Pennacook sachem Passaconaway, and his successor Wannalancet, worked to establish mutually beneficial relations with New England settlers who moved onto their lands during the early 1600s. The sachems did what they could to resist demands of land-hungry settlers, but devastated by epidemics that reduced their population from as much as twenty-four thousand at the time of initial contact to a few thousand by 1674, Indian people could actually do little to stop colonists intent upon acquiring their lands.

After selling most of their ancestral lands, many native people of the area moved to the Puritan Praying Town at Wamesit in modern Lowell and to other missions established along the borders of the Massachusetts Bay Colony. Wherever they lived, most Pennacook and Pawtucket Indian people either remained neutral or aided New England colonists against their Indian enemies when King Philip's War broke out in 1675. Worsening relations following the end of the war ultimately forced many to join family and friends in exile farther from the expanding New England towns.

A Pennacook community was noted near Albany, New York, in 1687. Other Pennacook people followed Passaconaway's grandson Kancamagus to new homes along the upper reaches of the Merrimack and Androscoggin Rivers. This latter group briefly supported the French when war broke out with England in 1689. Taking vengeance on Englishmen like Richard Waldron who had betrayed, cheated, or lied to them in earlier negotiations, they subsequently made a separate peace with the New Englanders after a raiding force led by Benjamin Church during the late summer

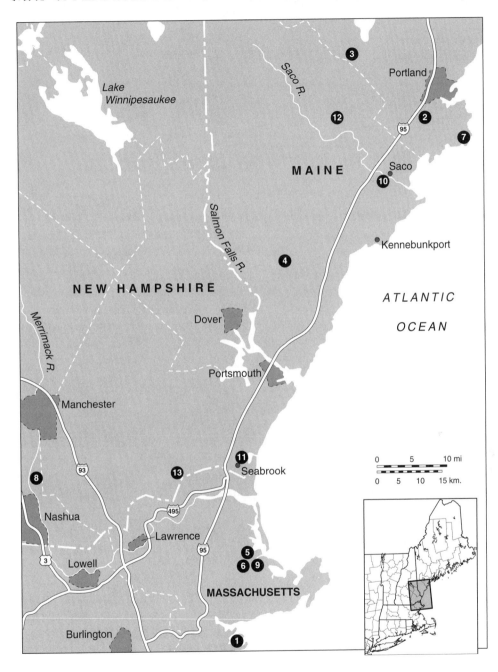

Map 7 Historic Contact Sites

Map Number	Site Name	County	State	Date	NR	Source
1	Isaac Wyman	Essex	MA	1575–1620		Hadlock 1949
2	ME 8.001	Cumberland	ME	1500s		MPASI
3	Quick Water	Cumberland	ME	1500s(?)		MPASI
4	Bonny Bake Pond Farm (ME 315-1)	York	ME	1600s		MHASI
5	Indian Ridge	Essex	MA	1600s		Willoughby 1924
6	Ipswich Burial	Essex	MA	1600s		Hadlock 1949
7	ME 076-3	Cumberland	ME	1600s		MHASI
8	Campbell (NH45-73)	Hillsborough	NH	Early 1600s		Kenyon 1983
9	Clark's Pond	Essex	MA	Early 1600s		Bullen 1949
10	College of New England	York	ME	Early 1600s		MHASI
11	Rocks Road (NH47-21)	Rockingham	NH	Mid-1600s		B. Robinson and Bolian 1987
12	Indian Cellar (ME 205-3)	York	ME	1600s–1700s		MHASI
13	Harvey Mitchell	Rockingham	NH	1700–1749		Holmes 1982

of 1690 destroyed their fort on the upper Androscoggin while most of its defenders were elsewhere.

Intact deposits containing diagnostic artifacts dating to the seventeenth century have not yet been found in large numbers in Pennacook-Pawtucket Country. As elsewhere, graves represent the most numerous type of archaeological site in this area. Generally unearthed during construction projects, most such sites have, in effect, been destroyed by the time of their discovery.

Extensive deposits documenting Indian habitation have been found at two locales. Substantial evidence of contact in the form of European white-clay trade pipes, iron knives and axes, copper or brass triangular projectile points, and a lead-sheet animal cutout have been found with shell and bone tools and ornaments, collared pottery, and triangular, chipped-stone projectile points at the now-destroyed Rocks Road site. This coastal site, located at a place known as Winnacunnet by early colonists, is believed to be the locale of a major Agawam town. Terminal dates of many European artifacts found at Rocks Road corroborate written evidence affirming Indian abandonment of the place sometime before English settlers first moved to the area in 1636 (B. Robinson and Bolian 1987).

Some 238 historic artifacts, including glass beads and a copper disc, were excavated with Late Woodland pottery, fire-cracked rocks, and chipped-stone flakes from upper levels of the Campbell site located on the banks of the Merrimack River between Nashua and Manchester, New Hampshire. This site evidently was the locale of a small camp. First used by Indian people during Middle Woodland times, it continued to be occupied intermittently until 1633, when English settlers constructed a cattle pen there.

THE EIGHTEENTH CENTURY

Few Indian people remained in this area after 1700. Most Pawtucket people driven from their homes during King

Philip's War never returned. Lands of Pennacook and other native people living farther north became a constantly bleeding frontier as Anglo-French hostilities that resumed with the outbreak of Queen Anne's War in 1702 dragged on in one form or another with only brief respite until 1762.

Most of the area's native people moved to new homes in Eastern or Western Abenaki countries. Small groups of these people periodically returned to hunting and fishing camps along the upper reaches of the Merrimack, Androscoggin, Saco, and other rivers during times of peace. Others shipped out on New England whalers, merchantmen, and privateers or worked for settlers in coastal towns and farms. Little archaeological or archival documentation records their lives during these years. Today people tracing descent to the original inhabitants of Pennacook-Pawtucket Country continue to live at various locales in the area.

SOURCES

Most of the data presented in this section appear in Calloway (1988, 1990); Conkey, Boissevain, and Goddard (1978); Salwen (1978); and Snow (1978a, 1980). Reports on individual archaeological sites may been seen in Holmes (1982), Kenyon (1983), and B. Robinson and Bolian (1987).

MASSACHUSETT COUNTRY

Massachusett Country extends along the shores of Massachusetts Bay from the Mystic and Charles Rivers south across the Neponsit River Valley to the present line separating Norfolk from Bristol and Plymouth counties. The Greater Boston area encompasses the heart of Massachusett Country today.

THE SIXTEENTH CENTURY

Almost nothing is known about the lives of the people who lived in Massachusett Country during the 1500s. Fragmentary archaeological evidence recovered from the Winthrop Burials and the Stepping Stones site indicates that people living in the area during the sixteenth century lived much as their ancestors had hundreds of years earlier.

Aboriginal ceramics and stone tools found at these sites generally resemble others found in terminal Late Woodland sites in southern New England. As elsewhere, small amounts of European metalware and glassware found in these deposits date them to the 1500s.

Very few radiometric samples dating to the sixteenth century have been recovered from sites in this area. One of

the few that has, a sample drawn from heartwood within the center of the hull of a wooden dugout canoe with an iron chain affixed to its bow recovered from the mud of a South Weymouth pond, almost certainly more accurately reflects the age of an early phase of the tree's growth than the period of its use (Dincauze 1991).

THE SEVENTEENTH CENTURY

As many as twenty-four thousand people may have been living in communities lining the banks of rivers flowing into Massachusetts Bay before 1634, by which time periodic epidemics and attacks by Micmacs and other "Northern Indians" had killed or driven away more than 90 percent of the area's native inhabitants (Salisbury 1982a). Europeans chronicling early relations with Massachusett Country people noted that they located their major communities on the Mystic River, at Nonantum in modern Newton, at Shawmut in Boston, at Neponset, and at Wessagusset in Weymouth during these plague years.

Plymouth colony settlers moving among Massachusett people at Wessagusset established the first English settlement in the area in 1622. These and other early settlers established close relations with influential Massachusett leaders like the Squaw Sachem. Although her name has not yet been found in English records, the Squaw Sachem rose to prominence as the most important Massachusett leader of her era. Succeeding to leadership after her husband, Nanepashemet, was killed by Northern Indians, she extended her authority through her sons. One of these, a man named Wonohaquaham but known to the English as Sagamore John, led a Massachusett community on the Mystic River. Two others, Montowampate (called Sagamore James by the English) and Wenepoykin (also known as Sagamore George), were chiefs of Pawtucket communities at Saugus and Salem, respectively.

Only one Massachusett leader, a Wessagusset sachem named Obtakiest, is known to have organized armed resistance against English settlers moving into Indian lands on and around Massachusetts Bay. He and his followers were defeated by a force of Plymouth soldiers who raided Wessagusset in 1623.

Squaw Sachem, her sons, the Neponset sachem Chicataubut, and his successor Cutchamakin all struggled to live peacefully with the thousands of Puritan settlers who poured onto their lands after 1630. But, devastated as they were by epidemic disease, they were unable to stop the Great Migration. Realizing that their lands would be seized if they did not sell them, Massachusett leaders had put their marks to deeds that conveyed both title and sovereignty to most of their homeland by 1650. Displaced and demoralized, they and their followers began moving to Praying Indian

towns built at Natick and other locales at that time (Bowden and Ronda 1980; Jennings 1971; Salisbury 1972, 1974).

Living under the supervision of John Eliot and other missionaries, they provided both food and furs to Boston merchants as they guarded the Massachusetts Bay frontier. Learning to read and write in Massachusett, they helped to produce one of the first Bibles translated into a North American Indian language (Goddard and Bragdon 1988).

The piety and faithfulness of these Praying Indians neither protected them from harassment from hostile English neighbors nor shielded them from further epidemics. Maintaining neutrality or openly siding with the English when King Philip's War broke out in 1675, many Massachusetts were interned under appalling conditions on Deer Island in Boston Harbor. Most returned to the few "praying towns" not destroyed in the fighting when the war ended. Pressed by the colonists to sell portions of their lands at Natick and other places, many of them gradually moved elsewhere toward the end of the century.

Most sites documenting seventeenth-century Indian life in this area have been damaged or destroyed by more than three centuries of development extending outward from Boston's urban core. Surveys funded by the Massachusetts Historical Commission have inventoried known archival and archaeological information associated with the seven original seventeenth-century Massachusetts Bay Praying Indian towns (Carlson 1986). Archaeological testing has recorded deposits associated with the Natick and Punkapoag Praying Indian towns in Massachusett Country.

Surveyors working along the Charles

MAP 8: MASSACHUSETT COUNTRY

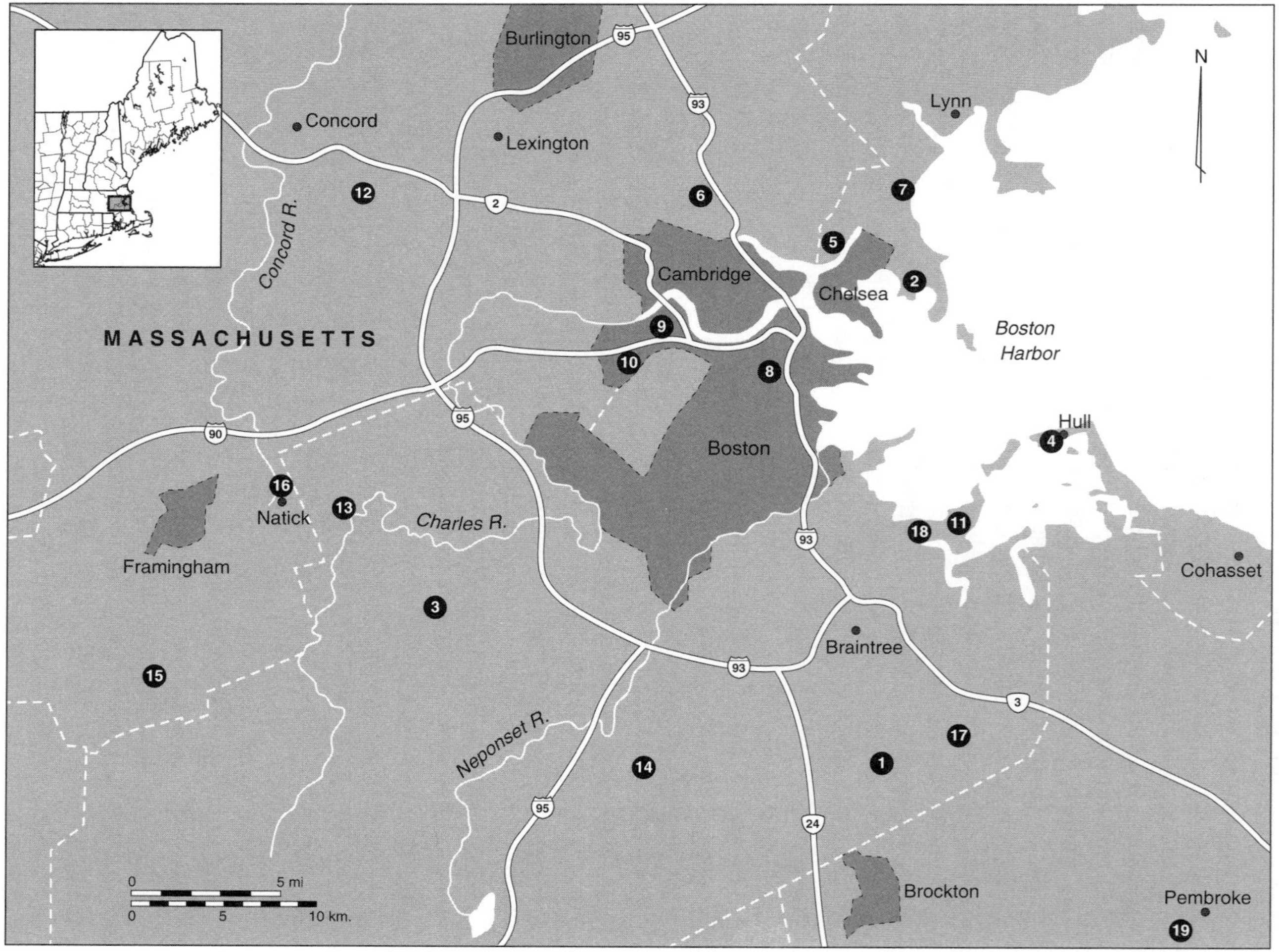

N

Boston Harbor

Cohasset

Pembroke
19

Hull
4

Lynn
7
11
18
2
5
Chelsea

17

3

Braintree
1

93
Brockton
24

Cambridge
6
8
Boston
9
10
93

95
93
14

Burlington
Lexington
2

Charles R.
3
95

Neponset R.

Concord
12

Concord R.
13
16
Natick
MASSACHUSETTS

90

Framingham
15

0   5 mi
0   5   10 km.

Map 8 Historic Contact Sites

Map Number	Site Name	County	State	Date	NR	Source
1	Stepping Stones	Norfolk	MA	1500s		C. Hoffman 1986
2	Winthrop Burials	Essex	MA	1575–1600		Willoughby 1924, 1935
3	Powissett Rock Shelter	Norfolk	MA	1580–1650		Dincauze and Gramly 1973
4	Atlantic Hill	Plymouth	MA	1600s		Bradley 1983
5	Chelsea Beach	Essex	MA	1600s		Bradley 1983
6	Indian Necropolis	Middlesex	MA	1600s		Corey 1899
7	Revere Beach	Essex	MA	1600s		Hadlock 1949
8	Savin Hill Park	Suffolk	MA	1600s		Willoughby 1935
9	Lemon Brook	Middlesex	MA	Early 1600s		Dincauze 1968
10	Hemlock Gorge Rock Shelter	Middlesex	MA	Early 1600s		Dincauze 1968
11	Moswetuset Hummock	Norfolk	MA	Early 1600s	X	Bradley 1983; Hale 1971
12	Indian Grave	Middlesex	MA	1600–1650		R. Barber 1984
13	South Natick	Middlesex	MA	1650–1700	X	Dincauze 1968; Bradley 1983; Fitch 1983
14	Chapman Street Praying Indian Burial Ground	Norfolk	MA	1660–1713		Carlson 1986; MHAS; Simon 1990
15	Cutler Morse	Middlesex	MA	Late 1600s		Dincauze 1968
16	Reverend Badger House	Middlesex	MA	1753–present	X	Carlson 1986; B. Pfeiffer 1979
17	Dugout Canoe	Norfolk	MA	Historic		Kevitt 1968
18	Squantum Burial	Norfolk	MA	Historic		MHC
19	Mattakeesett	Plymouth	MA	1500s–1800s		Gardner 1987, 1992; MHC

River also have discovered a brass triangular projectile point and an English gunflint at the Hemlock Gorge Rock Shelter and an engraved iron axehead at the Cutler Morse site (Dincauze 1968). White-clay pipe stems and other objects of European origin have been found with Late Woodland ceramics and stone tools in features within the Powissett Rock Shelter (Dincauze and Gramly 1973).

Archaeological deposits containing datable seventeenth-century diagnostic European goods are most frequently encountered in human burials in this area. As Dincauze (1974) notes in another report, the prevalence of mortuary sites in and around the Greater Boston area grimly reflects the disastrous depopulation of Indian communities documented in European records of the period (also see Bradley 1983, 1987b).

THE EIGHTEENTH CENTURY

Most of the few Indian communities remaining in Massachusett Country continued to shrink in size during the eighteenth century. Only two "praying towns" established in their country before King Philip's War, Natick and Punkapoag, endured into the 1700s.

Living close by the center of British colonization in New England, Indian people remaining in Massachusett Country managed to avoid the worst effects of border violence that ravaged Indian communities farther north throughout most of this period. But such proximity proved to be mixed blessing. Nearness to colonial towns increased exposure to epidemic contagion. A significant number of Indian people living in the area were killed by the many smallpox, measles, malaria, and influenza epidemics that struck Indian communities everywhere during the 1700s.

Missionaries and overseers appointed by town governments or provincial authorities continued to dominate Indian communities in Massachusett Country during these years. Although Indian people generally maintained permanent settlements in towns, many used other tracts located beyond reservation or mission boundaries for foraging, fishing, hunting, and other uses.

Despite attempts to dominate their lives, Indian people generally retained control over their day-to-day affairs during the eighteenth century. Quickly learning what was and was not acceptable to their non-Indian neighbors, the remaining Indian communities in Massachusett Country drew up and enforced ordinances regulating internal relations. Maintaining records in their own language, mission communities like Natick were even guided at times by their own leaders. Daniel Takawampait, for example, succeeded John Eliot as minister to Natick from 1690 until his death in 1716.

Takawampait and other Indian leaders had to be approved and supervised by colonial officials appointed by Massachusetts Bay Colony magistrates. Colonial authorities also insisted on approving all laws and ordinances enacted in Indian communities. They also regulated all relations between Indian people and non-Indians. Bodies of law systematizing Puritan-Indian legal relations were drawn up to adjudicate disputes over land and deal with other issues of importance to both peoples. Such disputes over land occurred with increasing frequency as settlers ac-

quired title to most remaining Indian lands in the province.

Under intense pressure to adopt British ways, native people in Massachusett Country outwardly abandoned many aspects of their own culture during the eighteenth century. Many continued to live at least some of the time in wigwams, but most moved into wooden-frame houses built within planned towns along the British model. British dress and decoration were adopted. Nearly all tools, implements, and weapons were acquired from local merchants or crafted from European models.

Even so, most Massachusett Indians struggled to adopt such aspects of British material culture on their own terms. Although native people increasingly adopted European fabrics, glass beads, and metal ornaments, they continued to fashion these materials into clothes and ornaments that satisfied their own sense of style and fashion. And, while their tools and implements came to be nearly indistinguishable from those used by European neighbors, few Indians employed them to amass large amounts of capital or to control the labor of others.

Other aspects of their lives changed more drastically as the eighteenth century wore on. Although many elders continued to speak the native tongue, English had come into common usage as the primary language of Indian people living in Massachusett Country by midcentury. Perhaps the single most important factor accounting for this transition was the increasing prevalence of marriage between Indian people and English-speaking settlers of European or African descent. Although the Indians who moved in with their non-Indian spouses rarely abandoned their Indian heritage, dwindling numbers passed this heritage intact to their children. Even so, many children born to such unions continued to acknowledge their Indian ancestry and identity.

Indian identity survived in other ways during these years. As anthropologist William S. Simmons has shown, several native communities in and around Massachusetts maintained extensive bodies of oral literature. Supporting ongoing community cohesiveness, these texts and narratives also preserved ancestral knowledge. Indian herbalists and healers continued to serve Indian and non-Indian clients. And many Indian men and women continued to produce baskets, woodcarvings, and other artifacts.

Mortuary sites constitute much of the known archaeological record of eighteenth-century Indian life in Massachusett Country. Surveys conducted at such places as the Chapman Street Indian burial ground in Canton and the Christian Indian burial ground at Natick show that Massachusett Indian people increasingly used wooden coffins to bury community members in clearly marked cemeteries. The Reverend Badger House at Natick represents one of the few surviving standing structures associated with Christian missionaries working in Massachusett Country during the 1700s.

SOURCES

Much of the historical information presented in this section has been drawn from Brenner (1980, 1984, 1988); Carlson (1986); Conkey, Boissevain, and Goddard (1978); Goddard and Bragdon (1988); Jennings (1975); Kawashima (1986); Salisbury (1982a); Salwen

(1978); Simmons (1986); and Vaughan (1979).

No single overview of Indian life in Massachusett Country currently exists. The best general summary of early Historic Contact period archaeological research in southern New England continues to be Snow (1980). Dena F. Dincauze's earlier-mentioned study (1974) notes how the high percentage of burial sites in the Greater Boston area reflects the consequences of direct contact with Europeans around Massachusetts Bay during the seventeenth century. Other summary information appears in Bradley (1982b). A number of archaeologists address the question of "Where are the Woodland Villages?" in Kerber (1988–1989).

Daniel Gookin's (1970) historical collection and John Winthrop's (1908) journal represent particularly significant sources of primary documentation describing developments in this area. Other pertinent primary sources include Thomas Morton's 1637 *New English Canaan* (T. Morton 1883), Mourt's 1622 *Relation* (Mourt 1963), and William Wood's 1634 *New England's Prospect* (W. Wood 1977).

Many secondary sources using these data focus on warfare in the area. A number of these studies examine Indian and colonial military technology and tactics in the area before and during King Philip's War (Hirsch 1988; Malone 1973, 1991). Others address the events of the war itself (Bourne 1990; Jennings 1975; Leach 1958; Vaughan 1979). Less work has been devoted to understanding Indian life in Massachusett Country after King Philip's War. Conkey, Boissevain, and Goddard (1978), Goddard and Bragdon (1988), Kawashima (1986), Mandell (1992), Simmons (1986), and Von Lonkhuyzen (1990) provide particularly useful surveys of known documentary information.

Although many Indian burying grounds from the period are listed on current inventories, only a few are known to contain extensive, intact deposits (Carlson 1986). One of these, the Chapman Street Praying Indian burial ground, contains remains associated with the people of the Punkapoag Praying Indian town (Carlson 1986; Simon 1990). Others are located within the borders of the former Praying Indian town of Natick (Brenner 1980, 1984, 1988). One of these properties is a much-disturbed community cemetery plot containing graves of many Natick Indian people. The other, a frame house that originally served as home to the last missionary to the Natick Indian community, is one of the few surviving aboveground structures associated with early contact between Indian people and colonists in Massachusetts (Carlson 1986; B. Pfeiffer 1979).

WAMPANOAG COUNTRY

Wampanoag Country stretches across southeastern Massachusetts and adjacent portions of Rhode Island from Cape Cod's Barnstable County west across Plymouth and Bristol Counties to Nantucket Island, Martha's Vineyard, the Elizabeth Islands, and the eastern shore of Narragansett Bay. This area encompasses the historic homeland of the Wampanoag people. Like Abenaki, the name Wampanoag comes from an Algonquian word meaning "Easterner." Pokanoket, another name used to identify these people, was originally the name of the home of the early seventeenth-century Wampanoag leader Massasoit at Mount Hope in present-day Bristol, Rhode Island.

THE SIXTEENTH CENTURY

As elsewhere, archaeological deposits provide the only material evidence of sixteenth-century life in Wampanoag Country. Although most archaeologists believe that large numbers of sites dating to the 1500s survive in the area, relatively few intact deposits have thus far been found. Those that have been found indicate that most area residents were a mobile people who moved from large, decentralized towns to smaller hunting, fishing, and foraging camps at various times of the year (Kerber 1988–1989; Little 1988b; Thorbahn 1988).

Analyses of ceramics found in these sites indicate that sixteenth-century residents of Wampanoag Country continued to produce variants of Late Woodland pottery similar to types first appearing in the area several hundred years earlier. Many of these people made or used Sebonac-series conoidal wares resembling pottery produced by people living along the shores of Long Island Sound (Lavin 1987; Luedtke 1986; K. McBride 1984). Potters working in this area also manufactured globular pottery similar to Niantic-series wares produced by Indian people living farther north and west.

As elsewhere, human burials constitute the most numerous type of site found in Wampanoag Country dating to the 1500s (Bradley 1983, 1987b). The few known sixteenth-century habitation sites in the main represent small, short-term occupations.

Mixed assemblages of Late Woodland and European artifacts have been found in radiometrically assayed deposits at the Marshall site (Dincauze 1991; Pretola and Little 1988) and the Hayward's Port-animicutt locale (Eteson 1982). European trade goods have not yet been found in the more intact, radiometrically assayed deposits dating to the sixteenth century that are preserved within the Nauset National Historic Landmark.

THE SEVENTEENTH CENTURY

Records of Europeans note that most Indians in Wampanoag Country belonged to a loose confederation led by Massasoit, the sachem of Pokanoket, at the time Plymouth settlers established the first permanent English colony in the area in 1620. At various times, this coalition embraced communities at Nauset, Manomet, Cummaquid, Monomoy, and Mashpee on Cape Cod; Pawtuxet and Nemasket in present-day Plymouth County; Capawack and other places on Martha's Vineyard; communities on Nantucket Island; and Aquidneck and Massasoit's town of Pokanoket in eastern Rhode Island. Recent estimates indicate that as many as twenty-four thousand people may have lived in these communities before epidemics ravaging the region devastated settlements throughout Wampanoag Country between 1616 and 1620.

The career of Squanto, an English-speaking Pawtuxet Indian also known as Tisquantum, exemplifies some of the creative ways inhabitants of the Wampanoag Country responded to the challenges of contact. Kidnapped by English slavers in 1614 and sold in Spain, Squanto managed to make his way to London by 1617. Shortly thereafter, he contrived his return to Massachusetts by promising to guide gold-hungry adventurers to deposits of the precious metal allegedly located near his home.

Squanto returned in 1619 to find his people's lands had been abandoned in a 1616 epidemic. Subsequently captured by warriors from nearby Indian communities when Epinow, another former English captive, led a successful attack on the English landing party he was guiding, Squanto later emerged in English annals as the bilingual intermediary who established relations between Massasoit and the English in the spring of 1621 (Salisbury 1981, 1982a). He is credited with saving the Plymouth settlers during that first grim spring, teaching them how to manure their fields with fish, a skill he may have picked up from English settlers while in Newfoundland (Ceci 1975). He also may have played an important role in arranging the first Thanksgiving, a modest feast hosted by the settlers in the fall of 1621.

This feast helped cement relations between the Wampanoags and Plymouth colonists at a time when both people needed each other. The few settlers surviving the winter at Plymouth lived isolated and almost defenseless among strangers on a coast open to attack by French and Dutch raiders. The Wampanoags, once a populous people whose influence had extended outward to the Massachusett and Nipmuck Countries, had not yet recovered from the epidemics that had killed thousands of their people just before the arrival of the colonists. In need of allies to help his people defend themselves against attacks from Narragansett enemies on the east, restive Massachusett and Nipmuck peoples on the north, and Tarrantine Micmac raiders from Maine and the Maritimes, Massasoit actively worked through Squanto to develop an alliance with the Plymouth settlers. Although the colonists refused to

MAP 9: WAMPANOAG COUNTRY

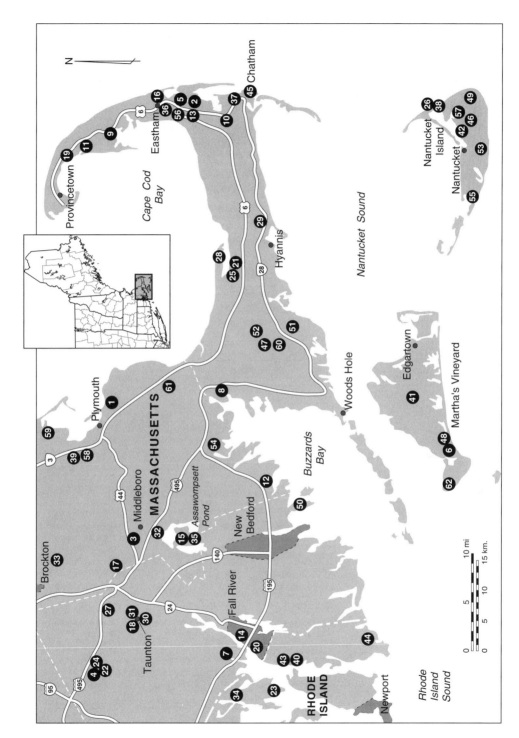

Map 9 Historic Contact Sites

Map Number	Site Name	County	State	Date	NR	Source
1	Eel River	Plymouth	MA	1500s		Brewer 1942
2	Hayward's Portanimicutt	Barnstable	MA	1500s		Eteson 1982
3	Nemasket	Plymouth	MA	1500s		Bradley 1987b
4	Newcomb Street	Bristol	MA	1500s		Thorbahn 1982
5	Peck	Barnstable	MA	1500s		Bradley 1987b
6	Peterson	Dukes	MA	1500s		W. Ritchie 1969b
7	South Swansea	Bristol	MA	1500s		Phelps 1947
8	Buttermilk Bay	Barnstable	MA	1500–1575		Bradley 1987b
9	Indian Neck	Barnstable	MA	1500–1575		Bradley et al. 1982
10	Muddy Cove	Barnstable	MA	1500–1575		Bradley 1987b
11	Railroad	Barnstable	MA	1500–1575		Moffett 1946
12	Herring Weir	Plymouth	MA	1575–1620		Bradley 1987b
13	Namequoit Point	Barnstable	MA	1575–1620		Bradley 1987b
14	Skeleton in Armor	Bristol	MA	1575–1620		Phelps 1947
15	Bettys Neck	Plymouth	MA	1500s–1600s		MHC
16	Nauset NHL Coast Guard Beach (19BN374) North Salt Pond (19BN390) South Salt Pond Complex (19BN274/339 and 19BN341) Fort Hill Complex (19BN308 and 19BN323)	Barnstable	MA	1500s–1600s	X	McManamon 1984
17	Titicut Complex Fort Hill Bluff Seaver Farm Taylor Farm Titicut Burials	Plymouth	MA	1500s–1600s		Dodge 1953, 1962; Fowler 1974; Jeppson 1964; Robbins 1967; Taylor 1976, 1982
18	Bay Street 1	Bristol	MA	1600s		Thorbahn 1982
19	Corn Hill	Barnstable	MA	1600s		Robbins 1968
20	Fall River Burial	Bristol	MA	1600s		Chapin 1927
21	Follins Pond	Barnstable	MA	1600s		Pohl 1960
22	G. B. Crane	Bristol	MA	1600s		Thorbahn, Cox, and Ritchie 1983
23	Mount Hope Farm	Bristol	RI	1600s	X	Warren 1976
24	Plain Street	Bristol	MA	1600s		Thorbahn 1982
25	Purcell	Barnstable	MA	1600s		Schambach and Bailey 1974
26	Quidnet	Nantucket	MA	1600s		Little 1977
27	Rozenas 2	Bristol	MA	1600s		Thorbahn 1982
28	Sandy Neck	Barnstable	MA	1600s		Bullen and Brooks 1948
29	Sandy's Point	Barnstable	MA	1600s		Mrozowski and Bragdon 1993
30	Snake River East	Bristol	MA	1600s		Thorbahn 1982
31	Snake River West	Bristol	MA	1600s		Thorbahn 1982
32	Wapanucket	Plymouth	MA	1600s	X	Robbins 1959
33	Old Fish Weir	Plymouth	MA	1649		MHC
34	Burr's Hill	Bristol	RI	1655–1680		L. Cook 1985; Gibson 1980
35	Wampanoag Royal Cemetery	Plymouth	MA	1676–1812	X	Robbins 1975
36	Hemenway	Barnstable	MA	Mid-1600s		F. Johnson 1942
37	Mattaquason Purchase	Barnstable	MA	Mid-1600s		Eteson, Crary, and Chase 1978

Map Number	Site Name	County	State	Date	NR	Source
38	Sesapana Will's Cellar Hole	Nantucket	MA	1680–1725		MHC
39	Patuxet Hotel	Plymouth	MA	Late 1600s		Bradley 1983
40	Stone Bridge/Tiverton Burials	Newport	RI	Late 1600s		Chapin 1927, L. Cook 1985
41	Christian Indian Burial Ground	Dukes	MA	1600s–1700s		MHC
42	Abrams Point 2	Nantucket	MA	1700s		MHC
43	Beattie Point Burials	Newport	RI	1700s		Bullen and Bullen 1946; L. Cook 1985
44	Pottersville Burials	Newport	RI	1700s		L. Cook 1985; Wilbour 1970
45	RM-27	Barnstable	MA	1700s		MHC
46	NAN-HA-11	Nantucket	MA	1700s–1800s		MHC
47	Santuit Pond Road Cemetery	Barnstable	MA	1700s–1800s	X	MHC
48	Experience Mayhew House	Dukes	MA	1700–1745		MHC
49	Tashime's Cellar Hole	Nantucket	MA	1720–1780		MHC
50	Scontuit Neck	Bristol	MA	1750s		MHC
51	Simons House	Barnstable	MA	1750–1900		Savulis 1991
52	Gideon Hawley House	Barnstable	MA	1758–1807	X	MHC
53	Miacomet Burial Ground	Nantucket	MA	1763–1764		MHC
54	Car-Tracks	Plymouth	MA	Historic		Stockley 1962
55	Eel Point	Nantucket	MA	Historic		Fowler 1973
56	Ford	Barnstable	MA	Historic		MHC
57	Marshall	Nantucket	MA	Historic		Pretola 1973; Pretola and Little 1988
58	Powers Shell Heap	Plymouth	MA	Historic		Sherman 1948
59	Valley	Plymouth	MA	Historic		MHC
60	Mashpee Old Indian Church and Cemetery	Barnstable	MA	1600s–present		MHC
61	Herring Pond/ Cumassacumhanet	Plymouth	MA	1600s–present		MHC
62	Gay Head/Old South Road	Dukes	MA	1600s–present		Glover and McBride 1992; MHC

attack the Narragansetts on his behalf, their connections with Massasoit evidently discouraged attacks on Wampanoag communities.

Massasoit and his people soon found themselves paying a high price for this protection. Requests for land turned into demands as settlers pouring into Plymouth expanded outward in search of new homes in Wampanoag territory. Requiring Wampanoag people to accept English authority, provincial administrators extorted often exorbitant fines for infractions of laws having little meaning to Indian people.

Unwilling to abandon their homeland, the Wampanoags soon found themselves restricted to limited tracts set aside for them by Plymouth authorities. In 1660, for example, magistrates established a fifty-square-mile reservation at Mashpee for Indian people living on Cape Cod. Other communities were established elsewhere on Cape Cod by Puritan missionaries like John Eliot and Thomas Mayhew, on the Elizabeth Islands, on Martha's Vineyard, and on Nantucket Island. Struggling to maintain autonomy at Pokanoket, Massasoit and his successor, Metacomet or Matacam—known among the English as King Philip—found themselves and their people hemmed in by settlers clamoring for more land.

Plymouth magistrates and missionaries gradually began to exert control over most aspects of Wampanoag life. Social conduct was strictly regulated. Polygamy, for example, was outlawed. Offended by what they regarded as "nakedness," colonists passed laws requiring Indian people to dress more like English settlers. They demanded the right to approve appointments of all Indian leaders. Taxes were levied on Wampanoag communities. Requiring natives and settlers to submit disputes to colonial courts, provincial authorities allowed certain Indian communities to establish courts of their own to adjudicate internal disputes. Indian people taught to read and write by missionaries soon began keeping court records in their own language (Goddard and Bragdon 1988).

Unable or unwilling to move elsewhere, Wampanoag people patiently struggled to endure loss of land and autonomy. Resentment finally spilled into war in 1675. Named for King Philip—the sachem Metacomet—the war gradually expanded to embroil nearly every Indian and European community in New England. It split Wampanoag communities already fragmented by colonial penetration. Swept up in the general conflict, most Wampanoag people were forced to choose one side or the other. The struggle assumed the dimensions of a civil war as Christian and non-Christian Indians fought with and against one another. Only Cape Cod townsfolk and offshore islanders escaped the general conflagration.

The war was a disaster for the Wampanoag people. Many, including King Philip, were dead by the time the fighting in Massachusetts Bay stopped in 1676. Those who had not surrendered or been killed by the English and their Mohawk and Praying Indian allies were in hiding or living in exile. Many fled to the Schaghticoke, New York, Indian refugee community and places farther west. Others moved north to New France or Acadia. Large numbers of Indian people surrendering to colonists were sold into slavery.

Colonial authorities closely supervised the lives of those Indian people remaining in Wampanoag Country after the war ended. Devastated by epidemics throughout the remainder of the century, survivors increasingly married European and African neighbors or Indian people from other places. Diminished by disease, poverty, emigration, and intermarriage, total Indian population in Wampanoag Country had shrunk to less than two thousand by the end of the century.

Most known archaeological sites containing identifiable evidence of seventeenth-century Indian occupation in Wampanoag Country predate King Philip's War. As elsewhere, most of these sites are cemeteries or individual graves. Several, such as the Purcell site burials containing the remains of women and children evidently pierced by bone and bronze arrow points, testify to violent happenings in the area. Statistical analyses of large grave populations, such as those found at the Pokanoket cemetery at Burr's Hill or the graves on both banks of the Nemasket River in the Titicut complex site area around North Middleboro, can provide potentially informative demographic documentation and other forms of data.

Most of the few habitation sites preserved in the area contain remains of small camps or households. One of the most extensive of these areas, the earlier-mentioned Nauset National Historic Landmark, contains deposits associated with the early–seventeenth-century Indian community sketched by Samuel de Champlain after his visits in 1605 and 1606 (McManamon 1984). Unusually intact remains of cornfields have been found during salvage excavations at Sandy's Point (Mrozowski and Bragdon 1993).

Little physical evidence documenting the English side of relations with Indian people in Wampanoag Country has been found. Archaeological deposits identified as remains of the first Plymouth colony trading post at Aptuxet in Bourne, Massachusetts, for example, may date to later periods of occupation. The still-standing Benjamin Church House in Bristol, Rhode Island, preserves the home of a New England soldier who became a formidable adversary to Indian people by adopting and then adapting their way of making war.

THE EIGHTEENTH CENTURY

Indian communities throughout Wampanoag Country continued to shrink in size during the eighteenth century. Only a few of the Massachusetts Bay "praying towns" established before King Philip's War endured into the 1700s. Some, like Mashpee and Gay Head, persist to the present day. Most others had collapsed by the end of the eighteenth century.

Like their Massachusetts neighbors on the north, Indian people in Wampanoag Country lived in the heart of the English settlement. As a result, they managed to avoid the worst effects of the border violence that ravaged Indian and colonial households in more exposed frontier communities. At the same time, the nearness of English towns increased exposure to epidemic contagion. One episode, a yellow fever epidemic, killed most of the Indian people living in Nantucket between 1763 and 1764. Hundreds of other native people were killed by the many smallpox, measles, malaria, and influenza epidemics that struck Indian communities everywhere during the 1700s.

Missionaries and overseers appointed by town governments or provincial authorities continued to dominate life in most Indian communities in Wampanoag Country during these years. Although the Indians generally maintained their most substantial permanent settlements in these towns, many used other tracts located beyond reservation or mission boundaries for foraging, fishing, and hunting. And like their neighbors in Massachusett Country, they managed to retain control over their day-to-day affairs during the eighteenth century, drafting and enforcing ordinances that regulated internal relations and keeping written records in their own language.

But Massachusetts provincial authorities continued to insist on appointing or approving all Indian leaders and on approving all laws and ordinances enacted by Indian people. In effect, they regulated all relations between native people and non-Indians. Colonists were appointed to oversee Indian communities. Provincial assemblies drew up bodies of law to adjudicate disputes over land and deal with other issues of importance to both peoples.

Increasingly constrained by colonial law and subjected to other pressures, the native people choosing to remain in

Nauset Archeological District National Historic Landmark

The Nauset Archeological District consists of two sites and two site complexes on the northern and northwestern shores of Nauset Marsh, which lines Nauset Harbor, a large tidal lagoon on the east coast of the Cape Cod National Seashore in Eastham Township, Barnstable County, Massachusetts. Nauset sites were located and tested from 1978 to 1985 during a survey of sites within Cape Cod National Seashore boundaries conducted by National Park Service North Atlantic Regional Office archaeologists supervised by Francis P. McManamon. The overall distribution of these sites roughly corresponds to the dispersed pattern of individual wigwams and cornfields depicted by Samuel de Champlain on his 1606 map of the area. Running from north to south, these properties include the Coast Guard Beach site (19BN374), the North Salt Pond site (19BN390), the South Salt Pond site complex (19BN274/339 and 19BN341), and the Fort Hill site complex (19BN308 and 19BN323).

Some or all of these sites may have been occupied when Samuel de Champlain drew his map of the locale. Sailing to Cape Cod in a ship commanded by Sieur de Poutrincourt, Champlain noted in his journal entry for July 21, 1605, that they arrived off Nauset where "they perceived a bay with wigwams bordering it all around." He further observed fields of corn, beans, squash, tobacco, "and roots which they cultivate." Naming the harbor Mallebarre, "bad bar," after its many shoals, the French sailed away on July 25 after one of the ship's sailors was killed in a fight with local inhabitants.

Excavations at 19BN323, Fort Hill Site Complex, Nauset Archeological District National Historic Landmark. Photograph by Francis P. McManamon. Courtesy Cape Cod National Seashore, National Park Service.

Returning to Nauset in October 1606, Champlain and his shipmates met "some 150 Indians, singing and dancing in accordance with their custom." Leaving after a brief visit, these French voyagers never returned to Cape Cod thereafter. This left the field open to the English, who first arrived in force aboard the Mayflower in late November 1620. Anchoring in what today is called Provincetown Harbor, the Brownist Separatists (today known as Pilgrims) aboard the ship made three short journeys to see if Cape Cod had sufficient amounts of freshwater and fertile soil to support a new colony. The last of these journeys, undertaken between December 16 and 17, took the Brownists to Nauset Harbor.

Their journals record that they passed by several fallow cornfields and four or five unoccupied native wigwam frames stripped of their mat coverings. Finding and emptying two storage pits containing parched acorns, they entered "a great burying place" partially enclosed by a palisade wall. Digging into the graves, as they had done during their earlier forays, they noted that burials beyond the palisade wall were "not so costly" as those within.

Attacked the next day by native people evidently enraged by the violation of their graves and storage pits, the Brownists quickly left. Sailing away from Provincetown, they subsequently established their colony at Plymouth.

Although data are scant, Indian people continued to live in and around Nauset until several chiefs put their marks to a deed conveying land in the area to Plymouth settlers in March 1645. The Indian signatories insisted on reserving their rights to collect shellfish and retained a share of the blubber of whales washing up on Nauset beaches, but most of the native people moved away from Nauset shortly after seven families of English colonists established the first permanent European settlement on the western shore of Town Cove.

Discoveries of deposits containing diagnostic Late Woodland period triangular, chipped-stone projectile points and shell-tempered pottery in Nauset site plow-zone soils, middens, pits, and hearths corroborate written records documenting Indian occupation. Radiocarbon samples recovered from deposits containing terminal Late Woodland lithics and ceramics at site 19BN323 in the Fort Hill site complex have produced dates of A.D. 1440 +/- 110 and A.D. 1770 +/- 115. Although the latter date is regarded as too recent and may reflect contamination caused by slopewash redeposition of later materials into earlier deposits, the former assay corroborates written records of Historic Contact period native occupation at Nauset. Floral and faunal evidence recovered from this and other Nauset locales further suggests that most sites were occupied year-round.

Nauset site deposits represent the

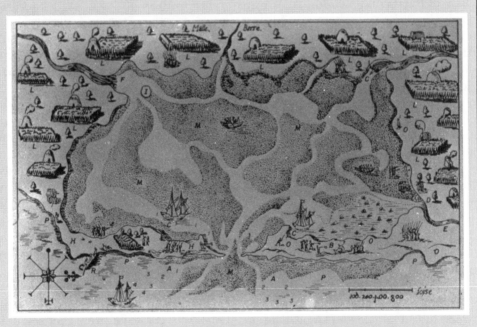

Samuel de Champlain's 1606 map of Nauset. Courtesy Newberry Libary, Chicago.

largest known single body of intact archaeological resources dating to Late Woodland times in the Cape Cod region. It is located in one of the few areas on the North Atlantic coast containing deposits collectively preserving an almost unbroken six-thousand-year-long record of human occupation. It is also one of the few areas still able to provide extensive information on past and present coastal environments and adaptations. Because of this, Nauset assemblages provide unparalleled opportunities to assess causes, consequences, patterns, and processes of development of the Indian culture documented at Nauset by early–seventeenth-century European visitors. Preserving a unique record of the initial phases of intercultural relations in southern New England, Nauset site deposits have yielded—and continue to possess the potential to yield—nationally significant information.

The Nauset Archeological District was designated a National Historic Landmark on April 19, 1993. Archaeological materials gathered from Nauset and other Cape Cod locales during National Park Service surveys are curated in laboratory facilities maintained at the Cape Cod National Seashore.

Information presented here is abstracted from McManamon (1984).

Wampanoag Country had to give up many vestiges of their ancestral ways of life during the eighteenth century. Although many of them continued to live in wigwams, increasing numbers moved into frame houses built and placed in accordance with current British style. British dress and decoration were adopted. Nearly all tools, implements, and weapons were acquired from English merchants or crafted from British models. As floor plans of wigwams and a frame house found together at the eighteenth-century Simons site in Mashpee show, interior house plans of many Indian frame houses enclosed single, unpartitioned spaces more reminiscent of wigwams than colonial houses (Savulis 1991).

As elsewhere, English came into common usage as the primary language of most native people in Wampanoag Country by midcentury. Marriage between Indian people and English-speaking settlers of European or African descent speeded adoption of English in Indian households. Despite this fact, many children born into these households maintained awareness of and respect for their Indian ancestry.

Just as their ancestral skills and established identities survived during these years, so too did the Wampanoags manage to maintain their oral literature. These texts supported community cohesiveness and preserved ancestral knowledge.

As they do for earlier periods, mortuary sites constitute much of the known archaeological record of eighteenth-century Indian life in Wampanoag Country. But unlike the sites of earlier periods, many of them represent cemeteries containing numbers of people buried in coffins. As many as nineteen grave shafts and five burials thought to represent interments of Nantucket Indians killed by the 1763–1764 yellow fever epidemic have been found during archaeological excavations at Miacomet Burial Ground. Other surveys have been conducted at such places as the Santuit Pond Road cemetery and the Christian Indian burial grounds at Gay Head.

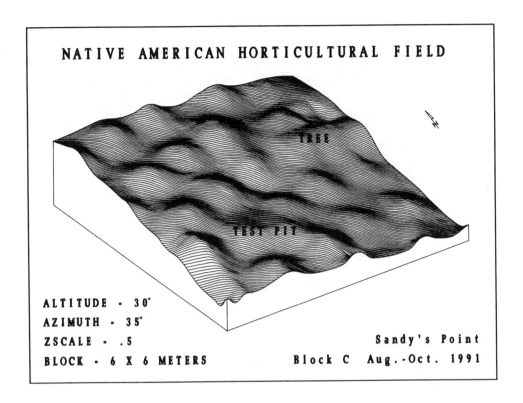

NATIVE AMERICAN HORTICULTURAL FIELD

TREE

TEST PIT

ALTITUDE - 30°
AZIMUTH - 35°
ZSCALE - .5
BLOCK - 6 X 6 METERS

Sandy's Point
Block C   Aug.-Oct. 1991

Computer-generated map of a portion of a cornfield excavated at the Sandy's Point site, Barnstable County, Massachusetts. *Courtesy Stephen A. Mrozowski.*

Archaeological remains of eighteenth-century habitation sites have been found at Fairhaven, Mashpee, Gay Head, and Nantucket Island. Standing structures associated with Christian Indian missionaries also survive on Cape Cod and Martha's Vineyard.

SOURCES

Much of the information presented in this section has been drawn from Bradley (1982a). Discussions of intercultural relations are largely based on information contained in Jennings (1975), Salisbury (1982a), Salwen (1978), and Vaughan (1979).

A number of archaeologists address the question of "Where are the Woodland Villages?" in Kerber (1988–1989). Daniel Gookin's (1970) historical collection and John Winthrop's journal (1908) provide primary documentary data on affairs in Wampanoag Country.

A substantial body of records document life in Wampanoag Country during the early seventeenth century. These include Champlain (1922–1936), T. Morton (1883), Mourt (1963), W. Wood (1977), Hirsch (1988), Malone (1973, 1991), Bourne (1990), Jennings (1975), Leach (1958), and Vaughan (1979).

Less work has been devoted to understanding Indian life in the area after King Philip's War. Conkey, Boissevain, and Goddard (1978), Goddard and Bragdon (1988), Kawashima (1986), and Simmons (1986) provide particularly useful surveys of known documentary information. Documentation describing the Nantucket Indian community is examined by Elizabeth A. Little (1977, 1979, 1981a, 1988a) and Vickers (1983). The early history of the Gay Head Wampanoag mission community is described in Ronda (1983).

Many documents analyzed in these studies mention one or more of the more than twenty Indian towns known to have existed in Wampanoag Country during the eighteenth century. Archaeological surveys conducted at the locales of several of these communities indicate that their inhabitants maintained dispersed settlement patterns rather than move into nucleated towns of the type occupied by neighboring colonists (Brenner 1984; Kerber 1988–1989).

Burying grounds associated with many of these communities are listed on current inventories. Extensive occupational evidence found at the Simons House site shows that similar archaeological deposits may be preserved at Mashpee and other surviving Indian communities in the area (Savulis 1991). Investigations conducted by Little (1977, 1979, 1981a, 1988b) have uncovered large bodies of written records and numerous housesites and have identified Indian graves associated with the native people of Nantucket Island. The Experience Mayhew House on Nantucket and the Gideon Hawley House on Cape Cod represent rare surviving frame houses occupied by missionaries working with Indian people in Wampanoag Country during the 1700s (MHC).

NARRAGANSETT COUNTRY

Narragansett Country extends across the southern two-thirds of the state of Rhode Island, from the Greater Providence area south to Rhode Island and Block Island Sounds. Encompassing Rhode, Prudence, Conanicut, and Block Islands, this area stretches from Narragansett Bay west to the Pawcatuck River boundary with Connecticut.

THE SIXTEENTH CENTURY

Very few archaeological sites in this area can be definitively dated to the sixteenth century. Rhode Island locales long thought to contain evidence of early contact, like the Newport Tower associated with Viking colonizers or the breech-loading cannon found at the Arnolda site believed to have been left by sixteenth-century Portuguese explorers, have since been shown to be of far more recent vintage (Anonymous 1922; L. Cook 1985; Feder 1990; Godfrey 1951).

Several sites in Narragansett Country contain terminal Late Woodland pottery or chipped-stone triangular projectile points possibly dating to the 1500s. Although modern oral narratives and other

texts recount stories of early contacts between Indian people and Europeans in Narragansett Country, written records of sixteenth-century events are few and are also equivocal. Several scholars believe that people described by Giovanni da Verrazzano during his visit to a broad New England bay in the spring of 1524 were encountered on Narragansett Bay (Verrazzano 1970), but verification of this and other evidence documenting sixteenth-century contacts in the area requires further research.

THE SEVENTEENTH CENTURY

The historic heart of Narragansett Country centered around southern Rhode Island in North and South Kingstown and Conanicut Island when Block made the earliest known, clearly documented European visit to this area in 1614. Although figures vary, many scholars today believe that as many as forty thousand Indian people were living on and around the shores of Narragansett Bay at the time of Block's visit (Salisbury 1982a).

Reaching its maximum extent during the mid-1600s, Narragansett Country embraced Coweset and Pawtuxet territory on the north, Niantic land on the east, and Manisean territory on Block Island on the south. Narragansett sachems also asserted authority over Montauks, Nipmucks, Wampanoags, and other neighbors at various times during these years. Several accounts indicate that Narragansett families frequently expanded the range of their power and influence through marriage and diplomacy.

Other documents show that Narragansett sachems also used force to extend the limits of their authority. Narragansett attacks mounted during the 1650s, for example, compelled Montauk and other eastern Long Island Indian people to pay tribute in the form of wampum and other products. Farther north, Narragansetts at war with Wampanoag people sold land claimed by Massasoit in what is today Providence, Rhode Island, to English purchasers. Poor relations with these and other neighboring Indian communities ultimately involved the Narragansetts in a seemingly interminable series of conflicts during the middle decades of the century.

Narragansett people vigorously resisted English penetration into their territories. Sending a bundle of arrows wrapped in snakeskin to Plymouth in 1622, Narragansett sachems signaled that they would resist English expansion. Wary of English intentions, the Narragansetts let fourteen years pass before allowing Puritan dissenters led by Roger Williams to establish the first permanent European settlements at the edges of the Narragansett heartland at Providence in 1636.

One year later, Narragansett leaders, pursuing their own foreign policy, sent men to join Mohegan warriors in helping the English in their war with the nearby Pequots. Shortly thereafter, the Narragansetts became embroiled in conflict with the Mohegans, who, under Uncas, rose as a major presence in the region following the Pequot defeat. Only strenuous diplomatic efforts by Rhode Island trader Samuel Gorton prevented war from breaking out after Narragansett sachem Miantonomi, who opposed English expansion into his country, was killed by Uncas with the covert approval of New England authorities in 1643.

Uneasy diplomatic relations did not stop commerce from developing between Narragansett people and the English settlers who opened up trading posts on their borders during these years. Narragansett traders exchanged furs, wampum, and other manufactures for European products at Williams's first trading post in Providence, at another post he established at the present-day Cocumscussoc National Historic Landmark in the North Kingstown village of Wickford in 1637, at Gorton's house in Warwick, and at various other posts.

As noted above, Samuel Gorton frequently played a major role in intercultural relations in Narragansett Country. Yet it is Roger Williams who today is better remembered as the frontier diplomat whose skill in statecraft helped keep the peace as increasingly overbearing New England magistrates demanded Narragansett submission to English authority.

As elsewhere in New England with other Indian peoples, peaceful relations between Narragansetts and the English ended when King Philip's War broke out in 1675. Initially neutral, the Indians of Narragansett Country were forced into the conflict after New England

MAP 10: NARRAGANSETT COUNTRY

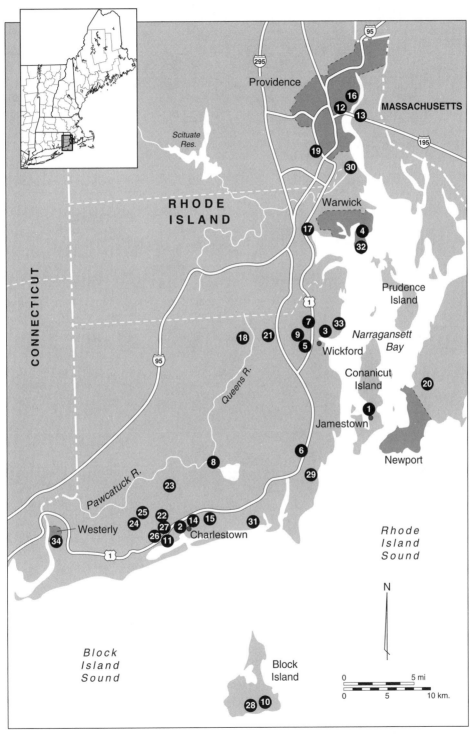

Providence

MASSACHUSETTS

Scituate
Res.

RHODE
ISLAND

Warwick

CONNECTICUT

Prudence
Island

Narragansett
Bay

Wickford

Queens R.

Conanicut
Island

Jamestown

Pawcatuck R.

Westerly

Charlestown

Newport

Rhode
Island
Sound

N

Block
Island
Sound

Block
Island

0   5 mi

0   5   10 km.

Map 10 Historic Contact Sites

Map Number	Site Name	County	State	Date	NR	Source
1	West Ferry I Burials (RI-84)	Newport	RI	1620–1660		L. Cook 1985; Simmons 1970
2	Fort Ninigret (RI-15)	Washington	RI	1620–1680	X	Salwen and Mayer 1978
3	Cocumscussoc NHL/ Smith's Castle (RI-375)	Washington	RI	1637–1692	X	P. Robinson 1989; Rubertone 1989; Rubertone and Fitts 1990, 1991
4	Samuel Gorton Housesite (RI-1767)	Kent	RI	1648–1675		Freedman and Pagoulatos 1989
5	RI-1000 Burials	Washington	RI	1650–1670		Kelley, Barrett, and Saunders, 1987; Kelley Sledzick, and Murphy, 1987; P. Robinson, Kelley, and Rubertone 1985; Turnbaugh 1984
6	Jireh Bull Blockhouse (RI-926)	Washington	RI	1657–1700	X	Zannieri 1983
7	Devil's Foot Cemetery (RI-694)	Washington	RI	–1672	X	Chapin 1927; L. Cook 1985; Hebert 1983
8	Great Swamp Fort (RI-2086)	Washington	RI	–1675		George, Jones, and Harper 1993
9	Whitford Burials (RI-1070)	Washington	RI	Mid-1600s		L. Cook 1985; Turnbaugh n.d.
10	Fort Island (RI-118)	Washington	RI	Late 1600s		K. McBride 1989
11	Arnolda (RI-1293)	Washington	RI	1600s		Anonymous 1992; L. Cook 1985
12	Bowen Street Burials (RI-1353)	Providence	RI	1600s		L. Cook 1985
13	Bullock's Point Burial (RI-1342)	Providence	RI	1600s		Chapin 1926; L. Cook 1985
14	Champlin Farm Burials	Washington	RI	1600s		Chapin 1927; L. Cook 1985
15	Indian Burial Hill	Washington	RI	1600s	X	Chapin 1927; L. Cook 1985
16	Mashpaug Pond Burial (RI-1351)	Providence	RI	1600s		Chapin 1927; L. Cook 1985
17	Matteson/Apponaug Burial (RI-1342)	Kent	RI	1600s		Chapin 1927; L. Cook 1985
18	Queen's Fort (RI-408)	Washington	RI	1600s	X	Cole 1980
19	Railroad Bridge Burials (RI-1370)	Providence	RI	1600s		Chapin 1927; L. Cook 1985
20	Railroad I Burials (RI-1362)	Newport	RI	1600s		Chapin 1927; L. Cook 1985
21	Dilon (RI-667)	Washington	RI	1600s–1700s		Morenon 1986
22	RI-1696	Washington	RI	1600–1700s		K. McBride 1990c
23	Narragansett Indian Reservation (RI-18)	Washington	RI	1709–present	X	Boissevain 1973
24	RI-1689	Washington	RI	Mid-1700s		K. McBride 1990b
25	RI-1691	Washington	RI	Mid-1700s		K. McBride 1990b
26	RI-1697	Washington	RI	Late 1700s		K. McBride 1990c
27	RI-1827	Washington	RI	Late 1700s		K. McBride 1990c
28	Block Island Indian Cemetery (RI-120)	Washington	RI	1700s		L. Cook 1985; E. Ritchie 1956
29	Narragansett Pier Burials (RI-1368)	Washington	RI	Historic		L. Cook 1985

Map Number	Site Name	County	State	Date	NR	Source
30	Pawtuxet Burial (RI-1367)	Providence	RI	Historic		Chapin 1926, 1927; L. Cook 1985
31	Potter Pond	Washington	RI	Historic	X	L. Cook 1985; Fowler and Luther 1950
32	Pumham's Fort (RI-696)	Kent	RI	Historic		P. Robinson 1992
33	Quonset Point (RI-1332)	Washington	RI	Historic		Chapin 1926; L. Cook 1985
34	West Side	Washington	RI	Historic		Chapin 1927; L. Cook 1985

troops, using Cocumscussoc as a forward base, attacked and destroyed their fort in the Great Swamp in the fall of 1675. Shortly thereafter, English soldiers and their Indian allies hunted down, killed, or captured Narragansett people all across New England. Hundreds of Narragansetts had died in the fighting or had been executed by colonists by the time hostilities ended in southern New England in 1676.

European records indicate that only a few hundred Indian people remained in the Narragansett Country at the end of the war. Although many present-day Narragansett Indian community members believe this figure to be far too low, most acknowledge the validity of English records showing that the Narragansetts known to have survived the war were, for the most part, forced to bind themselves out as indentured servants to Rhode Island settlers for varying lengths of time (J. B. Brown 1990).

Other records show that many Narragansetts refused to submit to this fate, choosing to leave New England altogether. Others joined Niantics who had stayed neutral or had actively supported Connecticut settlers during the war. Led by a succession of sachems bearing the name Ninigret, many of these Eastern Niantic people gradually came to be known themselves as Narragansetts.

Written records chronicling relations between Indians and Europeans in Narragansett Country in the years between the founding of the Rhode Island colony in 1636 and the end of King Philip's War in 1676 have been diligently collected and intensively studied. Less attention has been directed toward documented records of intercultural relations in the last quarter of the seventeenth century.

The physical record of seventeenth-century contact in Narragansett Country is both extensive and uneven. Archaeologist Lauren J. Cook's (1985) recent survey of Rhode Island archaeological records affirms long-standing knowledge that individual burials and cemeteries compose the overwhelming majority of known seventeenth-century archaeological sites in Narragansett Country. Contrasting the seventy-five sites identified in his sample, Cook charted a shift from single or small-group interments in agriculturally productive soils during Late Woodland and earlier times to increasingly larger cemeteries located on poor or marginally arable land during the Historic Contact period.

Studies conducted at places like the early–seventeenth-century West Ferry I cemetery on Conanicut Island (Simmons 1970) and the more recently excavated, later–seventeenth-century RI-1000 site (Kelley, Barrett, and Saunders 1987;

Cocumscussoc Historic Site National Historic Landmark

The Cocumscussoc site is located in North Kingstown, Washington County, Rhode Island. Cocumscussoc is the locale of the first English trading post established in Narragansett Country by Rhode Island's founder, Roger Williams, in 1637. Archaeological remains dating to the Historic Contact period found at the site document occupations of Narragansett frontier trader and diplomat Richard Smith, Sr., who purchased Cocumscussoc from Williams in 1651, and his son, Richard Smith, Jr., who operated the post from 1662 to 1692.

Richard Smith, Sr., and another trader named John Wilcox operated posts near Williams's establishment during the early 1640s. Buying Wilcox out in 1645, Smith purchased Roger Williams's "tradeing house at Narragansett" for fifty pounds in 1651. Extant records indicate that Smith moved into Williams's house. After his father's death in 1662, Richard Smith, Jr., continued to operate the property as a farm and trading post. His house also became an important center for adjudicating disputes, discussing land sales and trade issues, and concluding treaty agreements with Narragansett Indians.

By the time King Philip's War broke out in 1675, the younger Smith had fenced some of his land, built a dock on the shore of the site, and lived in a fortified house commonly called Smith's Castle. Smith's settlement became part of a line of border garrisons guarding English settlements on the Rhode Island frontier as the fighting spread. Initially using the place as a listening post to gather intelligence on Narragansett movements and intentions, provincial authorities later employed Cocumscussoc as a staging area for about a thousand United Colony troops who attacked and destroyed the Narragansett fort in the Great Swamp on December 19, 1675. The returning soldiers buried forty of their compatriots on Smith's property a few days later.

Narragansett warriors subsequently burned Smith's Castle after forcing the English to abandon Cocumscussoc and all other Rhode Island outposts south of Warwick during the spring of 1676. Returning to the area after the fighting stopped, Smith reputedly built his new home on the site of the old blockhouse. He undertook this construction sometime between 1677 and 1678, using salvaged timbers and other materials. This structure is the core of the present-day Smith's Castle. Although Smith continued to trade with his Narragansett neighbors after the war, plantation agriculture gradually supplanted commerce and was the dominant economic activity at Cocumscussoc by the time of Smith's death in 1692.

A local group of historic preservationists who incorporated themselves as the Cocumscussoc Association began buying up acreage in and around the site in 1949. Ultimately purchasing twenty-two acres, the association has maintained the property as a historic site open to the public. Restoring the building and landscaping the property, the association has encouraged research on the area's history and permitted archaeologists to conduct excavations. The first of these, undertaken in 1972 and 1973 by University of Rhode Island field crews under the direction of John Senulis, found a buried level consisting of structural mortar above a sealed deposit containing a coin dated 1652, a European gunflint, and a number of ceramic sherds possibly dating to the 1600s.

Aerial view of Cocumscussoc. The site appears in the center of the photograph. Photograph by Richard A. Gould. Courtesy Patricia A. Rubertone.

Brown University archaeologist Patricia E. Rubertone has supervised intensive archival and archaeological investigations at the site since 1989. Rubertone has found archival evidence affirming that Smith's Castle was indeed the site of Cocumscussoc and her field crews have systematically tested much of the area surrounding the Smith's Castle structure. Their excavations revealed a complex soil stratigraphy that varies considerably from one locale to another. A single layer of brown loam ranging from one to two feet in depth and containing diagnostic ceramics dating from the seventeenth to the nineteenth century occurs just below the lawn that covers most open areas at the locale.

Granite bedrock underlies the brown-loam layer at the southwesternmost extremity of the site. Several artifacts, including a blue glass bead dating to between 1660 and 1677, have been found within the brown loam layer at this locale. Artifacts dating from the Archaic period to the nineteenth century have been recovered from successive layers of dark-brown loam ranging from one foot to two feet in depth and a deep stratum of dense, gray-green marine clay beneath the brown-loam layer along the southern and eastern edges of the site deposit. A layer of olive-brown silty loam ranging in depth from six inches to one foot and containing artifacts dating to the Historic Contact period overlies yellow-tan, silty-clay subsoils beneath the brown-loam stratum in most other areas of the site.

One of the densest concentrations of Historic Contact period deposits thus far found at Cocumscussoc occurs in the olive-brown stratum above and below the layer of shell-tempered mortar first encountered by University of Rhode Island excavators. This layer is located about one foot below the ground surface along the southern half of a rectangular depression in the central portion of the southern part of the site area. Architectural debris such as chunks of mortar (some with lathe impressions), lead window cames, pane glass, and brick fragments is believed to represent structural remains. Delftware, lead-glazed slipware, and European white-clay tobacco-smoking pipe stems dating to the 1600s and early 1700s have been found within the mortar layer. Other pipe stems with bore diameters dating as early as 1620 to 1650 have been found below this level.

Remains of a large, stone-lined drain have been found on the north and east of these deposits. Lead-glazed slipware, westerwald stoneware, and a pipe stem with an 8/64-inch bore diameter dating to the early 1600s have been found within the drain trench. Delftware and pipe stems dating to the late seventeenth century have been found just above a cluster of stones and discolored soils in units about twenty feet to the north of these features. Seventeenth-century artifacts also have been found among another group of fieldstones believed to represent the remains of a structural footing on the north and west of the above-mentioned deposits.

These deposits represent some of the most extensively documented and best-preserved bodies of archaeological materials chronicling early contact between Indian and European people in Narragansett Country. Cocumscussoc was designated a National Historic Landmark on April 19, 1993. Archaeological materials recovered from the site are curated in the Brown University Department of Anthropology's Archaeology Laboratory and in the Rhode Island Historical Preservation Commission's storage facility.

Information presented here is abstracted from Rubertone and Fitts (1990, 1991).

Kelley, Sledzik, and Murphy 1987; Nassaney 1989; Turnbaugh 1984) have provided new information on Narragansett social life, mortuary customs, trade, spiritual beliefs, and patterns of health and disease. Other sites, like the extensively chronicled Indian Hill burial ground, continue to be particularly significant spiritual locales to present-day Narragansett Indians.

Few locales containing living floors or other evidence of Narragansett Indian dwellings or domestic life clearly dating to the 1600s have been found, though limited assemblages of diagnostic materials associated with seventeenth-century occupations have been recovered from intact archaeological contexts at the Fort Ninigret, Dilon, and RI-1696 sites.

More extensive evidence of seventeenth-century Narragansett domestic life is preserved in the Fort Island site on Block Island (K. McBride 1989). Field crews directed by archaeologist Kevin A. McBride have recovered glass beads; redware; European white-clay pipes; metal fragments; Shantok-ware ceramics; triangular, chipped-stone projectile points; and masses of debitage from hearths, pits, middens, and post-mold patterns believed to represent living floors at the site. Physical evidence of fortifications and wampum production at the site, however, has not yet been unearthed. More recently, Public Archaeology Survey Team investigators have discovered deposits associated with the Great Swamp Fort attacked by the English in 1675 (George, Jones, and Harper, 1993).

Several locales preserve evidence of the English side of contact in Narragansett Country. Remains of foundation walls and other deposits at the Jireh Bull blockhouse site, for example, document English garrison life on the Narragansett frontier during King Philip's War. Archaeological materials unearthed at the aforementioned Samuel Gorton housesite and the Cocumscussoc National Historic Landmark, for their part, amplify and affirm written records documenting seventeenth-century English trade and diplomacy along the shores of Narragansett Bay.

THE EIGHTEENTH CENTURY

At the beginning of the eighteenth century most Narragansetts Indians lived together in small communities at various places in southwestern Rhode Island. Although some lived in and around nearby colonial towns, most lived apart from increasingly intrusive settlers on sandy pinelands around Charlestown and North Kingstown, areas generally unwanted by colonists. Like many of their contemporaries in southern New England, Narragansett Indians had been compelled to acknowledge British sovereignty. Despite this fact, the Narragansetts continued to govern themselves as a sovereign people through their sachems and councils.

Continually pressed to concentrate his people's settlements in one place, Narragansett Indian leader Ninigret II finally exchanged all remaining Indian lands within Rhode Island for a sixty-four-square-mile reservation in Charlestown in 1709. But nearby colonists soon compelled Narragansett people to sell or lease even this land. Angered by the lies and the strong-arm tactics used by settlers, Narragansett leaders successfully petitioned the Rhode Island General Assembly to annul all sales of reservation land in 1713. Four years later, provincial authorities appointed three overseers to administer reservation lands for the tribe.

These overseers rarely intervened in tribal affairs. Most Narragansett people, for example, held fast to ancestral spiritual beliefs. Although Rhode Island officials encouraged conversion, none attempted to force Christianity upon the Narragansett community. The Narragansetts themselves began to accept the new religion when Joseph Park, a minister inspired by the Great Awakening, started preaching on the reservation in 1733. Large numbers of Narragansetts subsequently joined his congregation in Westerly, some ten miles west of the reservation.

Many of these converts joined the first Christian congregation established within the reservation in 1745. The founder of this church, Samuel Niles, was the first of many ordained Indian ministers to serve the Narragansett community. Initially meeting in reservation homes, Niles's followers built a wooden-frame church in 1750. The building quickly became the focal point of reservation life. A schoolhouse was subsequently built at Cockumpaug Pond in 1766.

Most Narragansett people made their living by farming, fishing, sheep raising, and lumbering during these years. Many also hired themselves out as wage laborers. More than a few augmented their incomes by working as sailors on whalers and merchantmen sailing out of New England ports.

Sales of large tracts of land to satisfy debts incurred by sachems George and Thomas Ninigret divided the Narragansett community during the 1740s and 1750s. Although many Narragansetts opposed the sales, they were unable to prevent the loss of much of their best remaining land by 1759. Finding it increasingly hard to make a living on what remained, many of them left their shrinking reservation to join Indian communities on the New Jersey coast or on Long Island. Some of them married men and women from these places and lived quietly among their neighbors. Others joined the Brothertown movement.

Organized during the 1760s by missionaries of Indian descent, like Mohegan minister Samson Occom, Brothertown leaders devoted themselves to removing Christian Indian people from what they regarded as the corrupting influences of neighboring colonists to new homes in Indian communities beyond the western frontier. Many Narragansett adherents of the movement joined Montauks, Mohegans, and other Indian emigrants on lands in New York set aside for their use by the Oneidas at the New Stockbridge and Brothertown communities. Remaining in New York through the turbulent years following the American War for Independence, most Brothertown Indians were finally forced to move farther west during the early decades of the nineteenth century. Today, descendants of many of these Brothertown people live on the Stockbridge-Munsee Reservation in north-central Wisconsin.

The Narragansett Indian Reservation, unilaterally dissolved by the state of Rhode Island in 1880 and reestablished by the federal government as a federal Indian reservation in 1985, is listed in the National Register of Historic Places. The sites of the 1750 church and 1766 schoolhouse are among the many properties found to be nationally significant that are located within the reservation. Recent surveys have located foundation walls and European goods at sites RI-1689, RI-1691, RI-1697, and RI-1827 within the bounds of the 1709 Charlestown Reservation (K. McBride 1990b, 1990c). These sites, not presently in Indian ownership, may contain evidence of eighteenth-century Narragansett wigwams, frame houses, and activity areas.

SOURCES

Much of the information presented in this section is abstracted from Campbell and LaFantasie (1978); Conkey, Boissevain, and Goddard (1978); L. Cook (1985); P. Robinson (1990); and Simmons (1970, 1978, 1986). Each of these studies draws upon information contained in Roger Williams's (1973) linguistic and ethnographic treatise on Narragansett culture, *A Key into the Language of America.* First published in 1643, and reprinted many times since then, this study contains the single best ethnographic description of southern New England Algonquian lifeways during the Historic Contact period. Williams's letters, which contain much of interest on life and events in Narragansett Country, have recently been edited and published (LaFantasie 1988).

MOHEGAN-PEQUOT COUNTRY

Mohegan-Pequot Country extends across the southeastern corner of Connecticut from the Thames River drainage west to the present Rhode Island line.

THE SIXTEENTH CENTURY

Nearly all of the few sites clearly associated with sixteenth-century Indian life in this area are located within the Mashantucket Pequot National Historic Landmark. Ceramics found at Mashantucket and contemporary locales indicate that people living in and around the Thames River Valley began making the distinctive terminal-Windsor-phase collared clay pots known as Niantic or Hackney Pond wares sometime during the late fourteenth century. Although permanent settlements dating to the century preceding intensive contact have not yet been clearly identified in this area, the rarity of objects of European origin in terminal Late Woodland sites in and around Mashantucket suggests that Indian people living along the eastern Connecticut coast took few foreign imports with them during hunting trips into the upland interior of the area.

THE SEVENTEENTH CENTURY

Reference to a people identified as "Pequatoos" on the 1614 Adriaen Block map represents the earliest known written mention of an Indian community by name in European records documenting Mohegan-Pequot Country. Block's map locates the Pequots within their historic heartland between the Thames and Mystic river valleys.

Subsequent research has shown that Pequot people stood at the center of a network of Coastal Algonquian communities stretching from Lower Connecticut Valley Country to eastern Long Island when Dutch and English settlers began moving into the area. Although direct records presently are lacking, researchers believe that as many as thirty thousand people may have been living in and around the Pequot heartland when the first few Europeans settled on the fringes of their territory during the late 1620s.

Scholars have long argued about the origins and affiliations of the Pequot people. Investigators contrasting the name of one of their affiliates, the Mohegans, with Mahican people in New York, once believed that the Pequots were recent immigrants to New England (De Forest 1851). More recent studies indicate that Pequot culture developed within its historic locale in Late Woodland times. Linguistic analyses contrasting the Mahican and Pequot languages show that both are distinct, if distantly related, Eastern Algonquian tongues (Goddard 1978a). Archaeologists tracing temporal, spatial, and stylistic distributions of aboriginal ceramics have shown that Hackney Pond wares found in terminal Late Woodland Indian occupations in Mohegan-Pequot Country most closely resemble pottery found in sites in eastern Long Island and Lower Connecticut Valley Country (K. McBride 1990e; Salwen 1969; L. Williams 1972).

Analyses of written and orally transmitted records affirm that Pequot people exerted often-resented influence over other Indian people living in these locales during the early decades of the seventeenth century. Many of these documents record Pequot levies of wampum and other goods on unwilling neighbors. Other records document Pequot attacks on recalcitrant tributaries. Such conduct helped earn Pequots a reputation for bellicosity that English settlers did little to discourage. Even today, as modern Pequots trace the etymology of their name to an Algonquian word for "ally," many people still accept earlier English translations asserting that the origins of the name lie in a word meaning "destroyers."

Although direct evidence is lacking, some Pequot people may have encouraged such a bellicose reputation. Facing formidable challenges during the early decades of the century, ravaged by new epidemic diseases and beset by foreign colonists, Pequot leaders did what they could to control restive tributaries, influence policies of diffident affiliates eager to align themselves with new Dutch or English neighbors, and deter aggressive settlers intent upon dominating or extirpating powerful Indian rivals.

Responding to the uncertainties of their situation, the Pequots began moving into fortified settlements at or about this time. Written records describing such settlements as the Mystic Fort show that major Pequot towns of the period consisted of large numbers of circular and oblong bark- or grass-mat-covered, sapling-framed houses surrounded by circular timber-palisade walls. Providing a measure of security against enemies waging war in established native Northeastern fashion, such settlements became death traps when attacked by European adversaries intent upon destroying entire communities and enslaving survivors. Between three hundred and six hundred Pequot people, for instance, may have been killed when English troops attacked and burned the Mystic Fort during the height of the Pequot War in 1637.

Largely precipitated by competition between Connecticut and Massachusetts colonies for Pequot lands, this war devastated the Pequot people and their allies. Support from Indian people hostile to the Pequots helped secure the colonial victory. Mohegan warriors led by Uncas, a local leader closely connected to several leading Pequot families, joined large numbers of Narragansett men in the assault on the Mystic Fort. Mohawks responding to English pleas for assistance killed hundreds of Pequot men, women, and children fleeing west after the Mystic Fort attack.

MAP 11: MOHEGAN-PEQUOT COUNTRY

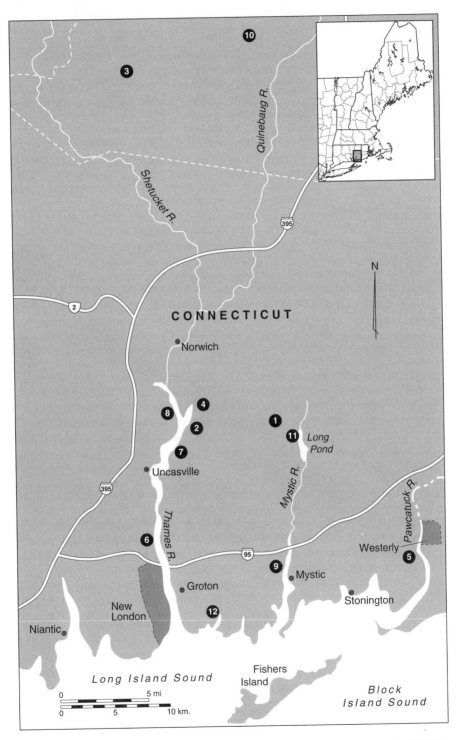

Map 11 Historic Contact Sites

Map Number	Site Name	County	State	Date	NR	Source
1	Mashantucket Pequot NHL	New London	CT	1500s–present	X	K. McBride 1990d
2	Aljen Heights	New London	CT	1600s		CAS
3	Ballymahack West	Windham	CT	1600s		K. McBride 1984
4	Calvin Main Complex	New London	CT	1600s		CAS
5	Davis Farm	New London	CT	1600s		K. McBride 1990d
6	Harrison's Landing	New London	CT	1600s		CAS
7	Stoddard's Cove	New London	CT	1600s		CAS
8	Fort Shantok NHL	New London	CT	1635–1750	X	Salwen 1966; L. Williams 1972
9	Pequot Fort	New London	CT	–1637	X	K. McBride 1990a
10	Pearl Harbor Rock Shelter	Windham	CT	Late 1600s		K. McBride 1984
11	Long Pond Cemetery	New London	CT	1660–1720		K. McBride 1990e
12	Trumbull Airport	New London	CT	Historic		CAS

Aided by their Indian allies, English troops relentlessly hunted down Pequot people throughout New England. All Pequot lands were confiscated. Those Pequots not killed outright were taken prisoner and enslaved. Some 200 of these captives were parceled out to English settlers moving onto appropriated Pequot lands. Others were transported to places like Bermuda, where modern descendants still retain the memory of their Pequot heritage (V. Mason 1938). Still others were divided among English Indian allies, becoming Montauk or Narragansett servants. Others had to settle among Uncas's Mohegans, who claimed their portion of the former Pequot heartland.

Most Pequots did not remain slaves for long. Although some were assimilated into colonial, Mohegan, Montauk, or Narragansett societies, most refused to give up their Pequot identity. Many of them gradually joined one or another of the two major Pequot communities that emerged during the middle decades of the century.

Led by Robin Cassasinamon, a group later known as the Western Pequots managed to establish small settlements under English supervision at Nameag near modern New London, Connecticut, soon after the end of the war. Gradually winning a degree of autonomy, many of these Pequots moved to the five-hundred-acre Noank reservation community south of Mystic in 1651. Another tract containing from two thousand to three thousand acres was reserved for their use at Mashantucket on the north of Mystic in the town of Ledyard in 1666. This community became, and remains, the central focus of Western Pequot life after most people living at Noank moved there in 1721.

Eastern Pequot people gradually moved to the Stonington reservation, which originally contained five hundred acres and was established for the Pequots by Connecticut authorities in 1683. Eastern Pequot people continue to live on and around this reservation on the eastern shore of Long Pond in Lantern Hill, Connecticut.

Several archaeological sites document seventeenth-century Pequot life. Archaeologists testing the area in the

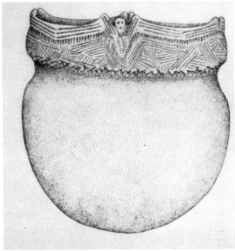

Terminal Late Woodland pottery from eastern Connecticut: *left,* Hackney Pond pot; *right,* Shantok-series pot. *Courtesy Kevin A. McBride.*

Pequot Hill district in West Mystic have found deposits associated with the Mystic Fort (K. McBride 1990a). Remains of a later fort dating to the period of King Philip's War have recently been found in the Mashantucket Pequot National Historic Landmark. Smaller sites containing Hackney Pond pottery, stone tools, and early–seventeenth-century diagnostic European goods have been found at various locales within the Mashantucket Pequot National Historic Landmark, the Aljen Heights site, and Poquetanuck Cove site in the nearby Calvin Main complex. Small upland campsites have been found at Mashantucket and at places like Ballymahack West and the Pearl Harbor Rock Shelter in the uppermost reaches of Mohegan-Pequot Country.

Several cemeteries used by the Mashantucket community have been archaeologically located in recent years. Three of these lie within the present bounds of the Mashantucket Pequot Indian Reservation. The fourth, a burial ground containing at least sixty graves and large numbers of aboriginal and European textiles, iron tools, earthenware, shell and brass beads, and other objects dating to the late seventeenth century, is located within the original bounds of the reservation on the western shores of Long Pond (K. McBride 1990e).

The main focus of Mohegan settlement centered upon the upper Thames River drainage. Mohegan people first appeared in early–seventeenth-century European records as tributaries closely related to their Pequot overlords. Led by Uncas, the Mohegan people won their independence from Pequot domination by aiding English colonists against the Pequots in 1637. Mohegan population, which probably did not number more than a few hundred before the war, subsequently swelled to nearly twenty-five hundred with the addition of enslaved

Mashantucket Pequot Indian Reservation Archeological District National Historic Landmark

The Mashantucket Pequot Indian Reservation Archeological District is located in the town of Ledyard, New London County, Connecticut. Situated in heavily glaciated rocky uplands covered by thin, poorly drained soils, Mashantucket is situated in the northern portion of a larger area historically called Wawarramoreke by Pequot Indians. All areas of Mashantucket except a large freshwater wetland today known as Cedar Swamp and historically known to Pequot people as Ohomowauke, "Owl's Nest," or Cuppacommock ("refuge or hiding place") are covered by a thick, mixed oak-hemlock forest.

Archival sources document Pequot occupation at Mashantucket since the early seventeenth century. In 1666 Connecticut authorities formally set aside some three thousand acres of land at Mashantucket west of Long Pond for the Western Pequot people living in a smaller tract at Noank south of Mystic. Agreeing to exchange their Noank lands for a survey and clear title to Mashantucket in 1721, the Pequots permitted surveyors commissioned by Connecticut provincial authorities to lay out two contiguous parcels for their community.

Non-Indian people increasingly encroached on reservation lands as the Masantucket population dwindled during the eighteenth century. In 1856, after disease, emigration, and deaths caused by seafaring and war service in colonial armies had drastically reduced Pequot numbers—from 322 in 1725 to less than fifty people living in six houses—the Connecticut legislature formally reduced the tribal land to 214 acres. Although they never gave up their reservation, only a few Western Pequot people were able to live on the much-diminished tract. By the early twentieth century, most Pequots were living elsewhere.

In 1976 the Mashantucket Pequot Tribe sued for the return of alienated reservation lands, and on October 18, 1983, the United States Congress gave federal recognition to the Mashantucket Pequot Indian Tribe and authorized the community to acquire up to 2,270 acres to be held in trust for them by the Secretary of the Interior as a federal Indian reservation. This land was to be acquired from a specially designated area known as Settlement Land, which was located within the original 1666 reservation.

Ongoing archaeological investigations sponsored by the tribe and begun in 1983 by the Public Archaeology Survey Team of the University of Connecticut have thus far located and tested fifteen sites dating to the Historic Contact period at Mashantucket. All materials removed from these sites presently are stored in research facilities located on the reservation and at the University of Connecticut's Laboratory of Archaeology in Storrs.

Twelve of the fifteen sites located in Mashantucket are multicomponent habitations. Eleven are small seasonal camps or homesteads. The other, a large twenty-five-acre nucleated townsite, contains deposits associated with Indiantown, the center of the eighteenth-century Mashantucket Pequot community. The site had been undisturbed since its abandonment during the early years of the nineteenth century, and archaeologists have located and mapped stone walls and foundations associated with as many as thirty dwellings.

The earliest Historic Contact period occupation, Site 72-31, contains aboriginal lithics, floral and faunal remains, and Windsor-phase Niantic-stamped vessels believed to date to the sixteenth or early seventeenth centuries. Aboriginal lithics and quartz crystals also have been found with a wide range of European ceramics, glass beads, and other materials dating to the late seventeenth century at Sites 72-34a, 72-54, and 72-62. Although direct evidence presently is lacking, contemporary archaeological and documentary data indicate that Pequot people probably erected small round or oblong bark- or grass-mat-covered, sapling-framed wigwams at these locales. Although all served to some extent as hunting and foraging camps, Site 72-62 has yielded archaeological materials that corroborate written sources suggesting that some members of the later-seventeenth-century Pequot community also planted small gardens and orchards within fieldstone-walled enclosures near settlements in and around the reservation.

Artifacts dating to the eighteenth century have been found in eleven of the twelve known Historic Contact period habitation sites. Most have been found within fieldstone walls, foundations, or other evidence of occupations ranging in size from small to moderately sized camps or farmsteads. Artifacts found at these sites corroborate documentary records reporting Pequot adoption of European tools, crops, and planting techniques. They also affirm that community members accepted these changes in different ways and at different times. In 1732, for example, a writer noted that many Mashantucket people still practiced traditional forms of shifting cultivation. Another chronicler writing in 1762 recorded that fifteen of twenty-four Pequot households

in Mashantucket continued to live in bark- or mat-covered wigwams. The rest lived in wooden-framed houses generally measuring sixteen feet by twenty-two feet.

Whatever form of housing they used, most Mashantucket Pequot people lived on three-to-four-acre houselots. Most were surrounded by low fieldstone walls that enclosed houses, outbuildings, wells, root cellars, planting fields, and orchards. Several wood roads capable of supporting wheeled vehicles were cut through reservation lands at this time.

Three cemeteries, Sites 72-34c, 72-49, and 72-78, also have been identified within district boundaries. Respecting the wishes of the Mashantucket Pequot community, archaeologists have not tested undisturbed marked graves within these bounds, but oral traditions and newspaper reports of looting incidents directly document Pequot use of these cemeteries. Discoveries of stone-cobble grave markers at these sites (markers identical to others on Indian graves found during salvage excavations at a mid-seventeenth-century Mashantucket Pequot cemetery at Long Pond on privately held lands located within original reservation boundaries) further indicate the three cemeteries served the needs of the Pequot Indian community at one time or another during the Historic Contact period.

The Mashantucket Pequot community is committed to maintaining the integrity of its culturally significant archaeological sites. Since 1980 the tribe has worked with federal, state, and local agencies to develop a comprehensive research and cultural resource management plan to study and protect their cultural heritage. Tribal regulations developed in accordance with this plan require that cultural resource

Pequot people and other immigrants following the end of the conflict.

Uniquely intact and well-preserved archaeological deposits associated with several occupation areas and at least three episodes of palisade construction at the Fort Shantok National Historic Landmark compose the remains of one of the several locales known to have been occupied by Uncas during these years. The assemblage excavated at this site constitutes one of the most extensive bodies of physical evidence documenting any seventeenth-century Indian community in the North Atlantic region (Salwen 1969; L. Williams 1972). Present-day Mohegan people continue to regard Fort Shantok as one of the most important sites marking their history and heritage, and they continue to use the meeting grounds and cemetery there.

People living at Fort Shantok and other locales in and around Mohegan-Pequot Country began making distinctive collared globular ceramics known as Shantok wares during the middle decades of the seventeenth century. Found in sites from Plymouth Bay to eastern Long Island, finely crafted Shantok wares are key diagnostic markers dating mid–seventeenth-century native occupations along the southern New England coast.

Periodically moving from Fort Shantok to other locales along the Thames River, Uncas and his people carefully cultivated their position as New England's closest Indian allies. Uncas provided a constant stream of information on real and supposed Indian plots and conspiracies against English settlers. In return, settlers made Mohegans subject to provincial law and maintained close trade relations.

Epidemic disease, incessant warfare with the Narragansetts, and emigration gradually reduced Mohegan population to fewer than a thousand by the time King Philip's War broke out 1675. Maintaining his alliance with the English, Uncas managed to prevent English settlers from attacking Mohegan communities during the war. Nevertheless, the war proved catastrophic to the Mohegan people. Many of their men were killed fighting other Indians during the war. No longer able to play off powerful Indian and colonial rivals against each other after the war, the Mohegan people found themselves increasingly powerless to resist settlers intent upon taking their remaining lands.

Colonists had managed to buy or lease most Mohegan lands by the time Uncas died in 1683. The struggle between local colonists and provincial

Stone foundations of a structure believed to be an animal pen at the Indiantown site in Mashantucket. *Courtesy Kevin A. McBride.*

authorities over title to these lands stretched well into the following century. Mohegan people tried to exploit this rivalry by favoring one claimant or another, but the ploy proved ill-advised. The controversies spawned during this struggle ultimately split the Mohegan community into rival factions, and these divisions deeply affected every aspect of Mohegan life throughout the remaining years of the colonial era.

THE EIGHTEENTH CENTURY

Pequot cultural developments during the 1700s largely paralleled those occurring elsewhere in southern New England. Pequot life initially continued to center around the small Noank, Stonington, and Mashantucket reservation communities established by Connecticut authorities during the preceding century. As mentioned earlier, Western Pequot people living at Noank finally moved to Mashantucket in 1721. The remaining two reservations subsequently dwindled in size as the declining Pequot population was unable to prevent colonists from taking their lands.

Most of the best acreage in the Mashantucket Pequot Reservation, for example, was leased or rented to settlers by mid-century. Other parts of the reservation gradually were purchased outright by colonists. More than half of the original Mashantucket reservation was owned by non-Indians by 1761. Trespassing settlers hunted or cut timber upon remaining

Fort Shantok Archeological Site National Historic Landmark

The Fort Shantok Archeological Site is located in Fort Shantok State Park on the west bank of the Thames River in the town of Montville in New London County, Connecticut. Archival and archaeological investigations carried out by field crews under the direction of Bert Salwen of Columbia University between 1962 and 1965 and New York University from 1966 to 1968 and again in 1970 corroborated earlier studies and local traditions associating the locale with the site of "Vncas his fort." The main Mohegan town from 1636 to 1682, this locale was the home of Uncas, the most prominent and influential Mohegan leader and statesman of his era (Salwen 1966, 1969, 1984; Salwen and Otteson 1972).

Although no known contemporary reference identifies any seventeenth-century Mohegan community by the name of Fort Shantok, several documents clearly locate Uncas's town at the Montville locale. Other evidence indicates that Mohegan people living at their main settlement in nearby Uncasville have continued to regard the site of Uncas's Fort as an important place. Many have interred community members in a cemetery that they maintain up to the present day. Purchasing land in and around the old fort site, Connecticut authorities established

Aerial view of Fort Shantok State Park. Photograph by Timothy O'Leary, 1968. Courtesy Connecticut Historical Commission.

Fort Shantok as their first state park in 1925.

Irving Rouse (1945, 1947) and Carlyle S. Smith (1944, 1947, 1950) first identified distinctive aboriginal ceramics from the site as Shantok wares. Noting that they occurred in sites containing large amounts of seventeenth-century European goods, both scholars named this complex the Shantok Tradition, a distinctive cultural development associated with Indian people living in southeastern Connecticut and adjacent portions of eastern Long Island during the mid- to late 1600s.

Shantok wares resemble other ceramics found in and around Mahican Country farther west in New York's upper Hudson Valley. Noting similarities between the names and the pottery, John De Forest (1851) and other investigators thought that Mohegan people and their Pequot neighbors were recent immigrants from upstate New York. Subsequent work by Salwen (1969) and Kevin A. McBride (1984) has shown that Shantok complex culture almost certainly developed in situ in eastern Connecticut.

Field crews led by Salwen conducted the first systematic test excavations at the site; they found an eight-to-ten-inch-thick, plowed midden layer containing substantial amounts of artifacts and floral and faunal remains. Rocky and gravelly yellow sandy subsoil underlay this midden layer. Investigators found that intact pits, post molds, stone foundations, and other features containing datable deposits intruded into this subsoil stratum from the midden layer.

Salwen's field crews recovered one of the largest Historic Contact period assemblages yet found in southern New England. A substantial variety of metal objects, such as hoes, axes, knives, wampum drills, pot hooks, scissors, hand-forged nails, finger rings, mouth

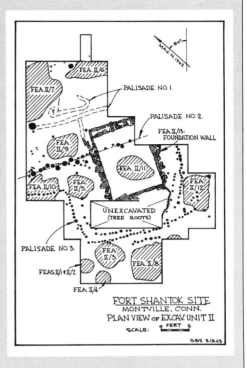

Plan view of Excavation Unit II at Fort Shantok, showing several pits, three episodes of palisade-wall construction, and the stone foundation walls of a structure within a bastion built during the last wall-construction episode. Drawn by Bert Salwen, 1963 (Salwen 1966, fig. 2).

harps, ladles, triangular arrowheads, a thimble, a hair comb, spoons, buttons, buckles, and scraps were retrieved from pits and hearths. Most were found alongside European earthenwares and delftwares, European white-clay tobacco-smoking pipes (primarily manufactured in England during the seventeenth century), and contemporary glass beads, bottle glass, and gunflints. Whelk and quahog shells were found with Shantok-ware sherds, aboriginal lithics, two ground-stone gunshot molds, and well-preserved animal remains.

Nearly all larger mammal bones found at Fort Shantok have been associated with white-tailed deer. A few bear and horse bones; numerous bones of dogs, smaller mammals, and birds; and substantial amounts of fish bones also have been recovered. Discoveries of sheep and cattle bones in several features containing artifacts dating to the later years of site occupation corroborate written records indicating that domesticated animals became increasingly important parts of the Mohegan diet during the 1660s and 1670s.

Most archaeological materials were found in the midden layer or in the fifteen storage pits; eleven "steaming" pits that contained concentrated layers of cobbles covered by dense masses of shell; five stone-lined hearths; and thirty-one other storage, cooking, or refuse pit features excavated by investigators. Narrow lines of post-molds and trench stains represent evidence of three episodes of palisade construction supporting a fortification wall built across the narrow neck joining the Fort Shantok peninsula to the mainland at or about the time Uncas moved to the locale in 1636.

The above-described concentration of datable post molds, trench lines, dry-laid fieldstone foundations, pits, and hearths within a small area periodically enclosed by palisade walls corroborates written accounts chronicling the existence of a large, nucleated, long-term settlement during the second and third quarters of the seventeenth century. Unlike the contemporary occupants of Fort Corchaug in eastern Long Island and of Fort Ninigret on the Rhode Island shore, who evidently used their forts as temporary places of refuge, Mohegan people lived within the walls of their fort for much of the year.

Fort Shantok presently is a state park providing picnicking facilities and other recreational opportunities to visitors. Mohegan Indian people continue to regard the place as one of their most spiritually significant sites. Maintaining their cemetery, they gather annually at the park for their August powwow. The Mohegan Indian community also continues to be an important part of Connecticut's cultural mosaic. Archaeological information preserved in Fort Shantok deposits represents nationally significant data capable of helping Mohegan people and others increase understanding of the continuing contributions of Indian people to America's heritage.

Listed in the National Register of Historic Places on March 20, 1986, the Fort Shantok Archeological Site was designated a National Historic Landmark on April 12, 1993. Archaeological materials recovered during Columbia and New York University field investigations are curated in the University of Connecticut's Laboratory of Archaeology in Storrs.

Unless otherwise cited, information presented here is abstracted from L. Williams (1972).

---

reservation tracts without regard for either Indian people or their land.

Epidemic disease repeatedly struck Pequot communities throughout the century. Other losses were suffered when men recruited into provincial armies or sailing off on whalers, merchantmen, and warships failed to return. Pequot population plummeted. Increasing numbers moved away from the dwindling Mashantucket and Stonington reservations as the century wore on. Many of these people settled at mission communities established at Schaghticoke, Connecticut; Stockbridge, Massachusetts; and Shekomeko, New York, during the 1730s and 1740s. Most of these people ultimately joined other New England Indian expatriates moving to Brothertown Movement mission settlements on the Oneida Reservation in New York that were established at New Stockbridge in 1785 and nearby Brothertown in 1788.

Although the population of both Pequot reservations continued to decline throughout the next 150 years, hundreds of Pequot people remained in and near their Connecticut homeland. Federal acknowledgment of the Mashantucket Pequot Indian community and establishment of the federally recognized Mashantucket Pequot Indian Reservation in 1983 has resulted in an unprecedented in-gathering of Pequot people from as far away as California. Today, several hundred Pequot people make their homes in the Mashantucket Pequot community.

The Mashantucket Pequot Reservation also contains the most extensive known body of archaeological evidence relating to eighteenth-century Pequot life. Many stone house foundations, walls, and other features associated with individual homesteads and the more concentrated long-lost Indiantown community have been found in recent surveys. Few aboriginal ceramics or stone tools have been found in these deposits. Discoveries of grass and bark textiles, a quartzite pestle, shell beads, and other materials in recently salvaged grave excavations at the earlier-mentioned Long Pond cemetery site show that Pequot people continued to use certain kinds of aboriginal manufactures well into the eighteenth century (K. McBride 1990e).

Mohegan people shared similar experiences. Like their Pequot neighbors, Mohegan settlements, economic pursuits, and spiritual beliefs gradually came to closely resemble those practiced by non-Indian neighbors. Like nearby Pequots, many Mohegan people put up wooden-frame buildings on stone foundations in the English manner. Abandoning Uncas's lifelong rejection of Christianity, many Mohegan people joined one or another Protestant sect after his death.

Several Mohegan Christians subsequently became prominent ministers. One, the already-noted Mohegan theologian Samson Occom, achieved worldwide fame for his oratory, piety, and devotion. Funds gathered for Indian education during his 1765–1767 speaking tour of Great Britain were used to finance the creation of Dartmouth College in Hanover, New Hampshire. Ironically, few Indian students received education at Dartmouth during the colonial era. Instead, those Indian children educated by Dartmouth's founder Eleazar Wheelock continued to be separately instructed in Moor's Indian School in western Connecticut.

Mohegan communities at Pamechaug and Massapeag encompassed from four thousand to five thousand acres of land along the Thames River between Groton and Norwich at the beginning of the eighteenth century. A portion of this land, originally purchased by John Mason and his associates during the 1640s and 1650s, was reconveyed to the Mohegans in perpetuity by Mason in 1671. However, none of this land was ever formally set aside as a reservation by provincial or local officials, who continued to assert their authority over Mohegan lands and lives. An ordinance passed by the Connecticut legislature in 1725 required all Indian people in Connecticut to accept provincial sovereignty. All land conveyances, marriages, and other legal actions involving Mohegan people subsequently fell under the jurisdiction of the governor and council.

Disagreements and other divisions split the Mohegan community throughout the century. On several occasions, individual Mohegans supported rival claimants to the tribal sachemship; sectarian disputes divided adherents of different Protestant denominations; and, most seriously, two separate camps supported one or the other of the contending colonial factions who claimed Mohegan lands.

One of these factions, known as Native Rights Men, based their claim upon Uncas's conveyance of jurisdiction over Mohegan lands to John Mason in 1659. The other faction, supporting the claims of the provincial government, sought sole control of Mohegan lands. These factions, and their Indian supporters, fought over this issue until a royal commission finally threw out the Native Rights claim in 1771.

Many Mohegan people subsequently began moving west to Stockbridge and other mission communities as the New England colonies drifted toward war with Great Britain. Occom, a founder of the Brothertown Movement and an active supporter of the defeated Native Rights faction, traveled back and forth between New York and Connecticut before moving his family to a new home in Oneida Country in 1784. After his death in 1792, Occom's followers were ultimately forced from Oneida Country into exile in Wisconsin. There, modern-day descendants of Brothertown settlers live with people tracing descent from other North Atlantic Indian people of the Stockbridge-Munsee Reservation.

Many Mohegans chose to remain in the Thames River Valley. Although some Mohegan lands ultimately were divided into individual allotments, the remainder, totaling nearly three thousand acres, remained under community control. Much of this land was sold to non-Indians as increasing numbers of Mohegan people left Connecticut during the nineteenth century. Today, most descendants of the Mohegans who stayed in Connecticut live in and around the towns of Uncasville and Montville.

SOURCES

Much of the information presented in this section has been drawn from articles published in a sourcebook containing papers first presented at a major symposium on Pequot history hosted by the Mashantucket Pequot Indian community on October 23–24, 1987 (Hauptman and Wherry 1990). Other major sources used include De Forest (1851), Jennings (1975), K. McBride (1990a), Salisbury (1982a), Salwen (1978), Speck (1928), Vaughan (1979), and L. Williams (1972).

Numerous specialized studies examine aspects of Pequot and Mohegan culture and history. Four of the most extensive primary accounts documenting the Pequot War have been compiled in Orr (1897). Blodgett (1935) has written a detailed biography of Samson Occom. More recently, Weinstein (1991, 1994) has produced several papers on eighteenth-century Mohegan affairs.

LOWER CONNECTICUT VALLEY COUNTRY

Lower Connecticut Valley Country encompasses the central and western portions of the state of Connecticut. Stretching from the shores of Long Island Sound north to the present Massachusetts border, this area extends across a region of heavily forested and hilly terrain from the broad Connecticut River Valley estuary on the east to the narrower streams draining into the Housatonic River on the west.

THE SIXTEENTH CENTURY

Numerous campsites, rockshelters, and shell middens containing terminal Late Woodland components have been found in this area. The few glass beads found with aboriginal stone tools and pottery in the remains of small campsites at the Beaver Meadow Brook, Fielding Rock Shelter, and Nick's Niche sites along the lower reaches of the Connecticut River Valley represent the only currently identifiable evidence of sixteenth-century Indian life in the area. Despite this paucity of evidence, most archaeologists believe that native people living in western Connecticut during the 1500s generally followed ways of life similar to those followed by neighbors on the south and east.

THE SEVENTEENTH CENTURY

Seventeenth-century European records indicate that a number of linguistically and culturally related Indian communities were located in this area when New Netherland and Plymouth traders began establishing their first posts in and around present-day Hartford during the early 1630s. These posts and the initial English colonial settlements built near them in 1636 were situated near communities identified by contemporary chroniclers as Sequin and Podunk towns. Tunxis communities were located farther west around Farmington. On the south, Wangunk, Hammonosett, Western Niantic, and other communities were situated along the Lower Connecticut River. Quinnipiac communities centered around the present site of New Haven. Farther west, Wepawaug, Naugatuck, Paugusset, Pootatuck, Tankiteke, and other communities were located at various places along the lower Housatonic drainage.

Archaeological and archival evidence

indicates that most people belonging to these communities lived in dispersed, decentralized towns extending across stretches of riverbank along secondary streams in wide, sheltered valleys and coves. Numerous small sites found throughout the area corroborate written records noting that these people maintained hunting, fishing, and foraging camps at various locales in community hinterlands. Most also took refuge in wooden-walled forts during times of war.

Although linguistic records are fragmentary, analyses of place-names and individual words and expressions noted by colonial chroniclers indicate that most, if not all, of the people living in this area spoke variants of an Eastern Algonquian language known among linguists as Quiripi (a variant spelling of the name Quinnipiac). This language was very similar to that spoken by Indian people living in Montauk Country on the south and by Pequot people on the east who claimed sovereignty over their lands at the time Europeans first settled among them.

Indian people living in this area and their Pequot overlords collectively may have numbered more than thirty thousand before wars and epidemic disease ravaged much of the North Atlantic region during the 1630s. The 1634 smallpox epidemic, for example, is thought to have killed almost half of the more than one thousand people reportedly taking refuge in a fortified town near Hartford. Fighting during the Pequot War in 1636 and 1637 further devastated this and many other Indian communities across the region.

Native people surviving these disasters soon found themselves pressed to sell their most productive agricultural lands to New Englanders flooding into Connecticut. Slowly conveying their lands in small parcels, they gradually withdrew to hilly or swampy lands not desired by colonists on the fringes of the settlements at Hartford, Fort Saybrook, New Haven, and other locales. Many of these people negotiated the rights to continue occupying their homes and planting fields for the remainder of their lives or the lives of their children as a condition of sale.

Relatively little was written about the lives of Indian people living in this area during the seventeenth century. More extensive evidence in the forms of metal tools, copper or brass triangular or conical projectile points, gun parts and flints, glass beads, European white-clay tobacco-smoking pipes, and other objects of European origin has been found with Hackney Pond or Niantic ceramics and chipped-stone, triangular projectile points at a number of archaeological sites.

Most of these sites cluster along the lower reaches of the Housatonic and Connecticut Valleys. Some, like the Tunxis Village and Little Pootatuck Brook sites, contain the remains of substantial communities. Others, like the radiometrically dated Coudert Ledge, Bluddee Rock, Bennett Rock Shelter, Cedar Lake, Costa's Cove, Devil's Hopyard Rock Shelter, and Kaiser I sites, represent the remains of less intensive occupations.

THE EIGHTEENTH CENTURY

Like their neighbors, most native people living in Lower Connecticut Valley Country during the 1700s struggled to adapt British custom to Indian usage.

MAP 12: LOWER CONNECTICUT VALLEY COUNTRY

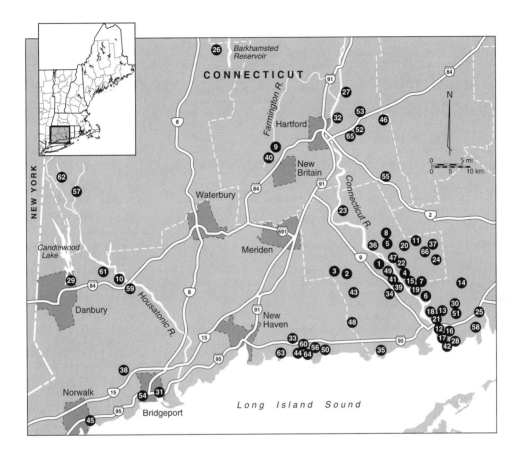

Map 12 Historic Contact Sites

Map Number	Site Name	County	State	Date	NR	Source
1	Beaver Meadow Brook 1	Middlesex	CT	Late 1500s		K. McBride 1984
2	Fielding Rock Shelter	Middlesex	CT	Late 1500s		K. McBride 1984
3	Nick's Niche	Middlesex	CT	Late 1500s		K. McBride 1984
4	Clark Creek	Middlesex	CT	1600s?		K. McBride 1984
5	Davison Farm	Middlesex	CT	1600s		K. McBride 1984
6	Costa's Cove	New London	CT	Early 1600s		K. McBride 1984
7	Coudert Ledge	New London	CT	Early 1600s		K. McBride 1984
8	Turkey Hill	Middlesex	CT	Early 1600s		K. McBride 1984
9	Tunxis Village	Hartford	CT	Mid-1600s		Feder 1981
10	Little Pootatuck Brook	New Haven	CT	1661–1761		K. McBride 1985
11	Bashan Road Rock Shelter	Middlesex	CT	Late 1600s		K. McBride 1984
12	Bennett Rock Shelter	New London	CT	Late 1600s		K. McBride 1984
13	Bluddee Rock	New London	CT	Late 1600s		K. McBride 1984
14	Cedar Lake Rock Shelter	New London	CT	Late 1600s		K. McBride 1984
15	Cold Spring	New London	CT	Late 1600s		K. McBride 1984

Map 12 Historic Contact Sites—*Continued*

Map Number	Site Name	County	State	Date	NR	Source
16	Kaiser I	New London	CT	Late 1600s		K. McBride 1984
17	Loctite	New London	CT	Late 1600s		K. McBride 1984
18	Lord Cove	New London	CT	Late 1600s		K. McBride 1984
19	Seldon Neck	New London	CT	Late 1600s		K. McBride 1984
20	Snell	Middlesex	CT	Late 1600s		K. McBride 1984
21	Whaleback	New London	CT	Late 1600s		K. McBride 1984
22	Brainard Rock Shelter	Middlesex	CT	1600s–1700s		K. McBride 1984
23	Indian Hill Avenue	Middlesex	CT	1600s–1700s	X	CAS; Clouette 1980
24	Devil's Hopyard Rock Shelter	Middlesex	CT	1700s		K. McBride 1984
25	Tubbs	New London	CT	Early 1700s		CAS
26	Lighthouse	Hartford	CT	1740–1860s		Feder 1993
27	Podunk Complex	Hartford	CT	1750–1799		M. Spiess 1960
28	Bartholomew Field	New London	CT	Historic		K. McBride 1984
29	Beaver Brook Mt	Fairfield	CT	Historic		CAS
30	Becket's Cave	New London	CT	Historic		CAS
31	Bridgeport Gas Works	Fairfield	CT	Historic		CAS
32	Burnham Cemetery	Hartford	CT	Historic		CAS
33	Christopher Reynolds	New Haven	CT	Historic		CAS
34	Chester Fairgrounds	Middlesex	CT	Historic		CAS
35	Clinton Nursery	Middlesex	CT	Historic		CAS
36	Copperhead Rock Shelter	Middlesex	CT	Historic		CAS
37	Early Road Rock Shelter	Middlesex	CT	Historic		K. McBride 1984
38	Easton Rock Shelter	Fairfield	CT	Historic		CAS
39	Fort Hill (Chester)	Middlesex	CT	Historic		CAS
40	Fort Hill (Farmington)	Hartford	CT	Historic		CAS
41	Goose Hill	Middlesex	CT	Historic		CAS
42	Griswold Circle	New London	CT	Historic		CAS; J. Pfeiffer 1982
43	Hackney Pond	Middlesex	CT	Historic		CAS
44	Hotchkiss Grove	New Haven	CT	Historic		CAS
45	Indian River Dam	Fairfield	CT	Historic		CAS; Rogers 1942
46	Kog's Hill	Hartford	CT	Historic		CAS
47	Kreiger Brook	Middlesex	CT	Historic		CAS
48	Manstan Rock Shelter	Middlesex	CT	Historic		CAS
49	Mazur City	Middlesex	CT	Historic		CAS
50	Menunketisuck	New Haven	CT	Historic		Russell 1942
51	Nehantic Rock Shelter	New London	CT	Historic		K. McBride 1984
52	Olcott Farm	Hartford	CT	Historic		CAS
53	Old Wapping Cemetery	Hartford	CT	Historic		CAS
54	Pequot Swamp	Fairfield	CT	Historic		CAS
55	Philip's Cave	Hartford	CT	Historic		CAS
56	Pine Orchard	New Haven	CT	Historic		CAS; Vescelius 1952
57	Pratt-Birches	Litchfield	CT	Historic		CAS
58	Rocky Neck Camp	New London	CT	Historic		CAS
59	Sandy Hook I	Fairfield	CT	Historic		CAS
60	Sheldon Creek	New Haven	CT	Historic		CAS
61	Shepaug Power Dam	Fairfield	CT	Historic		CAS
62	Sullivan	Litchfield	CT	Historic		CAS
63	Sunset Beach	New Haven	CT	Historic		CAS
64	Tennis Court	New Haven	CT	Historic		K. McBride 1984
65	West Cemetery	New Haven	CT	Historic		CAS
66	Ziobron Rock Shelter	Middlesex	CT	Historic		K. McBride 1984

Many of them adopted the tools, speech, and religion of their non-Indian neighbors as the century wore on. All ultimately embraced most aspects of British housing and houselife as foreign influences became pervasive in even the most conservative Indian communities.

Nowhere is this syncretic shift more poignantly apparent than in Ezra Stiles's earlier-mentioned 1761 sketches of the interiors of two mat-walled Western Niantic wigwams. Although both houses are constructed in the form of typical Late Woodland wigwams, each is filled with contemporary British furniture and housewares.

The few hundred Indian people remaining in the area during these years had to continue dealing with foreign diseases, wars, laws, avarice, and intolerance. Epidemics continued to sweep through their communities, and many Indian men who served in colonial armies fighting the French never returned. Expansionistic settlers, discriminatory laws, and unsympathetic courts dispossessed Indian families of their homes and belongings with depressing regularity throughout the period.

Most Indian people living in the Connecticut and Housatonic Valleys made every attempt to live unobtrusive, autonomous lives on their own lands for as long as possible during these years. Colonial chroniclers documented small settlements near Niantic, Farmington, Bridgeport, New Haven, Danbury, Kent, Barkhamstead, and other towns. Archaeologists excavating deposits preserved at the Indian Hill Avenue, Lighthouse, Tunxis, and Podunk sites have found physical evidence of several of these communities (Clouette 1980; Feder 1993; K. McBride 1984; M. Spiess 1960).

Colonial authorities ultimately set aside small tracts of land at Quinnipiac, Schaghticoke in the town of Kent, Turkey Hill in Derby, Coram Hill in Huntington, and the Bridgeport community at Golden Hill as reservations. Unable to make adequate livings on the plots allotted them in these tiny communities, many Indians continued to travel elsewhere in search of opportunities and work. Some found occasional employment in nearby towns or farms.

Forced to become itinerants, they traveled widely across the region from Quebec to Massachusetts to Pennsylvania. While in the North country, many stayed with friends and relatives in Eastern or Western Abenaki towns. Traveling to the nearby Hudson Valley, they visited with kinsfolk living in the other Indian community known as Schaghticoke or in the Wappinger or Esopus communities. Farther south, northern New Jersey colonists called these people "Pompton" or "Oping" Indians when they lived in small highland communities along the upper Passaic River drainage. The French lumped them together with other Eastern Algonquian "Loups," and British colonists living in the Susquehanna Valley of Pennsylvania identified these and other eastern Indian people as Mahicans or "Mahikanders."

These peripatetic people produced some prominent political figures. A man named Taphow, first mentioned in colonial documents as an Indian leader from Pequannock territory near Hartford, for example, became the most influential Indian sachem in northern New Jersey during the early decades of the eighteenth century (Grumet 1988). A kinsman named Gideon Mauwehu became even more widely known as a founder of the

Connecticut Indian community at Schaghticoke that endures to the present day.

The itinerant predilections of many members of these tiny communities led to increasing incidences of intermarriage with foreigners. More than a few married Indian people from other places. Others married European or African neighbors. Many children from such mixed marriages chose to maintain native identities. Pride in their heritage could not, however, halt depopulation, land loss, and poverty that compelled growing numbers of Indian people to abandon their ancestral homes along the lower reaches of the Connecticut, Quinnipiac, and Housatonic Valleys in the middle decades of the century.

Relentlessly pressed to sell, lease, or rent nearly all of their remaining lands, many Indian people from these communities joined other southern New England Algonquians in moving to Protestant missions established farther north at Schaghticoke, Connecticut; Shekomeko, New York; and Stockbridge, Massachusetts, during the 1730s and 1740s. Dispirited and impoverished by settlers clamoring for these lands, many then joined the Brothertown Movement and moved to Oneida Country after suffering grievous losses during the American War for Independence. Although some moved back to Connecticut, most ultimately were forced into exile farther westward, where their descendants remain today.

SOURCES

Much of the information presented in this section has been drawn from Conkey, Boissevain, and Goddard (1978), De Forest (1851), Orcutt (1882), Speck (1928), and Wojciechowski (1985). Kevin

McBride's analysis (1984) of his extensive site survey in the Lower Connecticut Valley summarizes much of what is known about the archaeology of the Historic Contact period in the area.

McBride (1985) uses archival documentation to identify and assess the significance of the limited amount of eighteenth-century artifacts excavated at the Little Pootatuck Brook site. Small amounts of other eighteenth-century European materials have been found in Indian burials within the Indian Hill Avenue Historic District. Other presently uninventoried archaeological properties dating to the period probably are located within the boundaries of the Schaghticoke reservation in Kent and other surviving Connecticut Indian communities.

Stone heaps and walls occur with some frequency in this stony country. Inundated lines of stones found in the Housatonic River are believed to represent historic Indian fish weirs (Coffin 1947). Other stone heaps found at intervals in woodlands are thought to represent offering sites or boundary markers (E. Butler 1946).

Perhaps the most exciting finds in recent years have occurred at the Lighthouse site in Barkhamstead. Large amounts of European goods have been found in and near stone foundations of a multiethnic community established there sometime around 1740. Documentary records indicate that community members of Indian, African, and European descent built as many as forty houses at the site before moving away by 1870. Analysis of materials excavated from this site will provide a unique glimpse into life in an early North Atlantic multiethnic community (Feder 1993).

MONTAUK COUNTRY

Montauk Country extends across eastern Long Island along the twin forks encompassing Peconic and Gardiners Bays from Orient Point in the north to Montauk Point in the south. This area then stretches westward across Suffolk County to the present Nassau County line.

THE SIXTEENTH CENTURY

Virtually nothing is known about sixteenth-century life in Montauk Country. Although archaeological evidence dating to the 1500s has been found on Block Island and in nearby Connecticut, no such deposits have yet been clearly identified anywhere in eastern Long Island.

THE SEVENTEENTH CENTURY

Dutch and English traders sailing to eastern Long Island shores first began writing about Indian people living at Montauk on the south fork of Long Island during the early decades of the 1600s. Settlers like Lion Gardiner established the first permanent English settlements in the area shortly after the end of the Pequot War. These colonists soon chronicled relations with Montauk people, with the Shinnecocks living just west of the Montauks, with members of the Cutchogue community on the north fork, with Setauket people on the north shore, and with people belonging to Unquachog or Patchogue communities on the banks of Great South Bay along the south shore.

Available evidence indicates that all of these people shared close political, social, and linguistic relationships with one another and with their Pequot and Lower Connecticut Valley Country neighbors on the far shores of Long Island Sound. Current estimates based on sparse documentary data suggest that the total Indian population of eastern Long Island may have been five thousand at this time. Extant records further indicate that some or all of these people had been living in some form of subjection to the Pequots before transferring allegiance to the English after 1637.

Both the Pequots and their English successors sought to control the manufacture of wampum shell beads produced by people living in these communities. Regarding the purple and white beads as a spiritually potent substance,

Indian people wove wampum strings and belts into mnemonic record-keeping devices and diplomatic instruments. Using wampum in diplomatic relations with native people, cash-poor colonists also used the beads as a type of money until sufficient amounts of specie became available. Increasing in popularity as the pace of intercultural contact quickened throughout the region, wampum assumed unprecedented political, social, economic, and spiritual significance throughout the Northeast during the seventeenth century.

English records affirm that most of the native people in Montauk Country confederated under the leadership of Montauk chief Wyandanch after the Pequot defeat. Organized for mutual support and defense against Niantic, Narragansett, and other Indian rivals interested in controlling wampum production, each of the confederacy's constituent communities was led by one of Wyandanch's brothers or sisters. Wyandanch further secured his position as paramount confederacy sachem by establishing close relations with Lion Gardiner and other English leaders in eastern Long Island in the years following the end of the Pequot War. He maintained this position until his death in 1659.

Pursuing their own domestic and foreign policies, Indian people living in Montauk Country managed to remain at peace with increasingly overbearing English neighbors through the turbulent years following Wyandanch's death. But Indian problems only increased as epidemics and attacks from Niantic and Narragansett warriors repeatedly devastated their communities.

Pressures had gradually subsided by the third quarter of the century, when availability of sufficient quantities of hard currency caused the wampum trade to temporarily collapse. Although wampum remained an important part of Indian trade and diplomacy, colonists employing industrial processes began replacing Indian producers by the end of the 1600s. Responding to these and other changes, Indian people living in Montauk Country found employment as whalers and seamen. Others peddled splint baskets, herbal remedies, and other goods door to door through English towns and back settlements. More than a few, driven by poverty or the desire to hone existing skills or develop new ones, bound themselves out as apprentices or servants.

Most Indian people living in this area continued to live on ancestral lands during these years. But, as elsewhere, increasing numbers began moving away as land sales and confiscations for debt or fines reduced their ancestral estate. Several families living along the more westerly reaches of Montauk Country moved to nearby Matinecock and Massapequa lands in western Long Island. Others relocated north to Indian towns in Connecticut, Rhode Island, and Massachusetts.

Few archaeological sites presently are known to contain clearly datable diagnostic artifacts associated with seventeenth-century Indian occupation in Montauk Country. The Fort Corchaug site, located in the town of Southold, is the most extensively studied and best preserved archaeological deposit in the area. Otherwise unobtainable information on Shinnecock demography, health, disease, and material culture of the period has been unearthed at the Pantigo Cemetery site.

MAP 13: MONTAUK COUNTRY

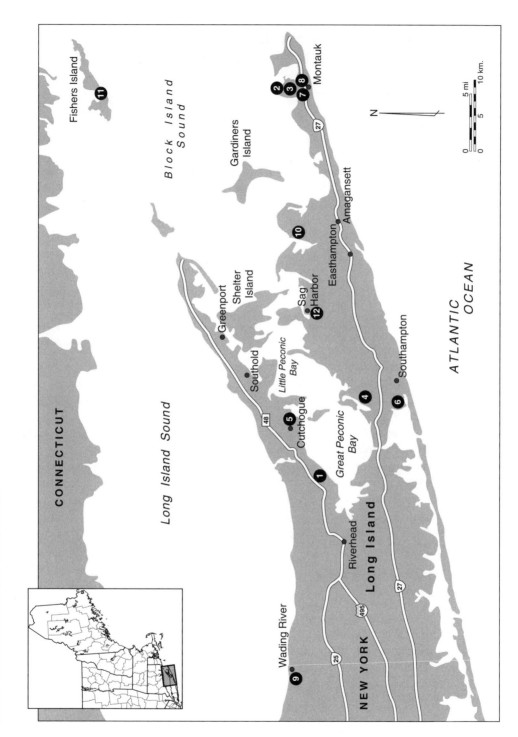

Map 13 Historic Contact Sites

Map Number	Site Name	County	State	Date	NR	Source
1	Brushes Creek	Suffolk	NY	1600s		Latham 1965
2	Burial Point (NYSM 6885)	Suffolk	NY	1600s		Latham 1957; NYSMAS
3	Montauk Fort Hill (NYSM 6882)	Suffolk	NY	1600s–1700s		Johannemann 1990; NYSMAS
4	Sebonac (NYSM 4903)	Suffolk	NY	1600s		M. R. Harrington 1924; NYSMAS
5	Fort Corchaug (NYSM 686)	Suffolk	NY	1640–1661	X	NYSMAS; Solecki 1950; L. Williams 1972
6	Pantigo Cemetery	Suffolk	NY	1600s–1700s		Saville and Booth 1920
7	Pharoah	Suffolk	NY	Late 1700s		Johannemann 1979
8	Cyrus Charles Cemetery	Suffolk	NY	1750–1799		Schroeder and Johannemann 1985
9	Cusano (NYSM 5588)	Suffolk	NY	Historic		NYSMAS; Wyatt 1990
10	Three Mile Harbor (NYSM 7306)	Suffolk	NY	Historic		Latham 1961
11	Turtle Pond No. 2 (NYSM 7148)	Suffolk	NY	Historic		Funk 1993; NYSMAS
12	Wegwagonock	Suffolk	NY	Historic		W. Tooker 1896

A copper-brass cutout bird effigy and small pieces of scrap found with post molds, stone tools, and finely crafted Late Woodland Niantic and Sebonac wares at the Turtle Pond No. 2 site on Fisher's Island may reveal new information on relations with people living in nearby Mohegan-Pequot Country. Sites at Montauk Fort Hill, Brushes Creek, and other locales await evaluative testing sufficient to determine their age and cultural affiliation.

THE EIGHTEENTH CENTURY

Indian life in eighteenth-century Montauk Country followed patterns similar to those described elsewhere in southern New England. Many Indian people adopted British customs and married non-Indian neighbors. Some eked out a living as fishers and farmers while others worked for non-Indians, being forced to accept low wages as laborers, servants, and farmhands. Although young and poor people often were bound out as apprentices or forced into indentured servitude, whaling and other shipborne commerce helped some families achieve a measure of prosperity.

As elsewhere, life near expanding colonial settlements created difficulties as well as opportunities for Indian people. Most had to sell their remaining land to local authorities during the first decades of the 1700s. Those refusing to live with colonists moved away. Several families moved to missions at Schaghticoke, Connecticut; Shekomeko, New York; and Stockbridge, Massachusetts, after 1730. Inspired by Samson Occom, the Mohegan missionary who worked among them for nearly twelve years between 1748 and 1760, large numbers of Indian people living in and around Montauk Point moved to Brothertown in upstate New York after 1785.

Those choosing to remain on ancestral lands had to make their homes on reservations. One reservation, the 175-acre Poosepatuck community, was set aside for the Unquachog Indians by manor lord William Smith in 1700. Suffolk County magistrates erected two other reservations. One was established for Montauk people on North Neck near the Great Pond on the eastern end of the town of Easthampton. The other drew members of the large Shinnecock community into a single reservation in Southampton.

Portions of all of these reservations were sold off or expropriated in succeeding years. Most Montauk people moved to the Shinnecock community after losing their lands at the end of the nineteenth century. The remaining two reservations, much diminished in size, survive today.

Several sites document aspects of eighteenth-century Indian life in Montauk Country. Artifacts dating to the 1700s have been found in several graves in the Pantigo Cemetery (Saville and Booth 1920). The Pharoah Site, situated within the Indian Fields archaeological complex, contains house foundations, features, and artifacts associated with a late eighteenth-century Montauk homestead.

Analyses of artifacts found in these and contemporary locales in Montauk Country corroborate written records indicating that most Indian people in the area had almost completely adapted European technology to their own purposes by midcentury. Each further documents patterns of cultural resilience that have enabled the native people of Montauk Country to endure to the present day.

SOURCES

Studies of the Montauk (Stone 1979), Shinnecock (Stone 1983), and Poosepatuck (Gonzalez 1986) communities provide much of the information presented in this section. Other information may be found in Conkey, Boissevain, and Goddard (1978), Salwen (1978), and J. Strong (1992). Ceci (1980b, 1982b) has surveyed wampum manufacture, use, and symbolism in and around Montauk Country.

Much of the archaeological data described in this section have been published in Ceci (1977), L. Williams (1972), C. Smith (1950), and Solecki (1950). Reports describing findings at particular archaeological locales include Mark Raymond Harrington's description (1924) of the Sebonac site, Saville and Booth's description (1920) of the Pantigo Cemetery burials, and Solecki's (1950) and L. Williams' (1972) studies of Fort Corchaug deposits.

MAHICAN
COUNTRY

Mahican Country extends across the upper Hudson and Housatonic Valleys from the Berkshires west to the Catskill and Heldeberg Mountains. Stretching from the westernmost reaches of Massachusetts across parts of southwestern Vermont and the upper Hudson Valley in New York, this area extends to northern borders demarcated by the Adirondack Mountains, Lake George, and the upper reaches of Lake Champlain.

THE SIXTEENTH CENTURY

Very little is known about the lives of people living in Mahican Country during the 1500s. Glass beads dating from 1570 to 1625 have been found with concentrations of lithic debitage and other remains in Mechanicsville Road site deposits discovered during mitigation operations along a proposed sewerline right-of-way in Waterford, New York (Fisher and Hartgen 1983). Most of these beads represent types dated at Cameron and other sites in Oneida Country to the late 1500s. Although other terminal Late Woodland sites doubtless survive in the area, these deposits presently constitute the only identifiable evidence of sixteenth-century native life in Mahican Country.

THE SEVENTEENTH CENTURY

The Mahican heartland centered around the upper Hudson River Valley when Europeans first began documenting visits to the area during the early 1600s. Frequently translated as an Algonquian term for wolf (an etymology evidently picked up by French colonists, who called Mahicans and other Coastal Algonquians "Loups" during Historic Contact times), the name "Mahican" more probably refers to tidal ebb and flow of the Hudson River.

The variety of uses and meanings of the term chronicled in European documents reflects changing social and cultural conditions of the era. Early Dutch maps and journals initially identified all Indian people living from Lake George south to the northern Catskill escarpment as Mahicans. The term subsequently was extended to include people from Western Abenaki Country and other Algonquian-speaking people living at the Schaghticoke, New York, settlement established for Indian refugees by New York governor Edmund Andros in 1676.

Colonists came to identify all Indian people on the Hudson as "River Indians." By 1700 both French and English settlers often used variants of the terms "Mahican" and "Mahikander" to identify River Indian people and their neighbors from the nearby Delaware and Connecticut Valleys.

Archaeological and documentary evidence indicates that people from Mahican Country encountered by early European travelers shared close social and cultural affinities with Algonquian-speaking people from Pocumtuck-Squakheag Country on the east, Wappinger and Munsee neighbors on the south, and Iroquois-speaking Mohawk townsfolk on the west. Fewer than five thousand people were probably living in this area when Dutch traders established their first permanent post at Fort Nassau in modern Albany, New York, in 1614.

Early Dutch chroniclers noted that many Indian people living in Mahican Country resided in large, fortified towns. Such settlements probably became necessary in the highly charged political climate dominated by trade rivalries and political competition between Indian contenders that emerged with the opening of the fur trade. But relations were not always hostile. Extant documents note that Mohawk people frequently traveled to Cohoes Falls and the Hudson River to fish and trade.

However, many Mahican townsfolk were killed fighting against Mohawk people seeking to control trade shortly after the Dutch West India Company established Fort Orange one mile north of the abandoned site of Fort Nassau in 1624. Defeated and forced to relocate their main towns away from the Mohawk frontier by 1628, Mahican people

were compelled to recognize Mohawk authority and allow them free access to markets at the Dutch fort (Trigger 1971).

Mahican people soon sold most of their land around Fort Orange to agents of Dutch West India Company director Kiliaen van Rensselaer between 1629 and 1630. Although some of these people stayed on to find work and take advantage of other opportunities offered by colonists settling in van Rensselaer's new domain, many Mahican people moved farther east to the Connecticut Valley, to more southerly parts of Western Abenaki Country, or to western Maine.

No matter where they moved, most of these Mahican expatriates were unable to find peace. Living on what ethnologist Theodore J. C. Brasser (1978b) has called a "moving frontier," they generally settled on contested borderlands separating often-hostile Indian and European communities. Frequently regarded as unwanted interlopers, Mahican people got into fights with roving Indian and European hunters and trappers traveling through such areas.

Not all Indian people left Mahican Country during these years. Many moved south among Catskill, Wappinger, and Esopus friends and kinsfolk. Others settled along the more northerly reaches of the Hoosic River Valley, along the main trade routes leading to New France. And most periodically returned to settlements on or near the Hudson River sometime every year.

Move where they may, Mahican people could neither escape the ravages of epidemic contagion nor avoid involvement in the series of wars that set entire communities against one another during the 1600s. Living directly in the path of European expansion along strategic

MAP 14: MAHICAN COUNTRY

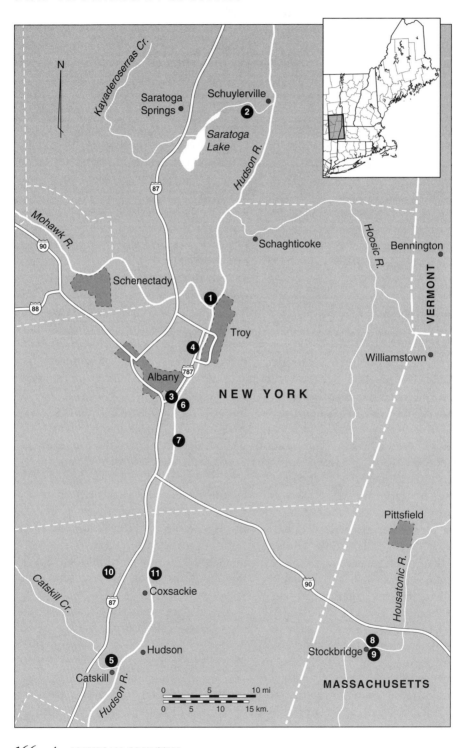

Map 14 Historic Contact Sites

Map Number	Site Name	County	State	Date	NR	Source
1	Mechanicsville Road	Albany	NY	1570–1625		Fisher and Hartgen 1983
2	Winney's Rift	Saratoga	NY	1620s–1630s		Brumbach and Bender 1986
3	Fort Orange NHL (NYSM 7645)	Albany	NY	1624–1689	X	Huey 1988a; NYSMAS; Peña 1990
4	Schuyler Flatts NHL (NYSM 1631)	Albany	NY	1642–1759	X	Huey 1985b; NYSMAS
5	Rip Van Winkle (NYSM 518)	Greene	NY	1630–1660		Funk 1976; NYSMAS
6	Fort Crailo	Rensselaer	NY	Mid-1600s		Huey, Feister, and McEvoy 1977
7	Papscanee Island	Rensselaer	NY	1600s		Huey 1989; Manley and Florance 1978
8	Mission House NHL	Berkshire	MA	1739–1804	X	NPS 1987
9	Christian Indian Burial Ground	Berkshire	MA	1734–1785		MHC
10	Bronck House Rock Shelter (NYSM 399)	Greene	NY	Historic		NYSMAS; W. Ritchie 1958
11	Little Nutten Hook (NYSM 422)	Columbia	NY	Historic		Funk 1976; NYSMAS

trade routes linking New York, New France, New England, and the Trans-Appalachian region, most Indian people living in Mahican Country suffered dreadfully from disease, alcohol abuse, and military attack.

Fewer than five hundred Indians were living in this area when southern New England Algonquian refugees fleeing from King Philip's War were resettled among them at Schaghticoke in 1676. Collectively called Mahicans or Upper River Indians by their English and Dutch neighbors, Schaghticoke townsfolk and their Mahican friends and kinsfolk became a peripatetic people whose travels periodically carried them to Maine, New France, Acadia, and westward to the Great Lakes and the Ohio and Mississippi Valleys.

European documents note that some of these people were living in the Maumee Valley with other Eastern Algon-

quian expatriates at the western end of Lake Erie in the early 1680s. Other chroniclers noted the presence of Mahican people at the multicultural Amesokanti mission town on the Sandy River in Maine's Kennebec River Valley from 1694 until its abandonment during the early years of Queen Anne's War.

Other Indian people moved to Mahican Country during these years. Mohawks anxious to take advantage of proximity to Fort Orange moved to a settlement at Niskayuna between Schenectady and Albany. The earlier-mentioned group of Pennacook people from Maine also moved near Albany in 1687. Seven years later, Mohawk people, reeling from the effects of a successful French attack on their towns, established a temporary fort at Schuyler Flatts ten miles north of Albany.

Archaeological deposits preserved at the Schuyler Flatts and Fort Orange National Historic Landmarks and other sites in the upper Hudson Valley document aspects of contact relations in seventeenth-century Mahican Country. Schuyler Flatts deposits preserve foundations of the home and trading post occupied by Dutch merchant-diplomat Arendt van Curler between 1643 and 1667 and equally influential Schuyler family members after 1672.

European goods dating to the 1620s and 1630s have been found with clay tobacco pipes and incised, collared ceramics similar to others often found in Mohawk Country at the multicomponent Winney's Rift site near Saratoga, New York (Brumbach and Bender 1986). Noting that "the site as a whole appears to represent a different social and ecological adaptation than that typical of the Iroquois villages of the Late Woodland period," Brumbach and Bender suggest that Winney's Rift deposits may represent remains of one of the many upper Hudson Valley locales known to have been used by Mohawk or River Indian people as fishing or hunting camps at various times during the seventeenth century (Brumbach 1991).

Farther south, Rip Van Winkle site deposits contain glass beads, European white-clay tobacco pipes, brass, copper, salt-glazed pottery, and other objects (Funk 1976). Deposits excavated at the Fort Crailo and Mechanicsville Road sites contain similar assortments of European goods (Fisher and Hartgen 1983; Huey, Feister, and McEvoy 1977). A triangular copper or brass projectile point and glass beads have been recovered on a site on Papscanee Island below Albany (Huey 1989). Archaeologists studying these collections believe that other sites dating to the period remain to be found.

THE EIGHTEENTH CENTURY

European records indicate that River Indians living in Mahican Country entered the eighteenth century as a devastated people. A census of New York's Indian allies indicates that fully half of the 180 River Indian warriors enumerated at the beginning of King William's War in 1689 were no longer living in the province when that war ended in 1697. Many of these men died in battle. Others probably were killed by the particularly virulent outbreak of smallpox that ravaged the colonial army sent against New France in 1690. Demoralized by their losses, a substantial number of people surviving the sickness and fighting probably simply left New York.

Many of these people returned to Saint Lawrence Valley communities at Caughnawaga, the Saint Francis mission at Odanak, and other now-familiar locales in New France. Others moved east, back toward the Merrimack River and the Acadian frontier. Still others probably traveled west to the Susquehanna and Ohio countries. No matter where they moved, most of them gradually returned to their Hudson Valley homes after peace was restored in 1697. Several rejoined families left behind in the Housatonic Valley, Dutchess County, and the Catskills. Many moved back to towns along the Hudson River. Others returned to Schaghticoke.

The Schaghticoke settlement extended for several miles along both banks of the Hoosic River. Although detailed descriptions of the community have not yet been located, it probably consisted of several scattered hamlets made up of bark, log, and wooden-

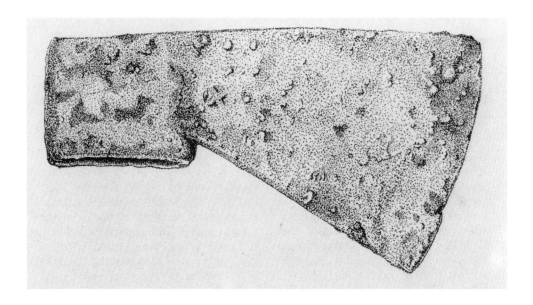

Drawing of iron axe found at the Winney's Rift site. Illustration by Sylvie Brown, 1985. *Courtesy Susan A. Bender and Hetty Jo Brumbach.*

frame houses. It was located astride one of the most volatile frontiers in the region, and thus Albany authorities administering town affairs considered it a vital outpost shielding their province's vulnerable northern border. Massachusetts, whose drive for western expansion was blocked by New York, saw Schaghticoke as its window to the west. Exploiting their relationship with Indian refugees from Mahican Country living along the Saint Lawrence, the French regarded the town as a vital source of information and smuggled supplies.

People living at Schaghticoke continually worked to play these colonial adversaries off against one another. Warriors from the town patrolled the border and hired on as scouts and spies to whoever paid the best wages. They also carried on an illicit trade between Albany and Quebec that continued without letup through peace, war, and prohibition. The steady stream of North Country beaver pelts hauled to Albany by Schaghticoke men helped New York merchants circumvent attempts by their Iroquois allies to control the western fur trade. The gunpowder, lead, cloth, ironware, and other English manufactures brought up to New France proved particularly important to people living in the often-blockaded and frequently poorly provisioned French colonies dependent on imports for nearly all supplies.

Life at Schaghticoke became increasingly more difficult as years passed. Renewed warfare with France in 1702 forced many townsfolk to again abandon their homes. When they returned at the end of the fighting in America in 1713, they found that Albany merchants had claimed the land for themselves. Outraged by the shady deals and cheating

Schuyler Flatts Archeological District National Historic Landmark

The Schuyler Flatts Archeological District is located in the town of Colonie, Albany County, New York. The district occupies 1.84 acres of archaeologically sensitive land located on the widest expanse of flat land on the Hudson River above Albany and astride the main communications route linking New York, New England, Iroquoia, and Canada. Schuyler Flatts was one of the most important trading, diplomatic, and military staging areas north of the Fort Orange/Albany area throughout much of the Historic Contact period.

Two sites preserved at this locale contain intact archaeological materials associated with figures who played significant roles in these activities. The earliest contains the remains of a residential, administrative, and commercial compound presided over by the influential Dutch frontier merchant-diplomat Arendt van Curler between 1643 and 1667. The second represents the archaeological remains of the Schuyler House. Built by Albany trader, soldier, and magistrate Philip Pieterse Schuyler, the house is best remembered as a hub of frontier activity first presided over by his son Peter and then by Margarita

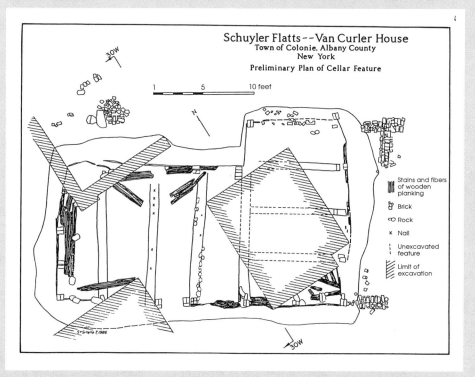

Plan view of the van Curler House cellar, Schuyler Flatts Archeological District. Drawn by Charles Gillette, 1986. Courtesy New York State Office of Parks, Recreation, and Historic Preservation.

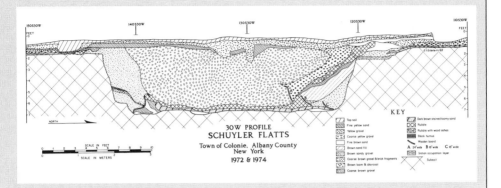

Profile view of the van Curler House cellar, Schuyler Flatts Archeological District. Drawn by Charles Gillette, 1983. Courtesy New York State Office of Parks, Recreation, and Historic Preservation.

Schuyler, the wife of his son Philip, who managed affairs at the Flatts from the time of Philip's death in 1758 until 1765.

The site briefly reassumed its old importance during the American War for Independence when it served as a crucially important staging area for American troops during the decisive 1777 Saratoga campaign. Remaining in the hands of the family until 1910, the Schuyler House was destroyed by a fire in 1962.

The ruins of the Schuyler House lay neglected for almost ten years until private developers threatened to destroy the site in 1970. Responding to the threat, local high school students and teachers belonging to the Heldeberg Workshop began conducting systematic excavations at the locale under the direction of New York State Office of Parks, Recreation, and Historic Preservation archaeologist Paul R. Huey in 1971.

Placing their first excavation units in and around the still-visible Schuyler House cellar, investigators encountered a brown-loam plow zone extending from six to eight inches below the ground surface. Plow-zone deposits were underlain by a layer of yellow gravel varying from six inches to one foot in thickness. A thin stratum of fine yellow sand directly

beneath this layer was discovered above layers of yellow and brown gravel that composed the cellar fill.

Investigators screening these soils quickly discovered diagnostic seventeenth-century artifacts in and around a dry-laid stone wall later identified as the foundations of the red-brick Dutch farmhouse constructed by Philip Pieterse Schuyler. Workers subsequently discovered a long, narrow soil stain that was identified as palisade-wall trench. This feature is believed to represent the remains of the stockade wall built around the farmhouse by British troops shortly after the outbreak of King George's War in 1744. A nearby stone foundation cut through the trench stain was identified as a possible kitchen wing built behind the main house sometime after the war ended in 1748.

Discoveries of layers and lenses of charred wood and fire-reddened soil mutely attest to documented accounts of a fire that destroyed this outbuilding and gutted the house interior in 1759. Excavations also revealed an extensive layer of cobblestones above the trench stain and the stone rear-wing foundation. These deposits proved to be the paving of a large courtyard built behind the house when it was restored during the early 1760s.

Intermittently working in the courtyard area from 1971 to 1974, investigators ultimately exposed six hundred square feet of cobblestone paving. Numerous artifacts dating to the middle decades of the eighteenth century, such as fragments of European white-clay tobacco-smoking pipes, lead musket balls (one bearing teeth marks), red earthenwares, and white salt-glazed stonewares, were found in this area. Wampum shell beads and glass beads also were found between paving stones.

The digging of sewer and power lines in the area just south of the Schuyler House excavations during the summer of 1972 prompted excavation of test units near these trenches. These excavations revealed remains of a six-to-seven-foot-deep rectangular cellar hole measuring fourteen feet on one side and twenty feet on the other filled with coarse yellow gravel. The cellar's walls were lined with horizontally placed wooden boards nailed to upright posts. Wooden-plank flooring was uncovered at the bottom of this cellar. Intrusive deposits of coarse brown gravel preserved evidence of two wall cave-ins. Artifacts found in the most recent of these associate the gravel with the filling of this cellar sometime between 1690 and 1710. Other artifacts found in a layer of fine yellow gravel overlying these deposits indicate that the cellar hole was completely filled in by 1730.

Excavations first conducted in the east end of the cellar revealed soft red-brick footings at the ends of each floor plank. Focusing attention on excavation units located north and east of this cellar in 1974, investigators discovered wooden wall and floor planks of a ten-foot by nineteen-foot cellar in an ell extending northeast of the rectangular cel-

ways of their colonial overseers, many Schaghticoke people began to move away from the precariously situated frontier town.

Some joined other River Indians living among the Mohawks along the Schoharie Valley southwest of Albany. Others moved south among Wappinger people pursuing a wandering life between the Hudson and Delaware Valleys. And more than a few moved north to Saint Lawrence Indian towns at Saint Francis, Bécancour, and other places.

Many Indian people still living in Mahican Country gradually moved to the Presbyterian mission founded by John Sargeant at Stockbridge, Massachusetts, in 1736. Moved from its original locale, the wooden-framed Mission House National Historic Landmark is the only surviving structure built for the Stockbridge Indian community. Numerous graves of Stockbridge's original inhabitants lie in the nearby Christian Indian burial ground. Although their general locations are known, specific identifications of Indian housesites and other features associated with contemporary missions in and around Shekomeko and Pine Plains, New York, await archaeological verification.

The above-mentioned physical evidence corroborates extensive bodies of documentation stating that Indian people moving to Stockbridge took up individual lots, built frame homes, and established their own form of New England townlife. Stockbridge Indian people tilled fields and orchards, raised livestock, and operated their own mills. Sargeant preached to his community in Mahican, taught them to lar. A set of wooden steps descending to the cellar floor was found along the southern wall of this ell. These findings match written accounts describing van Curler's house as either a New World variant of the Northern European Medieval Aisled House, which rarely had basements (Huey 1984), or an example of the Zeeland Barn Group, a later derivative of the Aisled House frequently underlain by cellars (Cohen 1992).

Like contemporary buildings at Fort Orange, the van Curler house was evidently a substantial, wooden-framed structure built atop an earthfast wooden-lined cellar that quickly rotted in soft wet soils. A wide variety of tin-glazed, salt-glazed, and other European ceramics, prunted roemer glassware, leaded window glass, glass beads, brass mouth harps, copper or brass tinkler cones, iron knives, gun parts, and European white-clay tobacco-smoking pipes found within lowermost cellar deposits document domestic life in this structure during the years of van Curler's occupancy. Discoveries of yellow ware pottery, glass beads, and European white-clay tobacco-smoking pipes bearing "RT" heel marks within slump deposits probably document later Schuyler family occupation of the house near the site. The absence of later artifacts in cellar deposits indicates that Schuyler House occupants finally stopped dumping trash in the abandoned cellar hole about 1700.

Listed in the National Register of Historic Places on January 21, 1974, the Schuyler Flatts Archeological District was designated a National Historic Landmark on August 11, 1993. Archaeological materials excavated from the locale between 1971 and 1974 are curated in the Archaeology Unit of the New York State Office of Parks, Recreation, and Historic Preservation's Bureau of Historic Sites in Waterford.

Unless otherwise cited, all information presented here is abstracted from Huey (1974).

read and write in both English and their own language, and oversaw the translation and printing of a Mahican Bible and other religious tracts.

Stockbridge prosperity soon attracted attention. Increasing numbers of Indian people from New York and New England moved to the town. Others regularly visited the settlement. Attracted by the success of the Presbyterian mission, Moravian ministers established missions of their own among Mahican settlements around Shekomeko in what is today eastern Columbia County in 1740. Presbyterian ministers erected a short-lived competing mission nearby at Kaunameek four years later. And, predictably, European settlers came to get what they could.

Some of these settlers denounced the Moravians and their Indian converts as French spies and had them evicted from the province in 1746 during King George's War. Some years later, powerful manor lords like Philip Philipse began to force other Mahican people off their remaining Hudson Valley lands (Handlin and Mark 1964; Nammack 1969). Aligning themselves with renters resisting manorial control and represented by an articulate leader from Wappinger territory named Daniel Nimham, many Mahican people challenged Philipse's claims in colonial courts. Nimham managed to take their case before the Lords of Trade in England in 1766. Referring the case back to New York's governor and Sir William Johnson, the colonial Superintendent of Indian Affairs in the region, for review, their lordships subsequently accepted the decision invalidating the Wappinger claim in 1767.

Other settlers intent on acquiring Stockbridge lands in Massachusetts managed to purchase much of the town when the Wappingers lost their case in New York. Forced from much of their remaining hunting and trapping lands, many Stockbridge Indians subsequently sold their property in the town to satisfy debts, needing the money to maintain a lifestyle that was becoming increasingly difficult to support. Taking over the community's mills and shops, settlers gradually dominated town government. Rising prices, fees, taxes, and other exactions levied by their new neighbors soon impoverished most Stockbridge Mahicans.

Ministers became increasingly unable to raise funds for their congregations as revivalistic fervor generated by the Great Awakening subsided. Local settlers sympathetic to the rebel cause, for their part, increasingly regarded their Indian neighbors with suspicion and growing fear as war with Great Britain began. Such fears were unfounded. Led by Daniel Nimham and his son Abraham, nearly all Stockbridge men fought with the patriots throughout the conflict.

But not all Mahicans supported the rebels. Many expatriates living in the west among the Munsees, Iroquois, and Shawnees fought for the British. Other Mahicans, living with Delawares in pacifistic Moravian missions in Pennsylvania and Ohio, for their part, tried to remain neutral during the fighting. They were not successful; most of the ninety men, women, and children murdered by American militia in Gnadenhütten, Ohio, on March 8, 1782, were from Mahican Country.

The war was a disaster for Mahican people. Many died in the fighting. The Stockbridge community suffered particularly devastating losses. Daniel Nimham and many other men were killed in battle or died from wounds or disease. Survivors returned to homes no longer their own. Unwelcome in their own community, they moved away. Most went to New Stockbridge and Brothertown in Oneida Country. Others were forced to move farther north and west as American settlers flooded across the Appalachians.

Those few people remaining in the area settled unobtrusively wherever they could in cities, towns, and countryside. Although today most descendants of the aboriginal people of Mahican Country live in exile with Delawares and other expatriates on the north and west, many people living in the Hudson Valley continue to trace their descent from the area's first inhabitants.

SOURCES

Much of the information presented in this section is drawn from Brasser (1978b) and Trelease (1960). A comprehensive history of the eighteenth-century Stockbridge Indian community may be found in Frazier (1992). Other information on Stockbridge appears in Colee (1977) and Mandell (1992). Detailed accounts of the Wappinger land claim appear in Handlin and Mark (1964) and Nammack (1969). Relations between Schaghticoke and Western Abenaki people are surveyed in Calloway (1990). The Amesokanti community is discussed in a paper by Prins (1988b). Summaries of archaeological site data are presented in Brumbach and Bender (1986); Fisher and Hartgen (1983); Funk (1976); Huey (1985a, 1988a, 1988b); Huey, Feister, and McEvoy (1977); and W. Ritchie (1958).

EUROPEAN-INDIAN CONTACT IN THE NORTH ATLANTIC REGION

THE SEVENTEENTH CENTURY

DUTCH-INDIAN CONTACT

Dutch merchants established the first permanent Dutch settlements in the colony they called New Netherland during the early 1600s. The Dutch colony stretched along the Atlantic coast from the "Fresh" (Connecticut) River across the "North" (Hudson) River to the "South" (Delaware) River. Although many settlers moving to this colony hailed from Dutch provinces, significant numbers of colonists came from Scandinavia, France, Belgium, and central Europe. English colonists moving westward from New England later settled along the eastern borders of the Dutch province at Westchester and western Long Island.

Dutch interest in the more northerly reaches of their colony largely centered upon trading outposts established in the Mahican and Lower Connecticut Valley Countries. A small permanent trading post named Fort Nassau was built on Castle Island in the heart of Mahican territory on the upper Hudson River near modern Albany, New York, in 1614. Prone to flooding and too far from the mouth of the Mohawk River, this post was soon abandoned.

Ten years later, Dutch West India Company employees established a new post named Fort Orange on the western shore of the river near where the main overland trail to Mohawk Country struck the Hudson in modern Albany. Situated near the head of navigation on the Hudson River along strategic crossroads linking New Netherland with New England, New France, and the eastern approaches to Iroquoia, the Fort Orange post became the major trading mart in the region.

Dutch traders at Fort Orange exchanged metal tools, textiles, glass beads, firearms, ammunition, and other European goods for furs with visiting Indian people. Disastrously involving themselves in a conflict between their Mahican neighbors and the Mohawks in 1626, the Dutch thereafter maintained a strict policy of neutrality in disputes between Indian peoples.

Intent upon establishing a self-supporting settlement capable of exploiting the Fort Orange trade mart, Dutch West India Company director Kiliaen van Rensselaer established his Rensselaerswyck patroonship between 1629 and 1630 on land surrounding Fort Orange that had been purchased from Mahican people. Several years later, Rensselaerswyck sheriff Adriaen van der Donck established a small, unauthorized post of his own several miles above Fort Orange. Carrying out van Rensselaer's order and evicting van der Donck from the premises, Rensselaerswyck resident director Arendt van Curler, a skilled frontier diplomat and canny trader, established his own post at the place in 1643. The locale, later known as Schuyler Flatts, rivaled Fort Orange as a major regional entrepôt and diplomatic center.

Encouraged by their success at Fort Orange, the Dutch turned their attention eastward toward the burgeoning Connecticut Valley fur market. In 1631 Dutch traders established a small post called Fort Good Hope near present-day Hartford, Connecticut. Built near competing New England trading posts, far from the main Dutch settlements, Fort Good Hope failed to prosper. Constantly embroiled in conflicts with nearby native and New England people, the Dutch finally surrendered the post to the English in 1653.

Though often cut off from resupply by English competitors and devastated by seemingly interminable wars with Munsee people farther downriver, the Fort Orange post remained a key source of supply for Mohawk traders. Muskets and ammunition obtained from Fort Orange during the 1640s and 1650s, for example, gave Mohawks and other Iroquois people receiving weapons from Mohawk trading partners crucial advantages in their wars against Huron, Neutral, and Erie rivals.

The Dutch surrendered their posts along the upper Hudson when New Netherland fell to an English expedition in 1664. Reoccupying the fort during their brief recapture of the province in

1673, the Dutch subsequently—and finally—agreed to return the colony to the English in 1674.

Both Fort Orange and Schuyler Flatts have recently been designated as National Historic Landmarks. Few other sites are known to contain deposits documenting Dutch relations with Indian people in this region.

FRENCH-INDIAN CONTACT

THE SIXTEENTH CENTURY

The first chronicled direct contacts between Indian and French people within the North Atlantic region in the present United States occurred when Italian navigator Giovanni da Verrazzano sailed to the region in the employ of King Francis I of France in 1524. Discoveries of artifacts possibly obtained from Verrazzano and other early French voyagers known to have sailed to North Atlantic shores during the sixteenth century have been found in Mashantucket Pequot National Historic Landmark sites and in several other locales.

THE SEVENTEENTH CENTURY

Establishment of permanent French settlements in the region followed explorations along the North Atlantic coast in 1604 and 1605 and subsequent movements into the Saint Lawrence Valley beginning in 1608. Both areas soon became centers of French expansion. Between 1604 and 1613 small settlements were established in northern Maine and adjacent sections of Nova Scotia and New Brunswick in an area that the French called Acadia. Expanding south and

MAP 15: NORTH ATLANTIC EUROPEAN-INDIAN CONTACT SITES

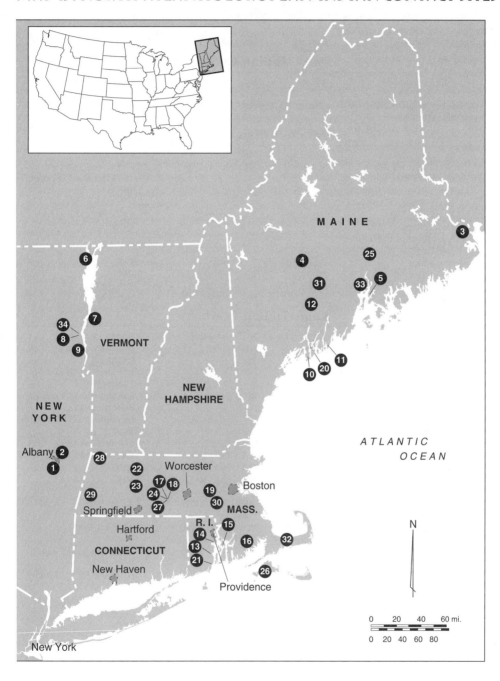

MAINE

3

25

6

4

31 33 5

12

34 7

8

9 VERMONT

11

10 20

NEW
HAMPSHIRE

NEW
YORK

ATLANTIC
OCEAN

Albany 2

1

28

22 Worcester

17 18

23

24 19 Boston

29 30

Springfield 27 MASS.

R. I. 15

Hartford 14

13 16 32

CONNECTICUT 21

New Haven 26

Providence

New York

N

0   20   40   60 mi.

0   20   40   60   80

Map 15 Historic Contact Sites

Map Number	Site Name	County	State	Date	NR	Source

Dutch-Indian Contact

Map Number	Site Name	County	State	Date	NR	Source
1	Fort Orange NHL (NYSM 7645)	Albany	NY	1624–1664	X	Huey 1988a; NYSMAS; Peña 1990
2	Schuyler Flatts NHL (NYSM 1631)	Albany	NY	1642–1664	X	Huey 1985b; NYSMAS

French-Indian Contact

Map Number	Site Name	County	State	Date	NR	Source
3	St. Croix NHS	Washington	ME	1604–1605		Cotter 1978
4	Norridgewock NHL Old Point (ME 069-2) Tracy Farm (ME 069-11) Sandy River (ME 069-24)	Somerset	ME	1614–1754	X	Cowie and Petersen 1992; Prins and Bourque 1987
5	Pentagoet NHL Fort Pentagoet (ME 084-3) Saint-Castin's Habitation (ME 084-7)	Hancock	ME	1635–1700	X	Faulkner and Faulkner 1985
6	Fort Anne	Grand Isle	VT	1665		VAI
7	Fort Cassin	Addison	VT	1690		VAI
8	Fort St. Frederic NHL	Essex	NY	1731–1760	X	NPS 1987
9	Fort Ticonderoga NHL	Essex	NY	1755–1757	X	NPS 1987

Anglo-Indian Contact

Map Number	Site Name	County	State	Date	NR	Source
10	Popham Colony	Phippsburg	ME	1607–1608	X	Briggs 1969
11	Pemaquid NHL (ME 058-1)	Lincoln	ME	1630–1759	X	Beard and Bradley 1978; Camp 1975
12	Cushnoc NHL (ME 021-2)	Kennebec	ME	1628–1670	X	Cranmer 1990; Prins 1986a, 1987
13	Cocumscussoc NHL/ Smith's Castle (RI-375)	Washington	RI	1637–1692	X	P. Robinson 1989; Rubertone 1989
14	Samuel Gorton Housesite	Kent	RI	1648–1675		Freedman and Pagoulatos 1989
15	Benjamin Church House	Bristol	RI	Late 1600s	X	P. Robinson 1992
16	Cooke's Garrison	Bristol	MA	Late 1600s		F. Howard 1907
17	Mark Garrison	Worcester	MA	Late 1600s		MHC
18	Philip Goss Garrison	Worcester	MA	Late 1600s		MHC
19	South Natick	Norfolk	MA	1651–present	X	Fitch 1983
20	Clarke and Lake (ME 015-1)	Knox	ME	1654–1676	X	Baker 1985
21	Jireh Bull Blockhouse (RI-926)	Washington	RI	1657–1700		Zannieri 1983
1	Fort Orange NHL (NYSM 7645)	Albany	NY	1664–1676	X	Huey 1988a; NYSMAS; Peña 1990
2	Schuyler Flatts NHL (NYSM 1631)	Albany	NY	1664–1759	X	Huey 1985b; NYSMAS
22	Old Deerfield Village NHL	Franklin	MA	1670–present	X	NPS 1987
23	West Street Palisade	Hampshire	MA	1670		Reinke 1990
24	Fort Gilbert	Worcester	MA	1686		MHC
25	Fort Hill	Penobscot	ME	1700s		MHASI
26	Experience Mayhew House	Dukes	MA	1700–1745		MHC
27	Jenning's Garrison	Worcester	MA	1704		MHC
28	Fort Massachusetts	Berkshire	MA	Mid-1700s		MHC
29	Mission House NHL	Berkshire	MA	1739–1804	X	NPS 1987
30	Reverend Badger House	Norfolk	MA	1753–present	X	B. Pfeiffer 1979
31	Fort Halifax NHL	Kennebec	ME	1754	X	NPS 1987
9	Fort Ticonderoga NHL	Essex	NY	1757	X	NPS 1987

east, Acadian traders, missionaries, and soldiers began to erect outposts like Fort Pentagoet on the New England frontier during the 1630s.

Along the Saint Lawrence, Samuel de Champlain established the capital of New France at Quebec in 1608. One year later, he and two other musket-bearing French soldiers helped a mixed force of Huron and Canadian Algonquian warriors defeat a Mohawk war party on the banks of the lake that today bears his name.

Focusing attention upon fur-rich lands to the north and west, New France colonists maintained close relations with their Huron and Algonquian allies. Sharing both their burdens and their wealth, the French found themselves continually embroiled in disputes between their native allies and the Iroquois. Anxious to protect the southern approaches to new Saint Lawrence Valley towns like the settlement established at Montreal in 1642, French authorities constructed Fort Anne and other fortifications near Indian towns along Lake Champlain. As with most defensive measures, these posts also served as offensive staging areas for attacks on colonial settlements along the New England and New York frontiers when war with England first broke out in 1689.

Moving outward from French frontier posts like Fort Anne and Fort Pentagoet, civil and military authorities bargained with Indian traders and provisioned Indian allies while Catholic priests ministered to proselytes and sought out new converts. Frequently built on lands already considered spiritually significant by Indian people, some missions like Sainte Anne de Beaupré in Vermont became sacred sites where Christian Western Abenaki and other Indian people came to pray.

French expansion into the upper reaches of the region was both extensive and spotty. Fewer than five hundred French people were living in the region by 1650. Stimulated by the possibilities of profit and supported by the French crown, their numbers grew dramatically along the Saint Lawrence Valley and the Acadian coast as the century wore on. Although written records show that the French erected several forts, missions, and settlements along the Acadian and Lake Champlain frontiers during this period, archaeologists have thus far located only a few of them.

One of the sites, Fort Anne, contains archaeological deposits associated with one of the earliest of the many French forts built along the strategic Lake Champlain–Richelieu River route connecting the Hudson and Saint Lawrence Valleys. Often built in or near existing Indian communities at strategic passes or "carrying places," posts like Fort Anne guarded New France's southern frontier from Mohawk attack during wars waged

Fort Orange Archeological Site National Historic Landmark

The Fort Orange Archeological Site is preserved in clay and alluvial silt strata beneath seventeen feet of fill below the intersection of Interstate 787 and U.S. Routes 9 and 20 at the approaches of the Dunn Memorial Bridge in the city of Albany, Albany County, New York. Built by the Dutch West India Company in 1624, Fort Orange was situated astride major east-west overland routes just below the heads of navigation of the Hudson River and its largest tributary, the Mohawk River.

This position along one of the most strategic crossroads in the region made Fort Orange the single most important center of diplomacy and trade between Dutch colonists and Indian people in Northeastern North America. Although the fort itself was abandoned by 1676, the city that grew alongside it continued to serve as a major focal point of regional social, political, and economic life throughout the colonial era. First called Beverwyck by the Dutch, it was given its modern name, Albany, when English forces sent by the Duke of York conquered New Netherland in 1664.

Fort Orange deposits preserve remains of a small, half-acre, fortified wooden-palisade-walled earthwork military post occupied by Dutch garrisons from 1624 to 1664 and from 1673 to 1674 and by British troops from 1664 to 1673 and again from 1674 to 1676. Several seventeenth-century written accounts and schematic drawings describe the post. One account noted that fort walls enclosed eight small houses dominated by "a handsome, large house with a flat roof and lattice work." Another, written in 1643, described the place as "a miserable little fort, . . . built of logs, with four or five pieces of Breteuil cannon, and as many pedereros [small swivel cannon]."

Other documents indicate that Fort Orange inhabitants were not preoccupied with security considerations. One order issued by the post commander prohibited "people from letting chickens, hogs, or other animals come on the bastions and [required] said bastions to remain properly closed." Another order politely denied the request of a trader asking permission to cut a door through the fort's curtain wall to ease passage from his house to the outside of the post.

Damaged by periodic flooding and neglected by occupants who were preoccupied with trade with Indians, the fort rapidly tumbled into ruin. Living in a place "considered no more than a nest," Fort Orange's inhabitants increasingly relied for protection against the threat of French, English, or Indian attack on the wall of flesh provided by their Mohawk allies. In return, New Netherland governor Peter Stuyvesant authorized fort personnel to establish "a moderate trade in munitions" with the Mohawks to be carried out as "secretly as possible." This trade helped the Mohawks and their Iroquois confederates defeat or drive away most of their trade competitors in the region. Mohawk traders funneled the proceeds of this briefly held trade monopoly to Fort Orange.

Cultural resources preserved in Fort Orange deposits compose one of the most significant bodies of data documenting the role played by Dutch traders in the region. As such, they provide a cultural and chronological benchmark for Northeastern North American historical archaeology. Intact features within the inner fort curtain have revealed new information on the dimensions and layout of the fort and its features as well as changes in diet, house construction, and type and range of furnishings and other materials used by fort occupants. These findings provide new insights into the continuing function of the site as a crossroads for trade and shed new light on relationships linking Fort Orange with other locales in America and Europe.

The exact location of Fort Orange had been long forgotten when archaeologists working under contract for the New York State Department of Transportation unexpectedly uncovered artifacts dating to the mid-1600s within discernibly stratified deposits in the proposed Interstate 787 right-of-way on October 20, 1970. More intensive salvage excavations were undertaken under the direction of New York State

Historic Trust (now the Division for Historic Preservation, New York State Office of Parks, Recreation, and Historic Preservation) archaeologist Paul R. Huey during through the winter of 1970–1971.

Findings made during these excavations corroborate written records describing the fort as a quadrangular earthwork with outward dimensions measuring 150 feet on each side. The fort earthwork was flanked on each corner by a bastion, surrounded by a moat, and surmounted by a wooden wall. Discoveries of a wheel lock part, a small section of chain mail, gunflints, lead shot, and two iron cannonballs further attest to the military character of the installation.

Portions of at least four buildings formerly flanking the inner wall of the fort's eastern curtain were identified. Archaeologists also uncovered parts of

Conjectural view of Fort Orange in 1635, based on archival and archaeological documentation. Oil painting by Len Tantillo. Courtesy Len Tantillo.

the clay-and-pebble-paved eastern post entrance roadway and the cobblestone-lined south moat. Excavators digging below the uppermost layer of stones believed to represent a 1648 moat-rebuilding episode found a deeper soil profile identified as the original moat of 1624. A wall covered with quarried stone believed to represent remains of the inner wall of an undocumented ravelin or outerwork was found along the moat's southern edge.

Glass beads and other datable diagnostic artifacts found among bricks, pan tiles, and other building debris in and around these features verify written records documenting several building and rebuilding episodes at the fort. Discoveries of wampum and glass beads, European white-clay tobacco-smoking pipes, glass-bottle receptacles for alcoholic beverages, lead shot, gunflints, and other goods in and around foundations of structures noted in extant documents as traders' houses or taverns affirm extensive written documentation recording Fort Orange's economic role in the regional Indian trade. Discoveries of ceramics and other wares imported from England, France, Germany, Italy, and Spain reveal the range and extent of Dutch and early English trade connections.

Other findings of delicately elegant roemer drinking glasses, glazed floor tiles, fired-clay roofing pan tiles, and leaded casement glass further suggest the extent to which fort merchants went to furnish luxury goods and building materials suitable for constructing a small-scale version of the home country along the upper Hudson River frontier bordering on Indian, Dutch, English, and French lands during the middle decades of the seventeenth century. The practice of building substantial, well-furnished brick buildings atop quickly rotting wooden cellar linings in soft, wet alluvial soils further attests to attitudes of Dutch traders regarding Fort Orange as temporary place of residence to be occupied only long enough to acquire sufficient wealth to move elsewhere.

Salvage excavators have examined 10 percent of the site area. Archival and field research conducted in conjunction with salvage operations further indicated that as much as 35 percent of the site remains intact. Working in close consultation with highway engineers, Huey supervised the reburial of uncovered stone and brick foundations and other features. Five to eight feet of clean brown sand was carefully laid above these features to both mark the site and act as a cushion to protect site deposits from compaction by the overlying ten-foot-high landfill layer supporting Interstate 787. Load-bearing concrete pillars placed at intervals along the highway right-of-way further reduce the amount of pressure on surviving deposits.

Archaeological materials removed during salvage excavations presently are on exhibit at the Fort Crailo State Historic Site and stored in the Division for Historic Preservation's Archaeological Laboratory Facility on Peebles Island in Waterford, New York. Listed in the National Register of Historic Places on January 31, 1980, the Fort Orange Archeological Site was designated a National Historic Landmark on November 4, 1993.

Unless otherwise cited, information presented here has been abstracted from Huey (1984, 1985a, 1988a, 1988b, 1991).

from the 1660s to 1701 and from English assaults during King William's War between 1689 and 1697. Regarding these posts as important trading centers and missions, Western Abenaki, Schaghticoke, and other Indian people also used them as way stations while carrying on illicit trade between Albany and Montreal.

Several other sites preserve remains of artifacts significant in seventeenth-century relations between French colonists and Indian people in the region. Saint Croix National Historic Site deposits preserve the remains of the first abortive French settlement attempt along the Maine coast in 1604 and 1605. Two other French-Indian contact sites have recently been designated as National Historic Landmarks. The Norridgewock National Historic Landmark is the site of an important French mission station and frontier post built at a major Eastern Abenaki town along Maine's upper Kennebec River during the 1690s. The Pentagoet National Historic Landmark, for its part, preserves the remains of two of the most significant French Acadian frontier posts of the period. Built near the Maine coast in the modern-day town of Castine, the strongly fortified Fort Pentagoet was first established in 1635. New Englanders occupied the post between 1654 and 1670. Returned to French sovereignty in 1670, it became the administrative center of French Acadia until its final destruction by Dutch privateers in 1674 during the Third Anglo-Dutch Naval War. The other site preserved at Pentagoet, Saint-Castin's Habitation, represents a small, unfortified Acadian trading and administrative center established by French merchant-diplomat Jean Vincent Abaddie de Saint-Castin in an Etchemin town in 1677.

THE EIGHTEENTH CENTURY

The first six decades of the eighteenth century were marked by nearly incessant wars between France and Great Britain. Vastly outnumbered by the British and generally poorly supported by their mother country, French colonists struggled to contain British expansion into their territories. Ceding Acadia to Great Britain at the end of Queen Anne's War in 1713, the French ultimately were forced to surrender New France to British troops in 1760.

Subsequent attempts by Great Britain to consolidate control over its new empire worsened relations with North Atlantic colonists. Finally breaking out into open conflict in 1775, this struggle eventually ended shortly after French military assistance helped the Americans defeat the British at Yorktown, Virginia, in 1781.

French and Indian relations were carried on within the context of these struggles. Accordingly, most sites associated with eighteenth-century contact between French and Indian people in the region generally represent forts or missions. As with earlier sites of this kind, most of these locales have been located and marked. Although several have been developed into parks, few of these sites have been systematically investigated by archaeologists. Those that have, like the Fort Saint Frederic National Historic Landmark and Fort Carillon within the Fort Ticonderoga National Historic Landmark, have largely been subjects of studies emphasizing European viewpoints and activities.

Pentagoet Archeological District National Historic Landmark

The Pentagoet Archeological District consists of two discontiguous sites located on the shores of the Bagaduce River estuary near the mouth of the Penobscot River in the town of Castine, Hancock County, Maine. Fort Pentagoet site deposits, dating from 1635 to 1674, lie in well-drained, sandy-clay loam soils beneath the back lawn of the Catholic Church of Our Lady of Holy Hope. Deposits preserving the remains of Saint-Castin's Habitation (ca. 1677–1690) are located one and one-half miles due north on privately owned property. Representing successive centers of French expansion into the Penobscot Valley, these sites collectively contain the largest, best preserved, and most intensively studied body of resources documenting relations between Indian people and French settlers on Maine's seventeenth-century Acadian frontier.

Warren K. Moorehead, who conducted limited excavations at the fort in 1915, and other collectors periodically dug at the site of Fort Pentagoet before the Diocese of Portland purchased the property for its historical value in 1920. Erosion, pothunting, and landscaping for the church, which was established in a remodeled residence on the property, have damaged some site deposits. Most of the site, however, lay intact and protected beneath the church lawn when University of Maine archaeologists under the supervision of Alaric Faulkner began test excavations in June 1980.

Surveying the locale with ground-penetrating radar, Faulkner's field crews uncovered a 922-square-foot area between 1981 and 1984. These excavations revealed coursed slate masonry

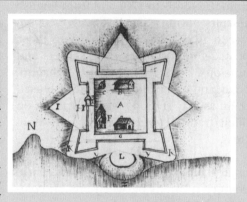

Detail of a plan of Fort Pentagoet, dated November 10, 1670. Photograph by Alaric Faulkner of an original in the Archives Nationales, Paris. Courtesy Alaric Faulkner, University of Maine.

foundations and other evidence of eight structures deeply buried beneath stone rubble. All were constructed during the two periods of French occupation (Pentagoet I: 1635–1654 and Pentagoet II: 1670–1674) in a compound seventy-nine feet long and seventy-seven feet wide. Contrasting their findings with maps and other archival information, project personnel were able to identify six of these foundations. Ironically, rubble heaped on the foundations by cannonfire from Dutch raiders, who razed the post by turning the fort's guns on its own stone walls before sailing away in 1674, preserved these deposits.

University of Maine excavators recovered an assemblage of 12,221 artifacts at Fort Pentagoet. Catalogued entries represent a wide range of iron, brass, and copper wares and European ceramics, glassware, and other artifacts produced primarily in what today are France, Germany, and the Low Countries. Few objects of English origin were found. Much of the site's ceramic and glassware assemblage comes from the section of southwestern France served by La

Rochelle, Pentagoet's primary supply port. Many of the European white-clay tobacco-smoking pipes, stonewares, tin-glazed wares, and firearms probably were made in Holland or Germany.

Analysis of diagnostic artifacts shows that much of the surviving assemblage dates to the Pentagoet I occupation. Analysis of the site's complex stratigraphy indicates that Pentagoet II occupations only slightly altered most Pentagoet I foundations. The abrupt disappearance of European white-clay tobacco-smoking pipes with bore-stem diameters postdating the third quarter of the seventeenth century corroborates archival records chronicling the final abandonment of the post in 1674.

Firearms, munitions, iron knives, axes, harpoons, and fishhooks; white-clay tobacco-smoking pipes; glass beads; and copper or brass tinkler cones, awls, and discs represent items probably used in trade with Indian people visiting the fort. Discoveries of fine glassware, tableware, wine bottles, elegant ceramics, cleaved bear skulls and other remains of elaborately prepared meals, and sword and spur fragments in a place where neither was needed mutely testify to the lengths the post's tiny twenty-man garrison went to maintain

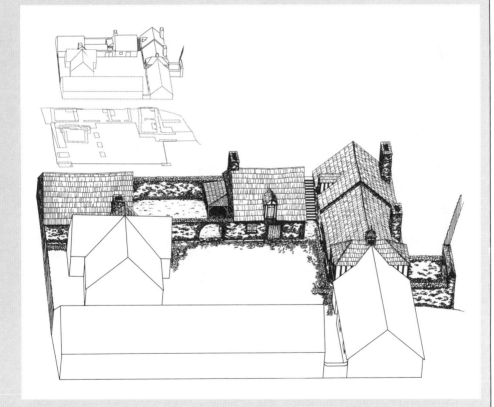

Reconstruction of the inner compound of d'Aulnay's original fort at Pentagoet, as it might have appeared in an aerial view looking south, ca. 1650. Courtesy Alaric Faulkner, University of Maine.

their genteel lifestyles as they barricaded themselves in their small fort along the volatile Acadian frontier.

A member of Fort Pentagoet's garrison named Jean Vincent Abaddie de Saint-Castin established a new post in the middle of a nearby Eastern Abenaki Etchemin town sometime between 1677 and 1680. A census taken in 1688 indicates that Saint-Castin's Habitation consisted of 160 Indian people and thirteen members of his own entourage (evidently Saint-Castin and three soldiers, their wives, seven children, and a priest) living in two houses and thirty-two wigwams.

Knowledgeable of Etchemin culture and fluent in their language, Saint-Castin married Mathilde, the daughter of Madockawando, the town's leader. Working as France's most influential agent among the Indians in Maine, Saint-Castin is remembered in both Canada and the United States as a romantic figure who became Acadia's first *capitaine des sauvages.* Playing a major role in the fighting that devastated Maine during King William's War, Saint-Castin abandoned his habitation a few years after helping his Indian allies take and destroy Pemaquid on August 13, 1696.

The site of Saint-Castin's Habitation lay buried and forgotten beneath underbrush and trees after its abandonment. Used as an apple orchard and never plowed, the site remained unknown and undisturbed until local residents discovered a charcoal lens, fired daub, and hand-forged nails eroding out of the riverbank in 1983. Archival and archaeological research directed by Alaric Faulkner in 1984 and again between 1990 and 1993 confirmed that deposits preserved at the locale were indeed the remains of Saint-Castin's Habitation.

Most deposits were found in undisturbed topsoil within a foot of the site

Cast brass acorn badge for a hat, recovered from the floor of the Fort Pentagoet workshop and believed to represent the crest of Sieur Charles d'Aulnay, the entrepreneur who built the post. Photograph by Steven Bicknell. Courtesy Alaric Faulkner, University of Maine.

surface. Faulkner's field crews found lead ingots, molten sprue, iron tongs, gunflints, and hundreds of musket balls aligned in parallel rows where they had fallen between the cracks of long-vanished floorboards within the faint outline of a single discontinuous course of field stones believed to represent the post's storehouse. Sheet refuse consisting of European white-clay tobacco pipes, glass beads, European ceramics, and other domestic debris has been found scattered outside this outline.

A second earthfast wattle-and-daub walled building was delineated by three stone-chinked post molds and rubble from a stone chimney and another feature identified as a bread oven. The distinctive type of slate used in the chimney appears to have been scavenged from the ruins of Fort Pentagoet. A substantial assemblage of iron fastenings and hardware, lead shot, and smaller amounts of European ceramics, glassware, gunflints, and glass beads has been found at this locale. Discovery of a number of reworked chamfered European white-clay tobacco-smoking pipe stems used as cylindrical wampumlike beads in deposits containing few European household objects within this structure suggests that it may have been one of the thirty-two Indian houses documented at the site.

English tin-glazed ceramics and Bristol-style white-clay tobacco-smoking pipes found in Saint-Castin's Habitation deposits materially corroborate reported clandestine trade with the English. The abrupt disappearance of white-clay tobacco-smoking pipes with bore-stem diameters postdating 1700 in this assemblage further supports archival records indicating that Saint-Castin and his Eastern Abenaki Etchemin neighbors left the place at or about the time King William's War ended in 1697.

Pentagoet Archeological District sites presently rank among the most intact known deposits of their type in the North Atlantic region. Fort Pentagoet deposits currently are closely monitored by landowners and protected from shore erosion by stone riprap placed on the site's southern scarp by the U.S. Army Corps of Engineers. Saint-Castin's Habitation is one of the few extensively studied Historic Contact period sites untouched by plowing or other disturbances.

Materials recovered from Pentagoet Archeological District sites currently are curated in the Historic Archaeology Laboratory of the University of Maine in Orono. Fort Pentagoet was listed in the National Register of Historic Places on February 23, 1973, as a contributing property in the Castine Historic District. The Secretary of the Interior designated both Fort Pentagoet and Saint-Castin's Habitation as the Pentagoet Archeological District National Historic Landmark on April 12, 1993.

Information presented here has been abstracted from A. Faulkner (1991) and Faulkner and Faulkner (1985, 1987).

Lead ingots, nippers, sprue, and musket balls representing shot manufacture, the principal product of a workshop located just outside Saint-Castin's truck house. Courtesy Alaric Faulkner, University of Maine.

ANGLO-INDIAN CONTACT

THE SIXTEENTH CENTURY

Chronicles recording the visits of voyagers like Sebastian and John Cabot who sailed to North Atlantic shores under English auspices during the 1500s indicate that all made their landfalls north of the present borders of the United States in Newfoundland and the Gulf of Saint Lawrence. Most encounters with native people were ephemeral contacts in which transactions were conducted on beachfronts or across a ship's railings. Although English mariners may have made their way farther south, no clear evidence of such encounters has yet been found in archaeological sites or archival sources.

THE SEVENTEENTH CENTURY

English people established their first short-lived settlements at Popham's Colony and other coastal locales in Maine during the early decades of the century. More sustained contact with Indians began farther south when Brownist Pilgrim settlers and Puritan colonists established the first permanent English colonies in the region at Plymouth and Massachusetts Bay during the 1620s and 1630s. Settlers from these colonies quickly spread out to found other settlements and trading posts in Maine, Connecticut, Rhode Island, and eastern Long Island.

The English achieved complete control over the region below Acadia following Richard Nicolls's conquest of New Netherland for the Duke of York in 1664. Although recurring epidemic disease and wars with Indian people—such as King Philip's War (1675-1676), struggles with the Dutch, and conflict with the French—caused loss and hardship, none of these events seriously challenged English hegemony in the North Atlantic.

Immigration, high birth rates, and importation of enslaved Africans caused populations in the English North Atlantic provinces to rise to more than 130,000 by 1700. Commerce played a major role in these settlements, much as it did in neighboring Indian, French, and Dutch communities.

Sites like the newly designated Cocumscussoc, Cushnoc, and Pemaquid National Historic Landmarks, the Samuel Gorton housesite, and the site of the Jireh Bull blockhouse graphically document the growing importance of Indian trade in the region.

Native people also played major roles in English frontier diplomacy. Trade and diplomatic negotiation with Indian allies initially were conducted in and around centers of English settlement at places like Cocumscussoc in Rhode Island. The sites of such activities gradually shifted to more peripheral locales like Cushnoc, Fort Orange, and Pemaquid as English settlers consolidated control over the coast by conquering or purchasing Indian land.

Expanding the scope of their commerce outward from Massachusetts, Plymouth traders had established a permanent post at Cushnoc on Maine's Kennebec River by the early 1640s. Operated at various times by Plymouth or Boston merchants, the post was abandoned by New Englanders sometime before the outbreak of King Philip's War, as corroborated by both archaeological evidence and written records.

Fort Orange was occupied and renamed Fort Albany by the English immediately after the Duke of York's fleet took Manhattan from the Dutch in 1664. Briefly recaptured during the Third Anglo-Dutch War in 1673, the post was abandoned in 1676, and English authorities built a new Fort Albany on a hill above the town that had grown up just north of the post. Both the fort and the nearby town continued to be the single most important center of Indian trade in Northeastern North America until other, more westerly posts like Oswego largely cut off the town's commerce during the 1720s.

Archaeologists conducting salvage excavations at the site of the first Fort Orange prior to its reburial beneath Interstate 787 in the 1970s uncovered extensive deposits associated with the earliest period of English occupation in New York. These included portions of the fort's southern moat and wall, the southeastern bastion, a tavern, and several traders' residences. Large amounts of artifacts reflecting every aspect of fort life were recovered in and around these features. Substantial amounts of European trade goods and wampum were also found.

Pemaquid was one of the most important seventeenth-century English outposts on the New England–Acadian frontier. Located on Penobscot Bay near several Indian towns, Pemaquid was the outermost English post facing French frontier stations at Pentagoet. The settlement served as a major English frontier military installation, trading post, and port. First settled on a year-round basis by English colonists sometime between 1625 and 1628, the place was abandoned in 1676 during King Philip's War. One year later, returning English colonists constructed Fort Charles at the southern end of the town. This fort, a large wooden redoubt, fell to a large force of Indian warriors advised by Saint-Castin at the beginning of King William's War in 1689.

The post was rebuilt by the English as a stone fort and rechristened Fort William Henry in 1692. Besieged by Penobscot and other Indian warriors who were once again advised by Saint-Castin and now supported by French warships, the fort was forced to surrender in 1696. The victorious attackers demolished it before returning to Acadia.

Negotiations and other activities carried on at Pemaquid, Fort Orange, and other frontier posts became increasingly important to the survival of English colonial enterprises as contending English and French administrators and merchants vied for Indian commerce and military support during this turbulent century.

THE EIGHTEENTH CENTURY

Anglo-American settlers along the coast maintained their dominant position over those Indian communities remaining near their settlements after the wars of the preceding century. Farther north and west, relations between Indian people and settlers were increasingly restricted to armed encounters along the frontier peripheries of New England and New York as settlers pouring into North Atlantic lands claimed by Great Britain gradually pressed into and overran territories defended by Indian warriors.

Schuyler Flatts, a gathering place for

Pemaquid Archeological Site National Historic Landmark

The Pemaquid Archeological Site is located in the Colonial Pemaquid State Historic Site in Pemaquid Beach in the village of New Harbor, Lincoln County, Maine. Administered by the Maine Bureau of Parks and Recreation since 1969, the site is situated on Pemaquid Harbor midway between Casco and Penobscot Bays.

Pemaquid had long been the site of shipborne trade between Indians and Europeans when English colonists established their first permanent settlements at the locale sometime around 1628. Carrying on a lively commerce extending from Virginia to Newfoundland, Pemaquid traders also smuggled firearms and other contraband interdicted by Boston authorities to Indian customers and French Acadian rivals. Serving as vital, if illicit, middlemen, Pemaquid traders successfully competed for Indian furs and pelts with Plymouth Colony traders at Cushnoc, French Acadian merchants at Pentagoet, and the many free traders living along the coast.

The Pemaquid community was said to consist of less than thirty houses when New York was granted control of the area in 1664. Massachusetts Bay magistrates counted as many as two hundred colonists living in more than forty frame houses at the locale when they reasserted authority over Pemaquid in 1673.

Boston magistrates, alarmed by the outbreak of King Philip's War in 1675, precipitated conflict in Maine by ordering town leaders to confiscate all firearms owned by Indians. Rendered defenseless by this edict and unable to provide adequately for their families without guns, embittered Indian warriors compelled to fight against the English forced Pemaquid settlers to abandon the town in August 1676.

New Yorkers reoccupied Pemaquid a year later. Building a wooden redoubt named Fort Charles on the west side of the peninsula, they instituted an elaborate set of ordinances regulating trade and other aspects of Indian relations. New Yorkers represented the most influential and fastest-growing part of a population that boasted more than three hundred permanent residents by 1686. The easternmost New England outpost, Pemaquid and its fort were taken by a force of Indians accompanied and advised by Saint-Castin shortly after fighting brought on by King William's War spread to America in 1689.

Massachusetts authorities built a large stone fortification named Fort William Henry at the locale in 1692. Garrisoned by sixty men, the post became the principal English bastion on the northern New England frontier. Angered by the seizure and murder of Indian leaders visiting the fort under flags of truce, a force of between five hundred and six hundred Eastern Abenaki Indians again aided by Saint-Castin and supported by three French warships attacked and seized Fort William Henry in 1696. Sending their prisoners back to Boston, the Indians razed the fort and burned the Pemaquid settlement to the ground.

Pemaquid had been abandoned by the British for more than thirty-five years when New England entrepreneur David Dunbar transported Scotch-Irish immigrants to the spot in 1729. Naming his short-lived colony Georgia, Dunbar erected a new post dubbed Fort Frederick on the foundations of old Fort William Henry. Periodically garrisoned after Massachusetts authorities forced Dunbar to abandon his colony in 1732, Fort Frederick was finally demolished in 1775 by local militiamen intent on denying it to the British.

Pemaquid remained largely unoccupied throughout the nineteenth-century as local farmers cleared fields for plowing by toppling stone walls and filling open cellar holes. Inspired by a wave of antiquarian interest that culminated in the nation's centennial celebration in 1876, nearby residents took renewed interest in the site.

Local folklore transformed fort ruins into the remains of Norse or Spanish settlements. Promoted as a patriotic shrine by John Henry Cartland, whose turn-of-the-century excavations uncovered fortress foundations and other deposits, the site was acquired by the state of Maine in 1903. In 1908, state workers used Col. Wolfgang William Romer's 1699 drawing of the ruins of Fort William Henry to erect an accurate reconstruction of the post's large western stone bastion atop its foundations.

Archaeologist Warren K. Moorehead

Aerial photograph of Fort William Henry, Colonial Pemaquid State Historic Site. Photograph by Nicholas Dean. Courtesy Maine Historic Preservation Commission, Augusta.

uncovered portions of stone-paved streets and dug up at least five cellar holes during an unsuccessful attempt to discover evidence of Viking occupation at Pemaquid in 1923. More than forty years passed before Helen B. Camp began conducting the first systematic archaeological excavations at the site in 1965. Excavators supervised by Camp recovered an assemblage of over forty thousand artifacts and other archaeological materials associated with intermittent English occupations at Pemaquid between 1628 and 1775. These artifacts came from intact deposits within stone foundations of fourteen structures and the site of Forts William Henry and Frederick.

Forty-four types of pots, plates, bottles, utensils, furnishings, and other household objects were identified. Redwares, tin-glazed earthenwares, and stonewares dominate the site's varied ceramic assemblage. A substantial variety of glasswares and utilitarian metalwares in the forms of iron cooking kettles and hooks; metal thimbles; pressing irons; buttons; drawer handles, latches, and hinges; latten, pewter, brass, and iron tableware; and other objects also have been found.

Archaeologists have identified twenty-two types of hoes, fishhooks, horseshoes, files, and other craft and activity artifacts; twenty types of shot, gun parts, and other military artifacts; seventeen types of personal artifacts, pieces of coinage, and other materials. Glass beads, European white-clay tobacco-smoking pipes, scissors, mouth harps, iron axes, lead clothing seals marking trade cloth type and quality, and other materials often traded to Indians also have been recovered.

Artifacts dating from the seventeenth century have been found in and around the foundations of nine buildings and the site of Fort William Henry. Fort Frederick foundations and five structures are known to contain objects associated with eighteenth-century occupation. All archaeological materials have been recovered from sandy topsoil strata overlying clay subsoils atop granite and basalt bedrock.

Objects removed from Pemaquid site deposits are curated in the Maine State Museum in Augusta and in the Fort House, a late–eighteenth-century structure converted into the site's laboratory and storage facility. A large display collection is on exhibit in the park museum. Outdoor exhibits interpret the reconstructed fort area and several stabilized and clearly labeled exposed structure foundations. Listed in the National Register of Historic Places on December 2, 1969, the Pemaquid Archeological Site was designated a National Historic Landmark on April 12, 1993.

Information presented here has been abstracted from Camp (1975) and DePaoli (1979, 1988).

armies, traders, and diplomats just above Albany, is one of the few National Historic Landmarks focusing upon the Indian side of eighteenth-century Anglo-Indian relations in the region. Most other sites preserve remains of military posts built to protect frontier settlers from Indian raiders during times of war; examples of these posts include Fort Massachusetts, Fort Pownall, and Jenning's Garrison. The Mission House National Historic Landmark in Stockbridge and the Experience Mayhew, Reverend Badger, and Gideon Hawley houses represent standing structures of missionaries primarily interested in less bellicose relations with Indian people in the region.

SOURCES

An extensive body of documentation chronicles European relations with Indians in the North Atlantic region. Most sources documenting New Netherland are noted in the Middle Atlantic regional summary. Feister (1985) and Huey (1974, 1984, 1985a, 1985b, 1988a, 1988b, 1991) report results of archaeological and documentary research at the Fort Orange and Schuyler Flatts National Historic Landmarks and other New Netherland sites.

The Jesuit Relations (Thwaites 1896–1901) provides the single most extensive source for published primary documentation on French expansion into this region. Useful studies summarizing information from this and other sources include Bailey (1969), Eccles (1969), and Wade (1988). Particularly detailed analyses of the archaeological and archival evidence for seventeenth-century French-Indian relations along the Acadian frontier may be found in Faulkner and Faulkner (1985, 1987).

Much of the literature based upon the documentary record of Anglo-Indian relations in the North Atlantic region has already been cited. Useful general summaries appear in Jacobs (1988) and Leach (1966). Documentation tracing developments in more northerly reaches of the region are covered in C. E. Clark (1970).

No general overview of the archaeological evidence of Anglo-Indian contact in the region currently exists. Excavation results from some of the larger sites like Pemaquid National Historic Landmark (Camp 1975) and the Clarke and Lake site (Baker 1985) have been published. Most other findings appear in graduate theses or dissertations, such as Paul R. Huey's (1985a) analysis of excavations at the Fort Orange National Historic Landmark, or as unpublished reports on file in state historic preservation office site inventories.

PART TWO

THE MIDDLE ATLANTIC REGION

MAP 16: THE MIDDLE ATLANTIC REGION

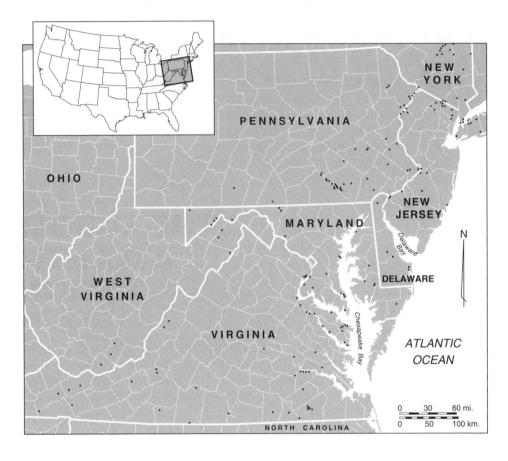

AN OVERVIEW
OF THE
REGION

The Middle Atlantic region stretches from southeastern New York to southwestern Virginia. Extending from the Atlantic coast west to inland Appalachian hills and valleys, the region encompasses all but the uppermost valleys of rivers flowing into New York Harbor, Delaware Bay, and Chesapeake Bay. The eastern reaches of this region are marked by flat coastal plains and low-lying hills that range westward from slender barrier beaches across sandy, barren lands to the deep, loamy soils of the inner coastal plain. A northeasterly line of hills, known as the Shawangunks in New York, the Kittatinies in New Jersey, and the Blue Mountains in Pennsylvania, rises above the piedmont area beyond the fall line to form the northwestern border of this region. Farther south, Appalachian highlands rising up beyond the Shenandoah, Roanoke, and New river valleys mark the westernmost limits of the region.

The Middle Atlantic region includes Delaware, Maryland, New Jersey, southeastern New York, southeastern Pennsylvania, Virginia, and the southernmost portion of West Virginia. This heavily forested region was the home to a diverse group of Indian communities at the time of initial contact. People then living in more northern parts of this region generally followed a comparatively mobile lifestyle. Most moved from large, dispersed settlements to smaller camps at different times of the year. The virtual absence of archaeological or archival documentation of large, nucleated settlements and elaborately furnished burials in northern parts of the region indicates that most people living in these areas belonged to largely egalitarian societies.

In contrast, both archaeological and written records of native life along the Maryland and Virginia coasts at contact suggest that the inhabitants of that area were members of larger and somewhat more stratified societies usually referred to as chiefdoms by scholars. People belonging to these chiefdoms generally lived in one or more large towns containing several round or oblong bark- or mat-covered houses. Several of the larger of these settlements were surrounded by stockade walls. Though townsfolk occupied these settlements year-round, they often moved to smaller camps or other communities at various times of the year. Farther west, people living in large, planned communities occupied lands beyond the fall line along the lower reaches of the Susquehanna River and the upper branches of the Potomac, Rappahannock, James, Nottoway, and Meherrin Rivers.

Many of the last speakers of the languages used by the inhabitants of these lands died during the early decades of this century, but by supplementing earlier vocabularies compiled by missionaries and other chroniclers, scholars working with the native people have been able to preserve the little that is known about the region's languages. Several linguistic studies indicate that people living along the Hudson River, the Delaware Valley, and the upper Delmarva Peninsula generally spoke closely related Eastern Algonquian dialects at the time of initial historic contact. Other linguistic sources suggest that the Piscataway, Potomac, or Powhatan people living in the Chesapeake Bay drainage also spoke Eastern Algonquian languages.

On the west, Iroquoian-speaking Susquehannocks moved south during the third quarter of the sixteenth century and supplanted Shenks Ferry people living in small towns along the lower Susquehanna Valley. Both Shenks Ferry and Luray-phase people living to the southwest along the upper branches of the Potomac River disappeared before European chroniclers arrived to record their languages. Farther south, Siouan-speaking Mannahoac, Monacan, Occaneechi, and Saponi people made their homes in piedmont valley communities west of the Virginian fall line. Indians living in the Nottoway and Meherrin Valleys of Southeastern Virginia during the Historic Contact period spoke Iroquoian

languages closely related to those used in nearby Tuscarora communities just south of the present-day North Carolina state line.

While speaking different languages, all of these people followed Late Woodland lifeways at the time of European contact. Each used stone, shell, bone, or antler tools hafted onto wooden or bone handles to cut, scrape, and pierce wood, skin, and other materials used for tools, food, shelter, and clothing. They also made and used stylistically distinctive clay pipes and pots, and most crafted ornaments from shell, bone, stone, and cold-hammered copper.

Europeans sailing to Middle Atlantic shores began settling on Indian lands during the early 1600s. As in the North Atlantic region, most newcomers settling on cleared Indian lands moved onto the same kinds of fertile and well-drained tracts favored by native people. Expanding outward from these settlements, colonists struggled to seize control over the region. Resisting colonial expansion, the native peoples fought for their lands and lives. But they were ravaged by epidemic disease and divided by old enmities and conflicting aspirations. Defeated in wars with settlers, they either submitted to colonial domination or moved away. Unwilling to face the uncertainties of life in exile among strangers, most Middle Atlantic people struggled to remain on their ancestral homelands whenever possible. But when forced to give up their best lands, they settled on small reservations or remote tracts unwanted by the colonists.

Increasingly dispossessed by European settlers, many of these people finally gathered in expatriate settlements along the Susquehanna and upper Delaware river valleys during the early 1700s. Resisting further expansion through the middle decades of the century, most of these people were finally forced to leave the region by 1800. Today, although most people claiming descent from Middle Atlantic Indian ancestors live elsewhere, many continue to make their homes at various locales throughout the region.

THE SIXTEENTH CENTURY

As in the north, most evidence of sixteenth-century Middle Atlantic Indian life survives in the form of artifacts, archaeological deposits, and orally transmitted narratives and texts. Information drawn from these sources indicates that Middle Atlantic lifeways during the 1500s closely paralleled those of coastal people living farther north and south. Although their lifeways may have differed in particulars, all of these people used similar Late Woodland types of tools, utensils, weapons, house forms, adornment, transportation, and storage. They also employed similar fishing, foraging, and hunting tools and techniques.

Like many of their neighbors, most of these people planted crops of corn, beans, squash, and tobacco wherever and whenever practicable. As elsewhere, plant cultivators produced largest yields when tilling deep soils located on lands exposed to warm, moist southerly winds. People living in northern parts of the region tended to live in small towns of scattered houses. People living farther south, for their part, often erected larger and more concentrated settlements near their fields.

As elsewhere in the Northeast, scholars studying these people use recon-structed settlement patterns; the presence or absence of distinctive features like house patterns, pits, or middens; and distinctive types of pottery, stone tools, and other temporally and geographically discrete evidence to identify particular archaeological complexes. Each complex is generally associated with particular cultural, social, or political groups within a given area.

Using these types of data, archaeologists believe that they have detected the emergence of several distinctive cultural complexes within the Middle Atlantic region during the centuries immediately preceding the 1500s. Correlating this information with later linguistic, documentary, and ethnographic evidence, scholars continue to try to link these complexes with historically chronicled people in the region.

Decorated and undecorated conoidal or globular pots have been found with Late Woodland triangular, chipped-stone projectile points in sites throughout the region. Although small amounts of pottery from nearby places are occasionally found in most locales, the greater bulk of pottery recovered in most sixteenth-century Middle Atlantic site deposits appears to have been made locally.

Many scholars interested in explaining this phenomenon believe that Middle Atlantic Late Woodland craftspeople had fewer opportunities to acquire or copy foreign wares after the collapse of exchange networks sometime between A.D. 1000 and 1300 (Custer 1986b, 1987). Other investigators think that these findngs show that members of Late Woodland Middle Atlantic communities in contact with other people simply did not readily adopt or adapt foreign pots, techniques, or design concepts.

Discoveries of European glass beads and smelted copper or brass hoops, spirals, and fragments in sites located in areas where little else had changed in two or three hundred years suggest that Late Woodland cultural traditions persisted into the 1500s in most areas of the region. Such findings corroborate Indian oral testimony affirming the antiquity of their occupation in their historic homelands. Several scholars believe that linguistic evidence suggesting close relationships between Delaware, Nanticoke, and Powhatan languages further confirms in situ hypotheses (Fiedel 1987; Goddard 1978a; Luckenbach, Clark, and Levy 1987).

Not all evidence supports these ideas. Many Delawares believe that their ancestors came from the west in recent times (Heckewelder 1819). Nanticoke oral literature states that their ancestors split from the Delawares and moved south some years before Europeans first sailed into the Chesapeake. Other records tell of further separations. In 1660, for example, the principal Piscataway *tayac* (their word for chief) reckoned that by 1636 thirteen generations of chiefs had passed away since an ancestor from the eastern shore moved west to the Potomac Valley (Feest 1978a; Merrell 1979).

Some archaeological evidence supports migration theories. Schultz ceramics found in large and densely occupied townsites located in or near the remains of smaller and less densely inhabited localities occupied by people making Shenks Ferry pottery, for example, are regarded as evidence of the movement of people later known as Susquehannocks from the northern part of the Susquehanna Valley to its lowermost reaches

during latter decades of the 1500s. Discoveries of snow whelks found only in coastal waters south of Delaware Bay in sites stretching from the Susquehanna and Monongahela Valleys northward to Ontario and the lower Great Lakes, for their part, are thought to represent physical evidence of the exchange network in the region chronicled by later colonial observers.

Known distributions of distinctive sand- or crushed-quartz-tempered Potomac Creek wares suggest somewhat earlier population movements. First found in Late Woodland sites along the Potomac and Rappahannock River fall lines, Potomac Creek wares came to dominate ceramic assemblages from upper tidewater locales farther down both rivers by the fourteenth century. Archaeologists finding such wares in places like the Accokeek Creek and Saint Mary's City National Historic Landmarks believe that they represent pottery made by the immediate ancestors of historically chronicled Doeg, Nacotchtanke (also known as Anacostia), Potomac, and Piscataway (known to the Iroquois as the Conoy) people.

Archaeologists contrasting known distributions of sites containing Potomac Creek and Shenks Ferry pottery suggest that people making the latter wares may have entered the lower Susquehanna Valley from the south sometime during the late 1300s. Discoveries of small numbers of Potomac Creek potsherds in somewhat later sites on Chesapeake Bay's eastern shore suggest subsequent northeastward movements of Potomac Creek people, pots, or design concepts.

Other data support in situ hypotheses. Farther south, for example, excavations of deposits dominated by Cashie-Branchville wares in sites along the Nottoway and Meherrin Rivers in southeastern Virginia suggest that their historically chronicled occupants had been living in this area since the late 1300s. Discoveries of assemblages dominated by Townsend-series wares in large, densely occupied locales containing many pits and other storage features in sites dating from 1000 to 1600, for their part, suggest that the ancestors of Tockwoghs, Assateague, Choptank, Pocomoke, and other people later collectively known as Nanticokes had been living on the Delmarva Peninsula for several hundred years when Potomac Creek pots, people, and ideas first appeared in the area sometime between 1350 and 1400.

Other discoveries of Townsend-ware-dominated assemblages in often densely occupied sites along the lower Chesapeake Bay drainage indicate that ancestors of historically chronicled Powhatan people and their neighbors also had been living in region during Late Woodland times. Farther north, stylistically similar Riggins or Minguannan wares dominate ceramic assemblages found in small, dispersed contemporary sites generally lacking pits and other storage features in the lower Delaware Valley. These diagnostic markers are associated with people belonging to historic Delaware or Lenape communities. Similar stylistic continuity has been observed in ceramic and settlement patterns discerned in Munsee Country sites.

Archaeologists have recovered a wide range of information on health, life expectancy, and biological community structure from human burials found at various places throughout the region. Although evidence of arthritis and peri-odontal disease occurs with some frequency, none of these burials contains clearly identifiable evidence of historically chronicled epidemic diseases like smallpox.

The fragmentary nature of human burial data also limits the ability of scholars to estimate total population numbers or densities. Some scholars upstreaming from early–seventeenth-century written records believe that as many as fifty thousand to one hundred thousand people may have lived in the region during the late 1500s (Dobyns 1983). Others believe that native populations were much smaller at the time. Scholars like E. Randolph Turner III, for example, have yet to find convincing evidence showing that more than thirteen thousand people lived on lands within the bounds of the Powhatan chiefdom in 1607 (Turner 1982).

As in the north, relations between Indians and Europeans began when voyagers from France, Spain, England, and other western European countries first traveled to the region during the early decades of the sixteenth century. As mentioned earlier, Giovanni da Verrazzano's journal of his 1524 voyage remains the earliest known written account documenting direct contact between Europeans and Indians along the Middle Atlantic coast or elsewhere in the Northeastern United States. Other sources note that Spaniards periodically ventured north from Florida along the coast and into the interior (P. Hoffman 1990; Hudson 1990; Quinn, Quinn, and Hillier 1979). Several sources mention recorded and unrecorded voyages of other Europeans to Chesapeake Bay during these years (Quinn, Quinn, and Hillier 1979; Pendergast 1991a). Many particulars of more recently documented Indian oral narratives recounting initial encounters with Europeans resemble those chronicled in early written reports.

Documents reporting early contacts in tidewater Virginia often record forcible abductions of children. One of these, a boy given the name Don Luis by his captors, was taken to Spain in 1559 or 1560. Like Squanto, the resourceful Don Luis also managed to find his way home. Catechized by Catholic priests, he subsequently guided a group of Jesuit missionaries back to the James River to a place near modern Yorktown, Virginia, called Ajacan in 1570. Rejoining his people shortly after his arrival, he subsequently led an attack that destroyed the mission settlement in February 1571 (Gradie 1988; P. Hoffman 1990; Lewis and Loomie 1953; Quinn, Quinn, and Hillier 1979).

Several Indians were killed or carried off during a subsequent reprisal raid on the James River towns led by Florida governor-general Pedro Menendez de Aviles. Far from their centers of settlement in the Caribbean, the Spanish did not attempt to reestablish another mission in the area.

Later well-known English attempts to colonize the region from their base on the North Carolina shore at Roanoke after 1584 also failed. Despite these failures, Europeans continued to sail to the coast throughout the 1500s. Searching for a way west to China, they traded with Indian people along the coast and raided their settlements for booty, provisions, and slaves. Although some may have stayed for months at a time, no Europeans settled permanently along the coast until Virginia Company colonists established Jamestown along the lower

reaches of James River in 1607 (Fausz 1985; D. Quinn 1985; Quinn, Quinn, and Hillier 1979).

Scholars presently do not fully understand the effects of these early contacts on Middle Atlantic native people or their communities. Not so long ago, for example, most scholars believed that historically chronicled, centrally directed coalitions such as the Powhatan, Piscataway, and Potomac chiefdoms were formed in response to European contact. More recently, scholars challenging this viewpoint are using growing bodies of archaeological data to show that the inclination to form chiefdoms may have first emerged locally during earlier Late Woodland times (Binford 1991; Potter 1993; Rountree 1989, 1990; Turner 1985).

Archaeologists also continue to debate whether or not long-distance exchange networks associated with chiefdoms existed during the 1500s. Glass beads, metal hoops and spirals, and other European imports believed to date to the earliest years of the Historic Contact period have been found in sites in Ontario and western New York. Archaeologists explaining the sources of these objects have long thought that Indian people acquired these goods from French or Basque mariners known to have visited the Saint Lawrence during the 1500s (Heidenreich 1971; Trigger 1980; Turgeon 1990).

Noting the absence of materials of European origin in Saint Lawrence Iroquoian sites, archaeologists James W. Bradley (1987a) and James F. Pendergast (1989, 1991a, 1992b) believe that discoveries of snow whelks from southeastern Atlantic shores in these sites constitute evidence of a late–sixteenth-century exchange network extending up the Susquehanna, Potomac, Monongahela, Allegheny, and Genesee Rivers. Contrasting the Ontario glass bead samples with others found in well-dated Iroquois sites, archaeologist William R. Fitzgerald (1990) believes that such regional exchange networks do not predate 1600. Contrasting these data with archival evidence, archaeologist James T. Herbstritt (1984) suggests that this exchange network only achieved regional significance after the 1630s.

Although the routes and relative time depths of exchange networks remain subjects of scholarly debate, few investigators doubt that such networks existed during the sixteenth century. And wherever they existed, such exchange networks probably served as effective avenues for transmitting the new ideas, goods, and diseases brought by Europeans visiting Atlantic shores.

The initial impact of these new ideas, goods, and diseases on Middle Atlantic Indians is neither fully known nor entirely understood. Several early Historic Contact period documents and many later Indian oral narratives record changing beliefs as they report on the effects of devasting epidemics. Records documenting numerous epidemic episodes in more northerly reaches of the region are preserved in written reports dating to the seventeenth and eighteenth centuries. Changes in burial practices observed in many sites, for their part, almost certainly reflect shifting meanings and patterns of belief.

Some investigators familiar with these data think that new diseases introduced by explorers probably ravaged Indian communities throughout the region during the 1500s. Although many scholars have looked for hard evidence of such contagions, none have yet found unequivocal documentation of their presence in sixteenth century Middle Atlantic communities. Tangible evidence revealing what Indian people thought or felt about the new European presence in the region also continues to elude investigators.

Scholars are working to develop new techniques capable of retrieving such information. Many, for example, are seeking ways to detect presently unrecognizable traces of damage caused by epidemic disease in bones of people interred in the many remaining gravesites preserved in the region. Such techniques have the potential to shed crucial new light on still poorly known aspects of Indian ways of life and death along the sixteenth-century Middle Atlantic coast.

THE SEVENTEENTH CENTURY

All evidence suggests that life began to change dramatically in Indian communities throughout the region after Europeans began establishing their first successful permanent settlements at various locales along the Middle Atlantic coast during the first decades of the seventeenth century. In the south, English colonists began settling at Jamestown, Virginia, in 1607. Both Indian and European sources confirm that relations between natives and newcomers around the new colony began uneasily. Searching for gold, slaves, or food, Virginians alternately tried to impress, beguile, and intimidate Indian neighbors. Crosses marked on John Smith's map of Virginia reflect the rapid rate of documented English penetration into the region by 1612.

Alarmed by the rapidity and rapacity of English penetration and increasingly certain of English intentions to drive their people from their homes, Powhatan leaders subsequently launched a series of three wars against the invaders between 1609 and 1646. Whether Powhatans saw themselves as equally matched combatants (Gleach 1992; Lurie 1959; Rountree 1990) or as oppressed freedom-fighters struggling against foreign domination (Fausz 1981, 1985), they were devastated by these struggles. Forced to sue for peace on English terms, they were ultimately compelled to acknowledge foreign sovereignty and move onto small, provincially supervised reservations.

Those not willing to live under such conditions, like many Nansemond and Weyanoke people from the James River Valley, moved southwest toward the Carolina border. Many of these people settled among Iroquoian-speaking neighbors living in the Nottoway and Meherrin Valleys. Others moved farther west to the towns of Occaneechi and other Siouian-speaking people in the piedmont.

Ironically, many of these people came to depend upon colonial assistance as native neighbors, hostile European settlers, and Iroquois and Cherokee raiders attacked their settlements. Formally submitting to provincial authority, these displaced people settling along the Virginian frontier helped defend the colony against incursions from the south and west.

Violence also often marked intercultural relations farther north in the Delaware and Hudson Valleys. Delaware-speaking Siconeysinck people, for example, obliterated the first Dutch colony established in their territories at a place named Swanendael near Lewes, Delaware, on the shores of Delaware Bay in 1632. The tempo of violence increased as Delaware people found themselves under attack by Susquehannocks anxious to dominate access to Dutch, English, and Swedish trading posts soon built farther upriver.

Using firearms obtained by exchanging pelts secured from northern Indian trading partners at these posts, the Susquehannocks drove the Delawares into the swampy pinelands east of the Delaware River. Farther south, Susquehannock warriors began their struggle with Maryland settlers and their Piscataway allies for control of the Chesapeake Bay trade in 1642.

Many Delawares devastated by Susquehannock attacks and ravaged by epidemic disease moved farther north to Raritan and Navesink lands nearer the center of Dutch colonial settlement around New York Harbor. The Dutch had established their first permanent posts in their new colony in 1626. Primarily interested in trade, they soon established other posts in an area stretching from the Connecticut River to Delaware Bay.

Open conflict with Dutch settlers broke out in 1640 after a series of unprovoked attacks in the area around the colony's main settlement at New Amsterdam at the southern tip of Manhattan Island. Although treaties temporarily ended hostilities for a time, fighting between Dutch settlers and Indian people in the Delaware and Munsee Countries continued to flare at various places in the Hudson Valley until the English captured New Netherland in 1664.

Violence also continued to flare farther south. Susquehannock warriors, for example, continued their war against the Piscataways and their Maryland clients until 1652. Other conflicts soon threatened as Wicomisse people driven south by Susquehannock attacks failed to get along with their new Maryland neighbors. Maryland authorities finally called on the Susquehannocks to drive them away in 1669, and many Wicomisses were killed as Susquehannock warriors mounted assaults on their settlements. Captured Wicomisse people were sold to the Marylanders, who then deported them to Barbados as slaves. Their community scattered, the few Wicomisse people avoiding capture settled in nearby Indian communities or moved elsewhere.

Weakened by losses caused by epidemic disease and these and other wars, the Susquehannocks were unable to refuse Maryland's demand that they relocate themselves closer to the center of the colony in 1675. Abandoning their main town along the Susquehanna, most of these people moved to the site of an old Piscataway fort on the banks of the Potomac River at the present Accokeek Creek National Historic Landmark.

They soon found themselves besieged by a large force of Virginian and Maryland settlers. Managing to escape after settlers murdered five of their chiefs at a parley, Susquehannocks accompanied by Doeg and other Indian neighbors fled to Occaneechi territory in southern Virginia.

Intent on vengeance, Susquehannock war parties ravaged Virginian frontier settlements. Alarmed by these raids and concerned by news of a general war with Indian people in New England, roving gangs of settlers resentful of the power and wealth of Virginia planters

and angered by what they regarded as the autocratic rule of royal governor William Berkeley and his retainers allied themselves with a charismatic local planter named Nathaniel Bacon, who promised power and vengeance. Unable to bring the Susquehannocks to battle, Bacon's men instead attacked the Occaneechis; large numbers of Virginia's Indians were killed before royal authorities restored order in 1676.

Piscataway and other Potomac Valley Indians joined English settlers in their war against the Susquehannocks. Seeking their own vengeance, Susquehannock warriors living with the Senecas joined a war party that forced the Piscataways to take refuge in a fort located in their marshy refuge in Zachiah Swamp during the summer of 1681. Taking nineteen prisoners, the raiders soon broke off their attack and withdrew.

Many Susquehannock people probably were among the large group of emigrants from Seneca Country who subsequently established a new community at Conestoga in the midst of the former Susquehannock heartland in Lancaster County sometime around 1690. Claiming sovereignty over the Susquehanna Valley, Iroquois confederacy sachems dominated Conestoga town affairs. They invited Delaware, Nanticoke, Piscataway, Potomac, Saponi, and other displaced Indians to settle nearby. Then, using these towns as springboards for attacks against Catawba, Cherokee, and other Indian enemies to the south, they turned the Susquehanna Valley into a frontier buffer zone, securing their borders against southern Indian counterattacks and European expansion from Pennsylvania, Maryland, and Virginia.

Iroquois strategy was facilitated by Bacon's Rebellion and other wars that depopulated vast areas of the region. Combined with disease, deportation, and migration, these wars had reduced Middle Atlantic Indian population by 90 percent by the end of the century.

Europeans were not immediately able to take advantage of the opportunities presented by the decline of native populations. Although large numbers of European people migrated to the region, the total number of settlers at first rose only slowly. Many writers have made much of war as a factor that restricted colonial population growth. Extant records, however, indicate that relatively few settlers were killed by Indian people. The high death rates are more easily laid to poor health. Unable to adjust easily to local climatic conditions, many settlers were carried off by disease and malnutrition during their first years of "seasoning" in the region. Fewer than thirteen thousand of the tens of thousands of colonists known to have settled around Chesapeake Bay during the first decades of colonization, for example, were still alive by 1650. Of these people, less than a thousand were of African origin or descent.

This situation changed as the pace of European colonization quickened during the middle decades of the century. Virginia and Maryland expanded rapidly. European population along the Hudson River also grew in the years following the English conquest in 1664. New settlements along the lower Delaware River Valley founded by Quakers like Richard Fenwick and William Penn increased the number of newcomers settling in the region after the defeat of the Susquehannocks and their Indian allies in 1675. Colonial population in the region had increased to more than 125,000 by 1700. Nearly two-thirds of the twenty thousand African people enumerated in this total lived in Maryland and Virginia.

Overwhelmed by this influx of new settlers, the total Middle Atlantic Indian population had dropped to less than a few thousand by the end of the century. Wars of extermination, epidemic disease, and mass deportations virtually annihilated many native communities. Devastated and dispossessed, large numbers of Munsee, Delaware, Nanticoke, and Piscataway people surviving such disasters moved west across the fall line into territory claimed by the Iroquois. Those remaining along the coast were forced to submit to colonial control. Like the Powhatans, nearly all were confined to reservations or driven to remote pine barrens, swamplands, or mountain valleys.

No matter where they lived, Indian people staying on ancestral lands were forced to endure growing hostility and deprivation. Most missionary projects ostensibly established to help Indian people did little to alleviate their suffering. Several early missionary enterprises, like the Henrico plan to establish an Indian school in Virginia, were actually little more than fund-raising schemes providing few, if any, benefits to native people (Axtell 1985; Jennings 1975).

Other missionary efforts were inspired by less mercenary motivations. Jesuit priests opening missions along the Potomac River in 1642 worked to establish strong economic and political relationships with Piscataway, Potomac, and other nearby Indian people. Attacked by Susquehannock raiders and suppressed by Protestant authorities, Jesuits, and the Franciscans who followed them, represented the only active missionaries among Middle Atlantic Indian people during the seventeenth century.

Although Indians found themselves increasingly drawn into the colonial cash economy, few had opportunities to establish dependable sources of income. Provincial authorities occasionally hired them as guides, messengers, interpreters, and warriors. Royal governors, for their part, distributed food and presents at treaty conferences and other meetings. Unwilling to depend upon such uncertain expressions of largesse, increasing numbers of Indian people worked as servants and laborers for cash or goods.

Rapacious settlers increasingly took advantage of their Indian neighbors. Many used liquor to pry land and peltry from their owners. Impoverished and dispossessed by settlers, most of the few Munsee, Delaware, Nanticoke, and Piscataway people remaining along the coast had finally joined friends and relatives living in exile farther north or west by 1700. Those refusing to leave their homelands struggled to live unobtrusively amid the hundreds of thousands of new immigrants from Europe and Africa who flooded into the region during the 1700s.

THE EIGHTEENTH CENTURY

Only a fraction of the precontact Indian population remained along the Middle Atlantic coast at the turn of the century. As in the north, most people choosing to live in their own communities had to settle in reservations or remote backcountry lots. Hemmed in on the west by Iroquois sachems closely aligned with provincial governments, Middle Atlantic native people were not able to play off contending adversaries in the manner so effectively used by other Indian communities in places along the heavily contested frontier separating the French colonies from New England, New York, and Pennsylvania. Instead, Middle Atlantic Indian peoples found themselves pressed between powerful nations intent upon their subjugation and relocation.

Iroquois diplomats persisted in their claim that they had the sole right to represent all but the southernmost Middle Atlantic Indians in negotiations with Anglo-American colonists. Determined to prevent British penetration of their exposed southern frontier, the Iroquois continued to relocate dispossessed Middle Atlantic Indians along the Susquehanna Valley.

British colonists, for their part, did what they could to fully exploit their technological and numerical advantages as they consolidated control over the coast. Total colonial population in the region rose to more than 560,000 during the first half of the century. More than one-quarter of these people were of African origin. In Maryland and Virginia alone, Africans came to constitute nearly 40 percent of the total population; nearly all of them were slaves.

By 1780 colonial population in the Middle Atlantic colonies had grown to more than 1,230,000. Only a small fraction of these people lived along the frontier west of the fall line. The rest resided on plantations and homesteads or in towns and cities on the coastal plain. By now nearly 350,000 of these people had been brought forcibly from Africa or were descendants of earlier African captives. As they had earlier in the century, most African American people lived among Europeans and native people along the Chesapeake coastal plains. European colonists made up the majority of the population settling in burgeoning urban centers like New York, Philadelphia, Annapolis, and Williamsburg. Few such centers developed in the rural plantation country of Virginia, where many Europeans found themselves living among black majorities.

Most Indian people remaining along the coast also lived in rural areas. After 1700 many of these people established close relations with European and African neighbors. As in the north, they continued to adapt many of their new neighbors' tools, customs, and ideas to their own purposes. No longer able to maintain established subsistence economies, most worked to earn their living as laborers, farmhands, and servants.

Nearly all of these people took European names. Most also joined Christian congregations. As their own numbers dwindled, many married Africans, native people from other communities, or Europeans. Some children from these mixed marriages moved among non-Indians, while others remained on their increasingly smaller reservations. The Pamunkey Indian community in Virginia represents one of the few reservations to survive to the present day.

Most surviving Munsee, Delaware, Nanticoke, Piscataway, or Saponi people were living farther north and west by the 1740s. Many Meherrin, Nottoway, and other Indian people from southern and western parts of Virginia, for their part, had moved south and west by this time. Only Chesapeake Bay Algonquian people managed to remain on ancestral lands in any numbers. Others who tried

to remain sometimes met a cruel fate. All Nanzatico reservation people above the age of twelve, for example, were enslaved for a period of years, deported to Antigua, and forbidden to return after several community members murdered local settlers in 1704. Their children were bound out as indentured servants to colonists. Today, intact archaeological deposits preserved within the Camden National Historic Landmark represent the only known body of physical evidence capable of enlarging upon the scant body of written documentation chronicling the final years of the ill-fated Nanzatico community.

Other Indian peoples remaining on ancestral lands were compelled to move to reservations after selling or ceding the last of their territories by the 1740s. Those refusing to sell held on for a time along the fringes of frontier settlement in places like Minisink territory along the upper Delaware River, Pennsylvania's Tulpehocken Valley, Fort Christanna on the southern Virginia frontier, or the Susquehanna Valley. Increasingly pressed to move on by provincial administrators, land speculators, and settlers flooding into their territories, Indian residents could do little more than slow expansion into their remaining lands.

Most resisted peacefully by selling as little as possible to prospective purchasers. Others, like the Delaware sachem Nutimus, vigorously challenged more controversial land appropriations such as the "Walking Purchase" signed in 1736 and carried out in 1737. Embittered by his failure to stop the seizure of their lands, Nutimus's people subsequently joined the Shawnees and their allies in a general attempt to roll back the tide of settlement when the Seven Years' War broke out between Great Britain and France in 1755.

Ravaging settlements of Europeans living on still-contested lands in the Susquehanna and Delaware Valleys, Delaware, Munsee, and other warriors controlled the western approaches to the French forts in the Ohio Valley. Anxious to end attacks on their frontier communities and to open a way west, British authorities concluded a series of treaties with their Delaware and Munsee adversaries at Crosswicks, New Jersey, and Easton, Pennsylvania, between 1756 and 1758. Adjudicating outstanding grievances, the British established a reservation for the Delawares of southern New Jersey at Edgepillock and purchased all but Indian hunting and fishing rights to northern New Jersey for one thousand Spanish dollars.

In return, Indian belligerents made peace with their erstwhile enemies and stepped aside as British soldiers and colonial militia marching from Philadelphia drove the French from the Upper Ohio Country by 1760. British troops and their Indian allies burned towns of any Indians refusing to come to terms with them along their line of march. The majority of the inhabitants of these towns along the Susquehanna and Allegheny Rivers moved farther westward as tens of thousands of settlers flooded across the Blue Mountains. Small groups of Indians who continued to live among the settlers, like the Conestogas, were murdered by roving frontier gangs reminiscent of Bacon's rebels.

Unable or unwilling to stop these attacks, provincial officials urged Indian people to move farther west. Most left the region. By 1765, only a few Indian communities remained in the region east of the Appalachian Mountains. Most of these communities were located on the few small reservation tracts not sold or abandoned by their inhabitants. Other peoples, like many Nanticokes, Piscataways, and Doegs, continued to occupy small tracts on or near ancestral lands. Unknown numbers of others lived with non-Indians in the region's towns, farms, and cities.

No matter where they lived, most of these people found their lives, lands, and labor regulated by colonists enforcing local and provincial laws. As elsewhere, Indian people received different degrees of justice in different provincial courts. Lower-level courts rarely found for the few Indian people admitted to their chambers, but some higher-level administrators enforced laws protecting Indians from abuse by settlers. In 1766, for example, Governor William Franklin of New Jersey saw to it that two of three settlers found guilty of raping and killing two Delaware women were executed. Neither Franklin nor most other colonial officials, though, openly supported Indian land claims against Europeans in the region.

Most Delaware people had abandoned the region by the first decades of the 1800s. Farther south, a few hundred Nanticokes, Pamunkeys, Chickahominys, Mattaponis, and Nansemonds lived almost unnoticed by provincial authorities on and around small reservations in Virginia and Maryland (Cissna 1986; Porter 1986). Wherever they lived, few of these people forgot their Indian heritage, and today their descendants preserve ancestral customs and beliefs in small communities and urban centers across the region.

SOURCES

Key sources presenting overviews of Indian life in various parts of this region include Binford (1991), Fausz (1985, 1988), Feest (1978a, 1978b), Flannery (1939), Gleach (1992), Goddard (1978b), Jennings (1975, 1984, 1988a), Kraft (1975a, 1975b, 1977, 1978, 1986, 1989a, 1989b), Pendergast (1991a), Potter (1982, 1989, 1993), Rountree (1989, 1990), Turner (1985), and Weslager (1972).

Articles appearing in Custer (1986c) provide the most comprehensive, up-to-date survey of Middle Atlantic Late Woodland archaeology. A collection of papers first presented in a symposium sponsored by the Council of Virginia Archaeologists and the Archaeological Society of Virginia in 1991 synthesize much of what is known about seventeenth-century Historic Contact period archaeology in Virginia (Reinhart and Pogue 1993). MacCord (1989a) provides a useful status report on the state of contact archaeology in Virginia. Dissertations by Potter (1982) and Turner (1976) also contain vital information. A succinct summary of Virginia Indian archaeology and history written for general audiences may be found in Egloff and Woodward (1992).

Useful documentary studies of early European penetration in the region may be consulted in Morison (1971) and D. Quinn (1977). The abortive Jesuit mission is discussed in Gradie (1988) and Lewis and Loomie (1953). Fausz (1985) and D. Quinn (1985) provide succinct accounts of relations between Indian people and early English explorers and colonists from the founding of Roanoke in 1585 to the establishment of Maryland in 1634.

European observers—Virginians Robert Beverley (1947), John Smith (Barbour 1986), and William Strachey (1953) and Dutch mariner and patroon David Petersz de Vries (in Jameson 1909 and Myers 1912)—recorded many aspects of seventeenth-century Middle Atlantic Indian life. Other accounts may be found in volumes edited by Hall (1910), Myers (1912), and Tyler (1907). Additional primary documentation appears in Browne et al. (1883–1970), Gehring (1977, 1981), Hazard et al. (1852–1949), McIlwaine (1918–1919, 1925–1945), Myers (1912), Quinn, Quinn, and Hillier (1979), and W. Robinson (1983a, 1983b).

Accounts of Bacon's Rebellion may be found in Jennings (1984), Webb (1984), and Washburn (1957).

MUNSEE
COUNTRY

Munsee Country stretches across the lower Hudson and upper Delaware river valleys. Bordered by the Catskill Mountains on the north and the Berkshire foothills on the east, this area extends from the lower Hudson Valley and western Long Island across southeastern New York and northern New Jersey to northwestern Pennsylvania above the Forks of the Delaware at present-day Easton.

THE SIXTEENTH CENTURY

Extant archaeological evidence indicates that Late Woodland lifeways similar to those documented in sixteenth-century Munsee Country archaeological sites first developed in this area between A.D. 900 and 1000. Discoveries of triangular, chipped-stone projectile points and other stone, bone, horn, and shell implements show that these Late Woodland people followed a way of life centering upon hunting, fishing, plant collecting, and, where possible, shell-fishing and plant cultivation.

Noting the low productive potential of many soils in the area, the scant nature of known deposits containing remains of corn, beans, or squash, and other nega-

tive evidence, several scholars believe that most people living in this area did not cultivate food plants before the European entrée (Ceci 1979; Becker 1987). Other scholars contest these assertions by emphasizing analyses of known discoveries of carbonized cultivated plant remains and results of pedological analyses establishing the presence of arable soils in various parts of Munsee Country (Kraft 1986; A. Silver 1981).

Pottery found at many locales in this area shows that the inhabitants of Munsee Country began producing a distinctive assemblage of ceramics during the final centuries of the Late Woodland period. Many of these people made grit-tempered globular, collared wares decorated with incised geometric linear designs similar to others found farther north in the Hudson and Mohawk Valleys (Kraft 1975b). Collar decorations of many of these pots display distinctive "ladder" motifs generally associated with pottery made by people living along the Hudson and upper Delaware river valleys (Bender and Brumbach 1992; Brumbach 1975; Brumbach and Bender 1986; Diamond 1991). Many potters in more southerly portions of Munsee Country

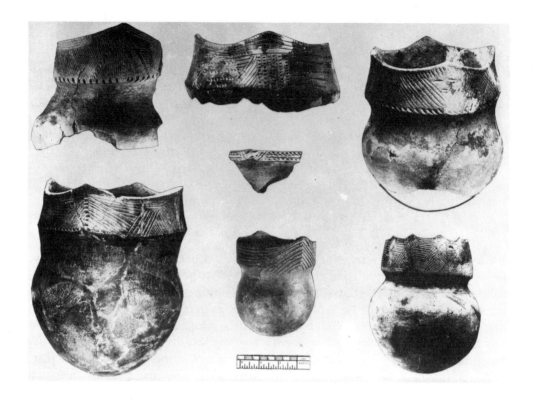

Minisink-phase pottery assemblage. All specimens are Munsee Incised wares except the center rim sherd, which is an example of Otstungo Notched ware. *Courtesy Herbert C. Kraft, Seton Hall University Museum.*

also produced Bowman's Brook, Overpeck, and other collarless conoidal wares more closely patterned after pottery used by people living along the Atlantic coast (Jacobson 1980; C. Smith 1950).

Other archaeological evidence indicates that people living in Munsee Country generally constructed and lived in longhouses similar to those built by their more northerly Mahican and Mohawk neighbors. Unlike their contemporaries living farther north and west, these people evidently did not live in large, fortified towns located in easily defensible uplands.

Systematic excavations conducted by avocational archaeologist George Van Sickle at the Wyncoop Farm/Grapes site near Kingston in Ulster County, New York, in anticipation of its destruction by a since-canceled road-construction project, for example, unearthed firepits, several human burials, and large numbers of post molds tracing the living floor and walls of a single round-ended longhouse measuring 110 feet by 25 feet (Van Sickle 1990). This structure's floor plan closely resembles the somewhat smaller and older longhouse post-mold pattern excavated by Herbert C. Kraft at the Miller Field site in the nearby upper Delaware River Valley (Kraft 1975b, 1986).

MAP 17: MUNSEE COUNTRY

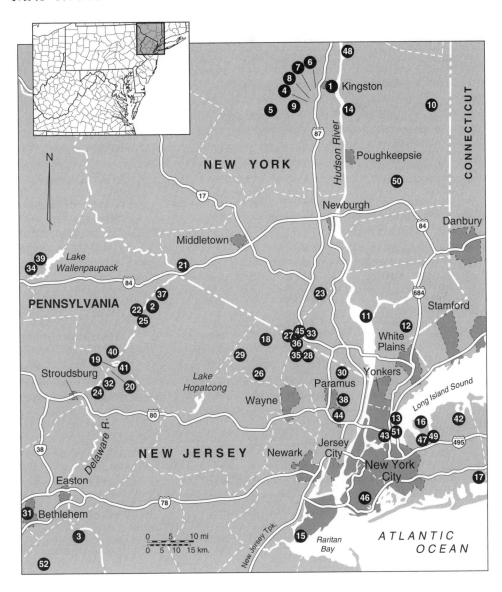

N

NEW YORK

48

6
7
8
4
5
9

1   Kingston

14

10

CONNECTICUT

87

Hudson River

Poughkeepsie

50

Newburgh

84

Danbury

Middletown

17

39
34

Lake
Wallenpaupack

21

84

PENNSYLVANIA

37
22 2
25

23

684

Stamford

11

12

White
Plains

18   27 45 33
36
35 28

29

26

40
19   41
32
24   20

Lake
Hopatcong

Wayne

30

Yonkers

Paramus

38

44

Stroudsburg

80

Delaware R.

NEW JERSEY

Newark

Jersey
City

13
51

16

42

47 49

495

43

New York
City

17

38

Easton

78

46

31 Bethlehem

3

52

0   5   10 mi
0   5 10 15 km.

15

Raritan
Bay

ATLANTIC
OCEAN

Long Island Sound

New Jersey Tpk.

Map 17 Historic Contact Sites

Map Number	Site Name	County	State	Date	NR	Source
1	Hendrickson	Ulster	NY	1400s–1600s		Eisenberg 1989
2	Minisink NHL	Sussex	NJ	1500s–1750s	X	Kraft 1977, 1978, 1986;
	Bell-Browning-Blair (28SX19)	Pike	PA			Marchiando 1972; Puniello and Williams 1978
	Bell-Philhower (28SX29)					
	Bena Kill-Mine Road (28SX256)					
	Manna (36PI4)					
	Minisink (28SX48)					
	Pratschler (28SX255)					
3	Overpeck (36BU5)	Bucks	PA	1550–1600		Fehr and Staats 1980; PASS
	Hurley Flats Complex	Ulster	NY	1500s–1600s		Diamond 1991; Van Sickle 1990
4	Wyncoop Farm/Grapes					
5	Beaver Lake Rock Shelter					
6	Spy					
7	Gill 1 and 2					
8	Hurley Rock Shelter					
9	Tongore Road					
10	Amenia	Dutchess	NY	1600s		Diamond 1992
11	Croton Point (NYSM 6868–6869)	Westchester	NY	1600s		M. R. Harrington 1925; NYSMAS
12	Finch Rock Shelter	Westchester	NY	1600s		M. R. Harrington 1909
13	Kaeser (NYSM 725)	Bronx	NY	1600s		NYSMAS; Rothschild and Lavin 1977
14	Shagabak Rock Shelter	Dutchess	NY	1600s		Diamond 1992
15	Ward's Point NHL	Richmond	NY	1600s	X	Jacobson 1980
16	Motts Point (IBM)	Nassau	NY	1600s(?)		Ceci 1982a; Salwen 1962
17	Fort Massapeag NHL	Nassau	NY	1630–1675	X	C. Smith 1950; Solecki 1991
18	Monksville Reservoir (28PA136)	Passaic	NJ	1630–1680		Lenik and Ehrhardt 1986
19	Miller Field	Warren	NJ	1650–1674		Kraft 1972
20	Calno School Burial	Warren	NJ	1650–1700		Puniello and Williams 1978
21	Van Etten (NYSM 4377)	Orange	NY	1650–1700		Heye and Pepper 1915; NYSMAS
22	Zimmermann (36PI14)	Pike	PA	1660–1690		Werner 1972
23	Tiorati Rock Shelter (NYSM 581)	Orange	NY	1660–1760		Funk 1976; NYSMAS
24	Harry's Farm	Warren	NJ	1660–1776		Kraft 1975a
25	Friedman II	Sussex	NJ	1680–1710		Puniello and Williams 1978
26	Apshawa Rock Shelter	Passaic	NJ	1680s		Lenik 1989
27	Spring House Rock Shelter (NYSM 7911)	Rockland	NY	1680s		Lenik 1993
28	LaRoe-Van Horn House	Bergen	NJ	Early 1700s		Lenik 1989
29	Echo Lake	Passaic	NJ	1730s		Lenik 1976
30	Wilder Mons Kerk-Hoff	Bergen	NJ	1730s		Demarest 1975
31	Gemeinhaus NHL	Northampton	PA	1733–	X	NPS 1987
32	Pahaquarra	Warren	NJ	Mid-1700s		Baird 1987; Kraft 1976, 1986
33	Potake Pond	Rockland	NY	1700s		Lenik 1987
34	36WY44	Wayne	PA	1700s		PASS

Map Number	Site Name	County	State	Date	NR	Source
35	Darlington Rock House	Bergen	NJ	Historic		Heusser 1923
36	Darlington Rock Shelter	Bergen	NJ	Historic		Bischoff and Kahn 1979
37	Davenport	Sussex	NJ	Historic		Leslie 1968
38	David Demarest House	Bergen	NJ	Historic		Lenik 1985
39	Dayton Pond (36WY125)	Wayne	PA	Historic		PASS
40	Faucett (36PI13A)	Pike	PA	Historic		Moeller 1975
41	Mill Brook Findspot	Warren	NJ	Historic		Becker 1990
42	Muskeeta Cove	Nassau	NY	Historic		Salwen 1968
43	Old Ferry Point	Bronx	NY	Historic		Ceci 1977
44	Prospect Street	Bergen	NJ	Historic		Lenik 1989
45	Ramapo Rock Shelter (NYSM 586)	Rockland	NY	Historic		Funk 1976; NYSMAS
46	Ryders Pond (NYSM 7459)	Kings	NY	Historic		Lopez and Wisniewski 1972-1973; NYSMAS
47	Soundview	Nassau	NY	Historic		C. Smith 1950
48	South Cruger Island (NYSM 505 and 7079)	Dutchess	NY	Historic		NYSMAS; W. Ritchie 1958
49	Spring Lake	Nassau	NY	Historic	X	Weaver and Rennenkampf 1973
50	Sylvan Lake Rock Shelter (NYSM 5923)	Dutchess	NY	Historic	X	Funk 1976; NYSMAS; W. Ritchie 1958
51	Throgs Neck (NYSM 714-715)	Bronx	NY	Historic		NYSMAS; Skinner 1919
52	Vermuhlen (36BU20)	Bucks	PA	Historic		PASS

Analyses of evidence found at these and other sites containing radiocarbon-dated deposits and glass beads dating to the sixteenth century suggest that their occupants preferred to live in less-densely occupied unfortified settlements located on well-drained terraces away from main river courses (Kraft 1972, 1975a, 1976, 1977, 1978; Diamond 1991; Van Sickle 1990).

Artifacts excavated from these sites and contemporary deposits preserved at the Hendrickson, Overpeck, and Minisink National Historic Landmark locales further show that people living in Munsee Country during the 1500s also produced new types of clay pipes, tubular shell beads, and effigies in the shapes of birds, people, and other creatures. Archaeologists analyzing this particular configuration of settlement patterns, features, and artifacts have named it the "Minisink horizon" or "phase." Beginning in the mid-1400s, Minisink horizon lifeways continued generally unchanged even after brass or copper beads and triangular projectile points, glass beads, and other artifacts of European origin or made from European materials began appearing during the late–sixteenth century. Scholars noting this pattern of continuity believe that Minisink horizon people were direct ancestors of archivally chronicled Munsee Indians (Grumet 1991; Kraft 1977, 1978).

THE SEVENTEENTH CENTURY

At least twelve thousand Indian people were living in Munsee Country when Adriaen Block, Cornelis May, Henry Hudson, and other western European mariners recorded the earliest documented seventeenth-century visits to the area

Minisink Historic District National Historic Landmark

The Minisink Historic District encompasses 1,320 acres of federally owned land in the northern portion of the Delaware Water Gap National Recreation Area located in Sussex County, New Jersey, and Pike County, Pennsylvania. Seven archaeological sites and a standing structure preserved within district boundaries contain information capable of corroborating written records that document Minisink as a major center of an Indian social network stretching from the Connecticut to the Ohio river valleys. It was the most prominent and best-documented Munsee Indian community of its era, and the single most important Indian community in the upper Delaware River Valley during the Historic Contact period. Today, Minisink remains one of the most extensive, best preserved, and most intensively studied archaeological locales in the Northeast.

Minisink is situated in and around Minisink Island in a broad, lowland area encompassing the largest expanse of arable level soils in the otherwise-constricted Delaware River Valley north of the Water Gap. The area's deep, fertile soils, moderate climate, abundant flora and fauna, and strategic location at the junction of trails passing over one of the region's major rivers caused Minisink to become the community it was.

Archaeological sites here comprise an almost-continuous deposit extending from the New Jersey shoreline across Minisink Island to the bottomlands below the line of steep cliffs that parallel the river on the Pennsylvania side. Singularly dense deposits preserved within the Bell-Browning-Blair (28SX19), Bell-Philhower (28SX29), and Minisink (28SX48) sites in the southernmost portion of the New Jersey side of the district contain intact features that date from Late Woodland to early Historic Contact period times and are associated with the archivally chronicled Minisink Indian community.

Located in rugged interior uplands initially considered stony wastelands by Europeans, the Minisink community was rarely visited by colonists and was almost unknown to Europeans until the late 1600s. A brief journal entry written by New York frontier agent Arendt Schuyler in February 7, 1694, represents the earliest known European eyewitness account of the place. Contemporary documents indicate that Minisink became a refuge for displaced Hudson and Delaware Valley Indian people. Increasingly unable to make their living on the poor lands left to them, these people became nomads in their own homeland. Moving from place to place, many of them came to regard Minisink town as an important waystation in a network of highland Indian settlements that stretched from the Connecticut Valley to Ohio (Grumet 1991). Written accounts document population shifts ranging from a few score to several hundred people and attest to the mobility of Minisink community members.

No detailed description of the settlement survives. Archaeological evidence of dispersed settlement patterns uncovered in and around Minisink corroborate eyewitness accounts describing Minisink as a community of bark- or mat-covered longhouses scattered across Minisink Island and the adjacent New Jersey and Pennsylvania shores. Much of what exists in the way of descriptions of Minisink town appears in deeds and other records that document disputes between Europeans claiming

Minisink lands for themselves during the second quarter of the 1700s.

One of these documents, a December 28, 1730, deed from "Scyacop, Indian of Minissinck," to Johannes Westbrook conveying, for the sum of five pounds, title to a hundred acres of previously surveyed land at and around Westbrook's house and barn represents the earliest known direct evidence of European settlement at Minisink. The building cited in this deed is today known as the Westbrook-Bell House and is the oldest standing structure in the upper Delaware Valley.

Extant records show that Indian people continued to live alongside Westbrook and other Europeans moving to Minisink for many years. The archaeological remains of Fort Westbrook, a fortified stone house built near Westbrook's home, provides evidence of the deteriorating relations that finally led to open war in 1755 (J. Carr 1969). Unable to drive settlers away, most Minisink people joined Munsee friends and families, moving to the Ohio Valley after selling all but their hunting and fishing rights in northern New Jersey for a thousand Spanish dollars at the Treaty of Easton in 1758.

Minisink has been a focal point of archaeological interest since the nineteenth century. Local residents like Charles A. Philhower and Branchville physician Edward S. Dalrymple have collected large numbers of artifacts from Minisink site locales. Field crews financed by George G. Heye, founder of what has become the National Museum of the American Indian, discovered extensive deposits associated with what was thought to be the historic Munsee cemetery at Minisink in 1914. Building from the baseline established by Heye, William A. Ritchie (1949) and later Herbert C. Kraft found that the Munsee cemetery was in fact a substantial habitation area where Indian people had made their homes and buried their dead throughout the Late Woodland period.

Excavations were conducted between 1967 and 1975 by Kraft, W. Fred Kinsey III, Patricia Marchiando, Lorraine E. Williams, and others in response to the projected inundation of the area by the since-canceled Tocks Island Dam project. The archaeologists found that the Minisink Historic District still contained intact cultural resources capable of providing information relevant to outstanding questions on the structure and relationships of the historic Minisink community.

Wide-area excavations conducted by Kraft, for example, showed that Minisink was a dispersed community rather than a crowded, walled fortress. Intensively excavating pit features, New Jersey State Museum investigators led by Lorraine E. Williams (Puniello and Williams 1978; L. Williams, Puniello, and Flinn 1982) sought to develop new ceramic identification techniques capable of dating previously undatable deposits. Studying floral and faunal remains recovered during their excavations, they were able to identify evidence indicating that corn, bean, and squash cultivation assumed increasing importance at Minisink during the terminal Late Woodland and early Historic Contact periods.

Archaeological investigations also uncovered the intact foundations of Fort Westbrook (J. Carr 1969). Both this site and the Westbrook-Bell House have yielded, and retain the potential to yield, information on relations between Indians and early European settlers at Minisink, regional construction techniques, and seventeenth-century western European architectural styles and methods.

during the first decades of the 1600s. Written records left by these and other voyagers represent some of the only clearly identifiable evidence of the many Indian communities that once ringed the shores of New York Harbor, western Long Island, and the lower Hudson River.

European colonists moving to the area during the second quarter of the century recorded the existence of small settlements at coastal locales like Canarsie, Rockaway, Massapequa, and Matinecock on western Long Island. Other settlements farther inland were documented in the Esopus, Walkill, and Rondout Valleys in southeastern New York and the Passaic, Hackensack, Raritan, and Musconetcong drainages in northern New Jersey. Europeans visiting more distant locales during the latter decades of the century noted other communities along the Delaware River from the falls at Trenton north to Minisink territory.

Linguistic studies contrasting historic texts with modern field data indicate that most people living in this area spoke variants of the Munsee dialect of the Delaware language. Indian people speaking other languages settled in various parts of Munsee Country during the late 1600s. People from Mahican Country and the lower Connecticut Valley who spoke closely related Eastern Algonquian languages, for example, began moving to the upper Passaic Valley during the 1690s (Grumet 1988). Many of the hundreds of Shawnee people moving east to escape intensified fighting in the Ohio Valley brought on by King William's War settled at Pechoquealin, their name for the Delaware Water Gap, sometime after 1692.

The coming of these immigrants helped slow but did not stop Munsee population decline. Untold thousands died in the no fewer than seven epidemics known to have swept around and through Munsee territory from 1633 to 1691 (Grumet 1990). Hundreds of other people were killed in wars with settlers, Mahicans, and Mohawks that ravaged communities throughout the Hudson Valley at various times between 1640 and 1676 (Trelease 1960).

The fighting began when Dutch troops looking for European hog thieves on Staten Island attacked and massacred the residents of a nearby Raritan Indian town. Outraged by the unprovoked assault, Indian warriors allied with the Raritans launched a series of attacks that drove colonists from Staten Island and other outlying settlements around Manhattan. The scope of this conflict, known today as Governor Kieft's War after the Dutch governor whose troops attacked the Raritan town, continued to widen as Raritan warriors and their friends threatened other Dutch settlements. Enlisting the help of English settlers living in New Netherland, Munsee communities on Long Island and Westchester closely allied to the Dutch, and Mahicans from the upper Hudson Valley, Kieft ultimately launched a series of attacks against the Raritans.

The fighting ended briefly when Raritan leaders sued for peace in 1642, but less than a year later, another unprovoked Dutch massacre brought on a more deadly phase of fighting. Gradually involving every community in the area, the war devastated New Netherland. Most communities beyond the center of Dutch settlement were pillaged and burned. Munsee towns on Long Island and in modern-day Westchester County were attacked and destroyed. Hundreds of settlers and as many as a thousand Munsee people may have been killed before most of the exhausted combatants signed a treaty affirming the antebellum status quo at Fort Amsterdam on August 30, 1645 (Trelease 1960).

Unwilling to make peace, unreconciled Wiechquaesgeck refugees from the lower Hudson Valley who had moved to Raritan territory in the northern reaches of Delaware Country continued to carry on the struggle. Dutch records of the period repeatedly report attacks on travelers journeying across central New Jersey between Sandy Hook and the falls of the Delaware at Trenton. These attacks continued until Kieft's successor, Peter Stuyvesant, signed a separate peace with the Wiechquaesgecks in 1649.

Treaties brought a measure of peace to the area, but they did not correct the trade abuses and other problems that had caused the violence in the first place. A new struggle, today known as the Peach War, soon broke out.

Striking during the fall of 1655 while the province's troops were away reducing the Swedish settlements on the Delaware River, Munsee warriors and their allies attacked Dutch settlements throughout the Hudson Valley. The warriors claimed that they attacked because they were angered by a Dutch settler's murder of an Indian woman who was picking peaches from his orchard. Modern scholars now believe that forewarned Swedes may have encouraged their Munsee allies to launch a diversionary attack to draw off the Dutch invaders (Gehring 1981). This struggle and the Esopus Wars, fought from 1658 to 1664 between Esopus people and settlers desiring their broad fertile lands above the Hudson Highlands, devastated Indian communities throughout Munsee Country.

Thousands of Europeans poured into the area as these and other struggles caused Indian numbers to dwindle. Many brought African slaves to work land bought or seized from Indian people. Colonists expanding their settlements from centers such as New York, Kingston, Newark, and Philadelphia increasingly pressed Indian people farther into the interior toward the highland frontiers bordering Mohawk Country.

Munsee relations with their Mohawk and Mahican neighbors often were uneasy during this century. Mahican warriors evidently attacked lower Hudson Valley Munsee communities during the winter of 1643. Mohawk people, for their part, evidently struggled with Munsees, Mahicans, and colonists for control of the Long Island wampum trade vital to the early economies of the region.

Pressed by the Mohawks on one side and colonists on the other, coastal Munsee people had sold as much as 40 percent of their ancestral homeland and moved inland by 1700. Many of these people settled at Minisink towns on the upper Delaware River for a time before leaving for new homes farther west. Most Minisink settlers had moved along the upper branches of the Susquehanna to places like Wyoming, Wyalusing, Tioga, and Ochquaga by the early 1700s.

Substantial deposits documenting seventeenth-century Indian life in Munsee Country have been found at various locales. Particularly extensive bodies of evidence are preserved in intact deposits in the Minisink National Historic Landmark, Harry's Farm site, and other places in the upper Delaware Valley. Other sites document life along the coast. Two of these locales, the Ward's Point and Fort Massapeag National Historic Landmarks, contain particularly well preserved deposits. Artifacts and features found at Ward's Point on the southern end of Staten Island preserve a record of nearly continuous human occupation ranging from Early Archaic times 8,000 years ago to the early 1600s. Deposits preserved at Fort Massapeag document Indian occupation of a stockade built during the mid-seventeenth century on western Long Island.

European white-clay tobacco-smoking pipes; gun barrels, locks, shot, and flints; coins; mouth harps;' and other objects of European origin have been found with Indian ceramics and stone tools at other seventeenth-century sites in Munsee Country. Several deposits containing such assemblages have been found in Hurley Flats complex sites. Smaller or more fragmentary deposits have been found in open sites and rockshelters in the New York counties of Ulster, Dutchess, Putnam, and Orange, the Greater New York area, and the Delaware Water Gap locale. Archaeologist Edward J. Lenik (1993) has found particularly well preserved masses of animal bone fragments and shells in radiometrically dated stratified deposits containing aboriginal ceramics, a small glass bead, and a European white-clay tobacco pipe dating to the third quarter of the seventeenth century at the Spring House Rock Shelter in Rockland County, New York.

In contrast to the record in more northerly areas, mortuary sites constitute a small part of the archaeological record in Munsee Country. The Van Etten site represents the only currently identified locale in Munsee Country used solely as a cemetery. Grave shafts and pits found among pits used to store food and other items at sites like the Minisink and Ward's Point National Historic Landmarks, for their part, are believed to represent evidence of interments beneath or near house floors.

THE EIGHTEENTH CENTURY

Indian population in Munsee Country continued to drop precipitously during the first decades of the eighteenth century as recurring outbreaks of smallpox, measles, and other diseases took their toll. Finding themselves directly in the path of colonial expansion and increasingly unable to resist the demands of the growing number of settlers flooding their territories, many Indian people remaining in Munsee Country parted with their last lands and moved elsewhere. Others, less willing to abandon ancestral lands, worked to develop somewhat subtler solutions to their problems.

Many Indians forced to sell their lands moved among friends and kinsfolk in more remote or less desirable swamplands or mountain valleys. Discoveries of contact components at the Tiorati Rock Shelter, the Potake Pond site, the Wilder Mons Kerk-Hoff, and other sites located in hilly, inaccessible areas of southeastern New York and northern New Jersey corroborate written records documenting Munsee relocations to such places after being forced from portions of their homelands near centers of European expansion.

Such moves were a temporary expedient at best. Continuing pressure from settlers ultimately forced most of these people to move to more remote settlements in and around Minisink. Today sites preserved at Minisink contain the best-preserved body of deposits documenting eighteenth-century Indian occupation in the area. Other deposits possibly associated with Shawnee occupation at Pechoquealin have been found at the Harry's Farm site. The graves of a man, woman, and child accompanied by remains of a musket, a medal bearing King George II's likeness, and a wooden box containing glass beads and other ornaments have been found in intrusive burials dug into earlier deposits at the Pahaquarra site. Farther north, glass beads and other datable artifacts indicate that Indian people continued to use the Van Etten site above Port Jervis, New York, as a cemetery into the first decade of the eighteenth century.

Indian leaders living at Minisink and other towns tried to assure the security of followers remaining in Munsee Country by weaving together complex webs of protective, interlocking alliances. They dispatched delegations carrying wampum belts and requesting friendship and protection to the Iroquois capital at Onondaga and worked to recognize the power and influence of the Iroquois League without surrendering control over their own lives and fortunes. Meeting regularly with British authorities in Albany, Kingston, and New York City, Munsee leaders like Taphow, Joris, Ankerop, and Renap continued to support the Covenant Chain alliance that linked them with New York and the Iroquois League.

Munsee leaders further worked to widen their base of support by encouraging displaced Indian people to live among them. Some of these attempts, like Ankerop's effort to obtain the permission of Covenant Chain allies to resettle Tuscarora refugees from North Carolina in Esopus territory during the 1720s, did not succeed. Other efforts were more successful as immigration

Ward's Point Archeological Site National Historic Landmark

The Ward's Point Archeological Site is located in Tottenville in Conference House Park (City of New York Department of Parks and Recreation) in the borough of Staten Island, Richmond County, New York. Situated at the southwestern corner of Staten Island, Ward's Point site deposits lie atop a high sandy bluff that rises above the waters of lower New York Harbor where the Arthur Kill and the Raritan River flow into Raritan Bay.

Also called Burial Ridge, in recognition of the many graves of Indian people found at the site since workmen unearthed the first reported human interments in the area in 1858, Ward's Point is the largest, best preserved, and most intensively studied archaeological locale associated with Indian people in the metropolitan New York area. The area's physical setting calls to mind Aquehonga, a Munsee name for Staten Island thought to mean "at the end of the rise of the landscape." Upland portions of bluff deposits around Ward's Point generally are overlain by black humus topsoils that extend from two to fourteen inches beneath the surface. A nine- to 12-inch-thick brown-loam plow zone lies below this humus layer. The plow zone in turn is underlain by brown and yellow layers of sand.

Avocationists like William Blackie and Albert J. Anderson and professional archaeologists like Mark Raymond Harrington, George H. Pepper, and Alanson B. Skinner have excavated site deposits at Ward's Point since the late 1800s. Publicity surrounding their discoveries has secured the site's enduring reputation as New York City's largest Indian cemetery. Surveying extant field records of these and other investigators while conducting test excavations at the site in 1960, Illinois Department of Transportation archaeologist Jerome Jacobson (then a Columbia University graduate student) found that at least seventy-seven individual human interments and one hundred twenty-seven pit features had been reported at Ward's Point since 1858. He further concluded that an equal number of burials and features may have been encountered by people not leaving records of their investigations.

Scattered cultural debris dating from Early Archaic times to the present has been found amid dense masses of roots and accumulations of oyster, hard clam, and other shells in humus and plow-zone strata at Ward's Point. Pit, midden, hearth, and burial features lie atop or intrude into the upper portions of underlying sand subsoils. Features containing diagnostic artifacts primarily date to Early Archaic, Middle Woodland, Late Woodland, and early Historic Contact times.

Triangular stone projectile points chipped from argillaceous shales from Delaware Valley quarries have been discovered alongside Bowman's Brook and Overpeck stamped or cord-marked pottery in and near graves of individuals facing south and southwest. Such discoveries provide archaeological corroboration of contacts with Munsee-speaking people in central and northern New Jersey during Late Woodland times. Findings of stone tools made from Normanskill or Onondaga cherts in deposits containing Munsee-series incised and cord-marked collared wares, for their part, document contacts linking Ward's Point inhabitants with Munsee and Mahican-speaking people living farther north and west along the Hudson and Delaware Valleys. Further corroboration of contact with people living farther west occurs in the form of grave orientations. Jacobson found that all graves dating to Late Woodland and Historic Contact times face south or west. This orientation, favored by Munsee people, was comparatively rare among more southerly Unami-speaking Delaware people. Joining these findings with available lithic, ceramic, floral, and faunal evidence from the site, Jacobson believes that Ward's Point probably was a Munsee community most extensively occupied during warmer months by people closely linked to others living farther north and west during the Late Woodland and early Historic Contact periods.

Discoveries of copper, brass, and iron triangular projectile points, white-clay tobacco-smoking pipes, iron knives, and other objects of European origin in deposits containing Late Woodland lithics and ceramics show that people at Ward's Point maintained these contacts as they established new relations with Europeans moving to their lands during the early 1600s. The absence of clearly identifiable artifactual evidence documenting Munsee occupation at Ward's Point postdating Christopher Billopp's August 5, 1675, patent that confirmed his purchase of more than thirteen hundred acres in the area affirms that most Indian people complied with European orders for their removal after signing the third and final Indian deed to Staten Island five years earlier on April 13, 1670.

Responding to recent reports of vandalism, Department of Parks and Recreation officials have authorized increased surveillance by park and city police at the site. Organizations like the Professional Archaeologists of New York City (PANYC) and the New York Archaeological Conference (NYAC) also are mounting new efforts to increase public awareness of the importance of preserving cultural resources in and around New York City. Site collections currently are curated in the American Museum of Natural History in New York, the National Museum of the American Indian in Washington, D.C., and the Staten Island Institute of Arts and Sciences in Saint George. Listed in the National Register of Historic Places on September 29, 1982, as a contributing property in the Ward's Point Conservation Area, the Ward's Point Archeological Site was designated a National Historic Landmark on April 19, 1992.

The information presented here is abstracted from Jacobson (1980).

Fort Massapeag Archeological Site National Historic Landmark

The Fort Massapeag Archeological Site is located in Fort Neck Park in the town of Oyster Bay, Nassau County, New York. A level expanse of sandy glacial outwash plain, Fort Neck is one of several lobes of land jutting from the southern shore of Long Island into south Oyster Bay, the westernmost part of a shallow thirty-five-mile-long saltwater lagoon called Great South Bay.

No known colonial record directly documents the existence of an Indian fortification at Fort Neck or anywhere else in central Long Island during the seventeenth century. Several written records, however, refer to forts in the area during these years. One of these, a deed to land in Fort Neck signed by "Maomy & Will Chippy, Indians & Chief proprietors of ye Indians Lands upon Massipeague or ffort Neck at ye south of Oysterbay" on July 13, 1696, mentions "ye Old ffort" at "ye Head of ye Meadows on sd. Neck." Another deed signed a year later documents the final sale of Indian lands in the area.

Local folk traditions identify Fort Massapeag as the site of a European massacre of Indian people in 1643 or 1653. Although colonial documents chronicle armed assaults upon Long Island Indian communities in both years, neither can be linked to an attack at Fort Neck.

Samuel Jones, a descendant of one of the settlers purchasing land at Fort Neck from the Indians, published the first account identifying Fort Neck as the site of an Indian town in a paper printed in 1821. Three years later, Long Island historian Silas Wood published

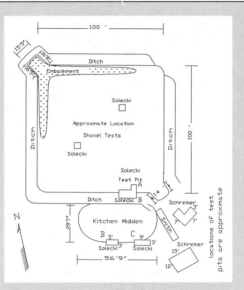

Fort Massapeag site map, showing excavations conducted by Ralph S. Solecki, Carlyle S. Smith, and Matt Schreiner in 1938. Courtesy Ralph S. Solecki.

the first description of earthworks at the locale.

Known as a good place to collect arrowheads by local enthusiasts, Fort Neck first came to wider public attention in 1933 when newspaper reports publicized the accidental discovery of several Indian graves during house foundation excavations at the Harbor Green development two thousand feet north of Fort Massapeag. Unable to prevent destruction of the Harbor Green site, local historian Charles E. Herrold managed to convince developers to preserve the small nearby Fort Massapeag locale.

Numerous avocational archaeologists were drawn to the site during these years. William Claude, for example, found a wooden mortar bowl containing a corn kernel, a blue glass bead, and two small white spherical glass beads within crevices lining the interior of the bowl while excavating at the locale between 1934 and 1935. James Burgraff excavated shell midden deposits just beyond the embankment wall. Finding no animal bones and few shells from edible oysters or soft clams, Burgraff suggested that the thousands of pieces of broken or cut quahog and whelk shells found with sandstone abraders, quartz and chert flakes, cut iron nails, glazed European stoneware sherds, and European white-clay tobacco-smoking pipes at the site represented remains of wampum shell bead production. Believing that Indians used the stone tools to cut and grind the shells, Burgraff thinks that the nails may have been used as drills to perforate the beads.

Ralph S. Solecki, later to achieve worldwide fame for his work at the Shanidar Cave Neanderthal site in Iraq, joined Carlyle S. Smith and other Flushing Archaeological Society members in excavating several test units at Fort Massapeag in 1938. Test excavation units placed at various locales in and around the embankment uncovered numerous broken or cut quahog and whelk shells, small amounts of Late Woodland pottery, quartz and chert triangular chipped-stone projectile points, quantities of debitage, several "EB" white clay pipe stems, two brass mouth harps stamped with the initial "R," copper arrow points, metal scraps, European glazed stoneware sherds, a piece of green glass, an iron fragment, a sandstone abrader, a grooved stone axe, and a number of sturgeon and deer bones.

Studying aboriginal pottery recovered from the site, Solecki and Smith found that terminal Late Woodland Bowman's Brook and Overpeck stamped or cord-marked pottery and Munsee-series incised and cord-marked collared wares overwhelmingly dominated the site ceramic assemblage. Identification of a number of particularly sensitive chronological-marker artifacts suggests more specific dates of occupation. Collared Shantok-series wares found at the site, for example, were produced by Indian women from eastern Connecticut and Long Island during the middle decades of the seventeenth century. Nearly all European white-clay tobacco-smoking pipe bowls recovered from site were attributed to Edward Bird, an Amsterdam pipemaker active from 1630 to 1683. The two brass mouth harps bearing distinctive "R" trademarks found in site shell midden deposits, for their part, resemble others found at the Power House site, a Seneca Indian town in western New York occupied between 1640 and 1655. The absence of artifactual evidence postdating 1700 in Fort Massapeag collections further corroborates written sources indicating that most Indian people moved elsewhere after putting their marks on the last deed to land at Fort Neck in 1697.

Analysis of these materials indicates that Fort Massapeag was built, occupied, and abandoned during the middle decades of the seventeenth century. The fort's size, shape, and method of construction suggest the fortified trading post and frontier refuge ordered built at Oyster Bay by Dutch authorities in 1656. It was a European-style quadrangular earthwork that measured one hundred feet on each side and was flanked at its northwestern and southeastern corners by bastions; it was further surrounded by a ditch and surmounted by an earth-fast stockade consisting of a single line of sharply pointed wooden palisade posts evidently cut by metal axes.

Late Woodland ceramics and lithics have been recovered alongside seventeenth-century European artifacts in a shell midden consisting almost entirely of cut or broken hard clam and whelk

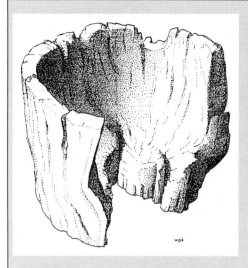

Wooden mortar that contained spherical glass beads and a corn kernel when found by William Claude at the Fort Massapeag site in 1934 or 1935. Presently curated in the Nassau County Museum, Garvies Point, New York. Courtesy Ralph S. Solecki.

Fort Massapeag NHL—*Continued*

shells just beyond what appears to have been the fort's southern entrance. These findings indicate that Indian people living at the since-destroyed, much-larger nearby Harbor Green habitation site two thousand feet to the northeast also used the locale as a place for manufacturing wampum shell beads and as a fortified refuge at various times between the 1630s and 1670s.

Artifacts from Fort Massapeag are currently curated in the Nassau County Museum at Garvies Point.

Fort Massapeag Archeological Site was designated a National Historic Landmark on April 19, 1992.

Information here is abstracted from Solecki (1991).

from Mahican Country and the Housatonic Valley, for example, continued through the first half of the eighteenth century. One of these immigrants to northern New Jersey, the earlier-mentioned Pequannock sachem Taphow, became a particularly influential Indian leader.

The presence of Shawnee refugees from Ohio moving to Pechoquealin settlements around the modern village of Shawnee-on-Delaware, Pennsylvania, in 1692 also strengthened negotiating positions of their Munsee hosts. Potent military allies with strong connections to powerful western nations, the Shawnees struggled to live peaceably near their Munsee friends. In the end, they lost this struggle. Worsening relations with the Iroquois and nearby colonists boiled into a series of killings that finally forced Pechoquealin Shawnees to abandon the valley and return west in 1727.

Munsee leaders worked hard to live peaceably with fractious local provincial authorities and greedy settlers. Several of their efforts, such as the more-or-less annual meetings at Kingston, New York, first instituted under the terms of the Nicolls Treaty cementing relations between the English and the Esopus in 1665, provided regular opportunities to renew friendship, and air grievances. But, the effectiveness of these strategies gradually diminished as steadily growing numbers of settlers began to overwhelm Munsee people. One strategy that had worked in the past—the delaying action that conveyed relatively small amounts of land to contending purchasers and forestalled larger and more damaging acquisitions—grew less effective as

Excavations in progress at the Spring House Rock Shelter, Rockland County, New York. Photograph by Edward J. Lenik, 1992. *Courtesy Edward J. Lenik.*

provincial governors like New York's Benjamin Fletcher and Pennsylvania's Thomas Penn seized great tracts and granted favorites and cronies patents to vast areas.

For example, Fletcher's most extensive grant, the 1708 Hardenburgh Patent, encompassed more than half a million acres of Munsee land in today's Catskill Mountains. And Pennsylvania's seizure, with Iroquois help, of land along the west bank of the Delaware River above the Forks at Easton, which was taken under the terms of the 1736 Walking Purchase deed, continues to rankle Munsee and Delaware people to the present day.

Many Munsees displaced by the Walking Purchase, which sanctioned an un-recorded 1686 deed, moved to Moravian mission settlements established in their country at the Forks of the Delaware in 1742. Joined by expatriates from Mahican Country and New England, they built stone and wooden-frame houses, tended fields, erected mills, and worshipped in Pennsylvania towns like Bethlehem and the first Gnadenhütten. Today, burying grounds and standing structures like the Gemeinhaus National Historic Landmark on the campus of the Moravian College in Bethlehem preserve physical evidence of the Moravian mission in this area.

Other Munsee people allied with powerful neighbors often received a surprising degree of protection. Minisink and Esopus Covenant Chain allies

A *Der Priester welcher tauft.*
BBB *Die Täuflinge.*

TAUFE
der Indianer
in America

C.C. *Die Arbeiter von ihrer Nation.*
D.D. *Die Indianer-Gemeine.*

Baptism ceremony at the Moravian mission in Bethlehem, Pennsylvania, ca. 1757. *Courtesy John Carter Brown Library at Brown University.*

threatened by border violence, for example, frequently were able to take refuge in towns closer to the center of colonial settlements. While it worked for a time, this system of protection gradually broke down as the century wore on. Panic-stricken settlers stampeded by rumors of impending French and Indian attacks at the beginning of King George's War in 1744, for instance, massacred several Esopus families who had fled to the Ulster County town of Walden. Twenty years later other settlers threatened to murder Indian refugees from the Susquehanna Valley town of Wyalusing, who were guarded by British troops.

Indian people continuing to live in Munsee Country during these years were increasingly forced to seek justice in British courts. Not surprisingly, Indian petitions were treated differently in different courts. Local courts usually found against Indian litigants. Higher provincial courts, administered by colonial officials anxious both to maintain Indian support and to retard the growth of provincial autonomy, often protected what they regarded as legitimate Indian interests. As Sir William Johnson's actions in the Wappinger case discussed earlier so convincingly showed, this system lasted until colonial officials found it more expedient to limit support to claims lodged by Mohawks and other powerful nations.

These and other actions worsened already-strained relations between Indians remaining in Munsee Country and their British neighbors. Despite continual renewals of friendship at treaty meetings, unavenged and unadjudicated assaults and other outrages committed by settlers nearly drove the Munsees and their neighbors to war against their British Covenant Chain allies in 1727 and 1744.

Title to most remaining Indian lands in Munsee Country passed into settlers' hands when Minisink and Esopus people finally agreed to validate Hardenburgh's claims to the Catskill uplands in two new deeds signed in 1746. Most Indian people in the Hudson Valley were forced from the last of their towns along the river shortly thereafter. Many of them moved east to new homes in or around missions at Schaghticoke, Connecticut, and Stockbridge, Massachusetts. Others moved farther west among Shawnee, Delaware, and Mahican friends and kinsfolk in the Susquehanna and Allegheny Valleys. No matter where they settled, Munsee people waited for an opportunity to avenge themselves on the people who had taken their lands and driven them from their homes.

The chance finally came in 1755 after Braddock's defeat at the beginning of the Seven Years' War between France and Britain. Pennsylvania, New Jersey, and New York frontier communities were now opened to attack. For two years, Munsee warriors supported with French arms and supplies ravaged border towns and outlying settlements along the upper Delaware Valley and Ulster County frontier. Caught in the middle, Moravian communities at Gnadenhütten and elsewhere were attacked by Indian enemies and vengeful colonists. Unable to obtain protection against such assaults, Moravian Indian converts and their missionaries moved farther west to more remote Susquehanna and Ohio Valley towns.

Poorly supplied by French allies because of the British blockade, Munsee, Mahican, Delaware, and Shawnee people, disheartened by counterattacks against Kittanning and other towns, finally began responding to British peace overtures carried by Teedyuscung and other frontier diplomats. Meeting in Easton, Pennsylvania, during the fall of 1758, their representatives made separate peace with the British. Using the meeting as an opportunity to arbitrate outstanding disputes, Munsee and Wappinger leaders surrendered all but hunting and fishing rights to lands in northern New Jersey for one thousand Spanish dollars.

A year later British troops seized the French posts at the Forks of the Ohio. Soon abandoning their homes east of newly renamed Fort Pitt, most Munsee people moved farther west to the Muskingkum and Beaver river valleys in Ohio. Though they resisted subsequent British and American efforts to expand into their territories, the Munsee and their neighbors were finally forced from Ohio Valley lands by the end of the century. People tracing descent to the original inhabitants of Munsee Country today live scattered from the Atlantic coast to Ontario, Wisconsin, Kansas, and Oklahoma.

SOURCES

Numerous studies publish the results of archaeological work conducted in Munsee Country. Those focusing upon work in the Hudson Valley and western Long Island include Ceci (1980a, 1982b), Funk (1976), Jacobson (1980), Lenik (1989), C. Smith (1950), Snow (1980), and Solecki (1991). Surveys of upper Delaware Valley archaeology appear in Heye and Pepper (1915), Kinsey (1972), Kraft (1975b, 1977, 1978, 1986), Marchiando (1972), Orr and Campana (1991), Puniello and Williams (1978), Schrabisch (1915), and L. Williams, Puniello, and Flinn (1982).

Significant primary sources for Munsee history include the many accounts compiled in Jameson (1909), the 1679–1680 journal of Labadist minister Jasper Danckaerts and its recently translated addendum on Indian life (Danckaerts 1913; Gehring and Grumet 1987), and the original and recent retranslations of Adriaen van der Donck's 1656 description of Indian life in New Netherland (van der Donck 1968; van Gastel 1990).

Studies by Grumet (1979, 1991), Thurman (1973), and Trelease (1960) exten- sively draw upon these and other sources. Ceci (1977) documents the economic impact of the wampum trade on seven- teenth-century intercultural relations. Studies written by Heckewelder (1819) and Zeisberger (1910) represent only two of the many sources chronicling Mora- vian mission work among Munsee and other Indian people.

The story of Munsee resistance and dispossession has long been a focus of intense scholarly interest. Goddard (1978b) and Weslager (1972) provide general summaries of Munsee sociocul- tural life of the period. Donehoo (1928); Kent, Rice, and Ota (1981); and P. A. W. Wallace (1965) locate many of their set- tlements in Pennsylvania. Jennings's (1984) revisionist studies of the Walking Purchase and the Covenant Chain alli- ance have exerted considerable influ- ence upon regional scholarship.

The little-known Nicolls Treaty re- newal process established in 1665 after the end of the Esopus Wars is surveyed in Scott and Baker (1953). Discussions of the Shawnee occupation at Pecho- quealin may be found in Callender (1978b), Donehoo (1928), Hanna (1911), and P. A. W. Wallace (1981).

DELAWARE COUNTRY

Delaware Country encompasses the lands drained by the lower Delaware River and its tributaries. Extending from the piedmont fall line around present-day Trenton to the north shore of Delaware Bay, it stretches across the lower Delaware Valley in what is now southern New Jersey, southeastern Pennsylvania, and the northern part of the state of Delaware.

THE SIXTEENTH CENTURY

Little more than scant deposits of stone tools and broken pottery have been found in most known sites dating to the 1500s in this area. Conoidal-to-globular grit-tempered Bowman's Brook, Overpeck, Riggins, and Minguannan wares, resembling Townsend ceramics found farther south, generally dominate pottery assemblages from deposits located in more southerly and westerly reaches of Delaware Country. Riggins wares are most frequently encountered in southern New Jersey. Minguannan wares are often found in terminal Late Woodland sites located between the lower reaches of the Delaware and the Susquehanna River.

Like the Munsee potters who made collared incised wares almost identical to those crafted by nearby Mohawk and Oneida people, makers of Minguannan wares used techniques and incised geometric motifs associated with Shenks Ferry ceramics made by Susquehanna Valley people who were destroyed, displaced, or absorbed by the Susquehannocks during the mid-1500s. Farther north and east, potters in central New Jersey often made Bowman's Brook and Overpeck wares resembling Sebonac pots found in sites along the North Atlantic coast.

Most known sites near the coast contain little more than scant evidence suggesting brief occupation. Larger sites located farther inland west and north of the Delaware River contain pits and other storage features believed to represent evidence of longer and more substantial forms of occupation.

Deposits containing small amounts of nondiagnostic metal fragments or unidentifiable pieces of glassware have been found with Overpeck wares, chipped-stone tools, and other terminal Late Woodland materials at the Abbott Farm National Historic Landmark and the Goods Field site. Schultz Incised pottery associated with Susquehannock Indian people also has been unearthed with

Overpeck and contemporary wares in Abbott Farm deposits. Such findings support suggestions that documented contact between the Susquehannock and Delaware peoples may date back to precontact times.

Archaeologists have found little evidence of food production, long-term community life, or social ranking in these sites. As mentioned earlier, several scholars, largely arguing from negative evidence, believe that the area's inhabitants organized themselves into small nomadic foraging bands during the Late Woodland and early Historic Contact periods (Becker 1987; Custer 1986c). Scholars taking this position believe that evidence of food production, town life, and other things associated with more complex social and economic forms chronicled by early colonial observers were by-products of European contact rather than local developments.

Other scholars question such findings. Many note that archaeological deposits found in Late Woodland sites differ little from those encountered in properties dating to the Historic Contact period. Both early and later sites generally consist of poorly preserved fragmentary deposits containing no evidence of storage pits and few, if any, European goods. Others point out that the distribution and composition of terminal Late Woodland sites closely resemble the dispersed Delaware settlement pattern chronicled by later colonial observers such as William Penn (Myers 1912). Rather than view basic developments of Delaware society as by-products of European contact, these scholars regard the charred corncobs, stone tools, ceramics, hearths, and other fragmentary remains found with European goods in many Late Woodland and early Historic Contact period sites in Delaware Country as possible evidence of continuity rather than change (Kraft 1986; Thurman 1973; Weslager 1972, 1991).

THE SEVENTEENTH CENTURY

Extant evidence indicates that people speaking the Eastern Algonquian Delaware language lived in communities along the lower Delaware Valley when Europeans first began settling in the area during the early 1600s. Identified today as the Unami dialect, this language is closely related to that spoken by Munsee people living farther north in northern New Jersey and southern New York. Although they spoke similar languages, significant differences in technology, settlement pattern, spiritual belief, social organization, and political affiliation distinguished Munsee from Delaware people.

As many as twelve thousand people lived in small hamlets along sheltered beaches and riverbanks from the New Jersey shore to the lower Delaware River Valley when Dutch settlers established their short-lived Swanendael settlement in Siconeysinck territory in 1631. Like their Munsee-speaking relatives to the north, most of these people did not live in large towns. Instead, they preferred to follow a less intensive settlement strategy centering around single structures sheltering up to one hundred maternally related kinsfolk and their families. Traveling widely, they hunted, fished, collected wild plants and animals, and visited relatives and friends. Delaware women aided by children, elders, husbands, and brothers planted and tended corn, beans, and squash wherever conditions favorable to cultivation were found.

Although Delawares destroyed the

MAP 18: DELAWARE COUNTRY

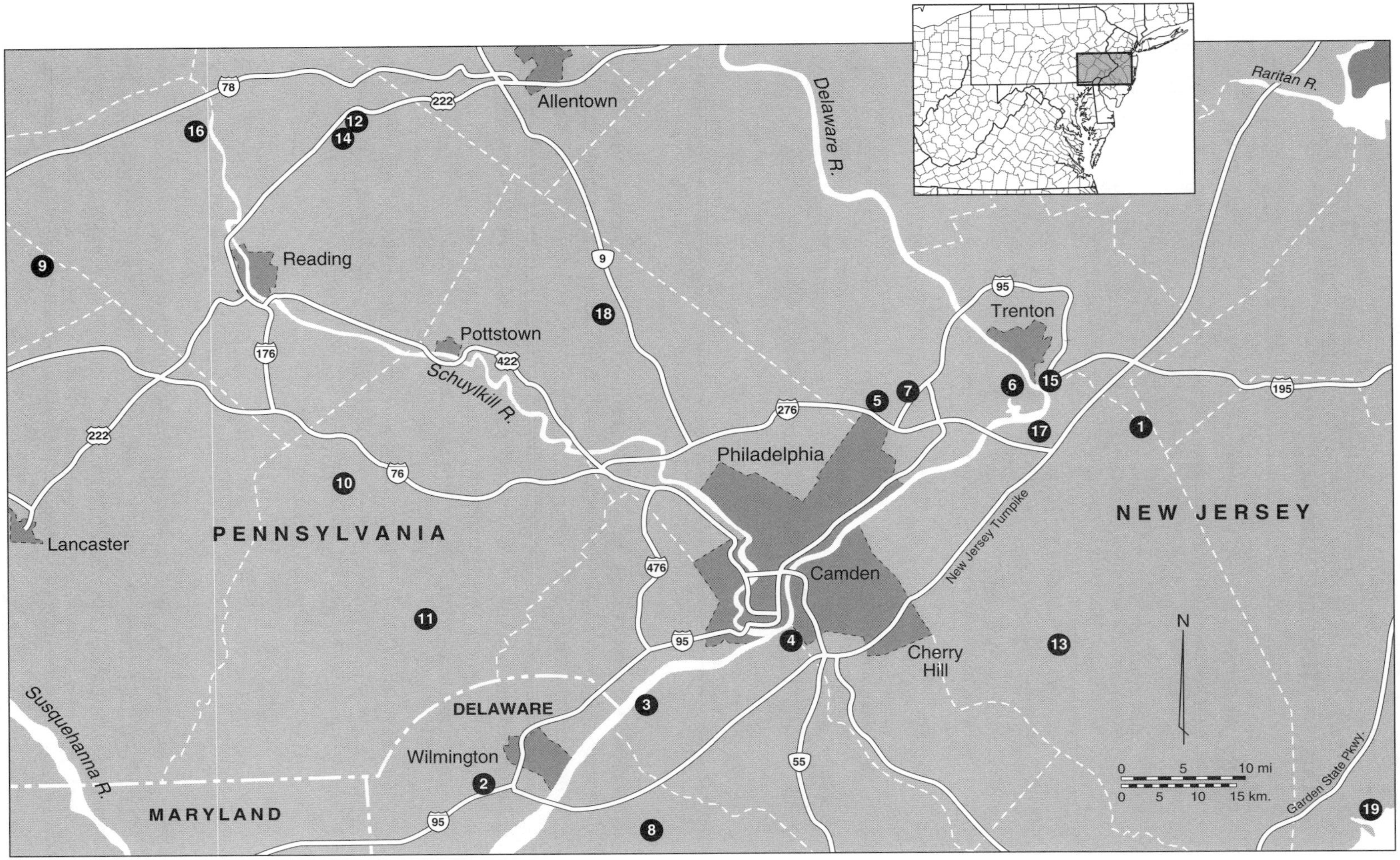

Map 18 Historic Contact Sites

Map Number	Site Name	County	State	Date	NR	Source
1	Lenhardt-Lahaway Hill	Burlington	NJ	1600s		D. Cross 1941
2	Clyde Farm	New Castle	DE	1600s	X	Custer and Watson 1985
3	Ware	Salem	NJ	1600s		D. Cross 1941
4	Gloucester City (28CA50)	Camden	NJ	Late 1600s		R. Thomas et al. 1985
5	Sweetwater (36BU57)	Bucks	PA	Late 1600s		PASS
6	Pemberton Family Cemetery (36BU179)	Bucks	PA	1680s–1705		Becker 1990; PASS; Witthoft 1951
7	Playwicky Farm (36BU173)	Bucks	PA	1600–1700s		R. M. Stewart 1993
8	Salisbury Farm	Gloucester	NJ	1600s–1700s	X	Batchelor 1976
9	36LE198	Lebanon	PA	1600s–1700s		PASS
10	Montgomery (36CH60)	Chester	PA	1720–1740		Becker 1978
11	North Brook (36CH61)	Chester	PA	1720s		Kent n.d.; PASS; Weslager 1953
12	Ingefield/Maxatawny (36BK450)	Berks	PA	1725		Becker 1980; PASS
13	Burr/Haines Mill (18BU414)	Burlington	NJ	1745–1765		Cosans-Zebooker 1992
14	36BK357	Berks	PA	Mid-1700s		PASS
15	Abbott Farm NHL	Burlington	NJ	Historic	X	D. Cross 1956
16	Bluebead (36BK590)	Berks	PA	Historic		PASS
17	Burlington Island	Burlington	NJ	Historic		Skinner and Schrabisch 1913
18	Goods Field (36MG124)	Montgomery	PA	Historic		PASS
19	West Creek (28OC45)	Ocean	NJ	Historic		Stanzeski 1993

Swanendael settlement in a dispute whose origins remain unclear, most other early relations with European colonists generally were peaceful. Early European documents state that people living in Delaware Country initially welcomed Dutch and English traders who sailed to the shores of their country. Claimed by the Dutch, this area was regarded by Europeans as a part of the colony of New Netherland after 1624.

The Dutch established most of their main settlements on the Hudson River. As a result, the few Dutch traders living along the Delaware River were unable to prevent local Delaware people from welcoming the Swedish settlers who established their New Sweden colony at Fort Christina in 1638. Dutch, Swedish, and Indian people lived amicably to-

gether for several years. Often cut off from resupply for years at a time, immigrants moving to New Sweden settled among their Delaware neighbors. More than a few of these settlers adopted Delaware housing, clothing, and food-ways.

Forced to live near one another in small isolated forts in the middle of Delaware territory, Dutch and Swedish authorities pledged their friendship to Delaware chiefs and bought land from Delaware people. Refusing to take sides in Indian conflicts, they stood by while Susquehannocks determined to dominate the river trade attacked their Delaware neighbors.

Unable to resist these assaults, most Delaware people on the west bank of the Delaware River withdrew eastward

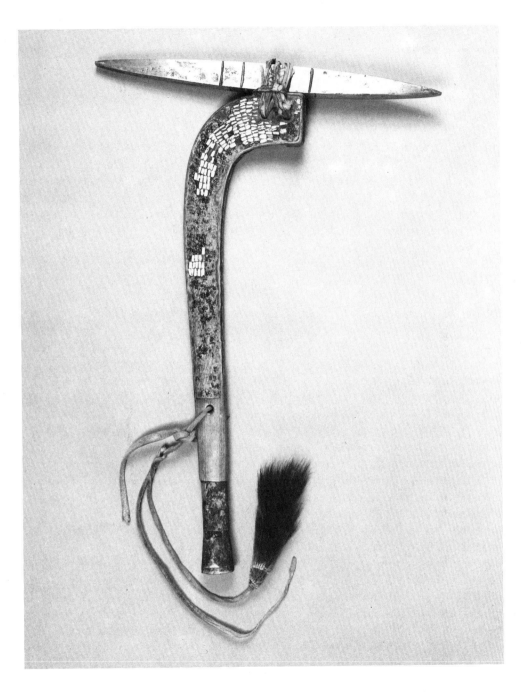

A steel-headed tomahawk hafted onto a wood handle decorated with inlaid wampum beads, reportedly collected on the Delaware River by Swedish colonists during the seventeenth century. *Courtesy New Jersey State Museum, Trenton, and the Folkens Museum, Stockholm, Sweden.*

to settlements along the lower reaches of Cohansey, Rancocas, Crosswicks, and other West Jersey creeks. Conceding the trade to their competitors, they subsequently made their peace with Susquehannocks just as Governor Kieft's War broke out with the Dutch along the northern borders of Delaware Country in 1640.

Living far from the center of fighting, most Indians living in Delaware Country managed to avoid direct involvement in this and subsequent conflicts with the Dutch. They quietly supported their Munsee brethren by discreetly sheltering warriors, their families, and their prisoners.

Able to escape conflicts along the Hudson, Delaware people could not avoid struggles closer to home. Many of them, for example, evidently supported former Susquehannock enemies in their wars with the Iroquois during the 1650s and 1660s. While figures are not currently available, references to large losses sustained by Susquehannock allies indicate that many of these people may have been killed or captured in the fighting.

Devastated by war losses and ravaged by malaria and smallpox epidemics sweeping the area between 1658 and 1664, Indian people living along the Delaware River submitted to English occupation when Dutch authorities surrendered New Netherland to a British force in 1664. Selling land to Quaker settlers moving to West Jersey, many of these people subsequently moved back to communities at Neshaminy, Okehocking, Perkasie, Playwicky, and other locales west of the Delaware River after the Susquehannocks abandoned the Susquehanna Valley in 1674.

Leaders from these and other Dela-ware communities acquiesced to the establishment of William Penn's proprietary colony on their lands along the west bank of the Delaware in 1682. Within the space of a very few years, Penn's agents purchased much of the riverfront from Neshaminy Creek to the Christina River from Delaware leaders.

The initial land transfers went peacefully enough, but imprecise deed boundaries, sometimes casually couched in terms of the length of time it took to walk or ride a horse in a certain direction, were to be an enduring source of friction between Delaware Indian people and Penn's descendants.

Unlike earlier colonists who frequently settled with Delaware people and adopted aspects of their culture, Quaker settlers lived apart from their Indian neighbors. Occupying lands already cleared by Indians in the most desirable locales in the area, the new colonists quickly fenced in large tracts of land. Prohibited from hunting, camping, or otherwise entering fenced tracts, most Delaware people soon withdrew inland toward still-unfenced lands along the upper reaches of the Brandywine, Schuylkill, and Tulpehocken Valleys.

Many Delaware people living on lands bought by West Jersey Quakers, for their part, moved deeper into the barren pinelands along the upper reaches of local creeks. Resenting the increasing tendency of colonial authorities to exert control over their lives or place their affairs in the hands of the Iroquois, many of these and other Delaware people began moving away. Most settled on former Susquehannock lands among native expatriates in the lower Susquehanna Valley. Others moved farther west to the Allegheny and Ohio drainages.

Those staying in Delaware Country struggled to live with English neighbors and their Iroquois clients. Unlike other native people on the north and south, many Delawares remaining in their homeland managed to maintain a considerable degree of autonomy during the last decades of the seventeenth century. Although Iroquois leaders claimed the right to control their affairs, the virtual absence of mention of the Iroquois in European records documenting transactions with Delaware people indicates that they did not openly try to dominate Delaware life within the Delaware heartland during these years.

Aware of their precarious position, Delaware people tried to avoid provocations whenever possible. Their leaders struggled to deal with provincial authorities who required conformance to English law and demanded the right to approve new sachems. Like other Indian people living directly in the path of massive colonial penetration, many of these people were able to pursue policies of accommodation. Living quietly on the borders of Quaker settlement, they managed to avoid being ordered off their land into Iroquois territory while sidestepping attempts to restrict them to reservations closely supervised by missionaries or provincially appointed overseers.

Often unable to obtain justice in lower courts, Delaware leaders pressed petitions to provincial governors and councils who were more sensitive to royal edicts requiring fair treatment of native peoples. Hearing native complaints, governors or their agents frequently saw to it that settlers accused of crimes against Indians were tried and sometimes punished.

During the seventeenth century provincial administrators also generally approved the appointment of sachems nominated by Delaware elders. Elders, for their part, rarely nominated leaders known to be objectionable to English authorities. Often called "kings" by the English, prominent Delaware leaders became influential culture brokers during the last decades of the century. Examples are Tamenend, Ockanickon, Sassoonan (also known as Allumapies), and Mechamiquon (or Big Feather, perhaps a play on the Delaware name for Penn, "Miquon," meaning both feather and quill) who was known to the English as King Charles. Acting as intermediaries between their followers and neighboring settlers, these leaders arbitrated local disputes, represented followers in meetings with governors and councils, and maintained close links with provincial authorities.

Although depopulation, relocation, and constant contact with non-Indian neighbors affected many aspects of Delaware life, few core elements of the culture changed appreciably during the 1600s. As elsewhere, Indian people throughout the area adapted European tools and ideas to their own established uses. While some Delaware people learned to speak Dutch, Swedish, or English, many used a trade jargon when conversing with settlers. Dutch, Swedish, and Quaker disinterest in Indian conversion, moreover, helped most Delawares preserve their spiritual heritage.

Several archaeological sites contain identifiable evidence of Indian life in Delaware Country during this turbulent century. Most are small, multicomponent sites located in areas long favored for settlement by Delaware Valley Indian people. All contain assemblages consisting of aboriginal pottery, stone tools, and objects of European origin or influence like white-clay tobacco-smoking pipes, glass beads, and stone artifacts knapped from local and European flints believed to be strike-a-lights or gunflints.

Distributions of deposits found in sites in Delaware Country containing clearly datable diagnostic early–seventeenth-century items—like the Lenhardt-Lahaway Hill, Salisbury Farm, and Ware locales in southern New Jersey and the Clyde Farm site in New Castle County, Delaware—suggest that Delaware Indian people clustered along Delaware Bay and the lower reaches of the Delaware River generally lived in decentralized communities. Discoveries of pits and hearths at Overpeck and other sites located farther upriver indicate that people living along the northern and western borders of Delaware Country frequently built more centralized towns. Other sites, like the Gloucester City locale in New Jersey, may contain materials documenting places where settlers and colonists lived or worked together.

Archaeologists have thus far been unable to unequivocally verify exact locales of Delaware Indian sites documented in seventeenth-century colonial records. Bolger (1989) has used West Jersey deeds to pinpoint the documented site of Alumhatta town in Burlington County, but no one has yet found clear material evidence of this occupation or of the Susquehanna Indian town in the upper Schuylkill River Valley noted in a 1689 map found by Charles E. Hunter (1983).

Archaeologist R. Michael Stewart (1993) has found at least two house patterns, a possible third structure, and a pit or hearth feature at what is believed to be the locale of the archivally documented late–seventeenth-century Delaware town of Playwicky. Radiometric analysis of charred wood from a burned house post found in the wall trench of Structure 1, an oval-shaped occupation encompassing an area of eighteen feet by twenty-five feet, has produced a date of 1780 plus or minus 60 years. Stewart has also found redware sherds and European white-clay tobacco-smoking pipe fragments in a stratum overlying Structure 2, a circular house pattern measuring forty feet in diameter.

THE EIGHTEENTH CENTURY

Much reduced by war and disease, the Delaware people nevertheless were the largest single Indian group remaining in the Middle Atlantic region in 1700. Although many Delaware people had already moved west into the Susquehanna and Ohio Valleys, most continued to live in small settlements scattered from the Raritan Valley south and west of New York Harbor to towns like Cohansey and Okehocking located along streams flowing into Delaware Bay.

Several factors account for this state of affairs. Unlike other people living elsewhere in the region, Delawares did not find their country threatened by massive influxes of European settlers until late in the century. The flexibility of their political systems and settlement strategies also served them well. Long accustomed to mobility, Delaware people were able to move away from places contested by more powerful rivals like the Susquehannocks. Delaware diplomats pursuing long-established strategies of flexible response also were often able to avoid involvement in wars that devastated nearby Indian communities.

However, such strategies could not stop the spread of epidemic contagion to Delaware communities. Although exact information is lacking, smallpox, measles, malaria, and other new diseases may have killed much of the precontact Delaware population by 1700.

Outnumbered and increasingly pressed by colonial proprietors to sell their lands, Delawares did what they could to avoid dispossession during these years. Resisting demands that they sell all of their land and move away, most Delaware people instead withdrew slowly by selling small parcels of land as they gradually moved up rivers into more mountainous and less accessible parts of their homeland.

European records locating major Delaware communities along upriver portions of the area's waterways reflect the success of this delaying strategy. Some of the largest of these communities were located along the upper Schuylkill River around Tulpehocken Creek near Reading, Pennsylvania. Led by Sassoonan, the second man to be recognized as king of the Delawares by Pennsylvanian officials, members of the Tulpehocken community were mostly Delaware Valley expatriates forced to move farther inland after selling their land to Penn's agents.

Other Delaware people living in the Raritan Valley slowly withdrew upriver as they sold their lands to East Jersey proprietors. Farther east, scattered groups of Delaware families led by Weequehela, known to settlers as the king of New Jersey, held on to their lands in the sandy pine-barren backcountry of present-day Middlesex, Monmouth, and Mercer counties. Nearly all of these people left their homes to join friends and relatives in the Lehigh Valley around the Forks of the Delaware when provincial authorities hanged Weequehela on June 24, 1727, for murdering a neighbor during a drunken dispute.

Farther south, small groups of Indians held onto their homes along the upper reaches of the Rancocas River and Cohansey Creek in southern New Jersey. Other Delaware families continued to make their homes along the Brandywine Creek in southeastern Pennsylvania and northern Delaware. Many Indians from New Jersey moved with their Brandywine friends and kinfolk to the town of Okehocking near Ridley and Crum Creeks after selling their land during the first decades of the 1700s. Living at Okehocking for a time, most of these people soon moved farther west to the Susquehanna Valley.

Anxious to secure title to as much land as possible, the Pennsylvanians pressed Delawares remaining along the Schuylkill River to join Okehocking residents or the other Delaware expatriates living in and around Shamokin in the heart of the Susquehanna Valley by 1724. Some years later, provincial officials used an unrecorded Indian deed allegedly written in 1686 to pressure Lehigh Delawares to sign what came to be called the Walking Purchase deed in 1736. Signing reluctantly, the Indians agreed to relinquish all the lands a man could walk in a day and a half from a starting point located in the lower Bucks County town of Wrightstown. On the morning of September 18, 1737, runners hired by provincial agents raced along a road cut straight into the heart of the Lehigh Valley. Leaving Indian witnesses far behind, the best of these runners paced off a line stretching fifty-five miles from the "walk's" starting place by noon of the next day.

Rather than run a line directly to the nearest point on the Delaware River, Penn's men insisted on tracing a right angle from the furthest point reached by their runner. Through this contrivance, they laid claim to all remaining Delaware land and most Munsee territory between the Delaware and Lehigh Rivers.

Outraged Delawares, expecting to lose only part of their lands under the terms of the 1736 deed, refused to abandon everything. Their protests fell on deaf ears. Onondaga sachem Cannasatego, speaking on behalf of the Iroquois confederacy at the urging of Pennsylvanian authorities, curtly ordered the Delawares off their lands at a meeting in Philadelphia in 1742.

Unable to resist such pressure, the Delawares left the Lehigh Valley. Many joined friends and relatives already living at Shamokin and other Susquehanna Valley towns. Others followed Presbyterian missionary David Brainerd back to New Jersey in 1746. Settling mostly between Cranbury and Crosswicks Creek, these Presbyterian Delawares struggled to live peacefully with their non-Indian neighbors for more than ten years, but most of them eventually moved to the Brotherton Reservation at Edgepillock near the present New Jersey pinelands community of Indian Mills, which was set aside for them by provincial authorities at the Easton treaty on August 29, 1758.

Like other Indian people remaining in the region, the Delawares living at Brotherton increasingly adopted European customs, language, and folkways. Many married Indian people from communities as far away as Rhode Island and Virginia. Others married non-Indians. Continuing to live in and around Edgepillock for more than forty years, most of these people joined Delawares and other displaced Coastal Algonquians moving to the Brothertown and New Stockbridge communities on the Oneida Reservation in New York in 1801.

Documents recording ongoing native occupation in Delaware Country reveal that many Indians stayed or returned to the area after the Brothertons moved away. More than a few elders, for example, chose to live out their days near the homes and graves of friends and relatives. Many children and spouses of mixed marriages, for their part, also refused to go. Others stayed because they simply did not want to live under the control of outsiders. But in the end, most people claiming Delaware ancestry in the east moved to non-Indian communities. A few lived as recluses in unwanted barren lands, back lots, and mountain hollows in various parts of their ancestral homeland.

Several workers—Donehoo (1928); Kent, Rice, and Ota (1981); and P. A. W. Wallace (1965)—have located the sites of historically documented eighteenth-century native communities in portions of Delaware Country presently within Pennsylvania state borders. Several of these communities, like Tulpehocken and Maxantawny in Berks County, Okehocking in Chester County, and Minguhanan and Queonemysing in Delaware County, have been listed in the state's archaeological inventory and assigned Smithsonian trinomial numbers.

Yet virtually no clearly identifiable

archaeological evidence documenting eighteenth-century native occupation has been found at most of these sites. Small numbers of European artifacts have been found among scattered debitage on the surface of the Tulpehocken site. Aboriginal artifacts and nondiagnostic materials are the only items thus far reported from other locatable places identified by name in Pennsylvania colonial records.

European artifacts were reportedly excavated from a documented trading post on Burlington Island near Trenton. Salvage excavations conducted at the Burr/Haines Mill site near Edgepillock, for their part, have uncovered deposits believed to represent the household of one of the many Indian families living close to the Brotherton Reservation during the middle decades of the eighteenth century. Archaeologist Andrew Stanzeski (1993) has found stonewares, redwares, delftwares, and other European ceramics alongside cut copper, lead beads, British coins, "RT" European white-clay tobacco-smoking pipes, masses of worked bone, and other objects in a dark, lens-shaped feature fifty feet from a historic house foundation at the West Creek site on the Jersey shore. These findings may corroborate archival references indicating that Indian people lived with European settlers at this locale during the eighteenth century.

At least four sites in Delaware Country provide information on eighteenth-century Delaware mortuary customs and beliefs. Investigators have found several Indian graves containing eighteenth-century glass beads, European white-clay tobacco-smoking pipes, and other imports at the Ingefield site near Kutztown, Pennsylvania, and at the North Brook site in the Brandywine Creek valley. The grave of an Indian person has also been discovered in a burial ground used before 1705 by the Pemberton family in Bucks County.

Excavations at the Montgomery site conducted by C. A. Weslager in 1952 and Marshall Becker in 1978 uncovered at least fourteen extended burials. Fragments of wooden coffins were found in two graves. Glass beads and other European goods were included as funerary offerings in most of these graves. Datable European white-clay tobacco-smoking pipes and glass beads recovered from this site indicate that it probably was a cemetery used by members of a still-unlocated Brandywine Delaware community sometime between 1720 and 1730.

SOURCES

Much of the information presented in this section has been drawn from Goddard (1978b), W. Hunter (1978b), Jennings (1984, 1988b), Kraft (1986), Newcomb (1956), and Weslager (1972). These sources, in turn, draw on the considerable body of primary documentation that has survived in this area. Much of this documentation may be found in compilations edited by Gehring (1977, 1981), Hazard et al. (1852–1949), A. Johnson (1911), Myers (1912), and O'Callaghan and Fernow (1853–1887). Histories and descriptions of seventeenth-century Delaware culture written by Swedish engineer Peter Lindeström (1925), New Sweden governor Johan Risingh (Dahlgren and Norman 1988), and Quaker proprietor William Penn (in Myers 1912) remain indispensable reading.

Several studies document events in particular Delaware communities or areas. Intercultural relations in the Lehigh Valley are surveyed in Becker (1987) and Grumet (1979). The Tulpehocken removal is examined in Jennings (1968a). Becker (1986) surveys the documentation of the Okehocking community. Documents chronicling the Siconeysinck community are analyzed in Weslager (1991). A survey of available documentation on the New Jersey Brotherton Reservation appears in Larrabee (1976).

Of all the events associated with contact between Delawares and colonists, none has sparked more controversy than the Walking Purchase. Much ink has been spilt by partisans arguing over the justice of the undertaking. Jennings, at present the foremost proponent of the view that the purchase was fraudulent, has observed that both sides of a controversy are controversial. He and Anthony F. C. Wallace have unearthed considerable bodies of documentation suggesting patterns of manipulation, fraud, and deception perpetrated by the Penn family and their agents (Jennings 1970, 1984, 1988b; A. F. C. Wallace 1990). William A. Hunter (1961) and Becker (1987) believe that, although the execution of the walk in 1737 was open to question, the 1736 deed was legitimate.

NANTICOKE COUNTRY

Nanticoke Country stretches across the central portion of the Delmarva Peninsula from southern Delaware to the Virginia state line.

THE SIXTEENTH CENTURY

No written records clearly document contacts between European voyagers and Indian people living in this area during the 1500s. Terminal Late Woodland pottery, tobacco pipes, triangular, chipped-stone projectile points, and other artifacts similar to those found in other sites around Chesapeake Bay dating to the 1500s and early 1600s have been recovered from pits, hearths, ossuaries, or other features preserved in the Killens Pond, Mispillion, Thomas, and Townsend sites on the Delmarva Peninsula.

Shell-tempered Townsend-series ceramics dominate the pottery assemblages found at the Mispillion and Townsend habitation sites. Similar in form to Riggins wares produced by people living across Delaware Bay in southern New Jersey, Townsend pottery is decorated with incised designs closely resembling others commonly seen on pots found in sites located elsewhere along the Middle Atlantic coast.

Archaeologists identify large coastal townsites and smaller temporary hinterland camps containing Townsend wares in the northern and central sections of the Delmarva Peninsula as components of the Slaughter Creek complex, which first emerged in the area sometime between A.D. 1000 and 1500. Larger Slaughter Creek complex locales like the Townsend and Mispillion sites often contain pits, midden layers, and other evidence of longer-term occupation. Antler and bone artifacts, unworked animal bones, and botanical remains (including occasional fragments of charred corncobs and corn kernels) have been found in some of these sites.

Smaller Slaughter Creek complex sites, like the Killens Pond locale, generally consist of thinly scattered fragments of cracked rock, hearths, or small concentrations of stone tools, cracked shells, and debitage. Believed to represent temporary camps, these sites usually are located along the coast or the banks of Delmarva Peninsula rivers and streams.

Like their neighbors on the south and west, Slaughter Creek people often bur-

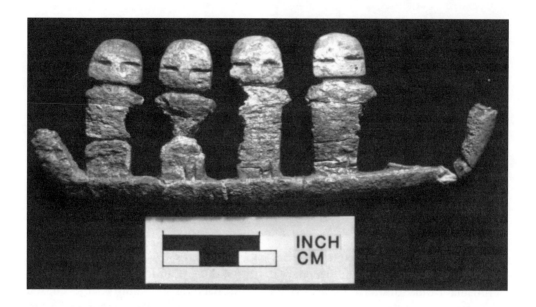

Carved bone object depicting four figures on a vessel, found at the Slaughter Creek site, Delaware. *Courtesy Delaware State Museums.*

ied their dead in ossuaries. Radiocarbon dates from one of these locales, the Thomas site, suggest that it was in use sometime during the sixteenth or very early seventeenth centuries.

Although several Slaughter Creek complex sites are believed to date to the sixteenth century, none is presently known to contain datable European goods or materials of European origin.

THE SEVENTEENTH CENTURY

Early European written records indicate that Algonquian-speaking people lived in towns located at various places in the central Delmarva Peninsula at the beginning of the seventeenth century. The largest and best known of these communities were located in places like Tockwogh, Wicomisse, Choptank, Pocomoke, and Nanticoke when John Smith visited the area in 1608.

Smith noted that Tockwogh people living at the northern end of the Delmarva Peninsula were Susquehannock clients. Wicomisse people evidently lived at the southernmost part of the area just above Accohannock and Accomac communities closely affiliated with the Powhatan chiefdom. In between, people living along the Choptank, Pocomoke, and Nanticoke Rivers came to be collectively known to colonists as Nanticokes by the end of the century.

Relatively little is known about the lives of people living on the Delmarva Peninsula during the 1600s. Occupying an area bypassed by most colonists, they do not appear in seventeenth-century documents as frequently as Indians living closer to centers of European expansion. Aware of the devastating impact of colonization elsewhere, Indian people living on the Delmarva Peninsula evidently

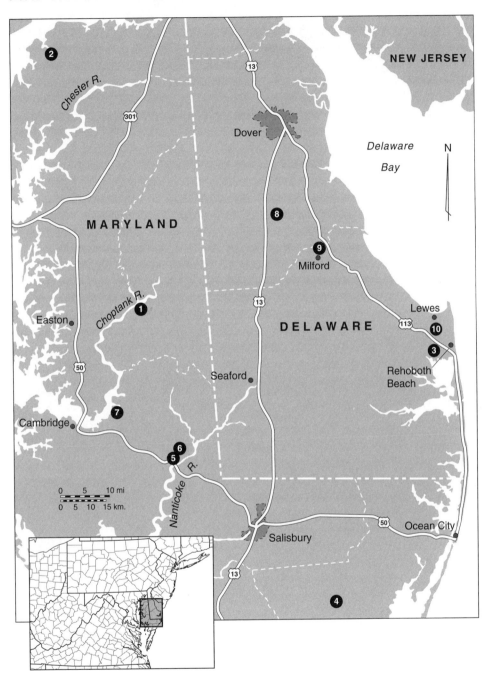

Map 19 Historic Contact Sites

Map Number	Site Name	County	State	Date	NR	Source
1	Thomas (18CA88)	Caroline	MD	1490–1656		Hughes 1991
2	Arrowhead Farm 1 (18KE29)	Kent	MD	1600s		Custer 1989
3	Warrington	Sussex	DE	1600s	X	Marine et al. 1964
4	Askiminikansen	Worcester	MD	1600s–1700s		Davidson 1982
5	Chicone No. 1 (18DO11)	Dorchester	MD	1600s–1700s		Davidson 1982; Davidson amd Hughes 1986; Davidson, Hughes, and McNamara 1985
6	18DO155	Dorchester	MD	1600s–1700s		Davidson, Hughes, and McNamara 1985; McNamara 1985
7	Locust Neck Village (18DO117)	Dorchester	MD	1600s–1700s		Davidson, Hughes, and McNamara 1985
8	Killens Pond	Kent	DE	Undated		Fithian 1993
9	Mispillion	Sussex	DE	Undated		BAHP 1990; Hutchinson et al. 1957
10	Townsend	Sussex	DE	Undated	X	BAHP 1990; T. D. Stewart et al. 1963

preferred to keep as low a profile as possible during this turbulent century.

No known reliable estimate of the early-seventeenth-century Indian population in Nanticoke Country presently exists. Feest (1978a) suggests that more than twelve thousand people may have lived on the Delmarva Peninsula and Maryland's eastern shore at the beginning of the 1600s, though fewer than a thousand Indians were living in the area by the end of the century.

The causes of this depopulation are not clearly known at present. Many people were probably killed by epidemic diseases known to have ravaged Indian and European communities farther north and west. Other records chronicling involvement of Indians from this area in such conflicts as the Second Powhatan War and the 1669 Wicomisse War indicate that numbers of Indian people on the eastern shore were killed or carried off into captivity during fighting that raged around Chesapeake Bay between 1609 and 1675. Still other documents reveal that increasing numbers of native people who were unwilling to live near settlers began moving to the Conoy Island refugee community (today known as Heater's Island near Point of Rocks, Maryland) in piedmont country along the upper Potomac River during the final decades of the century.

Indians electing to stay on their remaining lands in Nanticoke Country were compelled to accept English sovereignty by midcentury. Using treaties to establish and maintain authority, Virginian and Maryland colonists attempted to reduce these people to the status of subservient tributaries. Treaty protocols called on the Indians to make annual token payments in the form of bows and arrows or other symbolic objects, surrender fugitives, return escaping slaves, and submit names of prospective chiefs for approval. Provincial authorities also used treaty meet-

Aerial photograph of the Chicone site, Maryland. The site of the palisaded town is marked by the large donut-shaped dark soil stain at the lower right corner of the light-colored field. Photograph by Richard B. Hughes and Thomas E. Davidson. *Courtesy Maryland Historical Trust.*

ings as occasions to ask Indian people to move to reservations set aside for them on land unwanted by settlers.

Using this system, English settlers had managed to reduce Indian landholdings in Nanticoke Country to three small reservations by 1700. The earliest of these reservations, known as Gangascoe or Gingaskin, was established by Virginian authorities on the lower tip of the Delmarva Peninsula in 1641. The other two reservations were set aside by Maryland officials at Choptank and Chicone between 1669 and 1684. The latter settlement had become the principal Nanticoke town by the end of the century.

Archaeologists are currently working to unearth new information on life at these and other seventeenth-century Indian communities. Discoveries of stone tools, glass beads, Indian and European ceramics, and metal objects found in and around a circular midden ring at the Chicone site represent the single largest known, intact body of archaeological materials documenting seventeenth-century Indian life in the area.

Other sites contain more fragmentary remains. Gunflints evidently crafted from local stone, for example, have been excavated at the Arrowhead Farm 1 site in Kent County, Maryland. Other incompletely documented deposits containing aboriginal stone and ceramic artifacts, radiocarbon dated deposits, and presently unassociated or nondiagnostic European materials at places like the Warrington site, the Thomas ossuary, and the site of the archivally documented Pocomoke and Assateague communities at Askiminikansen may shed further light on poorly known aspects of seventeen-century Indian life in Nanticoke Country (Davidson 1982; Hughes 1991).

THE EIGHTEENTH CENTURY

Conditions in the small Delmarva Peninsula reservations progressively worsened as game disappeared and the fertility of already marginally productive soils was exhausted. Harassed by trespassers and non-Indian neighbors eager to see them move on, the Nanticokes in increasing numbers joined friends and relatives living elsewhere. Many moved to a refugee community known as Conejohela (the Iroquois term for Conoy Town) on the lower Susquehanna River after 1710. Others settled on new reservations established in 1711 at Indian River, Delaware, and Broad Creek, Maryland.

Gradually crowded out by the European settlers moving among them, most of these people moved to a new Conoy Town, ironically known today as Old Conoy Town, established on Haldeman's Island at the mouth of the Juniata River in 1744. Soon faced with yet another move considerably farther upriver from their ancient homeland, many Conoy Town inhabitants decided to take their chances and rejoined family and friends in and around their few remaining Chesapeake Bay reservations.

Many of these people had to move back to the Susquehanna Valley after provincial authorities sold the Chicone

and Broad Creek reservations in 1768. Some of those who stayed moved to the Choptank reservation. Others moved to unoccupied lands near their old homes. Many married non-Indians and lived quietly among their neighbors. Today most people tracing descent from those who refused to leave live in Nanticoke communities located from Maryland to southern New Jersey.

Very little is known about the archaeology of eighteenth-century Indian life in Nanticoke Country. Deposits preserved in sites at Chicone No. 1, the nearby 18DO155 site, and the Locust Neck Village at Choptank may date to this period. White-clay tobacco-smoking pipes, European ceramics, and other goods dating to the 1700s in locales not known to have been settled by Europeans during the eighteenth century also have been found at the Killens Pond, Mispillion, and Townsend sites in southern Delaware.

SOURCES

Much of the information presented in this section has been drawn from Boender (1988), Cissna (1986), Feest (1978a, 1978b), Marye (1935), and Porter (1986). Slaughter Creek complex archaeology is summarized in Custer (1986c), Custer and Griffith (1986), Griffith (1982), Griffith and Custer (1985), and Weslager (1939). The archaeology of contact in Nanticoke Country is discussed in Custer (1989) and Weslager (1948).

Transcripts of many of the major primary sources documenting relations between Indians and Europeans in Nanticoke Country have published in Browne et al. (1883–1970), Gehring (1977, 1981), Hall (1910), Myers (1912), and J. Smith (1624).

PISCATAWAY-POTOMAC COUNTRY

Piscataway-Potomac Country extends across tidewater sections of the Potomac and Rappahannock river valleys in Maryland and Virginia.

THE SIXTEENTH CENTURY

Archaeological evidence found at the Cumberland Palisaded Village site and Accokeek Creek National Historic Landmark in Maryland and the Boathouse Pond, Indian Town Farm, Potomac Creek, and De Shazo sites in Virginia indicates that most people living in this area at the time of initial contact with Europeans in the sixteenth century followed terminal Late Woodland lifeways that had first emerged during the 1300s.

All of these people hunted, fished, foraged, and tended fields and gardens. Most lived in mat- or bark-covered oblong-shaped houses in small hamlets or large, densely occupied towns. Several of these communities were surrounded by palisade walls. Like their neighbors on the south and east, people living in these towns buried the bones of their dead together in ossuaries.

Piscataway-Potomac Country people made and used triangular, chipped-stone projectile points and Late Woodland stone tools similar to those found elsewhere in the Northeast. They also used pottery types believed to reflect distinct social and political entities chronicled by Europeans moving into the area during the seventeenth century.

People primarily using grit-tempered Potomac Creek wares evidently began building large, densely settled fortified towns at the mouths of Potomac Creek, Accokeek Creek, and other streams flowing into upriver portions of the Potomac River estuary during the 1300s and 1400s. Discoveries of post-mold patterns indicating successive episodes of palisade-wall construction at several of these sites suggest that many were continuously occupied for long periods of time. Smaller locales, like the hamlet preserved at the Posey site at Indian Head on Mattawoman Creek in Maryland and campsite deposits at the Little Marsh Creek site in Virginia, were scattered throughout the area.

People using shell-tempered Rappahannock-complex wares similar to pottery found on sites 1,100 years old lived on the south and east of the Potomac Creek pottery makers on the Rappahannock and lower Potomac estuaries during the sixteenth century. Two wares produced by these people—a smoothed or scraped thin-bodied ware known as Yeocomico pottery and a type of Rappahannock ware decorated by hollow reed punctations—have been found in deposits radiocarbon-dated to the late sixteenth and early seventeenth centuries. Discoveries of such wares generally are regarded as indicators of early Historic Contact period occupation in sites where archaeologists have not yet found either European artifacts in intact contexts or undisturbed radiometrically datable deposits.

Several sites containing such wares have been found throughout the lower tidal reaches of the Rappahannock and Potomac Valleys. Substantial amounts of terminal Late Woodland Rappahannock-complex wares have been found in remains of large, dispersed communities in the Saint Mary's City National Historic Landmark in Maryland and at the multicomponent Boathouse Pond site in Virginia. Quantities of hand-wrought iron nails, gunflints, glass, white-clay tobacco-smoking pipes, and other European artifacts have been found in radiometrically dated deposits in the partially destroyed De Shazo site believed to be the locale of the archivally documented Cuttatowoman II town.

Shell middens containing Yeocomico and Rappahannock punctated pottery also have been found at Blue Fish Beach in the Chicacoan site complex, at White Oak Point, and in other locales. Glass beads thought by David I. Bushnell to date to the 1500s were found during plowing of a field at Leedstown near the north bank of the Rappahannock River at a place thought to have been the lo-cale of the archivally chronicled Pis-saseck town. More recently, Stephen R. Potter (1992) has identified most of these beads as the products of seventeenth-century Dutch factories. Noting that diagnostic aboriginal artifacts collected nearby primarily date from Archaic to Middle Woodland times, Potter believes that the Leedstown bead cache probably represents an isolated findspot rather than a Historic Contact period occupation.

THE SEVENTEENTH CENTURY

English colonists moving to Jamestown and other Virginia settlements during the first decades of the seventeenth century charted substantial numbers of Indian communities on maps of the lower Potomac and Rappahannock river valleys. Early mapmakers like John Smith located Potomac, Machotick, Nanzatico, Portobago, Doeg, Nacotchtanke, and other communities within the area occupied by Potomac Creek complex people. Piscataway, Patuxent, Mattapanient, and other people, for their part, lived in areas where Rappahannock-series pottery dominates the ceramic assemblages.

As many as ten thousand people may have been living in these towns when John Smith and other chroniclers first visited the area. Working with documents like Smith's map, archaeologists have associated several sites with archivally chronicled towns. The Potomac Creek and slightly later Indian Point sites, for example, are thought to represent successive locations of Patawo-meke, the main town of the principal werowance of the Potomac chiefdom during the early decades of the century.

MAP 20: PISCATAWAY-POTOMAC COUNTRY

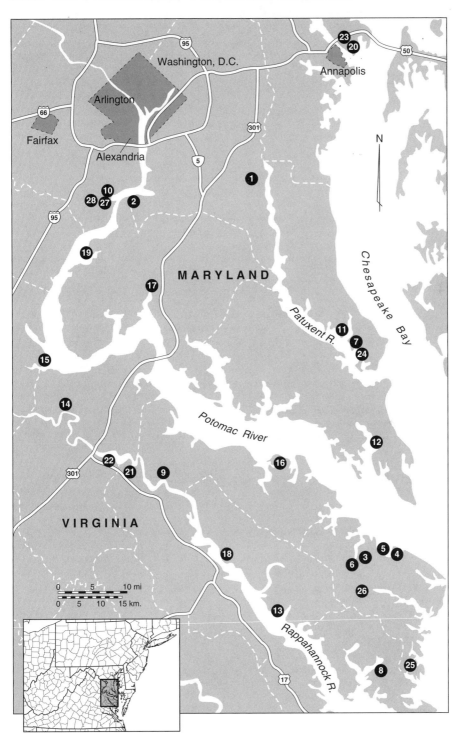

95

Washington, D.C.

Arlington

66

Fairfax

Alexandria

5

301

23

20

Annapolis

50

N

1

10

28 27

2

95

19

MARYLAND

17

Patuxent R.

11

7

24

Chesapeake Bay

15

14

Potomac River

12

22

21

9

16

301

VIRGINIA

18

5 4

3

6

26

13

8 25

Rappahannock R.

17

0   5   10 mi

0 5 10 15 km.

Map 20 Historic Contact Sites

Map Number	Site Name	County	State	Date	NR	Source
1	Nottingham South (18PR18)	Prince Georges	MD	Late 1500s	X	W. Clark 1974a
2	Piscataway Complex Accokeek Creek NHL (18PR8)	Prince Georges	MD	1500s	X	Potter 1980, 1993; Stephenson, Ferguson, and Ferguson 1963; Ferguson and Stewart 1940; Thurman 1972; Vrabel and Cissna n.d.
	Piscataway Park (18PR83 and 18PR248)			1600–1670		
	Ferguson Ossuary (18PR42)			1630–1660		
	Susquehannock Fort			1675		
	Chicacoan Complex	Northumberland	VA	1500s–1600s		Potter 1982, 1993; Turner 1990b; VDHR
3	Boathouse Pond (44NB111)			1500s–1600s		
4	Plum Nelly (44NB128)			1500s–1600s		
5	Blue Fish Beach (44NB147)			Mid-1600s		
6	44NB97					
7	Cumberland Palisaded Village (44CV171)	Calvert	MD	Late 1500s–early 1600s		Potter 1993; Smolek 1986
8	Indian Town Farm (44LA80)	Lancaster	VA	Late 1500s–early 1600s		Potter 1982, 1993
9	Leedstown Bead Cache	Westmoreland	VA	Late 1500s–early 1600s		Bushnell 1937; MacCord 1993
10	Little Marsh Creek (44FX1471)	Fairfax	VA	Late 1500s–early 1600s		L. Moore 1990; Potter 1993; Turner 1990b
11	Patterson's Archaeological District (18CT755)	Calvert	MD	Late 1500s–early 1600s	X	W. White, Dinsmoor and Clark 1981
12	St. Mary's City NHL (18ST1)	St. Marys	MD	Late 1500s–early 1600s	X	H. Miller 1983
13	Woodbury Farm No. 1 (44RD48)	Richmond	VA	Late 1500s–early 1600s		Potter 1982, 1993
14	De Shazo (44KG3)	King George	VA	1575–1615		MacCord 1965; Potter 1993; Turner 1990b; VDHR
15	Patawomeke Complex Potomac Creek (44ST2) Indian Point (44ST1)	Stafford	VA	1580–1610 1608–1630	X	MacCord 1991b; Potter 1989, 1993; Schmitt 1965; T. D. Stewart 1992; Turner 1990b; VDHR
16	White Oak Point (44WM119)	Westmoreland	VA	Early 1600s		Potter 1993; Turner 1990b; VDHR; Waselkov 1982
17	Port Tobacco Ossuary (18CH94)	Charles	MD	1630–1640		Graham 1935; MacCord 1993
18	Mount Airy (44RD3)	Richmond	VA	1630–1660		McCary 1950; Miller, Pogue, and Smolek 1983; Potter 1993; Turner 1990b
19	Posey/Indian Head (44CH281)	Charles	MD	1640–1660		Barse 1985; MacCord 1993; Potter 1993
20	Broadneck (18AN818)	Anne Arundel	MD	1640–1660		Luckenbach 1991
21	44EX3-5	Essex	VA	1650–1670		MacCord 1993; Turner 1990b; VDHR

Map Number	Site Name	County	State	Date	NR	Source
22	Camden NHL (44CE3-4, 13-15, 19-21, 30, 135, 139-156, 170, 178, 184, 217-218)	Caroline	VA	1650-1705	X	Hodges 1986; Hodges and McCartney 1986; MacCord 1969; Turner 1990b; VHLC 1969
23	Burle (18AN826)	Anne Arundel	MD	1675-1700		Luckenbach 1993
24	Compton	Calvert	MD	1675-1700		Luckenbach 1993
25	Owings (44NB1)	Northumberland	VA	Late 1600s–early 1700s		Dalton 1974; MacCord 1993; Potter 1977; Turner 1990b
26	Downing (44NB3)	Northumberland	VA	1700s		Miller, Pogue, and Smolek 1983; Potter 1982; Turner 1990b
27	Lazy Point	Fairfax	VA	Historic		L. Moore 1991b
28	Taft (44FX544)	Fairfax	VA	Historic		L. Moore 1988

Terminal Late Woodland deposits found at Accokeek Creek National Historic Landmark, for their part, have long been associated with Moyaone, the home community of an influential Piscataway tayac.

Deposits containing artifacts more clearly associated with early–seventeenth-century lower Potomac Valley community life have been identified at the Cumberland Palisaded Village site and the Saint Mary's City National Historic Landmark. Archaeologists working at the Cumberland locale on the banks of the Patuxent River believe that they may have found the remains of Opament town noted on John Smith's 1608 map. Findings of Yeocomico wares in intact deposits near the original center of Saint Mary's City, for their part, probably represent remains of the Yoacomaco town located on the spot where English settlers led by Leonard Calvert established their first colony in Maryland in 1634.

Contemporary documents written by English settlers moving into the area indicate that most Indian people living in these and other lower Potomac and Rappahannock river towns belonged to coalitions led by influential chiefs. Colonists often identified most people living in the area where archaeologists find Potomac Creek components as members of a Potomac chiefdom. Those people living in communities where archaeologists have found pottery assemblages dominated by Rappahannock wares, on the other hand, came to be known as Piscataways by settlers. As mentioned earlier, both people were called Conoys by the Iroquois.

Evidently basing their authority on political traditions established years before contact with Europeans, many of the most successful chiefs in this area probably increased their economic and political influence by serving as intermediaries between Europeans and populous and powerful interior fur suppliers like the Massawomecks. Competing with Susquehannock trade rivals to the north while fending off Powhatan efforts to incorporate them into their chiefdom farther south, rival Piscataway chiefs competed for furs and followers

Accokeek Creek Archeological Site National Historic Landmark

The Accokeek Creek Archeological Site is located on a low, sandy terrace south of Mockley Point between Piscataway and Accokeek Creeks on the south bank of the Potomac River in Prince Georges County, Maryland. Archaeological deposits preserved at the locale document between five thousand and six thousand years of human occupation in the lower Potomac River Valley. Analyses of materials uncovered during excavations conducted by local avocationists Alice and Henry Ferguson between 1935 and 1940 and former University of Maryland archaeologist Melburn Thurman in 1971 and 1972 show that the area was most intensively occupied during Late Woodland and early Historic Contact times.

Alice Ferguson conducted excavations between 1935 and 1939 in an area containing numerous pits, post molds of houses and stockade walls, three ossuaries, and other features indicative of intensive occupation. More than 150,000 potsherds and 9,000 chipped-stone projectile points were recovered from site features. Ferguson believed this locale to be the site of the town of Moyaone, which was visited by John Smith in 1608 and burned by English colonists during the mid-1620s and again around 1630.

Ferguson subsequently (from 1939 to 1940) excavated a stockaded fort with bastions and an ossuary containing forty-three interments within the fort's interior. This site was identified as the Susquehannock fort besieged by Maryland and Virginia militia in 1675.

During the 1960s, Robert L. Stephenson, then a University of Michigan doctoral candidate, systematically examined the seventy-five thousand artifacts donated by Ferguson to the University of Michigan Museum of Anthropology. Stephenson's stylistic analysis of these artifacts remains a chronological and cultural benchmark for Middle Atlantic regional archaeology.

Thurman (1972) found little evidence to support identification of the site as Moyaone. Reexamining Ferguson's data while conducting new excavations at the locale, he identified at least two episodes of Late Woodland occupation. The earliest appeared to be a small fortified community occupied during the early part of the Late Woodland period. The later occupation consisted of a larger stockaded townsite abandoned by 1550. Contrasting written documentation with Historic Contact period archaeological components from nearby sites, Thurman suggested that the site of Moyaone probably was located on or near the present-day Clagett Farm. Materials excavated by Thurman's field crews are curated in the University of Maryland's archaeology laboratory in College Park.

Designated a National Historic Landmark on July 19, 1964, the Accokeek Creek Archeological Site was listed in the National Register of Historic Places on October 15, 1966.

Unless otherwise cited, all information here is abstracted from Stephenson, Ferguson, and Ferguson (1963) and Weiss (1975).

along the lower Potomac and Rappahan- nock Rivers during the early years of contact.

Conflict with the expanding Pow- hatan chiefdom on the south may have led many Potomac communities to cre- ate what Maurice Mook (1943) believed was a defensive line of towns along the northern banks of the Rappahannock River. Although the largest of these towns, Nantaughtacund (later known as Nanzatico), was located on the southern bank of the river, most others were situ- ated between the Rappahannock and Potomac Rivers. These settlements, in turn, were separated from Powhatan towns on the south by a sparsely popu- lated buffer zone.

Farther north, Piscataway people and their neighbors were periodically visited after 1610 by Jamestown traders like Sam- uel Argall and Henry Spelman. Those who followed them, like Henry Fleet, who learned to speak the Nacotchtanke language while a captive among them from 1623 to 1628, established closer ties. Other Virginian traders, like William Claiborne, soon discovered that Sus- quehannocks controlling trade routes to the north could provide more and better pelts than those offered by Potomac Val- ley people. Knowing that Susquehan- nock leaders did not want English out- posts built in their country, Claiborne subsequently established his trading post seventy-five miles farther south on Kent Island in Chesapeake Bay, across from the present site of Annapolis, in 1631.

Claiborne initially hired an Algon- quian-speaking Accomack County resi- dent named Thomas Savage to deal with Susquehannocks bringing pelts to the new post, but most negotiations af- ter 1634 were conducted by one of Clai- borne's African slaves, a man who had learned the Susquehannock language while living among them. This man be- came the first of many people of Afri- can descent to play an important role as intermediary between Indian and European people in and around Chesa- peake Bay.

Casting an envious eye on the lucra- tive trade carried on by the Susquehan- nocks and the Virginians of Kent Island, Marylanders claiming the upper Chesa- peake for themselves by virtue of char- ter right moved to eject the Kent Is- landers shortly after establishing their Saint Mary's settlement at Yoacomaco in 1634. Aided by Piscataway people eager to revive their own faltering trade pros- pects, the Marylanders finally managed to seize both the Kent Island post and another establishment built on Palmer's Island at the mouth of the Susquehanna River by 1638.

Angered by this attack on their Virginian friends and resenting Mary- land's support for their Piscataway com- petitors, many Susquehannocks took their business to newly established Swedish trading posts on the Delaware. Armed with Swedish muskets and en- couraged by their Virginian clients, Sus- quehannock warriors began plundering Maryland and Piscataway settlements in 1642. These raids soon developed into something very much like a full-scale war, as Susquehannock warriors at- tacked Potomac Valley towns and car- ried off Indian and English captives. The presence of large numbers of Piscata- way prisoners forced to live in Sus- quehannock towns may account for the emergence of their language as a virtual lingua franca in subsequent trade trans- actions in the area.

Saint Mary's City Historic District National Historic Landmark

The Saint Mary's City Historic District National Historic Landmark is located on a neck of land extending southward into the Potomac River between Saint Mary's River and Saint Inigoe's, Broome, and Chancellor's Creeks in Saint Mary's County, Maryland. The district was originally designated a National Historic Landmark on August 4, 1969, as one of the nation's most significant archaeological sites associated with the themes of "European Exploration and Settlement" and "Architecture." Founded by colonists led by Gov. Leonard Calvert in 1634, Saint Mary's City was Maryland's first capital and the center of the only Roman Catholic English colony in British America from 1634 to 1694.

At the time of designation, archaeological remains of sixty seventeenth-century European buildings and structures were identified as contributing resources associated with the period of initial colonial settlement at Saint Mary's City. Since that time, archaeological surveys led by Henry M. Miller and Garry Wheeler Stone have identified six multicomponent sites containing archaeological resources dating to the Historic Contact period within the heart of the seventeenth-century central town area between Fisherman and Key Branch Creeks. Most of these sites are thought to have been localities within the large Piscataway Indian town of Yoacomaco, which was situated there at the time of initial English Catholic settlement in 1634.

Chipped-stone triangular projectile points, aboriginal clay tobacco pipes (several decorated with distinctive incised "running deer" motifs), Townsend, Potomac Creek, Yeocomico, and Colono pottery, lithic debitage, oyster shells, deer bones, and carbonized plant remains have been found with tin-glazed earthenwares, white-clay and terra-cotta tobacco-smoking pipes, bottle-glass fragments, glass beads, and iron implements in and around pits, midden layers, and post-mold patterns. Analyses of this assemblage affirm that the inhabitants of Yoacomaco were in contact with Europeans during Late Woodland and early Historic Contact times. These findings further corroborate written accounts stating that Maryland settlers built their capital in the heart of the Indian town.

Several written records document English impressions of the locale. Colonists Jerome Hawley and John Lewger, for example, wrote that Yoacomaco was "an Indian Towne, where they found ground cleered to their hands." Penning a more detailed description, Father Andrew White, the colony's spiritual leader, wrote that people living in Yoacomaco built their houses

> in an halfe ovall forme 20 foot long, and 9 or 10 foot high with a place open in the top, halfe a yard square, whereby they admit the light, and let forth the smoake, for they build their fire, after the manner of ancient halls of England, in the middle of the house, about which they lie to sleep upon mats, spread on a low scaffold halfe a yard from the ground. In one of these houses we doe celebrate [Mass], haveing it dressed a little better then by the Indians, till we get a better, which shall be shortly as may be.

Selecting Yoacomaco as the site of their new settlement, the colonists purchased all land within thirty miles of the town from the "Emperour of Pascatoway" on March 27, 1634. Immediately moving to the locale, settlers agreed to let the Indians remain in their homes long enough to harvest their corn. As Father

White noted, many English settlers moved into or adaptively reused Indian houses as they were vacated. In this way, Indian and English people lived and worked together through the summer of 1634.

Yoacomaco's original inhabitants had established a new community on the opposite bank of the Saint Mary's River by the fall of 1634. Soon afterwards, Saint Mary's settlers dismantled the last of their wigwams as they moved into new houses built in the English style. Surrounding their town with a fortified wall for protection against potential attacks from Indians or other English colonists living across the Potomac in Virginia, the new settlers farmed the land and carried on a modest trade with visiting Indian people.

Such visits became increasingly frequent as Maryland's Indian allies journeyed to the colony's capital to meet with provincial officials, worship with missionaries, or transact business with traders during the turbulent decades of the mid-1600s. Decreasing in frequency after Maryland's Indian community was devastated during Bacon's Rebellion (1675–1676), these visits ended when royal officials moved the capital to Anne Arundel Town (today's Annapolis) in 1695. Most of Saint Mary's City's public buildings were abandoned or destroyed following the transfer of the town's last governmental functions as a county seat to Leonardtown in 1708. Never a dense urban community, the locale remained a rural agrarian district into the twentieth century.

Yoacomaco's remains lay all but forgotten beneath fields and farms for

Aerial view of Saint Mary's City. Courtesy St. Mary's City Commission.

nearly 250 years before archaeologists first discovered evidence of historic Indian occupation within the area of Saint Mary's City's seventeenth-century town core during the early 1970s. Since that time, investigators working in this area have found objects and deposits associated with the historic Yoacomaco Indian community in the Village Center (18ST1-13), Van Sweringen (18ST1-19), Saint John's (18ST1-23), Gallow's Green (18ST1-112), and Mill Field complex (18ST1-116A and 18ST1-123A) sites.

Discoveries of intact deposits in these sites suggest that other intact deposits capable of yielding new information on early relations between Indian people and colonists survive at Saint Mary's City. The Saint Mary's City Commission, created in 1966 to preserve, study, and interpret the area's cultural resources, provides technical guidance and preservation assistance to landowners. St. Mary's College of Maryland, which owns some of the area containing known Historic Contact period resources, works with the St. Mary's City Commission in all undertakings potentially impacting cultural resources. The commission also manages the substantial tracts of land within the district that are owned and protected by the State of Maryland as a cultural and natural preserve.

Artifacts recovered from the above-mentioned sites currently are curated in research facilities maintained within the district by the Saint Mary's City Commission. An addendum incorporating Historic Contact period documentation into the Saint Mary's City Historic District National Historic Landmark nomination form was approved by the History Areas Committee of the National Park System Advisory Board on July 13, 1993.

Information presented here is abstracted from H. Miller (1983).

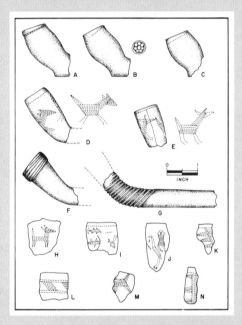

European- and Indian-made tobacco-smoking pipes from Saint Mary's City: (a–c) European white-clay tobacco-smoking pipes; (d, e, h, and m) Indian-made pipes decorated with roulete-incised running deer motifs (H. Miller 1983, fig. 21, p. 74). Courtesy St. Mary's City Commission.

The situation of Potomac and Piscataway people worsened when the Third Powhatan War broke out in Virginia in 1644 and they were forced by one belligerent or another to choose sides. Compelled to face enemies on both the north and south, many of these people turned to their new Maryland neighbors for support and protection.

Beleaguered themselves, the Marylanders could do little to help their Indian allies. Relief finally came in the form of Iroquois successes against the Hurons, Neutrals, and other interior Susquehannock fur-trade clients. Turning to meet this new threat to their main supply sources, Susquehannock leaders, feeling that they had profited all they could from their war in Maryland, shored up their southern flank by signing a peace treaty with their Indian and English enemies on the Potomac in 1652.

Resuming business at the end of hostilities, neither the Piscataways nor the Marylanders were able to fully revive the Chesapeake Bay trade. Continuing internecine conflicts between colonial rivals in the area depressed commerce, and continuing Iroquois successes farther north reduced the flow of northern furs to a trickle. More significantly, Iroquois warriors, who had defeated and dispersed the last of their western rivals by the mid-1650s, turned south to deal with suddenly isolated Susquehannock competitors.

Farther south, Potomac and Piscataway people had been impoverished by the collapse of the fur trade and devastated by the recent fighting. Increasingly, they turned to their Virginian and Maryland neighbors for material aid and spiritual guidance. Colonists extracted high prices for such support. Provincial officials, anxious to control all land and people within charter bounds, demanded that Indians submit formally to their authority. Forced to accede, Piscataway and Potomac leaders acknowledged their tributary status at treaty councils with colonial magistrates.

English settlers, for their part, increasingly demanded greater tracts of Indian land. Unable to stop the ever-growing number of colonists flooding into the area, most Indian people gradually sold their land along the main waterways and retired farther inland. Those refusing to move away camped on unoccupied lands or settled on reservations set aside for them by provincial authorities at places like Mattawoman near Indian Head in Maryland and Nanzatico in and around the Camden National Historic Landmark on the Rappahannock River in Virginia.

Missionaries exerted different degrees of influence in Potomac and Piscataway communities during these years. As the already-mentioned Henrico scheme showed, most Virginians gave little more than lip service to Indian conversion. Jesuit priests and their Franciscan successors, on the other hand, aggressively proselytized Indian people who visited their missions in and around Saint Mary's City after 1642. Operating as independent traders and freelance diplomats, many of these missionaries became important suppliers of trade goods as they interceded on behalf of their converts in colonial councils.

Temporarily forced to leave Maryland in 1655, the priests returned a few years later, gathered in new converts, and erected a new mission at Port Tobacco. A small, disc-shaped brass gorget dating to the mid-1600s and similar to others discovered in sites farther south has been discovered in an ossuary in the area. This discovery may materially corroborate written sources documenting contacts between Indian people and Catholic missionaries in other parts of the southeast.

Colonial administrators in Maryland and Virginia increased the extent of their authority over all Indian people living

Camden Historic District National Historic Landmark

The Camden National Historic Landmark is located on the southern shore of the Rappahannock River east of the city of Port Royal in Caroline County, Virginia. The Camden plantation manor house, built between 1857 and 1859, is regarded as one of the most complete and best preserved Italianate country houses in America. The plantation and manor house were listed in the National Register of Historic Places on November 17, 1969, and designated a National Historic Landmark on November 11, 1971.

Ninety-five sites dating from Early Archaic times (ca. 10,000 to 8,000 B.C.) to the mid–nineteenth century were discovered by archaeologists surveying 770 acres of the Camden estate between 1964 and 1984. Thirty of these sites contain deposits associated with the large, dispersed fifty-four-acre multicultural Nanzatico Indian community that was situated at the Camden locale between 1650 and 1704. The remains of at least eight houses and other occupation or activity areas associated with the main Nanzatico settlement are preserved in twenty sites located in a large field one-half mile to the east of Camden manor house. The other ten sites represent outlying community areas associated with this central town cluster.

Extant records indicate that displaced Portobago, Machotick, Nansemond, and Rappahannock Indian people moved among the Nanzaticos on lands set aside by Virginian provincial authorities at the Camden locale in or around 1650. Penning the only known description the Nanzatico Indian community, a visiting Frenchman named

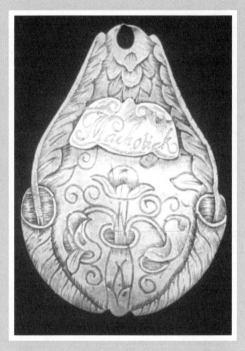

The reverse side of one of two silver medallions recovered from sites within the Camden National Historic Landmark. The front bears the legend "Ye King of." Courtesy Virginia Department of Historic Resources and the Virginia Historical Society.

Durand de Dauphine noted in 1686 that it consisted of "rather pretty houses, the walls as well as the roofs ornamented with trees, and so securely fastened together with deer thongs that neither rain nor wind causes them inconvenience." Noting that the Indians wore both cloth and deerskin garments, he went on to write that Indian townswomen made "pots, earthen vases and smoking pipes . . . the Christians buying these pots or vases fill them with Indian corn, which is the price of them."

Virginian settlers moving to the area during the middle decades of the 1600s came to own most Indian land at Nanzatico by the end of the century. Angered by the loss of their lands and livelihoods, Nanzatico people finally took matters into their own hands. On August 30, 1704, several men from the community killed a nearby family of colonists. Rounding up and jailing all the Nanzatico people they could find, the colonists executed five captives who had confessed to the killings. Determined to make an example, they sold all of the forty-four other Nanzatico people over twelve years of age into slavery in Antigua in the West Indies for a period of seven years. Prohibiting the exiles from returning to Virginia, authorities further ordered that all Nanzaticos younger than twelve be bound out as indentured servants until they reached the age of twenty-four.

A settler named John Pratt purchased the lands composing the present Camden tract between 1801 and 1802. He subsequently developed Camden into a large plantation that continues to operate under Pratt family ownership to the present day. Recovery of a silver badge inscribed with the legend "Ye King of Patomeck" by farmworkers plowing one of Pratt's fields in 1832 represents the earliest known record of archaeological discovery at Camden. More than one hundred twenty-five years passed before artifacts eroding from a logging road brought Camden's archaeological resources to the attention of Virginia's preservation community. Between October 1964 and March 1965, members of the Upper Rappahannock Chapter of the Archaeological Society of Virginia conducted a dig at the locale. Investigators found oyster and clam shells; deer and other animal bones; quantities of quartz, greenstone, and other debitage; two triangular, chipped-stone projectile points;

several bifaces associated with earlier occupations; ten scrapers; a sandstone abrader; several aboriginally produced clay tobacco-smoking pipes; and 9,055 aboriginal ceramic sherds within an area measuring thirty feet by fifty feet. Terminal Late Woodland Potomac Creek Plain (n = 5,329) and Cord-Marked (n = 3,394) wares and Camden Plain Colono ceramics (n = 177) composed the overwhelming majority of the site's aboriginal pottery assemblage.

Other artifacts found in this area included a silver medal inscribed "Ye King of Machotick," similar to the 1832 find; a small Colono-ware-type untempered-clay spoon and several small Colono-ware small cups; twenty-five European white-clay tobacco-smoking pipe fragments; a cylindrical white-clay bead; twelve pieces of majolica and thirty-eight fragments of Bellarmine salt-glazed Rhenish stoneware; nine gunflints and two small iron gun parts; a glass bead; eleven fragments of green bottle glass; and a clear-glass chipped triangular projectile point. Eighty-two hand-wrought iron nails; two iron files; five iron knife blades; three iron loops; an iron strap hinge; a piece of an iron door lock; a brass buckle; and a number of other copper, lead, pewter, brass, and iron objects also were found. The site was given the Smithsonian trinomial designation 44CE3.

Chronological-marker artifacts in the European portion of the site assemblage clearly date the deposit. The Bellarmine jug, for example, is similar to others manufactured between 1660 and 1680. Analysis of European white-clay tobacco-smoking pipe heelmarks and pipe-stem diameters indicates that most date to the period between 1650 and 1680.

The dates of manufacture of the Patomeck and Machotick silver medals remain subjects of debate. Some scholars believe that they may be two of several silver and copper badges Virginian officials ordered worn by tributary Indians visiting English settlements as signs of identification and submission in 1662 (McCary 1983). Others believe that they may be among the twenty silver badges distributed as gifts to tributary Indians signing the 1677 and 1680 Middle Plantation treaties (MacCord 1969).

Whatever their exact date, these medals and other diagnostic European artifacts found at 44CE3 provide evidence corroborating written records chronicling occupations of Indian people using both aboriginal products and European imports at Nanzatico between 1650 and 1704. The age, condition, and distribution of these artifacts, moreover, suggests that 44CE3 was the site of a small house occupied by Indian people sometime during the third quarter of the seventeenth century. Although the exact ethnic identity of the people associated with the site remains unclear, the name inscribed on the silver medal found at 44CE3 indicates an affiliation of some sort with the Machotick Indian community.

Virginia State Library archaeologists under the direction of Howard A. MacCord, Sr., surveying at Camden between 1964 and 1976 found Historic Contact period components at sites 44CE4 and 44CE19. In 1983 the Virginia Division of Historic Landmarks (the present Department of Historic Resources, which up to 1976 had been responsible for the state's historic sites) investigators supervised by Mary Ellen N. Hodges conducted a year-long survey of Camden. Hodges's fieldwork added twenty-one new Historic Contact period sites to the Camden site inventory. Artifacts recovered during these and earlier surveys currently are curated in facilities maintained by Virginia's State Historic Preservation Office.

Unless otherwise cited, information presented here is abstracted from Hodges (1986) and Hodges and McCartney (1986).

within their provincial boundaries during the last quarter of the century. In Virginia, Indian leaders formally submitting to provincial authority were given silver or copper medals symbolizing their status. Two of these medals, bearing inscriptions "Ye King of Patomeck" and "Ye King of Machotick," have been found within the former Nanzatico reservation in the Camden National Historic Landmark.

Maryland authorities also moved to control all Indians living within what they regarded as their charter limits. Claiming authority over Susquehannocks increasingly weakened by epidemic disease and decades of almost constant warfare, Maryland authorities ordered them to move to new settlements near the present site of Washington, D.C., on the province's exposed western borders in 1674. Unable to refuse Maryland's invitation but unwilling to settle in so insecure a location, Susquehannock leaders instead built a fortified town closer to the heart of English settlements at Accokeek Creek.

Settlers remembering earlier Susquehannock attacks quickly resolved to drive both the Susquehannocks and their provincial protectors from the area. The struggle that followed, known as Bacon's Rebellion, after Nathaniel Bacon, a Virginian planter who led the uprising, nearly toppled provincial governments on both sides of the Potomac.

It began when Virginian settlers, enraged when Doeg people seized several hogs from a Maryland trader who had refused to pay his debts, retaliated by murdering several Doeg people and fourteen Susquehannocks during the summer of 1675. Moving to preempt expected Susquehannock retaliation for these murders, more than a thousand Maryland and Virginia militiamen aided by Piscataway warriors besieged the Susquehannock fort.

When the settlers murdered five of their most important chiefs at a parley beyond the fort walls at the beginning of the siege, the Susquehannocks and their Doeg allies held off their assailants for several weeks, eventually breaking out and escaping to the southwest to a place near the Occaneechi towns along the Roanoke River. Seeking vengeance for the murder of their chiefs, Susquehannocks ranged from Roanoke territory to raid upcountry settlements along the Maryland and Virginia frontiers for more than a year before withdrawing farther north.

Devastated by years of seemingly endless warfare and forced to sell most of their remaining lands to settlers, Piscataway and Potomac peoples began moving away from their ancestral lands after Bacon's Rebellion ended. Some of them moved farther from the mouth of Piscataway Creek to more secure remote locales in the Zachiah Swamp. In 1681 people living in a fort there were attacked by a large force of Seneca and Susquehannock warriors who lived among them. Those who did not move to the swamplands settled farther up

the Potomac and Rappahannock Rivers, beyond the fall line, in new communities at places like Conoy Island. Still others began moving north to what until recently had been Susquehannock territory.

A substantial number of sites preserve archaeological evidence of seventeenth-century Indian life along the lower Potomac and Rappahannock river valleys. Significant deposits document Potomac townlife at sites like the aforementioned Potomac Creek and Indian Point locales and the Camden National Historic Landmark. Evidence associated with major Piscataway communities is preserved within the above-mentioned late–sixteenth- and early–seventeenth-century Cumberland Palisaded Village site, at early–seventeenth-century occupations at the Saint Mary's City National Historic Landmark, and in later–seventeenth-century deposits associated with the main Piscataway town preserved in Piscataway complex sites.

Deposits discovered at 44EX3–5 in Virginia contain an array of European stonewares, bottle-glass fragments, and white-clay pipes associated with plain and cord-marked Potomac Creek wares and aboriginal lithics. Diffusely scattered deposits indicative of campsites or activity stations found at White Oak Point and other locales indicate that Indian people forced to abandon major townsites along the area's rivers may have intermittently continued to use unoccupied portions of them as warm-weather oyster camps. Other deposits believed to represent remains of small hamlets or campsites dating to the 1600s have been found at the multicomponent Posey site at Indian Head Naval Ordnance Station in Maryland, the Little

Marsh Creek and Owings sites in Virginia, and other locales.

Fragments of aboriginal pottery believed to have contained corn traded by Indian people to settlers have been found at the sites of several late–seventeenth-century colonial Maryland homesteads. Late Woodland potsherds and fragments of aboriginal clay pipes have been found in unplowed midden deposits dating to the third quarter of the seventeenth century at the Burle site in Anne Arundel County. Other potsherds have been found at the nearby Broadneck site and at the Compton site in Calvert County.

Other information is preserved within seventeenth-century mortuary sites. Copper, glass beads, and other objects associated with power or influence sometimes found in individual graves of adults or very young children are rarely encountered in mass ossuary interments at Potomac Creek and Port Tobacco. Increased numbers of European objects found in later and larger mass interments at the Mount Airy site in Virginia and the Ferguson ossuary near Piscataway Park in Maryland may reflect higher mortality, increased economic opportunity, changing attitudes about suitable burial furnishings, or sociopolitical changes brought on by more intensive contact with Europeans.

THE EIGHTEENTH CENTURY

Relatively little is known about eighteenth-century Indian life in the lower Potomac and Rappahannock valleys. Many of the original occupants were already living as expatriates in Conoy or Nanticoke communities farther north, west, and east. Others, like Doeg people

chronicled on the Mattaponi River, had moved to more southerly locales. Still others, like the earlier-mentioned Nanzatico people caught in the dragnet set out by provincial authorities following the murder of several settlers in 1704, were condemned to indentured servitude or deported as slaves to the Caribbean.

Most Piscataway and Potomac Indians remaining in Virginia disappeared almost entirely from provincial records when colonial authorities began enumerating all native people as nonwhites in 1705. They are also lost track of in Maryland when that province adopted the same policy.

Ironically, provincial authorities, no longer distinguishing Indian people in census reports or other documents, continued to administer Indian reservations at Mattawoman, Pamunkey, and other locales. The Maryland Pamunkey reservation, unlike its Virginia counterpart of the same name, was a small place built on poor land. Unwilling to live on such bad land, most of the people settling there moved north to join friends and relatives at Conejohela in the lower Susquehanna Valley by 1712.

The colonists, for their part, often encouraged such emigrations, and chroniclers began to publish tracts affirming the legal fiction that no native people were still living within provincial boundaries. Robert Beverley (1947), for example, wrote that the Portobago and Rappahannock communities no longer existed in the first edition of his *History of Virginia*, published in 1705.

The continuing presence of people claiming descent from Rappahannock ancestors challenges the validity of such pronouncements. Although written documentation of their survival and that of other Piscataway and Potomac peoples in their homeland is spotty, extant sources indicate that people tracing Indian ancestry have lived unobtrusively throughout the area since colonial times.

Most places occupied by the area's eighteenth-century natives are difficult to identify archaeologically. Like other native people in the Northeast, the Piscataways and Potomacs had stopped making aboriginal tools and implements by the end of the preceding century. As a result, archaeological deposits left by such people differ little from those associated with non-Indians. Assemblages recovered from locales noted in colonial records as Indian habitation sites, for their part, are generally scant or fragmentary. The eighteenth-century component identified at 44NB97, for example, currently consists of a single glass bead recovered from the site's surface.

Written records and the oral literature hold that people living in places like 44NB97 and the few components believed to date to the middle decades of the century at the Camden National Historic Landmark increasingly married non-Indians or people from other native communities during these years. Working as farmers, fishers, laborers, servants, or artisans, most of these people gradually settled in provincial towns or villages.

Living and working with non-Indians, they became enmeshed in the area's cash economy. Most struggled to adjust to this situation by making old products yield new income. Selectively adopting and creatively adapting European and African tools, techniques, and materials, many of these people made and sold herbal remedies, baskets, straw brooms, and distinctive Colono wares to non-Indian customers.

Potters making Colono wares used aboriginal production techniques to create pottery incorporating what many scholars believe are European or African styles, shapes, and motifs. Citing information preserved in orally transmitted narratives and noting strong stylistic similarities with west African pots, scholars like James Deetz (1988) and Leland Ferguson (1992) believe that African potters produced most Colono wares found in eighteenth-century sites excavated in Georgia and the Carolinas.

Other scholars support Ivor Nöel-Hume's (1962) view that Colono wares are Indian products. Several note the discovery of such wares on sites known to have been the homes of Indian people. Noting that Indian people composed as much as one-third of South Carolina's slave population during the early 1700s, archaeologist L. Daniel Mouer (1991) suggests that native people probably produced much of the Colono ware found in the area's plantations.

Examining Colono wares found on sites in and around Piscataway-Potomac Country, Mouer and others (Binford 1965; Henry 1992) have found that all have turned up in locales associated with Indian people and that most appear to derive from aboriginal antecedents. Much remains to be learned about these wares. Discoveries of Colono pottery in sites containing otherwise undifferentiated assemblages of European materials, such as those found in the earlier-mentioned deposits in the Camden National Historic Landmark, have potential to yield information on com-

Colono-ware vessel forms from Chesapeake Bay area sites identified during research conducted by Susan L. Henry during the 1970s (Henry 1992, fig. 26, p. 98). *Courtesy Susan L. Henry.*

munity life in many otherwise poorly documented or now-forgotten Indian, African American, and Creole communities (Hodges 1986; Hodges and McCartney 1986).

SOURCES

Much of the information summarized in this section is abstracted from Fausz (1985, 1987, 1988), Feest (1978a, 1978b), and Potter (1980, 1982, 1993). Data suggesting contact at the late–seventeenth-century Broadneck, Burle, and Compton sites were provided by Luckenbach (1991, 1993).

Transcripts of records documenting political relations in the area may be found in Browne et al. (1883–1970), Gehring (1977, 1981), and W. Robinson (1983a, 1983b). Observations on Indian life written by early settlers, traders, and others may be found in Hall (1910), Myers (1912), and Tyler (1907).

Studies drawing on these and other primary sources include earlier analyses by Bushnell (1937), Graham (1935), and Marye (1935) and more recent examinations undertaken by Boender (1988), W. E. Clark (1980), Moore (1991a), and Turner (1976).

An analysis of the political ramifications of ossuary burial may be found in Jirikowic (1990). Axtell (1985) and Lewis (1988) briefly describe Jesuit and Franciscan missions in Maryland. A comprehensive analysis of studies examining Colono wares in area sites appears in Henry (1992).

Merrell (1979) suggests that Piscataway people used the fur trade and politics of accommodation to successfully adjust to European colonization. Archaeological, written, and oral documentation of enduring Piscataway identity and ethnicity is summarized in Cissna (1986) and Porter (1986).

POWHATAN COUNTRY

Powhatan Country extends across the Virginian tidewater lowlands from the York River Valley to the James River estuary.

THE SIXTEENTH CENTURY

Unlike other areas in the Middle Atlantic region, a number of written records document relations between native people and Europeans arriving in the Virginia lowlands during the sixteenth century. Several of these documents describe the establishment of a Jesuit mission at Ajacan in 1570 and subsequent Spanish reprisals following its destruction one year later. Others record the rescue of a Spanish boy by Indian people after the mission's destruction. Another group of documents chronicles visits made by Roanoke colonist Ralph Lane to the coastal town of Chesepiuc near modern Virginia Beach in 1585 and 1586.

Most other information documenting sixteenth-century Indian life in the area comes from archaeological sites excavated in the James River Valley. Archaeologists working in this area have discovered several ossuaries, numerous campsites, and remains of larger, occa-sionally fortified communities. Many of these sites contain diagnostic triangular, chipped-stone projectile points, shell beads and ornaments, and objects of un-smelted copper. Several also contain ceramic assemblages dominated by variants of shell-tempered terminal Late Woodland Townsend-series wares and sand- or crushed-quartz-tempered Cashie-Branchville pottery. A very small number of objects of European origin have been found in some of the sites otherwise dated to the 1500s or early 1600s in this area.

Pieces of smelted metal and glass beads have been found in assemblages recovered from the multicomponent Hatch site (the probable site of an early Historic Contact period Weyanoke town), Jordan's Journey, and the Tree Hill Farm site, believed to be the locale of Powhatan, home of the paramount sachem Wahunsonacock. Smelted copper objects have recently been identified in an ossuary found with house patterns, pits, and other deposits uncovered during test excavations at the locale of the Pasbehegh town noted on John Smith's 1608 map within the Governors Land at Two Rivers development at the confluence of the James and Chickahominy Rivers in James City County.

The number of sites believed to date to the 1500s along the James and York Rivers continues to dwindle as development obliterates surviving archaeological deposits in the area. Some properties on public lands, like Jamestown site deposits preserved within Colonial National Historical Park, are protected by federal law. Other deposits on private lands, like those located at Pasbehegh, can only be protected if landowners are dedicated to their preservation.

Although evidence found at these sites is fragmentary, Turner (1986) and other scholars currently believe that chiefdoms of the type chronicled by early European observers first developed at least three hundred years before Europeans sailed to the area. Archaeologist Lewis R. Binford (1991) was one of the first investigators to identify such continuities in the area. After surveying extant archaeological, environmental, and documentary records, Binford suggested that chiefdoms in the area emerged as a result of technological changes, population increases, and contacts with more complex Mississippian societies farther south and west.

THE SEVENTEENTH CENTURY

Wahunsonacock, the paramount werowance of the Powhatan chiefdom, exercised authority over the largest, last, and best-known chiefdom in the land between the James and York Rivers when English colonists established their settlement at Jamestown in the heart of his territories in 1607. Although estimates vary, most investigators believe that Wahunsonacock at the height of his power exerted authority over from twelve thousand to fourteen thousand Eastern Algonquian–speaking people living in communities stretching from the Rappahannock River and the lower tip of the Delmarva Peninsula south to the Blackwater River Valley. At least eight thousand of these people may have lived within the Powhatan heartland between the James and York Rivers.

Extant information indicates that most of these people spoke dialects of the Powhatan language. These same documents suggest that many of these people did not acknowledge Wahunsonacock's authority at all times. Some communities, like those in the Chickahominy Valley, regarded themselves as independent people. Other communities, like those on the farther edges of the chiefdom, did little more than pay tribute to Wahunsonacock's tax collectors.

Nevertheless, the Powhatan chiefdom was probably the most complex stratified native social order in the Northeast at the time of direct European contact. Surviving written accounts indicate that people belonging to this and other chiefdoms around the lower reaches of Chesapeake Bay organized themselves into a hierarchy of hereditary ruling families led by a paramount werowance. Each werowance was supported by a priesthood, councils of experienced hunters and warriors, and other people referred to simply as commoners.

Early English observers like John Smith and William Strachey wrote that Wahunsonacock controlled nearly every aspect of life in his domain. Intent upon weakening old loyalties and promoting new relationships with him and his family, Wahunsonacock rewarded loyal friends and punished opponents. Describing his control over Powhatan economic affairs,

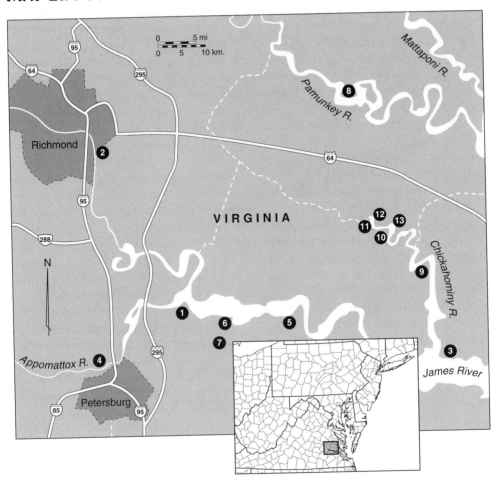

Map 21 Historic Contact Sites

Map Number	Site Name	County	State	Date	NR	Source
1	Jordan's Journey (44PG1)	Prince George	VA	Early 1600s		Mouer 1992b
2	Tree Hill Farm (44HE674)	Henrico	VA	Late 1500s–early 1600s		MacCord 1993; McLearen and Binns 1992
3	Pasbehegh (4JC308-10)	James City	VA	Late 1500s–early 1600s		JRIA 1990, 1992; Luccketti 1994
4	Kiser (44CF14)	Chesterfield	VA	1600–1610		Buchanan 1985; MacCord 1989a, 1993; Turner 1990b
5	Flowerdew Hundred Plantation (44PG64)	Prince George	VA	1600–1619	X	Barka 1975
6	Maycock's Point (44PG40)	Prince George	VA	1600–1620		MacCord 1989, 1993; Turner 1990b

Map Number	Site Name	County	State	Date	NR	Source
7	Hatch (44PG51)	Prince George	VA	1615–1622	X	Gregory 1980; Loth, Mc-Cartney, and Luccketti 1978; MacCord 1989a, 1993; Turner 1990b; Turner and Opperman 1989; VDHR
8	Pamunkey Reservation (44KW 14–15, 18, 21, 24–29)	King William	VA	1646–present	X	McCartney and Hodges 1982; Norrisey 1980; Turner 1990b
	Chickahominy Complex	Charles City	VA	1600s	X	McCary and Barka 1977; Turner 1990b; VHLC 1974
9	Buck					
10	Edgehill					
11	Harwood					
12	Osborne Landing					
13	Potts					

English chroniclers wrote that he exacted tribute from constituents in the form of corn, shell beads, skins, European goods, and forced labor.

One recent study indicates that the paramount chief may have extracted as much as 80 percent of the total production of some constituent communities in tribute (Barker 1992). Although most of this tribute was redistributed to followers, Powhatan leaders invested much of their people's resources in the burgeoning trade network based upon exchange of native furs, food, and other products for European glass beads; copper or brass hoops, spirals, and beads; and other items.

Like other people living in similar circumstances, members of communities in and around the Powhatan heartland accepted Wahunsonacock's overlordship uneasily. Although most of them probably appreciated his generosity to his followers and feared his vast power (the extent of both his generosity and his power has been well documented), many undoubtedly wished for their own autonomy. Enterprising colonists ignored contradictory directives from their home government calling on colonists to both respect and exploit the Indians, and took full advantage of cleavages in the Powhatan social fabric in a series of wars that followed English settlement in Wahunsonacock's country.

Concerned by English challenges to his authority and all-too-clearly appreciating the colonists' ultimate aim, Wahunsonacock led his people against the Virginians in the First Powhatan War in 1609. Although Powhatan warriors almost succeeded in destroying the Virginian settlements during the first year of the conflict, settlers were aided by Indian allies from the Piscataway-Potomac and Nanticoke Countries who were anxious to free themselves from Wahunsonacock's domination and helped them hold on.

Eventually, the tide of the war turned against the Powhatans. The English successfully attacked and burned major settlements like Powhatan itself and Pasbehegh. Those not killed or driven away during these assaults were captured and enslaved by the attackers.

The fighting also stunted colonial development. Unable to travel freely, and continually on guard, Virginians found their commerce grinding to a halt. Exhausted by the interminable struggle, the belligerents finally negotiated an uneasy peace on the occasion of the marriage of Wahunsonacock's daughter Pocahontas to Jamestown settler John Rolfe in 1614.

Although peace ended the violence and reopened commerce, it did not significantly improve relations between Powhatan people and their fractious English neighbors. Renewed English provocations angered the Powhatans and alienated their Indian allies. Abdicating in 1617, Wahunsonacock transferred his power to his brother Opitchapam and retired to a community on the Potomac River.

But Opitchapam was unable to consolidate his position and was soon supplanted by another brother, the Chickahominy chief Opechancanough, from the town of Pamunkey. Working with leaders from most of the James and York River towns, Opechancanough quickly forged a new coalition whose primary aim was the ejection of all English settlers from the shores of Chesapeake Bay. United as never before and outraged by the English murder of their warrior-prophet Nemattanew, coalition warriors launched a coordinated attack that succeeded in killing more than one-third of the colonists on March 22, 1622.

This second Powhatan war dragged on for more than ten years, as adversaries alternately traded with and fought against one another. Indian people repeatedly arranged truces to cultivate and harvest needed provisions. Virginians agreeing to such truces often broke them

just as the crops ripened. Years passed. Coalition warriors continually waylaid unwary English travelers while Virginian raiders adopted Indian tactics with growing effectiveness. Adversaries plundered each other's cornfields, destroyed their fishing weirs, and attacked their towns and villages.

Opechancanough's followers suffered dreadfully. Hundreds were killed when Pamunkey was burned and outlying communities like Moyaone and Patawomeke were razed to the ground. Demoralized, exhausted, and increasingly isolated, Opechancanough finally accepted an English offer to end hostilities in 1636.

The 1636 peace proved to be short-lived. Unwilling to accept English domination, Opechancanough once again assembled a coalition to strike the Virginian settlements. On April 18, 1644, his warriors killed or captured more than five hundred settlers. Recovering quickly, the colonists retaliated. Aided by Rappahannock and Accomac allies, Virginian columns soon defeated the much-reduced Powhatans. Opechancanough himself was murdered by an English guard shortly after being captured in 1646. Hundreds of other Indians taken prisoner in the fighting were sold into slavery. No longer able to resist, the Powhatans sued for a final peace in 1646.

Skillfully exploiting Indian rivalries, Virginians had successfully played contending native communities and factions off against one another. Outgunned, often outmaneuvered, and possibly suffering from epidemic diseases known to have struck other Indian communities farther north and south, chiefdom coalitions plagued by internal disputes could not effectively repel Virginian invasions. Repeatedly attacked by colonists and Indian enemies, the Powhatan chiefdom itself finally dissolved following Opechancanough's murder.

The Virginians dictated harsh terms of surrender in the treaties that ended hostilities. Indian leaders were forced to cede the heart of their people's territories. All had to acknowledge English sovereignty over their lands and lives. Powhatan people accepting these terms moved to small supervised communities established within ancestral lands.

The Pamunkey Indian Reservation typifies Virginian reservation life of the period. Established in 1653 at the site of the principal Pamunkey town, the reservation was then located in a remote part of the province. Pamunkey continues to encompass some two thousand acres of land on a marshy promontory jutting from the north bank of the Chickahominy River. Much of this tract was, and is, not only swampy but also heavily forested. Unable to adequately support themselves on such reservations and forced to compete in labor markets dominated by planters using slave labor, many Indians had to make their living by binding themselves out as indentured servants in the years following the end of the Third Powhatan War. Other Indians found themselves enslaved for debts or crimes against settlers.

Powhatan people also continued to be subjected to intermittent attacks from foreign enemies during these years. Susquehannock warriors, for example, killed or captured Powhatan people visiting or living with Potomac and Piscataway friends and relatives during their war with the Maryland colony and their Indian allies between 1642 and 1652. Other losses were suffered in 1656 when Pamunkey chief Totopotomoy and a large number of his warriors were killed while trying to drive away some seven hundred western Indian people—variously identified by investigators as Mannahoacs and Eries—who had settled at the falls of the James River in or near the present city of Richmond. Totopotomoy was succeeded by his widow, a descendant of Opechancanough, named Cockacoeske, who served her people as "Queen of Pamunkey" until the 1680s.

Powhatan people also suffered in the fighting during Bacon's Rebellion. Others were killed or carried off as captives by Iroquois raiders traveling south on the Great Warriors Path along the broad piedmont valleys from New York to northern Georgia after the Susquehannock dispersal in 1675.

Resenting Virginian domination and angered by the colonists' failure to protect them from foreign raiders, some Powhatan people abandoned old homes. Many Weyanoke and Nansemond people, for example, moved farther south and west to the Nottoway-Meherrin Country along the Virginia frontier. Others, refusing to leave Powhatan Country, moved to more remote portions of ancestral territory set aside for them by Virginian authorities. No longer owing allegiance to a chiefdom, many of these people revitalized earlier independent communities. Living quietly, members of Chickahominy, Mattaponi, Nansemond, Pamunkey, and Rappahannock communities tried to avoid contact with provincial authorities whenever possible. As a result, few documents record their presence in the area after Bacon's rebels dispersed and returned to their homes.

Surviving records do indicate that the number of Indian people living within the Powhatan heartland at the end of the century had dwindled to less than 5 percent of the 1607 population. Like other Middle Atlantic Indians, most of these people increasingly adopted English language, religion, clothing, tools, and weapons. Unable to find spouses in their own tiny communities, many married Indian and non-Indian people from other places.

Known archaeological deposits reflect these developments. Archaeologists surveying the surface of Tree Hill Farm fields have found stoneware, case glass, and English flint fragments among Late Woodland stone tools and pottery at the already-mentioned Powhatan town locale chronicled by John Smith and Gabriel Archer during the first decades of the century. Although objects of European origin have been reported in association with aboriginal deposits at a number of nearby early–seventeenth-century Chickahominy-complex properties, formal site reports detailing these findings have not yet been published. Farther east, clearly identifiable materials of European origin have not yet been found at the archivally chronicled Accomac and Accohannock locales.

Mixed deposits of Late Woodland Indian house patterns, stone tools, pottery, and European metal tools, weapons, and other materials dating from the late 1500s to the 1630s have been excavated at Flowerdew Hundred Plantation sites. Small numbers of European artifacts have also been found with aboriginal materials in intact features at the Hatch site, situated at a locale corresponding to the location of the principal Weyanoke town mapped by John Smith. Investigators believe that Hatch deposits chronicle initial Weyanoke relations with Virginians newly arrived at their most important community.

Gaston and Roanoke pottery found in English trash pits discovered during recent salvage excavations at the Jordan's Journey site graphically documents early intercultural relations. Dug by English settlers building a large, fortified community at the site of an earlier Weyanoke Indian town in 1620, the pits contain charred corn and pottery thought to represent fragments of pots containing produce obtained from Indian people visiting the locale to trade.

Deposits of clearly associated aboriginal stone tools, Colono wares, and objects of European origin such as glass beads and smelted metal have been excavated from sites located within the Pamunkey Indian Reservation. A shell bead necklace strung on iron wire found in one of several human burials discovered at Maycock's Point also may date to this century.

THE EIGHTEENTH CENTURY

Little archaeological or documentary evidence of Indian life in Powhatan Country during the 1700s has been found. Although written records document movements of Nansemond, Weyanoke, and other people farther south and west by midcentury, most reports affirm that the majority of native residents of Powhatan Country remained on or near the sites of ancestral settlements. Although individuals tracing descent from these and other local Indian groups continue to live in the state today, colonial Virginian authorities generally only recognized people living on provincial reservations at Gingaskin, Mattaponi, and Pamunkey as Indians after declaring all other native people nonwhites in 1705.

Most of these people continued to live unobtrusively in small rural enclaves scattered between the York and James river valleys. Difficult to identify archaeologically and almost undocumented in surviving archives, their houses and towns gradually came to closely resemble those built by non-Indians. As elsewhere, most of these people had stopped making Late Woodland–style tools and implements by the beginning of the eighteenth century. As a result, archaeological deposits left by these people differ little from those produced by non-Indians.

Deposits containing Colono wares, European ceramics, and a wide range of metal tools preserved intact within the Pamunkey Indian Reservation contain the only body of clearly identifiable archaeological evidence documenting eighteenth-century Indian life in Powhatan Country. Deposits dating to the 1700s may yet survive in or near other present-day Indian communities scattered between the York and James river valleys.

SOURCES

Much of the information presented in this section has been drawn from Barker (1992), Binford (1991), Fausz (1985, 1988), Feest (1978b), Gleach (1992), Potter (1982, 1989, 1993), Rountree (1989, 1990), and Turner (1985). Population figures generally follow Turner (1982). Material on Powhatan linguistics appears in Siebert (1975).

No general survey of Historic Contact period archaeology in the area currently exists. MacCord (1989a) and Reinhart and Pogue (1993) provide useful summaries on the state of contact studies in Virginia. Studies by Potter (1982, 1993) and Turner (1976) provide detailed information on specific portions of the area. Maps contrasting archaeological data with early cartographic projections in tidewater territory may be seen in Feest (1978b) and McCary and Barka (1977). Key site reports include Buchanan (1985); Gregory (1980); JRIA (1990, 1992); Loth, McCartney, and Luccketti (1978); McCartney and Hodges (1982); and Norrisey (1980).

European observers, like Virginians Robert Beverley (1947), John Smith (Barbour 1986), and William Strachey (1953), recorded information on aspects of Indian life in the area. Other primary sources include McIlwaine (1918–1919, 1925–1945); Quinn, Quinn, and Hillier (1979); W. Robinson (1983a, 1983b); and Tyler (1907). Information contained in these accounts provides insights into early Historic Contact period tidewater Virginian Indian social organization, spiritual beliefs, economic life, and political relations.

The abortive sixteenth-century Jesuit mission is discussed in Gradie (1988) and Lewis and Loomie (1953). Arguing from slender sources, Bridenbaugh suggests that the Don Luis who led the attacks that destroyed the Spanish Jesuit colony was the very same warrior and chief later known as Opechancanough (Bridenbaugh 1980, 1981). See Fausz (1981) for a biographical sketch of Opechancanough challenging Bridenbaugh's hypothesis. Fausz (1985) and D. Quinn (1985) provide succinct accounts of relations between Indian people and early English explorers and colonists from the founding of Roanoke in 1585 to the early years of the Virginia colony. McCartney (1989) presents a biographical sketch of the life and career of Cockacoeske, the Queen of Pamunkey.

MAP 22: NOTTOWAY-MEHERRIN COUNTRY

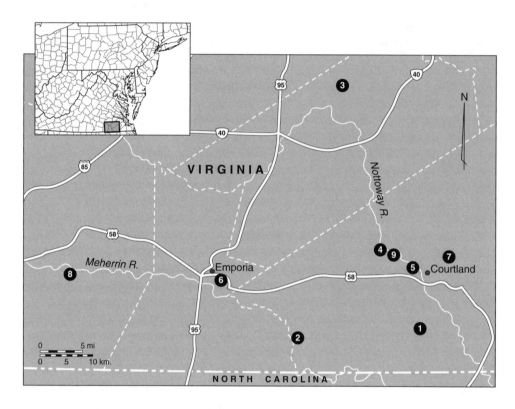

Map 22 Historic Contact Sites

Map Number	Site Name	County	State	Date	NR	Source
1	Hand (44SN22)	Southampton	VA	1590–1610		MacCord 1993; G. Smith 1984; Turner 1990b; VDHR
2	Ellis (44SN24)	Southampton	VA	1600s		Turner 1990b; VDHR
3	44SX198	Sussex	VA	1600s–1700s		Turner 1990b; VDHR
4	Rose Hill/C-1 (44SN4 and 44SN18)	Southampton	VA	1653–1700	X	Binford 1991; VHLC 1979
5	C-8	Southampton	VA	1700		Binford 1991
6	John Green (44GV1-2)	Greensville	VA	1700–1720	X	MacCord 1970, 1993; VHLC 1983; Turner 1990b; VDHR
7	C-3	Southampton	VA	1705–1745		Binford 1991
8	Fort Christanna (44BR3)	Brunswick	VA	1714–1732	X	Beaudry 1979; Hazzard and McCartney 1979; McCartney and Hazzard 1979; Turner 1990b; VDHR
9	C-10	Southampton	VA	1730–1770		Binford 1991

NOTTOWAY-MEHERRIN COUNTRY

Nottoway-Meherrin Country extends across valleys drained by the rivers of the same name in southern Virginia and adjacent portions of North Carolina. The area extends westward across the Atlantic coastal plain from the Dismal Swamp and the Blackwater River Valley west across the fall line into the eastern margins of the Virginian piedmont.

THE SIXTEENTH CENTURY

Very little is known about the lives of the Indians who lived here during the 1500s. Most evidently were descended from people who began living in towns, planting crops, and making the same types of triangular, chipped-stone projectile points and pottery at least a thousand years before Roanoke settler Ralph Lane became the first European reputed to visit the area in 1586.

Archaeologists have found little physical evidence of Indian life clearly dating to the sixteenth century along the Nottoway or Meherrin Rivers. Cashie-Branchville ceramics; Late Woodland triangular, chipped-stone projectile points; and smelted metal scraps have been found in features believed to date to the 1500s at the multicomponent John Green site complex near the fall line of the Meherrin River. Farther east, a pair of scissors, two scraps of sheet iron, and a worked chalcedony fragment broken from what is believed to have been a gunflint have been found in pits containing large amounts of shell-tempered pottery and stone tools at the Hand site along the Nottoway River on the Virginian coastal plain. Noting the absence of more recent diagnostic European artifacts, archaeologists believe that Hand site deposits probably date to the late sixteenth or very early seventeenth century.

THE SEVENTEENTH CENTURY

Edward Bland's 1650 account of his journey along the lower reaches of the Nottoway and Meherrin river valleys contains the earliest known written record of direct contact between Indians and Europeans in the area. Bland wrote that these people knew at least one interpreter from Fort Henry, the main Virginian southwestern frontier post, built near present-day Petersburg in 1646. He further noted that these people knew about the Powhatan Wars and were aware of other developments farther north. Noticing that they feared firearms, he stated that they had no such weapons themselves, owned few European goods, and gave little indication of contact with colonists.

Bland noted that people along the Nottoway River lived in towns named Rowantee, Tonnatorah, and Cohanahanhaka. He also noted another town, Meharineck, farther west on the banks of the Meherrin River. Evidence recovered from components believed to date to the middle decades of the 1600s in the John Green site complex has been associated with the slightly later Unote community.

Discovery of house-pattern post molds associated with later–eighteenth-century occupation at the John Green locale indicates that native communities in the area probably were dispersed plantations consisting of several dome-shaped roundhouses. Although direct evidence is lacking, some of the denser of these settlements may have been surrounded by palisade fortifications.

Linguistic analyses of these town names, the few words recorded by Bland and other observers, and two word lists compiled from nineteenth-century informants indicate that people living in this area spoke Northern Iroquoian languages. Most investigators further believe that these people spoke dialects similar to those used among their culturally similar Tuscarora neighbors on the south in North Carolina.

Powhatan-speaking Weyanoke refugees established their new principal village of Warekeck near the present-day town of Courtland on the south bank of the Blackwater River in 1653. They did not find peace in their new home. Repeatedly attacked by Nottoway neighbors supported by their Tuscarora allies, the Weyanokes had abandoned Warekeck by 1666.

Most of these Weyanokes took up a wandering life for several years. Some of them lived for a time at the recently abandoned site of Unote on the Meherrin River. Many of them eventually joined other Weyanoke refugees, moving closer to English settlements on the Blackwater River for protection when Bacon's Rebellion broke out.

Population records documenting native demography in the area at this time are incomplete. A census taken in 1669 listed 90 warriors representing as many as 450 people in three communities along the Nottoway River. The survey also enumerated 50 warriors representing a population of perhaps 250 people living in two towns on the Meherrin River. Farther east, several hundred Weyanoke people tried to find secure homes in the area.

Managing to avoid attack during Bacon's Rebellion in 1676, people living in the Nottoway and Meherrin Valleys formally acknowledged Virginian jurisdiction over their lands at the Treaty of Middle Plantation signed in 1677, shortly after the fighting ended. Under the treaty's terms, the Virginians pledged to live in peace with their Indian neighbors and halt expansion of their settlements at a line along the Blackwater River. In return, Nottoway, Meherrin, Weyanoke, and other Indians living within the charter bounds of the province agreed to recognize Virginian authority, make token tribute payments, patrol the province's exposed southwestern frontier, and limit their trade to provincial posts established in or near their territories.

Virginian colonists, no longer intimidated by the threat of Indian reprisal, soon began flooding across the Blackwater River border in defiance of the 1677 Middle Plantation agreement. Unwilling to live near aggressive and unfriendly new settlers, most Nottoway people gradually built a new town farther downriver in the Assamoosick Swamp.

People living along the Meherrin River also moved away from their towns at Unote and Cowinchahawkon at this time. Many of them moved farther south to Tuscarora towns. Others moved north and east toward the Nottoway and Blackwater Rivers. Most, however, evidently moved downriver to a new community called Tawarra near the present-day community of Boykins, Virginia.

Exiled Weyanoke people submitting to Virginian authority continued to have need of provincial protection during these years, as their Nottoway neighbors, aided by Tuscarora and Nansemond allies, continued to attack their towns. Unable to respond to these attacks, Weyanoke leaders continually appealed to Virginian authorities for help. As they had before Bacon's Rebellion, Virginians responded to these appeals by conducting reprisal raids on behalf of their Weyanoke clients.

But reprisals were no more effective after 1677 than they had been before. Disheartened when a 1681 Virginian reprisal raid against the Tuscaroras and Nottoways failed to stop further attacks, Weyanoke leaders finally made a separate peace with their enemies. Although the terms of this agreement are not known, later records indicate that the Weyanokes abandoned their towns along

the Blackwater River in 1693. Splitting up into several groups, most who chose to remain in the area moved in among their Nottoway neighbors.

Several sites are known to preserve deposits associated with seventeenth-century native communities in this area. Intact house patterns, hearths, pits, and human burials containing chipped-quartz triangular projectile points, Cashie-Branchville wares, European stonewares, wrought-iron nails, and glass beads dating from the mid- to late–seventeenth century have been found at John Green sites. Similar artifacts have been found mixed together on the surface of 44SX198.

Binford has found Colono wares in features containing stone tools at the Rose Hill site (identified as C-1 in the Binford survey). Analyzing findings from this site, Binford believes that they represent evidence associated with the archivally chronicled Warekeck community occupied by Weyanoke people between 1653 and 1666 and a later, briefly occupied Nottoway townsite built on or near the same spot in 1695.

THE EIGHTEENTH CENTURY

Indian people living along the Nottoway and Meherrin Rivers found themselves increasingly pressed by Virginian settlers moving south and west onto their lands. Disputes with settlers claiming Indian lands soon threatened to flare into violence. Anxious to head off conflict and to strengthen their control over the Nottoways, Virginian authorities set aside a circular-shaped tract measuring six miles in diameter as a reservation for them at Assamoosick Swamp in 1705. Another plot of land was reserved for their use just below Assamoosick south of the river.

Settlers immediately began moving onto lands given up by the Nottoways. Anxious to keep colonists from the heart of their settlements, Nottoway people looked on with alarm as settlers moved within three miles of their reservation borders by 1710.

War between the Tuscaroras and the North Carolinians broke out in 1711. Worried that embittered Nottoway people would join their allies in a general war against the colonists, Virginia Lt. Gov. Alexander Spotswood quickly arranged to visit their main town. William Byrd, a member of Spotswood's party, described the place as a collection of bark cabins situated in and around a square-shaped fort. Byrd further noted that Nottoway townsfolk cultivated fields, used European textiles for clothing, and raised hogs both for sale and for domestic consumption.

Agreeing to remain at peace, Nottoway warriors guarding the Virginian frontier helped keep the fighting from spilling across the North Carolina border. Thanking the Nottoways for their service, Virginia authorities then stood quietly by as settlers no longer fearing Tuscarora or Nottoway retaliation began moving onto and around Assamoosick Reservation lands after the worst of the fighting ended in 1713.

Reduced to fewer than two hundred people by war losses, smallpox, and the debilitating effects of alcohol abuse, in 1734 Nottoway people sold their Assamoosick Reservation and moved to their remaining tract of land south of the river. Living quietly there for the next ten years, they were eventually joined by a group of their old Nanse-

mond allies who left their lands near Newport News as King George's War broke out in 1744.

Few records document native life in this community during the remaining years of the Historic Contact period. Several deeds and other documents chronicle land sales, leases, and disputes. Other records note Nottoway service in the British armies that fought the French at various times between 1744 and 1760.

By 1772 the Nottoway people had leased or sold nearly all of their remaining lands. They all but disappeared from European documentary records for more than a century after state authorities dissolved their reservation in 1824. Yet, today hundreds of people tracing descent to Nottoway ancestors make their homes throughout the area.

Most Meherrin people were living at and around Tawarra at the turn of the seventeenth century. Many of them subsequently moved upriver, back to their old townsite at Unote, after a Virginian named Robert Hicks opened a trading post there in 1709. Supplying much of the food and most of the labor at the post, Meherrin people helped Hicks conduct transactions with visiting Catawba and Cherokee traders.

In 1711 these people moved south to support their Tuscarora allies when war broke out. Now distrusted by Virginian authorities, few of them were permitted to return to the province after the war ended. In 1720, nearly all Meherrin people gathered together at a new settlement at the confluence of the Meherrin and Chowan Rivers in North Carolina. Living there until 1731, they subsequently moved to Tuscarora communities along the lower Roanoke River. Today people tracing descent to Meherrin ancestors continue to live in this area of North Carolina, in or near the towns of Winton and Ahoskie.

Displaced Indians from other places moved into the area as Meherrin people left. More than three hundred Siouian-speaking piedmont people identified as "Saponis, Stuckanoes [evidently Mannahoac people], Occaneechees, and Totteros [Tuteloes]" moved to the newly established Fort Christanna outpost above the fall line of the Meherrin River, at Lt. Gov. Spotswood's request in 1714, just after the end of the Tuscarora War.

Collectively called Saponis by the Virginians, Indians belonging to this community joined Nottoway and Meherrin warriors patrolling the frontier, while their children, often referred to in Spotswood's correspondence as "hostages," attended classes taught by a schoolmaster hired by the governor in the fort. As described by John Fontaine, a Huguenot visiting Fort Christanna with Spotswood in 1716, the Saponi town consisted of a circular group of square, timbered, bark-roofed houses whose doors opened onto a central plaza.

Saponi people continued to live in this town after Virginian authorities abandoned Fort Christanna in 1718. But subject as they were to Nottoway and Iroquois raids, most of them soon moved within the fort walls. Most stayed on until one of their chiefs was executed by colonial authorities for murdering a local settler in 1728. Moving briefly among other Siouian refugees gathering together in Catawba territory in South Carolina, most Saponi people returned to homes along the upper reaches of the Roanoke or Appomattox Rivers after 1732.

Subjected to renewed Iroquois and Nottoway attacks, most of these people subsequently joined other Saponi and Tutelo people moving north to refugee Indian communities along the Susquehanna River or settled farther south among the Tuscaroras. People tracing descent from the few Saponi people who remained in Virginia after the main body moved away continue to live at various locales across southwestern Virginia.

Few archaeological sites are currently known to document eighteenth-century Indian life in Nottoway-Meherrin Country. Preliminary surface tests have recovered evidence that may be associated with late–seventeenth- or early-eighteenth-century Nottoway reoccupation of the earlier Warekeck townsite at Rose Hill. More substantial deposits dating to the early decades of the century have been excavated by archaeologists working at the John Green sites. Extensive testing has unearthed post molds associated with as many as five circular house patterns measuring from ten to fourteen feet in diameter.

Deposits located in and around these houses contain lead musket balls, spoons and other copper objects, glass beads, European white-clay tobacco pipes, gun parts, and other items of European manufacture. Archaeologists also have recovered well-preserved materials such as bone knife handles, small fragments of woolen blankets, pieces of split-cane matting, a gourd cup, and a copper-wrapped yarn belt decorated with woven diamond-shaped patterns. Analysis of this assemblage indicates that these houses probably were occupied by Meherrin people living near Robert Hicks's trading post between 1709 and 1720.

Binford has reported finding sand-

Copper-alloy kettle and spoon found at the John Green site, 44GV1, Greensville County, Virginia. *Courtesy Virginia Department of Historic Resources.*

tempered Courtland wares and shell-tempered Colono wares with other materials on the surface of sites C-3, C-8, and C-10. These properties may represent remains of Nottoway towns occupied from 1700 to 1770.

Archaeological excavations conducted at Fort Christanna have uncovered palisade post molds, glass beads, metal gun parts, European ceramics, Colono wares, and other occupational evidence. Excavators have also unearthed stone foundations and other features at the site of a mansion built by Spotswood near the fort in 1717. Other artifacts found nearby are believed to be part of de-posits associated with the still-unlocated Saponi town.

SOURCES

Information presented in this section generally draws on findings published in Binford (1967, 1991), Boyce (1978), Rountree (1973), and G. Smith (1984). Information chronicling Saponi occupations at Fort Christanna may be found in Beaudry (1979), Hazzard and McCartney (1979), and McCartney and Hazzard (1979). Studies reporting results of archaeological excavation at the John Green locale may be found in MacCord (1970) and Turner (1990b).

UPPER POTOMAC–
SHENANDOAH
COUNTRY

The Upper Potomac–Shenandoah Country extends across the piedmont regions of Maryland and Virginia west of the fall line along the upper Potomac and lower Shenandoah Valleys.

THE SIXTEENTH CENTURY

Intact remains of substantial sixteenth-century fortified towns have been excavated at places like Berryville (McNett and Gardner 1975), Keyser (Manson, MacCord, and Griffin 1943), Miley (MacCord and Rodgers 1966), and Quicksburg (MacCord 1973a) along the South Branch of the Potomac River.

Ceramic assemblages collected from these sites are dominated by Luray-phase Keyser-series ceramics similar to Monongahela wares used by native people living farther north and west. Small amounts of Townsend-series and Potomac Creek-like wares resembling pottery made by people living farther to the east also occur in some of these sites.

Archaeologists working beneath a large cliff overhang at the Bushey's Cavern locale during the late 1800s recovered substantial numbers of sherds of collared wares decorated with incised geometric designs along with several trumpet-shaped human and animal effigy clay pipes (R. M. Stewart 1980, 1982). MacCord (1991a) believes that these materials represent evidence of terminal Late Woodland or very early Historic Contact period Susquehannock occupation. Examining examples of this assemblage stored in Smithsonian Institution collections, R. M. Stewart (1990) identified these sherds as Munsee Incised wares almost exclusively found farther north and east in contemporary upper Delaware and lower Hudson valley sites. Similar ceramics have been found at the nearby Martin's Meadow site.

Whatever their identity, all of these wares have been found with local terminal Late Woodland ceramics and chipped-stone triangular projectile points. Substantial amounts of animal bone and a number of carbonized corncobs also were recovered from Bushey's Cavern site deposits. Discovery of a distinctively carved, drilled bear-molar "foot effigy" pendant, similar to others found in clearly dated early Historic Contact period sites in West Virginia, Seneca Country, and elsewhere in the Northeast, may provide chronological provenance for at least a portion of the since-destroyed deposit at this locale.

Neither Bushey's Cavern nor the above-mentioned South Branch townsites are known to contain objects of European origin dating to the late–sixteenth century. But such objects have been found at several sites along the North and South Branches of the Potomac River. Schultz Incised pottery has been found with glass beads and copper or brass hoops and spirals recovered from sites dating to the late–sixteenth or early-seventeenth centuries at the Herriott Farm Susquehannock townsite on the South Branch of the Potomac. Polychrome glass beads dating from the same period have been found with triangular, chipped-stone projectile points and Luray-phase ceramics at the Flanagan site on the North Branch of the river above the city of Cumberland, Maryland. Collectors also have found a copper "salamander" or "lizard" effigy, widely believed to be a marker representing a stylized beaver pelt, with Luray-phase artifacts at the nearby Barton site. Copper, brass, and shell versions of such effigies are found with some frequency farther west in early Historic Contact period Monongahela and Fort Ancient sites in the upper Ohio Valley.

Large numbers of glass beads and copper or brass ornaments have been found with Luray-phase ceramics and lithics on the surface of the Llewelyn site located on the Maryland side of the North Branch of the Potomac River between the Flanagan and Barton sites. Analysis of findings from each of these three North Branch locales affirms that Indian people continued to live along the upper branches of the Potomac long after Luray-phase people abandoned their earlier major towns sometime before 1590.

THE SEVENTEENTH CENTURY

Analysis of the date range represented in the glass bead assemblages recovered at the Llewelyn site affirms that it and its neighboring North Branch locales almost certainly had been abandoned by the time Henry Fleet's brother Edward paddled up the Potomac in 1632 while en route to Massawomeck towns, supposedly filled with furs, that were said to be seven days' journey upriver beyond the falls.

In contrast, dating estimates of glass beads and pottery found at the Herriott Farm and later Pancake Island sites indicate that Susquehannock people may have continued living in small towns along the South Branch until midcentury. Other evidence in the form of Washington Boro wares reportedly found with European trade goods in a site at the confluence of the north and south branches of the river further supports this hypothesis. Above-mentioned Munsee-series ceramics found at Bushey's Cavern and Martin's Meadow, for their part, may have been left by Delaware or Munsee hunters and travelers known to have visited the region during the middle years of the century.

Extant evidence indicates that most native people temporarily abandoned the area at about the time smallpox epidemics and warfare between the Susquehannocks and the Iroquois reached unprecedentedly high intensity during the 1660s. Other evidence documents the arrival of Indian refugees to the area during the last decade of the century. Maryland chroniclers report that

MAP 23: UPPER POTOMAC-SHENANDOAH COUNTRY

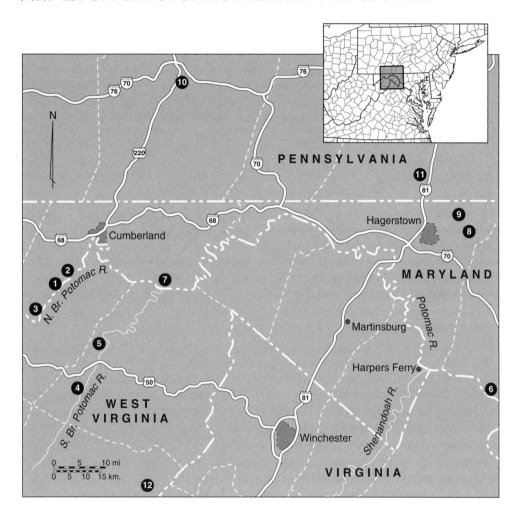

Map 23 Historic Contact Sites

Map Number	Site Name	County	State	Date	NR	Source
1	Llewelyn (18AG26)	Allegany	MD	1590–1630		Wall 1984
2	Barton (18AG3)	Allegany	MD	1590–1630		Wall 1984
3	Flanagan (18AG96)	Allegany	MD	1590–1630		Wall 1984
4	Pancake Island (46HM18)	Hampshire	WV	Early 1600s		Brashler 1987; MacCord 1993
5	Herriott Farm (46HM1)	Hampshire	WV	Early 1600s		MacCord 1952; Manson and MacCord 1941, 1944;
6	Heater's Island North (18FR72)	Frederick	MD	1699–1710		MacCord 1991a, 1993; Snyder 1967

Map 23 Historic Contact Sites—*Continued*

Map Number	Site Name	County	State	Date	NR	Source
7	Shawnee Indian Old Fields (18AG20)	Allegany	MD	1690s–1730s	X	W. Clark 1975; H. T. Wright 1973
8	Bushey's Cavern (18WA18)	Washington	MD	Historic		R. M. Stewart 1980, 1982
9	Martin's Meadow (18WA23)	Washington	MD	Historic		R. M. Stewart 1980, 1982
10	36BD90	Bedford	PA	Historic		PASS
11	36FR232	Franklin	PA	Historic		PASS
12	46HY62	Hardy	WV	Historic		WVAS

Piscataway people began emigrating up-river from their towns around Piscataway Creek and the Zachiah Swamp to new homes on Conoy Island during the 1690s. Farther west, other chroniclers noted the coming of 172 Shawnee refugees about the same time from Starved Rock, Illinois, to a place where the Warriors Path crossed the Potomac River. Later known as King Opessa's Town, the locale became both a major trade center and a place widely regarded as a safe haven for escaped prisoners and slaves fleeing tidewater servitude.

Archaeologists have discovered substantial amounts of European ceramics, ornaments, and munitions at this locale. Dating of glass beads and European white-clay tobacco-smoking pipe stems and bowls recovered from the site corroborates written records indicating that the place was first occupied by Shawnee people sometime during the 1690s.

Other deposits found at the Heater's Island North site affirm that increasing numbers of Piscataway, Potomac, and Nanticoke people began moving to the locale (then known as Conoy Island) at or about the same time. Small amounts of metal scrap found with chipped-stone triangular projectile points and terminal Late Woodland pottery at 36BD90, 36FR232, and 46HY62 may also preserve evidence of later-seventeenth-century Indian occupations in this area.

THE EIGHTEENTH CENTURY

Maryland records note that Indian people continued to live in their communities at Conoy Island and King Opessa's Town during the early decades of the eighteenth century. The latter locale was named after an important Shawnee leader who moved to the Potomac River community after losing influence in the Susquehanna Valley sometime after 1711. Contemporary accounts also note the presence of two other Shawnee towns and a Tuscarora community in the upper Potomac River Valley at this time.

The Heater's Island North and Shawnee Indian Old Fields locales remain the only sites known to contain clearly identifiable deposits capable of corroborating or contradicting early–eighteenth-century European accounts of relations with Indian people in the area. Complaints registered in several documents affirm that Shawnee communities continued to be regarded as havens for people fleeing bondage elsewhere. Other records note that Charles Anderson, a Maryland agent sent to negotiate the return of escaped slaves in 1722, established a trading post at King Opessa's Town some years later.

Analyses indicate that assemblages of glass beads and European white-clay tobacco pipe stems and bowls from the Heater's Island North site do not post-date 1710. This dating affirms reports of Maryland chroniclers noting the movement of most Indian people from Conoy Island and other locales to more northerly sites along the Susquehanna River during the early 1710s. Similar analyses indicate that people living in King Opessa's Town moved away sometime during the second quarter of the century.

No clear archival or archaeological evidence of later–eighteenth-century Indian occupation in the upper Potomac or Shenandoah Valleys is known to exist. European artifacts dating to the late 1700s have reportedly been found with aboriginal artifacts at the upper Poto-

mac Valley Conrad site. Closer examination of these findings indicates that this deposit most probably represents the mixing of materials from a much-earlier Indian site with later European tools in a refuse pit dug long after the last Indian people had abandoned the area (MacCord 1993).

SOURCES

Much of the archaeological data presented in this section is drawn from MacCord (1989a, 1993) and Wall (1984). A survey of area ceramics appears in R. M. Stewart (1982). Examples of site reports containing specific site information include Brashler (1987), MacCord (1952, 1973a), and H. T. Wright (1973).

Materials presented in Bushnell (1930, 1933, 1935), Briceland (1987), Fowke (1894), and Mooney (1894) furnish most of the documentary information presented in this section.

VIRGINIAN PIEDMONT COUNTRY

Virginian Piedmont Country extends from the fall line west to the Blue Ridge Mountains of central Virginia. An area of broad valleys and rolling hills, it stretches across the upper reaches of the Rappahannock, Rapidan, James, and Appomattox Valleys to the headwaters of the Roanoke and Dan Rivers.

THE SIXTEENTH CENTURY

Numerous sites and several mounds found in this area are believed to date to the 1500s. Several of these sites are situated at the approximate locales of Indian towns noted in early–seventeenth-century documents. Other records, like Thomas Jefferson's 1787 report of an earlier incident in which a group of native travelers walked miles out of their way to visit a mound he later excavated, suggest that such structures were known and used by Indian people during Historic Contact times.

Scholars like Bushnell (1930, 1933, 1935), Fowke (1894), Holland (1978), MacCord (1986), and, most recently, Hantman (1990a, 1990b) have looked for the locations of historic Indian communities throughout this area. All have found extensive deposits of aboriginal stone tools and ceramics at many of the locales indicated as Indian towns or gravesites in colonial documents. Late Woodland triangular, chipped-stone projectile points have been found with terminal Late Woodland Roanoke, Gaston, Cashie-Branchville, and Dan River–series wares at many of these multicomponent sites.

Several investigators have further noted the presence of small amounts of metal scrap, fragments of white-clay tobacco pipe bowls or stems, and other materials of European origin scattered across the disturbed surfaces of a number of locales in this area. None, however, have yet located such objects in intact deposits dating to the 1500s. As a result, all reconstructions of sixteenth-century native lifeways in this region remain based on earlier archaeological or later written and oral testimony.

Such reconstructions generally suggest that people making these and similar types of pots and stone tools began constructing large, decentralized communities along broad river floodplains at least five hundred years before Europeans first sailed to Middle Atlantic shores. Analyses of tools, seed, pollen, and bone found at these sites indicate that their occupants hunted deer, fished, collected uncultivated plants, and raised corn, beans, squash, and other crops. Assays of the small number of radiocarbon samples drawn from mounds erected by these people indicate that they generally buried their dead in such structures from a thousand to five hundred years ago.

THE SEVENTEENTH CENTURY

The veil of obscurity covering sixteenth-century Indian life in this area extends into the 1600s. For reasons still poorly understood, few Virginians appear to have ventured westward beyond the fall line before midcentury. Most were probably deterred by early reports recounting the hostile reception given a small party of Virginian adventurers led by John Smith at the falls of the Rappahannock River in August 1608. Others undoubtedly were discouraged by Christopher Newport's subsequent failure to find gold or precious stones in either of the two Monacan towns visited beyond the falls of the James River one month later.

Reports describing these encounters and similarly brief visits later made by such travelers as Edward Bland in 1650, John Lederer in 1670, and William Byrd I in 1688 provide much of the limited information presently available on seventeenth-century Indian life in Virginian Piedmont Country (Briceland 1987). These men described large and occasionally fortified villages surrounded by cornfields at various locales along the area's major rivers.

From five thousand to ten thousand people may have been living in these communities in 1600. Indian expressions and native names for towns, places, and individuals jotted down by European travelers further show that most of these people probably spoke related Eastern Siouian languages.

Information revealed in a conversation between Smith and Amoroleck, one of the four hundred or five hundred warriors who attacked the Virginian party at the falls of the Rappahannock, provides the earliest known account of Mannahoac communities along the upper reaches of the Rappahannock and Rapidan Rivers. Reporting the results of his conversation with the wounded Amoroleck through a hostile Potomac interpreter named Mosco years after the event, Smith wrote that "Mannahoacks" living along the upper Rappahannock River included "the Tauxsnitanias, the Shackaconias, the Outaponcas, the Tegoneaes, the Whonkentyaes, the Stegarakes, the Hassinnungas, and diverse others" (Barbour 1986; John Smith 1624). Amoroleck further apprised Smith of neighboring Monacans on the south and identified Massawomecks as people living "higher up in the mountaines."

Smith noted the locations of five Mannahoac settlements on the map accompanying his 1624 report. One of these, identified as Mahaskahod, was a large "hunting towne" on the banks of the Rappahannock just west of the fall line. Two communities, noted as Hassuiuga and Tanxsnitania, were located farther up the Rappahannock River. The remaining two towns, listed as Shackaonia and Stegara, were situated on the Rapidan River.

Almost nothing further is known about these communities. The German

MAP 24: VIRGINIAN PIEDMONT COUNTRY

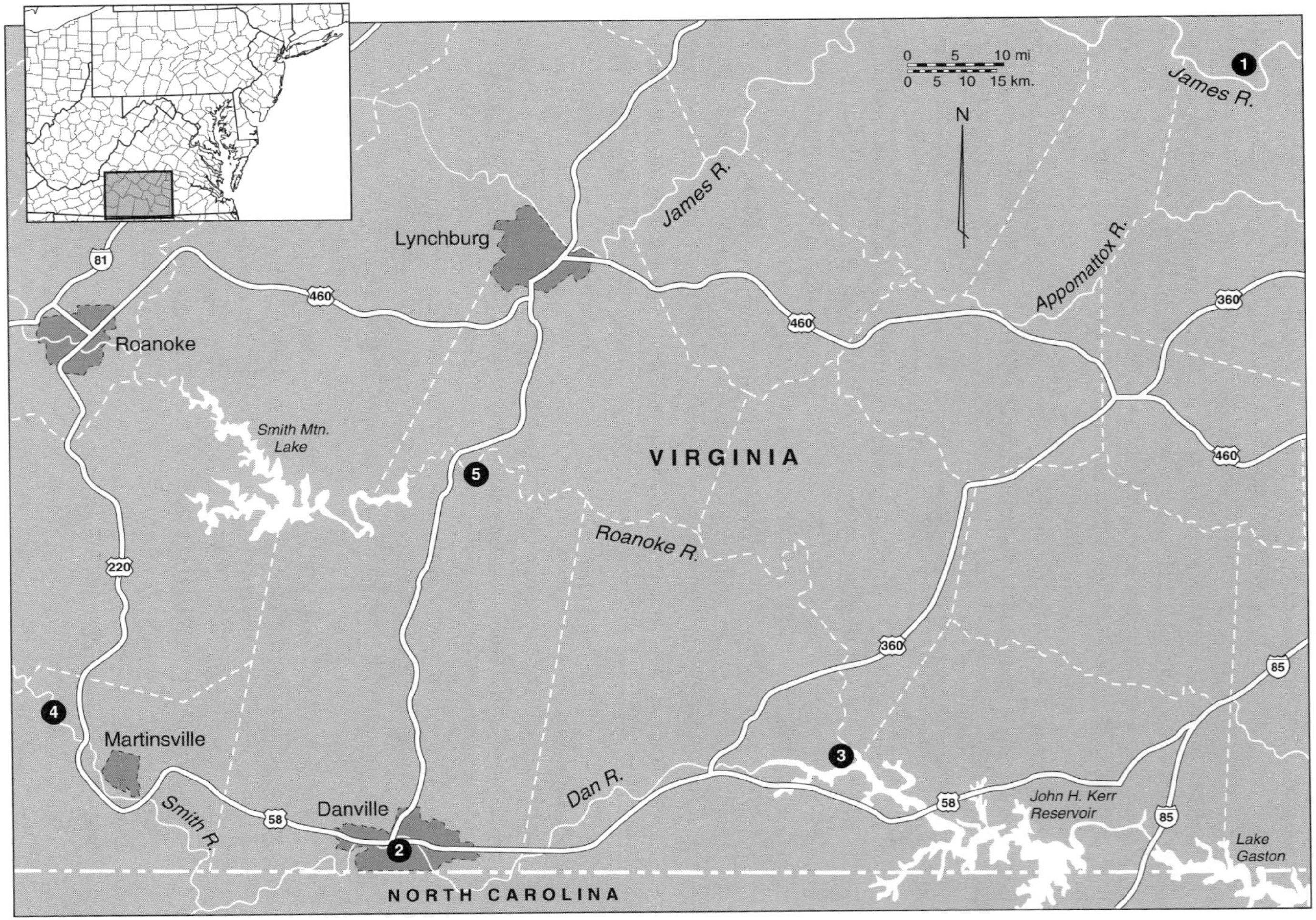

Map 24 Historic Contact Sites

Map Number	Site Name	County	State	Date	NR	Source
1	Wright	Goochland	VA	1600s		Mouer 1992b
2	Arey (44PY21)	Pittsylvania	VA	1620–1640		MacCord 1989a, 1993; Turner 1990b; VDHR
3	Occaneechi Town (44HA65)	Halifax	VA	1640–1660		MacCord 1989a, 1993; Turner 1990b
4	44HR4	Henry	VA	Mid-1700s		Egloff, Moldenhauer, and Rotenizer 1987; Turner 1990b; VDHR
5	Hurt Power Plant	Pittsylvania	VA	Early contact		M. Barber 1993

John Lederer encountered no Indian people while traveling through the area in 1670 (Cumming 1958). Earlier-mentioned documents listing Stuckanoes among several Siouian refugees settling at Fort Christanna in 1714 may represent references to displaced Stegara townsfolk.

Reports of another conversation, this one between Christopher Newport and a Monacan chief named Pawatah at the falls of the James in 1607, provide the earliest known references to Monacan Indian communities farther south along the upper James River. Two of these towns—variously identified as Massinacak or Massinnacock and Mowhemincke, Mowhemcho, or Mowhemenchouch—were subsequently visited by Newport. John Smith's 1624 map listed three more Monacan communities identified as Monahassanugh, Rassawek, and Monasukapanough farther upstream beyond the mouth of the Rivanna River.

Examining all available primary written records, Bushnell (1930) believed that Newport and Smith's Mowhemcho was the community known to subsequent visitors as Monacan Town. Bushnell further suggested that a town identified by Lederer in 1670 as Mahock was probably the earlier-mentioned Mas-

sinnacock community. Noted by Smith as Russawmeake, the principal Monacan community, Rassawek was evidently abandoned before presently documented European observers visited the locale.

Located farther up the Rivanna River just below Charlottesville, Monasukapanough is believed to have been the original home of people later identified as Saponis (Mooney 1894). Other analyses conducted by Mooney indicate that Smith's Monahassanugh community may have been the original home of people later identified as Nahyssans and better known as Tuteloes.

Farther south, Occaneechi communities strategically located near the confluence of the Roanoke and Dan Rivers came to dominate trade relations between coastal people and the inhabitants of populous Cherokee and Creek towns farther southwest in the interior uplands. Fighting off attacks by well-armed Westo raiders and others seeking captives to sell at Virginian and Carolinian slave markets, Occaneechi people struggled to defend themselves while maintaining their trade monopoly. Later they attempted to help Virginia settlers against the Susquehannocks who took refuge in their country at the height of Bacon's Rebellion. But frustrated when the Susquehannocks evaded their trap, the settlers turned their weapons on the hapless Occaneechis.

Now embittered against all Indian people, Virginian settlers began murdering native men, women, and children wherever they encountered them. Indian people living near English communities or even on their own reservations were especially vulnerable to these attacks. Devastated by Virginian assaults, most Occaneechis and many other Piedmont Siouian people abandoned their towns and moved south to new settlements along the Yadkin River in the Carolina piedmont. Finding themselves among strangers, they struggled to live amicably alongside Keyauwee and Catawba neighbors speaking related but mutually unintelligible Siouian languages. Passing through their country in 1700, John Lawson briefly described the Occaneechi community in South Carolina (Lawson 1967).

Very little else is known about the people who lived in Virginian Piedmont Country communities during the 1600s. Much of the information regarding their customs and forms of government was gathered from tidewater Algonquian people, who regarded their upriver neighbors with disdain. Because relations between coastal and interior people evidently were often hostile, much of this documentation probably more accurately records coastal Indian biases than actual ethnographic facts.

Physical evidence of seventeenth-century Indian occupation in Virginian Piedmont Country also is rare. University of Virginia investigators, for example, have been unable to find a single, clearly iden-tifiable site containing intact deposits dating to the Historic Contact period of Indian occupation in a 200-square-mile study area along the James and Rivanna river valleys (Hantman 1990a).

Four sites elsewhere in the area at present are known to contain deposits clearly dating to the 1600s. Glass and copper beads have been recovered from deposits believed to be associated with Occaneechi town (MacCord 1989a). Recent findings of Potomac Creek and Colono wares, chipped bottle glass, and English gunflints within a circular midden stain at the Wright site may represent the remains of the Monacan Massinnacock community (Mouer 1992b). A small number of glass beads dating to the seventeenth century have also been found in graves excavated at the since-destroyed Arey site in Danville (MacCord 1989a).

Several glass beads and some pieces of copper have recently been found with Dan River ceramics (some of it evidently painted) and triangular, chipped-stone projectile points in intact midden and pit deposits at the multicomponent Hurt site (M. Barber 1993), which is located in the southwestern reaches of the piedmont. Analysis of materials found at this site has the potential to reveal new information on changes that took place in native communities in the area from early Late Woodland times to the early years of the Historic Contact period.

Many scholars believe that future research will uncover other evidence of seventeenth-century Indian occupation in this and nearby areas. Others believe that the virtual absence of known archaeological and documentary evidence in Virginian Piedmont Country corroborates written records indicating that most native people had been destroyed or

Small pot decorated with six incised thunderbirds around the shoulder of the vessel, recovered in excavations at the Hurt Power Plant site, 44PY144, Pittsylvania County, Virginia. Vessels of this type are usually found in sites located south and east of Virginia. Photograph by Eugene B. Barfield. *Courtesy Preservation Technologies, Inc., Roanoke, Virginia.*

had moved away from the area by the late 1600s.

THE EIGHTEENTH CENTURY

The 1700s was a time of trouble for Virginian Piedmont Country natives. Siouian people were ravaged by epidemic disease, devastated by English or Shaw- nee slave raids, subjected to periodic Iroquois assaults, forced to contend with often-fractious neighbors, and increasingly pressed to move from lands claimed by European settlers. Living in a region convulsed by conflict and change, Siouian people moved from place to place to escape threats, find security, or live under more tolerable conditions.

Forced to abandon towns exposed to Iroquois assault, most Mannahoac and many Monacan people moved to more secure surroundings at the newly constructed Virginian frontier fort at Germanna built by Gov. Alexander Spotswood on the Rapidan River in 1714. Remaining at the fort for a time even after the Virginians abandoned it in 1734, most of these people later joined Saponi and Tutelo people moving north to refugee communities in the Susquehanna Valley.

Other Mannahoac people joined the Saponi, Tutelo, and Occaneechi people who were relocated on a six-square-mile reservation established around the newly built Fort Christanna outpost on the fall line of the Roanoke River in 1714 shortly after the end of the Tuscarora War. Cheated by Virginian traders, raided by Iroquois warriors and Nottoway neighbors, and pressed by settlers to leave their lands, many of these people moved among the Catawbas a year after Virginian authorities hanged one of their chiefs for the drunken murder of a settler in 1728.

Unable to find peace among the Catawbas, they had moved north by 1732 to the Roanoke or Appomattox Valleys in Virginia—or to a small community called Buttrum Town near Danville at the westernmost limits of Virginian Piedmont Country. Attacked in these new homes by Iroquois and Nottoway warriors, members of the Saponi and Tutelo communities split up. Some moved south to join the Tuscarora people. Others journeyed farther north into exile in the Susquehanna Valley. The few Siouian people remaining in Virginian Piedmont Country after midcentury largely became nomads, forced to move from place to place.

Most Siouian-speaking Virginian Piedmont Country people moving among strangers in Pennsylvania and North Carolina gradually gave up their language, customs, and identity, but people tracing descent to Siouian people who never left their piedmont homes continue to live today at various locales throughout the area.

European goods found in burials and organic materials radiometrically dated to the mid-1700s found in a refuse pit at 44HR4 preserve evidence of what is believed to be the site of the archivally chronicled Tutelo Buttrum Town settlement (Egloff, Moldenauer, and Rotenizer 1987). No other archaeological deposits clearly associated with the eighteenth-century native occupants of this area have thus far been identified.

SOURCES

Much of the archaeological data presented in this section is drawn from MacCord (1989a, 1993). Other archaeological sources include Evans (1955), Gardner (1980), and Wilson (1983).

Most of the documentary material presented herein comes from primary data published in Barbour (1986), Cumming (1958), Lawson (1967), W. Robinson (1983a), John Smith (1624), and Tyler (1907). Secondary sources consulted include Briceland (1987), Bushnell (1930, 1933, 1935), Fowke (1894), Hantman (1990a, 1990b), Merrell (1989), Mooney (1894), and Mouer (1983, 1992a, 1992b).

SOUTHERN APPALACHIAN HIGHLANDS COUNTRY

The Southern Appalachian Highlands Country encompasses the mountainous terrain along the present-day border separating West Virginia from the southwestern corner of Virginia. The New River, which drains the upper reaches of this area, flows north to the Ohio River. On the west, the Clinch and Holston Rivers flow southwest to the Tennessee Valley. Farther east, the James and Roanoke Rivers flow across the piedmont toward the Atlantic coast.

THE SIXTEENTH CENTURY

People belonging to what MacCord and Buchanan (1980) have defined as the Intermontane Tradition had been living in this area for at least seven hundred years when late–sixteenth-century glass beads attesting to indirect contact with Europeans first appeared in sites like Crab Orchard and Perkin's Point. Initially living in wigwams sheltering small groups of family and friends, most Intermontane Tradition people began living in large, nucleated towns during the late-fifteenth century (MacCord 1989b).

Groups of from five to twenty oval or circular houses were built in larger Intermontane Tradition towns. Many of these communities were surrounded by circular wooden palisade walls. Several were laid out in a concentric town plan in which houses surrounded a central plaza. People buried their dead just beyond house walls in flexed positions facing eastward.

Intermontane Tradition people raised corn, beans, and squash and crafted Late Woodland ceramics and stone, bone, shell, and horn tools and ornaments. Ceramic assemblages were dominated by limestone-tempered Radford wares and shell-tempered New River pottery. Radford wares resemble other limestone-tempered pottery found farther east in Virginian Piedmont Country sites. The appearance of shell-tempered New River wares similar to the Fort Ancient pottery found farther north after 1450 suggests contacts in that direction.

Very few objects of European origin have been found in deposits believed to date to the late–sixteenth century in area sites. Two glass beads dating to the late 1500s were recovered from features containing aboriginal artifacts during salvage excavations at the now-inundated Perkin's Point site. A third glass

MAP 25: SOUTHERN APPALACHIAN HIGHLANDS COUNTRY

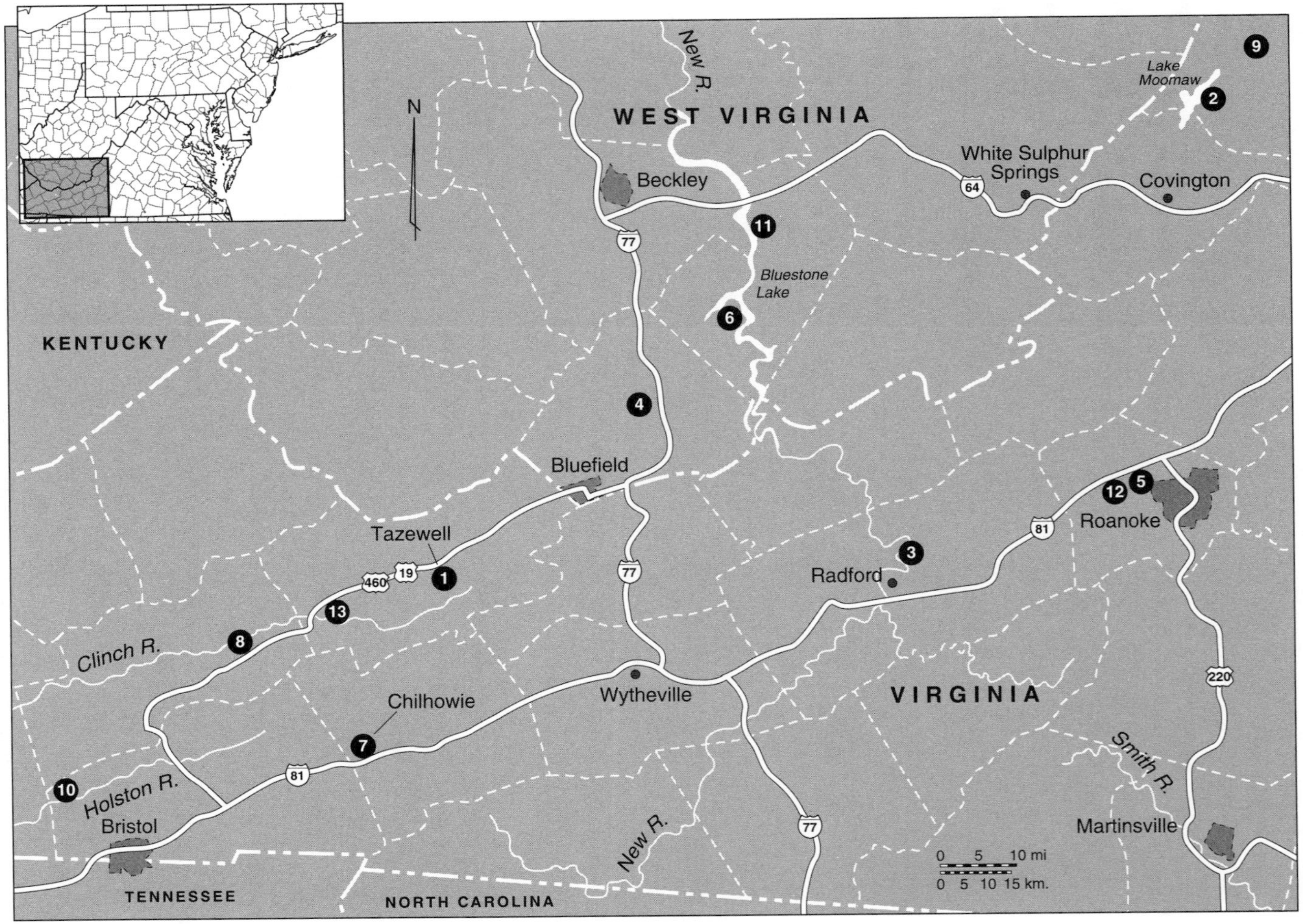

Map 25 Historic Contact Sites

Map Number	Site Name	County	State	Date	NR	Source
1	Crab Orchard (44TZ1)	Tazewell	VA	1590–1610	X	W. Clark and McCartney 1978; Egloff and Reed 1980; MacCord 1993; MacCord and Buchanan 1980; Turner 1990b
2	Perkin's Point (44BA3)	Bath	VA	1590–1610		L. Johnson 1985; Mac-Cord 1993; Turner 1990b; VDHR; Whyte and Geier 1982
3	Trigg (44MY3)	Montgomery	VA	1590–1625		Buchanan 1984; MacCord 1977, 1993; Turner 1990b; VDHR
4	Snidow 1/Shawnee Lake (46MC1)	Mercer	WV	Mid-1600s		Fuerst 1992
5	Graham-White (44RN21)	Roanoke	VA	Late 1600s		Turner 1990a; VDHR
6	Barkers Bottom (46SU3)	Summers	WV	Historic		Solecki 1949
7	Chilhowie School (44SM8)	Smyth	VA	Historic		Holland 1970; Turner 1990b; VDHR
8	Daugherty Cave (44RU14)	Russell	VA	Historic		Benthall 1990; MacCord 1993
9	Hidden Valley Rock Shelter (44BA31)	Bath	VA	Historic		MacCord 1973c
10	Mendota (44WG10)	Washington	VA	Historic		Holland 1970; Turner 1990b; VDHR
11	Sandstone Rock Shelter (46SU17)	Summers	WV	Historic		Solecki 1949
12	Thomas-Sawyer (44RN39)	Roanoke	VA	Historic		MacCord 1989a; Turner 1990b; VDHR
13	44TZ9	Tazewell	VA	Historic		Holland 1970; Turner 1990b; VDHR

bead was found on the site's surface. Two other late–sixteenth-century glass beads have been found in the plow zone at the large, multicomponent Crab Orchard townsite.

A large brass-disc gorget, similar to others dating from 1580 to 1650 in sites located from Tennessee to Florida, has been found with other goods of European origin at the Trigg site (MacCord 1977; Waselkov 1989). Other sites containing deposits possibly dating to the late-sixteenth or early-seventeenth centuries have been reported in the area. Excavators salvaging threatened archaeological remains at the Thomas-Sawyer site have recovered small numbers of glass beads in deposits containing terminal Late Woodland ceramics. Two other glass beads of uncertain age and style were reportedly found with twenty brass beads in a since-destroyed burial cairn at 44TZ9. Another glass bead was found at the large Barkers Bottom townsite in West Virginia.

Bronze ear plugs, unidentified glass beads, and an iron axe have been reported in features containing Radford-series wares and Late Woodland stone tools dug up by local residents at the Chilhowie School site. Another iron axe was found with aboriginal artifacts in

Knotted-net impressed variant of Dan River–series pottery found at the Trigg site, 44MY3, City of Radford, Virginia. *Courtesy Virginia Department of Historic Resources.*

one of over five hundred burials reportedly looted from terminal Late Woodland Mendota town deposits.

THE SEVENTEENTH CENTURY

Archaeological evidence recovered from above-mentioned sites and later occupations at the Trigg, Snidow 1, and Graham-White locales clearly show that Intermontane Tradition people continued to make their homes in the Southern Appalachian Highlands during the 1600s. Scholars have attributed Shawnee (Griffin 1943; Graybill 1981) or Siouian (Mooney 1894) identities to the people who lived in these and other contemporary sites, but little evidence exists at present to substantiate these attributions.

Archaeological evidence found at large townsites like those mentioned above and smaller camps like the Sandstone Rock Shelter indicates that the five thousand to ten thousand people living in this area at the dawn of the seventeenth century maintained contacts with native neighbors on the north and east. Virginian colonists living farther east are not known to have visited

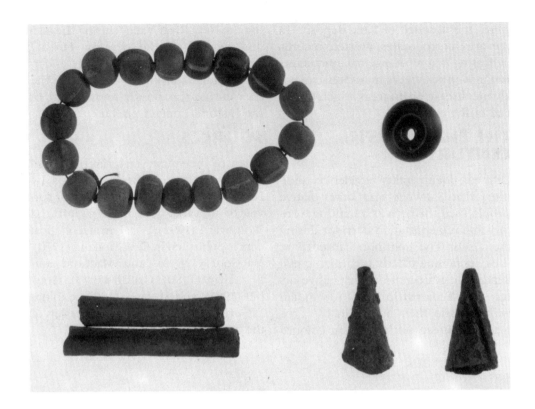

Glass beads *(top)* and copper beads *(bottom)* found at the Trigg site, 44MY3, City of Radford, Virginia. *Courtesy Virginia Department of Historic Resources.*

the area before traders Thomas Batts and Robert Fallam ventured into the New River Valley in search of native clients in 1671.

Both men traveled as far as the present site of Narrows, Virginia, on the West Virginia border before illness and fear of attack by Indian people vaguely identified as "Salt-Makers" compelled them to return to Fort Henry. Three years later, Gabriel Archer, a Virginia trader captured by Tomahitton Indians generally believed to be Cherokee people, described the Moneton community he stayed at somewhere in the area while en route to his captor's towns.

An iron gun trigger, several dozen glass beads, and iron and brass fragments found in features in the recently discovered Graham-White site represent the only clearly identifiable physical evidence of late-seventeenth-century Indian occupation in the area. Located near the earlier Thomas-Sawyer site, Graham-White may represent the remains of a small hamlet. Although construction activities have destroyed some of the known deposits at this locale, more than 70 percent of the site is preserved under landfill. A mouth harp, buckle, and other objects found at the Sandstone Rock Shelter also may date to the later 1600s.

Whoever the occupants of these sites

were, the absence of later deposits in the area corroborates written records indicating that most original inhabitants had moved elsewhere in response to epidemic disease or Iroquois attack by the end of the century.

THE EIGHTEENTH CENTURY

Limited documentary evidence indicates that Shawnee and other native people used this area as a hunting territory and transportation corridor during the 1700s. The continued absence of sites containing clearly identifiable evidence of eigthteenth-century native occupation further affirms that few Indian people made their homes in the area when European settlers began colonizing the New River Valley during the second quarter of the century. Further research is needed to more fully understand Indian-European relations in the area during this poorly known part of the Historic Contact period.

SOURCES

Much of the source material presented in this section has been provided by Fuerst (1992, 1993). A brief popular survey of the area appears in Egloff and Woodward (1992). Areal archaeological data is published in C. G. Holland (1970), MacCord (1989b), and MacCord and Buchanan (1980). Griffin (1943), Graybill (1981), and Mooney (1894) explore the evidence for ethnic identification of the area's people.

LOWER
SUSQUEHANNA
COUNTRY

Lower Susquehanna Country comprises the western portion of Pennsylvania's Piedmont physiographic province. A region of low rolling hills and broad plains, the area contains some of the most fertile soils in the state. Bordered on the north and west by the Blue Mountains, Lower Susquehanna Country is bounded on the south by the fall line and on the east by ridges separating the Susquehanna and Delaware watersheds.

THE SIXTEENTH CENTURY

Archaeological evidence indicates that people belonging to a culture known to archaeologists as the Shenks Ferry horizon or tradition were living in the lower Susquehanna Valley when Europeans first started sailing to Middle Atlantic shores during the early decades of the sixteenth century. These people had been living along the lower Susquehanna River in substantial fortified towns since the 1300s. They made collared pots decorated with incised motifs. Tempering their clay with crushed stone like Potomac Creek people on the south, Shenks Ferry potters also often used many decorative motifs popular among neighbors farther north and east.

Available evidence currently sheds little light on their social structure, religious beliefs, or language. Tools and implements found in their towns and camps indicate that Shenks Ferry people used Late Woodland hunting, foraging, fishing, and cultivation skills and techniques similar to those employed elsewhere in the region.

Shell-tempered Schultz wares, commonly associated with the direct ancestors of Susquehannock people living in the upper Susquehanna Valley during the 1300s and 1400s, first appear in Shenks Ferry sites during the early 1500s, just as they begin to disappear from upriver site deposits. Archaeologists generally agree that the gradual emergence of Schultz wares as the major pottery type in downriver deposits by 1575 reflects movements of Susquehannock people south into the land of Shenks Ferry people.

People making Schultz wares did not immediately supplant Shenks Ferry pottery makers along the lower Susquehanna. Schultz pottery has been found in pits containing Shenks Ferry wares and small numbers of brass hoops and

Shenks Ferry–series Funk Incised ware from the Schultz site
(Kent 1984, fig. 17). *Courtesy State Museum of Pennsylvania,
Pennsylvania Historical and Museum Commission.*

spirals at the mid-to-late–sixteenth-century Shenks Ferry site. This site, the
only Shenks Ferry locale known to contain goods of European origin, is also the
last known occupation associated with
Shenks Ferry culture.

Discovery of Schultz wares in Shenks

Ferry site deposits indicates the presence of Susquehannock captives, spouses,
or visitors. Further discoveries of increasingly smaller amounts of Shenks
Ferry ceramics in succeeding Schultz-
Funk and Washington Boro townsite pottery assemblages overwhelmingly domi-

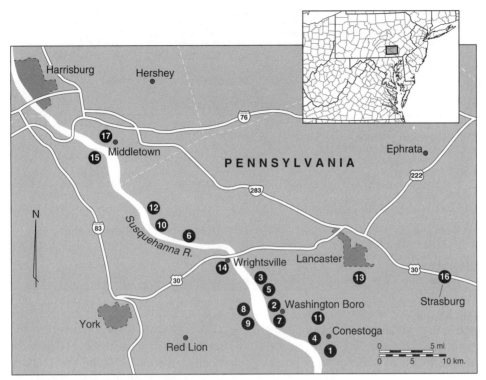

Map 26 Historic Contact Sites

Map Number	Site Name	County	State	Date	NR	Source
			Shenks Ferry			
1	Shenks Ferry (36LA2)	Lancaster	PA	1550–1575		Cadzow 1936; Kent 1984; PASS
			Susquehannock			
2	Schultz-Funk (36LA9/206)	Lancaster	PA	1575–1600	X	Cadzow 1936; Casselberry 1971; Kent 1984; PASS; I. Smith and Graybill 1977
3	Washington Boro Complex Daisy Cemetery (36LA956) Eshleman Cemetery (36LA12) Ibaugh Cemetery (36LA54) Keller Cemetery (36LA4) Reitz Cemetery (36LA92) Washington Boro Town (36LA8)	Lancaster	PA	1600–1625		Kent 1984; PASS
4	Roberts (36LA1)	Lancaster	PA	1625–1645	X	Kent 1984; PASS
5	Frey-Haverstick Cemetery (36LA6)	Lancaster	PA	1630–1645	X	Kent 1984; PASS

Map 26 Historic Contact Sites—*Continued*

Map Number	Site Name	County	State	Date	NR	Source
6	Billmyer (36LA10)	Lancaster	PA	1625–1645		Kent 1984: PASS
7	Strickler (36LA3)	Lancaster	PA	1645–1665	X	Kent 1984; PASS
8	Oscar Leibhart (36YO9)	York	PA	1665–1674	X	Kent 1984; PASS
9	Byrd Leibhart (36YO52)	York	PA	1676–1680		Kent 1984; PASS
10	Brand (36LA5)	Lancaster	PA	1600s		PASS

18th-Century Occupations

Map Number	Site Name	County	State	Date	NR	Source
11	Conestoga (36LA52)	Lancaster	PA	1690–1763	X	Kent 1984; PASS
12	Conoy Town Complex Conoy Town (36LA57) Conoy Town Cemetery (36LA40)	Lancaster	PA	1718–1743		Kent 1984; PASS
13	Lancaster County Park (36LA96)	Lancaster	PA	1720–1730	X	Custer, Carlson, and Doms 1986; Kinsey 1982; Kinsey and Custer 1982; PASS
14	Wrightsville	York	PA	1720s		Kent 1984; PASS
15	Bashore Island (36DA139)	Dauphin	PA	1700s		PASS
16	All Saint's Cemetery (36LA210)	Lancaster	PA	Historic		PASS
17	Middletown "Up" (35DA13)	Dauphin	PA	Historic		PASS

nated by Schultz wares, for their part, suggest that small numbers of Shenks Ferry potters or people emulating their style continued to make pottery in Susquehannock towns. The absence of later Shenks Ferry sites elsewhere in or outside of the Susquehanna Valley suggests that these people ceased to exist as a distinct community shortly after 1575.

Analyzing extant evidence from all known sites in the area, archaeologist Barry C. Kent (1984) has shown that the Susquehannocks established their first major settlement at the Schultz-Funk site at Washington Boro in the heart of Shenks Ferry country around 1575. Contrasting artifacts from the Schultz-Funk site with similar assemblages from Seneca sites, Sempowski (1992) believes that the town may have been built as late as 1600.

Whatever its initial date of occupation, the Schultz-Funk town was perhaps twice the size of earlier major Shenks Ferry communities. Post-mold patterns of at least twenty-seven longhouses have been found with three cemeteries and perhaps as many as three episodes of stockade construction at the site. Increasing in size over time, the town ultimately came to have the capacity to shelter as many as fifteen hundred inhabitants.

Unprecedentedly large numbers of European goods have been found in Schultz-Funk town deposits. These include several types of iron and brass artifacts and nearly three thousand glass beads. Existing evidence indicates that Schultz-Funk remained the principal Susquehannock town through the last quarter of the sixteenth century.

Other archaeological evidence shows that many Susquehannock people established residences elsewhere during these years. Discoveries of Schultz ceramics at various locales throughout the lower Susquehanna Valley and in the more distant Herriott Farm and Pancake Island townsites in West Virginia suggests that

Diorama of the Schultz-Funk site reconstruction in the Anthropology Gallery of the William Penn Memorial Museum, Harrisburg, Pennsylvania. *Courtesy State Museum of Pennsylvania, Pennsylvania Historical and Museum Commission.*

numbers of Susquehannock people periodically moved to different locales for varying periods of time during this phase of their history.

THE SEVENTEENTH CENTURY

Susquehannock people dominate the archaeological and archival record of Indian life in the lower Susquehanna Valley during the first three quarters of the seventeenth century. Substantial bodies of written records document trade relations, diplomatic contacts, and military encounters with European colonists and other native communities in the region. Archaeologists studying the remains of their towns have learned much about their material culture, but many aspects of their lives and language remain an enigma.

Prohibiting European settlement of any

type in their country, Susquehannock leaders allowed foreign diplomats and traders to visit their towns only briefly. Although many European travelers are known to have made the journey, few recorded accounts of their visits or noted Susquehannock customs, beliefs, or language. As a result, numerous aspects of their culture and whole periods of their history are almost wholly unknown; for instance, though some periods of early–seventeenth-century Susquehannock history are well documented, the Susquehannock people entirely disappear from archaeological and archival records during a ten-year period between 1680 and 1690.

The Susquehannocks first appear in European histories as the sixty tall men by that name who met John Smith at the head of Chesapeake Bay in 1608. The term "Susquehannock" has since been translated as an Algonquian word meaning "people or place at the roiling, muddy, long, or falling water." Investigators accepting this translation believe that it probably alludes to the many rock-strewn rapids along shallow sections of the Susquehanna River that flows past their main towns.

We do not know what Susquehannock people called themselves. Some scholars have shown that other Iroquoian-speaking people knew them as Gandastogues, Andastoeronnons, and Andastes. Later records of English settlers show the name "Conestoga," which probably best translates as "cabin pole people." Documents chronicling the presence of people identified as Andastes near Lake Erie suggest earlier origins or close connections in that direction (Pendergast n.d.).

Most scholars today believe that Dutch and Swedish settlers generally used the word "Minqua" as a term of identification for Susquehannock and other Iroquoian-speaking people living farther west. References to Black and White Minquas occur in colonial records. Many scholars believe that Susquehannocks were White Minquas, but the identity of the Black Minquas remains the subject of debate. Dutch chronicler Adriaen van der Donck (1968) wrote that the term referred to black "badges" worn by these people. Black cannel-coal ornaments have been found in sixteenth-century Fort Ancient and Monongahela sites farther west. Noting that such artifacts are not encountered elsewhere and pointing to the fact that almost no archaeological or archival evidence documents direct European contact with Fort Ancient people, archaeologist William C. Johnson (1993) suggests that Monongahelas may well have been the Black Minquas.

Records kept by Europeans also note Susquehannock associations with other Indian communities during these years. At least one Swedish source, for example, notes that Minqua people maintained affiliations with groups identified as Tehaques, Serosquackes, and Skonedidehagas (A. Johnson 1911). In 1661 Maryland authorities placed the Susquehannocks at the head of Sconondihago, Ohongeoguena, Unquehiett, Kaiquariegehaga, and Usququhaga communities identified as "united nations." Some or all of these terms may be Iroquoian names for Algonquian- or Siouian-speaking Susquehannock allies or tributaries. Several archaeologists believe that these terms also may identify Monongahela or other westerly Iroquoian communities. Information on these and other names associated with Susquehannock people and their affiliates is summarized in Pendergast (1991a).

Relationships between the Susquehannocks and their neighbors are presently unclear (Feest 1978a; Pendergast 1992a). Many of the above-mentioned people simply may have lived near Susquehannock towns. Some or all may also at various times have belonged to coalitions led by Susquehannock people. Others may have been defeated enemies subjugated by the Susquehannocks.

Extant data hint at the complexities of these relationships. Van der Donck and others suggest close relations between Black and White Minqua people. Although the Black Minquas are widely thought to have been destroyed by the Senecas sometime during the second quarter of the century, a note on the

1673 Augustine Herrman map states that Susquehannocks helped the Senecas destroy the Black Minquas.

Other records document earlier-mentioned Susquehannock attacks on Delaware communities during the 1630s and 1640s. Yet several chroniclers note that at least a hundred Delaware warriors may have helped Susquehannock people defend their town against a Seneca attack in 1663.

Maneuvering through this complicated and constantly shifting political landscape, Susquehannocks were able to draw upon the resources of perhaps as many as eight thousand people at the height of their power, and they generally dominated public affairs in and around their lower Susquehanna Valley heartland. Discoveries of Monongahela and Fort Ancient wares in Susquehannock sites affirm written records noting that many Susquehannock affiliates or adversaries probably moved to their main town after epidemic disease or catastrophic war losses forced abandonment of old homes and territories.

Archaeological evidence also corroborates historic records showing that most Susquehannock people generally lived together within the walls of one or two large fortified towns at this time. Discoveries of Schultz-phase and other Susquehannock wares at sites like Herriott Farm in West Virginia and smaller sites closer to their Susquehanna Valley towns affirm that Susquehannock people also continued to occupy smaller settlements beyond the walls of their main towns during these years.

Like other people in the region, occupants maintaining residences in a Susquehannock town moved together to new communities every ten to twenty years. The first such move chronicled in seventeenth-century archaeological records involved the relocation of Susquehannock people from the Schultz-Funk site to the somewhat larger Washington Boro town at or sometime after the turn of the century.

Archaeologists have uncovered portions of an oblong stockade wall, midden deposits, several hundred pits and hearths, and a substantial number of post molds at the Washington Boro site. Cemeteries associated with this community, formerly identified as the Daisy, Eshleman, Ibaugh, Keller, and Reitz sites, are located beyond the town's stockade wall. Although corroborative evidence presently is lacking, each of these locales may represent burial places of corporate kin groups or other distinctive community constituencies.

Estimates indicate that as many as seventeen hundred people may have made their homes within the six-acre enclosure encompassed within the Washington Boro site town palisade. Substantial numbers of glass beads, iron tools, and other European goods have been found in town deposits. Washington Boro residents also continued to produce large amounts of stone tools and clay pots and pipes. The most distinctive of these pots, a finely made and elaborately castellated shell-tempered globular ware, is known as Washington Boro Incised pottery. Often decorated with human effigies and widely regarded as the apogee of Susquehannock ceramic development, Washington Boro wares are identified by Kent (1984) as primary diagnostic artifacts dating Susquehannock sites from 1600 to 1625.

People living in the Washington Boro town established the first sustained contacts with Virginian colonists from Jamestown during this period. Working to dominate regional commerce, they struggled to hold onto their strategic position astride the trade route between Chesapeake Bay, the Ohio Valley, and the lower Great Lakes in the face of growing Iroquois opposition. Traveling west to bypass the Iroquois heartland, Susquehannock traders operating out of their Washington Boro town conducted business with Erie, Neutral, and Huron clients along the lower Great Lakes (Pendergast 1992a).

Contemporary Jesuit reports provide the earliest documentary corroboration of archaeological evidence revealing close relations between Canadian Iroquoian and Susquehannock trading partners. Jesuit records also contain some of the earliest known references to hostilities with the Iroquois League of Five Nations that would increasingly preoccupy the Susquehannocks and their allies.

Available evidence indicates that most Susquehannock people moved to the nearby Roberts and Billmyer sites sometime around 1625. Unlike its predecessors, Roberts is a relatively small, stockaded town located away from the main river on a branch of Conestoga Creek. Estimates based on site size indicate that nine hundred people could have lived in the town. Less intensively investigated Billmyer site deposits are located farther up the Susquehanna, opposite the point where Codorus Creek flows into the main river. Extant evidence indicates that Billmyer was also a relatively small Susquehannock town. Firearms, armor, a Rhenish stoneware jug dated to 1630, and other objects of European origin have been found in burials located in two cemeteries at the

contemporary Frey-Haverstick site located near the earlier Washington Boro locale. Dates derived from this assemblage indicate that Roberts and Billmyer town residents buried their dead in the Frey-Haverstick cemeteries.

Contrasting site deposits preserved at the Roberts and Billmyer sites, Kent (1984) believes that they represent a transition between the Washington Boro and later Strickler phases. No coins or other unequivocally chronologically diagnostic artifacts clearly date these sites to this intervening period. Discoveries of firearms and other European artifacts commonly found in later–seventeenth-century Susquehannock sites at the Roberts, Billmyer, and Frey-Haverstick locales indicate that they postdate 1625. Occurrences of aboriginal pottery, European glass beads, and other diagnostic artifacts chronologically straddling earlier and later phases of Susquehannock culture history in these site deposits more precisely date them to the years between 1625 and 1645.

Life in these towns began to change dramatically as epidemics and intensifying warfare increasingly affected Susquehannock society. Refugees and captives adopted into Susquehannock families only partially replenished losses. But trade and war also brought unprecedented prosperity to Susquehannock communities. European artifacts begin to substantially replace aboriginal manufactures at the Roberts, Billmyer, and Frey-Haverstick sites. Archaeological discoveries also corroborate documentation of a burgeoning munitions trade with Swedish, Dutch, and Virginian merchants who established posts on the eastern fringes of the Susquehannock heartland during this time. Other records recount Susquehannock military successes against Delaware and Piscataway trade rivals.

Susquehannock people erected a new and more imposing town at the Strickler site on or about 1645. Built a few years after the Susquehannocks went to war against the Piscataways and their Maryland allies, Strickler has been shown by archaeological excavations to be one of the largest and most densely populated Indian communities yet found in the Northeast. Archaeologists working at the site have discovered evidence of a bastioned stockade enclosing an area of 12.5 acres. Three community cemeteries have thus far been found just beyond Strickler town walls.

Archaeologists working at Strickler have exposed thousands of post molds believed to represent supporting elements of racks, platforms, and possibly as many as ninety longhouses. Hundreds of hearths and more than six hundred pits have also been found. Kent (1984) suggests that Strickler may have sheltered as many as three thousand people.

Substantial amounts of European goods also have been found at this locale. Aboriginal manufactures, by contrast, compose less than a quarter of the total site assemblage. Most of these are nonutilitarian clay tobacco pipes or shell beads. Several pipes and a number of bone combs found at Strickler are nearly indistinguishable from others found at the contemporary Dann site in Seneca Country.

Other aboriginal manufactures include small numbers of catlinite beads, some flaked and pecked stone tools, and a few sherds of a new type of pottery known as Strickler cord-marked ware. Relatively undecorated and poorly con-structed, this grit-tempered ware is the last type of pottery known to have been produced by Susquehannock potters. The disappearance of such pottery in later Susquehannock sites graphically documents its replacement by imported European brass, copper, iron, and ceramic wares.

Chronologically diagnostic beads and other artifacts found at Strickler indicate that the town was occupied during the height of Susquehannock power from 1645 to 1665. Susquehannock warriors striking Indian and English communities throughout Maryland brought prisoners and plunder back to their town. Contemporary European observers visiting the town noted that cannon mounted on stockade bastions commanded its approaches. Other documents report Susquehannock success in repelling a determined Seneca attack on the town in 1663.

European firearms and other support became vital to Susquehannock survival during these years. Colonists, for their part, regarded Susquehannock people as important trading partners and indispensable border guards. Pursuing their own interests, Susquehannock diplomats signed several treaties with nearby Swedish, Dutch, and English settlers during the 1650s and 1660s. Under the terms of these treaties, Susquehannocks secured arms; obtained ammunition and foodstuffs; and received promises of friendship, peace, and support. But colonial authorities were soon able to use these treaties to extend provincial boundaries and assert sovereignty over Susquehannock people and their confederates.

European support became increasingly essential as the tempo of Iroquois

Strickler cord-marked pot found at the Strickler site (Kent 1984, fig. 24) *Courtesy State Museum of Pennsylvania, Pennsylvania Historical and Museum Commission.*

attacks against neighboring peoples reached its height. Neither the Susquehannocks nor their European allies were able to stop Seneca and other Iroquois warriors from systematically attacking the towns and camps of long-established trading partners. One by one, the Hurons, Petuns, and Neutrals were defeated and dispersed. Looking north with increasing concern, Susquehannock diplomats shored up their southern frontier by making peace with Maryland in 1652 shortly after the Neutral defeat.

The Susquehannocks could do little after that to help the Neutrals and other old trading partners. Apprehension must

have given way to dismay when word of a Seneca victory over the Eries reached the Strickler community in 1656. Now cut off from their western supply sources, Susquehannock people girded for the blows that would inevitably rain down upon their town.

As expected, Seneca warriors quickly turned south against their last remaining rivals. Although they successfully fended off Seneca attacks like the one chronicled in 1663, Susquehannock people and their native allies suffered terribly. Many were killed or captured defending their town. Others never returned from retaliatory raids on Seneca, Cayuga, and other Iroquois communities. Hundreds more perished as smallpox epidemics repeatedly struck the Strickler community between 1661 and 1664, the worst years of the struggle.

Still, the weakened Susquehannocks continued to raid Iroquois towns, and answering a summons from their new Maryland allies, Susquehannock warriors also helped Chesapeake Bay settlers defeat and subjugate the Wicomisse people in a war fought on the Delmarva Peninsula in 1669.

In the midst of these troubles, the Susquehannock people moved to the Oscar Leibhart site. Excavators working there have found the remains of a town covering little more than five acres. Limited excavations have revealed numerous pits and a post-mold pattern of one of the community's longhouses within the town walls. Not surprisingly, Oscar Leibhart is much smaller than its immediate predecessors.

Analysis of artifacts found in town deposits and in three adjoining cemeteries mutely attest to the disruptive effects of war and disease on the population of this briefly occupied town. The gross numbers of all artifact classes found in Oscar Leibhart deposits are smaller than those found at the Strickler site. Almost all artifacts found in these features are European in origin. Although substantial numbers of glass beads seem to have accompanied the dead on their journey to the next world, overall numbers of most other European artifact types are much diminished.

Analyses of site size and longhouse length at Oscar Leibhart indicate that twelve hundred individuals could have lived in the town. English sources indicate that fewer than three hundred of

these people moved south to Maryland when the Oscar Leibhart town was abandoned in 1674. The comparatively small number of graves thus far found in site cemeteries corroborates these and other contemporary accounts documenting sharp Susquehannock population decline after 1664.

The reasons for the Susquehannock move to Maryland remain unclear. Francis Jennings (1984) believes that politically motivated Maryland authorities anxious to exert more control over Susquehannocks, who served as their border guards, forced them to move closer to their settlements along the Potomac River. Looking at the same data, Elisabeth Tooker (1984a) sees no reason to doubt the Jesuit reports citing continuing Seneca attacks as the cause for Susquehannock relocation.

Whatever their reasons, the consequences of the Susquehannock relocation are well documented. As shown in preceding sections, Virginian and Maryland settlers angered by the murder of a colonist attacked the Susquehannock refugees living within two miles of an old Piscataway fort on the banks of the Potomac on Piscataway Creek during the summer of 1675. Besieged for more than six weeks by settlers and their Piscataway supporters, the Susquehannocks finally slipped away and fled south, taking refuge with Occaneechi people living near the North Carolina border. Soon involved in incidents with local Virginian settlers, the Susquehannocks moved again. Virginian militiamen, arriving after the Susquehannock withdrawal, enlisted Occaneechi support in tracking them down. When they were unable to bring the Susquehannocks to battle, the Virginians took their frustrations out on the Occaneechis.

Susquehannocks remained on the Virginia frontier for only a short time. Intensifying hostilities brought on by the final phase of Bacon's Rebellion forced most to withdraw farther north. Some of these people evidently returned to the lower Susquehanna to build a new town at the Byrd Leibhart site in 1676.

Located near the Oscar Leibhart locale, this town was a fortified community encompassing something less four acres. As many as nine hundred people could have lived within the town's walls at one time. At least four cemeteries have been discovered beyond the stockade curtain.

Shell beads, a few catlinite beads, and clay or stone pipes compose most of the domestically produced assemblage found in Byrd Leibhart community deposits. Discoveries of Madisonville potsherds usually found in Ohio Valley sites associated with the final phase of Fort Ancient occupation suggest contacts with western Indian people.

Brass kettles, iron tools, gun parts, glass and ceramic wares, and other European imports constitute most of the site assemblage. Recovery of smaller numbers of such artifacts at this locale continues what appears to be the downward economic trend first observed in Oscar Leibhart site deposits.

Graves continue to contain substantial quantities of glass beads and other offerings, but departing from earlier practice, Byrd Leibhart people furnished few graves with guns, knives, or other utilitarian wares. This shift from earlier patterns indicates that European imports, especially firearms, lead, and edged iron tools, had become both too rare and too indispensable to be buried with the dead.

Although evidence is unclear, Susquehannock people probably abandoned Byrd Leibhart around 1680. Some of its inhabitants may have moved to a Susquehannock town in the upper Schuylkill Valley noted by Pennsylvania colonists. Others probably joined Seneca war parties settling old scores with Indian enemies farther south. Susquehannock warriors living among the Senecas, for example, are believed to have been part of a large war party that attacked Piscataway people who had taken refuge in their fort in the Zachiah Swamp during the summer of 1681.

Some of these people returned to the Susquehanna Valley under Seneca sponsorship sometime between 1690 and 1696. Paddling downriver, they debarked at a spot in the heart of former Susquehannock territory near the site of the old Washington Boro community.

Calling their community Conestoga, the new settlers were soon joined by other Indian refugees. From the east, small groups of Delaware people, who had been settling in the area at various times since the 1670s, began to establish more permanent communities. From the west came Shawnee refugees forced from their Ohio Valley towns by fighting brought on by the outbreak of King William's War in 1689.

French allies when the war broke out, the Shawnees had been driven from their lands by Iroquois warriors armed and supplied by New York authorities. Devastated by these attacks, the Shawnees asked the Delawares to help them make peace with the Iroquois and their English allies. Agreeing to live peacefully, groups of Shawnee people began

Pedestaled pot *(top)* and Madisonville-like pot *(bottom)* from the Byrd Leibhart site (Kent 1984, fig. 105). *Courtesy State Museum of Pennsylvania, Pennsylvania Historical and Museum Commission.*

moving east after 1692. Provincial records indicate that several of these groups subsequently settled near the newly built Conestoga community.

Like other settlements built after the Iroquois were forced to burn their compact fortified towns in front of invading French armies before and during King William's War, these lower Susquehanna towns were sprawling communities of widely spaced bark cabins surrounded by planting fields and orchards. Archaeological excavations conducted at the site of Conestoga affirm that its occupants almost totally relied upon imported European tools, ornaments, and weapons. Although town residents depended upon farm products and trade for their living, hunting, fishing, and foraging continued to play essential roles in lower Susquehanna Valley native economic life.

THE EIGHTEENTH CENTURY

Displaced people from a number of native communities moved to new settlements in and around the Conestoga and Pequehan locales during the early 1700s. On the north, increasing numbers of displaced Delaware people, forced from their homes at Tulpehocken, Okehocking, and other locales, settled around Conestoga and at places like Paxtang farther upriver, near present-day Harrisburg. Growing numbers of Shawnee people moved to Pequehan and other communities near the Delaware towns. Farther south, Conoy and Nanticoke people leaving their ancient homes joined Conoy Island expatriates gathering together at a new community named Conejohela Town between 1701 and 1710 on the east bank of the Susquehanna

across from the old Byrd and Oscar Leibhart townsites.

The area was well suited for such relocations. The lower Susquehanna lay astride a strategic trade route that had long connected coastal settlements with the interior. Situated on the broad frontier separating the Iroquois heartland from the rival Pennsylvania and Maryland colonies, the area also commanded the most easily accessible routes west into the Ohio Valley and lower Great Lakes.

Conestoga became the focal point of Indian settlement in this area during the first decades of the century. As many as 150 native people lived in the center of the town in 1700. Several hundred others lived within easy walking distance of the town center. Early–eighteenth-century observers like William Penn noted that Conestoga people initially lived in peak-roofed, bark-walled cabins. Archaeologists working at the site of the town more recently have found evidence indicating that most of these people began erecting log cabins in the town after 1730. Artifacts found in and around these housesites affirm written records indicating that nearly everything owned by Conestoga townsfolk was imported from European or other Indian communities.

Most of these records were written by Pennsylvanian traders like the Swede John Hans Steelman and the French Canadian emigré Martin Chartier who established trading posts at Conestoga shortly after the end of King William's War in 1697. Often marrying Indian women and frequently fluent in several languages, men like Martin Chartier and his son Peter worked as intermediaries between local townsfolk and traveling European merchants, missionaries,

Pipes made from catlinite imported from South Dakota, recovered from Conestoga site deposits (Kent 1984, fig. 31). *Courtesy State Museum of Pennsylvania, Pennsylvania Historical and Museum Commission.*

and dignitaries who journeyed to the Susquehanna to meet visiting Indian delegations.

Such meetings were held with increasing frequency as Conestoga became an important regional diplomatic and trade center. Struggling to secure their increasingly threatened southern frontier, Iroquois diplomats regarded Conestoga as their primary administrative center along the lower Susquehanna, asserting sovereignty over the region on the basis of their claim that they had conquered the Susquehannocks in 1675.

Negotiating with town leaders, Penn-

sylvania officials obtained title to all Conestoga lands in 1700, but they did not initially use their deed to uproot Conestoga townsfolk. Unable to colonize the area at the time, they instead used the town as a meeting place for councils with visiting Indian delegations, provincial traders, and contending Marylanders claiming the southern reaches of the Susquehanna for themselves.

Captain Civility, the Susquehannock Queen Cantowa, the Conestoga Seneca leader Sohaes, and other Conestoga town chiefs who had affixed their marks to Penn's deed hosted many of these meetings. Such assemblies became increasingly frequent as word of threatened attacks by French and Indian allies reached Conestoga shortly after Queen Anne's War broke out in 1702.

Firmly establishing themselves during the war as Pennsylvanian agents, Conestoga traders played a major role in extending provincial trade and influence farther west into Ohio. Their success helped Pennsylvania push westward in the years after the war ended in 1713. Then settlers moving into Lancaster County began forcing Conestoga townsfolk out. Those people remaining in the area ultimately were restricted to a five-hundred-acre reservation within a sixteen-thousand-acre tract known as Conestoga Manor. Increasingly pressed to leave by their new neighbors, Conestoga's native population drifted away. Gradually bypassed, Conestoga itself became frontier backwater.

Bending to the same pressures, Piscataway, Potomac, and Nanticoke expatriates living at nearby Conejohela moved north to Conoy Town in 1718. Located near the mouth of Conoy Creek in Lancaster County, Conoy Town remained the principal gathering place for Potomac Valley and Chesapeake Bay expatriates for more than twenty years. Excavations conducted at the site affirm that most town residents had largely adopted European technology by midcentury. Although quantities of shell beads and fragments of splint basketry testify to the persistence of some crafts, iron, glass, and European ceramics dominate assemblages recovered from this locale. Discoveries of ossuary burials, by contrast, affirm that Conoy community members maintained earlier-established spiritual beliefs and values during these years.

Relations between Delaware and Shawnee people living near one another around Conestoga and at various locales in the Paxtang area became particularly close at this time. Many Shawnees also maintained amicable relations with European traders living near their towns. Several continued to marry into Indian families.

Changing conditions gradually caused Shawnee and Delaware relations with the Iroquois and Pennsylvanian settlers to deteriorate. As mentioned earlier, hostilities with local colonists forced the Shawnees to abandon their settlements at the Delaware Water Gap in 1727. Many Delawares, for their part, were forced to leave their last homes in the Brandywine, Schuylkill, and Tulpehocken Valleys at this time. Selling the land from under them, the Iroquois ordered these and other dispossessed people to move farther north and west.

Many Shawnees and Delawares soon joined other people settling farther west in the upper Ohio Valley. Other Delawares and most Conoy and Nanticoke people moved farther upriver, above the Blue Mountains. Following their leader Sassoonan, most Delawares settled around the forks of the Susquehanna at Shamokin in present-day Sunbury. Conoy Town residents, for their part, joined other Piscataway and Nanticoke expatriates establishing a new town on Haldeman Island at the mouth of the Juniata River.

Most native people had left the lower Susquehanna Valley by the time the Seven Years' War broke out in 1755. All but two of the small group of twenty-two Conestoga people continuing to live in cabins in their old community were brutally murdered by Paxton rioters in December 1763. The remaining two, a married couple named Michael and Mary, lived quietly among the settlers until their deaths some years later.

Archaeologists have located the sites of several towns occupied during the 1700s by lower Susquehanna native emigrés. The locales of some of these communities, like Conestoga and Conoy Town, are extensively documented in colonial records. Documentation identifying the occupants of the Lancaster County Park site and other sites has not yet been located. Archaeological verification of documented communities like the Shawnee town of Pequehan also awaits results of future research.

SOURCES

Most information presented in this section has been abstracted from Kent (1984). Much of the documentation describing what is known about Shenks Ferry people is drawn from Heisey and Witmer (1964) and amplified by Herbstritt and Kent (1990). Other key sources for Susquehannock archaeology include Cadzow (1936); Casselberry (1971); Custer, Carlson, and Doms (1986); Handsman (1987); Kinsey (1982); Kinsey and Custer (1982); I. Smith and Graybill (1977); and Witthoft and Kinsey (1959).

Jennings (1967, 1968b, 1978) and E. Tooker (1984a) examine the causes and consequences of the Susquehannock dispersal. All of the numerous Indian towns along the lower Susquehanna mentioned in eighteenth-century colonial records are named and located in compilations put together by Donehoo (1928), Hanna (1911), W. Hunter (n.d.), Kent, Rice, and Ota (1981), Tanner (1987), and P. A. W. Wallace (1965). Studies by Callender (1978b), W. Hunter (1978b), Jennings (1984, 1988b), P. A. W. Wallace (1981), Weslager (1972, 1978a), and Witthoft and Hunter (1955) document many aspects of native life in these towns.

EUROPEAN-INDIAN CONTACT IN THE MIDDLE ATLANTIC REGION

THE SIXTEENTH CENTURY

Earlier-mentioned written records document brief visits in the region by mariners such as Verrazzano or short-lived settlements like that at Ajacan. No identifiable evidence directly attributable to these or other encounters known to have occurred along Middle Atlantic shores during the 1500s has yet been found by archaeologists.

THE SEVENTEENTH CENTURY

As the foregoing pages have shown, ever-increasing numbers of newcomers from Europe and Africa overwhelmed Indian communities, which consequently suffered devastating depopulation during the 1600s. Despite high epidemic mortality rates, total immigrant population in the region rose from nearly nothing to more than 125,000 at the end of the century. During the same period, the total Indian population in the region dropped from perhaps as many as 50,000 people to less than a tenth of that number. Desolated by such losses, Indian communities could do little to stop settlers from colonizing virtually every easily habitable portion of the Middle Atlantic area by 1700.

Most English colonists moving to the region during the seventeenth century settled at various locales in the Chesapeake Bay drainage. Like settlers elsewhere, many of these colonists first moved onto lands already cleared by Indian people. Only a few of the thousands of settlers colonizing Indian land in Virginia during the first decades of the century—and the colonists who arrived in Maryland after 1634—settled in small, compact towns like Jamestown and Saint Mary's City. The majority fanned out across the tidewater flatlands, establishing plantations or trading posts. Formed as largely self-supporting communities usually maintained by slave labor, most of these settlements were linked to regional administrative centers, markets, churches, and each another by the many channels, streams, and other waterways that coursed through the region.

English and Dutch traders had been sailing along the lower Delaware River for many years when Swedish colonists established their first posts along the river in 1638. Small trade forts were soon built at Fort Christina, Fort Elfsborg, Tinicum Island, and other locales. Close relations were established with neighboring Delaware people and Susquehannocks from towns farther west. Cut off from their home countries for years at a time, a number of impoverished settlers reportedly moved among Indian neighbors, largely adopting native dress, cuisine, and housing.

Farther north, Dutch colonists settled in small outposts and farms scattered throughout the Delaware and lower Hudson river valleys. Dutch interest in New Netherland, as the area between Virginia and New England became known, began when Henry Hudson, an English mariner in Dutch service, sailed into the Hudson River at the end of the summer of 1609. Subsequent voyages undertaken by explorers like Cornelis May and Adriaen Block resulted in the establishment of the first Dutch trade post at Fort Nassau on Castle Island on the upper Hudson River near modern Albany, New York, in 1614.

The Dutch built other posts in the Middle Atlantic region—Fort Nassau on the Delaware in 1626 and at the same time Fort Amsterdam on Manhattan Island at the mouth of the Hudson. Traders at these fortified truckinghouses exchanged metal tools, textiles, glass beads, firearms, ammunition, and other European goods for furs with visiting Indian people. Dutch privateers used New Netherland ports for attacks against enemy shipping during a series of three wars fought with England between 1653 and 1674. Several large feudal manors known as patroonships and large numbers of small independent farmholdings also were established at Rensselaerswyck and other locales.

New Netherland was a cosmopolitan colony stretching along the Atlantic coast from the Fresh (Connecticut) River across the North (Hudson) River to the South (Delaware) River. Although many settlers hailed from Dutch provinces, significant numbers of colonists came from Scandinavia, France, Belgium, and central Europe. Increasing numbers of English colonists moving from New England also settled along the eastern borders of the Dutch province at Westchester and western Long Island.

Many of these settlers, recruited and commanded by the same John Underhill who helped lead the assault on Mystic Fort during the Pequot War in 1637, participated in several devastating attacks on Munsee towns during Governor Kieft's War in 1644. Twenty years later, many of these same settlers served as a fifth column supporting the English conquest of the Dutch colony in 1664. Recapturing New York in 1673, the Dutch subsequently agreed to return the colony to the English for the last time in 1674.

On the Delaware, Dutch forces capturing New Sweden in 1655 surrendered the river to the English in 1664. Establishing their first settlements near the head of navigation below the falls of the Delaware, Quaker settlers moved to the east bank of the river in West Jersey after 1676. More intensive settlement of the region began several years later when Quaker William Penn established his proprietary government at Philadelphia in 1682. Penn's city was well on its way to becoming British America's largest urban settlement by the end of the century.

City life elsewhere in the region generally developed slowly. English New Yorkers taking over New Amsterdam maintained the city's twisting, medieval street plan. Recent analysis has shown that Saint Mary's City, built on the site of

MAP 27: MIDDLE ATLANTIC EUROPEAN-INDIAN CONTACT SITES

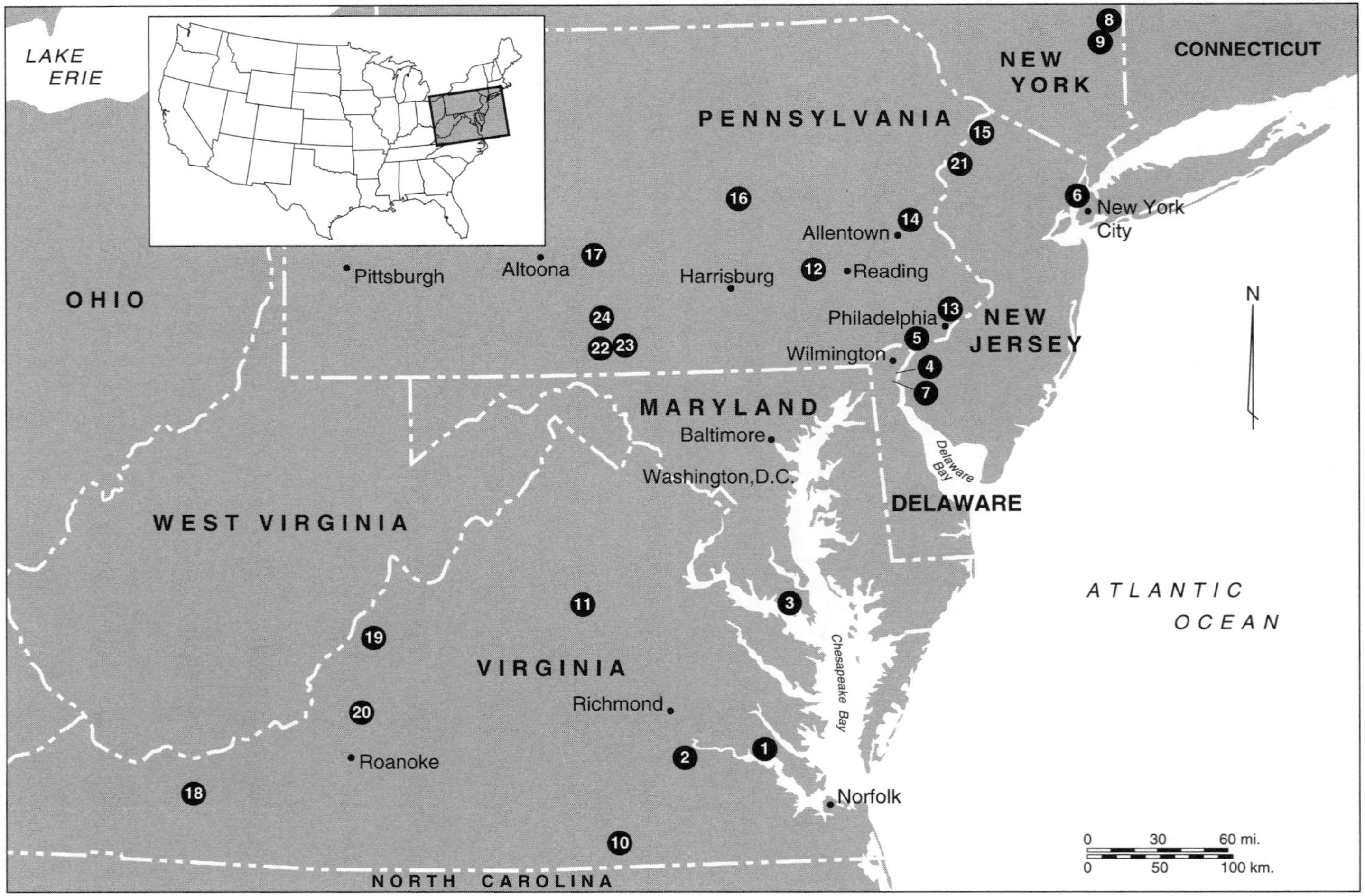

LAKE ERIE
OHIO
PENNSYLVANIA
NEW YORK
CONNECTICUT
NEW JERSEY
MARYLAND
DELAWARE
WEST VIRGINIA
VIRGINIA
NORTH CAROLINA
ATLANTIC OCEAN
Pittsburgh
Altoona
Harrisburg
Reading
Allentown
Philadelphia
Wilmington
New York City
Baltimore
Washington, D.C.
Richmond
Roanoke
Norfolk
Delaware Bay
Chesapeake Bay
N
0 30 60 mi.
0 50 100 km.
1
2
3
4
5
6
7
8
9
10
11
12
13
14
15
16
17
18
19
20
21
22
23
24

Map 27 Historic Contact Sites

Map Number	Site Name	County	State	Date	NR	Source
1	Colonial NHP	James City	VA	1500s–1600s	X	NPS 1987
2	Jordan's Journey (44PG1)	Prince George	VA	1620–1635		Mouer 1992b
3	St. Mary's City NHL (18ST1)	St. Mary's	MD	1615–1695	X	Chaney and Miller 1989, 1990; H. Miller 1983
4	Fort Christina NHL	New Castle	DE	1638–1664	X	NPS 1987
5	Printzhof NHL (36DE3)	Delaware	PA	1643–1655	X	Becker 1985; NPS 1987
6	Augustine Heermans' Warehouse	New York	NY	1650–1699		Grossman et al. 1985
7	Fort Casimir	New Castle	DE	1651–1654		Heite and Heite 1989
8	Hurley Historic District NHL	Ulster	NY	1653–present	X	NPS 1987
9	Huguenot Street NHL	Ulster	NY	1677–present	X	NPS 1987
10	Fort Christanna	Brunswick	VA	1714–1732	X	Beaudry 1979; Hazzard and McCartney 1979; McCartney and Hazzard 1979; Turner 1990b; VDHR
11	Germanna	Orange	VA	1714–1734	X	Sanford and Parker 1986
12	Conrad Weiser NHL	Berks	PA	1729–1760	X	NPS 1987
13	James Logan Home NHL	Philadelphia	PA	1730–1751	X	NPS
14	Gemeinhaus NHL	Northampton	PA	1733–present	X	NPS 1987
15	Minisink NHL Fort Westbrook Westbrook-Bell House	Sussex Pike	NJ PA	1735–1783	X	Kraft 1977, 1978, 1986; Marchiando 1972; Puniello and Williams 1978
16	Fort Augusta (36NB71)	Northumberland	PA	Mid-1700s		PASS
17	Fort Shirley (36HU94)	Huntingdon	PA	Mid-1700s		PASS
18	Fort Chiswell	Wythe	VA	1755–1760		MacCord 1973b
19	Fort Dinwiddie	Bath	VA	1755–1760		MacCord 1973b
20	Fort Fauquier	Botetourt	VA	1755–1760		MacCord 1973b
21	Fort Nomanock	Warren	NJ	1756–1758		Kraft 1977
22	Fort Loudon (36FR107)	Franklin	PA	1756–1765		PASS
23	Fort Armstrong (36FR49)	Franklin	PA	1756–1765		PASS
24	Fort Littleton (36FU42)	Fulton	PA	1756–1765		PASS

the Yoacomaco Indian town in 1634, was the region's first planned city (H. Miller 1988). Fully developed urban centers using modern grid plans did not fully emerge elsewhere in the Middle Atlantic colonies until Penn began constructing Philadelphia in 1682.

Most of the few standing structures clearly associated with seventeenth-century contact between Indian people and colonists in the Middle Atlantic region are located in the northernmost reaches of the area. Ulster County National Historic Landmarks like Kingston's Senate House and the New Paltz and Hurley Historic Districts preserve physical evidence documenting relations between Dutch colonists and Indian people after the fall of New Netherland. Most other seventeenth-century European-Indian contact sites in the region have been buried or destroyed.

A substantial number of archaeological sites preserve information associated with many of the now-demolished structures in the region. As mentioned earlier, Saint Mary's City National Historic Landmark contains the one of the best known and most extensively recorded assemblages of archaeological deposits documenting contact between Indian, European, and African people in the region (Chaney and Miller 1989, 1990; Hall 1910; H. Miller 1983).

Several archaeological sites preserve evidence of early English homesteads and other locales associated with the Jamestown settlement. Several of these sites, like Martin's Hundred within Colonial National Historical Park and Jordan's Journey, contain evidence of Indian trade and warfare.

Forts Christina and Casimir were sites of numerous treaty meetings and other encounters where Delaware and Susquehannock traders and diplomats met Swedish or Dutch counterparts. Recent testing of deposits at the Printzhof National Historic Landmark below modern Philadelphia has unearthed shell beads, European ceramics, and other artifacts possibly associated with the site's function as New Sweden governor Johan Printz's administrative center between 1643 and 1653.

THE EIGHTEENTH CENTURY

Great Britain had emerged as the sole colonial power in the Middle Atlantic region by 1700. Although Indian people did not abandon the region, increasingly fewer formal contacts occurred along the coast as the primary focus of intercultural relations shifted elsewhere in response to movements of many Middle Atlantic Indians farther north, west, and south by 1750. As a result, most contact sites built during these years are located on the peripheries of European settlement.

Archaeologists have found deposits associated with two frontier outposts built by Lieutenant Governor Spotswood. The Germanna site contains the remains of a mansion erected near a fort and town built to house German immigrants along the northwestern border of the province. Farther south, deposits unearthed at the site of Fort Christanna document the post that first attracted and then housed Saponi refugees guarding Virginia's southwestern border.

The Conrad Weiser and James Logan National Historic Landmarks are standing structures representing residences of influential eighteenth-century frontier diplomats. Weiser, who spoke Delaware, Mohawk, German, and English, was an intermediary between Pennsylvanian authorities and Indian people. James Logan, for his part, virtually ran the province while working as William Penn's secretary from 1699 to 1717. Logan is best known today among students of contact relations as a primary instigator of the 1736 Walking Purchase deed and the subsequent controversial boundary demarcation in 1737. He used his home at Stenton, built in 1730, as a place for meetings with the many Delaware, Iroquois, and other Indian delegations visiting Philadelphia during the late-seventeenth and early-eighteenth centuries.

Archaeologists have also located and tested a number of frontier fortifications built during the Seven Years' War in New Jersey, Pennsylvania, and Virginia. Particularly extensive excavations have been conducted at Forts Augusta and Loudon in Pennsylvania (PASS). Other investigations have been conducted at Forts Westbrook and Nomanock in New Jersey (Kraft 1977) and Forts Chiswell, Dinwiddie, and Fauquier in Virginia (MacCord 1973b).

SOURCES

A large body of documentary material records the European side of intercultural relations in the Middle Atlantic region. Useful summaries tracing various aspects of these encounters appear in Crane (1928), Craven (1949), Fausz (1988), Jacobs (1988), Jennings (1988b), Weslager (1967), and Weslager and Dunlap (1961).

Many studies documenting seventeenth- and eighteenth-century Middle Atlantic Anglo-American life consider relations with Indian people. Earlier surveys, like R. Morton's (1960), generally tend to focus upon archival records chronicling political and military relations. More recent studies, such as Leone and Potter's (1988), use archaeological evidence to verify archival data and address issues not documented in written records.

Scholars are increasingly employing sociological and anthropological theory to better understand the nature of British colonial society in the region. Isaac (1982), for example, traces the transformation of Virginia society from a relatively simple planting community to a more complex social order between 1740 and 1790. Edmund Morgan (1975) presents a comprehensive demographic analysis of Virginian colonial development. A case for the development of a syncretic culture combining aspects of European and African heritage in colonial Virginia is made in Sobel (1988). Other aspects of colonial Chesapeake life are examined in essays published in Carr, Morgan, and Russo (1988) and Craven (1971). Historical geographies of New Jersey (Wacker 1975) and southeastern Pennsylvania (Lemon 1972) also provide significant information.

Extensive studies continue to be carried out at Saint Mary's City National Historic Landmark (Chaney and H. Miller 1989, 1990; H. Miller 1983). Other studies have been conducted at Germanna (Sanford and Parker 1986) and the Printzhof National Historic Landmark (Becker 1985). Investigators conducting an ongoing survey of archaeological and archival data documenting seventeenth- and early–eighteenth-century life in Delaware are reexamining known sites and discovering new ones (Fithian 1992).

Basic sources of information on contact relations in the short-lived New Sweden colony include Dahlgren and Norman (1988) and A. Johnson (1911).

The most detailed current survey of New Netherland life and history appears in Rink (1986). Jennings (1988a) provides a succinct overview of the Dutch colony. Bachman (1969) examines New Netherland's role as a fur entrepôt, plantation colony, and privateers' lair. Nooter and Bonomi (1988) and Trelease (1960) summarize much of what is known about Dutch social contacts and political relationships with Indian people.

A large body of primary written records documents Dutch-Indian relations. Recent translations by linguist Charles T. Gehring (1977, 1980, 1981) correct errors in earlier compilations edited by archivists such as Edmund O'Callaghan and Berthold Fernow (1853–1887). Primary sources such as van der Donck (1968; also see van Gastel 1990) and narratives published in Jameson (1909) remain essential reading.

PART THREE

THE TRANS-APPALACHIAN REGION

MAP 28: THE TRANS-APPALACHIAN REGION

AN OVERVIEW OF THE REGION

The Trans-Appalachian region stretches across the central and western reaches of the Northeastern United States. Its eastern borders extend from the Lake Champlain Valley south to the Heldeberg, Catskill, Pocono, and Blue Mountains. Stretching west from the Mohawk and Susquehanna Valleys, the region extends west across present-day central and western New York and Pennsylvania to the headwaters of the Ohio Valley and the southern shores of Lake Erie. Extending from the Saint Lawrence lowlands on the north to the upper Susquehanna Valley in the east and the Allegheny, Monongahela, and upper Ohio Valleys on the west, this region includes western Maryland; western Vermont; central and western Pennsylvania; central and western Virginia; northern, central, and western New York; and northeastern West Virginia.

Most people living in the Trans-Appalachian region at the time of initial contact with Europeans are believed to have spoken Northern Iroquoian languages. Almost all, moreover, followed a variant of the widespread Late Woodland way of life called the "Northern Iroquoian cultural pattern" by William

N. Fenton (1978). Like other Late Woodland people, Northern Iroquoians lived lives based on hunting, fishing, foraging, and corn, bean, and squash cultivation. They generally used local materials—stone, bone, shell, antler, and wood—to craft tools, implements, and weapons. They also made the same small triangular projectile points and other chipped-stone tools used by Late Woodland people throughout the Northeast.

Unlike most of their neighbors, however, Northern Iroquoian people made and used a number of stylistically distinct globular clay pots and several forms of tobacco-smoking pipes. Many of these pipes were decorated with modeled effigies, and distinctive geometric motifs were incised into their collars, rims, and/or shoulders.

Northern Iroquoian settlement patterns also frequently differed from those of neighboring peoples. Northern Iroquoians tended to live in dense, nucleated communities of bark-walled longhouses that had doors at their ends rather than at their sides. Larger settlements could contain from 30 to 150 bark-covered buildings. More than a few

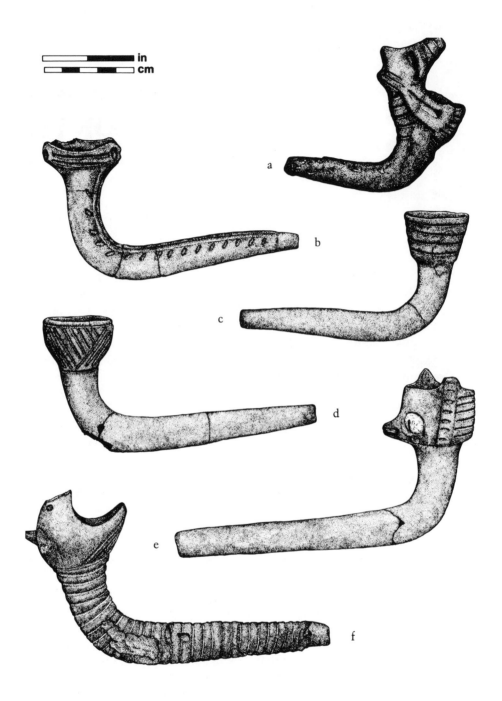

Clay tobacco-smoking pipes from sites in Onondaga Country: *(a)* a "pinch-face" effigy pipe, *(b)* a coronet trumpet pipe, *(c* and *d)* two rimless trumpet pipes, *(e)* an owl effigy with applied copper eyes, *(f)* an open-mouth effigy. The pipe in part *a* is from the Lot 18 site; the remainder are from the Carley site (Bradley 1987a, fig. 10, p. 124). *Courtesy of James W. Bradley.*

of these towns were surrounded by stockaded palisade fortifications.

People belonging to what archaeologists call the Monongahela cultural tradition lived in often-unfortified communities of round or oblong houses in and around the Monongahela Valley in southwestern Pennsylvania. Unlike most Northern Iroquoian towns, Monongahela communities were frequently laid out in concentric rings of houses fronting upon central plazas. Both Monongahela town plans and pottery types resemble those used in the Ohio Valley's Fort Ancient–Madisonville horizon communities and other towns farther south and west.

Exhausting nearby soils, using up local supplies of firewood, cultivating fields invaded by noxious insects and other pests, and increasingly stifled by the accumulated clutter of long occupation, people living in Trans-Appalachian towns generally moved to new locales every ten to twenty years (Fenton 1978; W. Ritchie and Funk 1973; Starna, Hamell, and Butts 1984; Sykes 1980). Though they usually relocated their towns only short distances away, under extraordinary circumstances Trans-Appalachian people were known to move their communities as far as several hundred miles away.

However they moved or wherever they lived, Trans-Appalachian townsfolk struggled to balance individual interest with social needs in order to maintain long-lasting alliances. People belonging to the five (later six) nations that composed the best-known of these coalitions, the Iroquois confederacy, gradually came to dominate affairs in the region during the eighteenth century after the dispersal and destruction of their Monongahela, Neutral, Wenro, and Erie rivals on the west. The League was unified through a ritual framework based on consensual participation of all confederated nations; sachems appointed by senior clanswomen met at their council fire at Onondaga to discuss policy and ratify decisions. Usually fulfilling largely symbolic roles, particularly effective confederacy leaders worked to maintain internal harmony and encourage unified action. The more successful of these leaders helped Iroquois nations exert economic and political influence far out of proportion to their relatively small numbers.

Most Iroquois nations struggled to gain influence in or assert authority over neighboring communities while playing colonial and Indian rivals off against one another. During what has been called the "golden age" of Iroquois diplomacy, from 1701 to 1755, Iroquois leaders worked hard to present a united front capable of stopping colonial expansion into the heart of their territories. Mohawk people living nearest to British settlements, for example, only grudgingly sold land along their frontiers. Cayuga and Oneida people, for their part, took leading roles in relocating and supervising displaced Indian refugees along the southeasternmost frontiers of Iroquoia. Farther west, Seneca people adopted foreigners and incorporated entire communities from conquered nations.

Strategies like these slowed rather than stemmed Iroquois population decline. Ever-increasing numbers of colonists pressed along the Iroquois borders, intent on possessing their land. Resisting as long as they could, Iroquois people were gradually outflanked by Europeans thrusting into their heartland from the north, south, and east. Indian communities guarding the eastern and southern approaches to Iroquoia were almost entirely swept away by colonists streaming into the Susquehanna Valley during the middle years of the eighteenth century. Outnumbered, outflanked, and finally divided by conflicting loyalties, the Iroquois could not prevent the devastation of their towns during the American War for Independence. Most Iroquois who had openly aligned themselves with the British had to sign a separate peace with the Americans at Fort Stanwix in 1784.

Both they and kinsfolk who had supported the American cause during the war were soon pressed to sell ancestral lands. Unable to resist mounting pressures, the Iroquois and other Trans-Appalachian Indians were finally compelled to convey title to most of their remaining lands to American purchasers in the first decades of the nineteenth century.

As used in this study, the term *Trans-Appalachia* refers to an area that was home to the Iroquois League of Five Nations and their culturally similar neighbors along the Susquehanna, Niagara, Erie, and Allegheny frontiers. The word *Iroquoian* identifies all Iroquoian-speaking people, while the term *Iroquois* specifically refers to the nations composing the Iroquois confederacy. The term *Iroquoia,* for its part, is used to identify the Iroquois heartland.

THE SIXTEENTH CENTURY

As elsewhere in the Northeast, nearly everything known about sixteenth-century life in the Trans-Appalachian region comes from archaeological sites or more recently collected Indian oral literature. Much of these data have been gathered in the form of European trade goods and other materials found in archaeological sites or from modern verbal accounts that present contemporary views of the effects of initial contacts. The few known written records from the period document visits by Basque mariners and French traders like Jacques Cartier to the Canadian Maritimes and lower reaches of the Saint Lawrence Valley beyond the boundaries of the United States.

Vocabularies gathered during Cartier's visit show that people living along the Saint Lawrence spoke Iroquoian languages at the time of first contact. Subsequent studies have shown that all other Iroquoian-speaking people living in the region spoke Northern Iroquoian variants (Lounsbury 1978). Iroquoian languages differ from Algonquian or Siouian tongues as much as Japanese differs from English and Bantu. Among themselves, Iroquoian languages can differ as much as English differs from German.

While speaking related languages, most Northern Iroquoian people belonged to communities maintaining distinctive cultural and social identities. At the same time, all Northern Iroquoians shared a generally similar way of life. The earlier-mentioned Northern Iroquoian cultural pattern consisted of comparable subsistence, technological, settlement, social, political, and ideological practices and beliefs (Fenton 1978).

Archaeologists analyzing data drawn from the hundreds of sites excavated in the Trans-Appalachian region during the past century and a half generally agree that these Northern Iroquoian cultural patterns first emerged in clearly discernible form between A.D. 800 and 1100. The transformation is signaled by initial appearances of triangular, chipped-stone projectile points; distinctive, domestically produced clay pots and tobacco pipes; and carbonized corn found in pits, hearths, middens, and roasting platforms unearthed among post molds of longhouses, stockade fortifications, and other remains of towns and camps. Later developments, such as incised, collared pottery production and more intensive settlement nucleation, first appear in sites dating from 1300 to 1400.

The causes of these transformations remain the subject of lively debate. Earlier in this century, most scholars believed that such changes signaled arrivals of new immigrants from other parts of the continent (Parker 1916). Seeing continuity rather than change in the available evidence, later investigators suggested that these transformations represented in situ developments (MacNeish 1952; W. Ritchie and MacNeish 1949).

Although in situ hypotheses continue to enjoy wide support, increasing numbers of scholars are challenging their validity. Using core-periphery and predatory-expansion models, archaeologists Dena F. Dincauze and Robert J. Hasenstab (Dincauze and Hasenstab 1987; Hasenstab 1987, 1990) believe that settlement shifts and evidence of increasing social, political, and economic complexity may reflect contact between town-dwelling Ohio River Valley Mississippian or Fort Ancient food producers and more easterly ancestors of Iroquoian people during periods of environmental stress.

Analyzing the same data, Snow (1991b) suggests that the appearance of Late Woodland Owasco culture in northeastern portions of the region, which were formerly occupied by people following a Middle Woodland Point Peninsula way of life, represents incursions of food-producing, Iroquoian-speaking town dwellers into Trans-Appalachian valleys occupied by hunting and gathering people. Examining extant paleoenvironmental evidence, Snow believes that these incursions occurred under environmental conditions favorable to expanding food producers. Citing recent linguistic studies that indicate Northern Iroquoian languages diverged from the Southern Iroquoian Cherokee language about A.D. 1000, and finding no evidence of Iroquoian cultural precursors elsewhere, Snow further proposes that initial appearances of triangular, chipped-stone projectile points and Owascoid pottery and pipes in sites associated with the poorly dated Clemson's Island Tradition along the lower Susquehanna Valley may represent a link in a migratory chain stretching north from somewhere in the southeast to the Saint Lawrence lowlands.

Whatever their origins, initial appearances of unprecedentedly larger and more nucleated townsites generally mark the shift from Middle Woodland hunting and gathering lifestyles to more settled ways of life in the region. The sites contain distinctive ceramic assemblages dominated by varieties of cord-marked, roughened, globular-bodied pots decorated with incised geometric motifs on their necks, collars, and rims. Archaeologists believe that sometime during the late fifteenth century people living in the more northern reaches of the region, in the Saint Lawrence lowlands and on the lower Great Lakes, began crafting distinctive forms of late-stage Ontario Iroquois Tradition pottery based on earlier Owasco and Pickering Tradition models.

Specialists are divided on the meaning of these discoveries. Most formerly thought that the appearance of pottery at particular sites represented the presence of their makers at these locales. More recently, increasing numbers of scholars are considering the possibility that such distributions may represent evidence of exchange networks or interaction spheres (Engelbrecht 1971; Petersen 1989; Pendergast 1991b; J. Wright 1966).

Most archaeologists believe that the immediate ancestors of Huron, Petun, Neutral, Wenro, and Erie people living farther west in Ontario, western New York, and northwestern Pennsylvania began making their own forms of late-stage Ontario Iroquois Tradition pottery based on preceding Pickering and Glen Meyer wares around 1400. Available evidence suggests that the cultural traditions of these people soon diverged. Direct ancestors of Huron and Petun potters living between Lakes Huron and Ontario quickly showed a preference for heavily decorated vessels that were often surmounted by carinated necks and shoulders. Available evidence also shows that flint knappers living with people making or using such pots frequently pressed notches into the sides of their triangular, chipped-stone projectile points.

Late-stage Ontario Iroquois Tradition people living farther west beyond the Genesee Valley in places later chronicled as Neutral and Erie territory made straight-sided, triangular, chipped-stone projectile points and crafted more simply decorated wares. Seriational analyses of pottery in this area indicate that many people living in its easternmost reaches began making stylistically distinct variants of Oakfield wares sometime during the 1500s. Small numbers of Richmond Incised and other wares found in Oakfield-phase sites suggest contacts with more easterly people believed to have been common ancestors of Senecas, Cayugas, and Susquehannocks.

People living in central New York on Seneca and Cayuga Country lands began making assemblages dominated by Richmond Incised wares that were based on earlier Owascoid prototypes. At about the same time people living farther north and west began crafting late-stage Ontario Iroquois Tradition pottery. Farther east, people living in the Onondaga and Oneida Country started producing pottery assemblages dominated by Chance-phase ceramics resembling distinctive Garoga-series wares made by Mohawks and other people living along the upper reaches of the Hudson, Delaware, and Susquehanna river valleys.

Potters living just south of this area began to produce their own, more elaborately decorated variants of Richmond Incised pots during the early 1500s. Discoveries of these wares in cemeteries like the Engelbert site or townsites like Murray Farm on the upper reaches of the East Branch of the Susquehanna River represent the first identifiable evidence of people later chronicled as Susquehannocks. Archaeological evidence indicates that people making or using these wares began to move south toward Chesapeake Bay sometime between 1550 and 1575. Supplanting, driving away, or assimilating Shenks Ferry people, the Susquehannocks learned to use shell tempering and other new techniques commonly employed by Monongahelas, Fort Ancient people, and other groups living farther west. Susquehannock potters subsequently developed new and distinctive incised wares of their own, which are known to archaeologists today as Schultz, Washington Boro, and Strickler pottery.

On the north, people making distinctive forms of Saint Lawrence Iroquoian pottery lived in towns stretching from Jefferson County, New York, and the upper Saint Lawrence Valley eastward to portions of northern New England extending from Lake Champlain to Maine. People crafting McFate and Quiggle wares lived along the upper branches of the Susquehanna and Allegheny drainages from the Wyoming Valley west to the Kiskiminetas River. Monongahela people southwest of the Kiskiminetas Valley, for their part, made shell-tempered pottery, often incorporating design elements or production techniques used by western or eastern neighbors.

As mentioned earlier, ways of life followed by most of these people generally resembled contemporary lifeways elsewhere in the Northeast. All of the region's inhabitants gathered locally available materials, collected wild foods, and fished, hunted, or tended crops for their livings. Deer and bear were major sources of meat and fur. Estimating that seven deerskins were needed to produce one set of women's clothing (five were needed for men), archaeologist Richard Gramly has suggested that occupants of larger communities in Trans-Appalachia had to take thousands of animals annually to clothe and feed themselves and their families, friends, and neighbors (Gramly 1977, but see Starna and Rel-

ethford 1985 for a cautionary note discussing problems associated with animal resource utilization estimates). Beaver, elk, birds, and other animals also were taken. Eels, pike, and other fish were netted, trapped, speared, or landed with barbless hooks.

Specific subsistence patterns varied regionally. Conrad Heidenreich (1971), for example, suggests that Hurons living close to swamps and large bodies of freshwater such as Lake Simcoe and Lake Huron generally concentrated on fishing and corn farming. Using these products as trade commodities, Hurons obtained meat and skins from more northerly hunting people. More southerly people living farther from northern boreal hunting country in less-well-watered lands, by contrast, often fished less and hunted more.

All people in the region hunted, trapped, or traded for beaver and other furbearing animals. Furs assumed new importance during the Historic Contact period as Indian people found that the earliest European visitors offered desirable new imports like glass beads, sheet copper, and woven textiles for food, furs, and favors.

Used by people in all but the southwesternmost reaches of the region, the longhouse became perhaps the most eloquent metaphor of Trans-Appalachian native life. Bark-covered frame structures generally ranging from sixty to one hundred feet long, and with doors at either end, were built in nearly all Iroquoian settlements. Some longhouses built in Mohawk territory during terminal Late Woodland times approached two hundred feet in length. Scholars "upstreaming" ethnographic and archival data believe that these longhouses, whatever their size or location, sheltered groups of matrilineally related families living in small apartments that flanked fireplaces located along the central corridor running through each structure. Changes in household population and composition were accommodated by adding or removing apartments at one end of the structure or the other. So compelling was this image of family, home, and community that even today members of the Iroquois confederacy call themselves "People of the Longhouse."

Post-mold patterns excavated by archaeologists indicate that nearly all ancestors of Iroquoian-speaking people were living in longhouses by 1100. After 1300 many of these structures were located within fortified towns atop defensible hills somewhat farther from rivers, lakes, and other potential avenues of assault. The largest of these towns could contain up to 150 longhouses sheltering as many as 3,000 people.

Life within the confines of such towns could present considerable challenges. Residents of even the smallest hamlets ultimately drove away nearby game animals and exhausted easily accessible supplies of timber, berries, other plants, and arable soil. Insects, rodents, and other pests gradually infested fields and homes. No matter how hard householders tried to keep things up, continuously occupied bark-covered homes lived in by large numbers of people for long periods of time ultimately became harder to keep clean, more difficult to repair, and increasingly flammable.

Relocation often presented a relatively direct answer to such problems. As mentioned earlier, archaeological evidence tends to corroborate archival and ethnographic data indicating that Iroquoian people generally moved townsites to new locales every ten to twenty years. But not all community members moved together or at the same time. In keeping with the enduring Iroquoian ethos of intracommunity cooperation and tolerance, people were free to move when they wanted to wherever they were welcome. Members of relocating communities could decide against joining old neighbors at new locales, and years could pass before rebuilding episodes were completed.

Individual and communal relocations probably played a major role in the formation of the Iroquois confederacy. Most modern Iroquois traditionalists regard their league as ancient. Scholars contrasting oral narratives recounting this tradition with archaeological, ethnographic, and archival data generally believe that Iroquois people formed their confederacy sometime during the fifteenth and sixteenth centuries.

Archaeological remains of terminal Late Woodland settlement patterns and practices present some of the most compelling physical evidence of confederacy formation in Iroquoia. Archaeologists have found numbers of unprecedentedly large, compact communities containing many longhouses on bluffs or hilltops along the escarpment running from the Mohawk Valley west to Lake Huron. Evidence of increasingly intensifying food production, initial appearances of town cemeteries, and discoveries of objects suggesting technological and aesthetic developments indicate population growth and rising sociopolitical complexity in these towns. Other evidence found in these communities suggests increasing trade and intermarriage among people living within the Iroquois heartland during this time.

Many towns are fortified, and most are located in defensible locales. Severed human heads and charred fragments of cut human bone have been found in pits and in large stone-filled fireplaces reminiscent of torture platforms described in written records at the late–fourteenth-century Genesee Valley Alhart site, the somewhat later Bloody Hill site in the heart of Onondaga Country, and other locales. These findings tend to corroborate orally transmitted texts attesting to the rising tide of violence that is said to have impelled Iroquois leaders to found their Great League of Peace before the coming of Europeans.

Ceramic analyses provide further clues to League origins. Contrasting similarities and differences in ceramics found in sites associated with the Iroquois and their neighbors, archaeologist William E. Engelbrecht (1971, 1974) has tried to correlate increasing rates of ceramic similarity with developments of closer community ties. Engelbrecht has found evidence suggesting that potters producing similar wares in the Onondaga and Oneida Countries may have begun to make pots resembling those made in Mohawk Country sometime during the fourteenth century. People living in the Genesee Valley, by contrast, may have only started making pots similar to those produced by more easterly neighbors during the sixteenth century. Affirmation of these tentative findings may corroborate oral accounts stating that Seneca and Cayuga people were the last of the original five nations to enter the Iroquois confederacy.

The first documented contacts between Iroquoian people and Europeans occurred when Saint Lawrence Iroquoians met Norman fishermen at the Strait of Belle Isle in 1520. More direct contact began on July 16, 1534, when a party of Saint Lawrence Iroquoians led by Donnacona, the chief of Stadacona (modern Quebec City), met Breton fishermen and French explorer Jacques Cartier while both were visiting the Gaspé Peninsula near the mouth of the Saint Lawrence River. This contact was marked by friendly conversation, some exchanges of gifts, a little thievery, and intimations that the river may have been the long-sought water route to China.

Quickly returning to France, Cartier brought two of Donnacona's sons back with him to see the country and learn French. Guided by these men when he returned the following year, Cartier sailed up the Saint Lawrence to Stadacona and on to the fortified town of Hochelaga at the present site of Montreal. Traveling upriver, he found the rapids of Lachine blocking the way west to Asia.

After living among his Saint Lawrence Iroquoian hosts during the winter of 1535–1536, Cartier again returned to France after kidnapping Donnacona and nine of his people. He subsequently returned to the area in 1542–1543 without his hostages, who had all died in France. Followed by Jean François de La Rocque de Roberval the next year, Cartier and other French colonists were soon forced to leave. Angered by the French predilection for seizing people against their will, and outraged by the deaths of their kidnapped kinsfolk while in French hands, Saint Lawrence Iroquoian people restricted direct trade with French sailors to brief shipboard encounters along the river below Tadoussac until the later 1500s.

Saint Lawrence Iroquoian resentment against the French may explain why few European goods seem to have made their way into the Trans-Appalachian region along the river during these years. Instead, most metal objects, glass beads, and other materials of European origin found in sixteenth-century Susquehannock, Iroquois, and late-stage Ontario Iroquois Tradition sites appear to have been brought into the region from more southerly points of contact in and around Chesapeake Bay. Other goods may have come from vessels visiting New England shores.

Some scholars believe that initial indirect contacts precipitated cataclysmic changes in Trans-Appalachian society during the 1500s. Dobyns (1983), for example, suggests that the first appearances of cemeteries in many Genesee and Susquehanna valley sites represent evidence of unprecedentedly high population losses caused by epidemic diseases introduced by sixteenth-century European visitors.

Other scholars challenge Dobyns's findings. Snow and Lanphear (1988), for example, see stability rather than change in early Historic Contact period Mohawk mortuary populations and settlement patterns. Describing what they believe to be the first clear osteological evidence of pre-Columbian treponematosis (indicative of syphilis) in the Northeast, Elting and Starna (1984) suggest that epidemic contagion was not unknown before European contact. Noting the telltale signs of nutritional deficiency, physical anthropologist Lorraine P. Saunders believes that famine rather than disease caused the unusually high number of multiple burials found at the sixteenth-century Seneca Adams and Culbertson sites (Wray et al. 1987). Other scholars, noting that famine often accompanies contagion, continue to debate the subject. Full resolution of this dispute, like so many others, awaits new discoveries and developments.

Although little of a definitive nature currently can be said about epidemiology in the Trans-Appalachian region during the 1500s, surviving site deposits do provide a great deal of information on regional settlement patterns and material culture. Aboriginally produced artifacts overwhelmingly predominate assemblages found in sites dating to this period everywhere in the region. European artifacts, by contrast, are almost wholly limited to small numbers of glass beads; copper and brass hoops, spirals, and tubular beads; iron knives and axes; and a smattering of brass kettles.

Archaeologists presently regard discovery of sixteenth-century Nueva Cadiz, Millefiori star chevron, and other glass beads in sites containing little or no other evidence of European contact as the most reliable indicator of occupation in the region during the initial phases of the Historic Contact period.

Patterns emerging from site deposits containing such diagnostic artifacts indicate that Indian life in the region began to change dramatically as the sixteenth century drew to a close. European materials appear with new types of ceramics and trade goods at a time when most people in the region begin to move into larger and more densely settled fortified townsites. Farther south, Monongahela culture people, abandoning the Kiskiminetas Valley, moved south to unfortified towns farther from Iroquoia in present-day Washington and Greene Counties in southwestern Pennsylvania.

Although we cannot yet discern the causes and effects of such changes, most archaeologists believe that they represent shifts in trade, warfare, and sociopolitical patterns. As mentioned in earlier sections, economic needs, for example, may have spurred Susquehannocks to move south toward Chesapeake Bay. Other deposits may reflect intensifying patterns of trade and warfare thought to have led Iroquois people to form their confederacy sometime before Europeans first encountered Mohawk warriors along the banks of Lake Champlain in 1609.

THE SEVENTEENTH CENTURY

Available records indicate that most Northern Iroquoian cultural patterns chronicled during the 1500s persisted with few changes into the next century. Roots, greens, fruits, and berries continued to be gathered in season. Strawberries, the first fruits to ripen, were ritually welcomed after long winters. Although investigators still disagree on its aboriginality, available evidence suggests that Northeastern Indian people may have made small amounts of maple sugar in clay pots before European copper, brass, and iron kettles made it easier to produce larger quantities for trade or domestic consumption (C. Mason 1986; Pendergast 1982).

Like most other native Northeasterners, people living in the Trans-Appalachian region also continued to cultivate corn, beans, squash, tobacco, and other plants. Archaeological evidence, European written records, and more recent native oral accounts affirm that the people of Trans-Appalachia generally employed more intensive cultivation

techniques than those used by native neighbors on the east. Cleared fields surrounded most major towns. Iron hoes supplemented but never entirely replaced digging sticks, wooden hoes, and deer and elk scapulae. Heidenreich (1971) estimates that the Huron nation, numbering 21,000 in 1630, annually harvested 189,000 bushels of corn from 7,000 acres of cleared ground in good years. Similarly high yields were reported by American troops burning Onondaga, Cayuga, and Seneca fields in 1779. Indian people throughout the region also adopted apples, peaches, pears, and other fruits brought by colonists as the seventeenth century wore on.

These developments generally paralleled those observed in documentation chronicling other native communities elsewhere in the Northeast. People throughout the region continued to make tools, weapons, and ornaments from stone, bone, shell, antler, copper, wood, sinew, and plant fiber through the first decades of the century. Chipped-stone implements and debitage associated with their manufacture are found in most contemporary regional sites. Triangular Madison and Levanna-style stone arrowpoints also are commonly found. These and other stone tools become increasingly rare in later sites as most people in the region gradually replaced locally available raw materials and domestically produced manufactures with European imports in the late seventeenth century.

Domestically produced pottery gradually fell from use as native people acquired brass, copper, and iron kettles and other cooking utensils. Native potters still producing pottery at the end of the century mostly crafted plain, undecorated, and comparatively poorly made wares. Ash and maple splint baskets largely patterned after new European prototypes also began to supplant woven and knotted containers by the end of the century. Although artisans using stone tools may have crafted small numbers of splint baskets prior to European contact, imported steel drawing knives and other metal tools now allowed native people to produce such baskets in great numbers.

New diseases devastated people living in the Trans-Appalachian region much as they ravaged native communities farther east. Europeans repeatedly recorded accounts of epidemic contagion among the region's native inhabitants during the 1600s. Fully half of all Huron people, for example, reportedly were killed by a single smallpox epidemic in 1639. Epidemics evidently struck native communities with ruthlessly implacable impartiality.

Repeatedly devastated by epidemic contagion and increasingly ravaged by warfare, native peoples tried to replenish dwindling numbers by marrying or capturing foreigners. Although records are fragmentary, more politically cohesive Iroquois groups seem to have been able to marry, capture, and assimilate larger numbers of foreigners than did other communities.

Numerous records show that Iroquois families gave names of deceased relatives to ritually adopted captives. Other documents attest to the fact that some adoptees fought against former friends and relatives. Until recently, most scholars analyzing these data have assumed that captives who were not sacrificed became enfranchised members of their new societies. Reexamining this documentation in light of new theories defin-

ing and explaining concepts and states of freedom and slavery, Starna and Watkins (1991) have shown that the available documentation can also be interpreted as evidence indicating that most adopted captives were enslaved.

Iroquois people occasionally adopted entire vanquished communities as they gradually forced neighboring nations to abandon ancestral territories. Turned into depopulated frontier zones, many of these former homelands subsequently became hunting and trapping preserves. Territories within a hundred-mile radius of the western and southern borders of the Iroquois heartland ultimately became buffer zones between Iroquois confederacy nations and other Indian people. Miamis, Ottawas, and other more westerly Indian people hunting and trapping on such lands during peacetime often were forced to travel around them in order to reach European traders whenever war broke out.

Their military success depended upon the Iroquois' ability to obtain better and more plentiful supplies of European firearms and munitions than those secured by Indian rivals. Dutch and English merchants began to trade muskets, powder, and lead to Iroquois customers during the 1630s. Iroquois raiders also captured guns from enemies like the French and Hurons. French policies limiting firearms to Christian converts frequently placed their Huron and other Indian allies at severe disadvantage in hostile encounters with Iroquois adversaries.

The nearly complete absence of gunflints, gun parts, and lead musket balls in early–seventeenth-century sites located beyond the borders of the Iroquois heartland attests to the growing military crisis confronted by groups having fewer arms. Only the Susquehannocks and their Erie allies appear to have achieved a degree of technological parity with their Iroquois adversaries. French chroniclers ascribed the Erie defeat in 1654, for example, to a shortage of ammunition rather than a deficiency of weapons.

More adequately supplied by nearby English, Swedish, and Dutch traders, Susquehannocks reportedly mounted small cannon on bastions along their town walls. But even with such weapons, the Susquehannocks were not able to overcome their adversaries. Forced to fight nearly continuous wars with the Senecas, their Iroquois confederates, and other Indian nations, the Susquehannocks were worn down and were ultimately dispersed by 1680.

The pace of change gradually increased as the effects of contact transformed life throughout the region. Cultural traditions in many areas of the region disappeared or were transformed beyond recognition; in the Iroquois heartland, those traditions underwent unprecedented growth and elaboration.

During these years, many Iroquois people came to enjoy a higher standard of living than any known by their ancestors. Trade goods flooded their towns. Although starvation still occasionally stalked their communities during wartime and drought years, or in early spring when winter stores ran out, produce from fields and orchards usually met local needs. If supplies failed, Dutch and English settlers provided provisions, though they might charge high prices.

The archaeological record mutely corroborates written accounts documenting this phase of history in the region. Entire societies located along the bor-ders of the Iroquois heartland that had developed in situ over the course of the preceding two hundred years suddenly disappeared in the mid–seventeenth-century. Communities within the heart of Iroquoia, by contrast, grew in size, content, and complexity during the same period.

John Smith's 1608 references to Massawomeck people represent the first known written references unequivocally identifying a Trans-Appalachian Indian nation by name within the present borders of the United States. Living beyond the piedmont foothills that separated them from European coastal beachheads, Massawomecks and other inland people were at first mentioned only briefly in colonial dispatches. But this situation gradually changed, and the Iroquois and their neighbors ultimately came to dominate colonial Indian affairs by the end of the century.

Iroquois people made their homes in towns located in central New York along the upper reaches of the Allegheny, Genesee, Oswego, Susquehanna, and Mohawk Rivers when Europeans first noted their existence in print during the early 1600s. The confederacy of five nations that had been formed by this time was, as mentioned earlier, likened by the Iroquois to a longhouse; Mohawks were regarded as keepers of the symbolic building's eastern door. Onondaga people, long regarded as having played a pivotal role in the confederacy's formation, tended the League's central fire in the hill country below Syracuse in central New York. Their "younger brothers," the Oneidas, lived south and east of Oneida Lake between Onondaga Country and the westernmost Mohawk towns. Farther west, Senecas and their "younger" brethren, the Cayugas, kept watch over the confederacy's western door.

Archaeological findings corroborate written records noting that each Iroquois nation comprised from one to four major towns, though smaller outlying settlements were often built near the larger communities. Mohawks and Cayugas each had from three to four major towns during the seventeenth century. Senecas generally had two large and two small towns. Onondagas and Oneidas usually had one large town and a smaller community.

Special circumstances, like the rebuilding episode necessitated by the French destruction of all Mohawk towns in 1666, sometimes compelled Iroquois people to simultaneously construct several new communities. Movements from old towns to new communities could be accomplished swiftly or drawn out over a span of years. Such variations in relocation rates may explain why seventeenth-century European observers like van den Bogaert and Wentworth Greenhalgh reported more than the above-mentioned numbers of towns during their visits.

The degree of protection provided by palisaded towns evidently outweighed their inconveniences in the years preceding European invasion, though these towns could become smoky death traps when attacked by assailants more intent on annihilating enemies than on capturing prisoners. When the threats of direct attack had receded after the burning of most Iroquois towns in front of the French columns invading their territories between between 1687 and 1696, the Iroquis tended to move from such places to more widely dispersed, unfortified settlements.

No matter how they lived, people belonging to Iroquois nations continually worked to take full advantage of their strategic position astride vital communication routes linking western trapping lands with growing markets of trade rivals in New France, New England, New York and the middle colonies. Rarely numbering more than twenty thousand at any one time, various nations of the Iroquois confederacy struggled to dominate this commerce. Mohawk people, who controlled the vital Hudson Valley and New England markets, for example, achieved particular influence and more than a small measure of affluence by the end of the century. Their power and prosperity rested in large part on the maintenance of advantageous trade ties, a willingness to wage war when necessary, and the organizational and diplomatic skills of their sachems.

Sachems and council members from each of the five Iroquois nations continually counted on mutual cooperation as they worked to play foreign and domestic rivals off against one another. Later in the century, the success of their efforts increasingly turned on vital alliances with powerful neighboring European colonies. Realizing this, Iroquois diplomats and traders established close ties with nearby Dutch, French, and English colonists. Farther west, Huron, Neutral, and Erie leaders aligned themselves with the French.

Sources like the spurious 1613 Tawagonshi Treaty are purported to document establishment of formal ties between Mohawk people and Dutch traders shortly after the erection of Fort Nassau in 1614 in the heart of Mahican Country beyond the eastern fringes of Iroquoia (Gehring, Starna, and Fenton 1987). Actual records show that early relations between both peoples were ambivalent. Mohawk warriors, for example, killed several Dutch soldiers accompanying a Mahican war party on its way to attack their towns shortly after the establishment of the Fort Orange post a mile or so north of the site of the then-abandoned Fort Nassau locale. Resolving their differences shortly thereafter, both peoples subsequently maintained peaceful relations throughout the remaining years of the Dutch regime.

Declining to support the Dutch when English troops conquered New Netherland in 1664, Mohawk leaders soon concluded an alliance with their new neighbors at the renamed town of Albany just north of the former Dutch post at Fort Orange. This alliance, formalized sometime between the 1670s and 1680s as the Covenant Chain (a metaphor commonly used to describe the alliance in councils), provided many benefits to Iroquois people.

Traders operating from the Covenant Chain's English fire at Albany, for example, usually offered better, cheaper, and more plentiful goods than did their French competitors. Firearms, ammunition, and repair facilities furnished by Albany traders, often in contravention of provincial laws prohibiting munitions trade with Indian people, gave Iroquois warriors important advantages over their adversaries.

This advantage became critical as Iroquois diplomats, warriors, hunters, and traders struggled to secure enough furs to trade for European goods and enough prisoners to atone for losses of friends and loved ones. Iroquois raiders searching for pelts, plunder, and vengeance attacked enemies wherever they were found. The most formidable of their rivals, the Hurons, forged increasingly close ties with the French during the 1630s when the Jesuits were establishing their missions. Relations were also strengthened as the Hurons and French sought to monopolize the northern fur trade.

Relations between the Iroquois and the French, by contrast, were marked by ambivalence and intermittent hostility. Initially unable to come to terms, the French waged war against the easternmost Iroquois nations between 1609 and 1615. An uneasy peace, repeatedly broken and renewed, was maintained throughout the remaining years of the century.

Unable or unwilling to drive the French away, the Iroquois focused attention on the Indian allies of the French. Possessing a decisive advantage over their less-well-armed rivals, Seneca warriors aided by their Iroquois confederates moved to destroy the Hurons in 1649. Striking deep into territories beyond the boundaries of their heartland, they soon defeated and dispersed nearby Neutral, Petun, and Erie people.

Some scholars believe that economic considerations impelled Iroquois warriors to destroy their enemies in these "Beaver Wars" fought between 1649 and 1657. Others think that Iroquois nations went to war for political or emotional reasons. Whatever the motivation, the outcome of these struggles is well known. Most survivors of Iroquois attacks abandoned their homelands. Some fled to the west. Others moved near French and Indian towns along the Saint Lawrence River, where their descendants remain today. More than a few were adopted into Iroquois families.

Settling in Iroquois towns, they saw their former homelands became Iroquois hunting and trapping territories.

Iroquois warriors fought on many fronts during these years. Mohawk warriors and their allies, for example, repeatedly tried to drive Western Abenaki, Mahican, and other North Atlantic Algonquian trade rivals eastward, away from the major European entrepôt established in modern-day Albany, New York. An important source of trade goods in its own right, the town also stood astride the strategic Hudson River–Lake Champlain–Richelieu River trade route. This route, dubbed the Mahican Channel by Francis Jennings (1988b), connected New York with Montreal. It also provided a conduit to English merchants willing to trade firearms, liquor, and wampum for pelts.

Iroquois warriors also fought Susquehannock rivals for control of the more southerly trade routes to the interior. Initially allied with the Hurons and other Ontario Indian people, Susquehannocks dominated access to English markets in and around Chesapeake Bay and Swedish posts along the lower Delaware River during the 1630s and 1640s. As mentioned earlier, Susquehannocks, unlike other Iroquois competitors, were well armed with muskets supplied by Swedish traders interested in pelts and Maryland authorities willing to exchange guns for land.

Colonial records indicate that the Senecas and Cayugas bore the brunt of the struggle with the Susquehannocks. Raiding each others' towns at intervals for more than forty years, many people on both sides were killed or taken prisoner. In 1652, for example, Iroquois warriors raiding Susquehannock terri-

tory reportedly carried from five hundred to six hundred captives back to their towns for adoption, execution, or exchange. Ten years later, Cayugas anxious to avoid further Susquehannock assaults fled to the northern shores of Lake Ontario. The war ended only when the dispersed and much-reduced Susquehannocks finally accepted Iroquois suzerainty after 1675.

Iroquois diplomats soon claimed Susquehannock lands and asserted sovereignty over former allies of the Susquehannocks, the Delawares. Turning westward, the Iroquois then tried to outflank New France by seizing control over vital western trade routes. Struggling to gain direct access to supply sources, Iroquois warriors launched forays into the Illinois and Ohio Valleys during the 1680s. Iroquois men traveled south along the Warriors Path to press their seemingly interminable war against the Cherokees, Catawbas, and other southern Indian nations. Although direct evidence is lacking, warriors traveling this path probably began to force many Mannahoac, Monacan, and other Siouian-speaking Virginian Piedmont people to move their homes farther from Iroquois lines of march.

Iroquois warriors may have enjoyed a formidable reputation, but they were not always successful in battle. Repeated attacks by Mohawk warriors, for example, failed to permanently dislodge Mahicans and their Western Abenaki allies. Farther west, Potawatomi and Illinois warriors turned back Seneca and Cayuga war parties, trappers, and traders. In Ontario, Mississaugas decisively defeated Seneca, Cayuga, and Onondaga colonists trying to establish settlements of their own on lands appropriated from vanquished Huron, Neutral, and Petun people during the 1660s.

Periodic outbreaks of fighting with the French also devastated Iroquois communities. The Mohawks, for example, were forced to burn every one of their towns as a French column advanced south from the Saint Lawrence Valley through the Mohawk Valley in 1666.

Many people living in these ravaged communities moved to new homes during the middle years of the century. Jesuits managed to establish briefly occupied missions within the Iroquois heartland at places like Sainte Marie Gannentaha (built on the shores of Onondaga Lake during the 1650s), but hostilities soon forced them to abandon such missions. Substantial numbers of Iroquois people followed the missionaries back to Canada. Some moved to new towns established along the Saint Lawrence River. Others joined Hurons and other Catholic Indian proselytes already living near French towns.

Redoubling their efforts to establish missions in Iroquoia soon after French officials signed a peace treaty with the Iroquois in 1667, Jesuit priests erected missions in every Iroquois nation. Needing peace on their northern borders as they turned their energies toward defeating the Susquehannocks, conservative Iroquois leaders tolerated the Jesuit missions. But when they claimed victory over their rivals in 1675, these same leaders came to regard the French as undesirable competitors standing in the way of their hard-won access to markets farther west in the Ohio Valley and the upper Great Lakes. They shared the English concern over growing French influence among their people. In 1683, at the very same time that New York

governor Thomas Dongan demanded the ejection of the Jesuits, many Iroquois leaders called for removal of all French missionaries and Indian proselytes from their towns. Shortly afterwards, war began between the French and the westernmost Iroquois nations. The Senecas were forced to burn their towns as they retreated in front of a French column marching through their settlements in 1687. More widespread fighting broke out in 1689 when France went to war with England in a struggle since known as King William's War.

Iroquois warriors, fighting both separately and alongside English troops, attacked Indian allies of the French and briefly besieged Montreal. Large numbers of Mahican and Western Abenaki people were forced to take refuge among relatives and friends in New France. Although the war officially ended in 1697, most refugees did not return to their homes until the Iroquois had signed a separate peace with the French in 1701.

The war had caused equally great suffering among the Iroquois. Many men were killed in the fighting, and the French army forced the Mohawks to burn their rebuilt towns in 1693. Three years later, another invading column compelled Onondaga and Oneida people to do the same.

Ironically, few Iroquois people were killed during these incendiary raids. Learning from hard experience, Iroquois townsfolk chose to evacuate and burn their towns rather than defend them. The French and their Indian allies also learned from experience. Unable to kill or capture large numbers of Iroquois people and not powerful enough to establish permanent garrisons in their country, French troops plundered Iroquois supplies and laid waste to their fields and orchards.

English authorities fed Iroquois refugees and replaced lost supplies. New communities were built. These rebuilding episodes, often replacing relatively new townsites, present modern archaeologists working in the region with a situation markedly different from that faced by colleagues working farther east. Scholars studying seventeenth-century native life along the North Atlantic coast, for example, have found only a few of the many towns documented by colonial observers. Archaeologists working in Trans-Appalachia, by contrast, have found many times the number of sites chronicled by Europeans.

Unlike the scattered settlements built by Indian people living farther east, most towns built by seventeenth-century Trans-Appalachian Indians were densely nucleated settlements, which are now easily discovered by excavators. Nearly all were built on hilltops or other locales often ill-suited for plow agriculture. Largely undamaged by subsequent farming activities and untouched until recently by most development, many of these sites have been discovered by archaeologists. Collectively, they represent one of most extensive assemblages of temporally, spatially, and culturally related archaeological deposits in native North America.

Towns destroyed during French invasions represent only a fraction of known townsites. Earlier-mentioned town relocation practices account for the proliferation of sites in most areas. Increased incidences of epidemic contagion probably accelerated relocation rates. A series of seven documented epidemic episodes devastated Iroquois towns from 1634 to 1691. The last of these, a particularly virulent smallpox epidemic, was accidently spread by warriors returning from an abortive English expedition against Canada. A census of warriors taken in 1697 suggests that as many as half of all Indian people living in the Iroquois heartland when King William's War started had died or moved away by the time the war ended.

As before, Indian people throughout the region tried to replace losses by adopting captives. Iroquois diplomats also stepped up efforts to relocate displaced Indian people among their own settlements. And, like many Hurons, Petuns, and others before them, increasing numbers of Iroquois people left their towns for new homes. Many moved farther south to towns like Tioga and Ochquaga among displaced Mahicans, Munsees, and Delawares along upper branches of the Susquehanna River during the waning years of the seventeenth century. Others turned north to Canada.

THE EIGHTEENTH CENTURY

Struggling to maintain internal cohesion as they worked to preserve their Covenant Chain alliance with the English, diplomats of the Iroquois confederacy sought to secure a firm peace with the French as the new century dawned. Surviving repeated episodes of epidemic contagion, interminable wars, and the contentions of the imperial powers to gain control over their lands and lives, the Iroquois finally concluded a lasting treaty of neutrality with French authorities in Montreal in 1701.

That treaty ushered in what more than one scholar has called the "golden age of Iroquois diplomacy." Enduring for more than fifty years, the pax Iroquoia maintained during this golden age allowed most Iroquois communities to experience a period of unprecedented prosperity. Iroquois diplomats like Daniel Garacontie had worked with Thomas Dongan, Edmund Andros, and other English administrators to forge the Covenant Chain into an effective alliance.

Now their success at the bargaining table allowed them to emerge as the dominant Indian military and economic power in the region. Restricting trade and most other contacts to posts situated along their frontiers, fewer than ten thousand Iroquois people asserted the right to control regional trade and influence political affairs of perhaps twice as many Delawares, Shawnees, Conoys, Tuteloes, and other Indian people resettled at their insistence on former Susquehannock lands.

Together, these people faced more than a quarter of a million colonists along a border stretching from Lake Champlain south to central Pennsylvania. Settlers had acquired most Indian lands to the east of that line by 1700. Some had pressed as far west as Schenectady. Farther south, Maryland and Pennsylvanian settlers moving onto former Susquehannock lands threatened the southern flanks of Iroquoia. Yet, despite these penetrations, no colonist could claim *clear* title to a single acre of land within the Iroquois heartland at the turn of the century.

English authorities could and did claim dominion over Iroquois lands on the strength of a deed negotiated by New York governor Thomas Dongan in 1684. But Iroquois subjection, and the vast Iroquois "empire" allegedly placed under English protection under the terms of the deed, were largely political affectations politely countenanced by both peoples. Few Iroquois were willing to needlessly alienate English allies by denying what did not exist. The reality was something else. Despite claims to the contrary, no English official, or any other European for that matter, was able to exercise direct authority over any Iroquois community before midcentury.

No longer living under nearly constant threat of attack, Iroquois people increasingly turned their attention to more peaceful pursuits. Iroquois hunters, trappers, and traders traveled widely through the Northeast. Closer to home, Iroquois diplomats worked to secure advantages for their people by exploiting divisions between powerful and fractious neighbors. Playing contending colonial factions off against one another, they obtained protection and gifts from rivals hoping to secure Iroquois support. In so doing, they were able to keep settlers out and let trade goods in. At peace, effectively organized, generally prosperous, and politically astute, Iroquois people seized and held the balance of power in the region throughout the first half of the 1700s.

Although the Iroquois joined other coalitions from time to time, they only formally admitted one other nation to their confederacy during the Historic Contact period. Tuscaroras, forced from their North Carolina homes after losing their war against British settlers and their Indian allies in the Tuscarora War of 1711–1713, had become the sixth Iroquois nation by 1722.

Substantial bodies of European documentation chronicle Iroquois diplomatic successes during this era. These same documents also reveal the Iroquois as a people who had changed greatly since the days of initial contact with Europeans. Epidemics and wars had probably reduced their population by more than 50 percent during the seventeenth century. Forced to marry or adopt people from other communities, more than a few Iroquois people surviving this calamitous century traced descent to foreign ancestors.

Intensive contact had also brought other changes. Increasing numbers of Christian converts moved to mission settlements in and around the Iroquois heartland. Though these missions had been generally short-lived and quickly abandoned during the preceding century, French and British authorities consolidating control over their colonies were able to establish more permanent missions, trading posts, and forts in or near many Iroquois towns as the eighteenth century progressed.

Settlement patterns in the region also changed dramatically during these years. As mentioned earlier, Iroquois people had moved from densely populated walled towns to more dispersed small farmsteads or hamlets. House size also diminished as families increasingly moved away from lineage longhouses into smaller bark houses or log cabins.

Change also characterized many aspects of Iroquois economic life. Although all people living in Trans-Appalachian communities continued to cultivate crops. hunt, fish, and collect wild foods and materials, most did so with imported tools and implements. Indian metalworkers fashioned iron, copper, and other new, imported materials into triangular projectile points and knives; they also put old materials to new uses.

As James W. Bradley (1987a) points out, flint knappers turned from producing projectile points and edged tools to making gunflints and strike-a-lights. Men making clay and stone tobacco-smoking pipes, for their part, increasingly crafted new and more elaborate forms from local clays, cast pewter, and imported stone like catlinite. Splint baskets and other new manufactures became important household items and trade commodities in most Indian homes.

Growing numbers of families living near newcomers in more easterly reaches of the region began to raise chickens, horses, cattle, pigs, and other domesticated animals brought over by Europeans during these years. Apple, peach, cherry, and pear trees also became popular. Harvested fruits and vegetables were dried and stored in pots, baskets, house eaves, and pits. Wooden cribs and barns similar to the surviving example preserved at the Brant Homestead in the Mohawk Upper Castle National Historic Landmark began to appear in Indian communities located near European settlements by the third quarter of the century.

Imported tools, techniques, and crops increasingly came to dominate domestic life. Despite this fact, very few Indian people in the region grew dependent on Europeans for basic foodstuffs. Nearly every Indian household in the region continued to rely on corn, bean, and squash cultivation; berry, greens, and nut gathering; hunting; fishing; and trapping for their food, furs, and clothing.

No matter how they made their living, almost all eighteenth-century TransAppalachian people became enmeshed in an international market economy centering around furs, diplomat gifts, and military service. Although many native people continued to produce stone and clay pipes; shell beads; stone, copper, and shell ornaments; wooden utensils; and bone and antler combs for export or domestic consumption, most of the region's inhabitants gradually fell under the influence of external market forces. Resisting attempts to increase involvement in local commodity markets, most Indian people struggled to make economic choices on their own terms during these years.

Many of these ideological, economic, and political developments are well reported in British and French archives. But archaeologists looking for physical evidence of these changes have encountered great difficulty in documenting patterns of native settlement, production, and consumption. As mentioned earlier, most of the region's people had stopped making temporally and culturally diagnostic artifacts from stone or clay by 1700. Deposits found in Indian sites dating after 1700, moreover, nearly always closely resemble those left by settlers. Movements from densely packed longhouse towns to widely scattered homesteads consisting of smaller structures resembling European dwellings also make it difficult to distinguish Indian sites from non-Indian settlements.

Occurrences of certain artifacts, such as wampum, catlinite beads, triangular metal projectile points, and Indian-made gunflints often reveal locations of eighteenth-century Indian settlements. Discoveries of German silver ornaments, pipe tomahawks, medals, and other objects specially produced for the purposes of Indian trade and diplomacy also represent identifiable indicators of native occupation. And, of course, dis-

coveries of the graves of Indian people provide evidence of native presence at particular sites.

Although some objects listed above, like gunlocks and European coins and medals, can be used to date site deposits, scholars have not yet determined precise date ranges for most eighteenth century European and Indian artifacts. More critically, while physical anthropologists can often identify indications of sex, race, and age of death in skeletal remains, no method capable of definitively determining social identity or ethnic affiliation has yet been devised.

Aware of these and other problems, archaeologists studying deposits thought to date to the later Historic Contact period generally rely on written documents to verify findings. Happily, European records directly document Indian occupation at many of the locales discussed in the following pages. Many other undocumented locales, for their part, contain Indian burials or Indian-modified tools, implements, ornaments, and weapons.

These artifacts document the Iroquois struggle to maintain the flow of trade goods into their communities. Prospering, but never fully completely controlling regional trade, more easterly Iroquois trappers and traders nevertheless managed to dominate commerce at major entrepôts like Albany and the post at Oswego constructed between 1722 and 1725 on the shores of Lake Ontario directly above Onondaga and Oneida territory. Farther west, Seneca people dominated access to French posts at Niagara established along the vital portage route between 1720 and 1726.

Diplomatic gifts and other payments made by British and French officials eager to maintain Iroquois friendship became increasingly important. Missionaries like Gideon Hawley who moved to upper Susquehanna Valley towns also brought hoes, knives, cattle, fruit trees, and other new wealth to converts. Jesuits enlarging already substantial settlements along the Saint Lawrence further enriched the lives of their many proselytes.

Anglican missionaries also provided aid and built chapels. Queen Anne sent two sets of silver communion services to the Iroquois during the first decades of the 1700s. The set originally sent to Mohawks living at the Lower Castle was divided between the Grand River and Tyendinaga Mohawk communities in Ontario after the end of the American War for Independence. A second set, brought to New York as a gift for the Onondagas and never delivered, remains in an Albany church.

New Light ministers inspired by the Great Awakening, such as the aforementioned Gideon Hawley, Henry Barclay, and Samuel Kirkland, often provided more tangible benefits to Indian people in various communities along the eastern periphery of the region. They frequently furnished resources needed to build log cabins and mills, fence fields, erect barns, and plant orchards. Increasing numbers of young men like Joseph Brant were educated in their Anglican schools. Translating religious tracts and other literature into the Mohawk language, missionaries printed and distributed this literature throughout eastern Iroquois towns.

More direct European penetration of the Iroquois heartland began when Mohawk leaders fearing possible French attacks permitted New York authorities to construct Fort Hunter at the mouth of Schoharie Creek by the Lower Mohawk Castle of Tiononderoge during the height of Queen Anne's War in 1710. Located near European settlements bordering the easternmost reaches of their country, this post quickly became a center for colonial expansion as provincial authorities and local entrepreneurs began purchasing land near the fort. Palatine German refugees were settled farther up the Schoharie River to the south of Fort Hunter by New York authorities shortly after the post's completion in 1712. Although their numbers remained small until 1723, the arrival of the Germans alarmed many Mohawk people.

Ten years later, anxiety gave way to anger as settlers began to move onto a large tract at Saratoga, north of Albany, known as the Kayaderosseras patent. Land speculators claimed this vast tract on the strength of a deed signed in 1704 by four Mohawk chiefs. Never paid the sixty pounds promised for the land, the Mohawks were alarmed to learn thirty years later that the New York government had granted the purchasers a patent to more than a half a million acres of their land. Refusing to surrender the territory, Mohawk leaders contested the deed for thirty more years. Supported by their neighbor and kinsman William Johnson, who became the Crown's Superintendent of Indian Affairs for the Northern Department in 1755, they finally agreed to accept five thousand dollars for already colonized eastern portions of the grant in 1768 (Nammack 1969).

Farther west, British and French interests vying for control of the Great Lakes and Ohio Valley pressed against the western door of the confederacy.

French authorities established a string of posts at Oswegatchie, Niagara, Detroit, Vincennes, Fort Ouiatenon, and Kaskaskia to strengthen their connection between the lower Great Lakes and the Mississippi. British traders began to move to Ohio Indian towns shortly thereafter.

French authorities countered the British move by building forts closer to the western frontier of Iroquoia at the forks of the Ohio and other locales in 1753. Combat between the contending colonial powers broke out one year later. Eventually spreading to the European continent and becoming known as the Seven Years' War, the conflict devastated the region. Following a policy that had held them in good stead for more than half a century, the Six Nations officially remained aloof from the struggle. Nevertheless, partisans favoring one side or the other created deep divisions within Iroquois councils. Closely aligned with William Johnson, most Mohawk Valley Indians openly sided with the British. Many Oneidas fought alongside them. Other Mohawks living in New France joined Seneca and Cayuga people in supporting the French.

As in earlier conflicts, Iroquois leaders formally maintained neutrality while individual warriors and nations pursued their own interests. Although the pretence of League solidarity helped prevent invasion of their territory during the war, differences widened by the conflict seriously divided Iroquois communities. These divisions grew as settlers and troops poured across the southern and eastern frontiers of the Iroquois heartland after the French defeat on this continent in 1760.

Neutrality became little more than an empty word as many western Iroquois people reacted violently to the British refusal to honor their promise to abandon former French forts in 1763. Substantial numbers of Seneca warriors, for example, openly fought against the British between 1763 and 1765 in what today is known as Pontiac's War. Iroquois unity collapsed for a time when communities split by conflicting loyalties brought on by the American War for Independence forced their leaders to ritually suspend confederacy activities in 1777.

The decision of these communities to follow different courses of action during the war diminished whatever chances a united front might have had to achieve either neutrality or military success. In 1778, local settlers drove away those Mohawks who had not already left their homes for Montreal or Fort Niagara. American armies guided by Oneida supporters burned Susquehanna settlements and destroyed Onondaga, Cayuga, and Seneca towns between 1778 and 1779. Iroquois people outraged by these attacks subsequently retaliated by burning American and Oneida settlements throughout the New York and Pennsylvania frontier.

Nearly every Iroquois community lay in ruins by the time the fighting stopped in 1783. Most Mohawk people moved to Canada after the fighting ended. Those Iroquois remaining on their lands were soon besieged by speculators anxious to acquire title to Indian properties. Finding themselves restricted to increasingly smaller plots of reservation land surrounding their towns, many Indians were gradually forced to leave their lands altogether. Although most of these people moved west to Oklahoma and Wisconsin or north to Canada, large numbers remained on their small reservations in New York and Pennsylvania. Today the descendants of Iroquois people still live in reservation communities in New York, Quebec, Ontario, Oklahoma, and Wisconsin, as well as in towns and cities throughout Canada and the United States.

Refugees who had moved to Trans-Appalachia during the eighteenth century were also forced from their homes during this period. Delawares, Shawnees, Nanticokes, Saponis, and other displaced Algonquian- and Siouian-speaking people living along the southern borders of the Iroquois heartland from the Susquehanna to the Allegheny began moving to the Ohio Valley during the 1750s and 1760s. Today people tracing descent from these groups live in small communities scattered across eastern North America.

SOURCES

A large body of material documents Indian life in the Trans-Appalachian region. Although much of it forms the basis of articles published in the *Northeast* volume of the Smithsonian Institution's *Handbook of North American Indians* (Trigger 1978b), few scholars have attempted to write overviews of the region's culture. William N. Fenton's already-cited survey article, "Northern Iroquoian Culture Patterns," which leads off the Saint Lawrence Lowlands section of the *Handbook,* provides one of the best and most accessible general guides to the subject (Fenton 1978). *Extending the Rafters,* a festschrift celebrating Fenton's contributions to Iroquois studies, contains a number of excellent general articles on Iroquoian ethnography, linguistics, and archaeology (Foster, Cam-

pisi, and Mithun 1984). Earlier surveys edited by Fenton (1951a) and Fenton and John Gulick (1961) also provide a range of information.

Studies of Indian life in the western portions of this region include those of W. C. Johnson (1993), Pendergast (1991a), and Wall (1984). Volumes written by Francis Jennings (1984, 1988b) and Paul A. W. Wallace (1981) are among the many studies of immigrant Indian people moving to the upper Susquehanna Valley during the 1700s.

Large amounts of information on Indian life in the region were included in dispatches sent by Jesuit fathers working in New France and Acadia to their superior in France during the colonial era. Much of this documentation is printed in *The Jesuit Relations* (Thwaites 1896–1901). Early information is provided in Father Joseph-François Lafitau's 1724 study of Iroquois culture (Lafitau 1974–1977). Other useful insights appear in journals written by such visitors as John Bartram (1751) and Augustus Spangenburg (1879).

Iroquois culture has attracted particular scholarly attention since Lewis Henry Morgan published the first modern ethnography, *League of the Ho-de'-no-sau-nee,* in 1851. Since then, hundreds of books and thousands of articles have examined nearly every aspect of Iroquois life. As a result of this attention, the Iroquois have become one of the most extensively studied native communities in North America.

Thousands of manuscript pages stored in archival repositories throughout North America and Europe document Iroquois treaty negotiations with Europeans. The sheer weight of this documentation attests to the significance

Iroquois held in colonial councils. Particularly significant groups of transcribed manuscript materials appear in published compilations edited by Leder (1956), O'Callaghan (1849–1851), O'Callaghan and Fernow (1853–1887), and Wraxall (1915). Retranslations of much of the Dutch material printed in these and other compilations may be found in New Netherland project research publications (Gehring 1977, 1980, 1981).

Much of this and other published and unpublished documentary material dating from 1613 to 1913 has been gathered together and microfilmed by *Documentary History of the Iroquois* project scholars. A reference guide, containing summary articles on Iroquois diplomacy and general lists of treaty meetings, prominent personalities, and locations of significant events and communities, introduces these materials (Jennings et al. 1985).

Scholars have been mining these documents since Cadwallader Colden used written records of Iroquois-English relations to write a history of the confederacy justifying English sovereignty over an Iroquois "empire" stretching from New York to the Mississippi Valley (Colden 1747). More recently, other studies, such as George T. Hunt's (1940) seminal inquiry into the possible economic causes of Iroquois warfare, George S. Snyderman's (1948) sociological slant on the subject, and Daniel K. Richter and James H. Merrell's recent studies on Iroquois conflict and diplomacy with other nations and each other (Richter 1983, 1985; Richter and Merrell 1987), have helped shape discourse on the subject.

Although criticized with much justification by Francis Jennings in recent years, the sweep, scope, and eloquence of Francis Parkman's accounts of the struggle for sovereignty and survival in the region still make them an indispensable if guilty pleasure to many scholars (Parkman 1865–1892). Useful discussions of seventeenth-century political affairs may be found in Fenton (1988), Richter (1983, 1988), Trelease (1960), and Trigger (1978a, 1980). Eighteenth-century developments are treated in Aquila (1983), Fenton (1988), Jennings (1984, 1988b), Downes (1940), Graymont (1972), and Trigger (1978a).

Numerous studies document other aspects of Iroquois life. Iroquois foodways, for example, are summarized in Parker (1910) and Waugh (1916). Settlement and town relocation are addressed in Fenton (1978); W. Ritchie and Funk (1973); Starna, Hamell, and Butts (1984); and Sykes (1980). Aspects of Iroquois ceremonial and religious life are examined in Beauchamp (1907), Fenton (1953, 1987), Parker (1968), E. Tooker (1970), and A. F. C. Wallace (1970).

Differing views of the status of Iroquois women are presented in J. K. Brown (1970) and E. Tooker (1984b). Contrasting Mohawk Revolutionary War loss claims and other documentation with archaeological evidence, David B. Guldenzopf (1986) has traced evidence for emerging economic, political, and social inequalities in late eighteenth-century Mohawk communities. Other studies seek to understand the social, economic, and spiritual motivations behind Iroquois torture and slavery (Knowles 1940; Starna and Watkins 1991).

The Trans-Appalachian region has been the site of intensive archaeological interest for many years. During that time, professional and avocational archaeologists have identified thousands of sites throughout the region. More than 450 of these locales contain deposits associated with Indian occupations dating from the Historic Contact period.

A vast literature documents the archaeology of the region. Papers published in the seventy-fifth anniversary issue of the New York Archaeological Association journal provide up-to-date summaries of the archaeological state of knowledge for Erie (Engelbrecht 1991), Seneca (Saunders and Sempowski 1991), Cayuga (Niemczycki 1991), Mohawk (Snow 1991a), Oneida (P. Pratt 1991), and Saint Lawrence Iroquoian people (Pendergast 1991b, M. Pratt 1991). Also see comprehensive overviews written by Bamann et al. (1992), Snow (1984), and Tuck (1978). Scholars like Arthur C. Parker (1922), Richard S. MacNeish (1952), William A. Ritchie (1969a; W. Ritchie and MacNeish 1949), and Robert E. Funk (W. Ritchie and Funk 1973) have made particularly significant contributions to New York Iroquois archaeology.

Other studies survey the archaeology of the Mohawks (Andrefsky 1980; Guldenzopf 1986; D. Lenig 1965; Rumrill 1985; Snow 1989b), the Oneidas (P. Pratt 1976), the Onondagas (Bradley 1987a; Tuck 1971), and people living in Seneca and Cayuga countries (Niemczycki 1984; Skinner 1921; Wray 1985).

The work of Marian E. White (1961, 1967, 1968, 1971, 1976, 1977, 1978a, 1978b) and James V. Wright (1966) has guided archaeological research in the Niagara-Erie frontier and nearby Ontario since the 1960s. Saint Lawrence Iroquoian archaeology is summarized by James F. Pendergast (1975, 1985, 1991b). Robert E. Funk and Bruce E. Rippeteau (1977) have surveyed late upper Susquehanna Valley prehistory. William C. Johnson (1992) has drawn together most of what is known about Monongahela culture archaeology in southwestern Pennsylvania.

These and most other studies generally focus attention upon more readily discernible, nucleated sixteenth- and seventeenth-century sites. Less is known about the archaeology of eighteenth-century life in the region. Investigators need to direct increased attention toward identifying and analyzing eighteenth-century locales throughout the region, which consist largely of decentralized towns and individual homesteads containing deposits similar to those found in contemporary colonial settlements.

MOHAWK COUNTRY

The Mohawk heartland stretches across the Mohawk Valley from the Schoharie Valley west to the valley of East Canada Creek. Mohawk people at various times have also claimed lands stretching from the Saint Lawrence lowlands across the Adirondack Mountains south to the upper branches of the Susquehanna River. Discoveries of pots resembling Garoga and other Mohawk wares in sites as far east as Maine and as far south as Munsee Country corroborate written and oral evidence attesting to the extent of Mohawk power and influence in the region during the Historic Contact period.

THE SIXTEENTH CENTURY

As elsewhere in the region, archaeological deposits represent the only body of physical evidence directly associated with life in Mohawk Country during the 1500s. Few orally transmitted texts clearly dating to this century have been documented. Scholars, for their part, have not yet found any clearly identifiable records written by Europeans journeying to the area before 1634.

Professional archaeologists like William M. Beauchamp (1900), Arthur C. Parker (1922), Richard S. MacNeish (1952), William A. Ritchie (1958, 1969a), Robert E. Funk (1976), and Dean R. Snow (1991a, 1993) have long studied the archaeology of this and subsequent centuries of occupation in the Mohawk Valley. As elsewhere, much work in the area has been done by avocationists. Some of these devoted amateurs, like Donald A. Rumrill (1985, 1992b) and Donald Lenig (1965), have written reports equal to any produced by professional investigators; others have produced less rigorous studies.

Large numbers of archaeological sites containing deposits dating from the Historic Contact period have been found. Ranging in size and complexity from large towns to smaller occupations, most (though not all) contain archaeological remains associated with single components. Rumrill (1985) developed the first published systematic sequence organizing Historic Contact period Mohawk Valley site data within a comprehensive chronological framework. Building from Rumrill's framework, Dean R. Snow, director of the State University of New York at Albany's multiyear Mohawk Valley Archaeological Survey, has since compiled the most complete site inventory for any area in the region (MDSI; Snow 1993). While differing in several particulars, Snow and Rumrill agree that not enough is presently known about the archaeology of Mohawk Valley Indian life to incontrovertibly trace specific relationships within or between Mohawk Valley native communities during the Historic Contact period.

Working with Rumrill during the 1980s, Mohawk Valley Archaeological Survey investigators, Dean R. Snow and William A. Starna inventoried a substantial number of sites dating from the sixteenth century. Located above the northern banks of the Mohawk River, diagnostic assemblages found at these sites contain chipped-stone, triangular projectile points and distinctive collared incised wares. Ceramic assemblages found at Otstungo, Wormuth, Cairns, and other early sixteenth-century sites containing no objects of European origin are dominated by late–Chance-phase wares. Small numbers of brass or copper beads and pieces of smelted metal have been found in later sixteenth-century Garoga-phase townsites like Cayadutta, Chapin/Wemple, Barker, England's Woods No. 1, Rice's Woods, Klock, Garoga, Smith-Pagerie, and Kilts and smaller sites like Bellinger, Crum Creek, Ganada No. 2, and Dewandalaer.

Sixteenth-century Mohawk Valley townsites generally range from two to four acres in size. Often fortified, most are located atop hills or ridges some distance from riverbanks. Studies of the locations and contents of these sites corroborate more recent Mohawk Indian oral narratives affirming that their ancestors were living in the valley bearing their name when Europeans first journeyed to North Atlantic shores.

Analyses correlating pottery attributes, site location, and other variables suggest that the tripartite Mohawk community organization documented by later European observers may have emerged during the 1500s. In the east, residents of Cayadutta town probably moved to the largely contemporary Chapin/Wemple and Barker sites sometime around 1580. The contemporary England's Woods No. 1 and Rice's Woods sites, for their part, represent the earliest identifiable communities associated with the central Mohawk Valley site sequence. Farther west, deposits dating from the sixteenth century have been found at the nearby western-sequence Klock, Smith-Pagerie, Kilts, Ganada No. 2, and Garoga sites.

Garoga, a townsite located atop a narrow bluff above Caroga Creek, currently is the most extensively studied sixteenth-century locale in the Mohawk Valley (W. Ritchie and Funk 1973). Long known to local collectors, it was first systematically excavated by Mark Raymond Harrington in 1905. Excavations directed by Robert E. Funk during the early 1960s unearthed extensive deposits of Garoga-phase wares, stone tools, small numbers of smelted-metal objects, and post-mold patterns of nine longhouses and two parallel wooden stockade walls.

Stretching along the bluff's narrowest point for seventy-five feet, these walls commanded the only level approach to a town sheltering people living in at least three clusters of three 100- to 200-foot-long longhouses placed parallel to one another within a two-and-one-half-acre habitation area. Noting ethnographic sources stating that Mohawk people generally belonged to one of

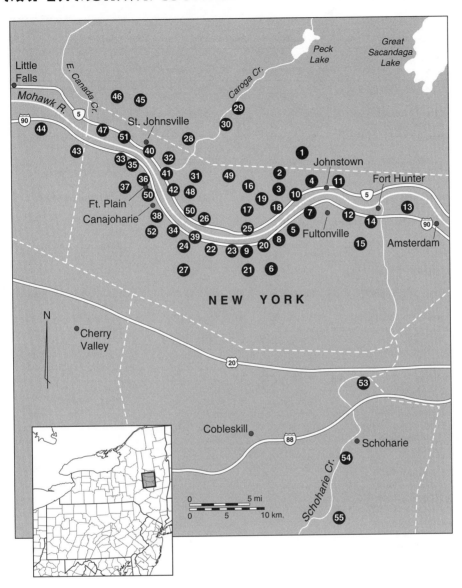

Little
Falls

Mohawk R.

St. Johnsville

Johnstown

Fort Hunter

Ft. Plain

Canajoharie

Fultonville

Amsterdam

Peck
Lake

Great
Sacandaga
Lake

Caroga Cr.

E. Canada Cr.

N E W   Y O R K

N

Cherry
Valley

Cobleskill

Schoharie

Schoharie Cr.

0   5 mi

0   5   10 km.

Map 29 Historic Contact Sites

Map Number	Site Name	County	State	Date	NR	Source

Eastern Series: Major Sites

Map Number	Site Name	County	State	Date	NR	Source
1	Cayadutta (NYSM 1115)	Fulton	NY	1525–1580		MacNeish 1952; MDSI; NYSMAS
2	Chapin/Wemple (NYSM 1125)	Montgomery	NY	1580–1614		MDSI; NYSMAS
3	Barker (NYSM 1137)	Montgomery	NY	1580–1614		MDSI; NYSMAS; Rumrill 1985
4	Martin (NYSM 1143)	Montgomery	NY	1614–1626		Engelbrecht 1971; Mac-Neish 1952; MDSI; NYSMAS
5	Cromwell (NYSM 1121 and 2340)	Montgomery	NY	1626–1635		MDSI; Rumrill 1985
6	Bauder (NYSM 1122)	Montgomery	NY	1635–1646		MDSI; NYSMAS; Rumrill 1985
7	Printup (NYSM 1124)	Montgomery	NY	1646–1666		MDSI; NYSMAS; Rumrill 1985
8	Freeman (NYSM 1145)	Montgomery	NY	1646–1666		MDSI; NYSMAS; Rumrill 1985
9	Janie (NYSM 5808)	Montgomery	NY	1646–1666		MDSI; NYSMAS; Rumrill 1985
10	Fox Farm (NYSM 1126)	Montgomery	NY	1666–1679		MDSI; NYSMAS; Rumrill 1985
11	Caughnawaga (NYSM 1116)	Montgomery	NY	1679–1693	X	Grassman 1952; Mc-Cashion 1975: MDSI; NYSMAS; Rumrill 1985
12	Milton Smith (NYSM 1092)	Montgomery	NY	1693–1712		MDSI; NYSMAS; Rumrill 1985
13	Bushy Hill (NYSM 1104)	Montgomery	NY	Early 1700s		MDSI; NYSMAS
14	Fort Hunter Complex Auriesville No. 1 (NYSM 1085) Auriesville No. 3 (NYSM 1087) Enders House Gravel Ridge Cemetery (NYSM 1105) Tehondaloga (NYSM 1112) Wemp No. 1 (NYSM 1100)	Montgomery	NY	1712–1776		Huey 1989; MDSI

Eastern Series: Small or Unevaluated Sites

Map Number	Site Name	County	State	Date	NR	Source
15	Kassen	Montgomery	NY	1600s		MDSI

Central Series: Major Sites

Map Number	Site Name	County	State	Date	NR	Source
16	England's Woods No. 1 (NYSM 1120)	Montgomery	NY	1580–1614		MDSI; NYSMAS
17	Rice's Woods (NYSM 1201)	Montgomery	NY	1580–1614	X	MacNeish 1952; MDSI; NYSMAS; Rumrill 1985
18	Briggs Run (NYSM 1118)	Montgomery	NY	1614–1626		MDSI; NYSMAS; Rumrill 1985

Map Number	Site Name	County	State	Date	NR	Source
19	Coleman-Van Deusen (NYSM 1119)	Montgomery	NY	1614–1626		MDSI; NYSMAS; Rumrill 1985
20	Yates (NYSM 1131)	Montgomery	NY	1626–1635		MDSI; NYSMAS; Rumrill 1985
21	Rumrill-Naylor (NYSM 5698)	Montgomery	NY	1635–1646		MDSI; NYSMAS; Rumrill 1985
22	Van Evera-McKinney Complex Van Evera-McKinney (NYSM 1232) Ford Cemetery (NYSM 1233)	Montgomery	NY	1635–1646		MDSI; NYSMAS; Rumrill 1985
23	Mitchell (NYSM 1248)	Montgomery	NY	1646–1666		MDSI; NYSMAS; Rumrill 1985
24	Allen (NYSM 1223)	Montgomery	NY	1646–1712		MDSI; NYSMAS; Rumrill 1985
25	Schenck (NYSM 1123)	Montgomery	NY	1666–1679		MDSI; NYSMAS; Rumrill 1985

Central Series: Small or Unevaluated Sites

Map Number	Site Name	County	State	Date	NR	Source
26	Turtle Pond	Montgomery	NY	1666–1680		MDSI; Rumrill 1985
27	Baker Farm	Montgomery	NY	Mid-1700s		MDSI

Western Series: Major Sites

Map Number	Site Name	County	State	Date	NR	Source
28	Klock (NYSM 2333)	Fulton	NY	1525–1580		Funk 1976; MDSI; NYSMAS; W. Ritchie and Funk 1973
29	Garoga (NYSM 2332)	Fulton	NY	1525–1580		MacNeish 1952; MDSI; NYSMAS; W. Ritchie 1969a
30	Smith-Pagerie (NYSM 2334)	Fulton	NY	1525–1580		Engelbrecht 1971; Funk 1973; MDSI; NYSMAS; W. Ritchie and Funk 1973
31	Kilts (NYSM 6297)	Montgomery	NY	1580–1614		MDSI; NYSMAS
32	Wagner's Hollow/Fox (NYSM 1202 and 1214)	Montgomery	NY	1614–1626		Engelbrecht 1971; Mac-Neish 1952; MDSI; NYSMAS
33	Failing Complex Failing (NYSM 1197) Crouse/Klemme Cemetery (NYSM 1175 and 1176)	Montgomery	NY	1624–1635		MDSI; NYSMAS; Rumrill 1985
34	Brown (NYSM 1204)	Montgomery	NY	1626–1635		MDSI; NYSMAS; Rumrill 1985
35	Sand Hill No. 1 (NYSM 1191)	Montgomery	NY	1635–1646		MDSI; NYSMAS
36	Fort Plain Complex Prospect Hill (NYSM 1207) Fort Plain Cemetery (NYSM 1196) Prospect Hill (NYSM 1207) Galligan No. 2 (NYSM 1192)	Montgomery	NY	1635–1646 1635–1646 1712–1755 1712–1755		MDSI; NYSMAS; Rumrill 1985, 1992
37	Oak Hill No. 1 (NYSM 1186)	Montgomery	NY	1635–1646		MDSI; NYSMAS; Rumrill 1985
38	Fisk (NYSM 1210)	Montgomery	NY	1646–1666		MDSI; NYSMAS; Rumrill 1985

Map 29 Historic Contact Sites—*Continued*

Map Number	Site Name	County	State	Date	NR	Source
39	Horatio Nellis (NYSM 1229)	Montgomery	NY	1646–1666		MDSI; NYSMAS; Rumrill 1985
40	Jackson-Everson Complex Jackson-Everson (NYSM 1213) Nellis Cemetery	Montgomery	NY	1666–1679		Kuhn and Snow 1986; MDSI; NYSMAS; Rumrill 1985
41	White Orchard Complex White Orchard (NYSM 1219) Gerstenberger Cemetery (NYSM 1218)	Montgomery	NY	1666–1693		MDSI; NYSMAS
42	Lipe Complex Lipe No. 2 (NYSM 1216) Katydid Burials (NYSM 1178)	Montgomery	NY	1679–1693		MDSI; NYSMAS; Rumrill 1985
43	Dekanohage Complex Mud Bridge Fort Hendrick	Herkimer	NY	1693–1755		MDSI
44	Upper Castle NHL (NYSM 1286)	Herkimer	NY	1755–1776	X	Guldenzopf 1986; W. Lenig 1977; MDSI; NYSMAS

Western Series: Small or Unevaluated Sites

Map Number	Site Name	County	State	Date	NR	Source
45	Bellinger (NYSM 2330)	Fulton	NY	1575–1590		NYSMAS; Rumrill 1991a
46	Crum Creek (NYSM 2327)	Fulton	NY	1575–1590		NYSMAS; Rumrill 1991a
47	Ganada Complex Ganada No. 2 (NYSM 2325)	Montgomery	NY	1575–1609		MDSI; NYSMAS
	Ganada No. 1 (NYSM 2324)			Mid-1700s		
48	Dewandalaer (NYSM 1206)	Montgomery	NY	1595–1610		MDSI; NYSMAS; Rumrill 1985
49	Christman	Montgomery	NY	1600s		MDSI
50	Rinehart Flats No. 3 (NYSM 1221)	Montgomery	NY	1600s		MDSI; NYSMAS
51	Timmerman No. 1	Montgomery	NY	1600s		MDSI
52	Swart-Farley (NYSM 1209)	Montgomery	NY	Historic		NYSMAS; Snow 1991a

Schoharie Valley Sites

Map Number	Site Name	County	State	Date	NR	Source
53	NYSM 6318/Site 154A-7-1	Schoharie	NY	Early 1600s		Peterson 1991
54	Mattice	Schoharie	NY	1600s		MDSI
55	Bohringer (NYSM 272)	Schoharie	NY	1712–1755		MDSI; NYSMAS

three clan groups often known among anthropologists as phratries, Funk and other archaeologists believe that Garoga's town plan may reflect this tripartite social organization.

Funk has further suggested that most people living at Garoga probably moved to the locale from the nearby Klock site on Caroga Creek sometime between 1550 and 1570. Funk also believes that many of Garoga's inhabitants probably began moving to the nearby Smith-Pagerie, Kilts, and Ganada No. 2 sites as early as 1580. Analyzing the

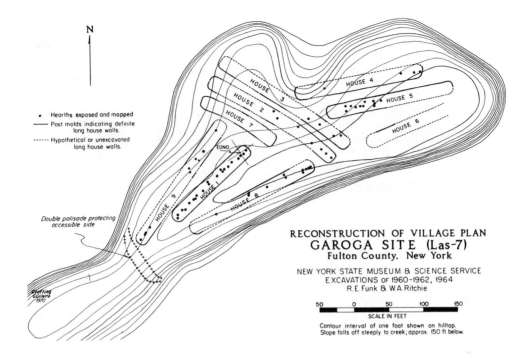

N

- Hearths exposed and mapped
- Post molds indicating definite long house walls.
- ----- Hypothetical or unexcavated long house walls.

HOUSE 4
HOUSE 3
HOUSE 5
HOUSE 2
HOUSE 7
HOUSE 6
EONO
HOUSE 9
HOUSE I
HOUSE 8

Double palisade protecting accessible side

Stotting Gallette 1970

RECONSTRUCTION OF VILLAGE PLAN
GAROGA SITE (Las-7)
Fulton County, New York

NEW YORK STATE MUSEUM & SCIENCE SERVICE
EXCAVATIONS OF 1960-1962, 1964
R.E. Funk & W.A. Ritchie

50   0   50   100   150
SCALE IN FEET

Contour interval of one foot shown on hilltop.
Slope falls off steeply to creek; approx. 150 ft. below.

Reconstruction of the Garoga site town plan (Ritchie and Funk 1973, fig. 30, p. 314). *Courtesy New York State Museum.*

same data, Rumrill believes that Cayadutta, Garoga, and Klock were simultaneously occupied sometime between 1560 and 1580.

Whatever the occupational sequence at these locales, documentation on all known sixteenth-century Mohawk Valley sites is recorded in the Mohawk Drainage Site Inventory at State University of New York at Albany (MDSI; Snow 1993) and reported in Snow (1989b, 1991a). Seeing continuity rather than change in the extant documentation, Snow believes that Mohawk Valley sites show few signs of forced relocations, settlement-pattern disruption, or abrupt changes in artifact types or assemblages. Noting that the few European materials found in late sixteenth-century Mohawk

Valley sites are not accompanied by discernible changes in the archaeological record, Snow believes that these patterns of technological conservatism reflect a period of general stability and continuity.

THE SEVENTEENTH CENTURY

Mohawk people first appeared in European records as they were defeated by the Algonquin, Montagnais, and Huron warriors accompanied by Samuel de Champlain and two other musket-bearing Frenchmen on the shores of Lake Champlain on July 29, 1609. Some years later, Dutch traders chronicled their first peaceful commercial transactions with visiting Mohawk fishing on the

Photograph of a longhouse post-mold pattern uncovered during wide-area excavations at the Smith-Pagerie site, 1960. *Courtesy Robert E. Funk.*

banks of the Hudson River near modern Albany, New York. These initial accounts, the first written records known to clearly identify Mohawks as a distinct people, begin the chronicle of commerce and conflict that would dominate much of Mohawk history during the seventeenth and eighteenth centuries.

The word "Mohawk" is not an Iroquoian term. Often written down as some variant of Maqua, Mohogg, or Mawhawke by Dutch and English chroniclers, the name appears to be an Algonquian term variously translated as "bear" or "man-eating cannibal monster." Frequently used

by Dutch scribes, the term "Maqua" may be derived from the name of the bear clan, one of the three major Mohawk matrilines first documented in written records during Historic Contact times.

Mohawk people generally call themselves *Kaniengehaga*. Long thought to mean "people of the place of the flint," the term, according to more recent studies, may come from the Mohawk word for "crystal," after the clear quartz crystals known as Little Falls or Herkimer diamonds found in abundance in the area (Hamell 1983). Whatever the word's meaning, Mohawk people continue to call their homeland "Kanienke" to the present day.

Surviving documentary sources affirm that Mohawk life generally centered around large, often fortified towns throughout much of the seventeenth century. The more prominent of these towns were frequently called "castles" by colonial chroniclers. Some writers, like Harmen Meyndertsz van den Bogaert, the Fort Orange surgeon who probably penned the earliest known firsthand European descriptions of Mohawk and Oneida communities in 1634, noted that Mohawk people lived in as many as eight towns during these years. Some of these communities almost assuredly were small towns associated with one or another of four major settlements. Others probably represented communities in transition.

Mohawk people retained the names of two of their three major communities through several relocations. Locales associated with the main westernmost Mohawk communities were repeatedly referred to as Tionnontoguen ("valley" or "between two mountains") or the Upper Castle. The middlemost town, for its part, was identified as Kanagaro, meaning "sticks" or "a pole in the water."

Inhabitants of the easternmost town, the Lower Mohawk Castle, by contrast, often changed the names of their main settlement. The largest of these communities was first identified in the 1634 van den Bogaert journal as a place called Onekahoncka. This community subsequently was identified as Ossernenon by French Jesuit Isaac Jogues in 1643 and as Asserue by Dutch domine Johannes Megapolensis, Jr., one year later. Writing in 1646, Jogues noted that its inhabitants had moved their town and changed its name to Oneugioure. Thirteen years later, other writers noted that Mohawks called the place Kaghnuwage ("at the rapids"). This town has since become better known as Caughnawaga.

Burned by its occupants before French raiders could plunder it in 1666, the community was soon relocated to the north of the Mohawk River. Both this group and a group of Christian Mohawks who established a new community on the banks of the Saint Lawrence River near Montreal in 1676 called their communities Caughnawaga.

Forty-three locales listed in the Mohawk Drainage Site Inventory contain components presently dated to the seventeenth century. Diagnostic European goods, such as glass beads and brass, copper, or iron objects dating from the late 1500s to the mid-1620s have been found at eleven of these locales. Like earlier sixteenth-century sites, all of these locales are situated north of the Mohawk River.

In the east, people living in the neighboring Chapin/Wemple and Barker locales continued to occupy their towns before moving to a new town at the Martin site in 1614. Most Martin townsfolk, for their part, moved to the Cromwell site south of the Mohawk River after 1626.

The inhabitants of the central Mohawk towns at England's Woods No. 1 and Rice's Woods moved eastward to the Briggs Run and Coleman-Van Deusen sites near the Martin locale after 1614. A French gunflint and a matchlock gun part found at Martin provide the first evidence of firearms at a Mohawk Valley site. Most of these people had subsequently moved south of the Mohawk River to the Yates site by 1626.

Farther west, people living at the Kilts site moved to the nearby Wagner's Hollow/Fox locale on Caroga Creek around 1614. Most Wagner's Hollow/Fox townsfolk subsequently relocated to the more southerly Brown and Failing sites near the south bank of the Mohawk River between 1624 and 1626.

Archaeologists have found unprecedentedly large and diverse assemblages of glass beads, European white-clay tobacco-smoking pipes, copper and brass triangular projectile points, and other metal implements and ornaments of European origin at these sites. These discoveries reflect the success of Mohawk raiders in using their towns as springboards for attacks against Canada to the north and of Mohawk traders in journeying eastward to do business with Dutch merchants along the upper Hudson River after 1614. The movement of these sites south of the river almost certainly reflects a response to fighting brought on by the outbreak of the First Mohawk-Mahican War in 1624.

Unlike their war against faraway Canada, Mohawk people suffered severe losses fighting against Mahican neighbors. Compelled to wage war on two fronts and suddenly exposed to attacks by Mahican warriors armed with Dutch muskets obtained from traders at newly established Fort Orange, Mohawk people strategically withdrew their towns to more secure locales south of the Mohawk River.

They were evidently living in towns relocated south of the river when van den Bogaert and his party left Fort Orange for Mohawk Country on a diplomatic mission to investigate reports of a Mohawk-French rapproachment in 1634. Locating archaeological sites associated with towns identified in the traveler's journal has become something of a Mohawk Valley cottage industry. Noting that diagnostic artifacts can rarely provide more than date ranges that vary from ten to twenty years, Starna (1992) believes that few locales can confidently be attributed to specifically described sites. Other investigators are less sanguine about such prospects.

Using poorly provenanced European white-clay tobacco pipes and other materials stored in private collections, avocationists Gilbert Hagerty (1985) and John McCashion (1991) asserted that the Bauder site was the locale of the large Onekahoncka town reported to have contained thirty-six houses within its precincts. But systematic surveys conducted by State University of New York at Albany archaeologists in 1986 showed that Bauder was a relatively small locale capable of containing no more than nine houses. Analysis of glass beads and other diagnostic artifacts found at the locale further indicated that Bauder was first occupied after van den Bogaert's party left the valley in early 1635.

Examining appropriately dated Cromwell site deposits situated at the approximate locale described by the Dutch diarist, both Snow and Rumrill agree that the large site is probably Onekahoncka. Snow suggests that the central-series Yates site is the probable locale of the documented major Mohawk town of Canagere. Believing Yates to be an earlier locale, Rumrill suggests that the Rumrill-Naylor site is the probable Canagere locale.

Snow goes on to propose that the western-series Brown and Failing sites represent the remains of the Schanidisse ("the town has been remade") and Tenotoge (also noted as Tenotoge-hage) castles. Discovering large amounts of pottery normally found in sites in more westerly Oneida Country, Snow believes that many Oneida women probably moved to the Failing locale during 1630s. Many of these women may have been among those who married Mohawk men after Huron and Algonquin warriors reportedly captured and killed many of the Oneida adult males in 1638.

Believing that the Oak Hill No. 1 site is Tenotoge, Rumrill suggests that the Sand Hill No. 1 site is the locale of Cawaoge ("a place where the road is submerged"). The locales of van den Bogart's smaller Canowarode ("a nail stuck in the wall"), Schatsyerosy ("one fingernail removed"), and Osquage ("on top of the roof") communities have not yet been clearly identified.

European trade goods found in deposits at sites dating to the early 1630s at the above-mentioned locales attest to documented Mohawk successes in their war against the Mahicans. Evidently forced from some of their easternmost towns at the beginning of the struggle, Mohawk warriors had defeated their Mahican adversaries by 1628. Negotiating from a position of strength after the commander of the Fort Orange post and three of his soldiers accompanying an unsuccessful Mahican raiding party had been killed, Mohawk diplomats subsequently concluded a lasting peace with the commander's replacement at the fort. Allying themselves with the colonists, the Mohawks managed to obtain nearly unlimited access to the vitally important Dutch market at Fort Orange.

Glass beads and other diagnostic artifacts found at the above-mentioned sites further indicate that most were abandoned shortly after van den Bogaert and his companions returned to the Dutch fort. In the east, most Cromwell site occupants probably moved to the smaller Bauder locale around 1635. Both Snow and Rumrill agree that Bauder probably was the site of the Ossernenon/Asserue locale documented between 1643 and 1644.

Snow and Rumrill also agree that most people living in the central area of Kanienke occupied the Rumrill-Naylor and Van Evera-McKinney sites after 1635. Snow suggests that the occupants of the Failing and Brown sites, for their part, moved to new homes at the Sand Hill No. 1 site, the Fort Plain–complex Prospect Hill locale, and the Oak Hill No. 1 site after 1635. Rumrill believes that Oak Hill No. 1 and Brown were occupied both before and after that date.

Whatever their differences, all investigators agree that these and other sites dating to the second quarter of the century contain unprecedentedly large quantities of glass beads; iron, brass, copper, and lead implements and ornaments; and European white-clay tobacco pipes.

The number of these imports grew during the next major phase of town relocation, which began in the mid-1640s. Snow and Rumrill generally agree that most eastern Mohawk people moved to the Printup, Janie, and Freeman sites at this time. Avocationist Kingston Larner has found evidence of palisade fortifications at the Freeman site. Rumrill further identifies Freeman as the site of the first Kaghnuwage town.

Both Snow and Rumrill also agree that many inhabitants of the central portion of Kanienke moved to the Mitchell site at this time. Snow believes that people living along the western reaches of

Mohawk Country established new communities at the Allen, Fisk, and Horatio-Nellis sites. Believing these sites to be later, Rumrill suggests that western Mohawk people probably continued to live at the Oak Hill No. 1 and Brown sites during this period.

Discoveries of large amounts of glass beads and European white-clay tobacco-smoking pipe fragments with lead musket balls, gunflints, and gun parts help date a Jesuit finger ring recovered from Janie site deposits to this period. Written records note that Jesuits established their first missions among the Mohawk people during the 1640s. The presence of such a ring in the small hamlet at Janie may represent an example of conversion, an incident of exchange, a piece of booty, the presence of a Jesuit captive, or the sojourn of a Huron or Algonquin Indian prisoner, visitor, or spouse.

Visits by Jesuit priests, initiated after 1643 during a brief interval of peace between the Mohawks and the French, ended abruptly in 1646 when Mohawk people, suspecting witchcraft, tortured and killed Father Jogues for allegedly causing an epidemic. Rumrill suggests the Rumrill-Naylor site contains the remains of the Canagere town where Jogues reportedly was killed. Snow, on the other hand, suggests Van Evera-McKinney or Mitchell as the possible locale.

Mohawk warriors from these and other towns helped the Senecas defeat the Hurons in 1649. Moving farther west, Iroquois warriors soon defeated and dispersed their Neutral and Petun neighbors. These victories secured the western approaches of Iroquoia for a time and opened up the possibility of unlimited access to the northern fur-producing areas. Free to concentrate on other matters, Mohawk warriors, diplomats, and traders turned their attention to the south. Playing important roles as intermediaries between warring Munsees and Dutch colonists in the Hudson Valley, Mohawk sachems made peace with Mahican people returning to their old homes. Aided by their Munsee and Mahican allies, Mohawk warriors subsequently joined Iroquois war parties raiding Susquehannock towns in 1651, but heavy losses compelled the Mohawks to break off the struggle the following year. They had little reason to continue the war. Mohawk policy of the period centered around controlling the vital trade route to Fort Orange. Susquehannocks did not trade at Fort Orange. Realizing few benefits from their participation in the war, the Mohawks subsequently let other Iroquois more threatened by Susquehannock competition bear the brunt of the struggle.

Other Iroquois warriors virtually blockaded the western approaches of New France during these years. Exhausted by the war and anxious to reopen trade, French authorities finally agreed to meet with Iroquois leaders in 1653. Those Iroquois chiefs willing to treat with the French exacted a high price for peace. While agreeing to stop fighting the French, they refused to end their wars against the Indian allies of the French. Cut off from supplies by the Iroquois blockade and unable to obtain sufficient support from the home country to break through it, French authorities gave in to Iroquois demands and signed the document.

The French treaty allowed the Senecas and other western Iroquois people to concentrate their efforts on eliminating remaining rivals like the Eries, whose towns were finally destroyed in 1656. The treaty did little else, however, to satisfy most Mohawks. Many still mourned friends and relatives killed by the French and their Indian allies. Others were concerned about the activities of French missionaries who were proselytizing in their communities and ministering to the many Christian Indians living as captives in their towns. Even Mohawk diplomats favoring a French alliance wished to keep French people and their influence at a safe distance. Angered by what they regarded as French intrigue in their towns, many Mohawks finally supported the efforts of several chiefs to expel the Jesuits from Onondaga in 1658. Soon afterwards, Mohawk war parties were again waylaying French convoys.

Anxious to maintain peaceful access to the Hudson River trade, Mohawk diplomats quickly concluded an alliance with the English conquerors of New Netherland in 1664. They did not, however, join the four other Iroquois nations in a peace treaty with the French a year later. Counting on the neutrality of their Iroquois confederates and assuming that the newly arrived English were too weak to effectively support their Mohawk friends, Canadian governor Daniel de Rémy de Courcelle marched a French army south toward the Mohawk towns that winter.

Ambushed by Mohawk warriors, Courcelle's army was forced to retreat. A second column commanded by Courcelle's successor, Alexandre de Prouville Tracy, set out the following fall. Advancing carefully, Tracy's men succeeded in breaking through to Mohawk Country.

Marching into the heart of Kanienke, the French destroyed four large abandoned Mohawk towns. Demoralized by this attack and angered by the failure of their new English allies to protect their homes, Mohawk leaders grudgingly agreed to put their marks upon a new peace treaty with the French in 1667.

Deposits found in sites dated to the years immediately following Tracy's raid indicate that the Mohawks quickly rebuilt their towns. Proposing that most Freeman site residents moved to Fox Farm, both Snow and Rumrill suggest that the Schenck site became the most important central Mohawk community. Both scholars further agree that most people living at the western end of Kanienke moved to the Jackson-Everson and White Orchard sites. The site of another Mohawk town noted by Dutch traveler Jasper Danckaerts at Niskayuna near Albany, New York, in 1679 has not yet been found.

All of these sites are located north of the Mohawk River. Fox Farm is almost certainly the site of the fortified Lower Mohawk Castle of Caughnawaga. Discoveries of Huron-like incised ceramics at Fox Farm corroborate a 1668 French account stating that two-thirds of Caughnawaga's inhabitants were Huron or Canadian Algonquian captives. Nearly ten years later, Wentworth Greenhalgh wrote that "Cahaniaga is double stockadoed round has four ports about four foott wide a piece, contayns about 24 houses, & is situate upon ye edge of an hill, about a bow shott from ye river side" (O'Callaghan 1849–1851).

The Schenck site probably represents the remains of Kanagaro town. Snow and Rumrill agree that the White Orchard

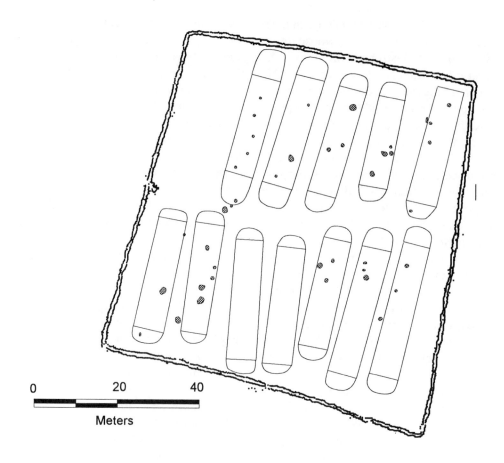

Reconstructed plan view of the Fox Farm site. *Courtesy Dean R. Snow.*

or Jackson-Everson sites may represent the site of the Upper Mohawk Castle of Tionnontoguen. Discoveries of late-stage Ontario Iroquois Tradition pottery in Jackson-Everson site deposits further affirm documented reports of mass movements of adopted Huron captives to the Mohawk Valley after 1659.

Large amounts of English and French imports—and correspondingly fewer domestically produced goods—have been found at these locales. The overall picture presented by these findings indicates that the Mohawk people had be-

come members of a prosperous trading nation. Findings of French coins and Jesuit rings may also corroborate documents recording both increased French influence and growing political factional conflict in Mohawk towns during the years following the 1667 treaty.

Extant documents show that growing numbers of Mohawks converted to Catholicism shortly after Jesuits began to reestablish missions throughout the Iroquois heartland after 1667. Jesuit successes at Caughnawaga indicate that they may have particularly appealed to the many adopted captives and slaves living in the town. Once again able to travel freely following the reestablishment of peace in the region, many adopted or enslaved proselytes may subsequently have left Mohawk Country and moved north to the Saint Lawrence Valley. Initially settling at La Prairie, most soon moved to the new Indian town also called Caughnawaga just west of Montreal.

Archival records note that Mohawk leaders, alarmed by the growth of Jesuit influence in their towns, ordered the ejection of missionaries and converts in 1683. Archaeological evidence further suggests that most Mohawk people moved to new town locations on both banks of the river at or about this time.

Snow and Rumrill believe that the people living in the eastern-sequence Fox Farm community split up during the early 1680s. The absence of Jesuit rings, medals, and other Catholic religious artifacts at the Caughnawaga archaeological site or any other later seventeenth-century Mohawk town in Kanienke suggests movement of non-Christian eastern Mohawk people to this locale. Ironically, these findings indicate that the Mohawk Valley Caughnawaga site presently preserved by the Franciscan order as a shrine to the devout Mohawk woman Kateri Tekakwitha, beatified by the Catholic Church in 1980, probably contains the remains of a town built by Mohawk people who expelled the Jesuits and their acolytes. Other findings affirm that Kateri and most other Catholic Mohawks probably moved north to New France at this time.

Snow has not yet found a site in the central reaches of Mohawk Country containing diagnostic assemblages clearly dating to these years. Looking at site materials from locales farther west, he suggests that Mohawk people continuing to live at the White Orchard site began moving to a new nearby locale now known as the Lipe No. 2 site. Agreeing that Caughnawaga site deposits date to these years, Rumrill suggests that other Mohawk people lived at the Allen and Horatio-Nellis sites from 1682 to 1693.

Wherever they lived in Kanienke, Mohawks experienced ever-worsening relations with the French during these years. Pledging to hold firmly to their end of the Covenant Chain, Mohawk and other Iroquois leaders symbolically recognized the authority of the English crown over their lands at a treaty conference convened by New York governor Thomas Dongan in 1684. Many Mohawk leaders established particularly close relations with the talented young New York diplomat Peter Schuyler at this time.

Son of a prominent Albany trader, Schuyler moved to the locale of earlier frontier-diplomat Arendt van Curler's post a few years after the prominent Dutchman's death in 1667. Like van Curler and other successful frontier diplomats, Schuyler quickly learned Indian languages and customs. And like van Curler, whose name was immortalized by Iroquois sachems ritually addressing all New York governors as Corlaer, Schuyler was soon known among Mohawk people as Quider, after the way the sound of his name fell on Mohawk ears. His home, known as Schuyler Flatts, became a major trading center, meeting ground, military staging area, and place of refuge.

Mohawk people soon had need of places like Schuyler Flatts. Concerned by the Iroquois tilt toward English interests and angered by renewed Seneca raids on western fur convoys, Tracy's successor, Jacques René de Brisay, marquis de Denonville, marched a French army into Seneca Country in 1687. Burning their own towns in front of the French, the Senecas moved back to their lands after Denonville's column withdrew.

Most Kanienke Mohawk people subsequently supported their Covenant Chain allies when King William's War broke out between France and England in 1689. Armed and provisioned by the English, Mohawk raiders began marching north to Canada. One of their raids, a particularly devastating surprise attack upon the Montreal suburb of Lachine made during the spring of 1689, spread terror throughout New France.

Responding to this and subsequent incursions, Louis de Buade de Frontenac, governor of New France, unexpectedly led a column of Canadian habitants and Caughnawaga Mohawk warriors into the Mohawk Valley during the winter of 1693. Although Canadian Caughnawagas reputedly warned their kinsfolk of the attack and refused to engage them in combat, Mohawk Valley people again forced to abandon their communities had to watch helplessly as Frontenac's force burned their towns.

Fighting disrupted community life throughout Iroquoia. Some eastern Mohawk people moved to a new town at the Milton Smith site. Those living in the central part of Kanienke moved to the locale of an earlier Mohawk town at the Allen site. Western Mohawk people, for their part, moved to a site known as Dekanohage.

But not all Mohawks moved to new towns. Large numbers fled north among relatives in Canada. Some joined Oneida, Onondaga, Mahican, Munsee, and other people settling in new towns along the northern branches of the Susquehanna River at Tioga, Ochquaga, and other places. A few moved farther west toward the West Branch of the Susquehanna and beyond.

More than sixty Mohawk refugees, fearing further attacks, quickly moved to a fortified town built near Peter Schuyler's house at Schuyler Flatts. Located close by the banks of the Hudson River in the heart of the area's English settlement, this locale remained a home to Mohawk people throughout the war. Events justified movement to such sites, for in 1696 French troops accompanied by Indian allies destroyed the Oneida and Onondaga towns just west of Kanienke. The violence did not end with the signing of a formal treaty in Europe between France and England in 1697, for the Mohawks and their Iroquois confederates were not able to conclude their own treaty with the French until 1701.

European census records indicate that fully half of the two thousand people believed to have been living in Kanienke when King William's War began in 1689 were not there when Europeans made peace among themselves in 1697. Analyzing archaeological and archival data, Starna suggests that the Mohawk population may have ranged from 4,129 to 5,134 at that time. Whatever their number, the Mohawk people were devastated by the war. Many were killed in the fighting. Other were killed by diseases like the smallpox epidemic spread by warriors returning from an abortive expedition against Canada in 1691. Moreover, all surviving Mohawks in Kanienke had been burned out of their homes.

Artifact assemblages found in sites associated with communities built by Mohawk people in Kanienke after Frontenac's 1693 raid reflect both change and continuity. Materials excavated from sites postdating 1693 indicate that most Mohawk people continued to utilize the same kinds of artifacts they had used before the war. Analysis of known site distributions and community plans suggests more dramatic changes. The disappearance of the central Mohawk town from European documents and the archaeological record after 1693, for example, indicates that its inhabitants moved to other Mohawk communities within or beyond the borders of Kanienke.

Unlike the compact and often fortified towns built before 1693, the two remaining centers of Mohawk occupation in Kanienke became decentralized, sprawling towns consisting of widely dispersed hamlets of one or more longhouses or cabins surrounded by cultivated fields and orchards. Mirroring similar settlement choices made by people living elsewhere in Iroquoia at this time, these changes show that Mohawk families, no longer forced to constantly be on guard against attack or invasion, generally chose to abandon close, cramped, indefensible, and often pestilential palisade-enclosed townsites when offered the opportunity.

THE EIGHTEENTH CENTURY

The Mohawks entered the eighteenth century a much-changed people. Although most of them continued to call Kanienke home, increasing numbers now lived in New France and elsewhere. Wherever they settled, most Mo-

hawks prospered in the years following the signing of the 1701 Montreal treaty. Mohawk trappers and traders ranged far into the interior in search of pelts, trading partners, and adventure. Closer to home, Mohawks and their Mahican and Munsee neighbors carried on a lucrative and illicit trade between Albany and Montreal.

This trade continued as a new war, known as Queen Anne's War, broke out between France and England in 1702. Officially maintaining their hard-won neutrality, Mohawks smuggled goods across the frontier with the tacit consent of the combatants. Although each adversary formally respected their neutrality, both worked tirelessly to enlist Mohawk support. Most Mohawks living in New France, for example, agreed to fight for their French allies. New York recruiters, for their part, initially encountered indifference in many Mohawk Valley communities. Remembering the devastation of the last war, most Mohawk people politely reminded recruiters that they were neutrals and refused to openly side with Great Britain. Still, they gradually came to actively support their British allies as the war ground on. Three Mohawk leaders, including the noted warriors Hendrick and Brant, grandfather of the famous Mohawk leader Joseph Brant, were among the four "Indian Kings" brought to Queen Anne's court to drum up support for an invasion of New France in 1710. Returning home the following year, these men encouraged their warriors to join the British army gathering above Albany.

The expedition broke up before any Mohawk warriors saw combat in New France. Knowing that the French were aware that they had taken sides in the conflict, Mohawk leaders fearing retaliation permitted the construction of British forts along their eastern frontier. Taking advantage of this unprecedented opportunity, New York authorities erected Fort Hunter at the mouth of Schoharie Creek between 1710 and 1712. The security and trade opportunities opened by the construction of the post prompted most Mohawk people to move from the Milton Smith locale to sites like Auriesville Nos. 1 and 2, Tehondaloga, and Wemp No. 1 on the west of Fort Hunter. Though it was known among the British as the Lower Castle, Mohawks called their new home Tiononderoge, "junction of two waterways."

Tiononderoge was not the only settlement established by Mohawk people along the eastern edges of Kanienke during these years. Another site one mile east of the fort at Bushy Hill may represent the remains of a small community established by returning Canadian Caughnawaga Catholic Mohawks. Other Mohawk people moved farther up the Schoharie River to new towns like the one known to archaeologists as the Bohringer site.

Farther west, Mohawk people continued to live at the Dekanohage locale at Canajoharie, "washed kettle." Also known as the Upper Castle, this community stretched for more than two miles along the southern banks of the Mohawk River. Although Mohawk people also established another community at Fort Plain in 1712, the Upper Castle locale would remain the center of western Mohawk life up to the time of the American War for Independence.

Queen Anne's War ended for the colonists and their Indian allies in 1713.

Leaving their other posts in Iroquoia, the British did not abandon Fort Hunter. Although some Mohawk people were alarmed by this development, most came to appreciate the convenience of a permanent post near their homes. Many did business with traders, gunsmiths, blacksmiths, and other fort residents. Others looked to the post for support and supplies when traplines or larders were empty. Still others came to take communion from the silver service sent to them by Queen Anne or to hear Anglican ministers preach from the pulpit of the chapel built for them within the post walls. Most Mohawks ultimately accepted this British outpost in their territory. Numbering fewer than a thousand people, they realized that they alone could no longer hold back colonial expansion, and they looked to the British authorities to safeguard their territory.

Although British diplomats promised security, colonial land speculators had other ideas. Anxious to expand settlements west of Schenectady, speculators had begun to press Mohawks to sell land even before the new fort was finished in 1712. Small numbers of Palatine German refugees were settled around Fort Hunter as early as 1713. Ten years later, hundreds of Palatine Germans poured into lower Mohawk Country. Most of these newcomers lived peacefully with their Mohawk neighbors. A few, like Kayaderosseras patentees anxious to claim much of eastern Kanienke for themselves, tried to defraud Mohawks out of tracts containing hundreds of thousands of acres.

Despite these problems, many Indian people living in Mohawk Country came to enjoy a measure of peace and prosperity during these years. Churchmen and traders brought new tools, skills, and ideas to Mohawk Country communities. Missionaries translated the Bible into Mohawk and taught congregants to read and write in English and their own language. They also supplied goods to adherents and advised congregants on a wide range of topics. Mohawk people learning how to use plows patronized mills and forges built in their towns.

Fur traders also settled among them. Some, like German immigrant Conrad Weiser and the Irish colonist William Johnson, learned the Mohawk language and customs. Working with powerful allies like Hendrick, these and other Mohawk Valley settlers pushed the fur trade deeper into the interior. As diplomacy followed trade, Johnson, Weiser, and other frontier entrepreneurs soon became accomplished forest diplomats.

Forest diplomacy became more critical as Europeans increasingly pressed into and around the Iroquois heartland. Construction of a new British post at the mouth of the Oswego River on Lake Ontario in 1722 allowed western traders to bypass Mohawk and other lower Iroquois towns. French and British authorities soon constructed other posts on the north and west of the Iroquois heartland. Farther south, thousands of settlers surged around the southern frontiers of Mohawk territory from the Delaware River to the Susquehanna Valley. The outbreak of a new war between France and Great Britain in 1744, known as King George's War, further increased tensions with Mohawk communities in Canada.

The total population of the Mohawk towns in New York had dwindled from one thousand to little more than four hundred by the time King George's War ended in 1748. Although Munsee and Mahican River Indians moved to the Schoharie River during these years, their total number was never very large.

Several factors account for Mohawk population decline. As had happened earlier, many people in Mohawk Country were killed by epidemics. Others moved to join family and friends already living in Canada at Caughnawaga or at the Saint Regis settlement built farther west on the banks of the Saint Lawrence. More than a few moved among Delawares, Mahicans, and other displaced Coastal Algonquians at burgeoning Susquehanna Valley communities like Tioga, Otsiningo, and Ochquaga.

Many Mohawk Valley Indian people supported the British in their final war with France on the North American continent between 1754 and 1760. William Johnson, who lived with the prominent Mohawk woman Molly Brant and who had been knighted and appointed Superintendent for Indian Affairs in the northern colonies for his service during the fighting, did what he could to keep the Mohawks in the British sphere. Distributing gifts as a hospitable host and powerful chieftain, Johnson hired Mohawks and other Indians living in Kanienke as soldiers, scouts, and laborers. Examinations of Johnson's account books affirm that he was generous with all who visited him or asked for his aid. He also helped see to it that Fort Hendrick—named for his friend and mentor who was killed at the Battle of Lake George in 1755 just as Johnson himself won the victory that would lead to his knighthood—was built near Hendrick's family home at the Upper Castle to secure the area from French attack.

Johnson also resettled many River

Mohawk Upper Castle Historic District National Historic Landmark

Excavations at the Brant Homestead in the Mohawk Upper Castle Historic District National Historic Landmark. The structure believed to be the Brant family barn is in the background. Courtesy Dean R. Snow.

The Mohawk Upper Castle Historic District is located in the village of Indian Castle, in the town of Danube, Herkimer County, New York. Two sites, the Brant Homestead and the Indian Castle Church, preserve archaeological and architectural evidence of Nowadaga, the most westerly part of this community. Called Canajoharie by Mohawk people, the Upper Castle was the most important western Mohawk Indian town during the 1700s.

Two stone foundations, a stratified midden deposit, and a wooden-framed Dutch barn situated on a level terrace overlooking the broad Mohawk River floodplain on the north represent what remains of the homestead of the influential Brant family built sometime around 1754. Nearby, the Indian Castle Church, a wooden-framed Anglican chapel built for the Canajoharie Mohawk Indian community in 1769, still stands atop a knoll near the edge of a terrace rising steeply above Nowadaga Creek.

The Brant Homestead was home to Molly Brant, best known as Sir William Johnson's consort, and her brother, Joseph Brant, the Mohawk war chief who led his people against American rebels during the War for Independence. Hoping to capitalize on the influence of this powerful Mohawk family, British authorities erected the Indian Castle Church near their homestead.

American rebels seized both sites after Mohawk people abandoned their Upper Castle homes in 1777. Extant evidence indicates that fires had destroyed all Brant Homestead structures except the barn by the second quarter of the 1800s. Turned ninety degrees on its axis during renovation operations in 1855, the nearby church survives today under the protection of the Indian Castle Church Restoration and Preservation Society.

A field crew led by Wayne Lenig conducted test excavations at the Indian Castle Church in July 1972. Field-workers uncovered elements of the original stone-foundation walls laid beneath the church when it was built in 1769 and newer stone foundations laid in place when workmen turned the church on its axis to its present position in 1855. Two artifacts, a copper George II half-penny minted in 1744 or 1757 and a set of metal carpenter dividers, were found in foundation deposits.

Analysis of the dimensions of the original 1769 stone foundation uncovered during these excavations suggests that the building's current framing columns, floorboards and joists, and other main structural elements probably date to the period of original construction. Contrasting nineteenth-century illustrations with the archaeological evidence, Lenig further found that workers changing building design elements and configurations from the Georgian to the Greek Revival styles in 1855 did little more than alter the structure's surface appearance. The basic shape, dimensions, and main structural features of the building remain essentially unchanged and intact.

State University of New York at Albany students under the general direction of Dean R. Snow conducted excavations at the Brant Homestead site during the summers of 1984 and 1985. Supervised on the site by David B. Guldenzopf, then a SUNY Albany graduate student, field crews placed excavation units at various places in and around two cellar-hole depressions. Measurements of stone-foundation walls lining the larger of these cellars indicate that they had originally supported a rectangular building at least forty feet long and twenty feet wide. A smaller foundation located thirty-five feet farther southeast evidently supported a building fifteen feet long and ten feet wide. Analyses of creamwares, salt-glazed stonewares, copper coins, and several wire-wound glass beads found within both cellars indicate that houses formerly resting above them were built sometime between 1762 and 1780.

Charred planks, many still embedded with hand-cut rosehead nails, were found just above a buried compacted layer of sand believed to represent the cellar floor of the larger structure. Bits of plaster found in the three-inch-thick layer of ash atop these boards suggests that the rooms of the house were lined with plaster walls. Analyses dating broken pieces of European ceramics thrown into the cellar hole above this ash layer further corroborate written records indicating that the house burned to the ground sometime between 1795 and 1820.

The Indian Castle Church in 1985. Courtesy Dean R. Snow.

Investigators also found a twenty-inch-thick stratified refuse midden between these cellar holes. Test excavations sampling the lowermost layer of this deposit uncovered catlinite and slate beads, a harness bell, a frizzen, European white-clay tobacco pipe bowls, bone-handled tableware, an iron-kettle fragment, and a variety of European ceramics dating from 1762 to 1780.

The Dutch barn near these deposits is a wood-framed four-bay structure fifty feet long and forty-six feet wide. Pinned and wedged, the structure's anchor beams have rounded tongues protruding up to twenty-one inches beyond their outer faces. A high-level, braced cross tie extends one foot beneath the horizontal purlin plate in the middle of the center bent. These features, widely considered diagnostic characteristics of eighteenth-century Dutch barn construction, support its identification as the structure mentioned in Molly Brant's Revolutionary War–loss claim inventory.

Neither barns nor stone-foundation-supported frame buildings are commonly found in contemporary Mohawk sites. Discoveries of such refined luxury ceramics as English Jackfield tewares, white salt-glazed stoneware plates,

Indian people forced from their Hudson Valley lands among their friends and relatives at Schoharie during the war. Although some stayed, most of these people returned to the Hudson Valley or moved farther westward when the fighting stopped in America in 1760. For their part, neither Johnson nor other prominent New Yorkers owning titles to large tracts of land in and around Kanienke were much interested in stopping thousands of colonists from buying their lands at Schoharie, the Upper Castle, or elsewhere after the conflict ended. By the time war broke out be

tween colonists and the crown in 1775, Indians living in Kanienke owned little more than the land beneath their towns.

Despite these problems, many Mohawks continued to prosper during the years between the Seven Years' and the Revolutionary Wars. They found employment in the carrying trade as bateaumen, transporting goods up and down the Mohawk River. Many also produced clothing, ornaments, and other items for use in the Indian trade.

Luxury items, such as stemmed glasswares, fine porcelain, leaded glass, and other objects excavated at the site of the

Brant homestead at the Nowadaga locale in the Mohawk Upper Castle National Historic Landmark show that the Brants and other close associates of Johnson benefited from his patronage. Written records reveal that the young Joseph Brant, Molly's brother, grew up in an affluent household. Educated in Eleazar Wheelock's Indian school, he later became Johnson's protégé. Drawn by the prestige of the Brant family, Anglican churchmen built the still-standing Indian Castle church near Molly's house in 1769. The only known example of an intact Indian mission chapel in Kanienke, the church is presently included within the Mohawk Upper Castle National Historic Landmark.

Other deposits recently found in the Ender's House site, at what is believed to have been the location of Mohawk war leader John Deserontyon's home, lend further support to documentary evidence indicating that many Mohawk people had a higher standard of living than most of their non-Indian neighbors during the years following the end of the Seven Years' War (Huey 1989). As mentioned earlier, David Guldenzopf's (1986) assessment of archival and artifactual evidence suggests that ambitious British clients like the Brant family and younger war leaders like Deserontyon amassed growing wealth and power as established Iroquois confederacy sachems grew poorer and less influential.

Led by the Brants and other British partisans, most Mohawk people continued to support their old Covenant Chain allies when war with the colonists broke out in 1775. Outnumbered by nearby settlers who supported the rebel cause, most of these Mohawk Loyalists had fled west to refugee camps around Fort Niagara by 1778. Those attempting to remain neutral, like the Fort Hunter leader Tigoransera, known to colonists as "Little Abraham," were badly treated by both sides.

Only four families were living at the Lower Castle when American troops, who had plundered the Mohawk towns in 1777, finally burned their homes to the ground in 1779. At the Upper Castle, settlers soon moved into Brant family houses spared from destruction by settlers fearing vengeance. Infuriated by the destruction or appropriation of their homes, Mohawk warriors relentlessly raided American frontier settlements everywhere in the Mohawk Valley until the war ended in 1783.

Virtually all Mohawk Valley Indians were living at Fort Niagara, Saint Regis, and other Canadian refugee centers when the war ended. Regarded with hostility and suspicion by their neighbors, the few Mohawks returning to their valley in the years following the war ultimately moved away. Border adjustments negotiated with the British during the 1790s subsequently brought the portion of the Saint Regis mission community south of the forty-fifth parallel within territorial limits claimed by the United States. Today, this settlement remains the only continuously occupied Mohawk community within the United States.

SOURCES

Dean R. Snow (1989a, 1990, 1991a, 1991c, 1992, 1993) and Donald A. Rumrill (1985, 1988, 1990, 1991a, 1991b, 1992) have provided much of the documentation presented in this section.

Individual site data may be consulted in the Mohawk Drainage Sites Inventory

(MDSI) on file in the Department of Anthropology at the State University of New York at Albany. The most complete Mohawk site report thus far published, the Jackson-Everson site study edited by Robert D. Kuhn and Dean Snow (1986), is one of a series of research monographs detailing findings based on materials in MDSI files. Site reports have also been written for excavations undertaken at Caughnawaga (Grassman 1952), Fort Hunter (Huey 1989), Garoga (W. Ritchie and Funk 1973), and the Mohawk Upper Castle National Historic Landmark (Guldenzopf 1986; W. Lenig 1977). Other archaeological studies have been published by Robert D. Kuhn (1985) and William A. Starna (Snow and Starna 1989).

Key studies based on written documentation include the recent retranslation of a 1634–1635 journal attributed to Fort Orange surgeon Harmen Meyndertsz van den Bogaert (Gehring and Starna 1988) and more general surveys of Mohawk history in Carse (1949) and Fenton and Tooker (1978). Starna (1980) revises pre- and postepidemic Mohawk population estimates. Documentation of the visit of the four "Indian Kings" to Great Britain in 1710 appears in Bond (1952) and Garratt and Robertson (1985).

The history of Anglican missionary efforts in Mohawk Country is presented in Lydekker (1938). Guldenzopf's (1986) study of Mohawk social relations and biographies of Joseph Brant (Kelsay 1984), John Deserontyon (Torok 1965), William Johnson (M. Hamilton 1976), and Conrad Weiser (P. A. W. Wallace 1945) also contain a range of information on the lives and times of some of the best-documented personalities noted in regional colonial records.

ONEIDA COUNTRY

Oneida Country extends across the present-day central New York counties of Oneida and Madison from the upper Mohawk Valley westward to the Oneida River drainage. Stretching at its greatest extent from the Saint Lawrence River to the upper Susquehanna Valley, the heart of Oneida Country is around the Oneida and Cowaselon creek valleys southeast of Oneida Lake.

THE SIXTEENTH CENTURY

Little is known about the origins or identities of people living in Oneida Country during the 1500s. No written, oral, or architectural evidence clearly dating to that time has yet come to light. As elsewhere, archaeological evidence of life in Oneida Country during the sixteenth century is fragmentary or inconclusive.

Investigations conducted by avocationists like New York State Archaeological Association Chenango Chapter founder Theodore Whitney (1964, 1967, 1970) and chapter members Monte R. Bennett (1973, 1981, 1983), Herman Weiskotten, Jr., and his son Daniel (1988) have unearthed much of what is known about Oneida historical archaeology.

Both they and professional archaeologists like Peter P. Pratt (1976) and William E. Engelbrecht (1971) believe that Oneida people probably share a common ancestry with neighbors from adjacent Onondaga and Mohawk countries.

Noting similarities in all eastern Iroquois Chance-phase ceramic and settlement patterns, Pratt (1976) suggests that the Oneida, Onondaga, and Mohawk cultures developed in situ in their homelands during later phases of the Late Woodland period. Finding evidence suggesting migration in similarities between Chance-phase Onondaga and Oneida pottery, Weiskotten (1988) proposes that Oneida people entered their country from a place just south of Cazenovia Lake in Onondaga Country.

Linguistic data suggest another migratory route. Noting uniquely close relationships between the Oneida and Mohawk languages, Dean R. Snow (1991c) believes that the Oneidas originally may have been Mohawk Valley people who moved upriver toward Oneida Creek sometime during Late Woodland times.

Whatever their points of view, all investigators agree that nearly all known sixteenth-century sites identified as residences of direct ancestors of Oneida people tightly cluster between Oneida and Cowaselon Creeks. Discoveries of glass beads and other European imports believed to date to the sixteenth century at the Vaillancourt, Diable, Cameron, Wilson, and Beecher (also known as Blowers) sites affirm later sources indicating that most Oneida people tended to make their homes in one or two large towns. Analyses contrasting occupation dates at these locales further confirm observations of Champlain and later European chroniclers that most Iroquois people moved to new town locales every ten to twenty years.

A large iron knife and small numbers of brass beads and buttons found with Chance-phase ceramics and triangular, chipped-stone projectile points at the mid–sixteenth-century Vaillancourt site represent the earliest evidence of European contact in Oneida Country. Small numbers of glass beads first appear in Diable site deposits. Larger numbers have been found with proportionately greater amounts of copper, brass, and iron artifacts at the later Cameron and Beecher sites. A copper "salamander" effigy, believed to represent a beaver and similar to others found farther west in Monongahela and Fort Ancient sites, has been found in Cameron site deposits.

Most of these sites are located atop high, defensible uplands. Relatively little is known about their site plans or layouts. Post-mold patterns preserving evidence of stockaded palisade walls have been unearthed at the Bach site (which contains no objects of European origin) and the Diable site (which does contain such objects). Other post molds found at the Bach site represent the remains of at least nine longhouses. Exca-vations unearthing one of these house-sites revealed a structure sixty-five feet long and eighteen feet wide (Whitney 1967).

Findings from Bach and other sixteenth-century sites in Oneida Country mirror those found elsewhere in Iroquoia. Scholars believe that the increasing density of these often-fortified sites reflects social and political changes associated with the rise of the Iroquois confederacy. Certain patterns indicate adoptions by Oneida pottery makers of stylistic elements from other Iroquois communities, which suggests intensification of contacts, which in turn suggests confederacy development (P. Pratt 1976; Engelbrecht 1985).

Ceramic data suggest other contacts during these years. A single sherd of Saint Lawrence corn-ear decorated ware has been found by Richard Hosbach in a sixteenth-century Oneida Country locale (Pendergast 1992b). Verification of similar wares reported from other Oneida sites may shed light on the identity, relationships, and fate of Saint Lawrence Iroquoian people whose Jefferson County towns just north of Oneida land disappeared sometime during the late 1500s.

THE SEVENTEENTH CENTURY

Archaeological evidence found at the Wilson and Beecher sites affirms that most early–seventeenth-century Oneida Country residents continued to live in towns first built during the last decade of the 1500s. Pits, hearths, and other features preserved within both sites contain substantial amounts of glass beads; white-clay tobacco-smoking pipe bowls and stems; copper, brass, and iron wares; imported and domestically

MAP 30: ONEIDA COUNTRY

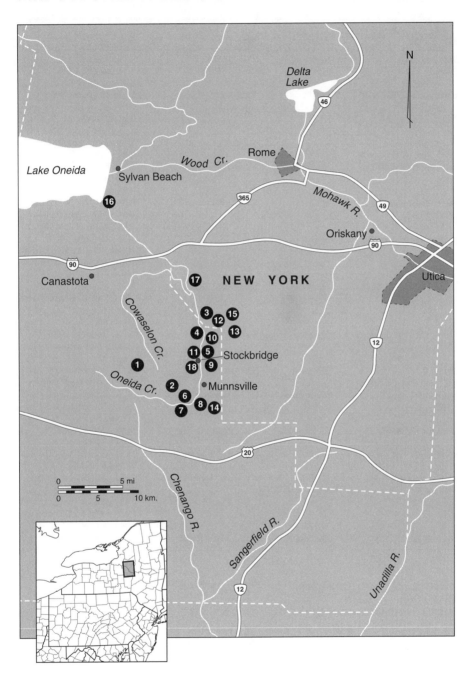

Map 30 Historic Contact Sites

Map Number	Site Name	County	State	Date	NR	Source
1	Vaillancourt	Madison	NY	1550–1575		P. Pratt 1976
2	Diable	Madison	NY	1555–1570		Engelbrecht 1985; P. Pratt 1976
3	Cameron (NYSM 648)	Oneida	NY	1570–1595		M. R. Bennett 1981, 1983; M. R. Bennett and Bigford 1968; M. R. Bennett and Clark 1978; M. R. Bennett and Hatton 1988; NYSMAS
4	Wilson (NYSM 644)	Madison	NY	1595–1625		M. R. Bennett 1983; Hosbach and Gibson 1980; NYSMAS
5	Beecher/Blowers (NYSM 643)	Madison	NY	1595–1625		P. Pratt 1976; M. R. Bennett 1979, 1983, 1984a, and 1991a; NYSMAS
6	Thurston (NYSM 670)	Madison	NY	1625–1637		M. R. Bennett 1983, 1984a, 1991a; McCashion 1991; NYSMAS; Whitney 1964
7	Marshall (NYSM 669)	Madison	NY	1637–1640		M. R. Bennett 1983, 1984a; M. R. Bennett and Cole 1976; McCashion 1991; NYSMAS
8	Stone Quarry (NYSM 668)	Madison	NY	1640–1650		M. R. Bennett 1983, 1984b; McCashion 1991; NYSMAS
9	Dungey (NYSM 666 and 667)	Madison	NY	1650–1660		M. R. Bennett 1983; McCashion 1991; NYSMAS
10	Sullivan/Moot (NYSM 645)	Madison	NY	1660–1677		M. R. Bennett 1983, 1984a; McCashion 1991; NYSMAS
11	March (NYSM 650)	Madison	NY	1660–1677(?)		M. R. Bennett 1991b; NYSMAS
12	Collins (NYSM 649)	Madison	NY	1677–1685(?)		M. R. Bennett 1991b; NYSMAS
13	Upper Hogan/Cody (NYSM 647)	Oneida	NY	1677–1685		Clark and Owen 1976; M. R. Bennett 1983, 1984a; M. R. Bennett and Cole 1974; McCashion 1991; NYSMAS
14	Prime's Hill (NYSM 671)	Madison	NY	1696–1720		M. R. Bennett 1988; Hasenstab 1990; McCashion 1991; NYSMAS; Snow 1990
15	Lanz-Hogan (NYSM 646)	Oneida	NY	1720–1750		M. R. Bennett 1982, 1983; NYSMAS
16	Sterling (NYSM 660)	Oneida	NY	1750–1767		M. R. Bennett 1991b; Hasenstab 1990; NYSMAS
17	Oneida Castle	Oneida	NY	1767–1779		M. R. Bennett 1991b
18	Brothertown	Madison	NY	Late 1700s		MDSI

produced pottery; and stone, bone, and antler tools and weapons.

The larger of these early–seventeenth-century Oneida towns probably sheltered from one thousand to three thousand people (Starna 1988). Beecher site findings clearly document patterns of continuity and change exemplified in contemporary sites. Believed to have been occupied sometime between 1595 and 1625, the Beecher site has yielded evidence suggesting the presence of a compact, densely settled, fortified town. Although large numbers of aboriginal ceramics and lithics have been found at the site, fully half of all triangular projectile points found there are cut from copper or brass sheets and kettles. White-clay tobacco-smoking pipes and stoneware sherds represent the earliest known discoveries of imported European ceramics in Oneida Country sites.

Discovery of a small group of graves just beyond the town's walls represents another first. Unlike earlier mortuary patterns that comprised single graves or small group interments in and around village areas, these graves represent the earliest known cemetery in Oneida Country. Local avocationists who discovered this cemetery believe that its appearance constitutes the first evidence of intensifying patterns of conflict, disease, and malnutrition associated with the early years of direct contact between colonists and Indian people in Oneida Country.

Local investigators have long believed that either the Beecher or the Nichols Pond (P. Pratt 1976) site represents the locale of the Entouhonoron fortress attacked by Indian warriors accompanied by Samuel de Champlain in 1615. A conventionalized engraving depicting the attack shows a town containing eighty-one longhouses laid out into neatly arranged groups surrounded by a six-sided multiple palisade wall. No such deposits have been found at Beecher. Showing that Nichols Pond deposits predate Champlain's attack by nearly a century, Pratt (1992) has since suggested a more westerly locale for the Entouhonoron fortress.

Oneida people first emerge in European written records as the residents of the town of Onneyuttehage visited by van den Bogaert and his party in 1634. Conventionalized into the form "Oneida," the name probably means "people of the erect or upright stone," after the boulder believed to always providentially appear at the site of newly relocated major settlements.

Like other Dutch recordists of the time, van den Bogaert often identified all Iroquois people living west of the Mohawks as "Sinnekens." Describing Onneyuttehage, the Dutch diarist wrote that the town contained sixty-six houses enclosed within double-palisaded walls measuring "767 steps in circumference" on a high hill overlooking Oneida Creek (Gehring and Starna 1988). Walking around the town walls, the chronicler further found that Onneyuttehage's inhabitants protected the graves of kinsfolk by surrounding individual interments with small stockades.

Archaeologists unearthing masses of domestically produced and imported goods dating to the 1620s and 1630s at the Thurston site have discovered evidence of a gate and a double-palisade wall matching van den Bogaert's description. Two cemeteries and the post-mold pattern of a single longhouse have also been found. Among the many objects recovered from town deposits are some of the earliest known examples found in Oneida Country of shell birds, crescents, and discs; brass kettles; blue glass beads; Jesuit finger rings; and lead shot.

Discoveries of artifacts at the four-and-one-half-acre Marshall site indicate that most Onneyuttehage town residents may have moved one mile south to this locale by 1637. Marshall may be the site of the Ononjote town chronicled in the contemporary *Jesuit Relations.*

Analysis of Marshall site assemblages reveals changes in Oneida technology and mortuary customs. Most European imports found in earlier sites were usually placed in graves. Departing from this pattern, most domestically produced lithics and ceramics unearthed at Marshall appear as funerary offerings in graves of older people. Although Oneida people continued to place mirrors, glass beads, and metal ornaments with their dead, most European imports discovered at this locale consist of utilitarian objects found within domestic contexts.

The presence of domestically produced tools and implements in graves may suggest the increasingly ceremonial role of formerly utilitarian objects. But such discoveries may also indicate that by this time only elders continued to make or be associated with Late Woodland–style clay and stone tools and implements.

European records may hold a key to the puzzle. *Jesuit Relations* reports that much of Ononjote's male population, including the Oneida war captain Ononkwaia, was captured and killed by Huron and Canadian Algonquian warriors shortly after the town was built.

The predominance of graves of older people at the site may thus reflect this documented loss of much of the town's younger adult male population.

Although Oneida widows rebuilt their shattered families by marrying Mohawk men, the smaller size of subsequent towns built at the Stone Quarry and Dungey sites indicates that the Oneidas were not able to completely make up for their losses after moving from the Marshall site in 1640. Discoveries of Oneida-type ceramics at the Mohawk Valley Failing site further suggest that some Oneida women may have moved in with the families of new Mohawk spouses.

Growing numbers of Oneida men and women died in subsequent Iroquois wars with the Eries, Susquehannocks, Mahicans, French, and Canadian Algonquians. Other Oneida people died in the epidemics that struck Iroquois towns at this time.

Deposits found at the later–seventeenth-century Sullivan, March, Collins, Upper Hogan, and Prime's Hill sites preserve evidence of Oneida responses to these challenges. European imports almost totally supplant aboriginally produced domestic manufactures at these sites. The English origin of many of these imports reflects increasingly close relations between Oneida people and their New York Covenant Chain allies.

Discoveries of Jesuit medals and rings in these sites also document the growth of French missionary influence in Oneida communities. Father Jacques Bruyas built the first permanent Jesuit mission in Oneida Country in 1667. The site was given the name Saint François Xavier. Sullivan or March site deposits may contain remains of this mission.

Evidence preserved within the Sullivan, March, and other later–seventeenth-century sites further documents Oneida responses to war losses and epidemic contagion during these years. Jesuit chroniclers writing in 1668, for example, assert that Huron and other adopted Indian captives made up more than two-thirds of the total Oneida population. Many adoptees probably chose to spend their lives in Oneida Country. Others, who had been forced into lives of servitude, almost surely left whenever opportunities presented themselves.

Although records are incomplete, large numbers of adoptees probably were among the many Oneida proselytes who followed their priests to Saint Lawrence mission communities in New France before 1683. Others may have started moving south to upper Susquehanna Valley towns on the fringes of Oneida territory when the Susquehannocks acknowledged Iroquois sovereignty over their lands after 1675.

Most people remaining in Oneida Country supported their English allies against the French during King William's War, fought between 1689 and 1697. Although few Oneida people were killed by French troops invading their country and destroying their towns in 1696, devastation left in the wake of the retreating French army brought hardship and poverty to their families. Distressed by such losses and outraged by their exclusion from negotiations ending the war between the European combatants in 1697, most Oneida people called for an end to the fighting in their homeland. Pressing their case at confederacy councils, Oneida diplomats played a major role in negotiations leading up to the signing of the French-Iroquois peace accord of 1701.

THE EIGHTEENTH CENTURY

Oneida diplomats and diplomacy figure prominently in eighteenth-century European records. Despite this, relatively little is known about their social and domestic life during the 1700s. Like that of other people elsewhere in the region, the Oneida way of life had changed considerably during the preceding century. Archaeological deposits found at the Prime's Hill and Lanz-Hogan sites corroborate written records indicating that all people living in Oneida Country had moved from walled towns to decentralized, unfortified communities.

The best known of these locales, the Lanz-Hogan site, is a large, dispersed community of cabins and longhouses that covers an area of at least twenty acres. Concentrations of European artifacts compose much of the occupational evidence found here. Although some domestically produced bone combs and clay pipes have been found, most site deposits consist of smelted metal axes, glass beads, and other imports.

Other evidence of eighteenth-century Oneida life has been found at Prime's Hill, Sterling, Oneida Castle, and Fishing Place. People living at Prime's Hill probably moved to the Lanz/Hogan site sometime around 1720. Surface finds at the documented locations of Oneida towns at the Sterling and Oneida Castle sites suggest that systematic excavations may yet reveal intact deposits at both locales.

Discoveries of artifact assemblages consisting almost wholly of English goods and materials at these sites further show that Oneida people continued to adapt European tools and clothing to their own purposes. They also learned to master new production techniques as the century wore on. Extant evidence indicates that many Oneida people came to accept new concepts like market commoditization and the Protestant religion during these years. And, like all people in the region, Oneida townsfolk had to continually adjust to the effects of war, disease, and out-migration.

Many responded to these changes by developing closer ties with their neighbors. Relations with nearby Onondaga townsfolk became particularly close. Like the Onondagas, many Oneida people had strong economic, social, and political contacts with the French colonial administrators, traders, and missionaries. Following reestablishment of peace in 1701, Oneidas frequently traveled to French markets. French missionaries and administrators, for their part, worked hard to bring Oneida and other Iroquois people within the French sphere of influence. Living near Lake Ontario, often sympathetic to French overtures, and aware that their communities lay open to French assault, many Oneida and Onondaga people publicly expressed strong pro-French sentiments in eighteenth-century councils.

Other Oneidas remained loyal to their British Covenant Chain allies. Unlike the Mohawks, who allowed the British to build fortified posts in their country during Queen Anne's War, Oneida leaders resisted all attempts to establish foreign forts near their principal towns. Forts farther from their towns were another matter. Many Oneidas, anxious to gain access to a convenient, strategically located marketplace, for example, evidently welcomed erection of the British post at Fort Oswego in 1722.

Pursuing Iroquois policies that played contending imperial powers and rival interest groups off against one another, Oneida leaders regarded the Fort Oswego post as a necessary counter to French influence. Others saw the post as a bulwark protecting their towns against potential attacks launched from the nearby French bastion at Fort Frontenac, built at the head of Lake Ontario along the headwaters of the Saint Lawrence during the preceding century.

Increasing numbers of Oneida people continued to move to upper Susquehanna Valley towns like Ochquaga and Otsiningo at this time. Joined by Mohawks unwilling to live near the European settlers who poured into their country after the end of Queen Anne's War, Oneida people soon found themselves living alongside dispossessed Delaware, Munsee, Mahican, and Tuscarora refugees forced from ancestral homelands elsewhere. Farther south, Oneida overseers administered affairs of other dispossessed Indian people relocated by Iroquois confederacy chiefs at such Susquehanna Valley towns as Wyoming and Shamokin. The most famous of these Iroquois regents, Shikellamy, played a particularly prominent role in frontier diplomacy during the middle years of the century.

Most upper Susquehanna Valley communities became cosmopolitan, multicultural centers. Formally maintaining neutrality in struggles between France and Great Britain, the upper Susquehanna Valley people tended to favor British interests throughout much of the century. Such tendencies set the tortuous course of Oneida foreign diplomacy as the century wore on. Oneida people walked a thin line between peace and war as France and Great Britain struggled for control of the continent.

Many pro-French Oneida people joined similarly inclined Onondaga and Cayuga townsfolk moving to the new French post of La Presentation that was established at Oswegatchie by Sulpician missionary François Picquet in 1749. Located at a strategic narrows in the Saint Lawrence River between Montreal and Fort Frontenac at the mouth of the Oswegatchie River in present-day Ogdensburg, New York, the Oswegatchie settlement grew from less than a hundred people in 1750 to more than a thousand by 1755 as Oneida, Onondaga, and other Iroquois alienated by British expansion into their territories moved to La Presentation to support the French in their war with Great Britain.

Fighting alongside the French throughout the war, these people had to reassess their political positions after the French defeat in America in 1760. Some threw their support behind western Indian nations in trying to drive the British from their country during Pontiac's War in 1763. Others fought against them, joining colonial troops often led by Indian commanders appointed by Sir William Johnson.

Feeling the need to cultivate powerful British clients, many hereditary Oneida chiefs openly threw their support behind Sir William Johnson during these years. Pressed by Johnson to establish a post in their territory, the chiefs finally allowed the British to build Fort Stanwix at the strategic carrying place between the Mohawk and Oswego Rivers in 1768. That decision angered many younger Oneida people. More than a few resented the presence of such a post in their territory; others, working as laborers carrying goods along the portage between the Oswego and Mohawk Rivers, feared losing their jobs to settlers.

Dissatisfied with established leaders and anxious to assert themselves, many of these young men and women supported Samuel Kirkland, an outspoken young "New Light" Presbyterian minister who settled among the Oneida people in 1767. Kirkland was a product of the Great Awakening. Rejecting spiritual values and social traditions sustained by the British establishment, he and his contemporaries became strident voices for rebellion and independence. Working closely with the Oneida people, Kirkland supplied provisions, established a school, and trained and employed converts. Having attracted a large following, he was able to convince many Oneidas to throw in with rebellious colonists when war broke out in 1775.

The split between pro-American and Loyalist factions in the Oneida community reflected similar divisions in most other Iroquois communities. Unable to achieve consensus, confederacy sachems symbolically covered the League's council fire and advised constituents to go their own way in 1777. Later that year, Oneida warriors accompanying Mohawk Valley militiamen on their way to relieve Fort Stanwix (known as Fort Schuyler during the war) fought against British troops and their Iroquois allies at Oriskany. Today, some Oneidas remember local stories affirming that their ancestors provided supplies for Washington's army during the following winter.

Not all people from Oneida Country

supported the colonists. Many Oneidas living at Oswegatchie declared for Britain. Oneidas at Ochquaga and other upper Susquehanna towns also remained loyal to the Crown. Iroquois war captains holding British commissions used towns like La Presentation at Oswegatchie and Ochquaga as staging areas for raids against American settlements.

Ochquaga was burned by American troops in 1778. La Presentation townsfolk helped beat back an assault on their town in early 1779, but later that year, American columns under the overall command of Maj. Gen. John Sullivan and James Clinton destroyed virtually every other Indian town along the upper Susquehanna while en route to the heart of Iroquoia.

Most Oneida families burned out of their homes fled to Fort Niagara. Warriors belonging to these families subsequently joined Iroquois war parties to avenge the devastation of their homeland and destroyed the homes of pro-American Oneida families during a raid through Oneida Country during the fall of 1780.

People driven from their homes by these raiders were compelled to accompany them back to Niagara. Some soon moved to temporary homes in the Genesee Valley near present-day Geneseo, New York. Others took shelter in rebel settlements farther east, around Schenectady. Confined to refugee camps and often short of provisions, most of these Oneida people lived under difficult conditions throughout the remaining years of the war.

Loyalist Oneida people generally moved north into Canada following the war. Pro-American Oneida community members, by contrast, returned to their country and rebuilt their homes. Encouraging Stockbridge, Brothertown, and other Indian refugees to settle in their country during the later 1780s, these Oneidas remained on their lands until American authorities convinced many to move elsewhere during the early decades of the 1800s. Most of the Oneida people who refused to leave their homeland today live in Madison and Oneida counties. Other Oneidas live in expatriate communities in Ontario, Wisconsin, and Oklahoma.

SOURCES

Much of the material presented in this section has been drawn from M. R. Bennett (1979, 1981, 1982, 1984a, 1984b, 1988, 1991a), Campisi (1978), P. Pratt (1976, 1991), and Whitney (1964, 1967, 1970). Archaeological analyses in Engelbrecht (1971, 1974, 1985) and Bradley (1987a) also contain documentation on Oneida material culture and settlement patterns.

Many aspects of Oneida history are extensively documented in European records. Much of this material is compiled in Leder (1956), O'Callaghan and Fernow (1853–1887), and Thwaites (1896–1901). Other information, largely focusing upon later phases of Oneida history, appears in Campisi and Hauptman (1988). Further documentation may be found in articles published in Jennings et al. (1985) and Richter and Merrell (1987).

ONONDAGA COUNTRY

Onondaga Country stretches across a section of central New York from the shores of Oneida and Cazenovia Lakes west to the eastern shore of Skaneateles Lake. It extends at its widest from the southern shores of Lake Ontario around the mouth of the Oswego River south to the forks of the Tioughnioga and Chenango Rivers above present-day Binghamton, New York, but the heartland of Onondaga Country is located between Limestone, Butternut, and Onondaga Creeks just south of the modern city of Syracuse in present-day Onondaga County.

THE SIXTEENTH CENTURY

People living in this area had been making their homes in a succession of large towns and smaller, nearby satellite communities for at least 150 years when the earliest known scraps of imported European brass and copper to enter Onondaga Country were deposited in Quirk and Sheldon site features sometime during the third quarter of the sixteenth century. Quirk was a large, densely settled town whose habitation area encompassed from four to five acres. The nearby Sheldon site contains the remains of a one-to-two-acre community.

Findings of glass beads at the large Chase and smaller Dwyer site locales indicate that Quirk and Sheldon site residents had moved to these new towns by the third quarter of the century. Little is presently known about the town plans or the residence composition of these late–sixteenth-century Onondaga communities. Most sites in the area have been investigated by local avocationists without access to resources available to professional researchers. As a result, few Onondaga Country sites have been subjected to the wide-area excavations needed to fully reveal individual houses or larger-scale town settlement patterns.

Working in small excavation units, investigators have nevertheless succeeded in delineating portions of palisade walls in nearly all known early Historic Contact period Onondaga townsites. Excavation of a single longhouse at the Temperance House site (which contains no objects of European origin) represents the only known discovery of a house pattern dating to the sixteenth century in the area. Analysis of ceramics found at this and contemporary locales in

Onondaga Country indicates that people in these communities produced pottery almost identical to wares made by Oneida and Mohawk people farther east.

Other ceramics present evidence of different contacts. Discoveries of small numbers of sherds of pots stylistically similar to others produced by northerly Saint Lawrence Iroquoians in several deposits dating to the late 1500s, for example, suggest contact with these people (Bradley 1987a). Recovery of marine shell beads, pendants, and gorgets; Schultz-type ceramics; and cold-hammered smelted copper or brass rings, hoops, and spirals suggests intensifying exchange or warfare with people living farther south.

An increase in the total volume of European goods imported into Onondaga communities during the final decades of the 1500s is evidenced by a proportionate decline in the number of marine shell artifacts found in Onondaga Country sites. Such artifacts disappear entirely from site inventories after new forms of tubular cylindric wampum beads appeared in the area during the early 1600s.

Tracing changes in the size and content of sites in Onondaga Country, archaeologist James A. Tuck (1971) believes that Onondaga Iroquois towns gradually came to contain larger numbers of small longhouses between 1300 and 1600. Tuck believes that this trend may reflect development of greater community cohesion, lineage segmentation, and preference for smaller family sizes associated with changing postmarital residence rules, settlement shifts, and depopulation. Attributing these changes to increasing incidences

of warfare and epidemic disease associated with demographic shifts and socioeconomic intensification, he and other scholars (Engelbrecht 1985) believe that these findings reflect processes that may have stimulated similar developments among other Iroquois people and their neighbors.

There presently is no evidence that the introduction of European imports by themselves sparked radical transformations in Onondaga life during the late 1500s. Although copper, brass, and iron began to replace some stone and shell objects, wholesale technological substitutions did not occur. As they would continue to do, sixteenth-century residents of Onondaga Country evidently selectively adopted those aspects of foreign technology that best accorded with their lives and tastes and rejected or ignored almost everything else.

THE SEVENTEENTH CENTURY

Written records and orally transmitted texts affirm that Onondaga was regarded as the capital of the Iroquois League by the time French, Dutch, and English explorers probed the fringes of the Trans-Appalachian region during the early-seventeenth century. Archaeological evidence further shows the Onondagas, "people of the great hill," continued to live in fortified towns within the heart of their homeland at this time.

Investigations by amateur excavators and avocational collectors indicate that the Pompey Center, Pratt's Falls, Shurtleff, Carley, and Lot 18 sites represent successive relocations of the main Onondaga community during these years. Most of these sites were stockaded towns covering areas ranging from three to

MAP 31: ONONDAGA COUNTRY

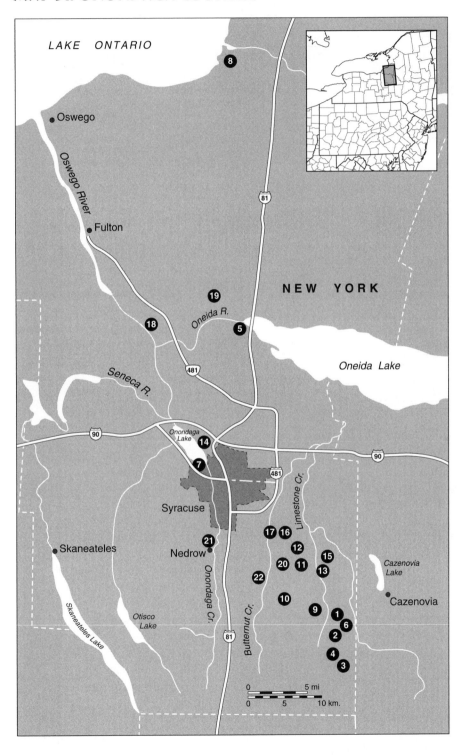

LAKE ONTARIO

• Oswego

Oswego River

• Fulton

NEW YORK

19

18

Oneida R.

5

Oneida Lake

Seneca R.

481

90

Onondaga Lake

14

7

Syracuse

Skaneateles

21

Nedrow

17 **16**

12

15

20 **11**

13

Cazenovia Lake

22

Onondaga Cr.

Butternut Cr.

Limestone Cr.

10

• Cazenovia

Otisco Lake

9

1

6

2

Skaneateles Lake

81

4

3

8

81

0   5 mi
0   5   10 km.

Map 31 Historic Contact Sites

Map Number	Site Name	County	State	Date	NR	Source
1	Quirk (NYSM 623)	Onondaga	NY	1550–1575		NYSMAS; Ricklis 1966
2	Sheldon (NYSM 624)	Onondaga	NY	1550–1575		NYSMAS; Ricklis 1966
3	Chase	Onondaga	NY	1575–1600		Bradley 1979
4	Dwyer	Onondaga	NY	1575–1600		Ricklis 1966
5	Brewerton	Onondaga	NY	1575–1600		Ricklis 1966
6	Pompey Center (NYSM 622)	Onondaga	NY	1600–1620		Bradley 1979; NYSMAS
7	Kaneenda (NYSM 4235)	Onondaga	NY	1600–1625		Beauchamp 1900; NYSMAS
8	Otihatanque	Oswego	NY	1600–1655		Beauchamp 1900; Bradley 1987a
9	Pratt's Falls (NYSM 621)	Onondaga	NY	1620–1630		Bradley 1979; NYSMAS
10	Shurtleff (NYSM 1075)	Onondaga	NY	1630–1640		Bradley 1979; NYSMAS
11	Carley (NYSM 1074)	Onondaga	NY	1640–1650		Bradley 1979; NYSMAS
12	Lot 18 (NYSM 1068)	Onondaga	NY	1650–1655		Bradley 1979; NYSMAS
13	Indian Castle (NYSM 620)	Onondaga	NY	1655–1663		Bradley 1987a; NYSMAS
14	Ste. Marie Gannentaha	Onondaga	NY	1656–1658		Connors, DeAngelo, and Pratt 1980
15	Indian Hill (NYSM 619)	Onondaga	NY	1663–1682		Bradley 1987a; NYSMAS
16	Bloody Hill II/Weston/ Western/Oley (NYSM 1070)	Onondaga	NY	1675–1700		Bradley 1987a; Hasenstab 1990; NYSMAS
17	Jamesville (NYSM 1067 and 2486)	Onondaga	NY	1682–1700		Bradley 1987a; NYSMAS
18	Phoenix	Onondaga	NY	1600s		Beauchamp 1900
19	Caughdenoy	Onondaga	NY	1600s		Beauchamp 1900
20	Sevier (NYSM 2761)	Onondaga	NY	1700–1720		Bradley 1987a; NYSMAS
21	Onondaga Castle	Onondaga	NY	1720–1779		Bradley 1987a
22	Coye	Onondaga	NY	1730–1750		Bradley 1987a

five acres. Smaller, nearby locales are thought to represent outlying hamlets or campsites.

Although the Entouhonoron fortress attacked by Champlain in 1615 may have been an Onondaga town, Onondaga people themselves do not clearly emerge in European written histories until 1635. Meeting with van den Bogaert and his compatriots at the main Oneida town in that year, a group identified as an Onondagan delegation told the visitors that their people were angered by the sharp business practices and high cost of goods at Fort Orange. Acknowledging that they were trading with French merchants who offered better wares at cheaper

prices, they said they would continue to travel to New France so long as Dutch authorities failed to establish more equitable conditions conducive to trade at Fort Orange.

In 1654, French Jesuit Simon Le Moyne became the first European known to visit Onondaga. One year later, Fathers Pierre Joseph Marie Chaumonot and Claude Dablon established the small chapel of Saint Jean Baptiste in the town, and the next summer the Onondagas allowed the Jesuits to establish a small, fortified mission colony on the banks of Onondaga Lake some miles to the north of their main town.

The new post was named Sainte

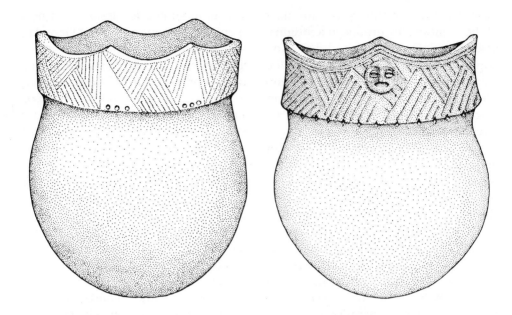

Historic Contact period Onondaga pottery: *left,* a Chance-phase pot; *right,* a Garoga-phase pot with a biconcave collar profile, notched collar base, and effigy face (Bradley 1987a, fig. 1, p. 18). *Courtesy James W. Bradley.*

Marie Gannentaha. Many Onondagas welcomed the establishment of a new trading mart only a few miles from their homes. Others were concerned by possible consequences of such an extension of French influence. In any event, the post did not last long. Worsening relations between the Iroquois League and the French finally led the Onondagas to eject all Jesuits in 1658.

People living in Onondaga communities had to deal with dramatic cultural and social changes during these years. Like other Iroquois people, Onondaga townsfolk were devastated by epidemic disease, and wars with Huron, French, and other enemies exacted heavy tolls. Although Onondaga communities remained largely self-sufficient during these years, written and archaeological sources

show that many Onondaga people increasingly came to prefer imported metalwares, firearms, and other European wares over their own domestic products as the century wore on.

Materials recovered from Indian Castle, the site of the Onondaga capital during the time of the short-lived Jesuit entrée, tellingly reveal the extent of this shift. European metalwares, ceramics, and glasswares dominate site assemblages. Stone axes, projectile points, and other chert, quartz, or jasper tools and weapons cease to appear in site deposits.

Bone and horn combs, clay pipes, native-made gunflints, catlinite beads and pendants, shell beads, runtees, effigies, and other ornaments, and a few poorly made, nondescript variants of incised collared wares constitute most of the domestically produced aboriginal assemblage recovered from site pits and burials. The large number of cold-hammered copper and brass bracelets and ear ornaments found at the locale further testifies to increasing Onondaga interest in metalwork.

The growing interest in European goods is evident in site deposits found within Onondaga towns built later in the century. Site distributions also reveal shifts in settlement patterns and residence choices. Indian Hill, the site of the main Onondaga town when the Jesuits returned in 1667, was a larger and less centralized town than its predecessors. Writing in 1677, Wentworth Greenhalgh failed to mention the stockade line later discovered by archaeologists at the site. Of great use while the Onondagas and other Iroquois nations were at war with the Susquehannocks from 1663 to 1675, this stockade may have been dismantled by the time Greenhalgh visited the town. The smaller, nearby Bloody Hill II site probably represents the town's outlying satellite community.

Deposits within a large, triple-palisaded town found at the Jamesville site (also known as the Pen site) probably represent remains of the site of the Iroquois capital between 1682 and 1700. Occupied during the turbulent years of the 1687 French invasion of western Iroquoia and King William's War (1689–1697), the Jamesville site today yields deposits that reflect the growing influence of their Covenant Chain ally.

Small numbers of Jesuit rings found at the site also provide evidence of the continuing influence of French missionaries and their Onondaga Indian converts in town politics. Jesuits continued to enjoy the support of many Onondaga people even after Iroquois sachems decided to eject French missionaries from their country in 1683. Pursuing long-established Iroquois policies of consensus and toleration, Onondaga leaders were initially unwilling to split their community into pro- and anti-Jesuit factions. War with France changed this situation. Unable to remain neutral after the French raid on Seneca Country in 1687, Onondaga leaders evicted all Jesuits from their territory. A substantial number of Onondaga people subsequently joined the priests as they returned to New France.

Although many Onondagas continued to support the French when war once again broke out between the colonial powers in 1689, most Onondaga warriors ultimately joined their English allies in raids against Canada. Suffering serious losses in the fighting, the Onondagas were forced to burn their town and retreat in front of the large army led by Gov. Louis de Buade de Frontenac of New France that swept through Oneida and Onondaga countries in 1696. Archaeological deposits at Jamesville postdating this event show that some Onondagas probably briefly reoccupied the town shortly after Frontenac's army returned to New France. Far more extensive deposits found at the nearby Sevier site indicate that nearly all Onondagas had subsequently moved north by 1700.

THE EIGHTEENTH CENTURY

Like many of their confederates, the Onondagas were a divided people in 1700. Nearly half of their population supported their English Covenant Chain allies. The other half favored the French. Despite these divisions, most Onondaga people continued to live together in their principal community at Sevier and subsequent townsites located farther west along Onondaga Creek in and around their present reservation below Nedrow throughout the first half of the eighteenth century. Sevier was a sprawling settlement stretching between Limestone and Butternut Creeks. Site deposits there have been found to contain antler combs and clay pipes as well as catlinite, red slate, shell, and glass beads; musket parts; and substantial amounts of imported European ceramics and glasswares and metal tools, weapons, and implements.

Archaeological deposits found at the Onondaga Castle and Coye sites corroborate European accounts recording the move to the Onondaga Creek drainage sometime after 1720. The Onondaga Castle site contains the remains of a large, dispersed community. Although house patterns have not yet been reported at the site, discoveries of small depositional concentrations at various places match written accounts describing the town as a substantial group of small hamlets and farmsteads extending for many miles along the banks of Onondaga Creek. Living in longhouses or log cabins, townsfolk constructed corncribs, small barns, and other outbuildings. Continuously occupied throughout much of the eighteenth century, the Onondaga Castle site was systematically destroyed by American troops in 1779.

Few known archaeological or written sources directly document domestic life at this or other Onondaga communities during these years. Descriptions penned by Moravian missionary David Zeisber-

ger and other Europeans visiting the Iroquois capital during the middle decades of the century provide some information. More detailed observations were recorded in the journals and reports of American troops who destroyed the Onondaga towns in 1779. Commanding one of four columns converging on Iroquoia that summer, Col. Goose van Schaik and his soldiers destroyed as many as fifty houses located along an eight-to-ten-mile stretch of Onondaga Creek.

All this was in the unforeseeable future when Onondaga diplomats assumed the major role in negotiating a lasting peace with the French at Montreal in 1701. Claiming neutrality while maintaining their English alliance, astute Onondaga diplomats like Teganissorens labored to restore Iroquois political preeminence in the region. Accepting presents from French and British agents seeking trade concessions or military assistance, they worked to play contending rivals off against one another.

As Covenant Chain allies of the British, they allowed New York authorities to station an agent, interpreter, and blacksmith at their main town more or less continuously from the 1680s to the early 1760s. Permitting the French to build a post at the town in 1711, they then stood quietly by while British authorities, incensed by this intrusion into what they regarded as their sphere of influence, pulled the post down. A second attempt to project French power into the Onondaga heartland in 1715 met with a similar response.

Upholding their end of the Covenant Chain, many Onondaga people secretly supported the British in their wars against France. Refusing to let Albany authorities—who openly flaunted British regulations forbidding trade with the French during Queen Anne's War (1702–1713)—to establish a post in their country, they subsequently allowed Crown officials to construct their own post at Oswego north of Onondaga between 1722 and 1725. Strategically located on the trade route joining the western country with coastal ports, Fort Oswego soon eclipsed Albany as the principal British trade emporium in the northern colonies.

Neither the Onondagas nor the British were able to completely control the Ottawas, Miamis, and other people from western Indian nations who traded at Fort Oswego. Iroquois claims of control over the western nations, and British assertions of dominion based upon these claims, were more symbolic than substantial. Such claims grew even more tenuous as French agents, working with Ohio Indian townsfolk alienated by the activities of unscrupulous Virginian traders, managed to significantly undermine British influence in the region, and both countries drifted toward another war during the 1740s.

Onondaga trade with the western nations finally collapsed when King George's War broke out in 1744. Pro-French Ohio Valley and Great Lakes Indian people traveling to Fort Frontenac or Montreal bypassed Fort Oswego. Increasingly cut off from their primary source of furs and divided by the war, the Onondaga community split along political fault lines.

Most pro-British Onondaga people remained in their ancestral country. The bulk of the pro-French faction, numbering nearly half of all Onondagas, gradually moved with like-minded Oneidas and Cayugas to the earlier-mentioned new settlement of La Presentation, founded by the Sulpician missionary François Picquet in 1749 on the southern shore of the Saint Lawrence River at the mouth of the Oswegatchie River. Located between Montreal and Fort Frontenac on land within the modern city limits of Ogdensburg, New York, Oswegatchie grew from less than a hundred people in 1750 to over five hundred families five years later; most of the immigrants were Iroquois people alienated by British expansion into their territories who now allied themselves with the French.

Although all Iroquois nations officially maintained neutrality during the Seven Years' War (1755–1762), most Onondaga people openly chose sides during the fighting. Many Onondaga warriors subsequently fought alongside Senecas and Cayugas in their unsuccessful bid to drive the British from Fort Niagara after the war ended in 1763. Almost all Oswegatchie Onondagas and more than a few of the eight hundred other Onondaga people remaining at their main town on Onondaga Creek supported the British war effort, despite formal assertions of neutrality when war broke out between Great Britain and the colonies in 1775. Both communities became staging areas for British and Indian border raids. La Presentation townsfolk were able to repel a rebel raid on their town in 1779. Confronted with an entire army a few months later, Onondaga Castle residents could do little more than abandon their town to the torches of American troops.

Many Onondaga people moved to Canada following the restoration of peace in 1783, but an estimated five hundred Onondagas elected to remain in their ancestral homes. Many of these people moved with their Seneca and Cayuga brethren to Buffalo Creek in western

New York during the 1790s. Dissatisfied with conditions there, many of them moved back to join the hundred or so Onondaga people who had refused to abandon their valley. Today most of the people living on the Onondaga Reservation trace their descent to those who refused to leave their ancestral homes.

SOURCES

Much of the material presented in this section has been drawn from Blau, Campisi, and Tooker (1978) and Bradley (1987a). James A. Tuck (1971) has extensively surveyed physical evidence documenting the early origins of Onondaga social and cultural life. Avocationist Robert Ricklis (1963, 1966) also has made significant contributions to the study of Onondaga archaeology. Compilations of information gathered by earlier archaeological investigators may be found in Beauchamp (1900) and Parker (1922).

Publications of direct, firsthand accounts of eighteenth-century Onondaga town life and culture may be seen in Bartram (1751), Beauchamp (1916), and Spangenburg (1879). Particularly detailed journal descriptions of Onondaga towns and countryside devastated by American soldiers during the 1779 Sullivan-Clinton expedition have been gathered together and published by F. Cook (1887). Other sources using significant eighteenth-century European writings on the Onondagas include Aquila (1983) and Graymont (1972).

CAYUGA COUNTRY

Cayuga Country is located in the eastern portion of the central New York Finger Lakes region. Bounded by Skaneateles Lake on the east, Cayuga Country extends westward to the rivers draining to and from Cayuga Lake. It encompasses at its maximal extent an expanse of land stretching from Lake Ontario south to the upper Susquehanna Valley, yet its heart is centered around portions of modern-day Cayuga and Tompkins counties between Owasco Lake and Cayuga Lake.

THE SIXTEENTH CENTURY

Cayuga Country has long been a locale of archaeological interest. As early as 1921, Alanson Skinner (1921) reported that most sites visited during his survey had been heavily damaged by looters or development. Although much has been lost, subsequent investigations conducted by Harrison C. Follett (1946–1947) and a number of local avocationists have since shown that intact deposits survive in many sites in the area.

Scholars analyzing information preserved in field notes and artifact collections gathered by Skinner, Follett, and others have worked to trace the origins and development of Cayuga culture. Using pottery to date and trace relationships between sites in the area, archaeologist Mary Ann Palmer Niemczycki (1984, 1991) believes that Richmond Incised collared ceramics first appearing in unprecedentedly nucleated settlements in the Finger Lakes region sometime around 1350 were made by the direct ancestors of Cayuga and Seneca people. Niemczycki further believes that the appearance of Genoa Frilled wares in early sixteenth-century fortified townsites like Klinko and Indian Fort Road indicates that the immediate ancestors of Cayuga people formed societies distinct from those of their Seneca kinsfolk or neighbors sometime between 1450 and 1550.

Further analyses of these and other contemporary sites indicate that people living in Cayuga Country during terminal Late Woodland times generally lived in one of three related communities. Corresponding to the archivally documented tripartite Cayuga settlement pattern, archaeological identification of this unique residence system further supports suggestions that the Cayuga people first emerged as members of a distinct society sometime in the late fifteenth or early sixteenth centuries (Niemczycki 1984).

More recently, archaeologist Adrian O. Mandzy (1992) has reexamined field notes and site collections to develop a framework capable of organizing and interpreting the archaeological record of Historic Contact period occupation in Cayuga Country. Contrasting glass beads and other European imports found in Cayuga Country sites with similar material from dated deposits elsewhere in the region, Mandzy has developed a systematic chronological sequence.

Mandzy found few artifacts clearly dating to the sixteenth century in museum or private collections. A piece of smelted metal identified as copper or brass found in a refuse pit at the fortified late–sixteenth-century Locke Fort site represents the earliest known evidence of European contact in Cayuga Country. Although Culver and several other nearby sites contain similar aboriginal ceramic and lithic assemblages, Locke Fort remains the only site known to contain European imports associated with the earliest phases of the Historic Contact period in Cayuga Country.

THE SEVENTEENTH CENTURY

More substantial evidence of Cayuga contact with Europeans first appears in early–seventeenth-century deposits preserved at the Genoa Fort 1 and 2 sites. Defensibly located atop a narrow peninsula rising from seventy-five to two hundred feet above Salmon Creek, the unfortified two-acre Genoa Fort 1 site contains post-mold patterns of several longhouses. The adjacent Genoa Fort 2 site encompasses a small area across from the narrow neck of land believed to have been the main approach to the Genoa Fort 1 town.

Substantial amounts of European imports have been found with domestically produced tools, utensils, weapons, and ornaments at both sites. Imports include large numbers of glass beads; a substantial array of iron knives, sword blades, celts, axes, chisels, scissors, saws, and needles; numerous copper and brass triangular projectile points; and a variety of brass and copper tubular beads, tinkler cones, kettles, hawk bells, mouth harps, and fishhooks. Large amounts of tubular shell wampum beads and at least two antler "September Morn" figurines almost exclusively found in graves of small Iroquois children dating to the early–seventeenth-century have been recovered with collared ceramics; triangular, chipped-stone projectile points; and other domestically produced wares at these sites.

Small amounts of European imports dating to the second quarter of the century have been found in Myer's Station, Culley's, and Garrett site deposits. Iron, brass, copper, and glass imports continue to be found with increasingly smaller amounts of native clay, stone, shell, bone, and antler manufactures at each of these locales. Firearms, European white-clay tobacco-smoking pipes, and Jesuit brass finger rings and medals appear for the first time.

Myer's Station is the last Cayuga town known to have been built in a naturally defensible locale. Cayuga people located Culley's, Garrett, and subsequent sites in low-lying, broad, level areas. Graves found at these sites generally contain larger amounts of funerary

MAP 32: CAYUGA COUNTRY

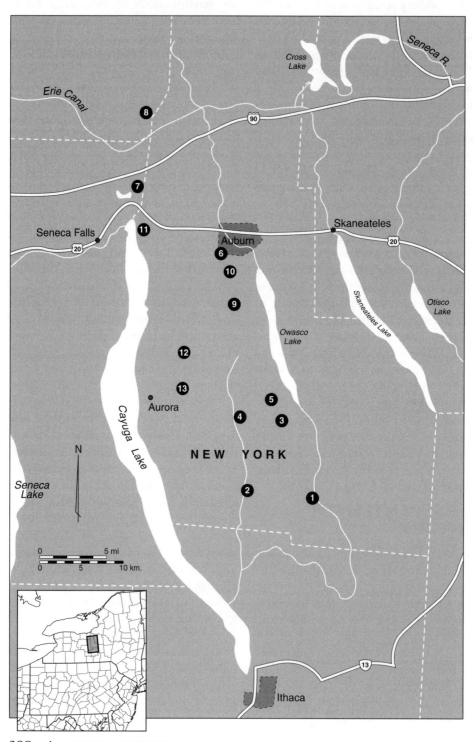

Map 32 Historic Contact Sites

Map Number	Site Name	County	State	Date	NR	Source
1	Locke Fort	Cayuga	NY	1575–1600		Mandzy 1992; Niemczycki 1984, 1991
2	Genoa Forts I and II (NYSM 2169)	Cayuga	NY	1610–1630		Mandzy 1992; Niemczycki 1984, 1991; NYSMAS
3	Myer's Station	Cayuga	NY	1620–1640		Mandzy 1992; Niemczycki 1984, 1991
4	Culley's/Venice	Cayuga	NY	1630–1650		Mandzy 1992
5	Garrett	Cayuga	NY	1640–1650		Niemczycki 1984, 1991
6	Crane Brook	Cayuga	NY	1640–1660		Niemczycki 1984
7	Kipp Island (NYSM 2083–2084)	Cayuga	NY	1600s		Mandzy 1992; NYSMAS
8	Rogers Farm (NYSM 2502)	Wayne	NY	1665–1685		Mandzy 1990, 1992; NYSMAS
9	Mead Farm	Cayuga	NY	1665–1685		Mandzy 1992; Snow 1990
10	Lamb	Cayuga	NY	1665–1685		Mandzy 1992; Niemczycki 1984
11	René Ménard Bridge Hilltop (NYSM 2085)	Cayuga	NY	1670–1690		Mandzy 1992; NYSMAS; Snow 1990
12	Young Farm/Great Gully (NYSM 2093)	Cayuga	NY	1690–1710		Mandzy 1992; Niemczycki 1984; NYAS; NYSMAS
13	Paddington	Cayuga	NY	1710–1730		Mandzy 1992; Niemczycki 1984, 1991

offerings than those placed in earlier interments. The presence of a cemetery plot containing at least one hundred graves at Myer's Station may represent the first evidence of the impact of epidemics known to have ravaged the region during the second quarter of the century.

Cayuga people probably were living at the Crane Brook and Kipp Island sites when French trader Pierre Esprit Radisson penned an account of his travels through the area as an Iroquois captive in 1653 (Radisson in M. White, Engelbrecht, and Tooker 1978). Recalling his captivity, Radisson noted that he traveled through three Cayuga towns located close to one another.

Arriving in Cayuga towns three years after Radisson passed through, Jesuit missionary René Ménard established a mission named Sainte Marie at or near one of the communities. Forced to abandon Sainte Marie in 1658, Jesuits subsequently established more permanent missions at each of the three main Cayuga towns in 1668. One of these missions, Saint Joseph, was built in a town identified as Oiogouen. Meaning "people of the swamp or marsh," the English form of this name, Cayuga, soon came to be used as a general term for the people of the area.

Archaeologists believe that the already-mentioned Myer's Station site, located near marshlands at the headwaters of Salmon Creek in the southern portion of the Cayuga homeland, represents the earliest identifiable location of the Oiogouen community. Although documentation is incomplete, Mandzy (1992) suggests that the nearby Mead Farm site contains the remains of the town occupied by Oiogouen townsfolk when Jesuit fathers established their Saint Joseph mission.

The Saint Stephen mission was established at Tiohero town, a substantial community located along the northern banks of Cayuga Lake. Mandzy (1992) suggests that the René Ménard Bridge Hilltop site contains archaeological deposits associated with this community. Farther north, the Jesuits built their mission of Saint René at the Cayuga town of Onontare. Substantial assemblages of diagnostic European goods found within intact deposits at the Rogers Farm site probably represent the remains of this community (Mandzy 1990). Although it has been disturbed by plowing and amateur collectors, the Rogers Farm site remains the most intact and best-preserved known archaeological locale documenting the Historic Contact period in Cayuga Country.

Deposits preserved at the above-mentioned Mead Farm, René Ménard Bridge Hilltop, and Rogers Farm sites indicate that each was still occupied when English visitor Wentworth Greenhalgh noted that "The Caiougos have three townes about a mile distant from each other" in 1677. Almost all tools, implements, and weapons used by people living in these locales were imported from European settlements. Large amounts of imported glass beads and white-clay tobacco-smoking pipes are found in site deposits. Small amounts of chipped-stone tools and larger numbers of bone and antler combs, wampum shell beads, catlinite beads and pendants, and turtle-shell rattles have been excavated from

most of these places. Although domestically produced smoking pipes still appear in site deposits, aboriginal ceramics vanish from these and subsequent Cayuga Country sites.

Only two sites, the René Ménard Bridge Hilltop and the Young Farm/Great Gully locales, are known to contain deposits dating to the final decades of the seventeenth century. The almost total absence of nonimported artifacts in site deposits found at these locales corroborates written records documenting the general Iroquois shift from domestic production to economic strategies based on more extensive trade, diplomacy, and warfare.

Demographic and social changes speeded this shift in Cayuga communities. Wars and diseases devastating Cayuga communities dramatically affected community life. Cayuga dependency on exports increased as skilled artisans and experienced producers died or moved away. Decreasing population levels also meant that ever-increasing amounts of trade goods, diplomat gifts, and war booty brought into Cayuga communities were redistributed to ever-diminishing numbers of people, and Cayuga townsfolk responded by sharing more and more of their goods with guests, family, friends, and the dead.

European firearms, lead, gunpowder, axes, and knives became particularly prized commodities as Cayuga warriors joined Iroquois compatriots in wars against Huron and Erie enemies. Fighting with the Susquehannocks became so severe that many Cayuga people temporarily moved to the Bay of Quinte on the north shore of Lake Ontario in 1662 to escape further attacks.

Emigration of substantial numbers of

Indian converts who followed the Jesuit missionaries expelled from all Iroquois communities after 1683 also caused severe demographic dislocations. Although the Jesuit expulsion strained French-Iroquois relations, Cayuga diplomats managed to preserve the peace with their Canadian neighbors. Successfully maintaining amicable relations when the French went to war with their Seneca neighbors, Cayuga communities were not attacked when Denonville's column invaded Seneca Country in 1687. Formally maintaining neutrality when King William's War broke out two years later, Cayuga people managed to avoid the attacks that had destroyed virtually every other Iroquois town east of their country by the time the conflict ended in 1697.

THE EIGHTEENTH CENTURY

Little is directly known about eighteenth-century life in Cayuga Country. Living far from centers of colonial expansion, the Cayugas were not extensively described by the few Europeans known to have traveled to their towns before the American War for Independence. Journal accounts, dispatches, and maps drafted by soldiers marching with the American army that devastated Cayuga Country in 1779 pinpoint the locations of Peach Town and other Cayuga communities. None of these communities, however, have been clearly identified by archaeologists. Although many investigators have looked for these and other contemporary Cayuga sites, only one locale, the early–eighteenth-century Paddington site, has thus far been found.

Analysis of Paddington site collections shows that the town's occupants continued to use the same types of imported tools, implements, weapons, and ornaments found in preceding late–seventeenth-century sites. Such findings tend to corroborate written records indicating that the Cayugas entered the eighteenth century with their homes and country largely intact and undisturbed. As mentioned earlier, Cayuga towns escaped destruction during the Iroquois-French war between 1687 and 1700. Signing the peace treaty that ended the fighting in 1701, most Cayuga people remained neutral when fighting between France and England resumed at the beginning of Queen Anne's War a year later. Refusing to openly choose sides in the struggle between the two powerful imperial rivals, the Cayugas instead turned their attention to trade with Great Lakes and Ohio Valley Indian people and war with more southerly Catawba, Saponi, and Cherokee adversaries.

Gradually making a lasting peace with the southern Indians, Cayuga chiefs joined other Iroquois sachems urging their former adversaries to move north. Taking up the invitation, a group of Saponi people subsequently moved to the Shamokin locale in the upper Susquehanna Valley during the 1740s. But they were soon forced to abandon Shamokin as Pennsylvanian settlers poured into the area in the years following the end of King George's War in 1748. Many moved upriver to new towns administered by Cayuga overseers. Formally adopted by the Cayugas in 1753, most of these people had moved to a town just south of Cayuga Lake in the heart of Cayuga Country by 1771.

While many Cayuga people themselves moved south to the Upper Susquehanna Country during these years, the same pressures that drove the Saponis north eventually drove them back to the Cayuga heartland, and by the time the Seven Years' War broke out in 1755, these Cayuga emigrés had returned to the towns along both shores of Cayuga Lake. Other Cayugas joined Seneca and Onondaga expatriates moving west to the Ohio Valley. Known as "Mingos," most of these Iroquois emigrants openly supported the French in the war; Cayugas who remained in their homeland generally fought alongside the French against British forces.

Acknowledging French defeat and responding to British promises that they would abandon the captured French posts following the signing of a treaty in Europe, most Cayuga people made their peace with the British following the French defeat in America in 1760. Subsequently angered by British failure to honor their promises, many Cayuga men joined Seneca warriors attacking British posts at Forts Pitt and Niagara. Failing to take either post, the Cayugas and their allies formally made peace with the British at a treaty meeting at Fort Niagara in 1765.

Like their neighbors, Cayugas generally continued to support their British allies when war broke out with American colonists in 1775. Most took refuge in Fort Niagara after American troops destroyed their towns in 1779. Although some moved to Canada with other Iroquois people when the war ended in 1783, the majority of Cayugas returned to their homeland around Cayuga Lake. Forced to sell their lands in the decades following the war, many of them then moved among Senecas and other Iroquois people settling at Buffalo Creek and other places in western New York. Today most of their descendants live in small communities in western New York, Ontario, and Oklahoma.

SOURCES

Much of the archaeological information used in this section was provided by Mandzy (1992). Other sources describing what is known about Cayuga archaeology include Beauchamp (1900), DeOrio (1978), Follett (1946-1947), Niemczycki (1984, 1991), and Skinner (1921). Information on eighteenth-century Cayuga town life and settlement structure has been preserved in accounts written by Moravian missionaries visiting the country between 1745 and 1766 (Beauchamp 1916). Other information was recorded by American troops led by General Sullivan, who chronicled the appearance of the countryside as they destroyed Cayuga towns and fields during the campaign against the Iroquois in 1779 (F. Cook 1887). A general survey based on these and other sources appears in M. White, Engelbrecht, and Tooker (1978).

SENECA COUNTRY

Seneca Country extends across western New York from Seneca Lake to the Genesee River Valley. It stretches from Lake Ontario south to the headwaters of the Allegheny and Cochocton river valleys. The Seneca heartland is centered around an area bordered by Canandaigua Lake on the east and the central Genesee Valley on the west within present-day Livingston, Ontario, and Monroe counties.

THE SIXTEENTH CENTURY

Archaeological evidence documenting Seneca origins is fragmentary and incomplete. The Genesee Valley appears to have been something of a cultural border during Late Woodland times. People making Richmond Incised collared pottery began living in large, often-fortified towns east of the river sometime during the fourteenth century. Farther west beyond the Genesee, townsfolk using late-stage Ontario Tradition wares similar to those found in western New York and adjacent portions of Pennsylvania and Ontario erected earthen-ringed enclosures and often buried their dead in ossuaries.

Analysts studying mid–sixteenth-century Seneca Country sites like Belcher, Harscher, and Richmond Mills have found evidence indicating that greater numbers of people gathered together in fewer, yet increasingly larger settlements during these years. Discoveries of marine shells from Chesapeake Bay, native copper from the Great Lakes, and other imports at these sites suggest revival of earlier, more widespread economic networks.

Richmond Incised wares dominate ceramic assemblages at mid–sixteenth-century Seneca Country sites. A tubular brass bead and a number of brass and iron fragments found at the Richmond Mills site represent the earliest known evidence of European contact in the area.

Distinctive Seneca-notched and Seneca-barbed collared pots first emerge as dominant wares in late–sixteenth-century Adams and Culbertson site ceramic assemblages. The appearance of quantities of such pots in these deposits marks the beginning of what archaeologist Charles F. Wray has termed the "Seneca sequence." Using diagnostic assemblages to work backward from sites destroyed during the 1687 French

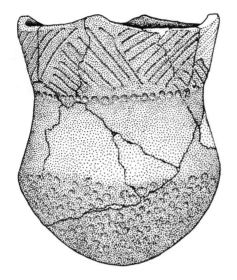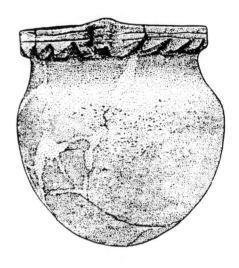

Historic Contact period Seneca-series pots: *left,* a Richmond Mills Incised pot (catalog no. 469/94) from the Adams site (Wray et al. 1987, figure 3-41d, p. 87); *right,* a Seneca Barbed pot (catalog no. 460/41) from the Cameron site (Wray et al. 1990, fig. 7–57b, p. 277). Both illustrations drawn by Patricia L. Miller. *Courtesy Rochester Museum and Science Center, Rochester, New York.*

invasion of Seneca Country, Wray tracked pairs of contemporary sites believed to represent successively relocated eastern and western Seneca towns and their satellites. Wray constantly adjusted the sequence during his lifetime, and his successors, Rochester Museum and Science Center archaeologists Martha Sempowski and Lorraine Saunders, continue to revise it. Investigators widely use this sequence as a comparative benchmark for dating artifact assemblages throughout the region.

The Adams site and the poorly known neighboring but smaller Johnston site are believed to represent the first identifiable western Seneca sequence towns. Culbertson and the small, nearby Alva

Reed site, for their part, are believed to represent the earliest identifiable eastern Seneca sequence communities.

Both Adams and Culbertson contain remains of large, fortified towns. Substantial quantities of aboriginal ceramics and lithics and bone, antler, and shell artifacts have been found in burials, pits, and other intact deposits at both locales. Small numbers of glass beads; copper and brass beads, hoops, and spirals; iron knives and axes; and other European imports also appear for the first time in these sites.

Ceramic and osteological analyses conducted by Saunders and Sempowski (Wray et al. 1987) reveal that certain Adams site burials differ from those

MAP 33: SENECA COUNTRY

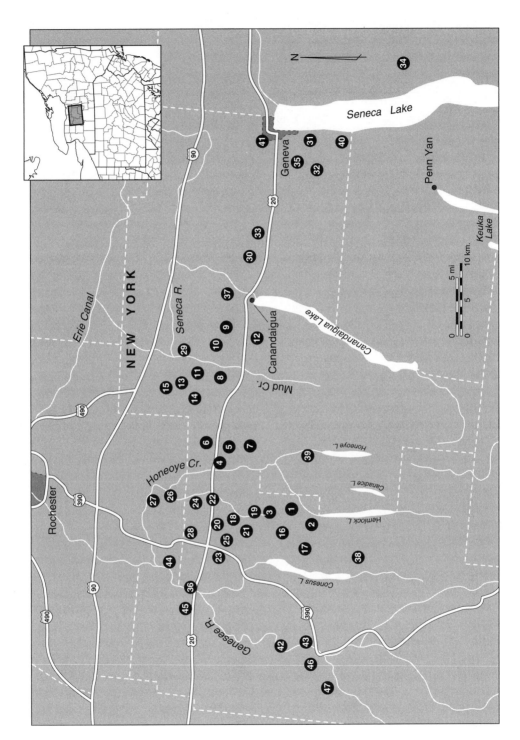

Map 33 Historic Contact Sites

Map Number	Site Name	County	State	Date	NR	Source

Eastern Sequence

Map Number	Site Name	County	State	Date	NR	Source
1	Culbertson	Livingston	NY	1575–1585		Wray et al. 1990
2	Alva Reed	Livingston	NY	1575–1585		Wray et al. 1990
3	Tram (NYSM 1037)	Livingston	NY	1585–1605		NYSMAS; Wray and Schoff 1953; Wray et al. 1990
4	Factory Hollow (NYSM 1023 and 2361)	Ontario	NY	1605–1625		NYSMAS; Wray et al. 1990
5	Conn (NYSM 1028 and 1392)	Ontario	NY	1605–1625		Hasenstab 1990; NYAS; NYSMAS; Wray et al. 1990
6	Warren (NYSM 1025)	Ontario	NY	1625–1640		NYSMAS; Wray et al. 1990
7	Cornish (NYSM 1024)	Ontario	NY	1625–1640		NYSMAS; Wray et al. 1990
8	Steele	Ontario	NY	1640–1655		Wray et al. 1990
9	Marsh (NYSM 1395)	Ontario	NY	1655–1670		NYSMAS; Wray et al. 1990
10	Fox/Wheeler Station (NYSM 1390)	Ontario	NY	1655–1670		Hamell and John 1987; NYSMAS; Wray et al. 1990
11	Bunce Burials (NYSM 1386)	Ontario	NY	1655–1670		Hamell and John 1987; NYSMAS; Wray et al. 1990
12	Hoffman	Ontario	NY	1655–1670		Wray et al. 1990
13	Ganondagan/Ganagaro Boughton Hill NHL (NYSM 1384)	Ontario	NY	1670–1687	X	Hamell 1980; NYSMAS; Wray 1985
14	Beale/Cherry Street	Ontario	NY	1670–1687		Hamell and John 1987; Wray et al. 1990
15	Fort Hill (NYSM 1383)	Ontario	NY	1685–1687		NYSMAS; Wray et al. 1990

Western Sequence

Map Number	Site Name	County	State	Date	NR	Source
16	Adams (NYSM 1030)	Livingston	NY	1575–1585		NYSMAS; Wray and Schoff 1953; Wray et al. 1990
17	Johnston	Livingston	NY	1575–1585		Wray et al. 1990
18	Cameron (NYSM 1019)	Livingston	NY	1585–1605		NYSMAS; Wray and Schoff 1953; Wray, et al. 1990
19	Brisbane	Livingston	NY	Historic		Wray et al. 1990
20	Dutch Hollow (NYSM 1006)	Livingston	NY	1605–1625		NYSMAS; W. Ritchie 1954; Wray and Schoff 1953; Wray et al. 1990
21	Feugle/South Lima (NYSM 1031)	Livingston	NY	1605–1625		NYSMAS; Wray and Schoff 1953; Wray et al. 1990
22	Lima (NYSM 1027)	Livingston	NY	1625–1640		NYSMAS; Vandrei 1986; Wray et al. 1990
23	Bosley Mills (NYSM 1800)	Livingston	NY	1625–1640		NYSMAS; Wray et al. 1990

Map Number	Site Name	County	State	Date	NR	Source
24	Power House (NYSM 1021)	Livingston	NY	1640–1655		NYSMAS; Wray et al. 1990
25	Menzis	Livingston	NY	1640–1655		Wray et al. 1990
26	Dann (NYSM 1022 and 3931)	Monroe	NY	1655–1670		NYSMAS; Wray et al. 1990
27	Rochester Junction (NYSM 1026)	Monroe	NY	1670–1687	X	NYSMAS; Wray et al. 1990
28	Kirkwood (NYSM 1020)	Livingston	NY	1670–1687		NYSMAS; Wray et al. 1990

Post-1687 Properties

Map Number	Site Name	County	State	Date	NR	Source
29	Damasky	Ontario	NY	1687–1710		Wray et al. 1990
30	Snyder-McClure (NYSM 2431)	Ontario	NY	1687–1710		NYSMAS; Wray 1983; Wray et al. 1990
31	White Springs (NYSM 1952 and 2442)	Ontario	NY	1687–1710		NYSMAS; M. White 1967; Wray 1983; Wray et al. 1990
32	Hazlet	Ontario	NY	1710–1745		Wray n.d.
33	Huntoon	Ontario	NY	1710–1745		Wray 1983, n.d.
34	Kendaia Complex (NYSM 4824)	Seneca	NY			Hasenstab 1990; NYAS; NYSMAS; Wray n.d.
	Kendaia I			1710–1745		
	Kendaia II			1745–1779		
35	Townley-Read (NYSM 2440)	Ontario	NY	1710–1745		Hasenstab 1990; NYAS; NYSMAS; Wray 1983, n.d.
36	Avon Bridge (NYSM 990)	Livingston	NY	1745–1779		NYAS; NYSMAS; Wray 1983, n.d.
37	Canandaigua (NYSM 1396)	Ontario	NY	1745–1779		NYSMAS; Wray n.d.
38	Conesus	Livingston	NY	1745–1779		Wray n.d.
39	Honeoye (NYSM 4305)	Ontario	NY	1745–1779		NYSMAS; Wray 1983, n.d.
40	Kashong (NYSM 4328)	Ontario	NY	1745–1779		NYSMAS; Wray n.d.
41	Kanadesaga (NYSM 4347)	Ontario	NY	1745–1779		NYSMAS; Wray n.d.
42	Ohagi 6 (NYSM 3656)	Livingston	NY	1775–1800		Hasenstab 1990; NYAS; NYSMAS; Wray n.d.
43	Fall Brook (NYSM 994 and 1000)	Livingston	NY	1754–1775		Hasenstab 1990; NYAS; NYSMAS; Wray 1983, n.d.
44	Big Tree (NYSM 1008)	Monroe	NY	1775–1820		NYSMAS; Wray 1983, n.d.
45	Canawaugus (NYSM 989)	Livingston	NY	1775–1820		Hasenstab 1990; Hayes 1965; NYSMAS; Wray 1983, n.d.
46	Little Beard's Town (NYSM 2196–2197)	Livingston	NY	1775–1820		NYSMAS; Wray 1983; n.d.
47	Squawkie Hill (NYSM 905)	Livingston	NY	1775–1820		NYSMAS; Wray 1983

encountered at the Culbertson, Johnston, and Alva Reed locales. Examinations of skeletons of women interred in Adams site graves show that many display distinctive physical attributes not observed in skeletons of women buried in Culbertson site graves or men interred in either locale. Late-stage Ontario Iroquois Tradition wedge-rimmed pottery sherds represent a large percentage of the Adams site ceramic assemblage. Few such wares, by contrast,

A "September Morn" antler figurine (catalog no. 5496/41) from the Cameron site. Height: 2 in. (Wray et al. 1991: Figure 7-4g). Drawn by Patricia L. Miller. *Courtesy Rochester Museum and Science Center.*

are found in contemporary Seneca Country locales. These findings collectively suggest that people living in the westernmost major Genesee Valley town of its time had closer relations with people living farther west than with their neighbors at the nearby Culbertson, Johnston, and Alva Reed sites.

Subsequent sixteenth-century sites in the area generally follow patterns identified at Adams and Culbertson. Recent research (Wray et al. 1990) suggests that

Cameron site deposits identified by Wray as remains of the relocated western-sequence Adams town may more properly represent the subsequent site of the late–sixteenth and early–seventeenth-century eastern-sequence Tram site. Whatever the precise affiliation, all known evidence indicates that both Tram and Cameron postdate the Adams and Culbertson sites.

Contemporary deposits found at the poorly known Brisbane site suggest that it may represent a western-sequence hamlet. Amounts and percentages of objects of European origin increase in this and other terminal–sixteenth-century Genesee Valley sites. New types of domestically produced artifacts, such as "September Morn" figurines and brass or copper triangular projectile points appear in deposits dating to these years. Perceived growth in site size further suggests earlier-recognized movements of expanding populations to increasingly larger and more nucleated towns and their satellites.

Whatever the precise chronological placement of the Tram and Cameron communities, locational analyses suggest that most people living in both places were descendants of townsfolk who had been moving their settlements in a northeastern direction down the Honeoye Creek drainage for more than fifty years when Europeans reportedly first began visiting the area during the early 1600s.

THE SEVENTEENTH CENTURY

Reports written by Samuel de Champlain and other chroniclers note visits by Frenchmen like Étienne Brûlé to Seneca Country during the early 1600s. Even so, Jesuit Father Pierre Joseph

Marie Chaumonot's 1656 account remains the earliest extant firsthand description of life in the westernmost Iroquois nation. Subsequent visitors, like French explorers René de Bréhant de Galinée and René-Robert Cavelier, Sieur de La Salle, who traveled along the western fringes of Seneca Country in 1669, and the already-mentioned English traveler Wentworth Greenhalgh, wrote little about what they saw in the Genesee Valley. As a result, much of what we know about seventeenth-century Seneca life comes from archaeological sources or oral literature.

French, Dutch, and English documents mentioning people from Seneca Country mostly chronicle visiting Seneca embassies or comment on activities of Seneca warriors, traders, and politicians. Some of these sources use variants of the terms "Seneca" and "Sinnekens" to collectively refer to the four Iroquois nations west of Mohawk Country. Others use the terms to refer specifically to the Sonnontouan town located in Seneca Country.

Although the origins of the name remain obscure, most scholars generally agree that the name "Seneca" translates as "people of the big hill." Many Seneca people believe that the Boughton Hill National Historic Landmark, in today's Ganondagan State Historic Site, is the locale of the original Sonnontouan town. Seneca people also believe that the grave of Jikohnsaseh is located at Sonnontouan (Parker 1926; R. Robinson 1976). Known as the "Peace Queen" and "Mother of the Nations," she is still revered by Iroquois people as one of the three founders of their confederacy.

Existing written records generally agree that Seneca people belonged to the most populous nation in the Iroquois confederacy. Several sources suggest that they may have represented half of the total Iroquois population during Historic Contact period times. Some written records indicate that the Senecas may have numbered in excess of ten thousand people during the 1600s. Extant archaeological evidence suggests a smaller population—from two thousand to three thousand individuals.

Whatever their actual numbers, hundreds of people living in Seneca Country were killed by war and disease during the 1600s. Like other Iroquois, Senecas struggled to replace such losses by adopting, marrying, or incorporating people from other communities.

Most major seventeenth-century Seneca towns were large settlements encompassing from eight to fifteen acres. A substantial number of these communities were surrounded by palisaded wooden stockade fortifications. As many as five cemetery plots have been identified at individual townsites. Like other Iroquois people, Seneca town residents generally moved to new locales every ten to twenty years. Factory Hollow, Warren, Steele, Marsh, and Boughton Hill National Historic Landmark presently are thought to represent successive relocations of major seventeenth-century eastern Seneca sequence towns. Dutch Hollow, Lima, Power House, Dann, and Rochester Junction, for their part, are believed to represent successively relocated contemporary major western Seneca sequence communities. Although relocation distances varied, general locations of all known Seneca sequence towns indicate that their inhabitants were moving their communities in a northerly direction prior to 1687.

Boughton Hill Archeological Site National Historic Landmark

The Boughton Hill National Historic Landmark is located in Ganondagan State Historic Site in the town of Victor, Ontario County, New York. Extensive archaeological deposits preserved within the Boughton Hill site represent the remains of the Seneca town of Gannagaro. Many Seneca people regard the locale as the site of important events in Iroquois history. Several Seneca narratives associate it with incidents leading to the formation of the Iroquois confederacy. Others state that the site contains the grave of Jikohnsaseh, an influential woman known as the "Mother of Nations" and the "Peace Queen" who helped Hiawatha and the Peace Maker found the League of Five Nations.

Analyses of archaeological materials recovered from the locale corroborate written records identifying Gannagaro as the largest and most prominent eastern Seneca community from 1670 to 1687. It was also the site of a contemporary Jesuit mission named Saint Jacques. Wentworth Greenhalgh penned the earliest known description of the town in 1677. Noting that neither it nor the four other Seneca towns were fortified, he wrote that "Canagorah lyes on the top of a great hill . . . contayning 150 houses."

More extensive descriptions were penned by French soldiers in Denonville's raiding column as they marched through Seneca Country in 1687. The most detailed of these, an account writ-

The view north toward the Boughton Hill site town area from the Ganondagan State Historic Site Visitor Center. Courtesy New York State Office of Parks, Recreation, and Historic Preservation, Ganondagan State Historic Site, Finger Lakes Region.

ten by a man known as L'Abbé de Belmont, described a town called "Gaensara" as

> the famous Babylon of the Tsonnontuans [Senecas], a city or village of bark, situated at the top of a mountain of earth, to which one rises by three terraces. It appeared to us, from a distance, to be crowned with wood towers, but these were only large chests, some five feet in diameter, in which they keep their Indian corn. . . . They had, outside this post, their Indian corn in a picket fort at the top of a little mountain, steep on all sides, where it was knee high, throughout the fort.

Observing that the retreating Senecas had burned the town in front of the invading army, Belmont further noted that the French looted both the town and its cemetery. Archival and archaeological evidence affirms that Seneca people abandoned the site of Gannagaro following the withdrawal of the French column.

Avocational archaeologists have collected large numbers of artifacts from Boughton Hill site deposits. Objects of European origin constitute as much as 75 percent of total artifact assemblages in known site collections. Rochester Museum and Science Center staff presently curate the largest publicly held collection of Boughton Hill site artifacts. Other collections are stored at the Buffalo Museum of Science and the New York State Museum.

The Boughton Hill site was designated a National Historic Landmark on July 19, 1964. In 1970 the site became the first property acquired by New York for the purpose of interpreting the Iroquois role in the state's history. Today Seneca people play an active role in managing, maintaining, and interpreting Ganondagan State Historic Site.

Antler effigy comb representing a man in European dress holding a musket and accompanied by a dog or other small animal. Found at the Boughton Hill site in 1919, this object is presently curated in the collections of the New York State Museum in Albany (catalog no. 74842). Photograph by Jack Williams. Courtesy Rochester Museum and Science Center, Rochester, New York, and New York State Office of Parks, Recreation, and Historic Preservation, Ganondagan State Historic Site, Finger Lakes Region.

Information presented here is abstracted from Hamell (1980).

Much of what we know about seventeenth-century Seneca diplomatic and military life centers around their wars with Europeans and other Indian nations. European sources affirm oral narratives stating that Seneca warriors often figured prominently in Iroquois military operations on the west and south. Often cooperating with warriors from other Iroquois nations, Seneca men scored strategic successes against Wenro, Huron, Petun, Neutral, and Erie adversaries during the middle years of the 1600s.

Other records show that Seneca arms did not always prevail against adversaries. Many Senecas were killed or captured in wars with Susquehannock and Erie enemies. Other Seneca people trying to colonize former Huron, Petun, and Neutral lands north of Lakes Ontario and Erie were driven away by Mississauga and other Canadian Algonquian warriors during the latter decades of the century.

European documents state that captives from as many as eleven Indian nations were living among the Senecas by 1656. Most were adopted by Seneca families and clans. The Seneca nation occasionally incorporated entire communities. The population of one Seneca community, Gandougarae, for example, almost wholly consisted of Huron, Neutral, and other people forced from their homes by Iroquois warriors. Chaumonot, who visited the town in 1656, named it Saint Michel in remembrance of the mission of the same name constructed at Scanoneanrat, the former home of most of Gandougarae's Huron residents. The Fox site (also known as Wheeler Station) contains deposits probably associated with this community. The nearby Bunce Burials, for their part, probably represent the community's cemetery.

Chaumonot further wrote that the easternmost Seneca town, which he identified as Gandagan, served as their national capital. Describing it as a large, fortified town, he observed that it contained no fewer than one hundred longhouses. Artifacts dating to the 1650s found at the Marsh site were probably left by Gandagan town residents.

Jesuit priests returned to establish three missions in Seneca Country in 1668. As mentioned earlier, Saint Michel was built at Gandougarae, the locale of present-day Fox site deposits. Establishing Saint Jacques at Gandagan, the priests erected La Conception mission at the western town of Gandachioragon, which may mean "fields in the valley." The Dann site probably contains the remains of this latter town.

Writing in 1677 while visiting the western Iroquois towns during an interval of peace following the Susquehannock defeat, Wentworth Greenhalgh observed that the newly relocated western Seneca town, renamed Totiakton, "where the stream bends," was an unfortified settlement containing more than one hundred longhouses. Rochester Junction site deposits almost surely contain the remains of this town and the relocated La Conception mission. The Kirkwood site, located five miles south, probably holds the remains of Totiakton's satellite community, Gannounata, "something beyond or behind another."

In 1672 Seneca people living at Gandagan and their Jesuit guests moved to their new town of Gannagaro at the modern site of Boughton Hill National Historic Landmark in Ganondagan State

Park. The Beale site (also known as the Cherry Street site), located near the state park, probably represents the remains of the relocated Gandougarae town and its associated Saint Michel mission.

The Senecas destroyed all of their towns as they retreated from Denonville's raiders in 1687. Returning immediately after the French withdrew, they quickly built less densely concentrated communities along the banks of Canandaigua and Seneca Lakes on the east and the central reaches of the Genesee Valley on the west.

Like other Iroquois people, Seneca families adopted many European tools, techniques, and materials during these years. Substantial amounts of metal implements, European ceramics, glasswares, Jesuit rings and medals, and other imports make up more than 75 percent of total artifact assemblages at Boughton Hill National Historic Landmark, Rochester Junction, and other late–seventeenth-century Seneca sites. Although domestic manufactures declined during these years, Seneca people continued to produce clay and stone pipes, chipped-stone tools, and shell beads and ornaments. While many of these products served utilitarian roles, their near-total absence in household deposits in these sites indicates that most aboriginally produced ceramic and stone tools and ornaments were serving their people as funerary offerings by the end of the seventeenth century.

THE EIGHTEENTH CENTURY

Seneca people still lived far from the expanding European frontier in 1700. Spared the insistent intrusions of settlers clam-

oring for land farther eastward, their distance from colonial centers did not insulate them from other effects of European contact. Like their neighbors, Seneca people had gained and lost much during the preceding century. New tools and ideas brought wealth and excitement to their towns. But such innovations came at a high price. Hundreds of Seneca people died in wars with Susquehannock, French, and other adversaries. Hundreds more died from disease.

Eastern Seneca people continued to live in their new towns along the shores of Canandaigua Lake and Seneca Lake during the early 1700s. Many western Seneca people, for their part, moved south and westward from the Genesee Valley into the Allegheny drainage. Traveling to Montreal from their new towns as the eighteenth century began, Seneca diplomats played major roles in negotiating the 1701 accord with the French that finally brought peace to Seneca Country after more than a half-century of war.

Seneca trappers and traders soon ranged widely through the Ohio Valley and beyond, peddling European wares in Ottawa, Miami, and Wyandot communities. Anxious to avoid involvement in European wars, Seneca diplomats played European rivals off against one another and stayed neutral when Queen Anne's War broke out in 1702. Seneca chiefs worked to manage affairs of displaced Indians settled at their invitation along their southern frontiers from Canasteo to the forks of the Ohio. Although officially neutral, many Seneca warriors secretly became involved in colonial wars or traveled south in search of plunder, prestige, and prisoners.

These pursuits brought a measure of

prosperity to Seneca towns during the early decades of the century, but changing conditions repeatedly challenged their ability to maintain a higher standard of living. Spoils and plunder became increasingly harder to get after Iroquois sachems made peace with the southern tribes in 1722. Peace created other problems. Seneca diplomats could not easily manipulate fears of colonial powers who lived together amicably during the "Long Peace" between 1714 and 1744. French posts established at Fort Detroit in 1701 and Fort Niagara in 1726 siphoned off much of their western commerce. Seneca trade was further threatened when New York authorities constructed a new post at Fort Oswego between 1722 and 1725. Cutting the Mohawks and Oneidas off from the trade in the east, the post also allowed Ottawa and other western Indian traders to bypass Seneca towns in their search for cheaper and better goods.

Responding to these challenges, Seneca entrepreneurs went further afield in search of clients and trapping grounds. Senecas moving around Fort Niagara and the trading post established by Louis-Thomas Chabert de Joncaire soon dominated the carrying trade along the Niagara portage. Business picked up when renewed conflict between France and Great Britain created new economic opportunities for warriors, diplomats, and traders between 1744 to 1748. This boom ended temporarily when French and British traders pushed past their towns to trade directly with Ohio Valley Indians in their own towns following the end of the war.

Many Senecas seeking greater economic and political freedom joined other Iroquois people moving to the Ohio Val-

ley during the 1750s. Often operating independently from Iroquois League councils, many of these people established close ties with the French and their Ohio Indian allies. Known as Mingos, they played major roles in subsequent developments in the Ohio Valley.

No matter where they lived, increasing numbers of Seneca people began building small log cabins in their towns during the mid-1700s. Leaded-glass windows, metal-hinged doors, wooden chests, and other imported furnishings ultimately became commonplace in Seneca homes. Large fields and orchards surrounded their towns. Farm animals —chickens, hogs, horses, and cattle— were raised. Archaeological evidence further corroborates written records showing that many Seneca people were able to afford woolen cloth, silver brooches, glass beads, and other expensive European imports.

International events compelled most Senecas to declare for Britain or France as both powers drifted toward a showdown during the early 1750s. Most western Senecas and many Mingos supported the French when fighting (precipitating a general war) broke out in 1754. Eastern Senecas, for their part, generally threw their support behind the British. Fighting alongside soldiers and patrolling the frontier, eastern Seneca people allowed the British to build, but not garrison, a fort at their town of Canadasaga in 1756.

Many Seneca warriors served in the British armies that took Fort Niagara and other French posts. Others fought alongside the French in defending Fort Niagara and those other posts. No matter what side they fought on, all Senecas were outraged when the British reneged on their promise to abandon the forts at the end of the war in 1762, and many joined other western Indians against the British in 1763. Successful for a time, their inability to drive the British from Niagara and other major posts ultimately forced the Senecas to sign a general peace treaty ending hostilities in 1765 at Fort Niagara.

Most Seneca people supported Great Britain when war broke out with the colonists in 1775. Refugees from other places, like Tuscaroras settling at the locale of the Ohagi 6 site, moved to Seneca Country for protection at this time. When Seneca warriors took part in attacks against American frontier forts and towns, American troops responded by invading Seneca Country from the south and east in 1779. Marching through their lands, these columns methodically destroyed nearly every town and field in Seneca Country.

Although some Seneca people joined other Iroquois expatriates moving north to Canada at the end of the war, most chose to stay in their homeland. Concluding a separate peace with the Americans at Fort Stanwix in 1784, the Senecas were gradually forced to sign away much of their land during the following decades. Today people who trace ancestry to the original inhabitants of Seneca Country continue to live in Seneca communities in western New York, Ontario, and Oklahoma, but many also reside in urban and rural communities throughout eastern North America.

SOURCES

Much of the material presented in this section has been drawn from the first of a projected series of volumes publishing analytic resumes of all known Seneca sequence townsites investigated by Charles F. Wray and his associates (Wray et al. 1987, 1990). The outline of the Seneca sequence is set out in Wray and Schoff (1953) and Wray (1973, 1985). Detailed information on the Seneca towns destroyed in 1687 may be found in Hamell (1980) and Hamell and John (1987). Other information is contained in Mary Ann Palmer Niemczycki's inquiry into the origins and development of the Seneca and Cayuga communities (Niemczycki 1984). Overviews of Seneca culture and history during the colonial era appear in Abler and Tooker (1978), Houghton (1912), Parker (1926), and A. F. C. Wallace (1970).

THE NIAGARA-ERIE FRONTIER

The Niagara-Erie Frontier extends across western New York and northwestern Pennsylvania from the southwestern end of Lake Ontario across the Niagara River to the southeastern shore of Lake Erie. Bordered on the east by Oak Orchard Creek and the headwaters of Tonawanda, Ellicott, and Buffalo Creeks, this area stretches westward across the Niagara and Portage escarpments to the present-day Pennsylvania-Ohio border.

THE SIXTEENTH CENTURY

Substantial numbers of archaeological sites containing ceramic assemblages dominated by late-stage Ontario Iroquois Tradition Neutral-Erie Branch wares have been found in this area. Although most such wares are relatively plain and unadorned, several types of Lawson-series pots have wedge-rim collars decorated with incised geometric designs. These and other Neutral–Erie Branch pots found in this area strongly resemble similar wares found in sites in nearby southwestern Ontario.

Other ceramics found in sixteenth-century assemblages in various locales in this area include small amounts of Whittlesey pottery made by people living in northeastern Ohio, a number of Madisonville and Monongahela pots from the south and west, McFate and Quiggle wares from the upper Susquehanna Valley, and Richmond Incised wares and vase-shaped or effigy-adorned clay tobacco-smoking pipes similar to those more commonly found farther east within the Seneca and Cayuga Countries.

Several sites in this area contain extensive deposits indicative of substantial towns. Many are associated with ossuaries or individual bundle burials. Most known secondary interments found in this area predate 1550. The reported discovery of brass or copper kettles from Gould Ossuary deposits near the present-day Tuscarora Reservation sometime during the nineteenth century suggests that the custom of ossuary burial may have persisted into Historic Contact period (Engelbrecht 1993).

Earthen rings also occur at several locales dating to terminal Late Woodland times in this area. The function and meaning of these rings are presently unknown. Some may represent ritually significant ceremonial locales; others may have been foundations of fortification walls.

Post-mold patterns representing remains of large, stockaded towns containing several longhouses have been exposed in wide-area excavations undertaken at sites in the heart of archivally chronicled Neutral lands in and around Hamilton, Ontario, on the northwest of Niagara-Erie territory. Similar excavations capable of revealing contemporary townsites have not yet been undertaken extensively on the American side of the international border.

Several sites in Niagara-Erie Frontier Country have been reported as Historic Contact period locales. Closer examination reveals that only a few date to the late–sixteenth or early–seventeenth centuries. The rest are either earlier or later or contain fragmentary, unanalyzed, or minimally reported deposits. No objects of European origin, for example, have been found in the mid–sixteenth-century Eaton site (Engelbrecht 1993; E. Hunt 1986; M. White 1961). Simmons site artifacts earlier dated to the late–sixteenth or very early–seventeenth centuries have since been found to date to the nineteenth century (Engelbrecht 1993; E. Hunt 1986). Intrusive human interments discovered at the sixteenth-century Buffum Street site (originally reported as eighteenth-century Seneca burials), have since been found to have been placed there by nineteenth-century Buffalo Creek reservation residents (Engelbrecht 1993; E. Hunt 1986; M. White 1961).

Copper or brass hoops, spirals, and fragments have been found with Late Woodland triangular, chipped-stone projectile points, terminal Late Woodland pottery, and glass beads believed to date to the late 1500s at the Newton-Hopper, Shelby, Goodyear, and Green Lake sites. Marian White (1961, 1977, 1978a) and other archaeologists analyzing differing clusters of attributes in Lawson-series wares found in these sites have identified what they believe are the beginnings of two site sequences. Newton-Hopper and Goodyear site deposits are thought to represent successive relocations of the late–sixteenth-century eastern-sequence community. The Green Lake site, for its part, is thought to represent the earliest known western-sequence community to contain European imports in its site deposits.

THE SEVENTEENTH CENTURY

Written records chronicling seventeenth-century events in the Niagara-Erie Frontier are fragmentary and unclear. Early commentaries indicate that men like Étienne Brûlé almost certainly traveled through the area during the first decades of the century. Other records chronicling Father Joseph de la Roche Daillon's 1626 visit to Neutral towns and Fathers Jean de Brébeuf and Pierre Joseph Marie Chaumonot's travels to the same area in 1640 do not describe communities east of the Niagara River.

French records note that a nation closely aligned with the Neutrals called Ahouenrochrhonons or Wenros, "people of the place of the floating scum," fled to the Hurons after being defeated in a war with the Senecas in 1638. Little more is known about this community. Utilizing scant written records suggesting that the Wenros were the easternmost Neutral people, archaeologist

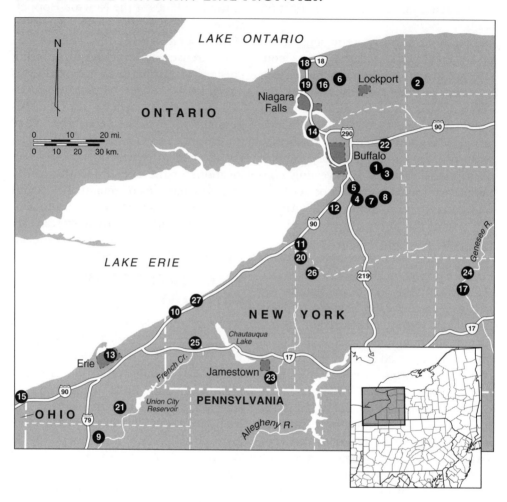

Map 34 Historic Contact Sites

Map Number	Site Name	County	State	Date	NR	Source
1	Newton-Hopper/ Rupp Farm	Erie	NY	1550–1575		E. Hunt 1986; NYAS
2	Shelby (NYSM 2382)	Orleans	NY	1550–1640		M. White 1977, 1978a
3	Goodyear (NYSM 2153 and 6213)	Erie	NY	1570–1590		E. Hunt 1986; NYAS; NYSMAS; M. White 1961
4	Green Lake/Orchard Park/ Yates (NYSM 2105)	Erie	NY	1580–1600		E. Hunt 1986; Hasenstab 1990; NYAS; NYSMAS; M. White 1961

Map Number	Site Name	County	State	Date	NR	Source
5	Ellis (NYSM 2104)	Erie	NY	1600–1625		E. Hunt 1986; Hasenstab 1990; NYAS; NYSMAS; M. White 1967
6	Gould Ossuary	Niagara	NY	Early 1600s		Engelbrecht 1993
7	Smokes Creek/R. Haas II	Erie	NY	1610–1635		Gramly 1993
8	Bead Hill/Crook (NYSM 1711 and 3214)	Erie	NY	1610–1640		E. Hunt 1986; NYAS; NYSMAS
9	Crowe/O'Conner	Crawford	PA	1610–1645		W. Johnson, Richardson, and Bohnert 1979
10	Ripley (NYSM 2490)	Chautauqua	NY	1620–1630		Parker 1907; Guthe 1958; W. Johnson, Richardson, and Bohnert 1979; NYSMAS; L. Sullivan 1992; J. Wright 1966
11	High Banks Complex High Banks Silverheels Burials	Erie	NY	1620–1640		Guthe 1958; Hasenstab 1990; NYAS; Schock 1976; M. White 1978b; J. Wright 1966
12	Kleis (NYSM 2159)	Erie	NY	1620–1640		Engelbrecht 1984; E. Hunt 1986; NYAS; NYSMAS; M. White 1967
13	East 28th Street	Erie	PA	1625–1640		Carpenter, Pfirman, and Schoff 1949; Cadzow 1936; W. Johnson 1993; W. Johnson, Richardson, and Bohnert 1979; Mayer-Oakes 1955
14	Van Son Farm	Erie	NY	1635–1645		E. Hunt 1986; Hasenstab 1990; NYAS; M. White 1968
15	Eastwall	Ashtabula	OH	Early 1600s		Brose 1977, 1993
16	Kienuka (NYSM 2478)	Niagara	NY	1600s		Beauchamp 1900; NYAS; J. Wright 1966
17	Caneadea Complex (NYSM 2798) Caneadea I Caneadea II	Allegany	NY	1710–1745 1745–1820		NYSMAS; Wray 1983, n.d.
18	Old Fort Niagara NHL	Niagara	NY	1720–1796	X	Dunnigan 1985; Dunnigan and Scott 1991; P. Scott 1991
19	Artpark	Niagara	NY	1720–1759		P. Scott 1991; S. Scott and P. Scott 1989; S. Scott et al. 1992
20	Burning Spring Fort (NYSM 2468 and 2863)	Cattaraugus	NY	Contact		Guthe 1958; NYAS; NYSMAS
21	Hemlock Tree (36ER74)	Erie	PA	Contact		PASS
22	Lehde Nursery	Erie	NY	Contact		Hasenstab 1990; NYAS
23	Richard Anderson Farm Number 1	Chautauqua	NY	Contact		Hasenstab 1990; NYAS
24	Ricotta-Winchip (NYSM 2058)	Allegany	NY	Contact		NYAS; NYSMAS
25	Scadden (NYSM 1638)	Chautauqua	NY	Contact		NYAS; NYSMAS
26	30CA3	Cattaraugus	NY	Historic		Hasenstab 1990; Mayer-Oakes 1955; NYAS
27	30CH6	Chautauqua	NY	Historic		Mayer-Oakes 1955

Marian E. White has proposed that Neutral-Erie Branch pottery found in deposits containing two iron tools at the Shelby site locale on Oak Orchard Creek may mark the place as the location of a Wenro town (M. White 1978a).

A map dated 1680 and attributed to Claude Bernou notes that a people identified as Niagagarega located along the Niagara River were a "Nation detruite," or destroyed nation (M. White 1978a). Believing Niagagarega to have been a community closely affiliated with the Neutrals, White and most other scholars believe that both nations were defeated and dispersed by the Senecas and their Iroquois League confederates in or about 1652.

The eastern-sequence Bead Hill and High Banks sites are believed to represent successively relocated towns occupied by Neutral people or their affiliates. Containing diagnostic artifacts dating from 1635 to 1645, the Van Son Farm site on Grand Island is thought to be the cemetery of a still-unidentified town occupied after High Banks townsfolk moved from their community in 1640. Kienuka site deposits also may preserve remains of a seventeenth-century eastern-sequence community.

Other records identify a nation variously referred to as Riquehronnons, Hereckeenes, Eriehronons, and la Nation du Chat ("raccoon nation," from the French for raccoon, *chat sauvage*), somewhere along the southeastern shores of Lake Erie. Most commonly known today as Erie people, they also may have been the Kakouagoga people, who were noted on the 1680 Bernou map at the approximate location of present-day Buffalo, New York, as another "Nation detruite." Extensively reviewing the scant available archival and archaeological evidence, Pendergast (n.d.) suggests that the Kakouagoga may have been among the people known to early–seventeenth-century Dutch, Swedish, and English chroniclers as Black Minquas.

Marian White (1967, 1971) and other investigators have found large amounts of glass beads dating to the early–seventeenth century with Lawson-series ceramics; triangular, chipped-stone and brass projectile points; brass and copper kettles; iron and stone axes, knives, awls, and other implements in pits, middens, hearths, and graves preserved in deposits at what are believed to be the successively occupied Ellis, Smokes Creek, and Kleis sites (Engelbrecht 1984; Gramly 1993; E. Hunt 1986). Contemporary deposits containing similar pottery assemblages have been identified farther west at the East 28th Street and Ripley sites. Even farther west, newly discovered artifacts dating to the earliest phases of contact have been found at the Whittlesey culture Eastwall site on the Pennsylvania-Ohio border (Brose 1993).

Most of these sites contain the remains of substantial towns. Recent work at the Smokes Creek locale, for example, has unearthed post-mold patterns of five or six longhouses within a small, unfortified habitation area (Gramly 1993). Substantial numbers of glass beads, a brass hoop, a cannel coal bead, and some brass or copper triangular projectile points have been found with Erie-Neutral Branch and Seneca-series ceramics in hearth features and a midden layer extending across much of the site.

Whatever the names or affiliations of the people occupying this and other early-seventeenth-century Niagara-Erie

Frontier sites, no diagnostic artifacts postdating 1650 have yet been found in these or any other known archaeological locales associated with earlier Indian inhabitants along the Niagara-Erie Frontier. The absence of later–seventeenth-century deposits corroborates written records stating that Neutral, Erie, and other area residents had been defeated and dispersed by Seneca and Onondaga warriors by the late 1650s.

Senecas and other Indian people are known to have lived around the Niagara portage at various times during the later decades of the century. Recently discovered deposits preserved at the Old Fort Niagara National Historic Landmark may contain remains of one of these occupations.

THE EIGHTEENTH CENTURY

Several sites corroborate written records documenting Indian reoccupation of this area during the early decades of the century. To the east, Caneadea site complex deposits contain evidence of Seneca movements westward beyond the Genesee Valley after 1710. Other evidence of Indian reoccupation has been found at Artpark, the site of the trading post established on the bluffs just below Niagara Falls by Louis-Thomas Chabert de Joncaire in 1720 and at the Old Fort Niagara National Historic Landmark. These deposits indicate that Seneca and other Indian people continued to occupy the area throughout the century.

SOURCES

Much of the information presented in this section has been drawn from the work of Engelbrecht (1991, 1993), Pendergast (n.d.), and M. White (1961, 1967, 1968, 1971, 1976, 1978a, 1978b). Recent studies assessing aspects of White's work have been published by E. Hunt (1986) and Milisauskas (1977).

A general compilation of sources for Neutral archaeology and archival history put together by Gordon K. Wright (1963) contains references to many of the numerous studies of Neutral sites in Ontario. James V. Wright's (1966) general survey of Ontario Iroquois Tradition archaeology continues to be the primary source on the subject. Roy Wright (1974) examines the linguistic evidence for the name Erie.

Descriptions of site deposits from the Burning Spring Fort, Ripley, and Silverheels sites appears in Guthe (1958). Other significant studies include Engelbrecht's (1984) analysis of Kleis site ceramics, Arthur C. Parker's (1907) monograph on the Ripley site, and site reports and histories of Artpark (Scott and Scott 1989; Scott et al. 1992) and the Old Fort Niagara National Historic Landmark (Dunnigan 1985, 1989; Dunnigan and Scott 1991; R. Howard 1968; and Severance 1917).

Old Fort Niagara Historic Site National Historic Landmark

The Old Fort Niagara National Historic Landmark is located on a triangular promontory where the Niagara River flows into Lake Ontario in the village of Youngstown, town of Porter, Niagara County, New York. Located along the international boundary with Canada fourteen miles north of Niagara Falls on the Ontario plain, the site occupies 29.9 acres in the northwesternmost portion of the 284–acre Fort Niagara State Park.

Old Fort Niagara is situated on a bluff rising thirty-one feet above Lake Ontario. A narrow shoreline strip running along the east bank of the Niagara River known as "The Bottoms" lies below the bluff's southwestern margin. Situated in a natural defensive position overlooking both western Lake Ontario and the lower Niagara River, the locale affords a commanding view that allowed post occupants to dominate one of the most critically important strategic lines of trade and communication in North America during the Historic Contact period.

The French first built two short-lived posts at the locale in 1678 and 1687. Establishing a permanent stone fort in 1726, they operated it as a trading post, communications center, and military bastion until they were forced to surrender it to a besieging British army in 1759. Becoming then a major British frontier post, it served as the headquarters of the British Indian department during the American War for Independence. Used as a base by Joseph Brant and other Iroquois warriors fighting alongside the British, the post also became a place of refuge for more than two thousand Iroquois and other Indian people driven from their homes during the war.

Many of these people moved to new homes in Canada when the war ended in 1783. Holding onto the post for a time, the British finally surrendered the fort to the American government in 1796.

Old Fort Niagara was designated a National Historic Landmark on October 9, 1960, under the theme of "European Colonial Exploration and Settlement," being labeled one of the best restored and preserved of America's historic military posts (Shedd 1958). A more recent boundary study notes that Old Fort Niagara contains the most complete collection of extant eighteenth-century military architecture in the United States (Conlin 1985).

Archaeologists conducting test excavations and salvage projects at the locale since 1979 have found artifacts documenting relations between Indian and European people within fort walls, in The Bottoms below the fort, and underwater in the riverbed of the adjacent cove. In Test Units 202–208 in the northwest corner of the fort's parade-ground, incised Late Woodland Iroquoian ceramics have been found in a hearth beneath a thin soil stratum that also contained debitage, stone tools, an early–seventeenth-century Jesuit finger ring, glass beads, and French-Canadian redwares. These artifacts represent the earliest evidence of contact thus far found in Old Fort Niagara. Analysis of the stratigraphic position of these deposits, which extend beneath the still-standing walls of the post's Castle (a two-story stone structure built in 1726) and the stone-foundation walls of a nearby bakehouse, indicates that these test units contain deposits dating to what site archaeologists term the "French trade period" (1720–1726).

Test Unit 352, a square-shaped excavation measuring six feet on each side and also located within the present paradeground, contains the largest and best-preserved assemblage of aboriginal and European artifacts found in Old Fort Niagara. Aboriginal stone tools have been found alongside charred wood, slag, metal scrap, masses of mammal and fish bones, European white-clay and terra-cotta tobacco-smoking pipes, Micmac-style stone pipes, glass beads, gunflints, lead shot, metal triangular projectile points, tin-glazed earthenwares, redwares, creamwares, Chinese export porcelain, scratch blue stonewares, and other materials. Dates derived from analyses of such artifacts found within intact features affirm that they document contact between Indian people and fort personnel from the 1740s to the 1760s in or near a building variously identified on contemporary maps as a lodging, a smithy, and an "artificer's hut."

Artifacts associated with contact between Indian people and colonists completely disappear in assemblages postdating the 1760s in Test Unit 352. This discovery, coupled with findings of artifacts representing later intercultural relations reported at The Bottoms and the adjoining cove, corroborates maps and written records noting that British authorities shifted the focus of Indian contact from the center of the fort compound to places beyond post walls after 1759.

These findings also identify specific locales containing the best-known intact physical evidence of archivally documented trade with Indian people at Old Fort Niagara. Shedding further light on French, and later British, use of the post as a military base, trading post, and administrative center, they materially corroborate written records documenting the ways Senecas and other Indian people regarded the place as a supply depot, a conference center, a refuge, and, on occasion, a military objective.

A local group of preservationists known as the Old Fort Niagara Association began restoring the Castle in 1926. Rehabilitating or reconstructing post buildings, grounds, and fortifications, they opened the Old Fort as a public museum in 1934. Briefly used by the U.S. Army during World War II, the Old Fort was reopened as a museum in 1946. The army surrendered title to the Old Fort to the State of New York between 1948 and 1949. Withdrawing the last military units from the adjoining New Fort Niagara installation in 1963, the government turned all portions of the post but the U.S. Coast Guard station at The Bottoms over to the State of New York in 1964.

Since that time, the New York State Office of Parks, Recreation, and Historic Preservation has administered the entire 284-acre area as Fort Niagara State Park. Park operations are managed by the Old Fort Niagara Association. Working with the State of New York, the association operates an active cultural resource protection and preservation program. Archaeologists employed by the association maintain an on-site archaeological laboratory and storage facility that supports ongoing cultural research and management programs.

Unless otherwise indicated, information presented here is abstracted from Dunnigan and Scott (1991) and P. Scott (1991).

UPPER SUSQUEHANNA COUNTRY

Upper Susquehanna Country embraces the ridge and valley regions and adjacent sections of the Catskill, Pocono, and Appalachian plateaus in present-day north-central Pennsylvania and south-central New York. Stretching southward from the upper reaches of the north and west branches of the Susquehanna, this area extends beyond the forks of the Susquehanna and Juniata Rivers to the Blue Mountain ridgeline just north of Harrisburg, Pennsylvania. Bordered on the east by the Delaware River watershed divide, the western boundaries of Upper Susquehanna Country extend along the uplands separating the Susquehanna Valley from the upper Ohio River drainage.

THE SIXTEENTH CENTURY

Archaeological evidence recovered from various locales in this area indicates that its residents began moving into concentrated communities by the mid-1300s. People making shell-tempered collared McFate-Quiggle ceramics similar to wares produced by potters living farther west in the Upper Ohio and Niagara-Frontier countries lived in communities from the West Branch of the Susquehanna to the Wyoming Valley around present-day Wilkes-Barre, Pennsylvania. McFate-Quiggle townsfolk lived in planned communities of oblong frame houses and semi-subterranean keyhole-shaped buildings. Most towns were laid out in circular arrangements facing a central plaza in a manner reminiscent of Monongahela and other westerly native communities. Many of these towns were further surrounded by palisaded fortification walls.

Farther north, people above present-day Scranton, living in towns laid out like contemporary Iroquois communities, began making shell-tempered variants of grit-tempered Seneca-Cayuga–series Richmond Incised wares sometime during the late 1400s. Known as Schultz-series pottery, these wares are associated with the direct ancestors of the Susquehannock people.

McFate-Quiggle wares and, presumably, the societies of the people who made them, evidently disappeared from the archaeological record just before European imports began appearing in regional sites after 1550. Small amounts of smelted copper scrap, some cold-hammered smelted copper hoops and spirals, and glass beads dating to the late-sixteenth century have been found with Schultz-series wares at the Comfort Station (Versaggi 1991), Engelbert (Beauregard 1991; Dunbar and Ruhl 1974; M. Stewart 1973), MacCaffee No. 2 (PASS), and Murray Farm (Skinner in Moorehead 1938) sites.

All of these locales are situated along a stretch of the North Branch of the Susquehanna between Athens, Pennsylvania, and the Greater Binghamton area in New York. Small amounts of Monongahela ware found at the multicomponent Engelbert site, a cemetery associated with a still-unidentified Schultz-phase townsite, document continuing connections with more westerly people. Interestingly, McFate-Quiggle wares have not yet been identified in these or other deposits known to contain Schultz-series ceramics in the area.

All presently recognizable evidence of occupation disappears from Upper Susquehanna Country at or about the time Schultz-phase ceramics and townsites supplanted Shenks Ferry occupations farther south. Most scholars agree that this southward movement reflects late–sixteenth-century Susquehannock emigration to the lower Susquehanna River Valley.

THE SEVENTEENTH CENTURY

Archaeologists have found little evidence of seventeenth-century occupation in Upper Susquehanna Country. Much of the area evidently became a buffer zone between Susquehannock and Iroquois rivals. Glass beads found with a stone maskette and Susquehannock pottery in a burial at the Ardenheim site in Huntingdon County along the westernmost reaches of Upper Sus-

quehanna Country suggest continuing Susquehannock connections with more westerly Monongahela people.

The Weist site, a small campsite in the Wiconisco Valley above Harrisburg, and the Johnston Farm site, another small occupation area in the Lycoming Valley along the West Branch of the Susquehanna, are the only other area sites presently known to contain deposits clearly dating to the century. An effigy pipe, gunflints, white-clay tobacco-smoking pipe fragments, and lead shot have been found with intact floral and fauna remains in a pit feature at the Weist site. A MASCA-corrected radiocarbon derived from a sample from this pit dates to 1640 (Basalik, Lewis, and Tabachnick 1991). A glass bead and a piece of eight dated 1671 found in Johnston Farm deposits (PASS), for their part, may represent physical evidence left behind by some of the many Delaware, Munsee, and Shawnee emigrés known to have moved into the area following the Susquehannock defeat in 1675.

THE EIGHTEENTH CENTURY

Archival records note that most Delawares and many Shawnee, Nanticoke, Conoy, and Saponi emigrants had joined earlier native expatriates at towns along the lower reaches of the North Branch of the Susquehanna between Shamokin (present-day Sunbury, Pennsylvania) and the Wyoming Valley by the 1740s. Farther north, Munsees, Mahicans, and Tuscaroras joined Mohawk and Oneida immigrants settling in log or bark-covered cabins at Tioga, Ochquaga, Otsiningo, and other multicultural communities between Athens, Pennsylvania, and Oneonta, New York.

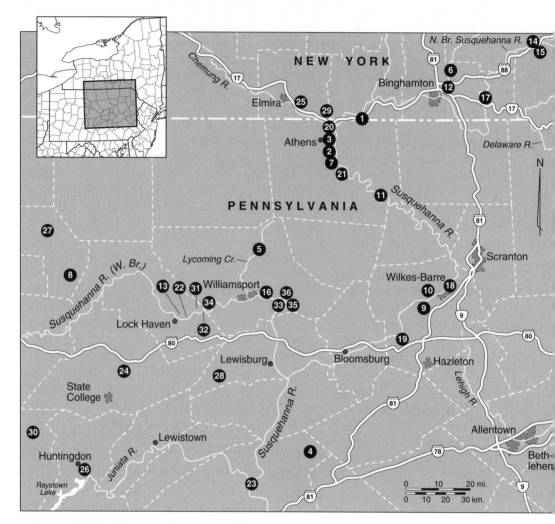

Map 35 Historic Contact Sites

Map Number	Site Name	County	State	Date	NR	Source
1	Engelbert	Tioga	NY	Late 1500s		Beauregard 1991; Dunbar and Ruhl 1974; Funk 1993; M. Stewart 1973
2	Murray Farm (36BR5)	Bradford	PA	1500s–1700s		Moorehead 1938; PASS
3	MacCaffee No. 2 (36BR130)	Bradford	PA	1500s–1700s		PASS
4	Weist (36DA148)	Dauphin	PA	Mid-1600s		Basalik, Lewis, and Tabachnick 1991
5	Johnston Farm (36LY232)	Lycoming	PA	Late 1600s		PASS

Map Number	Site Name	County	State	Date	NR	Source
6	Bowland	Broome	NY	1700s		Funk 1993; Versaggi 1991
7	Nagle Farm (36BR15)	Bradford	PA	1700s		PASS
8	Sinnemahoning 1 (36CM4)	Cameron	PA	1700s		PASS
9	Herold Farm (36LU59)	Luzerne	PA	Early 1700s		PASS
10	Bead Hill (36LU54)	Luzerne	PA	Mid-1700s		PASS
11	Biggin-McCarty (36BR80/81)	Bradford	PA	Mid-1700s		PASS
12	Comfort Station	Broome	NY	Mid-1700s		Elliott 1977; Funk 1993; Versaggi 1991
13	Dunnstown	Clinton	PA	Mid-1700s		Kent n.d.; Kent, Rice, and Ota 1981; Turnbaugh 1975
14	Egli	Chenango	NY	Mid-1700s		Funk 1993; Hesse 1975
15	Lord	Delaware	NY	Mid-1700s		Funk 1993; Hesse 1975
16	Montoursville Complex 36LY17 36LY56 36LY82 36LY83 36LY120 36LY121 (J. T. Roberts) 36LY182	Lycoming	PA	Mid-1700s		Kent n.d.; PASS
17	Ochquaga Complex	Broome	NY	Mid-1700s		Anthony 1991; Moorehead 1938
18	Sarf/O'Malia (36LU3/10)	Luzerne	PA	Mid-1700s		PASS
19	South Wapwallopen/ Knouse (36LU21/43)	Luzerne	PA	Mid-1700s		PASS
20	Tioga Point Farm (36BR1)	Bradford	PA	Mid-1700s	X	Beckerman 1980; PASS
21	36BR41/44	Bradford	PA	Mid-1700s		PASS
22	Great Island (36CN7)	Clinton	PA	1741-1776		Kent n.d.
23	Old Conoy Town	Dauphin	PA	1743-1750s		Kent, Rice, and Ota 1981; Witthoft, Schoff, and Wray 1953
24	Bald Eagle's Nest (36CE72)	Centre	PA	1779-		PASS
25	New Town Battlefield NHL	Chemung	NY	1779	X	NPS 1987
26	Ardenheim (36HU69)	Huntingdon	PA	Historic		PASS
27	Emporium (36CM21)	Cameron	PA	Historic		PASS
28	Gordon (36UN33)	Union	PA	Historic		PASS
29	Sod Farm	Chemung	NY	Historic		NYAS
30	36BL23	Blair	PA	Historic		PASS
31	36CN23	Clinton	PA	Historic		PASS
32	36CN32	Clinton	PA	Historic		PASS
33	36LY25	Lycoming	PA	Historic		PASS
34	36LY72	Lycoming	PA	Historic		PASS
35	36LY80	Lycoming	PA	Historic		PASS
36	36LY111	Lycoming	PA	Historic		PASS

Locations of many of these towns are indicated in contemporary land deeds, military maps, and other documents. A number of these sites have since been found to contain artifacts associated with earlier or later occupations. Others contain single gunflints, musket balls, or beads. Still others are little more than names on maps.

Coins, glass beads, and white-clay

tobacco-smoking pipe stems and bowls dating to the middle decades of the 1700s have been found with gunflints, brass kettles, lead shot, redwares, and other European imports at several locales. Blue-faceted glass beads and two onion-shaped bottles found in three graves at the Bead Hill site near Plymouth, Pennsylvania, have been associated with a documented Shawnee occupation. Contemporary deposits have also been identified at Sarf/O'Malia, Herold Farm, and other Wyoming Valley locales.

Montoursville complex sites around present-day Williamsport, Pennsylvania, contain deposits associated with a multicultural community known as Madame Montour's Village (also known as Ostonwakin or Ostuagy). Other evidence of more westerly Upper Susquehanna Country native occupations has been found at the Emporium site and the locale of the Sinnemahoning Indian town.

To the north, Biggin-McCarty site deposits mark the locale of the large Wyalusing Indian town and its associated Friedenshüetten Moravian mission. Glass beads and a brass triangular projectile point found at 36BR41/44 are thought to indicate Indian occupation of a town variously identified in European records as Ogehage and Newtychanning at the present locale of Towanda, Pennsylvania. Sheshequin town deposits are preserved just upriver at the Nagle Farm site.

MacCaffee No. 2 site deposits located below the modern city of Athens, Pennsylvania, for their part, are believed to contain the remains of Queen Esther's Town. The Tioga Point Farm site located just to the north may contain deposits documenting the large Mohawk-dominated Tioga town at the mouth of the Chemung River.

Farther north, eighteenth-century deposits found at the multicomponent Comfort Station site on the Chenango River above Binghamton, New York, have been identified as the remains of an expatriate Otsiningo Nanticoke community. Several sites associated with the very large multicultural Ochquaga community extend along a three-mile stretch of the North Branch around present-day Windsor, New York. Evidence of the Unadilla community is preserved at the Lord and Egli sites near Nichols, New York.

Missionaries, traders, and military men began to flock to sites like Wyalusing, Ochquaga, and Otsiningo during the 1740s. Moravian missionaries like David Zeisberger and John Heckewelder and Presbyterian ministers inspired by the Great Awakening such as John and David Brainerd moved to Upper Susquehanna towns or established their own communities. Erecting mills and barns as well as churches, they brought goods, seeds, and new knowledge to Indian immigrants struggling to build new lives among strangers.

Thus, new social, political, and religious movements arose as native people searched for ways to adjust to new locales. Regions surrounding places like Shamokin soon became multicultural centers, as Nanticoke, Tuscarora, and Saponi immigrants established separate communities or moved to enclaves of their own within large town complexes. Prophets emerged as nativistic religious revivals swept Susquehanna Valley towns.

Scattered communities of displaced Delaware emigrés tried to organize themselves into a unified nation on the Susquehanna under Sassoonan and other influential leaders. Shamokin, strategically located at the forks of the Susquehanna in modern Sunbury, Pennsylania, was widely regarded as the Delaware capital for a time. Sassoonan, the former Schuylkill Delaware leader recognized by Pennsylvania as the Delaware king, made his home there during the second quarter of the century. Shikellamy, the Oneida viceroy assigned by Iroquois sachems to oversee expatriate Susquehanna Indian communities, also made Shamokin his headquarters during these years. Drawn to the area for the same reasons, Pennsylvanian authorities erected Fort Augusta at the site of Shamokin.

Epidemic disease, intercolonial warfare, rivalries between Pennsylvania and New York authorities claiming the land for themselves, and the westward expansion of European settlement in the years following the end of King George's War in 1748 prevented Delawares from fully consolidating their reconstituted nation at Shamokin. Settlers moving into the area soon forced most Delawares and their Nanticoke, Tuscarora, and Saponi neighbors to relocate. Although many went west, most settled farther north in Wyalusing, Tioga, Otsiningo, Ochquaga, and other towns.

Moravian missionaries established Gnadenhütten, Friedenshüetten, and other missions at or near some of these towns as France and Britain drifted toward war during the 1750s. Prospering for a time, these Indian towns below Tioga were devastated by war parties sweeping through the region after widespread fighting broke out on the Pennsylvania frontier in 1755. Conditions deteriorated as Connecticut settlers claiming the upper Susquehanna for themselves under color of their provincial charter purchased land on the Pennsylvania side from Iroquois and Delaware sachems.

Dispossessed by the Iroquois and threatened with annihilation by Paxton rioters and their sympathizers, Wyalusing and other native townsfolk fled to new homes farther north and west during the 1760s. Those remaining behind often became victims of random assaults, thefts, and murders.

People living farther north and west weathered the storm. A small group of Shawnee people, in company with a number of Delaware, Munsee, and Mahican neighbors, held on at Great Island along the upper reaches of the West Branch of the Susquehanna. Residents of this town, the last known Shawnee community east of the Appalachian Mountains, finally abandoned the place sometime before the outbreak of the American War for Independence.

Otsiningo, Ochquaga, and Unadilla townsfolk living on land claimed by the Iroquois above the Pennsylvania–New York line also held onto their homes during these difficult years. Europeans visiting their towns during the 1760s reported prosperous settlements of log cabins surrounded by orchards, livestock, and fenced fields. More extensive descriptions of these towns were made by the American troops who burned Unadilla, Ochquaga, and the other river communities between 1778 and 1779. Fleeing to Fort Niagara and other locales for refuge, few of these townsfolk returned to the valley when the war ended in 1783.

SOURCES

Much of the documentation for this section has been drawn from Jennings (1984, 1988b), Kent (1984), Mancall (1991),

P. A. W. Wallace (1945, 1958, 1981), and Weslager (1972, 1978a). Eighteenth-century Indian town locations in the area are documented in Donehoo (1928); Hanna (1911); Hunter (n.d.); Kent, Rice, and Ota (1981); Tanner (1987); and P. A. W. Wallace (1965).

Delores Elliott's (1977) survey of written records documenting the changing locales of the Otsiningo community represents the most intensive look at eigh-teenth-century settlement patterns in the area. The Ochquaga community is described in Hinman (1975). Boyce (1987), F. R. Johnson (1967–1968), and Landy (1978) touch on aspects of Tuscarora life in the area. Much of what is known about Tutelo and Saponi occupations along the Susquehanna is summarized by Claude E. Schaeffer in Speck (1942).

UPPER OHIO COUNTRY

Upper Ohio Country stretches across the highest reaches of the Ohio River Valley from the Ohio River north of Wheeling, West Virginia, to the Allegheny and Monongahela river drainages above and below present-day Pittsburgh, Pennsylvnia. This area encompasses northern West Virginia and all of western Pennsylvania below the Lake Erie drainage.

THE SIXTEENTH CENTURY

People making distinctive shell-tempered Monongahela ceramics had been living in large and small towns throughout this area for more than six hundred years when cold-hammered smelted copper and brass hoops, spirals, and rolled beads indicative of European contact first appeared in late-sixteenth-century sites. The occupants of these and later towns belonged to what archaeologists call the Foley Farm-phase of the Monongahela culture.

First emerging during the middle years of the sixteenth century, Foley Farm-phase culture is marked by the appearance of distinctive pottery assemblages and settlement patterns. Foley Farm-phase pottery assemblages are dominated by undecorated, cord-marked, shell-tempered pottery. Small numbers of pots surmounted by "pie-crust" rims and low or bulbous Iroquoian-like collars found in several Foley Farm-phase locales suggest contacts with Ontario Iroquois Tradition and Seneca-Cayuga people on the north and Susquehannock people living farther east.

Occupants of sites containing earlier Monongahela culture components lived in communities scattered throughout much of western Pennsylvania between A.D. 900 and the early 1500s. Foley Farm-phase people, by contrast, concentrated most of their main settlements in a more limited area of southwestern Pennsylvania and adjacent portions of West Virginia. The majority of these sites were located between the lower Youghiogheny River, the middle Monongahela Valley, and the main stem of the Ohio River between Chartiers Creek and the Beaver River.

Foley Farm-phase towns were usually located on hilltop ridges and other upland locales. The larger of these townsites were surrounded by palisade-wall stockade fortifications and encircled by moatlike ditches. The majority enclosed level living areas ranging from one to four acres in extent. Fortifications surrounding the unusual Sony site encompassed some twenty-two acres of land set at an improbably steep angle of incline.

Single or double rings of circular or oval-shaped wattle-and-daub-walled houses have been found at many of these sites; the houses are generally arranged in a circular pattern around an open plaza. Structures containing large numbers of human burials have been found at some sites. Identified as "charnel houses," such structures probably served specific but still-unknown functions. Carbonized remains of corn, beans, squash, sunflowers, and nuts have been found in pits and semisubterranean features identified as storage structures adjoining town houses.

William C. Johnson (1992) has identified at least three clusters of Foley Farm–phase occupation. Howarth/Nelson, Moore/Ola, Spears, and other sites believed to date to the earliest years of Foley Farm-phase occupation cluster just south and west of Pittsburgh. Although Foley Farm-phase pottery occurs in each of these sites, no site is known to contain European imports.

Small numbers of the earlier-mentioned copper or brass beads, hoops, spirals, and fragments were found with Foley Farm-phase assemblages in Beazell School, Fullers Hill, Hartley, Household, Piersol, and Sony site deposits. All of these sites cluster around the lower reaches of the Youghiogheny drainage and adjacent portions of the Monongahela River. Contrasting assemblages from these sites with others in adjacent areas, Johnson suggests that most were probably occupied sometime during the last decades of the sixteenth century.

THE SEVENTEENTH CENTURY

Although the evidence presently is inconclusive, the occupants of most late-sixteenth-century Foley Farm–phase sites probably continued to live at various locales along the lower Youghiogheny and Monongahela drainages until 1615. The Throckmorton No. 1 and Sony sites are believed to be the last locales occupied by Foley Farm–phase people in this area. Throckmorton No. 1 assemblages contain an unusually high proportion of smelted copper and brass objects. An amber translucent glass bead found in a feature excavated at the Sony site, for its part, represents the only artifact of its type found in Foley Farm–phase deposits in this part of the Monongahela heartland.

Proportionately larger numbers of smelted metal artifacts have been found with small, spherical, blue glass beads or large, faceted, star or chevron glass beads in Delphine, Eisiminger/Jesse Lapping, Hughes Farm, Ingraham/Spragg, Lapoe No. 1, Rochester, R. T. Foley Farm, and White/Smith site deposits. Deposits found at the Ingraham/Spragg and R. T. Foley Farm locales differ in significant ways from those found in earlier Monongahela sites. Unlike most of their predecessors, both towns seem to have been completely unfortified. Each, moreover, was built on low-lying terrain. Site deposits in both locales contain the largest known assemblages of European imports thus far identified in Monongahela culture sites. Glass beads; copper or brass tinklers, beads, and discs; scrap-metal fragments; and a cut-out metal

MAP 36: THE UPPER OHIO COUNTRY

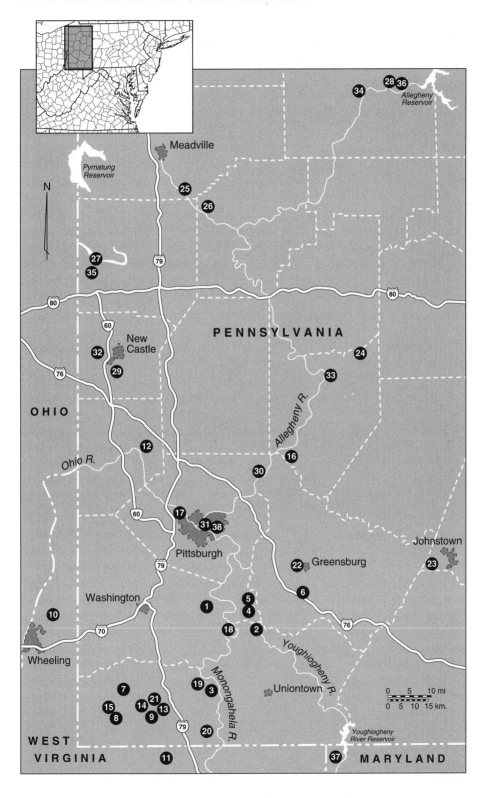

Map 36 Historic Contact Sites

Map Number	Site Name	County	State	Date	NR	Source
				Monongahela Culture		
1	Beazell School (36WH34)	Washington	PA	1580–1615		Gersna 1966; W. Johnson 1992
2	Fullers Hill (36FA17)	Fayette	PA	1580–1615		W. Johnson 1992
3	Hartley (36GR23)	Greene	PA	1580–1615		W. Johnson 1992
4	Household (36WM61)	Westmoreland	PA	1580–1615		George, Babich, and Davis 1990; W. Johnson 1992
5	Piersol (36WM68)	Westmoreland	PA	1580–1615		W. Johnson 1992
6	Sony (36WM151)	Westmoreland	PA	1580–1615		Davis 1993; W. Johnson 1992
7	Throckmorton No. 1 (36GR160)	Greene	PA	1580–1615		Herbstritt 1983; W. Johnson 1992
8	Delphine (36GR37)	Greene	PA	1610–1635		W. Johnson 1993
9	Eisiminger/Jesse Lapping (36GR2)	Greene	PA	1610–1635		W. Johnson 1992; Mayer-Oakes 1955; PASS
10	Hughes Farm (46OH9)	Ohio	WV	1610–1635		Dunnell 1962; W. Johnson 1993
11	Lapoe No. 1 (46MG20)	Monongalia	WV	1610–1635		Graybill 1989; W. Johnson 1992
12	Rochester (36BV80)	Beaver	PA	1610–1635		Alam 1957; W. Johnson 1992
13	White/Smith (36GR16)	Greene	PA	1610–1635		M. Butler 1936; W. Johnson 1992; Mayer-Oakes 1955; PASS
14	Ingraham/Spragg (36GR17)	Greene	PA	1620–1635		Bradley and Childs 1991; Herbstritt 1984; W. Johnson 1992; Mayer-Oakes 1955; PASS
15	R. T. Foley Farm (36GR52)	Greene	PA	1620–1635	X	Bradley and Childs 1991; Herbstritt 1982, 1984; W. Johnson 1992
16	Huffman Farm (36AR329)	Armstrong	PA	Early 1600s		W. Johnson 1993
17	McKees Rocks (36AL16)	Alegheny	PA	Early 1600s		W. Johnson 1993
18	Vesta (36WH26)	Washington	PA	Early 1600s		W. Johnson 1993
19	Bruckner (36GR15)	Greene	PA	Historic		W. Johnson 1992; Mayer-Oakes 1955
20	Donley (36GR60)	Greene	PA	Historic		W. Johnson 1992
21	Varner/John Lapping (36GR1)	Greene	PA	Historic		W. Johnson 1992; Mayer-Oakes 1955; PASS
				Later-17th- and 18th-Century Occupations		
22	Johnston (36WH705)	Westmoreland	PA	1600s		Beckman 1990
23	36CB6	Cambria	PA	1600s		W. Johnson 1992
24	Fishbasket (36AR134)	Armstrong	PA	1700s		PASS
25	Herrington Farm Cemetery (36CW232)	Crawford	PA	1700s		PASS
26	Heydrick	Venango	PA	1700s		Schoff n.d.
27	Stewart Farm/Hitchcock (36ME15)	Mercer	PA	1700s		Mayer-Oakes 1955; PASS
28	Penelec (36WA152)	Warren	PA	Mid-1700s		PASS

Map Number	Site Name	County	State	Date	NR	Source
29	West Pittsburgh (36LR1)	Lawrence	PA	Mid-1700s		Mayer-Oakes 1955; PASS
30	36AL276	Allegheny	PA	1734–1745		PASS
31	36AL303	Allegheny	PA	Mid-1700s		PASS
32	Chambers (36LR11)	Lawrence	PA	1748–1778		McConnell 1992a; PASS; Zakucia 1957
33	36AR12	Armstrong	PA	1751–1770		PASS
34	Buckahloons Park (36WA132)	Warren	PA	1700s		W. Johnson 1992; PASS
35	Denzinger 15/Margargee Run 1 (36ME200/202)	Mercer	PA	Historic		PASS
36	Ellsworth Hale (36WA294)	Warren	PA	Historic		W. Johnson 1992; PASS
37	Friendsville	Garret	MD	Historic		MacCord 1989a
38	31st Street Burial (36AL308)	Allegheny	PA	Historic		PASS

figure "salamander" beaver effigy have been found with shell-tempered ceramics and triangular, chipped-stone projectile points in pits, midden layers, and living floors.

Structural floor plans uncovered at these sites also differ from those found in most earlier locales. Large circular "flower petal" structures similar to two found at the Sony site have been excavated in the plazas of both sites. Semisubterranean teardrop-shaped structures extend beyond the tip of each structural "petal."

Unlike similar semisubterranean features found in earlier sites, these do not contain carbonized plant remains or other deposits suggestive of food storage. The location of these buildings within formerly clear plaza spaces suggests ceremonial functions; discoveries of fire-cracked rocks within otherwise immaculately clean semisubterranean features indicate that they may have served community members as sweat lodges.

Foreign imports continue to make up a very small percentage of total artifact assemblages found in these and other terminal Foley Farm–phase sites. Almost all such imports occur in funerary contexts as offerings or adornment. Metal hoops and spirals are found almost exclusively in graves of children. Several cut-brass "salamander" beaver effigies—resembling others found farther northeast in the Cornish and Feugle sites in Seneca Country, in the Cameron site in Oneida Country, and in Clover and other contemporary Fort Ancient site deposits farther west—also appear in early–seventeenth-century Monongahela site deposits. Several objects of this type initially reported as coming from the Eisiminger site have since been found to have been recovered from Ingraham/Spragg site deposits.

Other aspects of material culture appear little changed in these sites. Most people living here continued to use Late Woodland techniques to produce stone, wood, antler, horn, shell, and bone tools, implements, weapons, and ornaments. A carved antler ladle and several bone combs found in Ingraham/Spragg site deposits suggest continuing contacts with more easterly Iroquoian-speaking people. Discoveries of whelk shells further document contacts with Susquehannock or Luray-phase people on the east and Neutral-Erie Branch Ontario

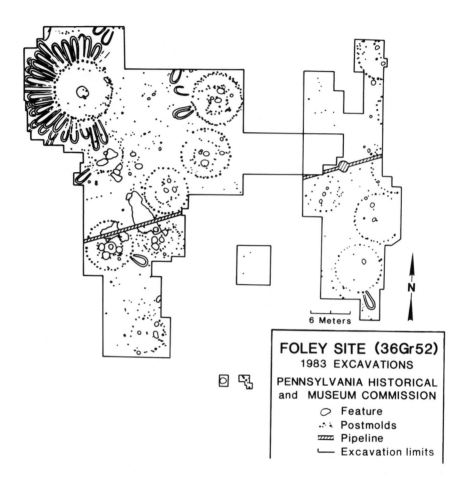

Plan view of the 1983 R. T. Foley Farm site excavations. *Courtesy State Museum of Pennsylvania, Pennsylvania Historical and Museum Commission.*

Iroquois Tradition people farther north. Distinctive conch-shell "ear spools," believed to have been produced by native people only during the late-sixteenth or early-seventeenth centuries, also have been found at several of these sites.

Iroquois pots and clay acorn or apple-ring tobacco-smoking pipes produced elsewhere only during the early-seventeenth century have been found in a number of terminal Foley Farm–phase lo-

cales. Such artifacts represent the only evidence of Historic Contact period occupation thus far found at the Foley Farm–phase Huffman Farm, McKees Rocks, and Vesta sites. Discoveries of pedestaled Madisonville pots at the early-seventeenth-century Vesta and R. T. Foley Farm sites, for their part, indicate continuing contacts with contemporary native communities farther north and west.

These and other terminal Foley Farm–

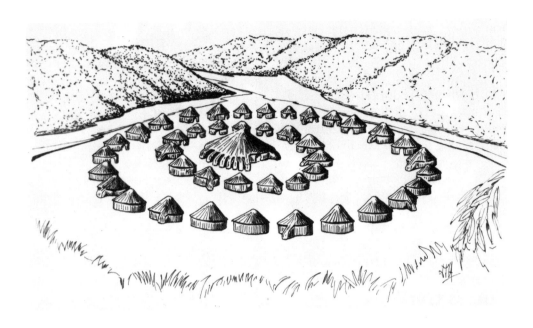

Reconstruction drawing of the R. T. Foley Farm site. Drawing by James Herbstritt. *Courtesy State Museum of Pennsylvania, Pennsylvania Historical and Museum Commission.*

phase sites cluster in Greene County, Pennsylvania, and adjacent areas of West Virginia south and west of earlier Monongahela-culture site concentrations. This shift occurred at a time when Neutrals, Senecas, and other people living in the westernmost reaches of the Trans-Appalachian region were evidently moving settlements farther from one another. The southwestward movement of Foley Farm occupations at this time may represent a Monongahela response to significant political, economic, social, and biological changes affecting people throughout the region during the early decades of the seventeenth century.

Analyses of the scant and equivocal documentary sources presently known for this area suggest that the occupants of terminal Foley Farm–phase towns probably were the powerful and pros-

perous people known to Virginian Indians as Massawomecks (Pendergast 1991a). Dutch and Swedish colonists probably knew them as Black Minquas. They may also be the Attiouandaron people noted on French maps as living midway between Lake Erie and the upper Ohio Valley (W. Johnson 1992). Johnson further suggests that people living farther north at the Sony, Piersol, and Household sites in Westmoreland County, for their part, may have been Heereckeen people identified in 1632 as living "three days' journey" beyond the Massawomecks.

Whatever the names of their towns or tribes, all Monongahela people disappeared after 1635. References dating from the 1640s and 1650s to people from the west moving into Virginian Piedmont Country may document the wanderings of some Monongahela expatriates. Sudden appearances of undecorated, cord-marked wares in Strickler site deposits dating from 1645 to 1665, for their part, may represent material corroboration of contemporary written references to movements of Black Minquas among the Susquehannocks.

Archaeologists have discovered several gunflints evidently knapped from triangular projectile points at a small campsite at the Johnston site near Greensburg, Pennsylvania (Beckman 1990). Little other unequivocal evidence of seventeenth-century Indian occupation has thus far been found in Upper Ohio Country.

THE EIGHTEENTH CENTURY

Discoveries of glass beads, white-clay tobacco-smoking pipes, musket locks and gun parts, gunflints, lead shot, and other European imports in sites throughout western Pennsylvania reflect documented movements of Delaware, Shawnee, Mingo, and other displaced native emigrés to the area during the middle decades of the eighteenth century.

A number of sites associated with these communities have been found. Extensive deposits associated with the large Kuskuskies Indian town have been located at the Chambers site. The Penelec site contains deposits documenting the Kananouagon town noted there in 1749. The 31st Street Burial and 36AL303 sites in Pittsburgh are believed to be parts of Shannopin's town at the forks of the Ohio.

Farther north, the Denzinger 15/Margargee Run 1 site contains deposits associated with the large town of Pymatuning. The Herrington Farm Cemetery, for its part, contains graves of people from nearby Custaloga's Town. Deposits associated with Seneca and other Iroquois people moving southwest into the region have been discovered farther up the Allegheny River at Buckhaloons Park, Fishbasket, Heydrick, and other locales.

Resisting European expansion into the area during the 1750s, most native people living in these and other Upper Ohio Country communities were finally forced to move farther west by the end of the American War for Independence. Although people tracing descent to Indian ancestors live throughout eastern North America, few make their homes in the upper Ohio Valley today.

SOURCES

William C. Johnson (1992, 1993) has provided the Monongahela data abstracted above. Documentation on Massawomeck identity and western Pennsylvanian whelk-shell trade is drawn from Pendergast (1991a, 1992a). Much of the substantial archival record of eighteenth-century expatriate Indian life in the area is analyzed in such sources as G. Dowd (1992), Downes (1940), and R. White (1992) and is mapped by Donehoo (1928); Hanna (1911); Hunter (n.d.); Kent, Rice, and Ota (1981); Tanner (1987); and P. A. W. Wallace (1965).

EUROPEAN-INDIAN CONTACT IN THE TRANS-APPALACHIAN REGION

THE SIXTEENTH CENTURY

Although Europeans traveled to the lower Saint Lawrence Valley and adjacent sections of the Atlantic coast during the sixteenth-century, none are known to have visited the Trans-Appalachian region at that time. Objects of European origin found in sites dating from the 1500s in this region are thus thought to represent evidence of indirect rather than direct contact with French, Basque, English, and other voyagers.

THE SEVENTEENTH CENTURY

Few of the hundreds of thousands of European settlers moving to Atlantic shores during the seventeenth century penetrated far beyond the easternmost fringes of the region. Even so, numbers of European explorers, missionaries, soldiers, and government officials traveled through eastern portions of Trans-Appalachia at various times during the 1600s. Only a few remained for more than a short time. Dutch explorations periodically penetrated the Trans-Appalachian frontier during this period. Examples are Kleyntie's 1614 expedition into the eastern portion of the region, Pieter Barentsz's diplomatic mission to Mohawk Country to reestablish the peace broken by Fort Orange commander van Crieckenbeeck's ill-fated support of the Mahicans in 1626, and the 1634-1635 mission to Mohawk and Oneida towns chronicled in a journal attributed to van den Bogaert. Later on, ethnic Dutch traders like Johannes Rooseboom pressed English trade interests deeper into the region and beyond.

Dutch traders generally limited their contacts to forts and posts situated along the eastern margin of the region at places like Fort Orange and Schuyler Flatts. French colonists made several abortive attempts to establish missions and forts in Iroquois territory. Rogers Farm is only one of several sites believed to preserve remains of Jesuit settlements established in the Iroquois heartland. Old Fort Niagara National Historic Landmark, for its part, is located at the site of the first short-lived French posts in the area, La Salle's Fort Conti (1678) and Fort Denonville (1687-1688).

English officials also were unable to establish permanent posts within the heartland of their Iroquois allies during the seventeenth century. Albany traders like Rooseboom and the French Huguenot

Arnout Viele began to travel west across the region to Upper Ohio Country during the final decades of the 1600s. During that time, small numbers of English settlers moving westward from the coast also began to purchase and settle territory along the extreme eastern and southern fringes of the region. Established along the lower reaches of the Mohawk and Susquehanna Rivers, these settlements would soon serve as jumping-off points for colonists moving deeper into the region during the first decades of the 1700s.

THE EIGHTEENTH CENTURY

FRENCH-INDIAN CONTACT

French authorities mounted repeated efforts to extend influence into the region. Jesuit and Sulpician missionaries proselytized widely in Iroquois communities. French traders peddled their wares and established posts near western Iroquois towns. French governors tried to flatter Iroquois leaders and gave gifts to draw them into their interest.

These efforts met with uneven success. Missionaries often won large followings in Iroquois towns, but Iroquois leaders alarmed by such successes repeatedly ordered priests to leave their territories. Proselytes left behind frequently formed themselves into pro-French political factions, factions that ultimately split many communities. Large numbers of Mohawk converts subsequently resettled at Caughnawaga. As many as one-half of all Onondaga people, for their part, moved to La Presentation when Father Picquet established his post at the mouth of the Oswegatchie River in 1749.

French traders—the coureurs de bois who traveled widely through the region—also encountered some success among western Iroquois people. Many of these traders served as French agents. Others, like Martin Chartier and James Le Tort, served themselves. One of these men, a former captive named Louis-Thomas Chabert de Joncaire, who was raised by a Seneca family, attained a high degree of influence among the Senecas during the last decades of the seventeenth century. Joncaire was especially successful in keeping many Senecas out of the fighting during King William's (1689-1697) and Queen Anne's (1702-1713) wars. He later built a trading post at the base of the Niagara escarpment, just below Niagara Falls, in 1720. This post, the only French settlement in the area until 1726, was maintained by the French until 1759. Drawn to the strategic locale, French troops soon built the bastion of Fort Niagara six miles downstream from Joncaire's post at the mouth of the Niagara River on the shores of Lake Ontario. Traders and diplomats traveling out from these posts extended French influence throughout the Great Lakes and the Ohio Valley.

Administrators encountered less success in their efforts to project French authority. Repeated efforts to build posts in Iroquois towns met with failure. Diplomatic gifts and flattery brought promises of support from many Iroquois leaders, but only the Catholic Iroquois living in New France openly helped the French in their subsequent wars against the British.

Unable to build forts in the Iroquois heartland, French authorities struggled to outflank the Iroquois by erecting Forts Niagara, Frontenac, Saint Frederic,

MAP 37: TRANS-APPALACHIAN EUROPEAN-INDIAN CONTACT SITES

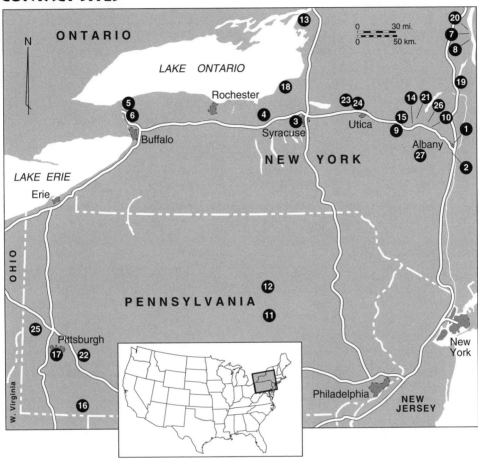

Map Number	Site Name	County	State	Date	NR	Source

Dutch-Indian Contact

Map Number	Site Name	County	State	Date	NR	Source
1	Schuyler Flatts NHL (NYSM 1631)	Albany	NY	1643–1664	X	Huey 1985
2	Fort Orange NHL (NYSM 7645)	Albany	NY	1624–1664	X	Huey 1988; Peña 1990

French-Indian Contact

Map Number	Site Name	County	State	Date	NR	Source
3	Ste. Marie de Gannentaha	Onondaga	NY	1656–1658		Connors, DeAngelo, and Pratt 1980
4	Rogers Farm (NYSM 2502)	Wayne	NY	1668–1682		Mandzy 1990
5	Old Fort Niagara NHL	Niagara	NY	1720–1759	X	Dunnigan 1985; Dunnigan and Scott 1991; P. Scott 1991

Map 37 Historic Contact Sites—*Continued*

Map Number	Site Name	County	State	Date	NR	Source
6	Artpark	Niagara	NY	1720-1759		P. Scott 1991; S. Scott and P. Scott 1989; S. Scott et al. 1992
7	Fort St. Frederic NHL	Essex	NY	1731-1760	X	NPS 1987
8	Fort Ticonderoga NHL	Essex	NY	1755-1762	X	NPS 1987

Anglo-Indian Contact

Map Number	Site Name	County	State	Date	NR	Source
1	Schuyler Flatts NHL (NYSM 1631)	Albany	NY	1664-1759	X	Huey 1974, 1985b
2	Fort Orange NHL (NYSM 7645)	Albany	NY	1664-1676	X	Huey 1988a; Peña 1990
9	Fort Plain Cemetery	Montgomery	NY	1600s		MDSI
10	Fort Hunter	Montgomery	NY	1711-1781		Moody and Fisher 1989
11	Fort Augusta (36NB71)	Northumberland	PA	Mid-1700s		PASS
12	Fort Brady (36LY23/196)	Lycoming	PA	Mid-1700s		PASS
13	Fort Haldimand	Jefferson	NY	Late 1700s		Bohn 1989
14	Fort Johnson NHL	Montgomery	NY	1749-	X	NPS 1987
15	Fort Klock NHL	Montgomery	NY	1750-	X	NPS 1987
16	Fort Necessity NB	Fayette	PA	1754	X	NPS 1987
17	Fort Duquesne/Pitt (36AL91)	Allegheny	PA	1755-		PASS
18	Fort Ontario	Oswego	NY	1755-1796		Workmaster 1969
8	Fort Ticonderoga NHL	Essex	NY	1755-1779	X	NPS 1987
19	Fort Gage	Warren	NY	1758		Feister and Huey 1985
5	Old Fort Niagara NHL	Niagara	NY	1759-1796	X	Dunnigan 1985; Dunnigan and Scott 1991; P. Scott 1991
20	Fort Crown Point NHL	Essex	NY	1760-1777	X	NPS 1987
21	Johnson Hall NHL	Montgomery	NY	1763-	X	Goring 1981; NPS 1987
22	Bushy Run Battlefield NHL	Westmoreland	PA	1763	X	NPS 1987
23	Fort Stanwix NHL	Oneida	NY	1768-	X	NPS 1987
24	Oriskany Battlefield NHL	Oneida	NY	1777	X	NPS 1987
25	Fort McIntosh (36BV147)	Beaver	PA	1778-		PASS
26	Guy Park Manor/ Claus Mansion	Montgomery	NY	Late 1700s		MDSI
27	Old Stone Fort	Schoharie	NY	1700s		MDSI

Carillon (at Ticonderoga), and other posts along their frontiers. French agents attempted to use these posts as bases to draw Iroquois people into their sphere of influence, but in the end, their efforts failed. The French never were able to outdo the British in the quantity or quality of their goods. Moreover, the efforts of British diplomats such as William Johnson and Conrad Weiser kept most Iroquois loyal to the Crown.

French inability to secure significant Iroquois support in their war against the British in 1755 was a major factor in their defeat. Achieving successes at the beginning of the war, French troops found themselves unable to stop subsequent British columns from advancing on their forts. Promised by the British that they would demolish and abandon captured posts, many Iroquois warriors joined the British armies and were instrumental in securing the surrender of the French posts, the last of which fell in 1760. The French were forced to cede New France to the British under the terms of the Treaty of Paris in 1763.

Substantial amounts of archival and archaeological research have been devoted to developing fuller knowledge of the posts erected on the borders of the region during the eighteenth century. Archival research to date has documented many aspects of French life at these posts; this research also has documented the conduct of Indian diplomacy and trade in the area. The posts have also been subjected to intensive archaeological inquiry. Much has been learned about their building history, military architecture, and layout, but until recently, almost nothing was known about the archaeology of Indian life at the posts. Now excavations at Old Fort Niagara National Historic Landmark have found the first known physical evidence of Indian relations with Europeans within that post. Some of this material predates the construction of the main fortification in 1726, and analysis of these materials promises to shed new light into Indian relations at the French posts of the period.

ANGLO-INDIAN CONTACT

Anglo-Americans generally enjoyed greater success among the Iroquois than did their French rivals. The Covenant Chain alliance established during the seventeenth century continued to bind both peoples together in the new century. English diplomats maintained their friendship while their goods circulated through Indian towns. Yet even the English could not establish a permanent post within the Iroquois heartland until Mohawk chiefs finally allowed New York authorities to erect a post at Fort Hunter in 1712 to protect their towns from French attack.

Fulfilling their promise to protect the Mohawk towns, British authorities also used the new post to project influence throughout the region. Traders began traveling west from Albany, though most New Yorkers preferred to let native people come to their posts. With the coming of peace in 1701, Ottawa, Miami, and other, more westerly Indian people began to visit these posts in increasing numbers. Eager to gain direct access to this trade, Pennsylvanian, Maryland, and Virginian frontiersmen traveled west to Ohio Valley Indian towns during the middle years of the century.

During the 1700s, contending commercial interests vied for control of the trade much as they had during the preceding century. French agents and many Iroquois traders did their best to discourage western Indian people from traveling to Albany. Determined to overcome such obstacles and anxious to gain more direct access to western trade routes, New York authorities erected Fort Oswego on the southern banks of Lake Ontario in 1722. The fort soon became the center of the northern British fur trade. Its isolated location and vulnerability to French attack, however, prevented it from becoming a center for British expansion into the region.

The Iroquois succeeded in limiting British expansion to the lower Mohawk and Susquehanna Valleys until the onset of the Seven Years' War when British troops and colonial settlers erected a chain of forts along the Appalachian foothills. Meant to protect their settlements from Indian and French attack, the chain ran from Forts Oswego and Stanwix in the north to Forts Chiswell, Dinwiddie, and Fauquier in the south.

Recovering from a series of defeats suffered at the beginning of the war, British forces subsequently captured and occupied all French posts on the west of the Iroquois heartland. Seneca and other western Iroquois warriors tried to drive the British from posts on their frontiers during the later, widespread struggle commonly known as Pontiac's War—and enjoyed some success for a time. However, their ultimate failure forced the Iroquois to accept the British military occupation of the western posts and acquiesce to a new general demarcation line between their territories and those of the eastern colonies at the Treaty of Fort Stanwix in 1768.

By the end of Pontiac's War the Trans-Appalachian frontier was ringed by British posts. Much of the Iroquois borderlands, so laboriously protected during the earlier years of the century, soon fell from their hands. By 1770, all but the uppermost branches of the Susquehanna along the eastern border was under British control. Farther west, the upper Ohio Valley around the forks of the Ohio was occupied by British troops, and settlers poured across the Cumberland Gap into Kentucky from Virginia. Yet few British settlers were living within the Iroquois heartland west of the 1768 demarcation line when war broke out between Great Britain and rebellious colonists in 1775.

Neither belligerent built new posts in the heart of Iroquoia during the American War for Independence. Instead, existing forts, like Fort Niagara, which became a haven for Iroquois continuing to support their old Covenant Chain allies, were strengthened and used to support military efforts and further Indian policies. American troops used posts like Fort Stanwix, rechristened Fort Schuyler during the war, to project influence into Iroquois country. Although the easternmost of these posts were surrendered to the Americans when the conflict ended, more westerly posts like Fort Niagara were not given up until 1796.

Like the French, British and American troops could raid but not occupy the Iroquois heartland during most of the eighteenth century. But the Iroquois eventually had to accede. Many did not return to their homes when the war ended in 1783; some moved west; those who remained were forced to sell their land and live on reservations. In the end, Americans found it more expedient to use business offices than forts to take Iroquois lands.

SOURCES

Indian-European relations in the region during the seventeenth century are summarized in Heidenreich (1971), Jennings (1984), Kent (1984), Trelease (1960), and Trigger (1978a, 1980). Information on the physical evidence of this encounter is summarized in Huey (1988a) and Peña (1990). A substantial body of literature documents Anglo-Iroquois relations.

Among the more prominent of these are Aquila (1983), Downes (1940), Graymont (1972), Jennings (1984, 1988b), McConnell (1992b), Richter (1992), Trigger (1978a), and R. White (1992).

A large number of archaeological sites contain deposits associated with European-Indian relations. Many of these are military or trade forts. Information illuminating various aspects of political, social, and economic relationships centering around these posts has been unearthed at the Fort Orange and Old Fort Niagara National Historic Landmarks. Other posts possess the potential to reveal further information.

CONSPECTUS

As the foregoing pages show, ethnographers, archaeologists, historians, and other scholars have made much progress in the forty years since William Fenton (1957) called for the ethnohistorical study of relations between Indian people and colonists in the Northeast. Many of the goals set by Fenton have since been realized. A system of regular interdisciplinary conferences and seminars, for example, has been put in place. Special study centers like the D'Arcy McNickle Center for the History of the American Indian, established with Fenton's help during the 1970s, have become major focal points for ethnohistorical research. Many of the projects called for, like the study of intercultural relations in New England and the examination of the Iroquois impact on American history, are now well under way.

These and other projects have revealed a great deal of new information on a wide variety of topics summarized in the preceding pages. Voices long still or never heard have found an audience. Much is now known about certain people, places, and periods. Vast amounts of archival and archaeological documentation recording many aspects of Iroquois life, for example, have been concentrated in several repositories. Much has also been learned about native Northeastern settlement patterns, technology, diplomacy, exchange, warfare, and social structure.

Although a good start has been made, much remains to be done. Greater attention needs to be placed on still poorly documented aspects of family, community, and spiritual life. Much more needs to be known about past and present Indian viewpoints on Historic Contact period issues and events. Although studies like those at the Lighthouse site in Connecticut reveal the potential in sites documenting African-Indian contact relations, far more needs to be done in this area as well. Increasing emphasis also needs to be directed toward more effective ways of interpreting meaning and other less-tangible elements of culture.

Archaeology's unique ability to provide otherwise-unobtainable tangible links with the past continues to make significant contributions to our understanding of these issues. Professional archaeologists in government, industry, and the academy continue to work with avocationists to verify locations of known sites and discover undocumented locales. Laboratory analysis of their findings is shedding new light on the lives and times of the people who lived at these sites. Better understanding of the archaeological evidence left behind by these people can provide new insights into health, the environment, politics, social relations, and other enduringly compelling human concerns.

Archaeologists must continue to develop or adapt new technologies. Increased use must be made of geomorphological and other noninvasive survey strategies that do little or no damage to archaeological resources. New techniques capable of dating deposits not containing European imports or other diagnostic artifacts must be developed. New markers of social and political identity must be sought.

Although great advances have been made in the archaeological understanding of seventeenth-century contact relations, further work must be done on sixteenth- and eighteenth-century life in the region. New archaeological data need to be sought out, analyzed, and combined with existing information into broader, more creatively interpretive studies. Poorly known areas, like Nipmuck Country and the Niagara-Erie Frontier, require systematic archaeological reconnaissance surveys. Even the better-documented areas, like the Mohawk and Seneca countries, need more intensive investigation. Information on file in existing site inventories needs to be updated and incorporated into computerized regional and national databases, and stronger and more effective tools are needed to preserve what is known and to protect still-undiscovered resources.

Much past work has focused upon the impact of contact on native people. Great opportunities exist to build upon a growing corpus of work documenting Indian contributions to America and the world. Corn, bean, squash, and tobacco cultivation are the best known of the many technological contributions made by Indian people to the rest of the world (Hallowell 1957). Colonists settling in the Northeast who adopted these crops tended to augment Indian planting methods with plows, manure, fertilizer, and other agricultural techniques (Ceci 1975). Popular foods such as succotash and hominy grits clearly originated at Northeastern Indian firesides. Scholars are less sure about the origins of maple sugaring in the region (C. Mason 1986; Pendergast 1982).

Many colonists in newly established settlements such as Saint Mary's City and Plymouth Plantation passed their first months in Indian wigwams. Today Northeastern Indian architectural ideas are incorporated in the forms of quonset huts and domes. Indian inventions, such as toboggans and snowshoes, continue to be used in snowy weather. Canoe designers using modern materials follow designs first laid out by Northeastern Indian people. Hard-soled moccasins similar to those adopted by frontier settlers today are worn throughout the world.

Museum collections, archaeological sites, and written records contain numerous examples of Indian contributions to decorative and fine arts in the Northeast. Both African and European settlers adopted or used Indian Colono wares throughout the eighteenth century. Settlers from New England to the Carolinas smoked from red terra-cotta tobacco pipes decorated with incised running deer and geometric designs of Indian origin. Floral and abstract design techniques and motifs used by native Northeastern people have long been popular. While scholars continue to debate the origins and cultural significance of these motifs (Brasser 1975; Speck 1914, 1947), decorative themes associated with Northeastern Indian people have significantly influenced American popular culture (Green 1988).

Many present-day Northeastern Indian people build on the aesthetic achievements of their ancestors. Gay Head Wampanoag potters from Martha's Vineyard, for example, craft clay pots popular with tourists and connoisseurs, while Iroquois artists in New York, Wisconsin, Quebec, and Ontario continue to carve, paint, and weave fine and folk arts. Widely appreciated throughout the world, their work is marketed in shops and museums across America (Johannsen and Ferguson 1983).

Northeastern Indian people have served as informants for non-Indians interested in their cultures for more than four centuries. Studies based upon data provided by such informants, like Joseph-François Lafitau's 1724 work favorably contrasting Iroquois society with classical Greek and Roman culture, have influenced thinkers of every social, political, and philosophical persuasion from Jean-Jacques Rousseau and John Locke to Friedrich Engels and Karl Marx (Berkhofer 1988; Lafitau 1974-1977).

Indian people have also played more indirect roles in developments in the Northeast. Most provincial charters called for the conversion of Indians to Christianity. Dartmouth College and several other schools ostensibly were founded to train Indian missionaries. Other institutions—among them Harvard, Princeton, and the College of William and Mary—ultimately devoted some degree of attention to Indian education. Fundraisers used such intentions as selling points to attract donations. The most successful of these, Mohegan Indian missionary Samson Occom, in company with the Rev. Nathaniel Whitaker, raised more than twelve thousand pounds for Eleazar Wheelock's Indian school in Connecticut during a two-year trip to England and Scotland between 1765 and 1767 (Blodgett 1935). However, little of this money was put toward Indian education. Most was instead spent to build Dartmouth College, a school largely catering to the educational needs of non-Indian people (Axtell 1981).

The image of the Indian represents the most enduring symbol of America (Berkhofer 1978, 1988). Real Northeastern Indian people like Squanto, other individuals documented in fact and fiction like Uncas, and totally mythical creations like James Fenimore Cooper's Chingachgook have come to symbolize the image of the "noble savage" in literature and art. Less appealing figures, such as Cooper's evil Huron warrior Magua and the Indian villains of a thousand captivity narratives, continue to typify the image of the "evil savage." More recently, Northeastern Indian imagery has been used by such divergent interests as sports teams, political parties, advertising agencies, and the environmental movement.

Perhaps the most significant, and most overlooked, contribution of Northeastern Indian people is the crucial role they played in the national and cultural formation of the United States. Indeed, as James Axtell reminds us, Indian people are indispensable to American history (Axtell 1987; De Voto 1953; Berkhofer 1973). Many native people fed, sheltered, and tutored newly arrived colonists during their first difficult years on American shores. Moreover, backwoods colonists moving beyond the periphery of European settlement incorporated Indian forms of dress, shelter, and subsistence. Categorizing the basic elements that compose what they term "backwoods colonization culture," cultural geographers Terry G. Jordan and Matti Kaups (1989) have shown that adaptation and adoption of Indian lifeways played a major role in development of frontier folklife and folkways in forested parts of Pennsylvania during the seventeenth and eighteenth centuries.

Most backwoods colonists settled along frontier peripheries separating powerful imperial European contenders. Growing centers of European colonization were arrayed along the coast. Occupying land desired by these settlers, powerful and vigorous native nations resisted all expansion attempts. The more successful of these nations, such as the Iroquois confederacy, the Abenakis, and the Shawnees, continued to hold the balance of power years after the first tiny European outposts grew into mighty centers of influence. Relations with these and other nations influenced political events on both sides of the Atlantic. More thoughtful European policymakers considered the friendship or hostility of Indian people when weighing questions of peace and war. Moreover, Indian military involvement in colonial conflicts frequently influenced outcomes of European wars. Francis Jennings (1975), for example, has convincingly shown that Mohawk warriors and Christian Indian converts secured an English victory over New England Indians fighting against the colonists in King Philip's War in 1676.

In these and other ways, the actions of native Northeastern warriors and diplomats influenced the course of history throughout the region and largely determined who would prevail in the struggle for empire that raged across eastern North America during the colonial era. Indian influence was also felt in the evolution of American law and custom. Colonial lawmakers were often forced to consider Indian interests when enacting, changing, or enforcing laws, ordinances, and regulations. Indian people also enduringly influenced diplomatic protocol. The Indian treaty system that was initially developed as a tool of Northeastern forest diplomacy, for example, survives today as the legal and moral basis for relations between the federal government and the various Indian nations.

However, assertions suggesting that Iroquois political concepts influenced and inspired the founders of the American republic remain the subject of considerable debate (Weatherford 1988). Some scholars, for example, think that both the philosophy and example of the Iroquois confederacy influenced the framers of the American Constitution. Grinde and Johansen (1991), in particular, believe that the Framers took from the Iroquois confederacy the concept that sovereignty derived from the people, the notion of separation of powers, and the idea of federalism. Other scholars note that such ideas were not limited to the Iroquois. Still others draw attention to the ethnocentric attitudes of the Framers and the overwhelming influence of Enlightenment thought among them. Elisabeth Tooker (1988), for one, has pointed out that the Constitution was written by people subscribing to a political culture not entirely well disposed toward Indian people. She has further shown that the document was based on principles little resembling Iroquoian concepts of consensus, matrilineal succession, clan representation, disproportionate national representation, and women's enfranchisement.

Awareness of the important role played by women in Iroquois decision making has had a profound impact upon Western thought. Both Lewis Henry Morgan (1877) and Friedrich Engels (1884), whose work was strongly influenced by Morgan, believed that the Iroquois exemplified an earlier matriarchical phase of human social evolution. Theirs and subsequent studies that took less unilinear and more balanced views of Iroquois gender roles have exerted a powerful influence on feminist thought and postmodernist theory. Several of the more prominent studies addressing this issue have been recently reprinted in a compilation edited by Spittal (1990).

Recent legal decisions bearing upon land issues originated during the Historic Contact period—such as the 1971 Maine Indian Land Settlement and recent land claim litigations in New York, Connecticut, and Massachusetts—have exerted significant influences upon the continuing development of American law. These and other actions show that the struggle over the legal issue of sovereignty first joined during the early years of the Historic Contact period continues to the present day.

Working with the vast body of data amassed in the forty years that have passed since William Fenton outlined the needs and opportunities for study in the Northeast, historians, ethnographers, ethnologists, archaeologists, and other specialists have had the opportunity to bring the hard-learned lessons of contact to audiences sorely in need of such knowledge. This knowledge promises to be all the more sorely needed as Americans and the rest of the world face the challenges of contact with unprecedentedly large numbers of "others" in an increasingly diverse cultural milieu.

BIBLIOGRAPHY

Abler, Thomas S., and Elisabeth Tooker
1978 Seneca. In *Northeast,* edited by Bruce G. Trigger, pp. 505-517. Handbook of North American Indians, vol. 15, William C. Sturtevant, general editor. Smithsonian Institution, Washington, D.C.

Alam, Emil A.
1957 A Preliminary Report on the Rochester Site. *Section of Man, Carnegie Museum Newsletter* 12:3-7.

Andrefsky, William
1980 Implications of the Contextual/Structural Approach for Archaeology: An Iroquois Illustration. Unpublished master's thesis. Department of Anthropology, State University of New York at Binghamton.
1922 Indian Graves Unearthed at Charlestown. *Rhode Island Historical Society Collections* 15(1): 18-19, 24.

Anonymous
Anthony, David W.
1991 Personal communication.

Aquila, Richard
1983 *The Iroquois Restoration: Iroquois Diplomacy on the Colonial Frontier, 1701-1754.* Wayne State University Press, Detroit.

Axtell, James
1981 *The European and the Indian: Essays in the Ethnohistory of Colonial North America.* Oxford University Press, New York.
1985 *The Invasion Within: The Contest of Cultures in Colonial North America.* Oxford University Press, New York.
1987 Colonial America without the Indians: Counterfactual Evidence. *Journal of American History* 73(4):981-996.
1989 *After Columbus.* Oxford University Press, New York.

Bachman, Van Cleaf
1969 Peltries or Plantations: The Economic Policies of the Dutch West India Company in New Netherland, 1623-1639. *The Johns Hopkins University Studies in Historical and Political Science,* 87th Ser., No. 2. Baltimore.

BAHP (Delaware Bureau of Archaeology and Historic Preservation)
1990 Delaware Bureau of Archaeology and Historic Preservation Archaeological Inventory. Ms. on file, Delaware State Historic Preservation Office, Newark.

Bailey, Alfred G.
1969 *The Conflict of European and Eastern Algonkian Cultures, 1504-1700: A Study in Canadian Civilization.* 2d ed. University of Toronto Press, Toronto.

Baird, Donald
1987 The Indian Trade Gun and Gunflints from Burial 8 at the Pahaquarra Site, Warren County, New Jersey. *Bulletin of the Archaeological Society of New Jersey* 42:1-9.

Baker, Emerson W.
1985 *The Clarke & Lake Company: The Historical Archaeology of a Seventeenth-Century Maine Settlement.* Occasional Publications in Maine Archaeology Vol. 4. Maine Historic Preservation Commission, Augusta.
1986. Trouble to the Eastward: The Failure of Anglo-Indian Relations in Early Maine. Unpublished Ph.D dissertation. Department of Anthropology, College of William and Mary, Williamsburg.
1989. "A Scratch with a Bear's Paw": Anglo-Indian Deeds in Early Maine. *Ethnohistory* 36(3):235-256.

Bamann, Susan, Robert Kuhn, James Molnar, and Dean Snow
1992 Iroquoian Archaeology. *Annual Review of Anthropology* 21:435-460.

Barber, Michael B.
1993 Personal communication.

Barber, Russell J.
1984 Treasures in the Peabody: A Button Mold with an Extraordinary Incised Figure. *Bulletin of the Massachusetts Archaeological Society* 45(2):49-51.

Barbour, Philip L. (editor)
1986 *The Complete Works of Captain John Smith [1580-1631].* 3 vols. University of North Carolina Press, Chapel Hill.

Barka, Norman F.
1975 Flowerdew Hundred Plantation National Register of Historic Places Registration Form. Ms. on file, U.S. Department of the Interior, National Park Service, National Register Branch, Washington, D.C.

Barker, Alex W.
1992 Powhatan's Pursestrings: On the Meaning of Surplus in a Seventeenth Century Algonkian Chiefdom. In *Lords of the Southeast: Social Inequality and the Native Elites of Southeastern North America,* edited by Alex W. Barker and Timothy R. Pauketat, pp. 61–80. Archeological Papers of the American Anthropological Association, vol. 3. Washington, D.C.

Barse, William P.
1985 A Preliminary Archeological Reconnaissance Survey of the Naval Ordnance Station, Indian Head, Maryland. Volume 1: Cornwallis Neck, Bullitt Neck and Thorofare Island. Report on file, Maryland Historical Trust, Crownsville.

Bartram, John
1751 *Observations on the Inhabitants, Climate, Soils, Rivers, Productions, Animals, and Other Matters Worthy of Notice, Made by Mr. John Bartram, in His Travels from Pensilvania to Onondago, Oswego and the Lake Ontario in Canada.* Printed for J. Whiston and B. White, London.

Basalik, Kenneth J., Thomas R. Lewis, and Alan D. Tabachnick
1991 Phase III Archaeological Survey: Weist Site (36DA148). Report on file, Pennsylvania Bureau of Historic Preservation, Harrisburg.

Batchelor, Nanci Kostrub
1976 Salisbury Farm National Register of Historic Places Registration Form. Ms. on file, U.S. Department of the Interior, National Park Service, National Register Branch, Washington, D.C.

Bawden, Garth
1977 Phase II/Intensive Archaeological Survey, EPA Project, Palmer, Mass. Report on file, Massachusetts Historical Commission, Boston.

Beard, Frank A., and Robert L. Bradley
1978 Colonial Pemaquid Archaeological District National Register of Historic Places Registration Form. Ms. on file, U.S. Department of the Interior, National Park Service, National Register Branch, Washington, D.C.

Beauchamp, William M.
1900 *Aboriginal Occupation of New York.* New York State Museum, Bulletin 32, Albany.
1907 *Civil, Religious, and Mourning Councils and Ceremonies of Adoption of the New York Indians.* New York State Museum, Bulletin 113, Albany.
1916 *Moravian Journals Relating to Central New York, 1745-1766.* Dehler Press, Syracuse, New York.

Beaudry, Mary C.
1979 Excavations at Fort Christanna, Brunswick County, Virginia. Ms. on file, Virginia Department of Historic Resources, Richmond.

Beauregard, Alan D.
1991 Personal communication.

Beaver, R. Pierce
1988 Protestant Churches and the Indians. In *History of Indian-White Relations,* edited by Wilcomb E. Washburn, pp. 430-452. Handbook of North American Indians, vol. 4, William C. Sturtevant, general editor. Smithsonian Institution, Washington, D.C.

Becker, Marshall J.
1978 Montgomery Site, 36-CH-60: Late Contact Lenape (Delaware) Site in Wallace Township, Chester County. Ms. in author's possession.
1980 Lenape Archaeology: Archaeological and Ethnohistoric Considerations in Light of Recent Excavations. *Pennsylvania Archaeologist* 50(4):19-30.
1985 The Printzhof (36DE3) Excavations of 1985, Final Report. Ms. on file, Pennsylvania Historical and Museum Commission, Harrisburg.
1986 The Okehocking Band of Lenape: Cultural Continuities and Accommodations in Southeastern Pennsylvania. In *Strategies for Survival: American Indians in the Eastern United States,* edited by Frank W. Porter III, pp. 43-83. Greenwood Press, Westport, Connecticut.
1987 The Moravian Mission in the Forks of Delaware: Reconstructing the Migration and Settlement Patterns of the Jersey Lenape during the Eighteenth Century through Documents in the Moravian Archives. *Unitas Fratrum* 21/22:83-172.
1990 The Origins of Trade Silver Among the Lenape: Pewter Objects from Southeastern Pennsylvania as Possible Precursors. *Northeast Historical Archaeology* 19:78-98.

Beckerman, Ira
1980 Tioga Point Farm Archaological District National Register of Historic Places Registration Form. Ms. on file, U.S. Department of the Interior, National Park Service, National Register Branch, Washington, D.C.

Beckman, Kristen A.
1990 Johnston Locus Data Recovery Report: Westmoreland County Greensburg Expressway. Report on file, Pennsylvania Bureau of Historic Preservation, Harrisburg.

Bender, Susan J., and Hetty Jo Brumbach
1992 Material Manifestations of Algonquian Ethnicity: A Case Study from the Upper Hudson. Paper presented at the 57th Annual Meeting of the Society for American Archaeology, Pittsburgh.

Bennett, Merrill K.
1955 The Food Economy of the New England Indians, 1605-75. *Journal of Political Economy* 63(3):369-397.

Bennett, Monte R.
1973 The Moot Site (Sullivans), OND 3-4. *Chenango Chapter New York State Archaeological Association Bulletin* 14(1):1-20.
1979 The Blowers Site, OND 1-4: An Early Historic

Oneida Settlement. *Chenango Chapter New York State Archaeological Association Bulletin* 18(2):1-25.

1981 A Longhouse Pattern on the Cameron Site, OND 2-4. *Chenango Chapter New York State Archaeological Association Bulletin* 19(2):1-23.

1982 A Salvage Burial Excavation at the Lanz-Hogan Site, OND 2-4. *Chenango Chapter New York State Archaeological Association Bulletin* 19(4): 1-25.

1983 Glass Trade Beads from Central New York. In *Proceedings of the 1982 Glass Trade Bead Conference,* edited by Charles F. Hayes III, pp. 51-58. Rochester Museum and Science Center Research Record 16.

1984a Recent Findings in Oneida Indian Country. *Chenango Chapter New York State Archaeological Association Bulletin* 21(1):1-17.

1984b The Stone Quarry Site MSV 4-2: A Mid-Seventeenth Century Oneida Iroquois Station in Central New York. *Chenango Chapter New York State Archaeological Association Bulletin* 21(2):1-35.

1988 The Primes Hill Site MSV 5-2: An Eighteenth Century Oneida Station. *Chenango Chapter New York State Archaeological Association Bulletin* 22(4):1-17.

1991a Onneyuttehage-Thurston-MSV 1: A Story of a Screened Sidehill Midden. *Chenango Chapter New York State Archaeological Association Bulletin* 24(3):1-19.

1991b Personal communication.

Bennett, Monte R., and Reginald Bigford

1968 The Cameron Site. *Chenango Chapter New York State Archaeological Association Bulletin* 10(2):1-40.

Bennett, Monte R., and Douglas Clark

1978 Recent Excavations at the Cameron Site, OND 8-4. *Chenango Chapter New York State Archaeological Association Bulletin* 17(4):1-35.

Bennett, Monte R., and Richard Cole

1974 The Upper Hogan Site, OND 5-4. *Chenango Chapter New York State Archaeological Association Bulletin* 15(2):1-16.

1976 The Marshall Site, MSV 7-2. *Chenango Chapter New York State Archaeological Association Bulletin* 16(3):8-14.

Bennett, Monte R., and Henry Hatton

1988 The Cameron Site, OND 8-4, Revisited. *Chenango Chapter New York State Archaeological Association Bulletin* 23(1):1-4.

Benthall, Joseph L.

1990 *The Daugherty Cave Site, Russell County, Virginia.* Special Publication, Archeological Society of Virginia. Richmond.

Berkhofer, Robert F., Jr.

1973 Native Americans and United States History. In *The Reinterpretation of American History and Culture,* edited by William H. Cartwright and Richard L. Watson, pp. 37-52. Washington, D.C.

1978 *The White Man's Indian.* Alfred Knopf, New York.

1988 White Conceptions of Indians. In *History of Indian-White Relations,* edited by Wilcomb E. Washburn, pp. 522-547. Handbook of North American Indians, vol. 4, William C. Sturtevant, general editor. Smithsonian Institution, Washington, D.C.

Beverley, Robert

1947 [1705] *The History of Virginia.* Edited by Louis B. Wright. University of North Carolina Press, Chapel Hill.

Binford, Lewis R.

1962 A New Method of Calculating Dates from Kaolin Pipe Stem Samples. *Southeastern Archaeological Conference Newsletter* 9(2):19-21.

1965 Colonial Period Ceramics of the Nottoway and Weanock Indians of Southeastern Virginia. *Quarterly Bulletin: Archeological Society of Virginia* 19(4):78-87.

1967 An Ethnohistory of the Nottoway, Meherrin, and Weanock Indians of Southeastern Virginia. *Ethnohistory* 14(3-4):103-218.

1981 *Bones: Ancient Men and Modern Myths.* Academic Press, New York.

1983 *In Pursuit of the Past: Decoding the Archaeological Record.* Thames and Hudson, London.

1991 *Cultural Diversity among Aboriginal Cultures of Coastal Virginia and North Carolina.* Garland Publishing, New York. Revised ed. of 1964 unpublished Ph.D dissertation, Department of Anthropology, University of Michigan, Ann Arbor.

Bischoff, Henry, and Michael Kahn

1979 *From Pioneer Settlement to Suburb: A History of Mahwah, New Jersey, 1700-1976.* A. S. Barnes & Co, South Brunswick, New Jersey.

Black, Glenn A.

1967 *Angel Site: An Archaeological, Historical, and Ethnological Study.* 2 vols. Indiana Historical Society, Indianapolis.

Blau, Harold, Jack Campisi, and Elisabeth Tooker

1978 Onondaga. In *Northeast,* edited by Bruce G. Trigger, pp. 491-499. Handbook of North American Indians, vol. 15, William C. Sturtevant, general editor. Smithsonian Institution, Washington, D.C.

Blodgett, Harold

1935 *Samson Occom.* Dartmouth College Manuscript Series 3, Hanover, New Hampshire.

Bock, Philip K.

1978 Micmac. In *Northeast,* edited by Bruce G. Trigger, pp. 109-122. Handbook of North American Indians, vol. 15, William C. Sturtevant, general editor. Smithsonian Institution, Washington, D.C.

Boender, Debra Ruth

1988 Our Fires Have Nearly Gone Out: A History of Indian-White Relations on the Colonial Maryland Frontier, 1633-1776. Unpublished Ph.D dissertation, Department of History, University of New Mexico, Albuquerque.

Bohannon, Laura

1987 Shakespeare in the Bush. In *Conformity and Conflict: Readings in Cultural Anthropology.*

6th ed. Edited by James P. Spradley and David W. McCurdy, pp. 35–45. Little, Brown, and Company, Boston. Originally published in 1966 in *Natural History Magazine.*

Bohn, Nels
1989 Personal communication.

Boissevain, Ethel
1973 Historic Village of the Narragansetts National Register of Historic Places Registration Form. Ms. on file, U.S. Department of the Interior, National Park Service, National Register Branch, Washington, D.C.

Boisvert, Richard A.
1993 The 17th Century Native American Presence at the Hormell Site, Freedom, New Hampshire. Paper presented at the 60th Annual Meeting of the Eastern States Archaeological Federation, Bangor, Maine.

Bolger, William C.
1989 Personal communication.

Bond, Richmond P.
1952 *Queen Anne's American Kings.* Clarendon Press, Oxford.

Bonine, Chesleigh A.
1952-1964 The Bastion of the De Vries Palisade of 1631. *The Archeolog* 4(1-2); 8(3); 16(2).

Bourne, Russell
1990 *The Red King's Rebellion: Racial Politics in New England, 1675-1678.* Oxford University Press, New York.

Bourque, Bruce J.
1975 Cobbosseecontee Dam Site National Register of Historic Places Registration Form. Ms. on file, U.S. Department of the Interior, National Park Service, National Register Branch, Washington, D.C.
1989a Ethnicity on the Maritime Peninsula, 1600-1759. *Ethnohistory* 36(3):257-284.
1989b Personal communication.

Bowden, Henry W., and James P. Ronda (editors)
1980 *John Eliot's Indian Dialogues: A Study in Cultural Interaction.* Greenwood Press, Westport, Connecticut.

Boyce, Douglas W.
1978 Iroquoian Tribes of the Virginia–North Carolina Coastal Plain. In *Northeast,* edited by Bruce G. Trigger, pp. 282–289. Handbook of North American Indians, vol. 15, William C. Sturtevant, general editor. Smithsonian Institution, Washington, D.C.
1987 "As the Wind Scatters the Smoke": The Tuscaroras in the Eighteenth Century. In *Beyond the Covenant Chain: The Iroquois and Their Neighbors in Indian North America, 1600-1800,* edited by Daniel K. Richter and James H. Merrell, pp. 151-163. Syracuse University Press, Syracuse, New York.

Bradley, James W.
1979 The Onondaga Iroquois: 1500-1655. A Study in Acculturative Change and Its Consequences. Unpublished Ph.D dissertation, Interdisciplinary Program in Social Science, Syracuse University, Syracuse, New York.
1983 Blue Crystals and Other Trinkets: Glass Beads from 16th and Early 17th-Century New England. In *Proceedings of the 1982 Glass Trade Bead Conference,* edited by Charles F. Hayes III, pp. 29–39. Rochester Museum and Science Center Research Record 16.
1987a *Evolution of the Onondaga Iroquois: Accommodating Change, 1500-1655.* Syracuse University Press, Syracuse, N. Y.
1987b Native Exchange and European Trade: Cross-Cultural Dynamics in the Sixteenth Century. *Man in the Northeast* 33:31-46.

Bradley, James W. (editor)
1982a Historic and Archaeological Resources of Southeast Massachusetts. Report on file, Massachusetts Historical Commission, Boston.
1982b Historic and Archaeological Resources of the Boston Area. Report on file, Massachusetts Historical Commission, Boston.
1984 Historic and Archaeological Resources of the Connecticut Valley. Report on file, Massachusetts Historical Commission, Boston.
1985 Historic and Archaeological Resources of Central Massachusetts. Report on file, Massachusetts Historical Commission, Boston.

Bradley, James W., and S. Terry Childs
1987 Analysis of a Copper Artifact from the Palmer Site, Westfield, Massachusetts. *Bulletin of the Massachusetts Archaeological Society* 48(2): 53-57.
1991 Basque Earrings and Panther's Tails: The Form of Cross-Cultural Contact in 16th-Century Iroquoia. In *Metals in Society: Theory beyond Analysis,* edited by Robert Ehrenreich, pp. 7-17. MASCA Research Papers in Science and Archaeology 8(2), Philadelphia.

Bradley, James W., Francis P. McManamon, Thomas F. Mahlstedt, and A. L. Magennis
1982 The Indian Neck Ossuary: A Preliminary Report. *Bulletin of the Massachusetts Archaeological Society* 43(4):47-59.

Brashler, Janet G.
1987 Excavations at a Sixteenth-Century Susquehannock Village. *West Virginia Archeologist* 39(2): 1-30.
1988 Excavations at a Late Prehistoric Site in Hardy County, West Virginia. Paper presented at the 1988 Annual Meeting of the West Virginia Archeological Society.

Brashler, Janet G., and Ronald W. Moxley
1990 Late Prehistoric Engraved Shell Gorgets of West Virginia. *West Virginia Archeologist* 42(1):1-10.

Brasser, Theodore J. C.
1975 *A Basketful of Indian Culture Change.* Mercury Series, No. 22, Ethnology Division, National Museum of Man, National Museums of Canada, Ottawa.
1978a Early Indian-European Contacts. In *Northeast,* edited by Bruce G. Trigger, pp. 78–88. Handbook

of North American Indians, vol. 15, William C. Sturtevant, general editor. Smithsonian Institution, Washington, D.C.

1978b Mahican. In *Northeast*, edited by Bruce G. Trigger, pp. 198-212. Handbook of North American Indians, vol. 15, William C. Sturtevant, general editor. Smithsonian Institution, Washington, D.C.

1988 The Coastal Algonkians: People of the First Frontiers. In *North American Indians in Historical Perspective*, edited by Eleanor Burke Leacock and Nancy Oestreich Lurie, pp. 69-91. Waveland Press, Prospect Heights, Illinois. Originally published in 1971 by Random House, New York.

Brenner, Elise M.
1980 To Pray or to Be Prey, That Is the Question: Strategies for Cultural Autonomy of Massachusetts Praying Towns. *Ethnohistory* 27(2):135-52.

1984 Strategies for Autonomy: An Analysis of Ethnic Mobilization in Seventeenth Century Southern New England. Unpublished Ph.D dissertation, Department of Anthropology, University of Massachusetts, Amherst.

1988 Sociopolitical Implications of Mortuary Ritual Remains in 17th-Century Native New England. In *The Recovery of Meaning: Historical Archaeology in the Eastern United States*, edited by Mark P. Leone and Parker B. Potter, Jr., pp. 147-181. Smithsonian Institution, Washington, D.C.

Brewer, J.
1942 Camp Sites near Plymouth, Mass. *Bulletin of the Massachusetts Archaeological Society* 3(4):55-57.

Briceland, Alan V.
1987 *Westward from Virginia: The Exploration of the Virginia Frontier, 1650-1710*. University Press of Virginia, Charlottesville.

Bridenbaugh, Carl
1980 *Jamestown, 1544-1699*. Oxford University Press, New York.

1981 *Early Americans*. Oxford University Press, New York.

Briggs, John W.
1969 Popham Colony Site National Register of Historic Places Registration Form. Ms. on file, U.S. Department of the Interior, National Park Service, National Register Branch, Washington, D.C.

Brose, David S.
1977 Archaeological Reconnaissance and Sub-Surface Investigation of the Proposed United States Steel Corporation Greenfield Steel Plant, Ashtabula County, Ohio; Erie County, Pennsylvania. Report on file, Cleveland Museum of Natural History, Cleveland.

1978 Late Prehistory of the Upper Great Lakes Area. In *Northeast*, edited by Bruce G. Trigger, pp. 569-582. Handbook of North American Indians, vol. 15, William C. Sturtevant, general editor. Smithsonian Institution, Washington, D.C.

1985 RP3 Study Unit: Late Prehistoric and Protohistoric Periods in Northeast Ohio, Study Unit B. Report on file, Ohio Historical Society, Columbus.

1993 Personal communication.

Brose, David S. (editor)
1976 *The Late Prehistory of the Lake Erie Drainage Basin: A 1972 Symposium Revisited*. Cleveland Museum of Natural History, Cleveland.

Brown, John B.
1990 Personal communication.

Brown, Judith K.
1970 Economic Organization and the Position of Women among the Iroquois. *Ethnohistory* 17(2): 151-67.

Brown, M. L.
1980 *Firearms in Colonial America: The Impact on History and Technology, 1492-1792*. Smithsonian Institution, Washington, D.C.

Browne, William H., et al. (editors)
1883-1970 *Archives of Maryland*. 73 vols. Maryland Historical Society, Baltimore.

Brumbach, Hetty Jo
1975 "Iroquoian" Ceramics in "Algonquian" Territory. *Man in the Northeast* 10:17-28.

1991 Personal communication.

Brumbach, Hetty Jo, and Susan J. Bender
1986 Winney's Rift: A Late Woodland Village Site in the Upper Hudson River Valley. *The Bulletin and Journal of Archaeology for New York State* 92:1-8.

Buchanan, William T., Jr.
1984 *The Trigg Site, City of Radford, Virginia*. Special Publication 14, Archeological Society of Virginia. Richmond.

1985 The Kiser Site, Colonial Heights, Virginia. In *Falls Zone Archeology in Virginia*, edited by Howard A. MacCord, Sr., pp. 41-142. Privately printed, Richmond.

Bullen, Adelaide K., and Ripley P. Bullen
1946 Two Burials in Tiverton, Rhode Island. *Bulletin of the Massachusetts Archaeological Society* 8(1):5.

Bullen, Ripley P.
1949 Excavations in Northeastern Massachusetts. *Papers of the R. S. Peabody Foundation for Archaeology* 1(3).

Bullen, Ripley P. and Edward Brooks
1948 Shell Heaps on Sandy Neck, Barnstable, Massachusetts. *Bulletin of the Massachusetts Archaeological Society* 10(1):7-13.

Bushnell, David I.
1908 *Native Villages and Village Sites East of the Mississippi*. Bureau of American Ethnology, Bulletin 60, Washington, D.C.

1930 The Five Monacan Towns in Virginia, 1607. *Smithsonian Miscellaneous Collections* 82(12): 1-38.

1933 Evidence of Indian Occupancy in Albemarle County, Virginia. *Smithsonian Miscellaneous Collections* 89(7):1-24.

1935 The Mannahoac Tribes in Virginia, 1608. *Smithsonian Miscellaneous Collections* 94(8):1-56.

1937 Indian Sites below the Falls of the Rappahannock, Virginia. *Smithsonian Miscellaneous Collections* 96(4):1-65.

Butler, Eva L.
1946 The Brush or Stone Memorial Heaps of Southern New England. *Bulletin of the Archeological Society of Connecticut* 19:2-12.

Butler, Mary
1936 Recent Archaeological Work in Southwestern Pennsylvania. *Pennsylvania Archaeologist* 6(3): 55-58.

Byers, David S., and Irving Rouse
1960 A Re-examination of the Guida Farm. *Archaeological Society of Connecticut Bulletin* 30: 3-38.

Cadzow, Donald A.
1934 Report on Archaeological Explorations in Western Pennsylvania. Report on file, Pennsylvania Historical and Museum Commission, Harrisburg.
1936 *Archaeological Studies of the Susquehannock Indians.* Safe Harbor Report 2, Pennsylvania Historical Commission, Harrisburg.

Caldwell, Joseph R.
1964 Interaction Spheres in Prehistory. *Illinois State Museum Papers* 12(6):133-143.

Callender, Charles
1978a Great Lakes-Riverine Sociopolitical Organization. In *Northeast,* edited by Bruce G. Trigger, pp. 610-621. Handbook of North American Indians, vol. 15, William C. Sturtevant, general editor. Smithsonian Institution, Washington, D.C.
1978b Shawnee. In *Northeast,* edited by Bruce G. Trigger, pp. 622-635. Handbook of North American Indians, vol. 15, William C. Sturtevant, general editor. Smithsonian Institution, Washington, D.C.
1978c Fox. In *Northeast,* edited by Bruce G. Trigger, pp. 636-647. Handbook of North American Indians, vol. 15, William C. Sturtevant, general editor. Smithsonian Institution, Washington, D.C.

Calloway, Colin G.
1988 Wanalancet and Kancagamus: Indian Strategy and Leadership on the New Hampshire Frontier. *Historical New Hampshire* 43(4):264-290.
1990 *The Western Abenakis of Vermont, 1600-1800: War, Migration, and the Survival of an Indian People.* University of Oklahoma Press, Norman.

Calloway, Colin G. (editor)
1991 *Dawnland Encounters: Indian and European Relations in the North Country.* University Press of New England, Hanover, New Hampshire.

Camp, Helen B.
1975 *Archaeological Excavations at Pemaquid, Maine: 1965-74.* Maine State Museum, Augusta.

Campbell, Paul R., and Glenn W. LaFantasie
1978 Scattered to the Winds of Heaven: Narragansett Indians, 1676-1800. *Rhode Island History* 37(3): 67-83.

Campbell, Tony
1965 *New Light on the Jansson-Visscher Maps of New England.* The Map Collectors' Circle, No. 24, London.

Campeau, Lucien
1988 Roman Catholic Missions in New France. In *History of Indian-White Relations,* edited by Wilcomb E. Washburn, pp. 464-471. Handbook of North American Indians, vol. 4, William C. Sturtevant, general editor. Smithsonian Institution, Washington, D.C.

Campisi, Jack
1974 Ethnic Identity and Boundary Maintenance in Three Oneida Communities. Unpublished Ph.D dissertation, Department of Anthropology, State University of New York at Albany.
1978. Oneida. In *Northeast,* edited by Bruce G. Trigger, pp. 481-490. Handbook of North American Indians, vol. 15, William C. Sturtevant, general editor. Smithsonian Institution, Washington, D.C.

Campisi, Jack, and Laurence M. Hauptman (editors)
1988 *The Oneida Indian Experience: Two Perspectives.* Syracuse University Press, Syracuse, New York.

Carlson, Catherine C.
1986 Archival and Archaeological Research Report on the Configuration of the Seven Original 17th Century Praying Indian Towns of the Massachusetts Bay Colony. Report on file, Massachusetts Historical Commission, Boston.

Carpenter, Edmund S., K. R. Pfirman, and Henry L. Schoff
1949 The 28th Street Site. *Pennsylvania Archaeologist* 19(1-2):3-16.

Carr, Christopher G., and Robert F. Maslowski
1991 Cordage and Fabrics: The Relationships between Form, Technology, and Social Processes. In *Style, Society, and Person,* edited by Christopher G. Carr and Jill Neitzel. Cambridge University Press, New York.

Carr, J. Revell
1969 The Westbrook Fort Site, Sussex County, New Jersey. Report on file, Delaware Water Gap National Recreation Area, Bushkill, Pennsylvania.

Carr, Lois Green, Philip D. Morgan, and Jean B. Russo (editors)
1988 *Colonial Chesapeake Society.* University of North Carolina Press, Chapel Hill.

Carse, Mary (Rowell)
1949 The Mohawk Iroquois. *Bulletin of the Archaeological Society of Connecticut* 23:3-53.

Cartier, Jacques
1924 [1843] *The Voyages of Jacques Cartier.* Edited by Henry P. Biggar, Publications of the Public Archives of Canada, vol. 11, Ottawa.

CAS (Connecticut Archaeological Survey)
n.d. Connecticut Archaeological Survey. Ms. on file, Connecticut Historical Commission, Hartford.

Casselberry, Samuel Emerson
1971 The Schultz-Funk Site (36Ka7): Its Role in the Culture History of the Susquehannock and Shenks Ferry Indians. Unpublished Ph.D dissertation, Department of Anthropology, Pennsylvania State University, University Park.

Ceci, Lynn
1975 Fish Fertilizer: A Native North American Practice? *Science* 188(4183):26-30.

1977 The Effect of European Contact and Trade on the Settlement Pattern of Indians in Coastal New York, 1524-1655: The Archaeological and Documentary Evidence. Unpublished Ph.D dissertation, Department of Anthropology, City University of New York Graduate Center, New York.

1979 Maize Cultivation in Coastal New York: The Archaeological, Agronomical, and Documentary Evidence. *North American Archaeologist* 1(1):45-74.

1980a Locational Analysis of Historic Algonquin Sites in Coastal New York: A Preliminary Study. In *Proceedings of the Conference on Northeastern Archaeology,* edited by John Moore, pp. 71-91. Research Report 19, Department of Anthropology, University of Massachusetts, Amherst.

1980b The First Fiscal Crisis in New York. *Economic Development and Cultural Change* 28(4):839-847.

1982a The Motts Point Site Report: The Documentary and Archeological Evidence. Report on file, New York State Office of Parks, Recreation, and Historic Preservation, Waterford.

1982b The Value of Wampum among the New York Iroquois: A Case Study in Artifact Analysis. *Journal of Anthropological Research* 38(1):97-107.

1982c Method and Theory in Coastal New York Archaeology: Paradigms of Settlement Pattern. *North American Archaeologist* 3(1):5-36.

Champlain, Samuel de
1922-1938 [1626] *The Works of Samuel de Champlain.* Edited by Henry P. Biggar. 6 vols. The Champlain Society, Toronto.

Chaney, Edward, and Henry M. Miller
1989 Archaeological Reconnaissance and Testing at the Gallow's Green Site (18ST1-112), St. Mary's City, Maryland. Report on file, St. Mary's College of Maryland, St. Mary's City.

1990 An Archaeological Survey of the Fisher's Road Science Building Area (18ST1-23 and 18ST1-265), St. Mary's City, Maryland. Report on file, St. Mary's College of Maryland, St. Mary's City.

Chapin, Howard
1926 Unusual Indian Implements Found in Rhode Island. *Rhode Island Historical Society Collections* 19(4):117-127.

1927 Indian Graves: A Survey of the Indian Graves That Have Been Discovered in Rhode Island. *Rhode Island Historical Society Collections* 20: 14-32.

Cissna, Paul Byron
1986 The Piscataway Indians of Southern Maryland: An Ethnohistory from Pre-European Contact to the Present. Unpublished Ph.D dissertation, Department of Anthropology, American University, Washington, D.C.

Clark, Caven P.
1988 Preliminary Report of Archeological Investigations. Report on file, Midwest Archeological Center, National Park Service, Omaha, Nebraska.

Clark, Charles E.
1970 *The Eastern Frontier: The Settlement of North-*

ern New England, 1610-1763. Alfred A. Knopf, New York.

Clark, Douglas, and Allen Owen
1976 Excavations at the Cody Site OND 5-4. *Chenango Chapter New York State Archaeological Association Bulletin* 16(3):1-7.

Clark, Wayne E.
1974 The Nottingham Archeological Site National Register of Historic Places Registration Form. Ms. on file, U.S. Department of the Interior, National Park Service, National Register Branch, Washington, D.C.

1975 Shawnee Old Fields Village Site National Register of Historic Places Registration Form. Ms. on file, U.S. Department of the Interior, National Park Service, National Register Branch, Washington, D.C.

1980 The Origins of the Piscataway and Related Indian Cultures. *Maryland Historical Magazine* 75(1):8-22.

Clark, Wayne E., and Martha W. McCartney
1978 Big Crab Orchard Site National Register of Historic Places Registration Form. Ms. on file, U.S. Department of the Interior, National Park Service, National Register Branch, Washington, D.C.

Clouette, Bruce
1980 Indian Hill Historic District National Register of Historic Places Registration Form. Ms. on file, U.S. Department of the Interior, National Park Service, National Register Branch, Washington, D.C.

Coffin, C. C.
1947 Ancient Fish Weirs along the Housatonic River. *Bulletin of the Archaeological Society of Connecticut* 21:35-38.

Cohen, David Steven
1992 *The Dutch-American Farm.* New York University Press, New York.

Colden, Cadwallader
1747 *The History of the Five Indian Nations of Canada, Which Are Dependent on the Province of New-York in America, and Are the Barrier between the English and French in That Part of the World.* 2 vols. T. Osborne, London.

Cole, Stephen
1980 Queen's Fort National Register of Historic Places Registration Form. Ms. on file, U.S. Department of the Interior, National Park Service, National Register Branch, Washington, D.C.

Colee, Phillip S.
1977 The Housatonic-Stockbridge Indians, 1734-1749. Unpublished Ph.D dissertation, Department of History, State University of New York at Albany.

Conkey, Laura E., Ethel Boissevain, and R. H. Ives Goddard
1978 Indians of Southern New England and Long Island: Late Period. In *Northeast,* edited by Bruce G. Trigger, pp. 177-189. Handbook of North American Indians, vol. 15, William C. Sturtevant, general editor. Smithsonian Institution, Washington, D.C.

Conlin, John H.
1985 Old Fort Niagara National Historic Landmark Boundary Study. Report on file, History Division, National Park Service, Washington, D.C.

Connole, Dennis A.
1976 Land Occupied by the Nipmuck Indians of Central New England, 1600-1700. *Bulletin of the Massachusetts Archaeological Society* 38(1-2): 14-20.

Connors, Dennis J., Gordon DeAngelo, and Peter P. Pratt
1980 *The Search for the Jesuit Mission of Ste. Marie de Gannentaha*. Office of Museums and Historical Sites, County of Onondaga Department of Parks and Recreation, Liverpool, New York.

Cook, Frederick (editor)
1887 *Journals of the Military Expedition of Major General John Sullivan against the Six Nations of Indians in 1779*. Knapp, Peck, and Thomson, Publishers, Auburn, New York.

Cook, Lauren J.
1985 *The Rhode Island Burial Survey*. 2 vols. Office of Public Archaeology Report of Investigations, No. 28, Center for Archaeological Studies, Boston University, Boston.

Cook, Sherburne Friend
1973a The Significance of Disease in the Extinction of the New England Indians. *Human Biology* 45(3):485-508.
1973b Interracial Warfare and Population Decline among the New England Indians. *Ethnohistory* 20(1):1-24.
1976 *The Indian Population of New England in the Seventeenth Century*. University of California Publications in Anthropology, No. 12, Berkeley.

Cooke, Jacob Ernest (editor in chief)
1993 *Encyclopedia of the North American Colonies*. 3 vols. Charles Scribner's Sons, New York.

Cooper, James Fenimore
1826 *The Last of the Mohicans*. New York.

Corey, A. Deloraine
1899 *History of Malden, Massachusetts: 1633-1785*. Malden, Mass.

Cosans-Zebooker, Betty
1992 A Cultural Resource Survey of the Burr/Haines Mill Site (Site 18BU414), Tabernacle Township, Burlington County, New Jersey. Draft report on file, New Jersey Historic Preservation Office, Trenton.

Cotter, John L.
1978 Premier Etablissement Francais en Acadie Sainte Croix. *L'Dossiers de Archeologie* 27:60-71.

Cowie, Ellen R., and James B. Petersen
1992 Archaeological Phase II Testing of the Weston Project (FERC No. 2325), Somerset County, Maine. Draft report on file, Maine Historic Preservation Commission, Augusta.

Cox, Deborah, Joan Gallagher, Allan Leveillee, and Duncan Ritchie
1982 Site Examination of the Bear Hollow, Black Bear, Cracker, Dead Dog, and Hartford Avenue Rock Shelter Sites: State Highway Route 146, Sutton to Uxbridge, Massachusetts, Construction Contract 2. Report on file, Massachusetts Historical Commission, Boston.

Crane, Verner W.
1928 *The Southern Frontier, 1670-1732*. Durham, North Carolina.

Cranmer, Leon E.
1990 *Cushnoc: The History and Archaeology of Plymouth Colony Traders on the Kennebec*. Occasional Publications in Maine Archaeology, No. 7. The Maine Archaeological Society, Fort Western Museum, and the Maine Historic Preservation Commission, Augusta.

Craven, Wesley Frank
1949 *The Southern Colonies in the Seventeenth Century, 1607-1689*. Louisiana State University Press, Baton Rouge.

Craven, Wesley Frank (editor)
1971 *White, Red, and Black: The Seventeenth-Century Virginian*. University Press of Virginia, Charlottesville.

Cronon, William
1983 *Changes in the Land: Indians, Colonists, and the Ecology of New England*. Hill and Wang, New York.

Crosby, Alfred W., Jr.
1969 The Early History of Syphilis: A Reappraisal. *American Anthropologist* 71(1):218-227.
1972 *The Columbian Exchange: Biological and Cultural Consequences of 1492*. Greenwood Press, Westport, Connecticut.
1986 *Ecological Imperialism: The Biological Expansion of Europe, 900-1900*. Cambridge University Press, New York.

Cross, Dorothy
1941 *The Archaeology of New Jersey: Volume I*. The Archaeological Society of New Jersey and the New Jersey State Museum, Trenton.
1956 *Archaeology of New Jersey: The Abbott Farm: Volume II*. The Archaeological Society of New Jersey and the New Jersey State Museum, Trenton.

Cumming, William P.
1958 *The Discoveries of John Lederer*. University Press of Virginia, Charlottesville.

Custer, Jay F.
1986a *A Management Plan for Delaware's Prehistoric Cultural Resources*. Monograph No. 2. University of Delaware Center for Archaeological Research, Newark.
1986b Late Woodland Cultural Diversity in the Middle Atlantic: An Evolutionary Perspective. In *Late Woodland Cultures in the Middle Atlantic Region*, edited by Jay F. Custer, pp. 143-172. University of Delaware Press, Newark.
1987 Problems and Prospects in Northeastern Prehistoric Ceramic Studies. *North American Archaeologist* 8(2):97-123.
1989 Personal communication.

Custer, Jay F. (editor)
1986c *Late Woodland Cultures in the Middle Atlan-*

tic Region. University of Delaware Press, Newark.

Custer, Jay F., Janice Carlson, and Keith Doms
1986 Archeometric Analysis of Materials from the Lancaster County Park Site (36LA96). *Pennsylvania Archaeologist* 56(3–4):22–24.

Custer, Jay F., and Daniel R. Griffith
1986 Late Woodland Cultures of the Middle and Lower Delmarva Peninsula. In *Late Woodland Cultures in the Middle Atlantic Region,* edited by Jay F. Custer, pp. 29–57. University of Delaware Press, Newark.

Custer, Jay F., and Scott Watson
1985 Archaeological Investigations at 7NC-E-42, a Contact Period Site in New Castle County, Delaware. *Journal of Middle Atlantic Archaeology* 1.

Dahlgren, Stellan, and Hans Norman
1988 *The Rise and Fall of New Sweden: Governor Johan Risingh's Journal 1654–1655 in Its Historical Context.* Almqvist and Wiksell International, Stockholm.

Dalton, Joseph F.
1974 The Owings Site, Northumberland County, Virginia. *Quarterly Bulletin: Archeological Society of Virginia* 28(3):162–168.

Danckaerts, Jasper
1913 *Journal of Jasper Danckaerts, 1679–1680.* Edited by Bartlett B. James and J. Franklin Jameson. Charles Scribner's Sons, New York.

Davidson, Thomas E.
1982 Historically Attested Indian Villages of the Lower Delmarva. *Maryland Archeology* 18(1): 1–8.

Davidson, Thomas E., and Richard B. Hughes
1986 Aerial Photography and the Search for Chicone Indian Town. *Archaeology* 39(4):58–59, 76.

Davidson, Thomas E., Richard B. Hughes, and Joseph M. McNamara
1985 Where Are the Indian Towns? Archaeology, Ethnohistory, and Manifestations of Contact on Maryland's Eastern Shore. *Journal of Middle Atlantic Archaeology* 1:43–50.

Davis, Christine E.
1993 A Unique 17th-Century Settlement Pattern and Exchange Network in Western Pennsylvania: The Sony Site. Paper presented at the 58th Annual Meeting of the Society for American Archaeology, St. Louis.

Day, Gordon M.
1953 The Indian as an Ecological Factor in the Northeastern Forest. *Ecology* 34(2):329–346.
1962 Roger's Raid in Indian Tradition. *Historical New Hampshire* 17:3–17.
1975 *The Mots Loups of Father Mathevet.* Canadian National Museum of Man Publications in Ethnology, No. 8, National Museums of Canada, Ottawa.
1978 Western Abenaki. In *Northeast,* edited by Bruce G. Trigger, pp. 148–159. Handbook of North American Indians, vol. 15, William C. Sturtevant, general editor. Smithsonian Institution, Washington, D.C.

1981 *The Identity of the St. Francis Indians.* Canadian Ethnology Service Paper 71, Mercury Series, National Museums of Canada, National Museum of Man, Ottawa.

Deetz, James
1988 American Historical Archeology: Methods and Results. *Science* 239:362–367.

De Forest, John W.
1851 *History of the Indians of Connecticut: From the Earliest Known Period to 1850.* William James Hamersley, Hartford.

Demarest, Thomas
1975 The Last Indians in the Upper Hackensack Valley. *Bergen County History Annual,* pp. 73–87. Hackensack, New Jersey.

DeOrio, Robert N.
1978 A Preliminary Sequence of the Historic Cayuga Nation within the Traditional Area: 1600–1740. *New York State Archaeological Association, Beauchamp Chapter Newsletter* 9(4).
1980 Perspectives on the Prehistoric Cayuga, Post Owasco Tradition, through the Correlation of Ceramic Types with Area Development. In *Proceedings of the 1979 Iroquois Pottery Conference,* edited by Charles F. Hayes III, pp. 65–85, Rochester Museum and Science Center Research Record 13.

DePaoli, Neill
1979 The New England Settler's Perception of the Amerindian, 1640–89: A Case Study of the Impact of Conflict and Locale. Unpublished master's thesis, Department of Anthropology, Brown University, Providence.
1988 Beaver, Blankets, Liquor and Politics: Pemaquid, Maine's Participation in the 17th and 18th Century English Fur Trade. Ms. in author's possession.

De Schweinitz, Edmund
1870 *The Life and Times of David Zeisberger, the Western Pioneer and Apostle to the Indians.* Philadelphia.

De Voto, Bernard
1953 Preface. In *Strange Empire: A Narrative of the Northwest,* edited by Joseph Kinsey Howard, pp. 8–9. New York.

Diamond, Joseph E.
1991 Personal communication.
1992 Personal communication.

Dincauze, Dena F.
1968 A Preliminary Report on the Charles River Archaeological Survey. Report on file in the North Atlantic Regional Office, National Park Service, Boston.
1974 An Introduction to Archaeology in the Greater Boston Area. *Archaeology of Eastern North America* 2(1):39–67.
1976a *The Neville Site: 8000 Years at Amoskeag.* Peabody Museum of Archaeology and Ethnography Monograph 4, Cambridge.
1976b Lithic Analysis in the Northeast: Resume and Prospect. *Man in the Northeast* 11:31–37.

1991 Personal communication.

Dincauze, Dena F., and R. Michael Gramly

1973 Powissett Rockshelter: Alternative Behavior Patterns in a Simple Situation. *Pennsylvania Archaeologist* 43(1):43–61.

Dincauze, Dena F., and Robert J. Hasenstab

1987 Explaining the Iroquois: Tribalization on a Prehistoric Periphery. In *Comparative Studies in the Development of Complex Societies, Vol. 3,* edited by T. C. Champion, pp. 67-87. Proceedings of the World Archaeological Congress, September 1986, Southampton, England, Part 4: Centre-Periphery Relations. Allen and Unwin, Boston.

Dobyns, Henry F.

1983 *Their Number Become Thinned: Native American Population Dynamics in Eastern North America.* University of Tennessee Press, Knoxville.

Dodge, Karl S.

1953 Preliminary Report on Field Activities at Fort Hill. *Bulletin of the Massachusetts Archaeological Society* 14(2):79–82.

1962 The Seaver Farm Site. *Bulletin of the Massachusetts Archaeological Society* 23(3–4):24–29.

Donehoo, George P.

1928 *A History of the Indian Villages and Place Names in Pennsylvania.* Pennsylvania Historical Commission, Harrisburg.

Dowd, Anne S.

1990 Vermont Historic Preservation Plan: Historic Context for the Contact Period. Report on file, Vermont Division for Historic Preservation, Montpelier.

Dowd, Gregory Evans

1992 *A Spirited Resistance: The North American Indian Struggle for Unity, 1745-1815.* Johns Hopkins University Press, Baltimore.

Downes, Randolph C.

1940 *Council Fires on the Upper Ohio: A Narrative of Indian Affairs in the Upper Ohio Valley until 1775.* University of Pittsburgh Press, Pittsburgh.

Dragoo, Don W.

1955 Excavations at the Johnston Site, Indiana County, Pennsylvania. *Pennsylvania Archaeologist* 25(2):85-141.

Dunbar, Helene R., and Katherine C. Ruhl

1974 Copper Artifacts from the Engelbert Site. *The Bulletin: The New York State Archaeological Association* 61:1-10.

Dunnell, Robert C.

1962 *The Hughes Farm Site, 46-OH-9.* Publication Series 7, West Virginia Archeological Society, Moundsville.

Dunnigan, Brian Leigh

1985 *History and Development of Old Fort Niagara.* Old Fort Niagara Association, Youngstown, New York.

1989 *Forts within a Fort: Niagara's Redoubts.* Old Fort Niagara Association, Inc. Youngstown, New York.

Dunnigan, Brian Leigh, and Patricia Kay Scott

1991 *Old Fort Niagara in Four Centuries: A History of its Development.* Old Fort Niagara Association, Inc. Youngstown, New York.

Eccles, William J.

1969 *The Canadian Frontier: 1534-1760.* Holt, Rinehart, and Winston, New York.

1988 The Fur Trade in the Colonial Northeast. In *History of Indian-White Relations,* edited by Wilcomb E. Washburn, pp. 324-334. Handbook of North American Indians, vol. 4, William C. Sturtevant, general editor. Smithsonian Institution, Washington, D.C.

Eckstorm, Fannie H.

1934 The Attack on Norridgewock, 1724. *New England Quarterly* 7(4):541-578.

1978 *Indian Place Names of the Penobscot and the Maine Coast.* University of Maine Press, Orono. Originally published in 1941.

Edmondson, Paul W.

1976 The Parker Farm and Indian Road Sites. Ms. on file, Honors Committee, Department of Anthropology, Cornell University, Ithaca.

Egloff, Keith T., Joey T. Moldenhauer, and David E. Rotenizer

1987 The Otter Creek Site (44FR31), A Late Woodland Hamlet along the Blue Ridge Escarpment. *Quarterly Bulletin: Archeological Society of Virginia* 42(1):1-15.

Egloff, Keith T., and Stephen R. Potter

1982 Indian Ceramics from Coastal Plain Virginia. *Archaeology of Eastern North America* 10: 95-117.

Egloff, Keith T., and C. Reed

1980 The Crab Orchard Site: A Late Woodland Palisaded Village. *Quarterly Bulletin: Archeological Society of Virginia* 34(3):130-148.

Egloff, Keith T., and Deborah Woodward

1992 *First People: The Early Indians of Virginia.* Virginia Department of Historic Resources, Richmond, in cooperation with the Jefferson National Forest, Roanoke.

Eisenberg, Leonard

1989 The Hendrickson Site: A Late Woodland Indian Village in the City of Kingston, Ulster County, New York. *Man in the Northeast* 38:21-53.

Eliade, Mircea

1959 *Cosmos and History: The Myth of the Eternal Return.* Harper and Row, New York.

Elliott, Delores

1977 Otsiningo, An Example of an Eighteenth Century Settlement Pattern. In *Current Perspectives in Northeastern Archeology: Essays in Honor of William A. Ritchie,* edited by Robert E. Funk and Charles F. Hayes III, pp. 93-105. *Transactions of the New York State Archaeological Association,* vol. 17, no. 1.

Elting, James J., and William A. Starna

1984 A Possible Case of Pre-Columbian Treponematosis from New York State. *American Journal of Physical Anthropology* 65(2):267-273.

Endrei, Walter, and Geoff Egan
1982 The Sealing of Cloth in Europe, with Special Reference to the English Evidence. *Textile History* 13(1):47-75.

Engelbrecht, William E.
1971 A Stylistic Analysis of New York Iroquois Pottery. Unpublished Ph.D dissertation, Department of Anthropology, University of Michigan, Ann Arbor.

1974 Cluster Analysis: A Method for the Study of Iroquois Prehistory. *Man in the Northeast* 7:57-70.

1984 The Kleis Site Ceramics: An Interpretive Approach. In *Extending the Rafters: Interdisciplinary Approaches to Iroquoian Studies,* edited by Michael K. Foster, Jack Campisi, and Marianne Mithun, pp. 325-339. State University of New York Press, Albany.

1985 New York Iroquois Political Development. In *Cultures in Contact: The European Impact on Native Cultural Institutions in Eastern North America A.D. 1000-1800,* edited by William W. Fitzhugh, pp. 163-183. Smithsonian Institution, Washington, D.C.

1990 Personal communication.

1991 Erie. *The Bulletin: Journal of the New York State Archaeological Association* 102:1-12.

1993 Personal communication.

Engels, Friedrich
1884 *The Origin of the Family, Private Property, and the State.* London.

Erikson, Vincent O.
1978 Maliseet-Passamaquoddy. In *Northeast,* edited by Bruce G. Trigger, pp. 123-136. Handbook of North American Indians, vol. 15, William C. Sturtevant, general editor. Smithsonian Institution, Washington, D.C.

Eteson, Marie O.
1982 The Hayward's Portanimicutt Site. *Bulletin of the Massachusetts Archaeological Society* 43(1):6-30.

1985 Thermoluminescent Dating Analysis of a Cape Cod Potsherd. *Bulletin of the Massachusetts Archaeological Society* 46(2):61-62.

Eteson, Marie O., Marilyn D. Crary, and Mary F. Chase
1978 The Mattaquason Purchase Site (M48N6), North Chatham. *Bulletin of the Massachusetts Archaeological Society* 39(1):1-39.

Evans, Clifford
1955 *A Ceramic Study of Virginia Archeology.* Bureau of American Ethnology, Bulletin 160, Washington, D.C.

Ewald, Johann
1979 *Diary of the American War: A Hessian Journal.* Edited by John P. Tustin. Yale University Press, New Haven, Connecticut.

Fairbanks, Jonathan L., and Robert F. Trent (editors)
1982 *New England Begins: The 17th-Century.* 3 vols. Museum of Fine Arts, Boston.

Faulkner, Alaric
1988 Historic and Prehistoric Archaeological Research at Fort Hill, Veazie, Maine, Phase 1 and 2 Research, 1987-1988. Report on file, Maine Historic Preservation Commission, Augusta.

1991 The Lower Bagaduce Historic Sites Survey-Phase 3: Further Definition of St-Castin's Habitation, 1990-1991. Report on file, Maine Historic Preservation Commission, Augusta.

Faulkner, Alaric, and Gretchen Faulkner
1985 Acadian Maine in Archaeological Perspective. *Northeast Historical Archaeology* 14:1-20.

1987 *The French at Pentagoet, 1635-1674: An Archaeological Portrait of the Acadian Frontier.* The Maine Historic Preservation Commission and the New Brunswick Museum, Augusta, and Saint John, New Brunswick.

Fausz, J. Frederick
1981 Opechancanough: Indian Resistance Leader. In *Struggle and Survival in Colonial America,* edited by David Sweet and Gary B. Nash, pp. 21-37. University of California Press, Berkeley.

1985 Patterns of Anglo-Indian Aggression and Accommodation along the Middle Atlantic Coast, 1584-1634. In *Cultures in Contact: The European Impact on Native Cultural Institutions in Eastern North America, A.D. 1000-1800,* edited by William W. Fitzhugh, pp. 225-270. Smithsonian Institution, Washington, D.C.

1987 The Invasion of Virginia—Indians, Colonialism, and the Conquest of Cant: A Review Essay on Anglo-Indian Relations in the Chesapeake. *The Virginia Magazine of History and Biography* 95(2):133-156.

1988 Merging and Emerging Worlds: Anglo-Indian Interest Groups and the Development of the Seventeenth-Century Chesapeake. In *Colonial Chesapeake Society,* edited by Lois Green Carr, Philip D. Morgan, and Jean B. Russo, pp. 47-98. University of North Carolina Press, Chapel Hill.

Feder, Kenneth L.
1981 The Farmington River Archaeological Project: Focus on a Small River Valley. *Man in the Northeast* 22:131-146.

1984 Metal Tools for Stone Age New Englanders: Trade and Warfare in Southern New England. *Man in the Northeast* 27:51-65.

1990 *Frauds, Myths, and Mysteries: Science and Pseudoscience in Archaeology.* Mayfield Publishing Company, Mountain View, California.

1993 *A Village of Outcasts: Historical Archaeology and Documentary Research at the Lighthouse Site.* Mayfield Publishing, Mountain View, California.

Feest, Christian F.
1978a Nanticoke and Neighboring Tribes. In *Northeast,* edited by Bruce G. Trigger, 240-252. Handbook of North American Indians, vol. 15, William C. Sturtevant, general editor. Smithsonian Institution, Washington, D.C.

1978b Virginia Algonquians. In *Northeast,* edited by Bruce G. Trigger, pp. 253-270. Handbook of North American Indians, vol. 15, William C. Sturtevant, general editor. Smithsonian Institution, Washington, D.C.

Fehr, Elinor, and F. Dayton Staats
1980 The Overpeck Site (35BY5). *Pennsylvania Archaeologist* 50(3):1–46.
Feister, Lois M.
1985 Archaeology in Rensselaerswyck: Dutch 17th-Century Domestic Sites. *New Netherland Studies: An Inventory of Current Research and Approaches—Bulletin Koninklijke Nederlandse Oudheidkundige Bond* 84(2–3):80–88.
Feister, Lois M., and Paul R. Huey
1985 Archaeological Testing at Fort Gage, a Provincial Redoubt of 1758 at Lake George, New York. *The Bulletin and Journal of Archaeology for New York State* 90:40–59.
Fenton, William N.
1940 Problems Arising from the Historic Northeastern Position of the Iroquois. In *Essays in Historical Anthropology in Honor of John R. Swanton, Smithsonian Miscellaneous Collections* 100:159–251.
1948 The Present Status of Anthropology in Northeastern North America. *American Anthropologist* 50(4):494–515.
1951a Iroquois Studies at the Mid-Century. *Proceedings of the American Philosophical Society* 95(2):296–310.
1953 *The Iroquois Eagle Dance: An Offshoot of the Calumet Dance.* Bureau of American Ethnology, Bulletin 156, Washington, D.C.
1957 *American Indian and White Relations to 1830: Needs and Opportunities for Study.* The Institute of Early American History and Culture, University of North Carolina Press, Chapel Hill.
1978 Northern Iroquoian Culture Patterns. In *Northeast,* edited by Bruce G. Trigger, pp. 296–321. Handbook of North American Indians, vol. 15, William C. Sturtevant, general editor. Smithsonian Institution, Washington, D.C.
1987 *The False Faces of the Iroquois.* University of Oklahoma Press, Norman.
1988 The Iroquois in History. In *North American Indians in Historical Perspective,* edited by Eleanor Burke Leacock and Nancy Oestreich Lurie, pp. 129–168. Waveland Press, Prospect Heights, Illinois. Originally published in 1971 by Random House, New York.
Fenton, William N. (editor)
1951b *Symposium on Local Diversity in Iroquois Culture.* Bureau of American Ethnology, Bulletin 149, Washington, D.C.
Fenton, William N., and John Gulick (editors)
1961 *Symposium on Cherokee and Iroquois Culture.* Bureau of American Ethnology, Bulletin 180. Washington, D.C.
Fenton, William N., and Elisabeth Tooker
1978 Mohawk. In *Northeast,* edited by Bruce G. Trigger, pp. 253–270. Handbook of North American Indians, vol. 15, William C. Sturtevant, general editor. Smithsonian Institution, Washington, D.C.
Ferguson, Alice L., and T. Dale Stewart
1940 An Ossuary near Piscataway Creek with a Report on the Skeletal Remains. *American Antiquity* 6(1):4–18.
Ferguson, Leland
1978 Looking for the "Afro" in Colono-Indian Pottery. *Conference on Historic Site Archaeology Papers [1977]* 12:68–86.
1992 *Uncommon Ground: Archaeology of Early African America, 1650–1800.* Smithsonian Institution, Washington, D.C.
Fiedel, Stuart
1987 Algonquian Origins: A Problem in Archaeological-Linguistic Correlation. *Archaeology of Eastern North America* 15:1–12.
Fisher, Charles, and Karen Hartgen
1983 Glass Trade Beads from Waterford, New York. *Pennsylvania Archaeologist* 53(1–2):47–52.
Fitch, Virginia A.
1983 South Natick National Register of Historic Places Registration Form. Ms. on file, U.S. Department of the Interior, National Park Service, National Register Branch, Washington, D.C.
Fithian, Charles M.
1992 On the West Side of the Delaware Bay: Current Research in Early Colonial Delaware. Paper presented at the Annual Middle Atlantic Archaeological Conference, Ocean City, Maryland.
1993 Personal communication.
Fitzgerald, William R.
1990 Chronology to Cultural Process: Lower Great Lakes Archaeology, 1500–1650. Unpublished Ph.D dissertation, Department of Anthropology, McGill University, Montreal.
Fitzhugh, William W., ed.
1985 *Cultures in Contact: The European Impact on Native Cultural Institutions in Eastern North America, A.D. 1000–1800.* Smithsonian Institution, Washington, D.C.
Flannery, Regina
1939 *An Analysis of Coastal Algonquian Culture.* Catholic University of America, Anthropological Series No. 7, Washington, D.C.
Fliegel, Carl J. (editor)
1970 *Index to the Records of the Moravian Missions among the Indians of North America.* Research Publications, New Haven, Connecticut.
Florance, Charles
1982 Ward's Point Conservation Area National Register of Historic Places Registration Form. Ms. on file, U.S. Department of the Interior, National Park Service, National Register Branch, Washington, D.C.
Follett, Harrison C.
1946–1947 Following the Cayuga Iroquois Migration in Cayuga County, New York. *The Bulletin of the Archaeological Society of Central New York* 1(5)–2(2).
Forbes, Jack D.
1988 *Black Africans and Native Americans: Color, Race and Caste in the Evolution of Red-Black Peoples.* Blackwell, New York.

Foster, Donald W., Victoria B. Kenyon, and George P. Nicholas II
1981 Ancient Lifeways at the Smyth Site NH38-4. *New Hampshire Archeologist* 22(2).

Foster, Michael K.
1974 *From the Earth to Beyond the Sky: An Ethnographic Approach to Four Longhouse Iroquois Speech Events.* Ethnology Division Paper No. 20, Mercury Series, National Museums of Canada, National Museum of Man, Ottawa.
1984 On Who Spoke First at Iroquois-White Councils: An Exercise in the Method of Upstreaming. In *Extending the Rafters: Interdisciplinary Approaches to Iroquoian Studies,* edited by Michael K. Foster, Jack Campisi, and Marianne Mithun, pp. 183-208. State University of New York Press, Albany.

Foster, Michael K., Jack Campisi, and Marianne Mithun (editors)
1984 *Extending the Rafters: Interdisciplinary Approaches to Iroquoian Studies.* State University of New York Press, Albany.

Fowke, Gerald
1894 *Archaeological Investigations in the James and Potomac Valleys.* Bureau of American Ethnology, Bulletin 23, Washington, D.C.

Fowler, William S.
1973 Metal Cutouts in the Northeast. *Bulletin of the Massachusetts Archaeological Society* 34(3-4): 24-30.
1974 Two Indian Burials in North Middleboro. *Bulletin of the Massachusetts Archaeological Society* 35(3-4):14-18.

Fowler, William S., and Herbert A. Luther
1950 Cultural Sequence at the Potter Pond Site. *Bulletin of the Massachusetts Archaeological Society* 11:91-102.

Francis, Convers
1836 *Life of John Eliot, the Apostle to the Indians.* Boston.

Franklin, Benjamin
1764 *A Narrative of the Late Massacres, in Lancaster County, of a Number of Indians, Friends of This Province, by Persons Unknown. With Some Observations on the Same.* Anthony Armbruster, Philadelphia.

Frazier, Patrick
1992 *The Mohicans of Stockbridge.* University of Nebraska Press, Lincoln.

Freedman, Janet, and Peter Pagoulatos
1989 Phase I and Phase II Archaeological Testing at Marina View Estates, Warwick, Rhode Island. Occasional Papers in Archaeology, No. 59, Public Archaeology Program, Rhode Island College, Providence.

Fuerst, David N.
1992 A Preliminary Report on the Protohistoric Component at the Snidow Site (46MC1), Mercer County, West Virginia. Paper presented at the Society for Historical Archaeology Annual Meeting, Kingston, Jamaica.

1993 Personal communication.

Funk, Robert E.
1976 *Recent Contributions to Hudson Valley Prehistory.* New York State Museum, Memoir 22, Albany.
1993 Personal communication.

Funk, Robert E., and Bruce E. Rippeteau
1977 *Adaptation, Continuity, and Change in Upper Susquehanna Prehistory.* Occasional Publications in Northeastern Anthropology, No. 3.

Gardner, Paul S.
1980 An Analysis of Dan River Ceramics from Virginia and North Carolina. Unpublished master's thesis, Department of Anthropology, University of North Carolina, Chapel Hill.

Gardner, Russell Herbert (Great Moose)
1987 The Mattakeesetts of Pembroke. In *Pembroke, Evolution of a New England Township, 1712-1987,* edited by Robert G. O'Hara and Elizabeth A. Bates. Claremont Press, Pembroke, Massachusetts.
1992 The Last Royal Dynasty of the Massachusett. Unpublished manuscript in author's possession.

Garratt, John G., and Bruce Robertson
1985 *The Four Indian Kings.* Public Archives of Canada, Ottawa.

Gehring, Charles T. (editor and translator)
1977 *New York Historical Manuscripts: Dutch, Volumes XX-XXI, Delaware Papers (English Period).* Genealogical Publishing Company, Baltimore.
1980 *New York Historical Manuscripts: Dutch, Volumes GG, HH, and II: Land Papers.* Genealogical Publishing Company, Baltimore.
1981 *New York Historical Manuscripts: Dutch, Volumes XVIII-XIX, Delaware Papers (Dutch Period).* Genealogical Publishing Company, Baltimore.

Gehring, Charles T., and Robert S. Grumet (editors)
1987 Observations of the Indians from Jasper Danckaerts's Journal, 1679-1680. *William and Mary Quarterly* 44(1):104-120.

Gehring, Charles T., and William A. Starna (editors)
1988 *A Journey into Mohawk and Oneida Country: The Journal of Harmen Meyndertsz van den Bogaert.* Syracuse University Press, Syracuse, New York.

Gehring, Charles T., William A. Starna, and William N. Fenton
1987 The Tawagonshi Treaty of 1613: Final Chapter. *New York History* 68(4):373-393.

George, David, Brian Jones, and Ross Harper
1993 Report on an Archaeological Reconnaissance Survey, South Kingstown, Rhode Island. Prepared for the Town of South Kingstown, Rhode Island, by Public Archaeology Survey Team, Storrs, Connecticut.

George, Richard L., Jay Babich, and Christine E. Davis
1990 The Household Site: Results of a Partial Excavation of a Late Monongahela Village in Westmore-

land County, Pennsylvania. *Pennsylvania Archaeologist* 60(2):40-70.

Gersna, Charles
1966 Notes on a Series of Nine Burials from the Beazell Site, Washington County, Pennsylvania 36WH34. *SPAAC Speaks* 6(1):7-18.

Ghere, David Lynn
1988 Abenaki Factionalism, Emigration, and Social Continuity: Indian Society in Northern New England, 1725 to 1760. Unpublished Ph.D dissertation, Department of Anthropology, University of Maine, Orono.

Gibbs, Virginia
1989 Personal communication.

Gibson, Stanford
1971 An Elevation Comparison of Iroquois Sites in Three Valleys of Central New York. *Chenango Chapter New York State Archaeological Association Bulletin* 12(2).
1986 A Report on Two Oneida Iroquois Indian Sites, OND 12, OND 16. *Chenango Chapter New York State Archaeological Association Bulletin* 22(1).

Gibson, Susan G. (editor)
1980 *Burr's Hill: A 17th Century Wampanoag Burial Ground in Warren, Rhode Island.* Studies in Anthropology and Material Culture, No. 2, The Haffenreffer Museum of Anthropology, Brown University, Providence.

Gipson, Laurence Henry
1936-1970 *The British Empire before the American Revolution.* 15 vols. Caldwell, Idaho.

Gleach, Frederic W.
1992 English and Powhatan Approaches to Civilizing Each Other: A History of Indian-White Relations in Early Colonial Virginia. Unpublished Ph.D dissertation, Department of Anthropology, University of Chicago.

Glover, Suzanne, and Kevin A. McBride
1992 Intensive (Locational) Archaeological Survey and Additional Testing, Parcels I, IIA, IIB, III, and Easements: Tribal Trust Lands, Gay Head, Massachusetts. Report prepared by the Public Archaeology Laboratory, Inc., for the Wampanoag Tribe of Gay Head (Aquinnah). On file, Massachusetts Historical Commission, Boston.

Goddard, R. H. Ives
1978a Eastern Algonquian Languages. In *Northeast,* edited by Bruce G. Trigger, pp. 70-77. Handbook of North American Indians, vol. 15, William C. Sturtevant, general editor. Smithsonian Institution, Washington, D.C.
1978b Delaware. In *Northeast,* edited by Bruce G. Trigger, pp. 213-239. Handbook of North American Indians, vol. 15, William C. Sturtevant, general editor. Smithsonian Institution, Washington, D.C.

Goddard, R. H. Ives, and Kathleen Bragdon
1988 *Native Writings in Massachusetts.* 2 vols. American Philosophical Society, Memoir 185, Philadelphia.

Godfrey, W.
1951 The Archaeology of the Old Stone Mill in Newport, Rhode Island. *American Antiquity* 17:(2): 120-129.

Gonzalez, Ellice B.
1986 Tri-Racial Isolates in a Bi-Racial Society: Poospatuck Ambiguity and Conflict. In *Strategies for Survival: American Indians in the Eastern United States,* edited by Frank W. Porter III, pp. 113-137. Greenwood Press, Westport, Connecticut.

Gookin, Daniel
1970 [1792] *Historical Collections of the Indians in New England.* Edited by Jeffrey H. Fiske. Towtaid, Massachusetts.

Goring, Rich
1981 An Archaeological Testing Project at Johnson Hall State Historic Site, Johnstown, New York. *The Bulletin and Journal of Archaeology for New York State* 82:25-38.

Gould, Richard A., and Patricia E. Rubertone
1991 One if by Land, Two if by Sea: The Historical Archaeology of Colonial Competition and Expansion. Paper presented at the Society for Historical Archaeology Annual Meetings, Richmond.

Gradie, Charlotte M.
1988 Spanish Jesuits in Virginia: The Mission That Failed. *Virginia Magazine of History and Biography* 96(2):131-156.

Graham, William J.
1935 *The Indians of Port Tobacco River, Maryland, and Their Burial Places.* Privately printed, Washington, D.C.

Gramly, Richard Michael
1977 Deerskins and Hunting Territories: Competition for a Scarce Resource of the Northeastern Woodlands. *American Antiquity* 42(4):601-605.
1993 Personal communication.

Grassman, Thomas
1952 The Mohawk-Caughnawaga Excavation. *Pennsylvania Archaeologist* 22:33-36.

Gray, Elma E., and Leslie Robb Gray
1956 *Wilderness Christians: The Moravian Mission to the Delaware Indians.* Cornell University Press, Ithaca.

Graybill, Jeffrey R.
1981 The Eastern Periphery of Fort Ancient (A.D. 1050-1650): A Diachronic Approach to Settlement Variability. Unpublished Ph.D dissertation, Department of Anthropology, University of Washington, Seattle.
1986 West Virginia Late Prehistoric Period Study Unit, A.D. 1050-1690. Ms. on file, West Virginia State Historic Preservation Office, Charleston.
1989 Late Prehistoric Period Historic Context. Draft ms. on file, West Virginia State Historic Preservation Office, Charleston.

Graymont, Barbara
1972 *The Iroquois in the American Revolution.* Syracuse University Press, Syracuse, New York.

Green, Rayna D.
1988 The Indian in Popular American Culture. In *History of Indian-White Relations,* edited by

Wilcomb E. Washburn, pp. 587–606. Handbook of North American Indians, vol. 4, William C. Sturtevant, general editor. Smithsonian Institution, Washington, D.C.

Greene, Lorenzo J.
1942 *The Negro in Colonial New England, 1620–1776.* New York.

Gregory, Leverette B.
1980 The Hatch Site: A Preliminary Report (Prince George County). *Quarterly Bulletin: Archeological Society of Virginia* 34(4):239–48.

Griffin, James B.
1943 *The Fort Ancient Aspect, Its Cultural and Chronological Position in Mississippi Valley Archaeology.* University of Michigan Press, Ann Arbor.

Griffith, Daniel R.
1982 Prehistoric Ceramics in Delaware: An Overview. *Archaeology of Eastern North America* 10:46–68.

Griffith, Daniel R., and Jay F. Custer
1985 Late Woodland Ceramics of Delaware: Implications for the Late Prehistoric Archaeology of Northeastern North America. *Pennsylvania Archaeologist* 55(3):5–20.

Grinde, Donald A., Jr., and Bruce E. Johansen
1991 *Exemplar of Liberty: Native America and the Evolution of Democracy.* UCLA American Indian Studies Center, Los Angeles.

Grossman, Joel W., Karen Bluth, Bonnie A. Bogumil, Diane Dallal, et al.
1985 The Excavation of Augustine Heermans' Warehouse and Associated 17th-Century Dutch West India Company Deposits: The Broad Street Financial Center Mitigation Report. 4 vols. Draft report on file, New York State Historic Preservation Office, Waterford.

Grumet, Robert S.
1979 "We Are Not So Great Fools": Changes in Upper Delawaran Socio-Political Life, 1630–1758. Unpublished Ph.D dissertation, Department of Anthropology, Rutgers University, New Brunswick.

1980 Sunksquaws, Shamans, and Tradeswomen: Middle Atlantic Coastal Algonkian Women during the Seventeenth and Eighteenth Centuries. In *Women and Colonization: Anthropological Perspectives,* edited by Mona Etienne and Eleanor Burke Leacock, pp. 43–62. Praeger Scientific, New York.

1981 *Native American Place Names in New York City.* Museum of the City of New York, New York.

1988 Taphow: The Forgotten "Sakemau and Commander in Chief of all Those Indians Inhabiting Northern New Jersey." *Bulletin of the Archaeological Society of New Jersey* 43:23–28.

1990 A New Ethnohistorical Model for North American Indian Demography. *North American Archaeologist* 11(1):29–41.

1991 The Minisink Settlements: Native American Identity and Society in the Munsee Heartland, 1650–1778. In *People of Minisink: Papers from the 1989 Delaware Water Gap Symposium,* edited by David G. Orr and Douglas V. Campana, pp. 175–250. Mid-Atlantic Region, National Park Service, Philadelphia.

1992 Historic Contact: Early Relations between Indian People and Colonists in Northeastern North America, 1524-1783. Ms. on file, Cultural Resources Planning Branch, National Register Programs Division, Mid-Atlantic Region, National Park Service, Philadelphia.

Guldenzopf, David B.
1986 The Colonial Transformation of Mohawk Iroquois Society. Unpublished Ph.D dissertation, Department of Anthropology, State University of New York at Albany.

Guthe, Alfred K.
1958 *The Late Prehistoric Occupation in Southwestern New York: An Interpretive Analysis.* Research Records of the Rochester Museum of Arts and Sciences, No. 11.

Hadlock, Wendell
1949 Three Contact Burials from Eastern Massachusetts. *Bulletin of the Massachusetts Archaeological Society* 10:63–71.

Hagerty, Gilbert
1963 The Iron Trade Knife in Oneida Territory. *Pennsylvania Archaeologist* 33(1–2):93–114.

1985 *Wampum, War, and Trade Goods West of the Hudson.* Heart-of-the-Lakes Publishing, Interlaken, New York.

Hale, Richard W.
1971 Moswetuset Hummock National Register of Historic Places Registration Form. Ms. on file, U.S. Department of the Interior, National Park Service, National Register Branch, Washington, D.C.

Hall, Clayton C. (editor)
1910 *Narratives of Early Maryland, 1633–1684.* Charles Scribner's Sons, New York.

Hallowell, A. Irving
1957 The Backwash of the Frontier: The Impact of the Indian on American Culture. In *The Frontier in Perspective,* edited by W. D. Wyman and C. D. Kroeber, pp. 229–258. University of Wisconsin Press, Madison.

Hamell, George R.
1976 Preliminary Report on the Alhart Site Archaeology. Report on file, Rochester Museum and Science Center, Rochester, New York.

1980 Gannagaro State Historic Site: A Current Perspective. In *Studies on Iroquoian Culture,* edited by Nancy Bonvillain, pp. 91–108. Occasional Publications in Northeastern Anthropology, No. 6.

1983 Trading in Metaphors: The Magic of Beads; Another Perspective upon Indian-European Contact in Northeastern North America. In *Proceedings of the 1982 Glass Trade Bead Conference,* edited by Charles F. Hayes III, pp. 5–28. Rochester Museum and Science Center Research, Record 16.

1987 Mythical Realities and European Contact in the Northeast during the Sixteenth and Seventeenth Centuries. *Man in the Northeast* 33:63–87.

1988 Arent Van Curler and the Underwater Grandfather. Ms. in author's possession.

Hamell, George R., and Hazel Dean John

1987 Ethnology, Archeology, History, and "Seneca Origins": Some Preliminary Interpretations of the Chieftain Title, Clan, and Moiety Associations of the Seneca Villages, c. 1650-1687. Paper presented at the 1987 Conference on Iroquois Research, Rennselaersville, New York.

Hamilton, Milton

1976 *Sir William Johnson: Colonial American, 1715-1763.* Kennikat Press, Port Washington, New York.

Hamilton, T. M.

1985 The Spall Gunflint. In *Selected Papers: Proceedings of the 1984 Trade Gun Conference, Parts I and II,* edited by Charles F. Hayes III, pp. 73-83. Rochester Museum and Science Center Research Record 18.

Handlin, Oscar, and Irving Mark (editors)

1964 Chief Daniel Nimham versus Roger Morris, Beverly Robinson, and Philip Philipse: An Indian Land Case in Colonial New York, 1765-1767. *Ethnohistory* 11(3):193-246.

Handsman, Russell G.

1987 The Sociopolitics of Susquehannock Archaeology. Paper presented at the New Approaches to the Past Symposium, Franklin and Marshall College, Lancaster, Pennsylvania.

Hanna, Charles A.

1911 *The Wilderness Trail: or, the Ventures and Adventures of the Pennsylvania Traders on the Allegheny Path with Some New Annals of the Old West, and the Records of Some Strong Men and Some Bad Ones.* 2 vols. G. P. Putnam's Sons, New York.

Hantman, Jeffrey L.

1990a Monacan History and the Contact Era in Virginia. *Society for American Archaeology Bulletin* 8(2):14.

1990b Between Powhatan and Quirank: Reconstructing Monacan Culture and History in the Context of Jamestown. *American Anthropologist* 92(3):676-690.

Hare, Lloyd C.M.

1932 *Thomas Mayhew, Patriarch to the Indians (1593-1682).* New York.

Harrington, Faith

1985 Sea Tenure in Seventeenth-Century New Hampshire: Native Americans and Englishmen in the Sphere of Maritime Resources. *Historical New Hampshire* 40(1-2):18-33.

Harrington, Jean C.

1954 Dating Stem Fragments of Seventeenth and Eighteenth Century Clay Tobacco Pipes. *Quarterly Bulletin: Archeological Society of Virginia* 9(1).

Harrington, Mark Raymond

1909 The Rock-Shelters of Armonk, New York. In *Indians of Greater New York and the Lower Hudson,* edited by Clark Wissler, pp. 123-138. Anthropological Papers of the American Museum of Natural History, vol. 3.

1921 *Religion and Ceremonies of the Lenape.* Indian Notes and Monographs, 2d ser., vol. 19, Museum of the American Indian, Heye Foundation, New York.

1924 An Ancient Village Site of the Shinnecock Indians. *Anthropological Papers of the American Museum of Natural History* 22(5).

1925 Indian Occupation of Croton Neck and Point. *Quarterly Bulletin of the Westchester County Historical Society* 1(4):3-19.

Harris, R. Cole, and Geoffrey J. Matthews (editors)

1987 *Historical Atlas of Canada. Volume 1: From the Beginning to 1800.* University of Toronto Press, Toronto.

Hasenstab, Robert J.

1987 Canoes, Caches, and Carrying Places: Territorial Boundaries and Tribalization in Late Woodland Western New York. *The Bulletin: Journal of the New York Archaeological Association* 95: 39-49.

1990 Agriculture, Warfare, and Tribalization in the Iroquois Homeland of New York: A G.I.S. Analysis of Late Woodland Settlement. Unpublished Ph.D dissertation, Department of Anthropology, University of Massachusetts, Amherst.

Hauptman, Laurence M., and James D. Wherry (editors)

1990 *The Pequots in Southern New England: The Fall and Rise of an American Indian Nation.* University of Oklahoma Press, Norman.

Haviland, William A.

1988 *Anthropology.* Holt, Rinehart, and Winston, New York.

Haviland, William A., and Marjory W. Power

1981 *The Original Vermonters: Native Inhabitants, Past and Present.* University Press of New England, Hanover, New Hampshire.

Hayes, Charles F., III

1965 *The Orringh Stone Tavern and Three Seneca Sites of the Late Historic Period.* Research Records of the Rochester Museum of Arts and Sciences, No. 12.

Hayes, Charles F., III (general editor)

1980 *Proceedings of the 1979 Iroquois Pottery Conference.* Rochester Museum and Science Center Research Record 13.

1983 *Proceedings of the 1982 Glass Trade Bead Conference.* Rochester Museum and Science Center Research Record 16.

1985 *Selected Papers: Proceedings of the 1984 Trade Gun Conference, Parts I and II.* Rochester Museum and Science Center Research Record 18.

1989 *Proceedings of the 1986 Shell Bead Conference: Selected Papers.* Rochester Museum and Science Center Research Record 20.

Hazard, Samuel, et al. (editors)

1852-1949 *Pennsylvania Archives.* 138 vols. Joseph Severns, Harrisburg, Pennsylvania.

Hazzard, David K., and Martha W. McCartney

1979 Fort Christanna, Archaeological Reconnaissance Survey. Report on file, Virginia Department of Historic Resources, Richmond.

Hebert, Michael
1983 Devil's Foot Cemetery Archeological Site National Register of Historic Places Registration Form. Ms. on file, U.S. Department of the Interior, National Park Service, National Register Branch, Washington, D.C.

Heckewelder, John
1819 *An Account of the History, Manners, and Customs of the Indian Nations, Who Once Inhabited Pennsylvania and the Neighbouring States.* Transactions of the American Philosophical Society, No. 1, Philadelphia.

Heidenreich, Conrad E.
1971 *Huronia: A History and Geography of the Huron Indians, 1600-1650.* McClelland and Stewart, Toronto.
1978 Huron. In *Northeast,* edited by Bruce G. Trigger, pp. 368-388. Handbook of North American Indians, vol. 15, William C. Sturtevant, general editor. Smithsonian Institution, Washington, D.C.

Heisey, Henry W., and J. Paul Witmer
1964 The Shenks Ferry People: A Site and Some Generalities. *Pennsylvania Archaeologist* 34(1):1-34.

Heite, Louise B., and Edward F. Heite
1989 Saving New Amstel: A Proposed City of New Castle Archaeological Preservation Plan. Report on file, Delaware Bureau of Archaeology and Historic Preservation, Dover.

Helms, Mary W.
1988 *Ulysses' Sail: An Ethnographic Odyssey of Power, Knowledge, and Geographical Distance.* Princeton University Press, Princeton, New Jersey.

Henry, Susan L.
1992 *Physical, Spatial, and Temporal Dimensions of Colono Ware in the Chesapeake, 1600-1800.* South Carolina Institute of Archaeology and Anthropology, Volumes in Historical Archaeology 23. Revised ed. of 1980 master's thesis, Department of Anthropology, The Catholic University of America, Washington, D.C.

Herbstritt, James T.
1982 Richard T. Foley Site National Register of Historic Places Registration Form. Ms. on file, U.S. Department of the Interior, National Park Service, National Register Branch, Washington, D.C.
1983 Excavation at Two Monongahela Sites: Late Woodland Gensler (36GR63) and Protohistoric Throckmorton (36GR160). Report submitted to Consolidated Coal Company, Pittsburgh and on file at the Bureau of Historic Preservation, Harrisburg.
1984 The Mystery of the Monongahela Culture: Archaeology at Foley Farm. *Pennsylvania Heritage* 10(3):26-31.

Herbstritt, James T., and Barry C. Kent
1990 Shenks Ferry Revisited: A New Look at an Old Culture. *Pennsylvania Heritage* 16(1):12-17.

Hesse, Franklin J.
1975 The Egli and Lord Sites: The Historic Component—"Unadilla" 1753-1778. *The Bulletin: The New York State Archaeological Association* 63:14-31.

Heusser, Albert H.
1923 *Homes and Haunts of the Indians.* Paterson, New Jersey.

Heye, George G., and George H. Pepper
1915 Exploration of a Munsee Cemetery near Montague, New Jersey. *Contributions to the Museum of the American Indian, Heye Foundation,* 2(1).

Hinman, Marjory
1975 *Onaquaga: Hub of the Border Wars.* Valley Offset, Deposit, New York.

Hirsch, Adam J.
1988 The Collision of Military Cultures in Seventeenth-Century New England. *Journal of American History* 74(4):1190-1200.

Hodges, Mary Ellen Norrisey
1986 Camden: Another Look Seventeen Years after Registration. *Notes on Virginia* 29:21-25.

Hodges, Mary Ellen Norrisey, and Martha W. McCartney
1986 Archaeological Addendum to the Camden National Historic Landmark Registration Form. Ms. on file, U.S. Department of the Interior, National Park Service, History Division, Washington, D.C.

Hoffman, Bernard G.
1955 The Historic Ethnography of the Micmac of the Sixteenth and Seventeenth Centuries. Unpublished Ph.D dissertation, Department of Anthropology, University of California, Berkeley.
1961 *Cabot to Cartier: Sources for a Historical Ethnography of Northeastern North America, 1497-1550.* University of Toronto Press, Toronto.
1964 Observations on Certain Ancient Tribes of the Northern Appalachian Province. *Bureau of American Ethnology Bulletin* 191:195-245.
1967 Ancient Tribes Revisited: A Summary of Indian Distribution and Movement in the Northeastern United States from 1534 to 1779. Parts I-III. *Ethnohistory* 14(1-2):1-46.

Hoffman, Curtiss
1986 Stepping Stones Condominium Archaeological Survey, Holbrook, Massachusetts. Report on file, Massachusetts Historical Commission, Boston.
1987 A Preliminary Report on the Excavation of Cedar Swamp 4. *Archaeological Quarterly of the W. Elmer Ekblaw Chapter, Massachusetts Archaeological Society* 9(1):1-25.

Hoffman, Paul E.
1990 *A New Andalusia and a Way to the Orient: The American Southeast during the Sixteenth Century.* Louisiana State University Press, Baton Rouge.

Holland, C. G.
1970 *An Archaeological Survey of Southwest Virginia.* Smithsonian Contributions to Anthropology, No. 12, Washington, D.C.
1978 Albemarle County Settlements: A Piedmont Model. *Quarterly Bulletin: Archeological Society of Virginia* 33(1):29-44.
1982 The Silver Frontlet. *Quarterly Bulletin: Archeological Society of Virginia* 37(1):24-30.

Holm, Thomas Campanius
1702 *Kort Beskrifning om Provincien Nya Swerige uti America.* J. H. Werner, Stockholm.
Holmes, Paul
1982 The Harvey Mitchell Site (NH 46-12), Newton Junction, N.H. *New Hampshire Archaeologist* 23:64-90.
Holstrom, Donald
1969a Damariscotta Shell Heap National Register of Historic Places Registration Form. Ms. on file, U.S. Department of the Interior, National Park Service, National Register Branch, Washington, D.C.
1969b Fort Pownall Memorial National Register of Historic Places Registration Form. Ms. on file, U.S. Department of the Interior, National Park Service, National Register Branch, Washington, D.C.
Hosbach, Richard E., and Stanford Gibson
1980 The Wilson Site (OND 9), A Protohistoric Oneida Village. *Chenango Chapter New York State Archaeological Association Bulletin* 18(4A).
Houghton, Frederick
1912 The Seneca Nation from 1655-1687. *Bulletin of the Buffalo Society of Natural Sciences* 10:363-476.
Howard, Franklyn
1907 *History of the Town of Acushnet.* New Bedford, Massachusetts.
Howard, Robert West
1968 *Thundergate: The Forts of Niagara.* Prentice-Hall, Englewood Cliffs, New Jersey.
Huden, John C.
1965 *Indian Place Names of New England.* Contributions from the Museum, Museum of the American Indian, Heye Foundation, New York.
Hudson, Charles
1862 *History of the Town of Marlborough, Middlesex County, Massachusetts.* Boston.
Hudson, Charles M.
1990 *The Juan Pardo Expeditions: Exploration of the Carolinas and Tennessee, 1566-1568.* Smithsonian Institution, Washington, D.C.
Huey, Paul R.
1974 *Archeology at the Schuyler Flatts, 1971-1974.* Town of Colonie, Colonie, New York.
1984. Dutch Sites of the 17th Century in Rensselaerswyck. In *The Scope of Historical Archaeology: Essays in Honor of John L. Cotter,* edited by David G. Orr and Daniel G. Crozier, pp. 63-85. Laboratory of Anthropology, Temple University, Philadelphia.
1985a Archaeological Excavations in the Site of Fort Orange, A Dutch West India Company Trading Fort Built in 1624. In *New Netherland Studies: An Inventory of Current Research and Approaches—Bulletin Koninklijke Nederlandse Oudheidkundige Bond* 84(2-3):68-79.
1985b An Historic Event at the Schuyler Flatts in 1643. Ms. in author's possession.
1988a Aspects of Continuity and Change in Colonial Dutch Material Culture at Fort Orange, 1624-1664. Unpublished Ph.D dissertation, Department of American Studies, University of Pennsylvania, Philadelphia.
1988b The Archeology of Colonial New Netherland. In *Colonial Dutch Studies: An Interdisciplinary Approach,* edited by Eric Nooter and Patricia U. Bonomi, pp. 52-77. New York University Press, New York.
1989 Personal communication.
1991 The Dutch at Fort Orange. In *Historical Archaeology in Global Perspective,* edited by Lisa Falk, pp. 21-67. Smithsonian Institution, Washington, D.C.
Huey, Paul R., Lois M. Feister, and Joseph E. McEvoy
1977 Archeological Investigations in the Vicinity of Fort Crailo during Sewer Line Construction under Riverside Avenue in Rensselaer, New York. *Bulletin of the New York State Archaeological Association* 69:19-42.
Hughes, Richard C.
1991 Personal communication.
Hunt, Eleazer D.
1986 Marian E. White: Researching Settlement Patterns of the Niagara Frontier. *North American Archaeologist* 7(4):313-328.
Hunt, George T.
1940 *The Wars of the Iroquois: A Study in Intertribal Trade Relations.* University of Wisconsin Press, Madison.
Hunter, Charles E.
1983 A Susquehanna Indian Town on the Schuylkill. *Pennsylvania Archaeologist* 53(3):17-19.
Hunter, William A.
n.d. Eighteenth Century Western Pennsylvania Sites. Ms. on file, Pennsylvania Historical and Museum Commission, Harrisburg.
1956 Pymatuning, an Identified Delaware Townsite in Western Pennsylvania. *Pennsylvania Archaeologist* 26(3-4).
1961 *The Walking Purchase and the Pennsylvania Proprietors.* Pennsylvania Historical and Museum Commission Leaflet. Harrisburg.
1974 Moses (Tunda) Tatamy, Delaware Indian Diplomat. In *A Delaware Indian Symposium,* edited by Herbert C. Kraft, pp. 71-88. Anthropological Series 4, Pennsylvania Historical and Museum Commission, Harrisburg.
1978a History of the Ohio Valley. In *Northeast,* edited by Bruce G. Trigger, pp. 588-593. Handbook of North American Indians, vol. 15, William C. Sturtevant, general editor. Smithsonian Institution, Washington, D.C.
1978b Documented Subdivisions of the Delaware. *Bulletin of the Archaeological Society of New Jersey* 35:20-40.
Huston, Geraldine
1950 *Oratam of the Hackensacks: An Account of Indian and Dutch in Seventeenth-Century Northern New Jersey.* Highway Printing Company, Paramus, New Jersey.

Hutchinson, Henry, et al.
1957 Report on the Mispillion Site, 7S-A-1. *The Archeolog* 9(2).

Isaac, Rhys
1982 *The Transformation of Virginia, 1740-1790.* University of North Carolina Press, Chapel Hill.

Jacobs, Wilbur R.
1950 *Diplomacy and Indian Gifts: Anglo-French Rivalry along the Ohio and Northwest Frontiers, 1748-1763.* Stanford University Press, Stanford, California.
1988 British Indian Policies to 1783. In *History of Indian-White Relations,* edited by Wilcomb E. Washburn, pp. 5-12. Handbook of North American Indians, vol. 4, William C. Sturtevant, general editor. Smithsonian Institution, Washington, D.C.

Jacobson, Jerome
1980 *Burial Ridge: Archaeology at New York City's Largest Prehistoric Cemetery.* Staten Island Institute of Arts and Sciences, St. George, New York.

Jameson, J. Franklin (editor)
1909 *Narratives of New Netherland, 1609-1664.* Charles Scribner's Sons, New York.

Jennings, Francis
1967 The Indian Trade of the Susquehanna Valley. *Proceedings of the American Philosophical Society* 110(6):406-424.
1968a Incident at Tulpehocken. *Pennsylvania History* 35(4):335-355.
1968b Glory, Death, and Transfiguration: The Susquehannock Indians in the Seventeenth Century. *Proceedings of the American Philosophical Society* 110(6):406-424.
1970 The Scandalous Indian Policy of William Penn's Sons: Deeds and Documents of the Walking Purchase. *Pennsylvania History* 37(1):19-39.
1971 Goals and Functions of Puritan Missions to the Indians. *Ethnohistory* 18(2):197-212.
1975 *The Invasion of America: Indians, Colonialism, and the Cant of Conquest.* University of North Carolina Press, Chapel Hill.
1978 Susquehannock. In *Northeast,* edited by Bruce G. Trigger, pp. 362-367. Handbook of North American Indians, vol. 15, William C. Sturtevant, general editor. Smithsonian Institution, Washington, D.C.
1984 *The Ambiguous Iroquois Empire: The Covenant Chain Confederation of Indian Tribes with English Colonies from Its Beginning to the Lancaster Treaty of 1744.* W. W. Norton, New York.
1988a Dutch and Swedish Indian Policies. In *History of Indian-White Relations,* edited by Wilcomb E. Washburn, pp. 13-19. Handbook of North American Indians, vol. 4, William C. Sturtevant, general editor. Smithsonian Institution, Washington, D.C.
1988b *Empire of Fortune: Crowns, Colonies, and Tribes in the Seven Years War in America.* W. W. Norton, New York.

Jennings, Francis, William N. Fenton, Mary A. Druke, and David R. Miller (editors)
1985 *The History and Culture of Iroquois Diplomacy: An Interdisciplinary Guide to the Treaties of the Six Nations and Their League.* Syracuse University Press, Syracuse, New York.

Jeppson, Britta D.
1964 A Study of Cordage and Rolled Copper Beads, Burial #6, Titicut Site. *Bulletin of the Massachusetts Archaeological Society* 25(2):37-38.

Jirikowic, Christine
1990 The Political Implications of a Cultural Practice: A New Perspective on Ossuary Burial in the Potomac Valley. *North American Archaeologist* 11(4):353-374.

Johannemann, Edward
1979 Indian Fields Site: Part I, Montauk, Suffolk County, Long Island, New York. In *The History and Archaeology of the Montauk Indians,* edited by Gaynell Stone, pp. 175-195. Stony Brook, New York.
1990 Personal communication.

Johannsen, Christina B., and John P. Ferguson (editors)
1983 *Iroquois Arts: A Directory of a People and Their Work.* Association for the Advancement of Native North American Arts and Crafts, Warnerville, New York.

Johnson, Amandus
1911 *The Swedish Settlements on the Delaware: Their History and Relation to the Indians, Dutch, and English, 1638-1664, with an Account of the South, the New Sweden, and the American Companies, and the Efforts of Sweden to Regain the Colony.* 2 vols. University of Pennsylvania Press, Philadelphia.

Johnson, Eric S.
1993 "Some by Flatteries and Others by Threatenings": Political Strategies among Native Americans of Seventeenth-Century New England. Unpublished Ph.D dissertation, Department of Anthropology, University of Massachusetts, Amherst.

Johnson, Eric S., and James W. Bradley
1987 The Bark Wigwams Site: An Early Seventeenth-Century Component in Central Massachusetts. *Man in the Northeast* 33:1-26.

Johnson, Eric S., and Thomas F. Mahlstedt
1985 Report of Salvage Excavation of Unmarked Burials at the Palmer Site (19HD97) Westfield, Massachusetts. Report on file, Massachusetts Historical Commission, Boston.

Johnson, Frank R.
1967-1968 *The Tuscaroras: Mythology, Medicine, Culture.* 2 vols. Johnson Publishing Company, Murfreesboro, North Carolina.

Johnson, Frederick
1942 The Hemenway Site M42/42, Eastham, Massachusetts. *Bulletin of the Massachusetts Archaeological Society* 3(3):27-30.

Johnson, L. Dean
1985 The Perkins Point Site, Bath County, Virginia. In *Prehistory of the Gathright Dam Area, Virginia.* Privately printed.

Johnson, William C.
1992 The Protohistoric Monongahela and the Case for an Iroquoian Connection. Paper presented at the 57th Annual Meeting of the Society for American Archaeology, Pittsburgh.
1993 Personal communication.

Johnson, William C., James B. Richardson III, and Allen S. Bohnert
1979 Archaeological Site Survey in Northwestern Pennsylvania, Region IV. Report on file, Bureau of Historic Preservation, Harrisburg.

Johnston, John
1873 *History of the Towns of Bristol and Bremen, including the Pemaquid Settlement.* Albany, New York.

Jordan, Terry G.
1985 *American Log Buildings: An Old World Heritage.* University of North Carolina Press, Chapel Hill.

Jordan, Terry G., and Matti Kaups
1989 *The American Backwoods Frontier: An Ethnic and Ecological Interpretation.* Johns Hopkins University Press, Baltimore.

JRIA (James River Institute for Archaeology, Inc.)
1990 Phase I Archaeological Survey of the Governor's Land at Two Rivers, James City County, Virginia. Report submitted to Governor's Land Associates, Inc., Williamsburg, and on file in the Virginia Department of Historic Resources, Richmond.
1992 Archaeological Treatment Plan for Sites 44JC308 and 44JC159 at Governor's Land at Two Rivers, James City County, Virginia. Report submitted to Governor's Land Associates, Inc., Williamsburg, and on file in the Virginia Department of Historic Resources, Richmond.

Justice, Noel
1987 *Stone Age Spear and Arrow Points of the Midcontinental and Eastern United States.* Indiana University Press, Bloomington.

Kawashima, Yasuhide
1986 *Puritan Justice and the Indian: White Man's Law in Massachusetts, 1630-1763.* Wesleyan University Press, Middletown, Connecticut.
1988a Colonial Government Agencies. In *History of Indian-White Relations,* edited by Wilcomb E. Washburn, pp. 245-254. Handbook of North American Indians, vol. 4, William C. Sturtevant, general editor. Smithsonian Institution, Washington, D.C.
1988b Indian Servitude in the Northeast. In *History of Indian-White Relations,* edited by Wilcomb E. Washburn, pp. 404-406. Handbook of North American Indians, vol. 4, William C. Sturtevant, general editor. Smithsonian Institution, Washington, D.C.

Kehoe, Alice B.
1991 Personal communication.

Kelley, Marc A., Gail Barrett, and Sandra D. Saunders
1987 Diet, Dental Disease, and Transition in Northeastern Native Americans. *Man in the Northeast* 33:113-125.

Kelley, Marc A., Paul S. Sledzik, and Sean P. Murphy
1987 Health, Demographics, and Physical Constitution in Seventeenth-Century Rhode Island Indians. *Man in the Northeast* 34:1-25.

Kelsay, Isabel Thompson
1984 *Joseph Brant, 1743-1807: Man of Two Worlds.* Syracuse University Press, Syracuse, New York.

Kent, Barry C.
1984 *Susquehanna's Indians.* Anthropological Series, No. 6. Pennsylvania Historical and Museum Commission, Harrisburg.
n.d. 18th-Century Sites and Collections from the West Branch. Ms. on file, Pennsylvania Museum and Historical Commission, Harrisburg.

Kent, Barry C., and Charles Douts, Jr.
1977. Exploratory Excavations at the Site of Fort Loudon, Peters Township, Franklin County, Penna. (36FR107). Ms. on file, Pennsylvania Museum and Historical Commission, Harrisburg.

Kent, Barry C., Janet Rice, and Kakuko Ota
1981 A Map of 18th Century Indian Towns in Pennsylvania. *Pennsylvania Archaeologist* 51(4):1-18.

Kenyon, Ian T., and Thomas Kenyon
1983 Comments on 17th Century Glass Trade Beads from Ontario. In *Proceedings of the 1982 Glass Trade Bead Conference,* edited by Charles F. Hayes III, pp. 59-74. Rochester Museum and Science Center Research Record 16.

Kenyon, Victoria
1983 Campbell Site Survey Report. Report on file, New Hampshire Division of Historic Resources, Concord.

Kerber, Jordan E. (editor)
1988-1989 Where Are the Woodland Villages? *Bulletin of the Massachusetts Archaeological Society* 49(2):44-82; 50(1):24-28.

Kevitt, Chester B.
1968 Aboriginal Dugout Discovered at Weymouth. *Bulletin of the Massachusetts Archaeological Society* 30(1):105.

Kidd, Kenneth E.
1955 A Statistical Analysis of Trade Axes. *Bulletin of the New York State Archaeological Association* 5(5):6.

Kidd, Kenneth E., and Martha A. Kidd
1970 A Classification System for Glass Beads for the Use of Field Archaeologists. *Canadian Historic Sites: Occasional Papers in Archaeology and History* 1:45-89. Ottawa.

Kinsey, W. Fred, III
1982 Park Site 36LA96 National Register of Historic Places Registration Form. Ms. on file, U.S. Department of the Interior, National Park Service, National Register Branch, Washington, D.C.

Kinsey, W. Fred, III (editor)
1972 *Archaeology in the Upper Delaware Valley: A Study of the Cultural Chronology of the Tocks*

Island Reservoir. Anthropological Series 2. Pennsylvania Historical and Museum Commission, Harrisburg.

Kinsey, W. Fred, III, and Jay F. Custer
1982 Lancaster County Park Site 36LA96: Conestoga Phase. *Pennsylvania Archaeologist* 52:25-57.

Knowles, Nathaniel
1940 The Torture of Captives by Indians of Eastern North America. *Proceedings of the American Philosophical Society* 82(2):151-225.

Kraft, Herbert C.
1972 The Miller Field Site, Warren County, New Jersey. In *Archaeology in the Upper Delaware Valley: A Study of the Cultural Chronology of the Tocks Island Reservoir,* edited by W. Fred Kinsey III, pp. 1-54. Anthropological Series 2, Pennsylvania Historical and Museum Commission, Harrisburg.
1975a *The Archaeology of the Tocks Island Area.* Archaeological Research Center, Seton Hall University Museum, South Orange, New Jersey.
1975b The Late Woodland Pottery of the Upper Delaware Valley: A Survey and Reevaluation. *Archaeology of Eastern North America* 3(1):101-140.
1976 *The Archaeology of the Pahaquarra Site.* Archaeological Research Center, Seton Hall University, South Orange, New Jersey.
1977 *The Minisink Settlements: An Investigation into a Prehistoric and Early Historic Site in Sussex County, New Jersey.* Archaeological Research Center, Seton Hall University, South Orange, New Jersey.
1978 *The Minisink Site: A Reevaluation of a Late Prehistoric and Early Historic Contact Site in Sussex County, New Jersey.* Archaeological Research Center, Seton Hall University Museum, South Orange, New Jersey.
1986 *The Lenape: Archaeology, History, and Ethnography.* New Jersey Historical Society, Newark.
1989a Evidence of Contact and Trade in the Middle Atlantic Region and with the Minisink Indians of the Upper Delaware River Valley. *Journal of Middle Atlantic Archaeology* 5:77-102.
1989b Sixteenth and Seventeenth Century Indian/White Trade Relations in the Middle Atlantic and Northeast Regions. *Archaeology of Eastern North America* 17:1-29.

Kuhn, Robert D.
1985 Trade and Exchange among the Mohawk-Iroquois: A Trace Element Analysis of Iroquoian Ceramic Smoking Pipes. Unpublished Ph.D dissertation, Department of Anthropology, State University of New York at Albany.
1989 The Trace Element Analysis of Hudson Valley Clays and Ceramics. *The Bulletin: Journal of the New York Archaeological Association* 99:25-30.

Kuhn, Robert D., and William A. Lanford
1987 Sourcing Hudson Valley Cherts from Trace Element Analysis. *Man in the Northeast* 34:57-69.

Kuhn, Robert D., and Dean R. Snow (editors)
1986 *The Mohawk Valley Project: 1983 Jackson-Everson Excavations.* Institute for Northeastern Anthropology, State University of New York at Albany.

Kupperman, Karen Ordhal
1980 *Settling with the Indians: The Meeting of English and Indian Cultures in America, 1580-1640.* Rowman and Littlefield, Totowa, New Jersey.

LaFantasie, Glenn W. (editor)
1988 *The Correspondence of Roger Williams.* 2 vols. University Press of New England, Hanover, New Hampshire.

Lafitau, Joseph-François, S.J.
1974-1977 [1724] *Customs of the American Indians Compared with the Customs of Primitive Times.* 2 vols. Edited by William N. Fenton and Elizabeth L. Moore. Publications of the Champlain Society, Nos. 48-49, Toronto.

Lamson, D. F.
1895 *History of the Town of Manchester, Essex County, Massachusetts.* Manchester.

Land, Aubrey C., Lois Green Carr, and Edward C. Papenfuse (editors)
1977 *Law, Society, and Politics in Early Maryland.* Johns Hopkins University Press, Baltimore.

Landy, David
1978 Tuscarora among the Iroquois. In *Northeast,* edited by Bruce G. Trigger, pp. 518-524. Handbook of North American Indians, vol. 15, William C. Sturtevant, general editor. Smithsonian Institution, Washington, D.C.

Larrabee, Edward M.
1976 Recurrent Themes and Sequences in North American Indian-European Culture Contact. *Transactions of the American Philosophical Society* 66(7).

Latham, Roy
1957 Seventeenth-Century Graves at Montauk, Long Island. *New York State Archaeological Association Bulletin* 9.
1961 Three Mile Harbor Sites. *New York State Archaeological Association Bulletin* 23.
1965 Late Indian Graves in Laurel, Long Island, N.Y. *New York State Archaeological Association Bulletin* 33.

Lauber, Almon W.
1913 *Indian Slavery in Colonial Times within the Present Limits of the United States.* Columbia University Studies in History, Economics, and Public Law, No. 134, New York.

Lavin, Lucianne M.
1983 Patterns of Chert Acquisition among Woodland Groups within the Delaware Watershed: A Lithologic Approach. 2 vols. Unpublished Ph.D dissertation, Department of Anthropology, New York University.
1986 Pottery Classification and Cultural Models in Southern New England Prehistory. *North American Archaeologist* 7(1):1-14.
1987 The Windsor Ceramic Tradition in Southern New England. *North American Archaeologist* 8(1):23-40.

Lawson, John
1967 [1709] *A New Voyage to Carolina.* Edited by Hugh Talmadge Lefler. University of North Carolina Press, Chapel Hill.
Leach, Douglas Edward
1958 *Flintlock and Tomahawk: New England in King Philip's War.* Macmillan, New York.
1966 *The Northern Colonial Frontier, 1607-1763.* Holt, Rinehart, and Winston, New York.
1988 Colonial Indian Wars. In *History of Indian-White Relations,* edited by Wilcomb E. Washburn, pp. 128-143. Handbook of North American Indians, vol. 4, William C. Sturtevant, general editor. Smithsonian Institution, Washington, D.C.
Leacock, Eleanor Burke
1954 The Montagnais "Hunting Territory" and the Fur Trade. *Memoirs of the American Anthropological Association* 78.
Leacock, Eleanor Burke, and Nancy Oestreich Lurie (editors)
1988 *North American Indians in Historical Perspective.* Waveland Press, Prospect Heights, Illinois. Originally published in 1971 by Random House, New York.
Leder, Lawrence H. (editor)
1956 *The Livingston Indian Records, 1666-1723.* Pennsylvania Historical Association, Harrisburg.
Lemon, James T.
1972 *The Best Poor Man's Country: A Geographical Study of Early Southeastern Pennsylvania.* Johns Hopkins University Press, Baltimore.
Lenig, Donald
1965 The Oak Hill Horizon and Its Relation to the Development of Five Nations Iroquois Culture. *Researches and Transactions of the New York State Archaeological Association* 15(1):1-114.
Lenig, Wayne
1977 Archaeology, Education and the Indian Castle Church. *The Bulletin and Journal of Archaeology for New York* State 69:42-51.
Lenik, Edward J.
1976 A Silver Brooch from Echo Lake. *Newsletter of the Archaeological Society of New Jersey* 102:6-7.
1985 Archaeological Investigations at the David Demarest House Site, River Edge, New Jersey. Ms. on file, Sheffield Archaeological Consultants, Wayne, New Jersey.
1987 Cultural Resource Reconnaissance Survey of the Pierson Lakes Estates Property, Town of Ramapo, Rockland County, New York. Ms. on file, Sheffield Archaeological Consultants, Wayne, New Jersey.
1989 New Evidence on the Contact Period in Northeastern New Jersey and Southeastern New York. *Journal of Middle Atlantic Archaeology* 5:103-120.
1993 Personal communication.
Lenik, Edward J., and Kathleen L. Ehrhardt
1986 Data Recovery Excavations in the Monksville Reservoir Project Area, Passaic County, New Jersey. Ms. on file, Sheffield Archaeological Consultants, Wayne, New Jersey.

Leone, Mark P., and Parker B. Potter, Jr. (editors)
1988 *The Recovery of Meaning: Historical Archaeology in the Eastern United States.* Smithsonian Institution, Washington, D.C.
Lescarbot, Marc
1907-1914 [1618] *The History of New France.* Edited and translated by W. L. Grant, 3 vols. The Champlain Society, Toronto.
Leslie, Vernon
1968 The Davenport Site: A Study in Tocks Island Reservoir Archaeology. *The Chesopiean* 6(5): 109-139.
Levernier, James A., and Hennig Cohen (editors)
1977 *The Indians and Their Captives.* Greenwood Press, Westport, Connecticut.
Lewis, Clifford M.
1988 Roman Catholic Missions in the Southeast and the Northeast. In *History of Indian-White Relations,* edited by Wilcomb E. Washburn, pp. 481-493. Handbook of North American Indians, vol. 4, William C. Sturtevant, general editor. Smithsonian Institution, Washington, D.C.
Lewis, Clifford M., and Albert J. Loomie
1953 *The Spanish Jesuit Mission in Virginia, 1570-1571.* University of North Carolina Press, Chapel Hill.
Lindeström, Peter
1925 [1691] *Geographia Americae with an Account of the Delaware Indians Based on Surveys and Notes Made in 1654-1656.* Edited by Amandus Johnson. The Swedish Colonial Society, Philadelphia.
Little, Elizabeth A.
1977 Report on 1976 Excavation at Site Q-6, Quidnet, Nantucket, Massachusetts. Report on file, Massachusetts Historical Commission, Boston.
1979 An Inventory of Indian Sites on Nantucket. Ms. on file, Nantucket Historical Association, Nantucket.
1981a Historic Indian Houses of Nantucket. *Nantucket Algonquian Studies* 4.
1981b The Indian Contribution to Along-Shore Whaling at Nantucket. *Nantucket Algonquian Studies* 8.
1988a Nantucket Whaling in the Early 18th Century. In *Papers of the Nineteenth Algonquian Conference,* edited by William Cowan, pp. 111-131. Carleton University Press, Ottawa.
1988b Where Are the Woodland Villages on Cape Cod and the Islands? *Bulletin of the Massachusetts Archaeological Society* 49(2):72-82.
Lohse. E. S.
1988 Trade Goods. In *History of Indian-White Relations,* edited by Wilcomb E. Washburn, pp. 396-406. Handbook of North American Indians, vol. 4, William C. Sturtevant, general editor. Smithsonian Institution, Washington, D.C.
Lopez, Julius, and Stanley Wisniewski
1972-1973 The Ryders Pond Site, Kings County, New York. *New York State Archaeological Society Bulletin* 53 and 55.

Loth, Calder, Martha W. McCartney, and Nick Luccketti

1978 Weyanoke National Register of Historic Places Registration Form. Ms. on file, U.S. Department of the Interior, National Park Service, National Register Branch, Washington, D.C.

Lounsbury, Floyd

1978 Iroquois Languages. In *Northeast,* edited by Bruce G. Trigger, pp. 334-343. Handbook of North American Indians, vol. 15, William C. Sturtevant, general editor. Smithsonian Institution, Washington, D.C.

Lowenthal, David

1985 *The Past Is a Foreign Country.* Cambridge University Press, New York.

Luccketti, Nick

1994 Personal Communication

Luckenbach, Alvin H.

1991 Personal communication.

1993 Personal communication.

Luckenbach, Alvin H., Wayne E. Clark, and Richard S. Levy

1987 Rethinking Cultural Stability in Eastern North American Prehistory: Linguistic Evidence from Eastern Algonquian. *Journal of Middle Atlantic Archaeology* 3:1-33.

Luedtke, Barbara E.

1979 The Identification of Sources of Chert Artifacts. *American Antiquity* 44(4):744-757.

1986 Regional Variation in Massachusetts Ceramics. *North American Archaeologist* 7(2):113-135.

Lurie, Nancy O.

1959 Indian Cultural Adjustment to European Civilization. In *Seventeenth-Century America: Essays in Colonial History,* edited by James Morton Smith, pp. 33-60. University of North Carolina Press for the Institute of Early American History and Culture, Chapel Hill.

Lydekker, John W.

1938 *The Faithful Mohawks.* Macmillan Press, New York.

MacCord, Howard A., Sr.

1952 Susquehannock Indians in West Virginia, 1630 to 1677. *West Virginia History* 13(4):239-253.

1965 The DeShazo Site, King George County, Virginia. *Quarterly Bulletin: Archeological Society of Virginia* 19(4):98-104.

1969 Camden: A Postcontact Indian Site in Caroline County. *Quarterly Bulletin: Archeological Society of Virginia* 24(1):1-55.

1970 The John Green Site, Greenville County, Virginia. *Quarterly Bulletin: Archeological Society of Virginia* 25(2):97-138.

1973a The Quicksburg Site, Shenandoah County, Virginia. *Quarterly Bulletin: Archeological Society of Virginia* 27(3).

1973b Fort Dinwiddie Site, Bath County, Virginia. *Quarterly Bulletin: Archeological Society of Virginia* 27(3).

1973c The Hidden Valley Rock Shelter, Bath County, Virginia. *Quarterly Bulletin: Archeological Society of Virginia* 27.

1977 Trade Goods from the Trigg Site, Radford, Virginia. *Conference on Historic Site Archaeology Papers [1975]* 10:60-68.

1986 *The Lewis Creek Mound Culture in Virginia.* Privately printed, Richmond.

1989a The Contact Period in Virginia. *Journal of Middle Atlantic Archaeology* 5:121-128.

1989b The Intermontane Culture: A Middle Appalachian Late Woodland Manifestation. *Archaeology of Eastern North America* 17.

1991a Personal communication.

1991b The Indian Point Site, Stafford County, Virginia. *Quarterly Bulletin: Archeological Society of Virginia* 46(3):117-140.

1993 Personal communication.

MacCord, Howard A., Sr., and William T. Buchanan

1980 *The Crab Orchard Site, Tazewell County, Virginia.* Special Publication 8, Archeological Society of Virginia, Richmond.

MacCord, Howard A., Sr., and C. L. Rodgers

1966 The Miley Site, Shenandoah County, Virginia. *Quarterly Bulletin: Archeological Society of Virginia* 21(1):9-20.

MacNeish, Richard S.

1952 *Iroquois Pottery Types: A Technique for the Study of Iroquois Prehistory.* National Museum of Canada, Bulletin 124, Anthropological Series, No. 31, Ottawa.

Malone, Patrick M.

1973 Changing Military Technology among the Indians of Southern New England, 1600-1677. *American Quarterly* 25(1):48-63.

1991 *The Skulking Way of War: Technology and Tactics among the New England Indians.* Madison Books, Lanham, Maryland.

Mancall, Peter C.

1991 *Valley of Opportunity: Economic Culture along the Upper Susquehanna 1700-1800.* Cornell University Press, Ithaca.

Mandell, Daniel R.

1992 Behind the Frontier: Indian Communities in Eighteenth-Century Massachusetts. Unpublished Ph.D dissertation, Department of History, University of Virginia, Charlottesville.

Mandzy, Adrian O.

1990 The Rogers Farm Site: A Seventeenth-Century Cayuga Site. *The Bulletin: Journal of the New York State Archaeological Association* 100: 18-25.

1992 History of Cayuga Acculturation: An Examination of the 17th Century Cayuga Iroquois Archaeological Data. Unpublished master's thesis, Department of Anthropology, Michigan State University, East Lansing.

Manley, Doris, and Charles Florance

1978 *Joachim Staats House National Register of Historic Places Registration Form.* Ms. on file, U.S. Department of the Interior, National Park Service, National Register Branch, Washington, D.C.

Manson, Carl P., and Howard A. MacCord, Sr.

1941 An Historic Iroquois Site near Romney, West Virginia. *West Virginia History* 2(4):290-293.

1944 Additional Notes on the Herriott Farm Site. *West Virginia History* 5(3):201-211.

Manson, Carl P., Howard A. MacCord, Sr., and James Griffin

1943 The Culture of the Keyser Farm Site. *Papers of the Michigan Academy of Science, Arts, and Letters* 29:375-418.

Marchiando, Patricia

1969 The Bell-Browning Site, Sussex County, New Jersey. Report on file, Mid-Atlantic Region, National Park Service, Philadelphia.

1972 Bell-Browning Site 28-SX-19. In *Archeology in the Upper Delaware Valley,* edited by W. Fred Kinsey III, pp. 131-158. Pennsylvania Historical and Museum Commission, Anthropological Series 2. Harrisburg.

Marine, David, et al.

1964 Report on the Warrington Site, 7S-G-14. *The Archeolog* 16(1).

Marye, William

1935 Piscattaway. *Maryland Historical Magazine* 30(3):183-240.

Mason, Carol I.

1986 Prehistoric Maple Sugaring: A Sticky Subject. *North American Archaeologist* 7(4):305-311.

Mason, John

1736 *A Brief History of the Pequot War: Especially of the Memorable Taking of Their Fort at Mistick in Connecticut in 1637.* S. Kneeland and T. Green, Boston.

Mason, Van Wyck

1938 Bermuda's Pequots. *Bulletin of the Archaeological Society of Connecticut* 7:12-16.

Mayer, Susan N.

1977 Niantic-European Contact at Fort Ninigret, Rhode Island. Paper presented at the 42d Annual Meeting of the Society for American Archaeology, New Orleans.

Mayer-Oakes, William J.

1955 *Prehistory of the Upper Ohio Valley.* Annals of the Carnegie Museum 34, Pittsburgh.

McBride, Bunny, and Harald E. L. Prins

1991 Micmacs and Splint Basketry: Tradition, Adaptation, and Survival. In *Our Lives in Our Hands: Micmac Indian Basketmakers,* edited by Bunny McBride, pp. 3-23. Tilbury House Publishers, Gardiner, Maine.

McBride, Kevin A.

1984 The Prehistory of the Lower Connecticut Valley. Unpublished Ph.D dissertation, Department of Anthropology, University of Connecticut, Storrs.

1985 Little Pootatuck Brook Site Report. Ms. on file, Connecticut Historical Commission, Hartford.

1989 Great Salt Pond Archaeological District, Block Island National Register of Historic Places Registration Form. Ms. on file, U.S. Department of the Interior, National Park Service, National Register Branch, Washington, D.C.

1990a Pequot Fort Archaeological Site National Register of Historic Places Registration Form. Ms. on file, U.S. Department of the Interior, National Park Service, National Register Branch, Washington, D.C.

1990b Phase II Intensive Archaeological Survey, Sites RI-1689, 1690, and 1691, Kingswood Sub-Division, Charlestown, Rhode Island. Report on file, Rhode Island Historic Preservation Commission, Providence.

1990c Phase II Archaeological Investigations, Long Ridge Sub-Division, Charlestown, Rhode Island. Report on file, Rhode Island Historic Preservation Commission, Providence.

1990d The Historical Archaeology of the Mashantucket Pequots, 1637-1900: A Preliminary Analysis. In *The Pequots in Southern New England: The Fall and Rise of an American Indian Nation,* edited by Laurence M. Hauptman and James D. Wherry, pp. 96-116. University of Oklahoma Press, Norman.

1990e Personal communication.

n.d. Mashantucket Pequot Indian Reservation Archaeology Survey Field Notes. Ms. on file, Laboratory of Archaeology, University of Connecticut, Storrs.

McCartney, Martha W.

1989 Cockacoeske, Queen of Pamunkey: Diplomat and Suzeraine. In *Powhatan's Mantle: Indians in the Colonial Southeast,* edited by Peter H. Wood, Gregory A. Waselkov, and M. Thomas Hatley, pp. 173-195. University of Nebraska Press, Lincoln.

McCartney, Martha W., and David K. Hazzard

1979 Fort Christanna National Register of Historic Places Registration Form. Ms. on file, U.S. Department of the Interior, National Park Service, National Register Branch, Washington, D.C.

McCartney, Martha W., and Mary Ellen Norrisey Hodges

1982 Pamunkey Indian Reservation Archaeological District National Register of Historic Places Registration Form. Ms. on file, U.S. Department of the Interior, National Park Service, National Register Branch, Washington, D.C.

McCary, Ben C.

1950 The Rappahannock Indians. *Quarterly Bulletin: Archeological Society of Virginia* 5(1):1-15.

1983 The Virginia Tributary Indians and Their Metal Badges of 1661/62. *Quarterly Bulletin: Archeological Society of Virginia* 38(3):182-196.

McCary, Ben C., and Norman F. Barka

1977 The John Smith and Zuñiga Maps in the Light of Recent Archaeological Investigations along the Chickahominy River. *Archaeology of Eastern North America* 5:73-86.

McCashion, John

1975 The Clay Tobacco Pipes of New York State Part 1: Caughnawaga 1667-1693. *New York State Archaeological Association Bulletin* 65.

1979a *A Preliminary Chronology and Discussion of Seventeenth Century Clay Tobacco Pipes from New York State Sites.* British Archaeological Reports, No. 60, Oxford.

1979b A Unique Clay Tobacco Pipe from the Blowers Site and a Preliminary Statement on the Seventeenth Century Oneida Site Sequence Based on the Pipe Data. *Chenango Chapter New York State Archaeological Association Bulletin* 18(1).
1991 Personal communication.

McConnell, Michael N.
1987 Peoples "In Between": The Iroquois and the Ohio Indians, 1720-1768. In *Beyond the Covenant Chain: The Iroquois and Their Neighbors in Indian North America, 1600-1800,* edited by Daniel K. Richter and James H. Merrell, pp. 93-112. Syracuse University Press, Syracuse, New York.
1992a Kuskusky Towns and Early Western Pennsylvania Indian History, 1748-1778. *The Pennsylvania Magazine of History and Biography* 116(1): 33-58.
1992b *A Country Between: The Upper Ohio Valley and Its Peoples, 1724-1774.* University of Nebraska Press, Lincoln.

McCusker, John J., and Russell R. Menard
1985 *The Economy of British America, 1607-1789.* University of North Carolina Press, Chapel Hill.

McIlwaine, Henry R. (editor)
1918-1919 *Legislative Journals of the Council of Colonial Virginia.* Virginia State Library, Richmond.
1925-1945 *Executive Journals of the Council of Colonial Virginia.* 5 vols. Virginia State Library, Richmond.

McLearen, Douglas C., and Beverly Binns
1992 Description and Analysis of Controlled Surface Collections of the Tree Hill Farm Site, Henrico County, Virginia. Report on file, Virginia Department of Historic Resources, Richmond.

McManamon, Francis P. (editor)
1984 *Chapters in the Archeology of Cape Cod, I: Results of the Cape Cod National Seashore Archeological Survey, 1979-1981.* 2 vols. Cultural Resources Management Study 8. North Atlantic Regional Office, National Park Service, Boston.

McMullen, Ann, and Russell G. Handsman (editors)
1987 *A Key into the Language of Woodsplint Baskets.* American Indian Archaeological Institute, Washington, Connecticut.

McNamara, Joseph M.
1985 Excavations on Locust Neck: The Search for the Historic Indian Settlement in the Choptank Indian Reservation. *Journal of Middle Atlantic Archaeology* 1:87-95.

McNett, Charles, and William Gardner
1975 Archaeology of the Lower and Middle Potomac. Ms. on file, Department of Anthropology, American University, Washington, D.C.

McNeill, William H.
1976 *Plagues and Peoples.* Doubleday, New York.

MDSI (Mohawk Drainage Sites Inventory)
n.d. Mohawk Drainage Sites Inventory. Computerized database on file at the Department of Anthropology, State University of New York at Albany.

Melvoin, Richard Irwin
1989 *New England Outpost: War and Society in Colonial Deerfield, Massachusetts.* W. W. Norton, New York.

Merrell, James H.
1979 Cultural Continuity among the Piscataway Indians of Colonial Maryland. *William and Mary Quarterly* 36(4):548-570.
1989 *The Indians' New World: Catawbas and Their Neighbors from European Contact through the Era of Removal.* University of North Carolina Press, Chapel Hill.

MHC (Massachusetts Historical Commission)
n.d. Massachusetts Historic Resources Survey: Historic Archeologic Sites. Ms. on file at the Massachusetts Historical Commission, Boston.

MHASI (Maine Historic Archaeological Sites Inventory)
n.d. Maine Historic Archaeological Sites Inventory. Ms. on file at the Maine Historic Preservation Commission, Augusta.

Milisauskas, Sarunas
1977 Marian Emily White, 1921-1975. *American Antiquity* 42(2):191-195.

Miller, David R. (editor)
1979 *A Guide to the Ohio Valley-Great Lakes Ethnohistory Archive.* Research Report 4, Glenn A. Black Laboratory of Archaeology, Indiana University, Bloomington.

Miller, Henry M.
1983 *A Search for the "Citty of Saint Maries": Report on the 1981 Excavations in St. Mary's City, Maryland.* St. Mary's City Commission, St. Mary's City.
1988 Baroque Cities in the Wilderness: Archaeology and Urban Development in the Colonial Chesapeake. *Historical Archaeology* 22:57-73.

Miller, Henry M., Dennis J. Pogue, and Michael A. Smolek
1983 Beads from the Seventeenth Century Chesapeake. In *Proceedings of the 1982 Glass Trade Bead Conference,* edited by Charles F. Hayes III, pp. 127-144. Rochester Museum and Science Center Research Record 16.

Miller, Jay
1973 Delaware Clan Names. *Man in the Northeast* 9:57-60.

Moeller, Roger W.
1975 Seasonality and Settlement Pattern of Late Woodland Components at the Faucett Site. Unpublished Ph.D dissertation, Department of Anthropology, State University of New York at Buffalo.
1990 Personal communication.

Moffett, R.
1946 Some Shell Heaps in Truro, Massachusetts. *Bulletin of the Massachusetts Archaeological Society* 7(2):17-22.

Moody, Kevin, and Charles L. Fisher
1989 Archaeological Evidence of the Colonial Occupation at Schoharie Crossing State Historic Site,

Montgomery County, New York. *The Bulletin: Journal of the New York State Archaeological Association* 99:1–13.

Mook, Maurice A.
1943 The Ethnological Significance of Tindall's Map of Virginia, 1608. *William and Mary College Quarterly Historical Magazine* 23(4):371–408.

Mooney, James
1894 *The Siouan Tribes of the East.* Bureau of American Ethnology, Bulletin 22, Washington, D.C.
1928 The Aboriginal Population of America North of Mexico. John R. Swanton, ed. *Smithsonian Miscellaneous Collections* 80(7). Washington, D.C.

Moore, Larry E.
1988 Archaeological Investigations at the Taft Site. *Fairfax Chronicles* 12(3):1, 5–8.
1990 The Little Marsh Creek Site: Mason Neck National Wildlife Refuge, Lorton, Virginia. Report on file in the Fairfax County Environmental and Heritage Resources Office, Falls Church.
1991a A Little History of the Doeg. *Quarterly Bulletin: Archeological Society of Virginia* 46(2):77–85.
1991b Personal communication.

Moorehead, Warren K.
1922 *A Report on the Archaeology of Maine.* Andover, Massachusetts.
1938 A Report of the Susquehanna River Expedition Sponsored in 1916 by the Museum of the American Indian, Heye Foundation. The Andover Press, Andover, Massachusetts.

Morenon, E. Pierre
1986 Archaeological Sites at an Ecotone: Route 4 Extension, East Greenwich and North Kingstown, Rhode Island. Report Prepared for the Federal Highway Administration and the Rhode Island Department of Transportation by the Public Archaeology Program. Rhode Island College, Providence.

Morgan, Edmund S.
1975 *American Slavery, American Freedom: The Ordeal of Colonial Virginia.* New York.

Morgan, Lewis Henry
1851 *League of the Ho-De'-No-Sau-Nee.* Sage and Brother, Rochester, New York.
1877 *Ancient Society or Researches in the Lines of Human Progress from Savagery through Barbarism to Civilization.* Henry Holt, New York.
1881 *Houses and House-life of the American Aborigines.* Contributions to North American Ethnology 4, U.S. Geological and Geographical Survey of the Rocky Mountain Region, Washington, D.C.

Morison, Samuel Eliot
1971 *The European Discovery of America: The Northern Voyages, A.D. 500–1600.* Oxford University Press, New York.

Morrison, Kenneth M.
1984 *The Embattled Northeast: The Elusive Ideal of Alliance in Abenaki-Euramerican Relations.* University of California Press, Berkeley.

Morton, Richard L.
1960 *Colonial Virginia.* 2 vols. University of North Carolina Press, Chapel Hill.

Morton, Thomas
1883 [1637] *New English Canaan or New Canaan: Containing an Abstract of New England Composed in Three Books.* Edited by Charles Francis Adams, Jr. The Prince Society, Boston.

Mouer, L. Daniel
1983 A Review of the Archeology and Ethnohistory of the Monacans. In *Piedmont Archaeology: Recent Research and Results,* edited by J. Mark Wittkofski and Lyle E. Browning, pp. 21–39. Special Publication 10, Archeological Society of Virginia, Richmond.
1991 Rebecca's Children: A Critique of Old and New Myths concerning Indians in Virginia's History and Archaeology. Paper presented at the 24th Annual Meeting of the Society for Historical and Underwater Archaeology, Richmond.
1992a Chesapeake Creoles: An Approach to Colonial Folk Culture. Paper presented at the 25th Annual Meeting of the Society for Historical and Underwater Archaeology, Kingston, Jamaica.
1992b Personal communication.

Mourt, G.
1963 [1622] *A Journal of the Pilgrims at Plymouth: Mourt's Relation.* Edited by Dwight Heath. Corinth Books, New York.

MPASI (Maine Prehistoric Archaeological Sites Inventory)
n.d. Maine Prehistoric Archaeological Sites Inventory. Ms. on file at the Maine Historic Preservation Commission, Augusta.

Mrozowski, Stephen A., and Kathleen Bragdon
1993 Feast or Famine: Native Agriculture and Population Stress on 17th Century Cape Cod. Paper presented at the Annual Meeting of the Northeastern Anthropological Association, Danbury, Connecticut.

Mulholland, Mitchell T., Ellen-Rose Savulis, and D. Richard Gumaer
1986 Archeological Remote Sensing and Historic Records for the Yeardon Parcel at the Hassanomisco Indian Burying Ground, Grafton, Massachusetts. Report on file, Massachusetts Historical Commission, Boston.

Murdock, George Peter, and Timothy J. O'Leary (editors)
1975 *Ethnographic Bibliography of North America: Volume 4, Eastern United States.* 4th ed. Human Relations Area Files Press, New Haven, Connecticut.

Myers, Albert Cook (editor)
1912 *Narratives of Early Pennsylvania, West New Jersey, and Delaware: 1630–1707.* Charles Scribner's Sons, New York.

Nabokov, Peter, and Robert Easton
1989 *Native American Architecture.* Oxford University Press, New York.

Nammack, Georgiana C.
1969 *Fraud, Politics, and the Dispossession of the*

Indians: The Iroquois Land Frontier in the Colonial Period. University of Oklahoma Press, Norman.

Nash, Gary B.
1982 *Red, White, and Black.* 2d ed. Prentice-Hall, Englewood Cliffs, New Jersey.

Nassaney, Michael S.
1989 An Epistomological Enquiry into Some Archaeological and Historical Interpretations of 17th Century Native American–European Relations. In *Archaeological Approaches to Cultural Identity,* edited by Stephen Shennan, pp. 76-93. Unwin Hyman, London.

Newcomb, William W., Jr.
1956 *The Culture and Acculturation of the Delaware Indians.* University of Michigan Museum of Anthropology, Anthropological Paper 10.

Nicholas, Andrea Bear, and Harald E. L. Prins
1989 The Spirit in the Land: The Native People of Aroostook. In *The County: Land of Promise,* edited by Anna Fields McGrath, pp. 18-37. The Donning Company, Norfolk, Maine.

Niemczycki, Mary Ann Palmer
1984 *The Origin and Development of the Seneca and Cayuga Tribes of New York State.* Rochester Museum and Science Center Research Record 17.
1986 The Genesee Connection: The Origins of Iroquois Culture in West-Central New York. *North American Archaeologist* 7(1):15-44.
1988 Seneca Tribalization: An Adaptive Strategy. *Man in the Northeast* 36:77-87.
1991 Cayuga Archaeology: Where Do We Go from Here? *The Bulletin: Journal of the New York State Archaeological Association* 102:27-33.

Nietfeld, Patricia K. L.
1981 Determinants of Aboriginal Political Structure. Unpublished Ph.D dissertation, Department of Anthropology, University of New Mexico, Albuquerque.

Nöel-Hume, Ivor
1962 An Indian Ware of the Colonial Period. *Quarterly Bulletin: Archeological Society of Virginia* 17:2-14.

Nooter, Eric, and Patricia U. Bonomi (editors)
1988 *Colonial Dutch Studies: An Interdisciplinary Approach.* New York University Press, New York.

Norrisey, Mary Ellen
1980 The Pamunkey Indians Retrieve Their Past. *Notes on Virginia* 20:24-27.

Norton, Thomas E.
1974 *The Fur Trade in Colonial New York, 1686-1776.* University of Wisconsin Press, Madison.

NPS
1987 Catalog of National Historic Landmarks: 1987. U.S. Department of the Interior, Washington, D.C.

NYAS (New York Archaeological Survey)
n.d. New York Archaeological Survey. Computerized database compiled by Robert J. Hasenstab and John Knoerl, on file, New York State Office of Parks, Recreation, and Historic Preservation, Waterford.

NYSMAS (New York State Museum Anthropological Survey)
n.d. New York State Museum Anthropological Survey. Computerized database on file, New York State Museum Anthropological Survey, Albany.

O'Callaghan, Edmund B., (editor)
1849-1851 *Documentary History of the State of New York.* 4 vols. Weed, Parsons, Albany.

O'Callaghan, Edmund B., and Berthold Fernow (editors)
1853-1887 *Documents Relative to the Colonial History of the State of New York; Procured in Holland, England and France, by John R. Brodhead.* 15 vols. Weed, Parsons, Albany.

Omwake, H. Geiger
1972 Report on the Examination of Four White Kaolin Pipes from the Ryders Pond Site, Brooklyn, Kings County, New York. *New York State Archaeological Society Bulletin* 56.

Opperman, Antony F., and E. Randolph Turner III
n.d. Searching for Virginia Company Period Sites: An Assessment of Surviving Archaeological Manifestations of Powhatan-English Interactions, A.D. 1607-1624. Draft ms. on file, Virginia Department of Historic Resources, Richmond.

Orcutt, Samuel
1882 *The Indians of the Housatonic and Naugatuck Valleys.* Case, Lockwood, and Brainard, Hartford, Connecticut.

Orr, Charles (editor)
1897 *History of the Pequot War.* The Helman-Taylor Company, Cleveland.

Orr, David G. and Douglas V. Campana (editors)
1991 The People of Minisink: Papers from the 1989 Delaware Water Gap Symposium. Mid-Atlantic Region. National Park Service, Philadelphia, Pennsylvania.

Parker, Arthur C.
1907 *Excavations in an Erie Indian Village and Burial Site at Ripley, Chautauqua County, New York.* New York State Museum Bulletin 117.
1910 Iroquois Uses of Maize and Other Plant Foods. *New York State Museum Bulletin* 144(482): 5-113.
1916 The Origin of the Iroquois as Suggested by Their Archaeology. *American Anthropologist* 18(4):479-507.
1922 *The Archaeological History of New York.* 2 pts. New York State Museum Bulletins 235-238.
1926 An Analytic History of the Seneca Indians. *Researches and Transactions of the New York State Archaeological Association* 6(1-5).
1968 *Parker on the Iroquois.* Edited by William N. Fenton. Syracuse University Press, Syracuse, New York.

Parkman, Francis
1865-1892 *France and England in North America: A Series of Historical Narratives.* 9 vols. Little, Brown Publishers, Boston.

PASS (Pennsylvania Archaeological Site Survey)
n.d. Pennsylvania Archaeological Site Survey.

Computerized database on file at the Bureau of Historic Preservation, Harrisburg.

Peña, Elizabeth Shapiro
1990 Wampum Production in New Netherland and New York: The Historical and Archaeological Context. Unpublished Ph.D dissertation, Department of Anthropology, Boston University.

Pendergast, James F.
1975 An In-Situ Hypothesis to Explain the Origin of the St. Lawrence Iroquoians. *Ontario Archaeology* 25:47-55.
1982 *The Origin of Maple Sugar.* Syllogeous 36, National Museum of Natural History, Ottawa.
1983 Proto-Historic European Trade Routes into Iroquoia with Particular Emphasis on Ontario. Paper presented at the 10th Annual Symposium of the Ontario Archaeological Society, Toronto.
1985 Huron-St. Lawrence Iroquois Relations in the Terminal Prehistoric Period. *Ontario Archaeology* 44:23-39.
1989 The Significance of Some Marine Shells Excavated on Iroquoian Archaeological Sites in Ontario. In *Proceedings of the 1986 Shell Bead Conference: Selected Papers,* edited by Charles F. Hayes III, pp. 97-112. Rochester Museum and Science Center Research Record 20.
1990 Native Encounters with Europeans in the Sixteenth Century in the Region Now Known as Vermont. *Vermont History* 58(2):99-123.
1991a The Massawomeck: Raiders and Traders into Chesapeake Bay. *Transactions of the American Philosophical Society* 81, pt. 2, Philadelphia.
1991b The St. Lawrence Iroquoians: Their Past, Present and Immediate Future. *The Bulletin: Journal of the New York State Archaeological Association* 102:47-73.
1992a Susquehannock Trade Northward to New France Prior to A.D. 1608: A Popular Misconception. *Pennsylvania Archaeologist.*
1992b Personal communication.
n.d. *The Kakouagoga or Kahkwas: An Iroquoian Nation Destroyed in the Niagara Region c. 1652. Proceedings of the American Philosophical Society.* In press.

Penn, William
1912 [1683] Letter from William Penn to the Committee of the Free Society of Traders. In *Narratives of Early Pennsylvania, West New Jersey, and Delaware, 1630-1707,* edited by Albert Cook Myers, pp. 217-244. Charles Scribner's Sons, New York.

Petersen, James B.
1989 Evidence of the St. Lawrence Iroquois in Northern New England: Population Movement, Trade, or Stylistic Borrowing? Paper presented at the Annual Meeting of the Northeastern Anthropological Association, Montreal.

Petersen, James B., and David Sanger
1989 An Aboriginal Ceramic Sequence for Maine and the Maritime Provinces. In *Prehistoric Archaeology in the Maritimes: Past and Present Research,* edited by Michael Deal, Council of Maritime Premiers, Fredericton, New Brunswick. In Press.

Peterson, Mark
1991 Site 154-7-1. In *IGTS Phase 2 Archaeological Evaluations, Volume 2: The Mohawk/Schoharie Region.* Report submitted to the Iroquois Gas Transmission System by Garrow and Associates, Inc., Atlanta.

Pfeiffer, Brian
1979 Rev. Stephen Badger House National Register of Historic Places Registration Form. Ms. on file, U.S. Department of the Interior, National Park Service, National Register Branch, Washington, D.C.

Pfeiffer, John
1982 Remote Sensing: Archaeological Applications in Southern New England. *Bulletin of the Archaeological Society of Connecticut* 45:75-84.

Phelps, M. M.
1947 The South Swansea Burials. *Bulletin of the Massachusetts Archaeological Society* 8(3):33-38.

Piersen, William D.
1988 *Black Yankees: The Development of an Afro-American Subculture in Eighteenth-Century New England.* University of Massachusetts Press, Amherst.

Pohl, Frederick J.
1960 Further Proof of Vikings at Follins Pond, Cape Cod. *Bulletin of the Massachusetts Archaeological Society* 21(1):48-49.

Poirier, David
1990 Personal communication.

Porter, Frank W., III
1979 *Indians of Maryland: A Critical Bibliography.* Indiana University Press, Bloomington.

Porter, Frank W., III (editor)
1986 *Strategies for Survival: American Indians in the Eastern United States.* Greenwood Press, Westport, Connecticut.

Potter, Stephen R.
1977 Ethnohistory and the Owings Site: A Re-Analysis. *Quarterly Bulletin: Archeological Society of Virginia* 31(4):169-175.
1980 A Review of Archeological Resources in Piscataway Park, Maryland. Report on file, National Capital Region, National Park Service, Washington, D.C.
1982 An Analysis of Chicacoan Settlement Patterns. Unpublished Ph.D dissertation, Department of Anthropology, University of North Carolina, Chapel Hill.
1989 Early English Effects on Virginia Algonquian Exchange and Tribute in the Tidewater Potomac. In *Powhatan's Mantle: Indians in the Colonial Southeast,* edited by Peter H. Wood, Gregory A. Waselkov, and M. Thomas Hatley, pp. 151-172. University of Nebraska Press, Lincoln.
1992 Personal communication.
1993 *Commoners, Tribute, and Chiefs: The Development of Algonquian Culture in the Potomac Valley.* University Press of Virginia, Charlottesville.

Potter, Stephen R., and Gregory A. Waselkov
n.d. Whereby We Shall Enjoy Their Cultivated Places. In *The Historic Chesapeake: Archaeological Contributions,* edited by Paul Shackel and Barbara Little. Smithsonian Institution, Washington, D.C. In press.

Pratt, Marjorie K.
1991 The St. Lawrence Iroquois of Northern New York. *The Bulletin: Journal of the New York State Archaeological Association* 102:43-46.

Pratt, Peter P.
1976 *Archaeology of the Oneida Indians.* Occasional Publications in Northeastern Anthropology 1.
1991 Oneida Archaeology: The Last Quarter Century. *The Bulletin: Journal of the New York State Archaeological Association* 102:40-42.
1992 Personal communication.

Pretola, John
1973 The Marshall Site: An Early Contact Shell Midden from Nantucket Isle. Unpublished master's thesis, Department of Anthropology, University of Massachusetts, Amherst.
1985 The Fort Hill Site. Paper presented at the 51st Annual Meeting of the Archaeological Society of Connecticut, Milford.

Pretola, John, and Elizabeth A. Little
1988 Nantucket: An Archaeological Record from the Far Island. *Bulletin of the Archaeological Society of Connecticut* 51:47-68.

Prins, Harald E. L.
1984 Foul Play on the Kennebec: The Historical Background of Fort Western and the Demise of the Abenaki Nation. *The Kennebec Proprietor: Magazine of the Fort Western Museum* 1(3):4-14.
1986a "The Most Convenientest Place for Trade": A Discussion of the Kenibec/Cushnoc Controversy. *The Kennebec Proprietor: Magazine of the Fort Western Museum* 3(1):4-9.
1986b Micmacs and Maliseets in the St. Lawrence River Valley. In *Actes du Dix-Septieme Congres des Algonquinistes,* edited by William Cowan, pp. 263-275, Carleton University Press, Ottawa.
1987 The Search for Cushnoc: A 17th-Century Pilgrim Trading Post in the Kennebec Valley of Maine. *The Kennebec Proprietor: Magazine of the Fort Western Museum* 4(1):8-13.
1988a Tribulations of a Border Tribe: A Discourse on the Political Ecology of the Aroostook Band of Micmacs, 16th-20th Centuries. Unpublished Ph.D dissertation, Graduate Faculty of Political and Social Science, New School for Social Research, New York.
1988b Amesokanti: Abortive Tribe Formation on the Colonial Frontier. Paper presented at the Annual Conference of the American Society for Ethnohistory, Williamsburg.
1991a Turmoil on the Wabanaki Frontier, 1524-1678. In *The History of Maine,* edited by Richard Judd et al., University of Maine Press, Orono. In press.
1991b Children of Gluskap: Wabanaki Indians on the Eve of the European Invasion. In *American Beginnings: Exploration, Culture, and Cartography in the Land of Norumbega,* edited by Harald E. L. Prins et al., University of Nebraska Press, Lincoln.

Prins, Harald E. L., and Bruce J. Bourque
1987 Norridgewock: Village Translocation on the New England-Acadian Frontier. *Man in the Northeast* 33:137-158.

Puniello, Anthony J., and Lorraine E. Williams
1978 Late Woodland Occupations in the Upper Delaware Valley: Final Report: 1974 Investigations at the Bell-Browning, Zipser Lower Field, Beisler, Heater II and Heater V Sites. Report on file, Interagency Archaeological Services, Atlanta.

Purchas, Samuel
1625 *Hakluytus Posthumus, or Purchas, His Pilgrimes.* 4 vols. Henry Fetherstone, London.

Puype, Jan Piet
1985 Dutch and Other Flintlocks from Seventeenth Century Iroquois Sites. *Proceedings of the 1984 Trade Gun Conference, Part I,* edited by Charles F. Hayes III. Rochester Museum and Science Center Research Record 18.

Quinn, David B.
1977 *North America from Earliest Discovery to First Settlements: The Norse Voyages to 1612.* Harper and Row, New York.
1981 *Sources for the Ethnography of Northeastern North America to 1611.* Canadian Ethnology Service Paper 76, Mercury Series, National Museums of Canada, National Museum of Man, Ottawa.
1985 *Set Fair for Roanoke: Voyages and Colonies, 1584-1606.* University of North Carolina Press, Chapel Hill.

Quinn, David B., Alison Quinn, and Susan Hillier (editors)
1979 *New American World: A Documentary History of North America to 1612.* 5 vols. Arno Press and Hector Bye, Inc., New York.

Raber, Paul A. (editor)
1985 *A Comprehensive State Plan for the Conservation of Archaeological Resources.* 2 vols. Pennsylvania Historical and Museum Commission, Harrisburg.

Ramenofsky, Ann F.
1987 *Vectors of Death: The Archeology of European Contact.* University of New Mexico Press, Albuquerque.

Redman, Charles L.
1991 Distinguished Lecture in Archeology: In Defence of the Seventies—The Adolescence of New Archeology. *American Anthropologist* 93(2):295-307.

Reeve, Stuart A., Jean B. Russo, Dennis J. Pogue, and Joseph M. Herbert
1991 *Myrtle Point: The Changing Land and People of a Lower Patuxent River Community.* Jefferson Patterson Park and Museum Occasional Paper 3, St. Leonard, Maryland.

Reichel, William C.
1860 A Memorial of the Dedication of Monuments

Erected by the Moravian Historical Society, to Mark the Sites of Ancient Missionary Stations in New York and Connecticut. C. B. Richardson, New York; J. B. Lippincott, Philadelphia.

Reinhart, Theodore R., and Dennis J. Pogue (editors)

1993 *The Archaeology of 17th-Century Virginia*. Special Publication 30, Archeological Society of Virginia, Richmond.

Reinke, Rita

1990 17th Century Military Defenses Uncovered. *Preservation Advocate, Magazine of the Massachusetts Historical Commission* 17(3–4):3.

Richter, Daniel K.

1983 War and Culture: The Iroquois Experience. *William and Mary Quarterly* 40(4):528–559.

1985 Iroquois versus Iroquois: Jesuit Missions and Christianity in Village Politics, 1642–1686. *Ethnohistory* 32(1):1–16.

1988 Cultural Brokers and Intercultural Politics: New York-Iroquois Relations, 1664–1701. *The Journal of American History* 75(1):40–67.

1992 *The Ordeal of the Longhouse: The Peoples of the Iroquois League in the Era of European Colonization*. University of North Carolina Press, Chapel Hill.

Richter, Daniel K., and James H. Merrell (editors)

1987 *Beyond the Covenant Chain: The Iroquois and Their Neighbors in Indian North America, 1600–1800*. Syracuse University Press, Syracuse, New York.

Ricklis, Robert

1963 Excavations at the Atwell Fort Site, Madison County, New York. *Bulletin of the New York State Archaeological Association* 28:2–5.

1966 A Preliminary Report on Some Late Prehistoric and Early Historic Onondaga Sites Near Syracuse, New York. *Morgan Chapter New York State Archaeological Association Newsletter* 6:1–13.

Rink, Oliver

1986 *Holland on the Hudson*. Cornell University Press, Ithaca.

Ritchie, Duncan

1985 Archaeological Investigations at the Hartford Avenue Rockshelter, Uxbridge, Massachusetts: The Data Recovery Program. Report on file, Massachusetts Historical Commission, Boston.

Ritchie, Ethel Colt

1956 *Block Island Lore and Legends*. F. Norman Associates, Block Island, Rhode Island.

Ritchie, William A.

1949 *The Bell-Philhower Site, Sussex County, New Jersey*. Indiana Historical Society, Prehistory Research Series 3(2).

1954 Dutch Hollow, An Early Historic Period Seneca Site in Livingston County, New York. *Researches and Transactions of the New York State Archaeological Association* 13(1).

1958 *An Introduction to Hudson Valley Prehistory*. New York State Museum Science Service, Bulletin 372.

1969a *The Archaeology of New York State*. Revised ed. Natural History Press, Garden City, New York. Originally published in 1965.

1969b *The Archaeology of Martha's Vineyard*. Natural History Press, Garden City, New York.

1971 *A Typology and Nomenclature for New York Projectile Points*. New York State Museum Science Service, Bulletin 384, 2d ed. Originally published in 1961.

Ritchie, William A., and Robert E. Funk

1973 *Aboriginal Settlement Patterns in the Northeast*. New York State Museum and Science Service, Memoir 20.

Ritchie, William A., and Richard S. MacNeish

1949 The Pre-Iroquoian Pottery of New York State. *American Antiquity* 15(2):97–124.

Robbins, Maurice

1959 Some Indian Burials from Southwestern Massachusetts, Part I. *Bulletin of the Massachusetts Archaeological Society* 20:17–32.

1967 The Titicut Site. *Bulletin of the Massachusetts Archaeological Society* 28(3–4):33–76.

1968 A Brass Kettle Recovery at Corn Hill, Cape Cod. *Bulletin of the Massachusetts Archaeological Society* 29(3–4):62–68.

Robbins, Maurice, and Christine Boulding

1975 Wampanoag Royal Cemetery National Register of Historic Places Registration Form. Ms. on file, U.S. Department of the Interior, National Park Service, National Register Branch, Washington, D.C.

Robinson, Brian S., and Charles E. Bolian

1987 A Preliminary Report on the Rocks Road Site (Seabrook Station): Late Archaic to Contact Period Occupation in Seabrook, New Hampshire. *The New Hampshire Archeologist* 28(1):19–51.

Robinson, Paul A.

1987 The Indian Use of the Salt Pond Region between 4000 B.P. and 1750 A.D. National Register of Historic Places Registration Form. Ms. on file, U.S. Department of the Interior, National Park Service, National Register Branch, Washington, D.C.

1988 The Social Context of Historical Research: Archaeological Investigations of the Contacts between the English and the Narragansett in 17th-Century Rhode Island. Paper presented at the "Presenting the Past" Symposium, University of Minnesota Center for Ancient Studies, Minneapolis.

1989 Personal communication.

1990 The Struggle Within: The Indian Debate in Seventeenth-Century Narragansett Country. Unpublished Ph.D dissertation, Department of Anthropology, State University of New York at Binghamton.

1992 Personal communication.

Robinson, Paul A., Marc A. Kelley, and Patricia E. Rubertone

1985 Preliminary Biocultural Interpretations from a Seventeenth-Century Narragansett Indian Cemetery in Rhode Island. In *Cultures in Contact: The*

European Impact on Native Cultural Institutions in Eastern North America, A.D. 1000-1800, edited by William W. Fitzhugh, pp. 107-130. Smithsonian Institution, Washington, D.C.

Robinson, Rosemary
1976 Gannagaro: Strongbold of the Senecas. Wolfe Publications, Pittsford, New York.

Robinson, W. Stitt (editor)
1983a Virginia Treaties, 1607-1722. Early American Indian Documents: Treaties and Laws, 1607-1789, vol. 4. University Press of America, Frederick, Maryland.
1983b Virginia Treaties, 1723-1775. Early American Indian Documents: Treaties and Laws, 1607-1789, vol. 5. University Press of America, Frederick, Maryland.

Rogers, Edward H.
1942 The Indian River Village Site, Milford, Connecticut. Bulletin of the Archaeological Society of Connecticut 15:7-78.

Ronda, James P.
1983 Generations of Faith: The Christian Indians of Martha's Vineyard. William and Mary Quarterly 31(1):30-42.

Rothschild, Nan A., and Lucianne Lavin
1977 The Kaeser Site: A Stratified Shell Midden in the Bronx, New York. The Bulletin and Journal of Archaeology for New York State 70:1-27.

Rountree, Helen C.
1973 Indian Land Loss in Virginia. Unpublished Ph.D dissertation, Department of Anthropology, University of Wisconsin, Milwaukee.
1989 The Powhatan Indians of Virginia: Their Traditional Culture. University of Oklahoma Press, Norman.
1990 Pocahontas's People: The Powhatan Indians of Virginia through Four Centuries. University of Oklahoma Press, Norman.

Rouse, Irving
1945 Styles of Pottery in Connecticut. Bulletin of the Massachusetts Archaeological Society 7(1):1-8.
1947 Ceramic Traditions and Sequences in Connecticut. Bulletin of the Archaeological Society of Connecticut 21:10-25.

Rubertone, Patricia E.
1989 Personal communication.
1990 Archaeology, Colonialism, and 17th-Century Native America: Towards an Alternative Interpretation. In Conflict in the Archaeology of Living Traditions, edited by Robert Layton, pp. 32-43. Unwin Hyman, London.

Rubertone, Patricia E., and Robert K. Fitts
1990 Historical Archaeology at Cocumscussoc: A Pilot Study for Local Preservation Planning. Report on file, Rhode Island Historical Preservation Commission, Providence.
1991 Smith's Castle (Amendment) National Register of Historic Places Registration Form. Ms. on file, U.S. Department of the Interior, National Park Service, National Register Branch, Washington, D.C.

Rumrill, Donald A.
1985 An Interpretation and Analysis of the Seventeenth Century Mohawk Nation: Its Chronology and Movements. The Bulletin and Journal of Archaeology for New York State 90:1-39.
1988 Art Form or Artifact Type? The Bulletin and Journal of Archaeology for New York State 96:19-25.
1990 Personal communication.
1991a The Evolution of Firearms and Its Relationship to Seventeenth Century Mohawk Chronological Analysis. Ms. in author's possession.
1991b The Mohawk Indian Glass Trade Bead Sequence and Chronology c. 1560-1760 A.D. Beads: The Journal of the Society of Bead Researchers 3:5-45.
1992 Personal communication.

Russell, Lyent W.
1942 The Menunketisuck Site. Bulletin of the Archaeological Society of Connecticut 14:3-55.

Salisbury, Neal
1972 Conquest of the "Savage": Puritans, Puritan Missionaries, and Indians, 1620-1680. Unpublished Ph.D dissertation, Department of History, University of California at Los Angeles.
1974 Red Puritans: The "Praying Indians" of Massachusetts Bay and John Eliot. William and Mary Quarterly 31(1):27-54.
1981 Squanto: Last of the Patuxets. In Struggle and Survival in Colonial America, edited by David G. Sweet and Gary B. Nash, pp. 228-246. University of California Press, Berkeley.
1982a Manitou and Providence: Indians, Europeans, and the Making of New England, 1500-1643. Oxford University Press, New York.
1982b The Indians of New England: A Critical Bibliography. Indiana University Press, Bloomington.

Salwen, Bert
1962 Field Notes: IBM Site, Port Washington, L.I., N.Y. New York State Archaeological Association Bulletin 25.
1966 European Trade Goods and the Chronology of the Fort Shantok Site. Bulletin of the Archaeological Society of Connecticut 34:5-39.
1968 Muskeeta Cove 2: A Stratified Woodland Site on Long Island. American Antiquity 33(3):322-340.
1969 A Tentative "In-Situ" Solution to the Mohegan-Pequot Problem. In An Introduction to the Archaeology and History of the Connecticut Valley Indian, edited by William K. Young, pp. 81-88, Springfield Museum of Science, Springfield, Massachusetts.
1978 Indians of Southern New England and Long Island: Early Period. In Northeast, edited by Bruce G. Trigger, pp. 160-176. Handbook of North American Indians, vol. 15, William C. Sturtevant, general editor. Smithsonian Institution, Washington, D.C.
1984 Fort Shantok National Register of Historic Places Registration Form. Ms. on file, U.S. Depart-

ment of the Interior, National Park Service, National Register Branch, Washington, D.C.

Salwen, Bert, and Susan N. Mayer
1978 Indian Archaeology in Rhode Island. *Archaeology* 31:57-58.

Salwen, Bert, and Ann Otteson
1972 Radio-Carbon Dates for a Windsor Occupation at the Shantok Cove Site, New London County, Connecticut. *Man in the Northeast* 3:8-19.

Sanford, Douglas W., and Scott K. Parker
1986 From Frontier to Plantation: The Archaeological Reconnaissance of the Germanna Area, Orange County, Virginia. Report on file, Virginia Department of Historic Resources, Richmond.

Sanger, David
1975 Big Black Site National Register of Historic Places Registration Form. Ms. on file, U.S. Department of the Interior, National Park Service, National Register Branch, Washington, D.C.

Sappey, Sally
1989 Personal communication.

Sargeant, Howard R.
1974 The Weirs (NH26-1) National Register of Historic Places Registration Form. Ms. on file, U.S. Department of the Interior, National Park Service, National Register Branch, Washington, D.C.

Saunders, Lorraine P.
1986 Biological Affinities among Historic Seneca Groups and Possible Precursive Populations. Unpublished Ph.D dissertation, Department of Anthropology, University of Texas, Austin.

Saunders, Lorraine P., and Martha L. Sempowski
1991 The Seneca Site Sequence and Chronology: The Baby or the Bathwater. *The Bulletin: Journal of the New York State Archaeological Association* 102:13-26.

Saville, Foster H., and Nat Booth
1920 *A Montauk Cemetery at Easthampton, Long Island.* Indian Notes and Monographs 2(3), Museum of the American Indian, Heye Foundation, New York.

Savulis, Ellen-Rose
1991 Continuity and Change in Historic Native American Settlement and Subsistence Traditions: The Simons Site, Mashpee, Massachusetts: Statement of Field. Ms. in author's possession.

Scammell, G. V.
1981 *The World Encompassed: The First European Maritime Empires, c. 800-1650.* Methuen, London.

Schambach, Frank, and Howard L. Bailey
1974 The Purcell Site: Evidence of a Massacre on Cape Cod. *Bulletin of the Massachusetts Archaeological Society* 34(30-4):18-23.

Schiffer, Michael B.
1987 *Formation Processes of the Archaeological Record.* University of New Mexico Press, Albuquerque.

Schmitt, Karl
1965 Patawomeke: An Historic Algonkian Site. *Quarterly Bulletin: Archeological Society of Virginia* 20(1):1-36.

Schock, Jack M.
1976 Southwestern New York: The Chautauqua Phase and Other Late Woodland Occupation. In *The Late Prehistory of the Lake Erie Drainage Basin: A 1972 Symposium Revisited,* edited by David S. Brose, pp. 89-109, Cleveland Museum of Natural History, Cleveland, Ohio.

Schoff, Harry L.
1938 Activities of the Archaeological Division of Frontier Forts and Trails Survey, 1937. *Pennsylvania Archaeologist* 13(3).
n.d. Archaeological Report on the Opening of Three Indian Graves in the Old Heydrick Farm, Venango County, Pa. Report on file, Pennsylvania Historical and Museum Commission, Harrisburg.

Schoolcraft, Henry Rowe
1851-1857 *Historical and Statistical Information Respecting the History, Condition, and Prospects of the Indian Tribes of the United States.* 6 vols. Lippincott, Grambo Publishers, Philadelphia.

Schrabisch, Max
1915 *Indian Habitations in Sussex County, New Jersey.* Geological Survey of New Jersey, Bulletin 13.

Schroeder, Laurie, and Ed Johannemann
1985 Cyrus Charles Cemetery. Report on file, New York State Office of Parks, Recreation, and Historic Preservation, Waterford.

Scott, Kenneth, and Charles E. Baker
1953 Renewals of Governor Nicolls' Treaty of 1665 with the Esopus Indians at Kingston, N.Y. *New York Historical Quarterly* 37(3):251-72.

Scott, Patricia Kay
1991 Fort Niagara And Artpark—Contact Period. Draft report on file, New York State Office of Parks, Recreation, and Historic Preservation, Waterford.

Scott, Stuart D., and Patricia Kay Scott
1989 State-Funded Archaeological Work at Old Fort Niagara, July–August 1988. Draft report on file, Old Fort Niagara Association, Youngstown, New York, and New York State Office of Parks, Recreation, and Historic Preservation, Waterford.

Scott, Stuart D., Patricia Kay Scott, Christopher J. Hughes, Paul Nasca, and David Mauzy
1992 *Artpark: The Lower Landing.* Mellon Press, Lewiston, New York.

Seaver, James E.
1992 [1824] *A Narrative of the Life of Mrs. Mary Jemison.* Edited by June Namias. University of Oklahoma Press, Norman.

Secor, Harold
1987 *Pre-history of the Savannah, New York Area 9000 B.C. to 1700 A.D.* Wayne County Historical Society, Lyons, New York.

Sempowski, Martha L.
1986 Differential Mortuary Treatment of Seneca Women: Some Social Inferences. *Archaeology of Eastern North America* 14.
1989 Fluctuations through Time in the Use of Marine Shell at Seneca Iroquois Sites. In *Proceedings of*

the 1986 Shell Bead Conference: Selected Papers, edited by Charles F. Hayes III, pp. 81–96, Rochester Museum and Science Center Research Record 20.

1992 Preliminary Observations on Early History Period Exchange between the Seneca and the Susquehannock. Paper presented at the 25th Annual Meeting of the Canadian Archaeological Association, London, Ontario.

Severance, Frank H.
1917 An Old Frontier of France. 2 vols. Dodd, Mead, and Company, New York.

Shedd, Charles F., Jr.
1958 Old Fort Niagara. National Survey of Historic Sites and Buildings Inventory Form. Ms. on file, History Division, National Park Service, Washington, D.C.

Sherman, Charles F.
1948 A Preliminary Report of the Powers Shell Heap in Kingston, Massachusetts. Bulletin of the Massachusetts Archaeological Society 9(4):75–76.

Siebert, Frank T., Jr.
1967 The Original Home of the Proto-Algonquian People. Contributions to Anthropology: Linguistics I, National Museum of Canada Bulletin 214:13–47.

1973 The Identity of the Tarrantines, with an Etymology. Studies in Linguistics 23.

1975 Resurrecting Virginia Algonquian from the Dead: The Reconstituted and Historical Phonology of Powhatan. In Studies in Southeastern Indian Languages, edited by James M. Crawford, pp. 285–453. University of Georgia Press, Athens.

Silver, Annette
1981 Comments on Maize Cultivation in Coastal New York. North American Archaeologist 2(2):117–130.

Silver, Timothy
1990 A New Face on the Countryside: Indians, Colonists, and Slaves in South Atlantic Forests, 1500–1800. Cambridge University Press, New York.

Simmons, William S.
1970 Cautantowit's House: An Indian Burial Ground on the Island of Conanicut in Narragansett Bay. Brown University Press, Providence, Rhode Island.

1978 Narragansett. In Northeast, edited by Bruce G. Trigger, pp. 190–197. Handbook of North American Indians, vol. 15, William C. Sturtevant, general editor. Smithsonian Institution, Washington, D.C.

1986 Spirit of the New England Tribes: Indian History and Folklore, 1620–1984. University Press of New England, Hanover, New Hampshire.

Simon, Brona G.
1990 Native American Culture Change and Persistence in Contact Period New England: Analysis of Mortuary Data from a Praying Indian Burial Ground in Massachusetts. Paper presented at the 55th Annual Meeting of the Society for American Archaeology, Las Vegas.

Simpson, Scott
1984 Human Skeletal Remains from Concord, New Hampshire. New Hampshire Archaeologist 25(1):66–72.

Sipe, C. Hale
1927 The Indian Chiefs of Pennsylvania. Ziegler Printing Company, Butler, Pennsylvania.

Skinner, Alanson Buck
1909 The Lenape Indians of Staten Island. In The Indians of Greater New York and the Lower Hudson, edited by Clark Wissler, pp. 1–61, Anthropological Papers of the American Museum of Natural History, No. 3.

1919 Exploration of Aboriginal Sites at Throgs Neck and Clasons Point, New York City. Museum of the American Indian, Heye Foundation, Contributions from the Museum 5(4).

1921 Notes on Iroquois Archaeology. Museum of the American Indian, Heye Foundation, Miscellaneous Series 18:5–216.

Skinner, Alanson Buck, and Max Schrabisch
1913 A Preliminary Report of the Archaeological Survey of the State of New Jersey. Geological Survey of New Jersey, Bulletin 9.

Smith, Carlyle Shreeve
1944 Clues to the Chronology of Coastal New York. American Antiquity 10(1):87–98.

1947 An Outline of the Archaeology of Coastal New York. Bulletin of the Archaeological Society of Connecticut 21:2–9.

1950 The Archaeology of Coastal New York. Anthropological Papers of the American Museum of Natural History 43(2).

Smith, Gerald P.
1971 Protohistoric Sociopolitical Organization of the Nottoway in the Chesapeake Bay–Carolina Sounds Region. Unpublished Ph.D dissertation, Department of Anthropology, University of Missouri, Columbia.

1984 The Hand Site, Southampton County, Virginia. Special Publication 11, Archeological Society of Virginia, Richmond.

Smith, Ira F., III, and Jeffrey R. Graybill
1977 A Report on the Shenks Ferry and Susquehannock Components of the Funk Site, Lancaster County, Pennsylvania. Man in the Northeast 11:45–65.

Smith, James
1799 An Account of the Remarkable Occurrences in the Life and Travels of Col. James Smith, during His Captivity with the Indians in the Years 1755, '56, '57, and '59 . . . John Bradford, Lexington, Virginia.

Smith, James Morton (editor)
1959 Seventeenth-Century America: Essays in Colonial History. W. W. Norton, New York.

Smith, John
1624 The Generalle Historie of Virginia, New England, and the Summer Isles. Michael Sparks, London.

Smolek, Michael A.
1986 The Cumberland Palisaded Village Site: A

(Very) Preliminary Report. Paper presented at the Annual Meeting of the Archaeological Society of Maryland, St. Leonard.

Snow, Dean R.

1968 Wabanaki "Family Hunting Territories." *American Anthropologist* 70(6):1143-1151.

1978a Late Prehistory of the East Coast. In *Northeast*, edited by Bruce G. Trigger, pp. 58-69. Handbook of North American Indians, vol. 15, William C. Sturtevant, general editor. Smithsonian Institution, Washington, D.C.

1978b Eastern Abenaki. In *Northeast*, edited by Bruce G. Trigger, pp. 137-147. Handbook of North American Indians, vol. 15, William C. Sturtevant, general editor. Smithsonian Institution, Washington, D.C.

1980 *The Archaeology of New England*. Academic Press, New York.

1984 Iroquois Prehistory. In *Extending the Rafters: Interdisciplinary Approaches to Iroquoian Studies*, edited by Michael K. Foster, Jack Campisi, and Marianne Mithun, pp. 241-257. State University of New York Press, Albany.

1989a Mohawk, Seneca, and Ontario Iroquois Trade Good Chronology. Ms. in author's possession.

1989b Mohawk River Drainage Archaeological Context. Ms. on file, New York State Office of Parks, Recreation, and Historic Preservation, Waterford.

1990 Personal communication.

1991a Mohawk. *The Bulletin: Journal of the New York State Archaeological Association* 102:34-39.

1991b Great Lakes Archaeology and Paleoecology: Exploring Interdisciplinary Initiatives for the Nineties—Paleoecology and the Prehistoric Incursion of Northern Iroquoians into the Lower Great Lakes Region. Ms. in author's possession.

1991c Personal communication.

1992 Evolution of the Mohawk Iroquois. Paper presented at the 57th Annual Meeting of the Society for American Archaeology, Pittsburgh.

1993 Sequence of Major Mohawk Villages Known as of August, 1992. Ms. in author's possession.

Snow, Dean R., and Kim M. Lanphear

1988 European Contact and Indian Depopulation in the Northeast: The Timing of the First Epidemics. *Ethnohistory* 35(1):15-33.

Snow, Dean R., and William A. Starna

1989 Sixteenth Century Depopulation: A View from the Mohawk Valley. *American Anthropologist* 91(1):142-149.

Snyder, Joseph J.

1967 The Heater's Island Site—A Preliminary Report. *Journal of the Archaeological Society of Maryland* 3(2):154-161.

Snyderman, George S.

1948 Behind the Great Tree of Peace: A Sociological Analysis of Iroquois Warfare. *Pennsylvania Archaeologist* 18.

Sobel, Mechal

1988 *The World They Made Together: Black and White Values in Eighteenth-Century Virginia*. Princeton University Press, Princeton, New Jersey.

Solecki, Ralph S.

1949 An Archaeological Survey of Two River Basins in West Virginia, Illustrations (Concluded). *West Virginia History* 10(4):319-432.

1950 The Archaeological Position of Historic Fort Corchaug, Long Island, and Its Relation to Contemporary Forts. *Bulletin of the Archaeological Society of Connecticut* 24:5-35.

1991 The Archaeology of Fort Massapequa. Ms. in author's possession.

South, Stanley

1972 Evolution and Horizon as Revealed in Ceramic Analysis in Historical Archaeology. *The Conference on Historic Site Archaeology Papers* 6(1-2):71-116.

Spangenburg, Augustus Gottlieb

1879 [1745] Bishop Spangenburg's Notes of Travel to Onondaga in 1745. *Pennsylvania Magazine of History and Biography* 3(1):56-64.

Speck, Frank G.

1914 *The Double-Curve Motif in Northeastern Algonkian Art*. Department of Mines, Geological Survey of Canada, Memoir 42.

1915 The Eastern Wabanaki Confederacy. *American Anthropologist* 17(3):492-508.

1928 Native Tribes and Dialects of Connecticut. *Annual Report of the Bureau of American Ethnology* 43:199-287.

1931 A Study of the Delaware Indian Big House Ceremony. *Publications of the Pennsylvania Historical Commission* 2.

1940 *Penobscot Man: The Life History of a Forest Tribe in Maine*. University of Pennsylvania Press, Philadelphia.

1942 *The Tutelo Spirit Adoption Ceremony*. Pennsylvania Historical Commission, Harrisburg.

1947 *Eastern Algonkian Block-Stamp Decoration: A New World Original or an Acculturated Art*. Archaeological Society of New Jersey, Research Series 1, Trenton.

Spicer, Edward H. (editor)

1961 *Perspectives in American Indian Culture Change*. University of Chicago Press, Chicago.

Spiess, Arthur E.

1980 The Hogdon Site National Register of Historic Places Registration Form. Ms. on file, U.S. Department of the Interior, National Park Service, National Register Branch, Washington, D.C.

1983 Allen's Island National Register of Historic Places Registration Form. Ms. on file, U.S. Department of the Interior, National Park Service, National Register Branch, Washington, D.C.

1986 Caratunk Falls Archeological District National Register of Historic Places Registration Form. Ms. on file, U.S. Department of the Interior, National Park Service, National Register Branch, Washington, D.C.

1987 The Pejepscot Site National Register of Historic Places Registration Form. Ms. on file, U.S. Department of the Interior, National Park Service, National Register Branch, Washington, D.C.

Spiess, Arthur E., and Robert L. Bradley
1979 Nahanada Village Site National Register of Historic Places Registration Form. Ms. on file, U.S. Department of the Interior, National Park Service, National Register Branch, Washington, D.C.

Spiess, Arthur E., and Bruce D. Spiess
1987 New England Pandemic of 1616-1622: Cause and Archaeological Implications. *Man in the Northeast* 34:71-83.

Spiess, Matthias
1960 Podunk Indian Sites. *Bulletin of the Archaeological Society of Connecticut* 5:9-11.

Spittal, W. G. (editor)
1990 *Iroquois Women: An Anthology.* Iroqrafts, Oshweken, Ontario.

Springer, James Warren
1986 American Indians and the Law of Real Property in Colonial New England. *The American Journal of Legal History* 30(1):25-58.

Stahle, David W., and Daniel Wolfman
1985 The Potential for Archaeological Tree-Ring Dating in Eastern North America. In *Advances in Archaeological Method and Theory, Vol. 8,* edited by Michael B. Schiffer, pp. 279-302. Academic Press, New York.

Stanzeski, Andrew
1993 Personal communication.

Starna, William A.
1980 Mohawk Iroquois Populations: A Revision. *Ethnohistory* 27(4):371-382.
1988 The Oneida Homeland in the Seventeenth Century. In *The Oneida Indian Experience: Two Perspectives,* edited by Jack Campisi and Laurence M. Hauptman, pp. 9-22. Syracuse University Press, Syracuse, New York.
1992 Personal communication.

Starna, William A., George R. Hamell, and William L. Butts
1984. Northern Iroquoian Horticulture and Insect Infestation: A Cause for Village Removal. *Ethnohistory* 31(3):197-207.

Starna, William A., and John H. Relethford
1985 Deer Densities and Population Dynamics: A Cautionary Note. *American Antiquity* 50(4): 825-832.

Starna, William A., and Ralph Watkins
1991 Northern Iroquoian Slavery. *Ethnohistory* 38(1):34-57.

Stephenson, Robert L., Alice L. L. Ferguson, and Henry Ferguson
1963 *The Accokeek Creek Site: A Middle Atlantic Seaboard Culture Sequence.* University of Michigan Museum of Anthropology, Anthropological Paper 20.

Stewart, Marilyn C.
1973 A Protohistoric Susquehannock Cemetery near Nichols, Tioga County, New York. *Bulletin of the New York State Archaeological Association* 58: 1-21.

Stewart, R. Michael
1980 Prehistoric Settlement and Subsistence Patterns and Testing of Predictive Site Location Models in the Great Valley of Maryland. Unpublished Ph.D dissertation, Department of Anthropology, Catholic University of America, Washington, D.C.
1982 Prehistoric Ceramics of the Great Valley of Maryland. *Archaeology of Eastern North America* 10:69-94.
1989 Personal communication.
1990 Personal communication.
1993 Interim Report of Archaeological Investigations: Snodgrass Farm, Lower Southampton Township, Bucks County, Pennsylvania. Report on file, Bureau of Historic Preservation, Harrisburg.

Stewart, R. Michael, Chris C. Hummer, and Jay F. Custer
1986 Late Woodland Cultures of the Middle and Lower Delaware River Valley and the Upper Delmarva Peninsula. In *Late Woodland Cultures in the Middle Atlantic Region,* edited by Jay F. Custer, pp. 58-89. University of Delaware Press, Newark.

Stewart, T. Dale
1992 *Archeological Exploration of Patawomeke: The Indian Town Site (44St2) Ancestral to the One (44ST1) Visited in 1608 by Captain John Smith.* Smithsonian Contributions to Anthropology 36.

Stewart, T. Dale, et al.
1963 The Townsend Site Report. *The Archeolog* 15(1).

Stockley, Bernard H.
1962 The Car-Tracks Site, Wareham. *Bulletin of the Massachusetts Archaeological Society* 23(3-4): 41-45.

Stone, Gaynell (editor)
1979 *The History and Archaeology of the Montauk Indians.* Readings in Long Island Archaeology and Ethnohistory, vol. 3. Suffolk County Archaeological Association, Stony Brook, New York.
1983 *The Shinnecock Indians: A Culture History.* Readings in Long Island Archaeology and Ethnohistory, vol. 6. Suffolk County Archaeological Association, Stony Brook, New York.

Stothers, David M., and James R. Graves
1985 The Prairie Peninsula Co-Tradition: An Hypothesis for Hopwellian to Upper Mississippian Continuity. *Archaeology of Eastern North America* 13:153-175.

Strachey, William
1953 [1612] *The Historie of Travell into Virginia Britanica.* Edited by Louis B. Wright and Virginia Freund. Hakluyt Society, 2d series, vol. 103, Cambridge.

Strong, John A.
1992 The Thirteen Tribes of Long Island: The History of a Myth. *The Hudson Valley Regional Review* 9(2):39-73.

Strong, William Duncan
1940 From History to Prehistory in the Northern

Great Plains. *Smithsonian Miscellaneous Collections* 100:353-394.
1953 Historical Approach in Anthropology. In *Anthropology Today: An Encyclopedic Inventory,* edited by Alfred L. Kroeber, pp. 386-397. University of Chicago Press, Chicago.

Sturtevant, William C.
1975 Two 1761 Wigwams at Niantic, Connecticut. *American Antiquity* 40(4):437-444.

Sullivan, James, Alexander C. Flick, Almon W. Lauber, Milton W. Hamilton, and Albert B. Corey (editors)
1921-1965 *The Papers of Sir William Johnson.* 15 vols. University of the State of New York, Albany.

Sullivan, Lynne P.
1992 Personal communication.

Sykes, C.M.
1980 Swidden Horticulture and Iroquoian Settlement. *Archaeology of Eastern North America* 8:45-52.

Tanner, Helen Hornbeck
1979 Coocoochee: Mohawk Medicine Woman. *American Indian Culture and Research Journal* 3(3):23-42.
1987 *Atlas of Great Lakes Indian History.* University of Oklahoma Press, Norman.

Tanner, Helen Hornbeck, and Erminie Wheeler-Voegelin
1974 *Indians of Northern Ohio and Southeastern Michigan.* Garland Publishing, New York.

Taylor, William B.
1976 The Fort Hill Bluff Site. *Bulletin of the Massachusetts Archaeological Society* 38(1-2):7-12.
1982 The Taylor Farm Site. *Bulletin of the Massachusetts Archaeological Society* 43(2):40-47.

Thomas, David Hurst
1989 *Archaeology.* 2d ed. Holt, Rinehart, and Winston, New York.

Thomas, Peter Allen
1977 Contrastive Subsistence Strategies and Land Use As Factors for Understanding Indian-White Relations in New England. *Ethnohistory* 23(1):1-18.
1981 The Fur Trade, Indian Land and the Need to Define Adequate "Environmental" Parameters. *Ethnohistory* 28(4):359-379.
1985 Culture Change on the Southern New England Frontier, 1630-1665. In *Cultures in Contact: The European Impact on Native Cultural Institutions in Eastern North America, A.D. 1000-1800,* edited by William W. Fitzhugh, pp. 131-162. Smithsonian Institution, Washington, D.C.
1991 *In the Maelstrom of Change: The Indian Trade and Cultural Process in the Middle Connecticut Valley, 1635-1665.* Garland Publishing, New York. Revised ed. of 1979 unpublished Ph.D dissertation, Department of Anthropology, University of Massachusetts, Amherst.

Thomas, Ronald A., et al.
1985 Archeological Data Recovery at 28CA50, Gloucester City, New Jersey. Report on file, Mid-

Atlantic Region Office, National Park Service, Philadelphia.

Thompson, Stith
1955 *Tales of the North American Indians.* Indiana University Press, Bloomington.

Thorbahn, Peter
1982 Interstate 495 Archaeological Data Recovery Project: Final Report. Report on file, Massachusetts Historical Commission, Boston.
1988 Where Are the Late Woodland Villages in Southern New England? *Bulletin of the Massachusetts Archaeological Society* 49(2):46-57.

Thorbahn, Peter, Deborah Cox, and Duncan Ritchie
1983 Archaeological Investigations at the G. B. Crane Site, Norton, Massachusetts: The Data Recovery Program. Report on file, Massachusetts Historical Commission, Boston.

Thornton, Russell
1987 *American Indian Holocaust and Survival: A Population History since 1492.* University of Oklahoma Press, Norman.

Thurman, Melburn D.
1972 Re-excavation of the Accokeek Site: A Preliminary Report. Paper presented at the Annual Meeting of the Society for American Archaeology, Bal Harbour, Florida.
1973 The Delaware Indians: A Study in Ethnohistory. Unpublished Ph.D dissertation, Department of Anthropology, University of California, Santa Barbara.

Thwaites, Rueben Gold (editor)
1896-1901 *The Jesuit Relations and Allied Documents: Travel and Explorations of the Jesuit Missionaries in New France, 1610-1791; The Original French, Latin, and Italian Texts, with English Translations and Notes.* 73 vols. Burrow's Brothers, Cleveland.

Tooker, Elisabeth
1970 *The Iroquois Ceremonial of Midwinter.* Syracuse University Press, Syracuse, New York.
1978a History of Research. In *Northeast,* edited by Bruce G. Trigger, pp. 4-13. Handbook of North American Indians, vol. 15, William C. Sturtevant, general editor. Smithsonian Institution, Washington, D.C.
1978b Wyandot. In *Northeast,* edited by Bruce G. Trigger, pp. 398-406. Handbook of North American Indians, vol. 15, William C. Sturtevant, general editor. Smithsonian Institution, Washington, D.C.
1978c The League of the Iroquois: Its History, Politics, and Ritual. In *Northeast,* edited by Bruce G. Trigger, pp. 418-441. Handbook of North American Indians, vol. 15, William C. Sturtevant, general editor. Smithsonian Institution, Washington, D.C.
1978d *The Indians of the Northeast: A Critical Bibliography.* Indiana University Press, Bloomington.
1984a The Demise of the Susquehannocks: A 17th Century Mystery. *Pennsylvania Archaeologist* 54(3-4):1-10.
1984b Women in Iroquois Society. In *Extending the Rafters: Interdisciplinary Approaches to Iro-*

quoian Studies, edited by Michael K. Foster, Jack Campisi, and Marianne Mithun, pp. 109-123. State University of New York Press, Albany.

1988 The United States Constitution and the Iroquois League. *Ethnohistory* 35(4):305-336.

Tooker, Elisabeth (editor)

1979 *Native North American Spirituality of the Eastern Woodlands*. Paulist Press, New York.

Tooker, William Wallace

1896 The Indian Village of Wegwagonock. *Souvenir of the Sag Harbor Fire Department Fair,* June 1-6, 1896, pp. 27-31, Sag Harbor, New York.

Torok, Charles H.

1965 The Tyendinaga Mohawks: The Village as a Basic Factor in Mohawk Social Structure. *Ontario History* 57(2):69-77.

Trelease, Allen W.

1960 *Indian Affairs in Colonial New York: The Seventeenth Century*. Cornell University Press, Ithaca, New York.

Trigger, Bruce G.

1971 The Mohawk-Mahican War (1624-1628): The Establishment of a Pattern. *Canadian Historical Review* 52(3):276-286.

1978a Early Iroquoian Contacts with Europeans. In *Northeast,* edited by Bruce G. Trigger, pp. 344-356. Handbook of North American Indians, vol. 15, William C. Sturtevant, general editor. Smithsonian Institution, Washington, D.C.

1980 *The Children of Aataentsic: A History of the Huron People to 1660*. 2 vols. McGill-Queen's University Press, Montreal.

1981 Prehistoric Social and Political Organization: An Iroquoian Case Study. In *Foundations of Northeast Archaeology,* edited by Dean R. Snow, pp. 1-50. Academic Press, New York.

1985 *Natives and Newcomers: Canada's "Heroic Age" Reconsidered*. McGill-Queen's University Press, Montreal.

1991a Early Native North American Responses to European Contact: Romantic versus Rationalistic Interpretations. *The Journal of American History* 77(4):1195-1215.

1991b Distinguished Lecture in Archeology: Constraint and Freedom—A New Synthesis for Archeological Explanation. *American Anthropologist* 93(3):551-569.

Trigger, Bruce G. (editor)

1978b *Handbook of North American Indians 15: Northeast*. Smithsonian Institution, Washington, D.C.

Trigger, Bruce G., and James F. Pendergast

1978 Saint Lawrence Iroquoians. In *Northeast,* edited by Bruce G. Trigger, pp. 357-361. Handbook of North American Indians, vol. 15, William C. Sturtevant, general editor. Smithsonian Institution, Washington, D.C.

Trigger, Bruce G., L. Yaffe, M. Diksic, J. L. Galinier, H. Marshall, and James F. Pendergast

1980 Trace-Element Analysis of Iroquoian Pottery. *Canadian Journal of Archaeology* 4:119-145.

Tuck, James A.

1971 *Onondaga Iroquois Prehistory: A Study in Settlement Archaeology*. Syracuse University Press, Syracuse, New York.

1978 Northern Iroquoian Prehistory. In *Northeast,* edited by Bruce G. Trigger, pp. 322-333. Handbook of North American Indians, vol. 15, William C. Sturtevant, general editor. Smithsonian Institution, Washington, D.C.

Turgeon, Laurier

1990 Basque-Amerindian Trade in the Saint Lawrence during the Sixteenth-Century: New Documents, New Perspectives. *Man in the Northeast* 40:81-87.

Turnbaugh, Sarah Peabody, and William A. Turnbaugh

1987 Weaving the Woods: Tradition and Response in Southern New England Splint Basketry. In *A Key into the Language of Woodsplint Baskets,* edited by Ann McMullen and Russell G. Handsman, pp. 77-94. American Indian Archaeological Institute, Washington, Connecticut.

Turnbaugh, William A.

1975 *Man, Land, and Time: The Cultural Prehistory and Demographic Patterns of North-Central Pennsylvania*. Lycoming County Historical Society, Williamsport.

1984 *The Material Culture of RI 1000, A Mid-17th Century Narragansett Indian Burial Site in North Kingstown, Rhode Island*. Department of Sociology and Anthropology, University of Rhode Island, Kingston.

n.d. Whitford Collection of Artifacts from Narragansett Indian Graves, Cranston Corners, R.I. Ms. on file, Rhode Island Historical Preservation Commission, Providence.

Turner, E. Randolph, III

1976 An Archeological and Ethnohistorical Study on the Evolution of Rank Societies in the Virginia Coastal Plain. Unpublished Ph.D dissertation, Department of Anthropology, Pennsylvania State University, University Park.

1982 A Re-examination of Powhatan Territorial Boundaries and Population, ca. A.D. 1607. *Quarterly Bulletin: Archeological Society of Virginia* 37(2): 45-64.

1985 Socio-Political Organization within the Powhatan Chiefdom and the Effects of European Contact, A.D. 1607-1646. In *Cultures in Contact: The European Impact on Native Cultural Institutions in Eastern North America, A.D. 1000-1800,* edited by William W. Fitzhugh, pp. 193-224, Smithsonian Institution, Washington, D.C.

1986 Difficulties in the Archaeological Identification of Chiefdoms as Seen in the Virginia Coastal Plain during the Late Woodland and Early Historic Periods. In *Late Woodland Cultures of the Middle Atlantic Region,* edited by Jay F. Custer, pp. 19-28. University of Delaware Press, Newark.

1990a Personal communication.

1990b A Compilation of Virginia Native American Sites Dating to the Contact Period. Report on file, Virginia Department of Historic Resources, Richmond.

Turner, E. Randolph, III, and Antony F. Opperman
1989 Hatch Archeological Site/44PG51 National Register of Historic Places Registration Form. Ms. on file, U.S. Department of the Interior, National Park Service, National Register Branch, Washington, D.C.

Tyler, Lyon G. (editor)
1907 *Narratives of Early Virginia, 1606-1625.* Charles Scribner's Sons, New York.

Tylor, Edward S.
1889 On a Method of Investigating the Development of Institutions; Applied to Laws of Marriage and Descent. *Journal of the Royal Anthropological Institute* 18:245-269.

Ulrich, Thomas
1977 Prehistoric Archaeological Surveys (Phase II) of Portions of the I-391 Project Corridor including the Willimansett Bluffs and the Indian Crossing Prehistoric Site. Report on file, Massachusetts Department of Public Works, Boston.

VAI (Vermont Archaeological Inventory)
n.d. *Vermont Archaeological Inventory.* Ms. on file, Vermont Division for Historic Preservation, Montpelier.

van der Donck, Adriaen
1968 [1656] *A Description of the New Netherlands.* Syracuse University Press, Syracuse, New York.

Vandrei, Charles E.
1986 A Preliminary Report on the 1983 and 1984 Excavations at Bosley's Mills, A Seventeenth Century Seneca Iroquois Community. Report on file, New York State Office of Parks, Recreation, and Historic Preservation, Waterford.

van Gastel, Ada
1990 Van der Donck's Description of the Indians: Additions and Corrections. *William and Mary Quarterly* 47(3):411-421.

Van Sickle, George
1990 Personal communication.

Vaughan, Alden T.
1979 *New England Frontier: Puritans and Indians, 1620-1675.* Revised ed. W. W. Norton, New York. Originally published in 1964.

Vaughan, Alden T., and Edward W. Clark (editors)
1981 *Puritans among the Indians: Accounts of Captivity and Redemption, 1676-1724.* Harvard University Press, Cambridge.

VDHR (Virginia Department of Historic Resources)
n.d. Virginia Department of Historic Resources Archaeological Inventory Archives. Ms. on file, Virginia Department of Historic Resources, Richmond.
1991 Definition of Historic Contexts. Report on file, Virginia Department of Historic Resources, Richmond.

Verrazzano, Giovanni da
1970 [1524-1528] *The Voyages of Giovanni da Verrazzano, 1524-1528.* Edited by Lawrence C. Wroth. Yale University Press, New Haven, Connecticut.

Versaggi, Nina
1991 Personal communication.

Vescelius, Gary
1952 Excavated Material from Pine Orchard Swamp, Branford, Connecticut. *Bulletin of the Archaeological Society of Connecticut* 26:51-53.

VHLC (Virginia Historic Landmarks Commission)
1969 Camden National Register of Historic Places Registration Form. Ms. on file, U.S. Department of the Interior, National Park Service, National Register Branch, Washington, D.C.
1974 Moysonec National Register of Historic Places Registration Form. Ms. on file, U.S. Department of the Interior, National Park Service, National Register Branch, Washington, D.C.
1979 Rose Hill National Register of Historic Places Registration Form. Ms. on file, U.S. Department of the Interior, National Park Service, National Register Branch, Washington, D.C.

Vickers, Daniel
1983 The First Whalemen of Nantucket. *William and Mary Quarterly* 40(4):560-583.

Voegelin, Erminie W.
1944 Mortuary Customs of the Shawnee and Other Eastern Tribes. Indiana Historical Society, *Prehistory Research Series* 2(4).

Von Lonkhuyzen, Harold W.
1990 A Reappraisal of the Praying Indians: Acculturation, Conversion, and Identity at Natick, Massachusetts, 1646-1730. *New England Quarterly* 63(4): 396-428.

Vrabel, Deborah M., and Paul B. Cissna (editors)
n.d. Archeological Survey of Piscataway Park. Report on file, National Capital Region Office, National Park Service, Washington, D.C.

Wacker, Peter O.
1975 *Land and People, A Cultural Geography of Preindustrial New Jersey: Origins and Settlement Patterns.* Rutgers University Press, New Brunswick, New Jersey.

Wade, Mason
1988 French Indian Policies. In *History of Indian-White Relations,* edited by Wilcomb E. Washburn, pp. 20-28. Handbook of North American Indians, vol. 4, William C. Sturtevant, general editor. Smithsonian Institution, Washington, D.C.

Walker, Ian C.
1977 *Clay Tobacco-Pipes, with Particular Reference to the Bristol Industry.* 4 vols. History and Archaeology 11a-d, National Historical Parks and Sites Branch, Parks Canada, Department of Indian Affairs and Northern Development, Ottawa.

Wall, Robert D.
1984 Protohistoric Settlement of the Maryland Plateau Region: An Overview. In *Upland Archeology in the East: Symposium 2,* edited by Michael B. Barber, pp. 180-190. U.S. Department of Agriculture Forest Service Southern Region, Atlanta, Georgia.

Wallace, Anthony F. C.

1970 *The Death and Rebirth of the Seneca.* Alfred A. Knopf, New York.

1990 *King of the Delawares: Teedyuscung, 1700–1763.* Syracuse University Press, Syracuse, New York. Originally published in 1949 by University of Pennsylvania Press, Philadelphia.

Wallace, Paul A. W.

1945 *Conrad Weiser, 1696–1760: Friend of Colonist and Mohawk.* University of Pennsylvania Press, Philadelphia.

1958 *Thirty Thousand Miles with John Heckewelder.* University of Pittsburgh Press, Pittsburgh.

1965 *Indian Paths of Pennsylvania.* Pennsylvania Historical and Museum Commission, Harrisburg.

1981 *Indians in Pennsylvania.* Revised ed. Edited by William A. Hunter. Pennsylvania Historical and Museum Commission, Harrisburg.

Wallerstein, Immanuel

1974 *The Modern World-System.* Academic Press, New York.

Wallis, Wilson D., and Ruth S. Wallis

1955 *The Micmac Indians of Eastern Canada.* University of Minnesota Press, Minneapolis.

Warren, Elizabeth S.

1976 The Governor William Bradford House National Register of Historic Places Registration Form. Ms. on file, U.S. Department of the Interior, National Park Service, National Register Branch, Washington, D.C.

Waselkov, Gregory A.

1982 Shellfish Gathering and Shell Midden Archaeology. Unpublished Ph.D dissertation, Department of Anthropology, University of North Carolina, Chapel Hill.

1989 Seventeenth-Century Trade in the Colonial Southeast. *Southeastern Archaeology* 8(2):117–133.

Washburn, Wilcomb E.

1957 *The Governor and the Rebel: A History of Bacon's Rebellion in Virginia.* University of North Carolina Press, Chapel Hill.

1978 Seventeenth-Century Indian Wars. In *History of Indian-White Relations,* edited by Wilcomb E. Washburn, pp. 78–88. Handbook of North American Indians, vol. 4, William C. Sturtevant, general editor. Smithsonian Institution, Washington, D.C.

Washburn, Wilcomb E. (editor)

1975–1979 *The Garland Library of Narratives of North American Indian Captivities.* 111 vols. Garland Publishing, New York.

1988 *Handbook of North American Indians 4: History of Indian-White Relations.* Smithsonian Institution, Washington, D.C.

Waugh, Frederick W.

1916 *Iroquois Foods and Food Preparation.* Memoirs of the Canadian Geological Survey 86, Anthropological Series 12.

Weatherford, Jack

1988 *Indian Givers: How the Indians of the Americas Transformed the World.* Crown Publishers, New York.

Weaver, Lynn Beebe, and Lenore Rennenkampf

1973 James William Beekman Estate National Register of Historic Places Registration Form. Ms. on file, U.S. Department of the Interior, National Park Service, National Register Branch, Washington, D.C.

Webb, Stephen Saunders

1984 *1676: The End of American Independence.* Alfred A. Knopf, New York.

Wedel, Waldo Rudolph

1936 *An Introduction to Pawnee Archaeology.* Bureau of American Ethnology, Bulletin 112, Washington, D.C.

1938 The Direct-Historical Approach in Pawnee Archeology. *Smithsonian Miscellaneous Collections* 97(7):1–21.

Weinstein, Laurie

1991 Land, Politics, and Power: The Mohegan Indians in the 17th and 18th Centuries. *Man in the Northeast* 42:9–16.

1994 Samson Occom: A Charismatic 18th-Century Mohegan Missionary. In *Enduring Traditions: The Native Peoples of New England,* edited by Laurie Weinstein. Greenwood Press, Westport, Connecticut. In press.

Weiskotten, Daniel H.

1988 Origins of the Oneida Iroquois: Fact and Fallacy—Past and Present. *Chenango Chapter New York State Archaeological Association Bulletin* 22(4):1–20.

Weiss, Francine D.

1975 Accokeek Creek Site National Historic Landmark Registration Form. Ms. on file, U.S. Department of the Interior, National Park Service, History Division, Washington, D.C.

Welters, Linda M.

1985 Narragansett Bay Survey: Conservation and Analysis of European Textiles from RI 1000. Report on file at the Rhode Island Historical Preservation Commission, Providence.

Werner, David J.

1972 The Zimmerman Site, 36-PI-14. In *Archaeology in the Upper Delaware Valley: A Study of the Cultural Chronology of the Tocks Island Reservoir,* edited by W. Fred Kinsey III, pp. 1–54. Anthropological Series, Vol. 2. Pennsylvania Historical and Museum Commission, Harrisburg.

Weslager, C. A.

1939 An Aboriginal Shell Heap near Lewes, Delaware. *Bulletin of the Archeological Society of Delaware* 3(2):3–8.

1948 *The Nanticoke Indians: A Refugee Tribal Group of Pennsylvania.* Pennsylvania Historical and Museum Commission, Harrisburg.

1950 Indians of the Eastern Shore of Maryland and Virginia. In *The Eastern Shore of Maryland and Virginia,* edited by Charles B. Clark, vol. 1, pp. 39–69. Lewis Publishing Company, New York.

1953 *Red Men on the Brandywine.* Hambleton Company, Wilmington, Delaware.

1967 *The English on the Delaware: 1610-1682.* Rutgers University Press, New Brunswick, New Jersey.

1969 *The Log Cabin in America from Frontier Days to the Present.* Rutgers University Press, New Brunswick, New Jersey.

1972 *The Delaware Indians: A History.* Rutgers University Press, New Brunswick, New Jersey.

1978a *The Delaware Indian Westward Migration.* Mid-Atlantic Press, Somerset, Pennsylvania.

1978b *The Delaware Indians: A Critical Bibliography.* Indiana University Press, Bloomington.

1991 *The Siconese Indians of Lewes, Delaware: A Historical Account of a "Great" Bayside Lenape Tribe.* Lewes Historical Society, Lewes, Delaware.

Weslager, C. A., and Arthur R. Dunlap

1961 *Dutch Explorers, Traders and Settlers in the Delaware Valley, 1609-1664.* University of Pennsylvania Press, Philadelphia.

Wherry, James D.

1980 *The History of Maliseets and Micmacs in Aroostook County Maine.* Proposed Settlement of Maine Indian Land Claims, Hearings before the Select Committee on Indian Affairs, U.S. Senate, 96th Congress, pp. 506-622. U.S. Government Printing Office, Washington, D.C.

White, Andrew

1910 [1634] A Briefe Relation of the Voyage unto Maryland, by Father Andrew White, 1634. In *Narratives of Early Maryland, 1633-1684,* edited by Clayton C. Hall, pp. 27-45. Charles Scribner's Sons, New York.

White, Marian E.

1961 *Iroquois Culture History in the Niagara Frontier Area of New York State.* Museum of Anthropology, University of Michigan, Anthropological Paper 16.

1967 An Early Historic Niagara Frontier Iroquois Cemetery in Erie County, New York. *Researches and Transactions of the New York State Archaeological Association* 16(1).

1968 A Re-examination of the Historic Iroquois Van Son Cemetery on Grand Island. *Bulletin of the Buffalo Society of Natural Sciences* 24:7-48.

1971 Ethnic Identification and Iroquois Groups in Western New York and Ontario. *Ethnohistory* 18(1):19-38.

1976 Late Woodland Archaeology in the Niagara Frontier of New York and Ontario. In *The Late Prehistory of the Lake Erie Drainage Basin: A 1972 Symposium Revisited,* edited by David S. Brose, pp. 110-136. Cleveland Museum of Natural History, Cleveland, Ohio.

1977 The Shelby Site Reexamined. In *Current Perspectives in Northeastern Archeology: Essays in Honor of William A. Ritchie,* edited by Robert E. Funk and Charles F. Hayes III, pp. 85-91. Transactions of the New York State Archaeological Association 17(1).

1978a Neutral and Wenro. In *Northeast,* edited by Bruce G. Trigger, pp. 407-411. Handbook of North American Indians, vol. 15, William C. Sturtevant, general editor. Smithsonian Institution, Washington, D.C.

1978b Erie. In *Northeast,* edited by Bruce G. Trigger, pp. 412-417. Handbook of North American Indians, vol. 15, William C. Sturtevant, general editor. Smithsonian Institution, Washington, D.C.

White, Marian E., William E. Engelbrecht, and Elisabeth Tooker

1978 Cayuga. In *Northeast,* edited by Bruce G. Trigger, pp. 500-504. Handbook of North American Indians, vol. 15, William C. Sturtevant, general editor. Smithsonian Institution, Washington, D.C.

White, Richard

1991 *The Middle Ground: Indians, Empires, and Republics in the Great Lakes Region, 1650-1815.* Cambridge University Press, New York.

White, Richard, and William Cronon

1988 Ecological Change and Indian-White Relations. In *History of Indian-White Relations,* edited by Wilcomb E. Washburn, pp. 417-429. Handbook of North American Indians, vol. 4, William C. Sturtevant, general editor. Smithsonian Institution, Washington, D.C.

White, W., P. Dinsmoor, and Wayne E. Clark

1981 Patterson's Archeological District National Register of Historic Places Registration Form. Ms. on file, U.S. Department of the Interior, National Park Service, National Register Branch, Washington, D.C.

Whitehead, Ruth H.

1988 *Stories from the Six Worlds: Micmac Legends.* Nimbus Publishing Ltd., Halifax, Nova Scotia.

Whitney, Theodore

1964 Thurston, Onneyuttehage? MSV 1. *Chenango Chapter New York State Archaeological Association Bulletin* 6(1).

1967 The Bach Site. *Chenango Chapter New York State Archaeological Association Bulletin* 8(4).

1970 Buyea Site, OND-13. *Chenango Chapter New York State Archaeological Association Bulletin* 11(1).

Whitrow, G. J.

1988 *Time in History: The Evolution of our General Awareness of Time and Temporal Perspective.* Oxford University Press, New York.

Whyte, Thomas, and Clarence Geier

1982 *The Perkins Point Site (44BA3): A Protohistoric Stockaded Village on the Jackson River, Bath County, Virginia.* Occasional Papers in Anthropology 11. James Madison University, Harrisonburg, Virginia.

Wilbour, Benjamin Franklin

1970 *Notes on Little Compton.* College Hill Press, Providence, Rhode Island.

Williams, Lorraine E.

1972 Fort Shantok and Fort Corchaug: A Comparative Analysis of Seventeenth-Century Culture Contact in the Long Island Sound Area. Unpublished Ph.D dissertation, Department of Anthropology, New York University.

Williams, Lorraine E., and Susan Kardas
1982 Contact between Europeans and the Delaware Indians in New Jersey. In *New Jersey's Archaeological Resources: A Review of Research Problems and Survey Priorities, the Paleo-Indian Period to the Present*, edited by Olga Chesler, pp. 185-198. Office of New Jersey Heritage, Trenton.

Williams, Lorraine E., Anthony J. Puniello, and Karen A. Flinn
1982 *Reinvestigation of the Late Woodland Occupation in the Delaware Water Gap National Recreation Area, New Jersey*. Report on file, Mid-Atlantic Region, National Park Service, Philadelphia.

Williams, Roger
1973 [1643] *A Key into the Language of America*. Edited by John J. Teunissen and Evelyn J. Hinz. Wayne State University Press, Detroit.

Willoughby, Charles C.
1906 Houses and Gardens of the New England Indians. *American Anthropologist* 8(1):115-132.
1924 Indian Burial Place at Winthrop, Massachusetts. *Papers of the Peabody Museum of American Archaeology and Ethnology* 11(2).
1935 *Antiquities of the New England Indians*. Harvard University, Peabody Museum of Archaeology and Ethnology, Cambridge.

Wilson, Jack Hubert, Jr.
1983 A Study of the Late Prehistoric, Protohistoric, and Historic Indians of the Carolina and Virginia Piedmont: Structure, Process, and Ecology. Unpublished Ph.D dissertation, Department of Anthropology, University of North Carolina, Chapel Hill.

Wingerson, R., and R. Wingerson
1976 The Hunter Brook Rockshelter. *The Bulletin and Journal of the New York Archaeological Association* 68:19-28.

Wintemberg, W. J.
1931 Distinguishing Characteristics of Algonkian and Iroquoian Cultures. *National Museum of Canada, Annual Report for 1929, Bulletin* 67:65-125.

Winthrop, John
1908 [1630-1649] *Winthrop's Journal: History of New England*. Edited by James K. Hosmer. 2 vols. Charles Scribner's Sons, New York.

Witthoft, John
1951 The Pemberton Family Cemetery. *Pennsylvania Archaeologist* 21(1-2):21-32.

Witthoft, John, and William A. Hunter
1955 The Seventeenth-Century Origins of the Shawnee. *Ethnohistory* 2(1):42-57.

Witthoft, John, and W. Fred Kinsey III (editors)
1959 *Susquehannock Miscellany*. Pennsylvania Historical and Museum Commission, Harrisburg.

Witthoft, John, Harry Schoff, and Charles F. Wray
1953 Micmac Pipes, Vase-Shaped Pipes, and Calumets. *Pennsylvania Archaeologist* 33(1-2):89-107.

Wojciechowski, Franz
1985 *The Paugusset Tribes*. Catholic University of Nijmegen, the Netherlands.

Wolf, Eric R.
1959 *Sons of the Shaking Earth*. University of Chicago Press, Chicago.
1982 *Europe and the People without History*. University of California Press, Berkeley.

Wood, Alice
1974 A Catalogue of Jesuit and Ornamental Rings from Western New York State. *Historical Archaeology* 8:83-104.

Wood, William
1977 [1634] *New England's Prospect*. Edited by Alden T. Vaughan. The Commonwealth Series, Vol. 3, University of Massachusetts Press, Amherst.

Woodson, C. G.
1920 The Relations of Negroes and Indians in Massachusetts. *Journal of Negro History* 5:45-62.

Workmaster, Wallace F.
1969 *Fort Ontario: A New Look at the Past*. Oswego County Historical Society, Oswego, New York.

Wraxall, Peter (compiler)
1915 *An Abridgement of the Indian Affairs Contained in Four Folio Volumes, Transacted in the Colony of New York, from the Year 1678 to the Year 1751*. Edited by Charles H. MacIlwain. Harvard University Press, Cambridge.

Wray, Charles F.
1973 *Manual for Seneca Archaeology*. Cultures Primitive, Honeoye Falls, New York.
1983 Seneca Glass Trade Beads c. a.d. 1550-1820. In *Proceedings of the 1982 Glass Trade Bead Conference*, edited by Charles F. Hayes III, pp. 41-47, Rochester Museum and Science Center Research Record 16.
1985 Handbook of Seneca Archaeology. Ms. on file, Rochester Museum and Science Center.
n.d. Seneca Site Notes and Records. Ms. on file, Rochester Museum and Science Center.

Wray, Charles F., and Harry Schoff
1953 A Preliminary Report on the Seneca Sequence in Western New York. *Pennsylvania Archaeologist* 23(2):53-63.

Wray, Charles F., Martha L. Sempowski, and Lorraine P. Saunders
1990 *Two Early Contact Era Seneca Sites: Tram and Cameron*. C. F. Wray Series in Seneca Archaeology, vol. 2, Rochester Museum and Science Center, Research Record 21.

Wray, Charles F., Martha L. Sempowski, Lorraine P. Saunders, and Gian Carlo Cervone
1987 *The Adams and Culbertson Sites*. C. F. Wray Series in Seneca Archaeology, vol. 1, Rochester Museum and Science Center Research Record 19.

Wright, Gordon K.
1950 The Long Point Site. *Pennsylvania Archaeological Bulletin* 20(3-4).
1963 *The Neutral Indians—A Sourcebook*. Occasional Papers of the New York State Archaeological Association 4.

Wright, Harry Andrew
1895 Discovery of Aboriginal Remains near Springfield, Massachusetts. *Scientific American* 76(11):170.

Wright, Henry T.
1973 Site 18AG20. Ms. on file, Division of Archeology, Maryland Geological Survey, Baltimore.

Wright, James V.
1966 *The Ontario Iroquois Tradition.* National Museum of Canada, Bulletin 210.

Wright, Roy
1974 The People of the Panther: A Long Erie Tail. In *Papers in Linguistics from the 1972 Conference on Iroquoian Research,* edited by Michael K. Foster, pp. 47-118. Mercury Series, Ethnology Division Paper No. 10. National Museums of Canada, National Museum of Man.

WVAS (West Virginia Archeological Survey)
n.d. West Virginia Archeological Survey. Ms. on file at the West Virginia Historic Preservation Office, Charleston.

Wyatt, Ronald J.
1990 Personal communication.

Young, William R.
1969a A Survey of the Available Knowledge on the Middle Connecticut Valley Indians—Prehistoric and Historic. In *An Introduction to the Archaeology and History of the Connecticut Valley Indian,* edited by William R. Young, pp. 33-61. Springfield Museum of Science, Springfield, Massachusetts.

Young, William R. (editor)
1969b *An Introduction to the Archaeology and History of the Connecticut Valley Indian.* Springfield Museum of Science, Springfield, Massachusetts.

Zakucia, John A.
1957 Chambers Site (36LA11). Ms. on file, Pennsylvania Historical and Museum Commission, Harrisburg.

Zannieri, Nina
1983 Jireh Bull Blockhouse Historic Site (RI-296) National Register of Historic Places Registration Form. Ms. on file, U.S. Department of the Interior, National Park Service, National Register Branch, Washington, D.C.

Zeisberger, David
1910 *History of the North American Indians.* Edited by Archer B. Hulbert and William N. Schwarze. Ohio State Archaeological and Historical Quarterly 19.

INDEX

Arnold, Benedict, 80
Arnolda site, 129
Arrowhead Farm 1 site, 247
Arrows. *See* Projectile points
Artifacts, 36, 38–45, 47, 49; of Cayuga Country, 396, 397, 399–401, 416; of Delaware Country, 231, 238, 241; of Eastern Abenaki Country, 71, 75, 78–79, 82–84, 184–187, 192; at Fort Orange site, 182; of Lower Connecticut Valley Country, 153, 154, 158; of Lower Susquehanna Country, 301–302, 304, 306–309, 311, 312, 314; of Mahican Country, 164, 171–173, 183; of Massachusett Country, 110; of Middle Atlantic region, 322; misuse of (*see* Excavations, site: looting of); of Mohawk Country, 353, 354, 361–364, 366, 367, 369, 372–375, 382; of Mohegan-Pequot Country, 143, 145, 149–150; of Montauk Country, 160, 162, 163; of Munsee Country, 215, 217, 220–226, 353; of Nanticoke Country, 243, 247–248; of Narragansett Country, 134–136; of Niagara-Erie Frontier, 416, 417, 420–421, 423; of Nipmuck Country, 103, 105, 108; of North Atlantic region, 58, 59, 61; of Nottoway-Meherrin Country, 279, 281–282; of Oneida Country, 363, 378–384, 435; of Onondaga Country, 387–388, 391–393; of Pennacook-Pawtucket Country, 105, 108; of Piscataway-Potomac Country, 250, 253, 256, 258, 261–265; of Pocumtuck-Squakheag Country, 96–99; of Powhatan Country, 268, 274, 275; of Seneca Country, 283, 304, 309, 403, 404, 407–408, 411–413, 416, 435; of Southern Appalachian Highlands Country, 295–299; of Trans-Appalachian region, 331, 336, 347, 439; of Upper Ohio Country, 431–436, 438; of Upper Potomac-Shenandoah Country, 283, 284, 286, 287; of Upper Susquehanna Country, 424–425, 427–428; of Virginia Piedmont Country, 288–289, 292; of Wampanoag Country, 117–118, 122, 125; of Western Abenaki Country, 86–87, 89–91. *See also* Beads; Ornaments, Indian; Pipes, clay; Pottery; Projectile points; Tools; Utensils, Indian; Weapons, Indian
Artisans, Indian, 19, 48, 100, 160, 162, 265, 338, 400, 448. *See also* Basketry; Pottery
Artists, Indian, 448
Artpark site, 421
Askiminikansen site, 248
Assamoosick (reservation), 280
Assateague Indians, 201; town, 248
Asserue (Indian town), 361, 363
Attiouandaron Indians, 437
Auriesville sites, 370
Awashonks (Algonquian), 13

Bach site, 378
Backwoods colonization culture, 449
Bacon, Nathaniel, 205, 209, 262–263, 273
Bacon's Rebellion, 205, 206, 257, 262–263, 273, 278, 279, 292, 312
Ballymohack West site, 143
Barbados, Indian slaves to, 205
Barclay, Henry, 348

Barentsz, Pieter, 439
Barka, Norman F., 30
Barkers Bottom site, 297
Barker site, 354, 361
Barkhamstead, Conn., 157, 158
Bark Wigwams site, 97
Barns, Indian, 48, 346, 348, 372, 373, 393, 428
Barton site, 284
Bartram, John, 350
Bashaba (Mawooshen), 76
Basketry, Indian, 19, 39, 66, 115, 160, 265, 316, 338, 346
Basques, 10, 14, 56, 60, 202, 330, 439
Bauder site, 362, 363
Bead Hill site, 420, 428
Beads, 19; clay, 261, 309, 312, 347, 373, 391, 393, 400; glass, 8, 39, 61, 72, 79, 83, 84, 89, 97, 108, 114, 135, 136, 145, 149, 153, 164, 168, 172, 173, 182, 185–187, 192, 200, 202, 203, 215, 220, 221, 224, 238, 241, 247, 250, 256, 261, 263, 265, 268, 271, 274, 279, 281, 282, 284, 286, 287, 292, 295–297, 299, 304, 307, 308, 311, 312, 319, 333, 336, 361–364, 373, 378, 382, 383, 387, 393, 397, 400, 404, 414, 417, 420, 422–425, 427, 428, 432, 438; as medium of exchange (*see* Wampum); metal, 143, 241, 292, 297, 354, 378, 403, 404, 432; rolled, 431; rosary, 33; shell, 8, 15, 39, 45, 143, 151, 159–160, 172, 215, 268, 274, 309, 312, 316, 322, 347, 388, 391, 393, 413 (*see also* Wampum); slate, 393
Beale site, 413
Beans, 10, 15, 58, 72, 124, 199, 232, 289, 295, 327, 337, 346, 447; in archaeological deposits, 84, 211, 217, 432
Bear Hollow site, 103
Beaver, 15, 80, 91, 333, 341
Beaver Meadow Brook site, 153
Beazell School site, 432
Bécancour (mission), 81, 93, 172
Beecher (Blowers) site, 378, 381
Beekman projectile points, 45
Belcher site, 403
Belgium, colonists from, 175, 319
Bell-Browning-Blair site, 216
Bellinger site, 354
Bell-Philhower site, 216
Belmont, L'Abbé de, 411
Bennett Rock Shelter site, 154
Berkeley, William, 205
Berkhofer, Robert, 18
Bermuda, Indian slaves to, 142
Bernou, Claude, 420
Berryville site, 283
Beverley, Robert, 31, 210, 264
Bibles, Indian-language, 33, 111, 173, 371
Bibliographies: archaeological, 37; Historic Contact-related, 33
Biggin-McCarty site, 428
Billmyer site, 308
Billopp, Christopher, 223
Biographies, Historic Contact-related, 35
Bird, Edward, 225

Birds, as Indian food source, 333
Blackie, William, 222
Black Minquas, 420, 437, 438
Bland, Edward, 277-278, 289
Block, Adriaen, 13, 129, 215, 319
Bloody Hill site, 335
Bloody Hill II site, 392
Bluddee Rock site, 154
Blue Fish Beach site, 250
Boathouse Pond site, 249, 250
Bogaert, Harmen Meyndertsz van den, 340, 361-363, 376, 381, 390, 439
Bohringer site, 370
Bone(s): in archaeological deposits, 149-150, 220, 225, 243, 256, 261, 283, 289, 309, 404, 423; as Indian raw material, 58, 198, 211, 241, 295, 327, 337, 347, 378, 383, 391, 400, 435
Boston, Mass., 103, 111, 113. *See also* Massachusett Country
Boughton Hill Archeological Site and NHL, 5, 409-413
Boukins, Va., 279
Bowman's Brook pottery, 212, 222, 225, 231
Braddock, Edward, 229
Bradley, James W., 28-29, 202, 346
Bragdon, Kathleen, 47
Brainerd, David, 240, 428
Brainerd, John, 428
Brant, (Mohawk), 369
Brant, Joseph, 13, 35, 348, 369, 372, 375, 422
Brant, Molly, 371-373, 375
Brant Homestead site, 347, 372-375
Brasser, Theodore J. C., 29, 165
Brébeuf, Jean de, 417
Brenner, Elise M., 44
Bridgeport, Conn., 157
Bridges Point site, 75
Briggs Run site, 361
Brisay, Jacques René de, Marquis de Denonville, 368, 401, 410, 413
Brisbane site, 408
Bristol, R.I., 123
Brittany, adventurers from, 10, 335
Broad Creek, Md., 248
Broadneck site, 264
Brookfield, Mass., 103
Brothertown (Indian town), 138, 151, 162, 174, 240, 386
Brothertown Movement, 138, 151, 152, 158
Brotherton Reservation, 240, 241
Brown site, 362-364
Brûlé, Étienne, 408, 417
Brushes Creek site, 162
Bruyas, Jacques, 382
Buckhaloons Park site, 438
Buffum Street site, 417
Bunce Burials site, 412
Bureau of American Ethnology, 50
Burgraff, James, 225
Burial Ridge. *See* Ward's Point NHL
Burials, Indian, 19, 43-44, 66, 108, 113, 115-117, 124-126, 128, 133, 143, 145, 158, 201, 203, 212, 217, 220-224, 241, 243-244, 254, 264, 268, 274, 279, 288, 289, 292, 294, 295, 297, 298, 304, 307-309, 311, 312, 316, 332, 334, 336, 347, 381, 382, 392, 397-398, 403-405, 412, 416, 417, 425, 428, 432, 435, 438. *See also* Offerings, funerary
Burle site, 264
Burning Spring Fort site, 421
Burr/Haines Mill site, 241
Burr's Hill site, 65, 66, 70, 122
Bushey's Cavern site, 283, 284
Bushnell, David, 48, 250, 291
Bushy Hill site, 370
Buttrum Town (Indian town), 294
Byrd, William, 280, 289
Byrd Leibhart site, 29, 312, 314

Cabins, Indian log, 314, 346, 348, 369, 383, 414, 425, 429
Cabot, John, 10, 188
Cabot, Sebastian, 188
Cadzow, Donald A., 38, 47
Cairns site, 354
Calvert, Leonard, 253, 256
Camden Historic District, 5
Camden NHL, 208, 259-263, 265
Cameron site, 164, 378, 408, 435
Campbell, Tony, 30
Campbell site, 108
Campisi, Jack, 25
Canada, 3, 99, 344; French surrender of, 67, 84; Indian attacks on, 362, 368, 392; Indian refugees to, 95, 349, 386, 394, 402, 415, 422; Indians of, 33, 57, 335-336, 344, 365, 367, 371, 412. *See also* Maritime Provinces; New France; Ontario, province of; Quebec, province of
Canadasaga (Indian town), 414
Canadea site, 421
Canadian Heroic Age, 18
Canagere (Indian town), 362, 364
Canajoharie. *See* Upper Mohawk Castle
Canals, North American, 18
Canarsie (Brooklyn [N.Y.] area), 218
Caniba Indians, 72
Cannasatego (Onondaga), 240
Canoes, 66, 110, 447
Canowarode (Indian town), 363
Cantowa (Susquehannock), 315
Capawack (Indian town), 118
Captives: Indian, 16, 21, 342, 344, 366, 367, 399, 412; colonists as Indian, 31, 255; Indians as Indian, 246, 255, 273, 338, 383; Indians as colonist, 76, 111. *See also* Slaves
Carley site, 388
Cartier, Jacques, 59, 330, 335
Cartland, John Henry, 191
Cashie-Branchville pottery, 201, 268, 277, 279, 288
Cassasinamon, Robin, 142
Castine (Me.) Historic District, 187
Castles (towns), Mohawk, 361-363, 439
Catawba Indians, 205, 280, 281, 292, 294, 342, 401

Edgepillock, N.J., 209, 240
Education, of American Indians, 448. *See also* Schools, Indian
Effigies, carved, 215, 284, 327, 378, 391, 408, 416, 425, 435, 448
Egli site, 428
Egloff, Keith, 38
Eisiminger/Jesse Lapping site, 432, 435
Eliot, John, 32, 58, 104, 111, 114, 121
Ellis site, 420
Emporium site, 428
Ender's House site, 375
Englebert site, 332, 425
England, 151, 319; colonial independence from (*see* American War for Independence); France and, 62, 67, 75, 77, 80, 188. *See also* English (people)
England's Woods No. 1 site, 354, 361
English (lang.), Indian command of, 68, 114, 126, 157, 173, 237, 274, 371
English (people): Indians and (*see* Anglo-Indian relations); as New World invaders, 10, 14, 22, 56, 60, 159, 201-204
Entouhonoron (Indian town), 381, 390
Environment, as Historic Contact factor, 49-50, 60
EPA site, 96
Epinow (Wampanoag Country Indian), 118
Erie Indians, 38, 176, 273, 308, 310, 329, 332, 339-341, 365, 382, 400, 412, 420, 421
Erie-Neutral Branch pottery, 420
Eshleman site, 307
Esopus Indians, 165, 219, 221, 226-229; community, 157; wars, 219
Etchemins, *See* Maliseet Indians
Ethnoarchaeology, 51
Ethnography, 50-51
Ethnohistory, 6, 14, 18, 20, 51, 446
Europe, colonists from central, 175, 319, 322, 370. *See also* England; France; Scandinavia, visitors from
European-Indian relations, 8-13, 15-22, 27-28, 30-32, 46, 55-57, 59-70, 75-84, 89-96, 99, 105-114, 118-140, 153-159ff; in 18th century, 183-187, 189-192, 322-323, 440-444; in Middle Atlantic region, 318-323; in North Atlantic region, 175-193; in 17th century, 175-183, 188-189, 318-322, 439-440; in 16th century, 176, 188, 318, 439; in Trans-Appalachian region, 439-445. *See also* Anglo-Indian relations; Dutch-Indian relations; Europeans: Africans, Indians, and; French-Indian relations; Missionaries
Europeans: Africans and, 3, 8, 11-13, 15, 17-18, 21, 22, 208; Africans, Indians, and, 3, 8, 11, 13, 15, 17, 18, 21, 22, 208; "Indianization" of, 319, 371, 449; Indians and (*see* European-Indian relations; Indians, Northeastern: Europeanization of; Missionaries). *See also* Basques; Dutch, in Northeast; English; French; Portuguese; Spaniards; Swedes
Evans, Clifford, 38
Excavations, site, 35-38, 43-46, 48-49, 65-66, 71, 72, 159-163, 265, 297; in Cayuga Country, 396-397, 399-401; in Delaware Country, 231-232, 237, 240-241; in Eastern Abenaki Country, 71, 72, 74-

75, 78-79, 82-84, 184-187, 191-192; erosion of, 35, 38, 75, 184, 187; looting of, 35, 37, 38, 61, 66, 223, 396; in Lower Connecticut Valley Country, 153, 154, 157, 158; in Lower Susquehanna Country, 301-305, 307-309, 311, 312, 314, 316, 317; in Mahican Country, 164, 167-168, 170-173, 180-182, 189; in Massachusett Country, 110-113, 115, 116; in Middle Atlantic region, 199-203, 321, 322; in Mohawk Country, 353-354, 356-359, 361-367, 369, 370, 372-376, 382; in Mohegan-Pequot Country, 139, 142-146, 148-151; in Munsee Country, 211-218, 220-226, 353; in Nanticoke Country, 243, 246, 247-248; in Narragansett Country, 129, 132-138; on Niagara-Erie Frontier, 416-423; in Nipmuck Country, 102-104; in North Atlantic region, 178-179; in Nottoway-Meherrin Country, 276, 279, 281-282; in Oneida Country, 164, 363, 378-384, 435; in Onondaga Country, 387-388, 390-393; in Pennacook-Pawtucket Country, 105, 108; in Piscataway-Potomac Country, 249-250, 252-254, 256, 258-265; in Pocumtuck-Squakheag Country, 96, 97, 99; in Powhatan Country, 268-271, 274, 275; in Seneca Country, 403-408, 412, 413, 435; in Southern Appalachian Highlands Country, 295-299; threats to, 37-38; in Trans-Appalachian region, 330-332, 334, 336-338, 344, 347, 352, 439, 441-443, 445; in Upper Ohio Country, 431-438; in Upper Potomac-Shenandoah Country, 283-287; in Upper Susquehanna Country, 424-428; in Virginia Piedmont Country, 288-289, 291, 292, 295; in Wampanoag Country, 117-118, 120-126, 128; in Western Abenaki Country, 86-87, 89-91, 94. *See also* Artifacts; Pits, archaeological site
Experience Mayhew House, 128, 192

Factory Hollow site, 409
Failing site, 362, 363, 382
Fairhaven, Mass., 127
Fallam, Robert, 299
Farmers, Indians, 138, 145, 162, 172, 199, 211, 226, 232, 249, 265, 280, 289, 301, 314, 327, 329, 333, 337, 339, 346, 369, 371, 414, 429, 447. *See also* Barns, Indian; Crops, Indian; Livestock, Indian; Orchards, Indian; Plows
Farmhands, Indians as colonial, 162, 208
Farmington, Conn., 153, 157
Feder, Kenneth, 21
Fenton, William N., 18, 28, 29, 51, 327, 350, 446, 450
Fenwick, Richard, 206
Ferguson Ossuary site, 264
Fertilizers, 447
Feugle site, 435
Fiedel, Stuart, 47
Fielding Rock Shelter site, 153
Fine arts, Indian contributions to, 447-448
Finns, 234
Fish, 118, 333. *See also* Shellfish
Fishbasket site, 438
Fishing, Indian, 20-21, 58, 72, 80, 89, 100, 103, 105, 109, 114, 117, 123, 138, 154, 158, 162, 165, 168, 199,

Houses, Indian, 48-49, 56, 58, 65, 77, 79, 114, 126, 128, 140, 145, 151, 157, 168-169, 197, 199, 212-215, 227, 232, 234, 238, 249, 254, 256-257, 260, 275, 281, 295, 319, 329, 333-334, 346, 347, 362, 378, 381, 387, 393, 410, 414, 424, 432-435, 449. *See also* Cabins, Indian log; Longhouses; Wigwams
Howarth/Nelson site, 432
Howe Farm site, 94
Hudson, Henry, 69, 215, 319
Hudson River, 67, 69, 164, 179, 180, 234, 342; Africans on, 64; European colonists on, 11, 63, 64, 175, 206, 318, 319, 362, 364; Indians of, 24, 25, 56, 62, 86, 104, 149, 157, 164, 165, 168, 172-174, 198, 204, 211, 216, 219, 220, 223, 229-230, 236, 283, 332, 340, 360, 364, 365, 368, 374. *See also* Fort Orange; Schuyler Flatts NHL
Huffman Farm site, 436
Hughes Farm site, 432
Hunter Brook projectile points, 45
Hunters: colonial, 147; Indians as, 19, 58, 66, 72, 80, 84, 100, 103, 105, 109, 114, 117, 123, 139, 145, 154, 165, 168, 199, 209, 211, 217, 229, 232, 249, 269, 284, 289, 300, 301, 314, 327, 331, 333, 338, 341, 342, 345, 346
Huntington, Conn., 157
Hurley Flats complex sites, 220
Hurley NHL, 321
Huron Indians, 81, 176, 179, 259, 308, 310, 332, 333, 337-344, 359, 363, 364, 366, 382, 391, 400, 412, 417
Huron-like pottery, 365
Hurt site, 292

Ibaugh site, 307
Illinois Indians, 342
Implements. *See* Utensils
Indian Burial Hills site, 134
Indian Castle, N.Y., 372; Church, 372, 373, 374, 375; site, 391
Indian Claims Commission, 18
Indian Crossing site, 96
Indian Fields archaeological complex, 163
Indian Fort Road site, 396
Indian Hill Avenue site (Conn.), 157, 158
Indian Hill site (N.Y.), 392
Indian leaders, 13, 35, 45, 106, 111, 133, 137, 152, 157, 160, 200, 205, 207, 208, 226, 240, 250, 253, 263, 268, 269, 291, 315, 329, 335, 340, 348, 364, 365, 367, 369, 375, 385, 392, 401, 414, 429; councils, 58
Indian Mills, N.J., 240
Indian Point site, 250, 263
Indian Power, 18
Indian Reorganization Act of 1934, 18
Indian River, Del., 248
Indians, Northeastern, 8-11, 16, 31-35; Africans and, 3, 8, 11-13, 15, 17-18, 21, 22, 57, 64, 114, 126, 158, 208; Christianization of, 94, 100, 115, 122, 126, 137, 151, 157, 172, 179, 208, 226-227, 229, 240, 259, 274, 343, 346, 348, 361, 364-367, 370, 371, 383-385, 392, 401, 440, 448, 449 (*see also* Broth-

ertown Movement; Missionaries); contributions of, 447-450; and Dutch (*see* Dutch-Indian relations); enmeshed in debt, 160, 273; and English (*see* Anglo-Indian relations); Europeanization of, 10, 15, 100, 114, 126, 145, 157, 163, 208, 237, 240, 274, 280, 294, 314, 316, 346, 384, 391, 413, 414 (*see also* European-Indian relations; Missionaries); and French (*see* French-Indian relations); generosity to settlers, 448; as guides, 80, 84, 207, 289; idealization of, 10, 11, 448; as international factor, 449; literature on, 31, 33; nomadism enforced upon, 68, 157, 167, 172, 216, 294; population patterns of (*see* Population, patterns of Northeast Indian); today, 22, 448, 450; in U.S. politics, 11-12, 16, 22, 28, 85, 95, 386. *See also* Artisans, Indian; Farmers, Indian; Fishing, Indian; Foragers, Indians as; Houses, Indian; Hunters: Indians as; Laborers, Indians as colonial; Sailors, Indian; Servants, Indians as colonial; Soldiers, Indians as colonial; Towns: Indian; *and individual tribes by name*
Indiantown (Mashantucket Pequot NHL), 144, 151
Indian Town Farm site, 249
Influenza, 114, 123
Ingefield site, 241
Ingraham/Spragg site, 432, 435
Intermarriage, Indian: with Africans, 12, 21, 64, 122, 126, 158, 208; with Europeans, 95, 122, 126, 158, 208, 314, 316; intergroup, 68, 93, 122, 138, 158, 208, 240, 265, 274, 346, 363, 382; with non-Indians, general, 114-115, 162, 240, 248, 265, 274, 338
Intermontane Tradition, 295, 298
Interpreters, Indians as, 207
Iroquoia (term), 330
Iroquoian (lang.), 9, 24, 165, 198, 204, 306, 330, 334, 435. *See also* Northern Iroquoian; Southern Iroquoian
Iroquoian (term), 330
Iroquois (term), 330
Iroquois confederacy. *See* Iroquois League of Five Nations
Iroquois Indians, 13, 15-16, 22, 24, 25, 29, 33, 39, 45, 48, 49, 56, 57, 59, 175, 176, 179, 180, 200, 202-207, 221, 226, 227, 236, 237, 240, 259, 273, 281, 284, 293-294, 300, 306, 308-316, 322, 329-334, 341, 377, 378, 381-386, 388, 392, 394, 400-402, 409, 412-415, 420, 422, 424, 425, 429, 436, 439, 440, 442-446, 448-449; and feminism, 450; legacy of, 449-450; literature on, 350-352; today, 334, 341, 350, 448. *See also* Convenant Chain of Friendship; Iroquois League of Five Nations; Mingo Indians; Northern Iroquois Indians
Iroquois League of Five Nations, 22, 28, 29, 47, 308, 329, 339, 388, 391. *See also names of nations*
Iroquois League of Six Nations, 22, 29, 349. *See also names of nations*
Iroquois Pottery Conference, 38

Jackfield pottery, 373
Jackson-Everson site, 365, 366, 376

Jack's Reef projectile points, 45
Jacobson, Jerome, 222, 223
James Logan NHL, 322
Jamestown site, 269
Jamesville site, 392
Janie site, 363, 364
Jansson-Visscher maps, 30
Jargon, Indian trade, 68
Jefferson, Thomas, 288
Jemison, Mary, 31, 49
Jenning's Garrison, 192
Jesuits, 32, 33, 68, 193, 202, 206–207, 259, 268, 341, 343, 348, 350, 364, 366, 367, 382, 390–392, 399–401, 408–410, 412, 417, 439, 440. *See also* Jogues, Isaac; Râle, Sébastien
Jewelry, in archaeological deposits, 149, 274, 283, 297, 366, 382, 391, 392, 397, 413, 414, 422. *See also* Ornaments, Indian
Jewels, settler search for, 289
Jikohnsaseh (Iroquois), 409, 410
Jireh Bull Blockhouse site, 137, 188
Jogues, Isaac, 361, 364
Johansen, Bruce E., 449
John Green site complex, 277–279, 281
Johnson, William, 11, 17, 35, 173, 228, 348, 349, 371–375, 385, 442
Johnston Farm site (Upper Susquehanna Country), 425
Johnston site (Seneca Country), 404, 407, 408
Johnston site (Upper Ohio Country), 438
Joncaire, Louis-Thomas Chabert de, 414, 421, 440
Jones, Samuel, 224
Jones, William, 32
Jordan's Journey site, 268, 274, 322
Joris (Munsee), 221
Journals, scholarly, 35, 36

Kaghnuwage (Indian town), 361, 363
Kaiquariegehaga Indians, 306
Kaiser I site, 154
Kakouagoga Indians, 420
Kanagaro (Indian town), 361, 365
Kananouagon (Indian town), 438
Kancagamus (Pennacook), 35, 106
Kaniengehaga. *See* Mohawk Indians
Kanienke (Mohawk community), 363, 365, 367–371, 374, 375. *See also* Mohawk Country; Upper Mohawk Castle
Kaskaskia (French town), 349
Kaunameek, N.Y., 173
Kaups, Matti, 449
Kayaderosseras patent, 348, 370
Keller site, 307
Kennebec Indians, 80
Kent, Conn., 157
Keyauwee Indians, 292
Keyser site, 283
Keyser-series pottery, 283
Kieft (Dutch colonial governor), 219
Kienuka site, 420
Killens Pond site, 243, 248

Kilts site, 354, 358, 362
King George's War, 93, 171, 173, 228, 280, 371, 394, 401, 429
King Opessa's Town (Indian town), 286
King Philip. *See* Metacomet
King Philip's War, 21, 56, 62, 69, 70, 76, 79, 89, 92, 93, 99, 104, 106, 108–109, 111, 115, 122, 128, 130–131, 134, 137, 143, 146, 167, 188–190, 449
Kingsclear (Indian town), 81
Kingston, N.Y., 220, 221, 226
King William's War, 80, 93, 168, 183, 186, 187, 189, 190, 218, 312, 314, 343, 344, 368, 383, 392, 401, 440
Kipp Island site, 399
Kirkland, Samuel, 348, 385
Kirkwood site, 412
Kittanning (Indian town), 229
Kleis site, 420, 421
Kleyntie (Dutch explorer), 439
Klinko site, 396
Klock site, 354, 358, 359
Kuskuskies (Indian town), 438

Laborers, Indians as colonial, 18, 19, 68, 80, 100, 109, 162, 207, 208, 265, 371, 385
Labrador, 10
Lachine, Que., 368
La Conception (mission), 412
Lafitau, Joseph-François, 350, 448
Lake George, 164; Battle of, 371
Lancaster, Mass., 103
Lancaster County Park site, 317
Land grants, Indians and, 226
Lane, Ralph, 217, 268
Languages, Indian, 9, 24, 33, 47, 57, 59, 68, 69, 89, 111, 140, 154, 198, 218, 223, 232, 255, 269, 278, 281, 289, 292, 306, 322, 327, 330, 331, 348, 377. *See also* English, Indian command of
Lanz-Hogan site, 383
Lapoe No. 1 site, 432
La Presentation (French mission), 385, 386, 394, 440
Larner, Kingston, 363
La Salle, René-Robert Cavelier, Sieur de, 409, 439
Late Woodland Tradition, 10, 37, 45, 56, 57–59, 61, 84, 86, 87, 89, 96, 105, 110, 113, 117, 125–126, 129, 133, 139, 140, 153, 157, 162, 164, 168, 198–202, 210, 211, 216, 217, 223, 225, 231, 232, 243, 249, 250, 253, 254, 261, 264, 268, 274, 275, 277, 283, 286, 288, 292, 295, 297, 298, 301, 327, 331, 333, 334, 377, 382, 396, 403, 416, 417, 422, 435
Lauverjat, Etienne, 93
Lavin, Lucianne, 38
Law(s): 122, 157, 449, 450
Lawson-series pottery, 416, 417, 420
Leacock, Eleanor Burke, 18, 23, 29
Leases, on Indian lands, 94, 137, 146, 147, 158, 280
Lederer, John, 289, 291
Leedstown, Va., 250
Le Moyne, Simon, 390
Lenape Indians. *See* Delaware Indians
Lenhardt-Lahaway Hill site, 238

Mattawoman (reservation), 259, 264
Mauwehu, Gideon, 157-158
Mawooshen (Eastern Abenaki territory), 76
Maxantawny (Indian town), 240
May, Cornelis, 215, 319
Maycock's Point site, 274
Mayflower (ship), 124
Mayhew, Thomas, 32, 121
McCary, Ben C., 30
McFate pottery, 333, 416, 424, 425
McKees Rocks site, 436
Mead Farm site, 400
Measles, 15, 113-114, 123, 221, 239
Mechamiquon (Delaware Indian), 237
Mechanicsville Road site, 164, 168
Medals, as burial items, 221, 261-262, 347, 397, 413
Medicine, Indian, 35, 66, 115
Megapolensis, Johannes, Jr., 361
Meharineck (Indian town), 278
Meherrin Indians, 24, 208, 278, 280-281
Ménard, René, 399
Mendon, Mass., 103
Mendota site, 298
Menendez de Aviles, Pedro, 202
Messengers, Indians as colonial, 207
Metacomet (Wampanoag), 62, 92, 121, 122. *See also* King Philip's War
Metal (-ware/-work), in archaeological contexts, 162, 168, 184, 198, 241, 264, 268, 271, 274, 277, 284, 288, 292, 299, 301, 304, 312, 316, 333, 336, 337, 346, 354, 361, 363, 372, 378, 381, 382, 387, 388, 391-393, 397, 403, 416, 417, 420, 424, 428, 431-435. *See also* Beads: metal; Projectile points; Tools; Utensils, Indian; Weapons, Indian
Miacomet Burial Ground, 126
Miami Indians, 338, 394, 413, 443
Miantonomi (Narragansett), 130
Micmac Indians, 55, 62, 63, 72, 85, 110, 118, 423; language, 72
Middle Atlantic region, 24, 195-323; boundaries of, 197; overview of, 197-210
Middle Plantation treaties, 262, 278-279
Middle Woodland Period, 108, 222, 250, 331
Miley site, 283
Millefiori star chevron beads, 336
Miller, Jay, 51
Miller Field complex, 258; site, 212
Mills, 18, 19, 48, 172, 226, 348, 371, 428
Milton Smith site, 368, 370
Mines, 18
Mingo Indians, 402, 414, 438
Minguannan pottery, 201, 231
Minguhanan (Indian town), 240
Minisink (Indian town), 216-218, 221; NHL, 215-218, 220
Minisink horizon, 215
Minisink Indians, 208, 216-218, 220, 227, 229
Minqua Indians, 306-307
Mispillion site, 243, 248
Missionaries, 57, 70, 80, 114, 115, 123, 127, 138, 237, 257, 314-315, 371, 384, 439, 448; Catholic, 68, 77, 80-83, 179, 202, 206, 207, 259, 348, 365, 382, 384, 385, 390-392, 394, 399-401, 408-410, 412, 417, 440; existing structures of Historic Contact period, 192; fraudulent, 206; Protestant, 13, 32, 68, 104, 121-122, 162, 172, 173, 229, 240, 348, 385, 393, 402, 428, 429, 448 (*see also* Eliot, John; Occom, Samson). *See also* Indians, Northeastern: Christianization of
Mission House NHL, 49, 172, 192
Missions, 17, 32-33, 56, 65, 76, 106, 114, 128, 150-151, 162, 179, 346; Catholic, 64, 68, 81, 93, 99, 183, 206-207, 259, 268, 341, 343, 348, 350, 364, 366, 382, 383, 399-400, 410, 412, 439 (*see also* Norridgewock NHL); fraudulent, 206; Protestant, 57, 68, 158, 172-174, 229, 348, 428, 429 (*see also* Praying Indian Towns). *See also* Indians, Northeastern: Christianization of
Missisauga Indians, 342, 412
Missisquoi (Indian town), 81, 92-94
Mississippian Period, 269
Mitchell site, 363, 364
Moats, Indian use of defensive, 432
Mohawk Country, 59, 92, 168, 175, 220, 333, 353-377, 409, 447; boundaries of, 353. *See also* Johnson, William
Mohawk Indians, 16, 25, 32-33, 35, 48, 56, 59, 62, 76, 91, 92, 97, 122, 140, 165, 167, 168, 172, 175, 176, 179, 180, 212, 219, 220, 229, 231, 329, 332, 336, 337, 339-343, 348, 351, 353-376, 382, 384, 388, 414, 425, 428, 439, 440, 443, 449; language, 33, 322, 348, 360, 371, 377; name, 360; today, 26, 33, 360-361, 375. *See also* Mohawk Country
Mohawk-Mahican Wars, 97, 362, 363
Mohawk Upper Castle NHL, 372-376
Mohawk Valley Archaeological Survey, 353
Mohegan Indians, 13, 103, 130, 138-140, 142-152; today, 148, 150, 152. *See also* Fort Shantok NHL; Mohegan-Pequot Country; Occom, Samson; Uncas
Mohegan-Pequot Country, 55, 139-152
Monacan Indians, 198, 289, 291, 292, 294, 342
Monacan Town (Indian town), 291
Monahassanugh (Indian town), 291
Monasukapanough (Indian town), 291
Moneton Indians, 299
Monomoy (Indian town), 118
Monongahela Culture, 284, 329, 431, 435-437
Monongahela Indians, 306, 329, 333, 336, 352, 424, 425, 437-438
Monongahela pottery, 283, 307, 416, 425, 431
Montagnais Indians, 359
Montauk Country, 56, 154, 159-163
Montauk Fort Hill site, 162
Montauk Indians, 56, 130, 138, 142, 159-163; language, 69
Montgomery site, 241
Montoursville complex sites, 428
Montowampate (Massachusett), 111
Montreal, Que., 179, 183, 343, 369
Montville, Conn., 148, 152
Moore/Ola site, 432
Moor's Indian School, 151

New York, N.Y., 38, 208, 220, 221, 223. *See also* New Amsterdam

Niagagarega (Indian community), 420

Niagara, Ont., 347, 349. *See also* Fort Niagara

Niagara-Erie Frontier, 416–424, 447

Niantic, Conn., 49, 157

Niantic Indians, 59, 130. *See also* Eastern Niantic Indians

Niantic-series pottery, 117, 139, 154, 162

Nichols Pond site, 381

Nick's Niche site, 153

Nicolls, Richard, 188

Nicolls Treaty, 226

Niles, Samuel, 137

Nimham. Abraham, 174

Nimham, Daniel, 173, 174

Ninigret, George and Thomas, 138

Ninigret II (Narragansett), 137

Ninigrets (Eastern Niantic), 133

Nipmuck Country, 55, 102–104, 118, 447

Nipmuck Indians, 56, 99, 103, 104, 130

Niskayuna (Indian town), 167, 365

Noank (reservation), 142, 144, 147

"Noble savage," Indian as, 10, 448

Nomads, Indians as, 72, 89, 117, 197, 232. *See also* Indians, Northeastern: nomadism forced upon

Nonantum (Indian town), 110

Normandy, New World adventurers from, 335

Norridgewock: mission town, 65, 68, 77–84; NHL, 49, 75, 82–85, 183

North Atlantic region, 24, 53–193; boundaries of, 55; overview of, 55–70

North Brook site, 241

North Carolina, colony/state of, 3, 148, 265, 277, 278, 280–281, 292, 294

Northeast North America: defined, 3; dimensions of, 24–26

Northern Iroquoian: cultural pattern, 327; language, 278, 327, 330, 331

Northern Iroquois Indians, 327–331, 337

Northfield, Mass., 55, 96, 97

North Kingstown, R.I., 137

North Salt Pond site, 124

Northwest Passage, search for, 60, 202

Norwottuck (Indian town), 55, 96, 97

Nottoway Indians, 24, 208, 278–282, 294

Nottoway-Meherrin Country, 273, 276–282

Nova Belgii maps, 30

Nova Scotia, province of, 56, 64, 72, 77, 85, 122, 167, 176, 179, 183

Nowadaga (Indian town), 372, 375

Nueva Cadiz beads, 336

Nutimus (Delaware sachem), 208

Nuts, 346; artifactitious, 84, 97, 432

Oakfield pottery, 332

Oak Hill No. 1 site, 363, 364

Obtakiest (Massachusett), 111

Occaneechi (Indian town), 204, 292

Occaneechi Indians, 198, 205, 263, 281, 291–292, 294, 311–312

Occom, Samson, 13, 138, 151, 152, 162, 448

Ochquaga (Indian town), 220, 344, 368, 371, 384, 386, 425, 428, 429

Ockanickon (Delaware sachem), 237

Ockocagansett (mission town), 104

Odanak (mission town), 81, 93, 94

Offerings, funerary, 44, 66, 241, 413, 435

Ogehage (Indian town), 428

Ohagi 6 site, 415

Ohio, territory of, 28, 168, 174, 226, 349, 394, 414, 416

Ohio Country, 168. *See also* Upper Ohio Country

Ohongeoguena Indians, 306

Oiogouen (Indian town), 399–400

Okehocking (Indian town), 236, 238–240, 314

Oklahoma, territory/state of, 26, 51, 349–350, 386, 402, 415

Old Conoy Town, 248

Old Fort Niagara NHL, 5, 416, 421–423, 431, 436

Old Mine Road Historic District, 218

Old Point site, 82–84. *See also* Norridgewock

Old Town (Indian town), 81, 85

Oneida Castle site, 383

Oneida Country, 36, 152, 158, 164, 174, 332, 335, 363, 377–386, 392, 435. *See also* Brothertown Movement

Oneida Indian Reservation, 151, 240. *See also* Brothertown

Oneida Indians, 25, 138, 231, 329, 339, 340, 343, 347, 349, 361, 363, 368, 377–386, 388, 390, 394; language, 377; name, 381; today, 385, 386

Onekahoncka (Indian town), 361, 362

Oneugioure (Indian town), 361

Onneyuttehage (Indian town), 381, 382

Onondaga (Iroquois capital), 221, 329, 365, 388, 390, 392–394

Onondaga Castle site, 393

Onondaga Country, 332, 335, 339, 377, 387–395

Onondaga Indians, 13, 240, 337, 339, 340, 342, 343, 347–349, 368, 384, 385, 387–395, 402, 421, 440; reservation, 395; today, 393, 395

Ononjote (Indian town), 382

Ononkwaia (Oneida), 382

Onontare (Indian town), 400

Ontario, province of, 26, 33, 200, 202, 203, 332, 342, 348, 386, 402, 403, 415–417, 448

Ontario Iroquois Tradition, 332, 336, 366, 403, 407, 416, 421, 431, 436

Opament (Indian town), 253

Opechancanough (Powhatan), 35, 272–273, 275

Oping Indians, 157

Opitchapam (Powhatan), 272

Oral literature, Indian, 47–49, 115, 126, 129, 200, 202, 203, 265, 330, 334, 335, 354, 388, 409, 412

Oratam (Hackensack), 13

Orchards, Indian, 48, 145, 172, 314, 339, 348, 369, 414, 429. *See also* Fruit

Orient Point, 159

Oriskany, Battle of, 385

Ornaments, Indian, 15, 35, 56, 80, 89, 108, 114, 198, 268, 286, 295, 306, 314, 337, 347, 362, 363, 374,

Quicksburg site, 283
Quick Water site, 105
Quiggle pottery, 333, 416, 424, 425
Quinnipiac, Conn., 157
Quinnipiac Indians, 55, 153
Quinsigamond (Indian town), 104
Quiripi (lang.), 154
Quirk site, 387
Quonset huts, 447

R. T. Foley Farm site, 432, 437
Racism, Indians and, 157
Radford-series pottery, 295, 297
Radiocarbon assays, 27
Radisson, Pierre Esprit, 399
Râle, Sébastien, 68, 80–83
Rappahannock-complex pottery, 249, 250, 253
Rappahannock Indians, 260, 264–265, 272, 273
Raritan Indians, 204
Rassawek (Indian town), 291
Rattles, turtle-shell, 400
Reading, Pa., 239
Redwares, in archaeological contexts, 136, 192, 241, 374, 422, 423, 428
Reitz site, 307
Religion: Indian, 13, 57, 100, 136, 137, 269, 428. See also Indians, Northeastern: Christianization of; Longhouse religion; See also Bibles, Indian-language; Christianity, Indians and; Churches, Indian
Renaissance, 15
Renap (Munsee leader), 221
René Ménard Bridge Hilltop site, 400
Rensselaer, Kiliaen van, 165, 175–176
Rensselaerswyck, 175–176, 319
Reservations, Indian, 17, 57, 65, 67–68, 85, 114, 121, 123, 137, 138, 142–144, 151, 157, 163, 198, 204, 206–209, 237, 240, 247, 248, 259, 264, 273, 274, 279–280, 292, 294, 316, 349–350, 393, 416, 417, 444. See also Brothertown Movement; reservation names
Reverend Badger House site, 115, 116, 192
Revolution, American. See American War for Independence
Rhode Island, colony/state of, 55, 63, 103, 117, 118, 123, 133, 150, 160, 188, 240. See also Narragansett Country; Nipmuck Country; Wampanoag Country
Rice, Janet, 30
Rice's Woods site, 354, 361
Richmond Incised pottery, 332, 396, 403, 416, 424
Richmond Mills site, 403
Riggins pottery, 201, 231, 243
Ripley site, 38, 420, 421
Rippeteau, Bruce E., 352
Rip Van Winkle site, 168
Risingh, Johan, 241
"River Indians," 165, 168, 172
Roanoke, N.C., 202
Roanoke, Va., 210
Roanoke Indians, 263

Roanoke pottery, 274, 288
Roberts site, 308
Roberval, Jean François de La Rocque de, 335
Rochester Junction site, 409, 413
Rochester site, 432
Rocks Road site, 108
Rogers, Robert, 47, 94
Rogers Farm site, 400, 439
Rolfe, John, 272
Roman Catholic Church, 207, 259, 366, 367, 385, 394, 440. See also Jesuits; Saint Mary's City
Romer, Wolfgang William, 191
Rooseboom, Johannes, 439
Rose Hill site, 279, 281
Rousseau, Jean-Jacques, 448
Rowantee (Indian town), 278
Rumrill-Naylor site, 362–364
Runtees, 391
Russawmeake (Indian town), 291

Sailors, Indian, 21, 68, 84, 109, 138, 144, 150, 160, 162. See also Whalers, Indian
Saint-Castin, Jean Vincent Abaddie, 77, 183, 186, 187, 189, 190
Saint-Castin's Habitation, 75, 77, 183, 184, 186–187
Saint Croix National Historic Site, 183
Sainte Anne de Beaupré (mission), 179
Sainte Marie (mission town), 399
Sainte Marie Gannentaha (mission town), 343, 390–391
Saint Francis (Indian mission town), 47, 94, 172. See also Odanak
Saint François Xavier (mission), 382
Saint Jacques (mission), 410, 412
Saint Jean Baptiste (chapel), 390
Saint John's Indians. See Maliseet Indians
Saint John's site, 258
Saint Joseph (mission town), 399–400
Saint Lawrence (Iroquoian) pottery, 59, 333, 378
Saint Mary's City, 255–259, 318–321, 447; NHL, 5, 200, 250, 253, 256–258, 263, 321–322
Saint Michel, 412, 413
Saint Regis (mission town), 371, 375
Saint René (mission), 400
Saint Stephen (mission), 400
Salem, Mass., 111
Salisbury, Neal, 18
Salisbury Farm site, 238
Samuel Gorton House site, 137, 188
Sand Hill No. 1 site, 363
Sandstone Rock Shelter site, 298, 299
Sandy Point site, 75
Sandy River site, 82–84
Sandy's Point site, 123
Santuit Pond Road site, 126
Sapling (Iroquois), 28
Saponi Indians, 198, 205, 208, 281, 282, 291, 294, 322, 350, 401, 402, 425, 428–430; today, 281
Saratoga, N.Y., 348
Sarf/O'Malia site, 428
Sargeant, John, 172–173

INDEX / 509

Snow, Dean R., 44, 60, 85, 86, 331, 353-354, 359, 362, 364, 365, 367, 373, 375-377
Snow Hill site, 104
Snow whelks, 200, 202
Sohaes (Seneca Conestoga), 315
Sokoki Indians, 87, 89, 92, 97
Soldiers, Indians as colonial, 19, 66, 84, 144, 150, 157, 158, 174, 207, 280, 322, 371, 414, 449
Sonnontouan (Indian town), 409
Sony site, 432, 435, 437
Souriquois. See Micmac Indians
Southhampton, N.Y., 163
South Carolina, colony state of, 3, 265, 281, 292
Southern Appalachian Highlands Country, 15, 295-300
Southern Iroquoian (lang.), 331
Southold, N.Y., 160
South Salt Pond site, 124
Spain: England, Holland, and, 319. See also Basques; Spaniards
Spangenburg, Augustus, 350
Spaniards, 10, 14, 56, 60, 201, 268. See also Basques
Spears site, 432
Speck, Frank G., 51, 60, 85
Spelman, Henry, 255
Spicer, Edward H., 22
Spotswood, Alexander, 280-282, 294, 322
Spring House Rock Shelter site, 220
Squakheag (Indian town), 55, 96. See also Pocumtuck-Squakheag Country; Sokoki Indians
Squanto (Pawtuxet), 118-121, 202, 448
Squash, 10, 15, 58, 72, 124, 199, 232, 289, 295, 327, 346, 447; in archaeological contexts, 84, 211, 217, 432
Squaw Sachem (Massachusett), 111
Stadacona (Indian town), 335
Stafford Brook site, 104
Steele site, 409
Steelman, John Hans, 314
Stegara (Indian town), 289
Stegara Indians, 291
Stepping Stones site, 110
Sterling site, 383
Stiles, Ezra, 49, 157
Stockades. See Forts
Stockbridge, Mass., 33, 68, 150-151; mission at, 57, 70, 152, 158, 172-174, 229, 386. See also Mission House NHL
Stockbridge-Munsee Indian Reservation, 138, 152
Stone, Garry Wheeler, 256
Stone(ware): in archaeological contexts, 136, 172, 184, 192, 225, 241, 261, 263, 274, 279, 295, 308, 347, 381, 388, 391, 423 (see also Lithics, in archaeological contexts); as Indian raw material, 58, 198, 211, 327, 337, 378, 435
Stone Quarry site, 382
Stonington (reservation), 142, 147, 150
Strachey, William, 210, 269
Strickler pottery, 309, 333
Strickler site, 29, 308, 309, 310-311
Stuckanoe Indians, 281, 291

Stuyvesant, Peter, 180, 219
Sullivan, John, 386, 395, 402
Sullivan site, 382, 383
Sulpicians, 385, 394, 440
Sunflowers, in archaeological context, 432
Sunksquaws, 13, 111
Susquehanna Country, 168. See also Lower Susquehanna Country; Upper Susquehanna Country
Susquehanna Indians, 238, 349, 425, 429
Susquehannock Indians, 24, 29, 38, 47, 48, 198, 200, 204-206, 231-232, 234, 236, 238, 244, 253-255, 259, 262-263, 273, 283, 284, 291-292, 301, 302, 304-317, 319, 322, 332-333, 336, 337, 339, 342, 343, 345, 364, 382, 383, 392, 400, 412, 413, 424, 431, 435, 438; language, 255; name, 306. See also Lower Susquehanna Country
Swanendael (Dutch community), 204, 232-234
Sweat lodges, 435
Swedes, 204, 219, 234, 237, 255, 308, 309, 318-319, 322, 339, 342, 420, 437
Sphyilis, 15, 336

Tableware, in archaeological context, 373
Tadoussac, Que., 335
Takawampait, Daniel, 114
Tamenend (Delaware sachem), 237
Tankiteke Indians, 153
Tanxsnitania (Indian town), 289
Taphow (Munsee and Pequannock sachem), 35, 157, 221, 226
Tarrantine Micmacs, 118
Tatamy, Moses Tunda, 35
Tavern, as Fort Orange amenity, 182, 189
Tawagonshi Treaty, 340
Tawarra (Indian town), 279, 280
Taxes: on Indians, 122, 174; Indian-imposed, 269
Teedyuscung (Delaware leader), 229
Teganissorens (Onondaga diplomat), 13, 17, 393
Tehaque Indians, 306
Tehondaloga site, 370
Tekakwitha, Kateri (Mohawk), 367
Temperance House site, 387
Tennessee, state of, 297
Tenotoge(hage) (Indian town), 363
Terminus post quem (TPQ), 27
Textiles, 151, 175, 319
Thanksgiving, first, 118
Theme studies, 4
Thirty-first Street (Pittsburgh) Burial site, 438
Thirty Years' War, 15
Thomas, Jacob E., 51
Thomas-Sawyer site, 297, 299
Thomas site, 243, 244
Throckmorton No. 1 site, 432
Thurston site, 381
Tigoransera (Mohawk), 370
Time, cyclic vs. linear, 26-28
Tioga (Indian town), 220, 344, 368, 371, 425, 428, 429
Tioga Point Farm site, 428
Tiohero (Indian town), 400